WITH
PREJUDICE

WITH PREJUDICE

The War Memoirs

of Marshal of the Royal *Air Force*

Lord Tedder G.C.B.

with illustrations and maps

LITTLE, BROWN AND COMPANY · BOSTON · TORONTO

Preface

THIS is intended to be a true preface, and I do not propose to commence writing my Memoirs before it is complete. I want here to formulate broad principles which can serve me as a guide.

One of the most interesting relationships during the Second World War was that between Churchill and Smuts—a blend of mutual admiration and mutual respect somewhat akin to that between favourite uncle and favourite nephew, the nephew being Churchill. A sidelight on this relationship is provided by an anecdote which is so probable that it simply must be true. Smuts was calling on Churchill one afternoon—the first volumes of his *History of the Second World War* were out, and Churchill hoped to get Smuts's views on them. The afternoon wore on and Smuts began to make a move towards leaving, without having said a word about the books. Churchill asked directly, 'What did you think of my books?' to which Smuts replied— 'Oh, Winston, why? Why did you have to do that? You, more than anybody in the world, could have written as no one else could have written, the true history of the war, and instead of that you have produced these books,' to which Churchill replied: 'These are *my* story. If someone else likes to write *his* story, let him.'

I do not feel that Smuts was being quite fair. He implied first that Churchill's books did not give the whole truth, and also that Churchill had thrown away the priceless opportunity of writing the authoritative account of world-wide events in which he had held so commanding a position.

It seems to me that there are two ways of writing history— the impersonal and the personal. The impersonal method is adopted by, and rightly adopted by, the official historians; such histories are based on official documents and records, and, with the object of ensuring against any personal, technical or Service bias, they have in numerous cases been compiled by a team of two or three experts. In my innocence, I had thought that this method would definitely ensure that the histories told the truth, the whole truth and nothing but the truth. My knowledge of the histories of the First World War should have taught me better. I am inclined to think that we expect far too much from the official histories. After all, they are contemporary. The authors who compile them are almost certain to have been involved in some way or another with the events they describe. With the best will in the world they cannot be entirely unprejudiced. Moreover, in all probability they have been subjected to various pressures. Also, by the nature of things, they have been limited very largely to the use of official documents and orders, which are not perhaps the ideal, and certainly not the whole, source on which to have to rely. I expect that most of us have seen, sometimes with amusement and sometimes almost with anger, reports and orders obviously worded with an eye to the future historian, or, as we used to call them, 'for the record'. The wording of signals and orders 'for the record' is a very fine art and well calculated to fox the historian. The authors of the official Second World War Histories have done a good job in compiling and sifting the facts in so far as they were available to them. They have provided invaluable foundation for subsequent research, but I do not think that they were in a position to issue final judgment on any of the main issues.

There remains the alternative form of history—the personal, or as Churchill called it, 'his story'. As I have said, I do not think that Smuts was being quite fair to him. Objective history calls for a tight rein. Can one imagine Churchill writing under such a limitation? No. As I see it, his account of the late war is essentially a personal one, a story of the course of events as he saw them, not the history of the 1939–1945 Great War. That will have to wait for many years before it can be written, but his is nevertheless an unique and great contribution towards the ultimate history.

I was impressed by the exchange between Churchill and Smuts because it seemed to me to indicate a principle, a sound one, which might govern these Memoirs I am proposing to write. I mean to record the course of events as I saw them. I shall be as objective as I feel it possible to be, but I have no intention whatever of departing, for any reason, from my own honest opinion as to events and personalities. So often, people make great play about being completely unprejudiced. Frankly, I am completely prejudiced, and I accept as a guide and as a warning, Goethe's saying:

'I can promise to be upright but not to be unprejudiced.'

TEDDER

TO THE MEMORY

OF

R.T. AND M.T.

*without whose inspiration
this could never have been written*

Contents

Illustrations

The illustrations marked with an asterisk
are reproductions of sketches made by the
author.

Maps

Acknowledgments

I WISH to express my thanks to Mr. David Dilks and Mr. Anthony Paice for their help in the preparation of this volume. I am also grateful to Mrs. Marjorie Grover who again and again rescued me from certain chaos.

My thanks are also due to Mr. L. A. Jackets and his staff at Ministry of Defence (Air) Historical Branch for their help in research.

These pages have been read by friends who experienced the events which are described. They made suggestions which have been of great help to me, but since the responsibility for every word is properly mine, I do not give their names in acknowledgment.

I would also like to thank those friends and colleagues, authors and publishers, who have given me permission to use extracts from published sources in which they hold copyright. Such sources have been acknowledged in an abbreviated form in footnotes, while full publication details can be found in the Bibliography of Sources at the end of the book.

The official documents printed in this volume are Crown Copyright, which is legally vested in the Controller of Her Majesty's Stationery Office, and I am obliged for permission to reproduce them.

Overture

1932 – 1940

Chronology

1939
September:

1   Poland invaded.

3   Declaration of war on Germany by France, Great Britain, Australia and New Zealand.

29   Soviet–Germany treaty of friendship partitions Poland.

November:

3   U.S. Congress introduces 'Cash and Carry' clause into statute of Neutrality.

30   U.S.S.R. invades Finland.

1940
April:

15   British troops land near Narvik, Norway.

May:

2   Allied forces evacuate Namsos, Norway.

5   German troops advance north from Trondheim.

10   Germany invades Holland, Belgium and Luxemburg.
British troops land in Iceland.
Chamberlain resigns.
Coalition Government with Mr. Churchill as Prime Minister.

Overture

SHORTLY before the end of my third year as an instructor at the R.A.F. Staff College, the then Commandant, Air Marshal Joubert de la Ferté, told me that it was the normal custom for a Staff College instructor, at the end of his term of instructing, to be given a free choice (within reason) as to where he would wish to go and what job he would like to undertake. It so happened that I have always made it a rule, then and since, not to ask for a given appointment, but to leave it in the hands of the personnel authorities. I therefore suggested no particular post to which I wished to go. I did, however, request that I be not posted to another training unit. I suppose it was rather naïve of me to think that anyone would pay much regard to my request. Nor did they; and I was duly posted to the Air Armament School. For that posting I have no regrets.

In that year—1932—that ingenious rule which had served as a perfect alibi for inaction, the Ten Years Rule, at long last lost its authority. No longer would it be possible for the procrastinators to say there was no hurry whatever, and that there would not be war for at least ten years. What was urgently needed was a complete change of heart regarding air armament. Normally the armament staff were not regarded as part of the operational air staff but as another form of equipment officer, a lower form of life altogether. These were the men whose duty it should have been to ensure the proper use and maintenance of all forms of armament and examine and advise on new methods. It was the role of the Air Armament School at Eastchurch to train officers to carry out these duties, but this could only be effective if, when trained armament officers went out to serve in operational units, they were properly used. In practice this was rarely done.

One of the main functions of the School was to administer the Armament Training Camps and the various ranges which they operated. I have said that I did not regret my posting to armament training: I would go much further. To me, my two years in charge of the Armament Camps at Eastchurch was one of the most interesting periods in my service. The squadrons, led by their squadron commanders, would come in what I used to call 'a state of nature'—in other words stripped of all but their operational equipment—for three weeks to one month simply to carry out the various bombing and gunnery exercises set and supervised by the Armament Staff of the camp. There was no scope for 'adjusting' the figures or the results.

I would make it a habit, when possible, to visit a squadron in its first few days at camp, and at the end of its time. My report on each squadron's camp went direct to the Air Ministry with a copy to the C.-in-C. of the Command. It is not for me to say whether the Command found these reports useful (surprisingly enough I never had a come-back, even on a very adverse report), but to me they were intensely interesting and useful. Here one was seeing what one had almost lost sight of in the welter of peacetime regulations—the rare spectacle of a squadron commander commanding, and the flight commanders commanding. To me this was a very welcome sight. In a number of instances one felt that the individual commander or squadron commander had definitely grown in stature as a result of being able to exercise his own authority. The general situation, however, as revealed by the camp training, was far from welcome. During the Ten Years Rule moratorium, aircraft design had been making steady, albeit slow, progress, and by 1932 a major revolution was already in train. Wood and fabric were on their way out; the monoplane was replacing the old box kite; the undercarriage was retractable; and these and other developments all had a direct bearing on the armament position and called for corresponding development. The Royal Aeronautical Establishment at Farnborough were at work on one or two experimental jobs, but apart from that the Royal Air Force was almost wholly dependent on the Inter-Service Establishments at Woolwich, Enfield, and Borden, all of which were under the control of the War Office. There was no one executive authority, and the only co-ordinating body was the Ordnance Board, which itself had no executive authority. I shall never forget my first attendance at the Ordnance Board. One found it hard to believe that in the twentieth century there still existed such

[4]

organisations with traditions and methods so utterly unsuited to meet the need for rapid decisions essential in coping with the changing conditions of air warfare. The meeting of the Ordnance Board reminded me of nothing so much as of the tea party in *Alice in Wonderland*—except that there was certainly more than one dormouse.

In 1934, having served two years at Eastchurch, fathering air armament, I was appointed to be Director of Training under the Air Member for Personnel, Air Marshal Sir Frederick W. Bowhill. The Armament Branch came under my directorate, so I was able to give some support to that devoted little band of armament officers in their struggle against complacency and ignorance. The other main task before me in the new directorate was a more than tenfold expansion of the Flying Training Organisation, to meet the growing expansion of the Service. Over a period of years the Secretariat under the Air Member had acquired immense power, which was exercised quite justifiably to ensure maximum economy. The financial implications of the expansion must have appeared highly alarming to my civil servant opposite number, and frankly I foresaw some pretty tough battles ahead. In particular it appeared peculiarly difficult to convince the gentleman of a real, practical need for a reserve of pilots. Fortunately I had an inspiration. There were already a number of flourishing Flying Clubs which were, in fact, also Flying Schools, and I was always being told how much more efficient and economical civilian organisations were, 'run on business lines'. It occurred to me that we could make use of this idea. I told my opposite number that I accepted this principle of civilian organisations (Civil Flying Schools) as being the most economical method of providing for the necessary expansion, but subject to certain conditions. The conditions were that the instructors must be fully qualified and categorised Central Flying School Instructors, subjected to an examination at the outset and at intervals thereafter. The Central Flying School was to provide a travelling Examination Board, keeping continual check on the standard of instruction. At the outset I think I was regarded with considerable suspicion on both sides. The civil servant thought I had pulled a fast one. I had. The Service side was uncertain whether the standards would be adequate.

The key to this problem was, of course, the Central Flying School, that remarkable organisation which for years had set standards universally accepted as being A.1.

*

On 9 October 1936, I was posted to Singapore to command the Far Eastern Air Force—a wonderful tonic to be with squadrons again. The Command stretched from Hong Kong and Borneo in the east, to Siam and Burma in the north; all of which, when coupled with the Dutch East Indies, afforded wonderful scope for Cook's Tours, which could quite plausibly be called 'Showing the Flag'. My predecessor had made full use of his opportunities. I did not feel it incumbent on me to follow in his social footsteps, but rather to concentrate on training exercises, especially those in company with the Navy.

I doubt whether there were many people who realised, when they were enjoying the social activities of Singapore, Kuala Lumpur, and Rangoon, that they were seeing the last flickering lights of the way of life immortalised by Kipling. Whether Sir Shenton Thomas, Governor of Singapore, had any premonition of the tragedies in which he was later on to be involved, I know not, but he was in a most invidious position. As Governor, he was nominally Commander-in-Chief of all forces, but without any real authority. The three Service Chiefs took their orders direct from Whitehall, and this was at a time when one of the most bitter inter-departmental wrangles was going on in Whitehall—big guns versus big Navy and naval base versus aircraft.

Shortly before being recalled to the United Kingdom in 1938 for other employment, I attended two ceremonial occasions which, to some people, would appear to be further milestones on the road to ruin; the 'opening' of the naval base and the completion of the first of the big gun turrets. To me, even at that time, there was something pathetic about the 15″ gun turret. General William Dobbie was the 'fortress commander', and to him the completion of the first installation was really a Red Letter Day. I was invited to attend the ceremony. We first went underground to view the mechanism of the turret, the loading device and so on—an impressive sight which, however, lost a little of its effect when

[6]

one saw marked across the huge breach a broad arrow and the figures 1915. I am afraid I rather unkindly asked Dobbie whether 1915 was the best they could do for him. The first round was to be fired by a push button in the open, some way behind the line of fire. The General asked me if I would fire the first shot. I declined the honour, and am afraid I could not resist saying that I did not feel that the gun would ever fire in anger, for it covered the main entrance to the Singapore Straits, and one would not expect an enemy to break in the front door.

As regards aircraft, there was an extensive programme of new aerodromes covering Malaya, Sarawak, and British North Borneo. On the map, the ring of proposed airfields looked impressive. All but two or three had no ground defences, and as a result were simply hostages to fortune ready to be plucked by the Japanese at any time they wished.

I can see little justice in hunting in the Far East for scapegoats. To my mind there is no need to go farther than Whitehall to apportion the blame.

*

I first met Wilfrid Freeman when I was a flight commander in one of his squadrons, and subsequently squadron commander, in 1916 and 1917, in his wing. I think he was rather intrigued to come across one of his pilots busy in his spare time correcting the proofs of a small book on Naval History which the Cambridge University Press were about to publish[1], and for which Freeman promptly labelled me 'Tirpitz', after the German Grand Admiral—a name which he continued to use right through. He had a very quick, and sometimes impish, sense of humour, and whether playing chess or gossiping about books, music, politics, he was wonderfully refreshing and a relief from the general hearty cheerfulness of an R.F.C. mess. He was not willing to suffer fools gladly and could perhaps be a little intolerant at times, but his judgment of individuals was shrewd, and as Air Member for Development and Production in those critical days of 1938 to 1940 there was certainly no time to be wasted on fools. He was able to imbue the Ministry with a due sense of urgency

[1] *The Navy of the Restoration* (Cambridge University Press, 1916).

[7]

without panic. Freeman also possessed to a remarkable extent the gift of inspiring confidence and attracting loyalty. He established a team spirit of mutual confidence and understanding between the Air Ministry and Industry such as we never had before or since. On that foundation was built the whole of the expansion. Without it there would have been nothing but chaos. Few people appreciate the supreme debt that we all owe to Wilfrid Freeman for his courage and leadership during those three years.

In July 1938 I got my orders to report back to the United Kingdom 'forthwith'. Forthwith meant an immediate passage home in one of the Empire Flying Boats, the most comfortable air journey I have ever had. The ability to walk from one deck to another or to stand, leaning on the hand-rail, looking down at the passing scene below, gave one an air of luxury not to be experienced in any modern aircraft.

I was appointed to a new post, Director-General of Research and Development, virtually Deputy to Freeman, my role being to relieve him of all the research and development work so that he could concentrate on the immediate problems of production. Most of the subjects which concerned me in my new directorate were subjects with which I was already familiar from my experience as Director of Training, and very largely they consisted of air armament in one or other of its many branches. But the whole tempo of development had altered drastically. Scarcely a month would pass without some new demand for the adaptation of an existing weapon to meet some special condition; or alternatively, the development of a new weapon for such a purpose.

'Changed ideas', I wrote in a minute to Freeman, 'regarding operational requirements, have been accompanied by various *ad hoc* experiments carried out by commands, groups, and some units. Many of these were carried out without any reference to the Armament Directorate, some against the advice of the Armament Officers and the staff; examples are the modification of the arming of the G.P. (General Purpose) bomb and of the S.A.P. (Semi-Armour Piercing) bomb, and the low dropping of the 40-pound bomb. To carry out such experiments without using the technical knowledge and experience which is available, is not a short cut to anything except to casualties!' If instances such as these can

[8]

be put down to misjudged enthusiasm, what is less excusable is the ignorance which in September 1939 briefed a costly bombing attack on ships at Wilhelmshaven to be carried out at low altitude. This was a new operational requirement for which neither had any of the personnel been trained, nor had the appropriate equipment (bombs, fuses, or sights) been designed. Some, at least, of our casualties were due to aircraft being hit by their own bombs.

It must also be remembered that there were no facilities for testing ammunition or bombs to ascertain their effectiveness against the wide variety of targets which would present themselves in war; nor were there any means for developing gun and bomb sights to meet changing conditions. One priority project which suffered particularly from the lack of appropriate ranges was a stabilised bomb sight which Royal Aircraft Establishment were fathering—the Americans had for some years had their Nordern stabilised bomb sight which was very effective.

The fact was that during the years of peace we had let armament drag a long way behind aircraft development. I have always felt that our great mistake prior to the war was in thinking that it was possible soundly to consider tactics quite apart from armament. To my mind they are two sides of a coin. The aircraft with which we entered the war betrayed the fact that their armament, whether it be bomb gear or guns, was more or less of an afterthought. Not that afterthoughts are necessarily bad things. We had two prototypes of one of the three heavy bombers on which the rearmament programme was based. It was the Manchester—a twin-engine job with Rolls-Royce Vulture engines. For a reason which was obscure, the first prototype had spun in, so I went up with Freeman to Manchester to have a talk with Avros. The second prototype was running, and we both went up in the back seats for a couple of circuits (and afterwards were called fools for our pains!) We went in from the tarmac to the office of Roy Dobson, the chief designer, to talk over matters. It was clear that nobody liked the machine very much, and we gathered that Rolls were not at all happy about the Vulture. On the desk in Dobson's office there was a nice model of the Manchester. Before we got any farther on the subject, Dobson asked Freeman a direct question: 'I am told you have plenty of Merlins coming in. Is this right?' to which Freeman answered 'Yes'. 'Then what about this?' said Dobson, taking one of the wing tips off and adding an extra wing and an extra engine on one side and then repeating the process on the other side. 'How's that?' he asked. 'That' was the Lancaster—an afterthought that became one of the most successful and effective bombers of the war.

It was on the heavy bombers that the whole of our air strategy was based. The two remaining prototypes were the Stirling and the Halifax. Freeman and I had gone down to Shorts's aerodrome at Rochester, where the Stirling was being built. We were to see its first flight. When we got to the aerodrome there was the Stirling, looking huge, but somehow rather lop-sided. The undercarriage had collapsed. I don't know when I have seen a more pathetic sight, or more grown men on the verge of tears. The Stirling never became a real success owing to its extreme weight, and, consequently, its low ceiling. Freeman and I did not go and see the Halifax debut.

The Mosquito was another winner which was not in the book. The wooden 'uncatchable' bomber had sounded rather like a myth, but it was not. It was true. I remember Freeman ordering fifty Mosquitoes off the drawing board—a gamble, if ever there was one.

'Spot the winner' was one of the preoccupations of my Directorate. The trouble was, the field was so big and the number of potential winners so small. I found myself having to warn my staff that we could not afford to ignore any proposition. Many people would have dismissed as fanciful young Whittle's early claims. I can well remember Henry Tizard, on his way out with me to Lutterworth to see Whittle and his prototype of the first jet engine, trying to explain the difference between a jet engine and the old push-and-pull engine to which we were accustomed. I gathered that somehow the more difficult conditions got for the normal engine, the easier it was for the jet engine, and I remember remarking to Tizard that if anybody else had told me this story I would have regarded it as a confidence trick.

We went later to see the small machine shop which had been made available to Whittle on the first floor of the big shops of British Thomson-Houston. One of the Directors came round with us, and obviously was not particularly interested, if at all, in Whittle's idea, and kept on pressing us to come down on to the floor and see a *real* turbine—enormous things they were. His reaction made me think of an experienced ship builder (in oak) dismissing as foolish an early iron ship, and pointing to his latest wooden ship, saying—'Now, there is a *real* ship'.

My recollection of the first engine, or, rather, the test rig, was pure, unadulterated Heath Robinson. In an enclosure in one corner of what looked like, and I believe was, a derelict motor garage, was an iron framework on which was mounted a combustion chamber with an under-carriage connected to what looked like nothing so much as a giant trout-fisher's spring balance—a typical Emett design. But more impressive was the glowing combustion chamber and the blazing blue jet flame roaring out into the open, added to which the fact that the thrust developed was considerably more than optimism had suggested. Here was another gamble; a real war winner justifying the manufacture of an initial batch of engines and aircraft to match, straight off the drawing board.

At the other end of the scale, scores of allegedly war-winning devices were put up to us but, as I have said, we could not afford to ignore anything. There was always the possibility of a pearl hidden amongst the rubbish, but raking through the rubbish could be a very tedious job. Having adopted this policy of thorough investigation, it was, however, very frustrating to experience political pressure to continue with a project long after it had been proved practically useless. Mr. Churchill himself appeared to have a schoolboyish delight in gimmicks, 'war winners' as he called them. One particularly troublesome invention was what was called the aerial mine, of which there were two varieties; one a long mine to be dropped in front of enemy bomber formations, the other a short aerial mine, rocket launched, to provide defence against dive bomber attacks; the former soon proved impracticable, but the latter did appear to have some possibilities, and we proceeded with experiments until I heard from our team down in Devonshire that they were losing faith in the proposition; so I went down to see for myself. The very thorough and careful trials that I saw convinced me that it was a waste of time to continue, and I stopped the work in order to clear the way for other important and urgent tests. The Prime Minister ordered the trials of the mine to be resumed. In a fortnight's time, after further trials, the mine was discarded for good.

Another proposition which had been put direct to him, short-circuiting myself and my team, appeared to have a special fascination for Mr. Churchill. It was a floating mine weighing about 12 lbs. which was to be dropped in the upper reaches of the Rhine, float down, and interrupt the Rhine traffic by sinking the big Rhine barges. One of its best selling points was that it was going to be made out of bits and pieces which could be bought in a local ironmonger's shop. In fact, as regards its simplicity, in the form in which we saw it there were no less than 94 separate parts. The P.M. used to have special late-night sessions at which all the gadgetry was discussed and reported on—somewhat irreverently called 'midnight follies'. Time came when the finished mine was to be displayed, Winston bubbling over with delight at this exhibition of a new toy. It consisted of a cylinder with a buoyancy chamber and a charge of about 9 lbs. of high explosive, and on the top some spidery feelers to actuate the detonator. A fire bucket was brought into the room and placed on a rather attractive little round table. The bucket was filled with water, and the mine (uncharged!) placed carefully in the water. Winston proceeded to juggle the spider's legs up and down. To his obvious annoyance, nothing happened, and with a peevish comment it was removed. What finally happened to this gadget I don't know, except that it never did work.

There was one other famous potential war winner which, unfortunately, never came before me. In code it was known as Habbakuk. It was the scheme devised by Geoffrey Pyke for putting artificial ice floes in the Atlantic to serve as landing grounds. Since the idea was, I believe, primarily sponsored by Louis Mountbatten, there must have been something in the scheme. To the ignorant eye it looked like pure Jules Verne.

It is true that a number of the subjects which were pushed by Mr. Churchill at his 'midnight follies' were frustrating and time-consuming, and certainly did not merit the attention given to them, but let it not be forgotten that while some of his war winners proved to be non-starters, there were others which proved to be winners in every sense. It is possible that without his personal drive and enthusiasm behind the artificial harbours on the Normandy coast (Mulberry), that extraordinary operation would never have come to fruition. Indeed the whole question of the invasion of Europe might well have turned on the practicability of these artificial harbours in which Winston affirmed again and again his complete faith.

*

Throughout the whole of the Royal Air Force expansion, with its almost unlimited ramifications, there was a continual battle to establish and maintain priorities, the theory being that no effort should be expended on the subject unless it had been allocated a priority. This procedure was by no means infallible, but it did keep some pathways clear through the jungle of competing interests, operational, technical, scientific, financial, political and so on. There were some instances where one could sense a firm's long-term selfish interest at work, and on the other hand there were some remarkable examples of unselfish collaboration between rivals. I think, perhaps, that the most remarkable of these was the collaboration between I.C.I. and the Shell and Trinidad oil companies in designing and setting up a 100-octane petrol plant at Heysham.

One strange incident came to me. I was attending the Air Ministry Supply Board set up before the Ministry of Aircraft Production was inaugurated, when there was a proposal before the Board to establish a large Rolls-Royce factory near Glasgow. The Air Staff wanted it to get some effective dispersal. The production people wanted it to increase production on a scale required to meet the great expansion plan. During the brief sandwich-lunch interval, the Treasury official representative took me on one side and said, 'Look, does your department want this, or not? One of your people seems to try to think of every possible reason for not proceeding with this plan. I have come here with what is virtually a blank cheque.' A few minutes later our hostile Civil Servant buttonholed me and urged me to speak up against the proposition. He said it would take at least two years to get it going, and by that time we should have lost the war, and it would be foolish to waste money on military things now, from which we should never get benefit. The project was approved and the cheque completed.

*

A few days after the inauguration of the Ministry of Aircraft Production in May 1940, and the installation of Lord Beaverbrook as Minister, there was a story going round which was said to indicate the methods to be adopted by the new Minister. As the story goes, the Minister rang up half a dozen or so of the Managing Directors of big aircraft firms about three o'clock in the morning. He asked them where they were speaking from, and when they replied, quite naturally, that they were in bed, the Minister roared off at them for loafing about in bed when our fighter boys were fighting for their lives in the air. Whether or not this story is a true one, is, I think, immaterial. The parable is there, and the lesson is an obvious one. I have often been asked my opinion regarding the Beaverbrook régime. Did Beaverbrook really win the Battle of Britain by pouring out hundreds more Spitfires, or was it the reverse? My first answer to the story of three o'clock in the morning is to say that I think the shock treatment was worth a lot, and I think that for the first four weeks or more, Beaverbrook did a fine job in keying everybody up to a higher pitch of energy. As for the remainder of the Beaverbrook régime, that is a very different story, and it is sad that Beaverbrook's great qualities of drive and energy could not have been employed for the benefit of the Royal Air Force without descending to the depths disclosed in the letter which I wrote to the Secretary of State, Sir Archibald Sinclair, in November 1940, on leaving the Ministry of Aircraft Production and rejoining the Royal Air Force, and from which the following are extracts:

... I am compelled to state that while recognising to the full certain valuable steps that have been taken since the formation of the Ministry of Aircraft Production, the present organisation and working of the Ministry are such as gravely to threaten the efficiency of the Service and consequently the safety of the country.

Many measures which would have had disastrous results have been prevented after bitter argument; it has only been possible by devious methods to minimise the ill effects of other measures which could not be prevented. In May and June, the general instructions were that all research and development which could not produce results in the front line in a month was to stop, research and development staff were to be absorbed into production or disposed of. . . .

The wholesale withdrawal of development aircraft and pilots from the experimental establishments in May and June may have been justifiable in the emergency, but it, coupled with the continued opposition to work on Service aircraft in these establishments, has resulted in delaying developments of which the Service is in urgent need. . . . In such circumstances, the experimental establishments cannot properly meet their main responsibilities to the Service of clearing the new types. Some of the troubles now being experienced in squadrons with the Beaufighter, for example, could and would have been solved by A. and A.E.E. [Aeronautical and Armament Experimental Establishment] had they been allowed to carry out their proper function. . . .

More and more development has been handed over entirely or in part to the control of persons with no Service knowledge. . . . Various individuals, none with any knowledge of Service requirements, and most with no knowledge of the particular subject, have been placed in charge of specific items. . . .

The activities of these uninformed but well-meaning individuals are often harmless. . . . In general, the technical teams at the Ministry and the firms, thanks to their essential loyalty to the Service, carry on quietly with the work without undue regard to these 'comptrollers'. It is, however, necessary for me to point out that the definite and declared policy of the Minister and those in immediate authority round him is to pay no attention to the Service's requirements as stated by the Air Ministry. It is considered that the Ministry of Aircraft Production should be the judge as to what the Service should get. . . .

I have referred to the loyalty of the technical team, and I must emphasise that it is only that very remarkable loyalty which is keeping development going in the face of conditions calculated to undermine all team work and enthusiasm. Juniors are consulted and given instructions without reference to their responsible seniors, overriding decisions are made on external and irresponsible advice without consultation with those actually responsible for the work, conflicting instructions arrive from various sources; decisions, when wanted, are difficult and sometimes impossible to obtain because the chain of responsibility in the Ministry is rarely clear—in short, the present

[15]

organisation of the Ministry is chaotic and the methods employed by some of the principal authorities are such as to cause mutual distrust, friction and confusion. Work is done and urgent problems are cleared, but the effort involved is out of all proportion to the results achieved, the whole balance of the development programme is repeatedly disrupted with the inevitable resulting delays and an utterly unnecessary strain is placed on the staff. . . .

I do not underestimate the difficulties of obtaining absolute proof if an investigation is undertaken. The present administration of the Ministry of Aircraft Production is based on force and fear, threats are the very essence of its direction. Fear that overt opposition to the present régime would result in professional ruin will almost certainly prevent many individuals both in the department and in the industry from telling the whole truth and nothing but the truth. Nevertheless, it is, I submit, essential in the interests of the Service and the country that a drastic change be made with a view to a return to a rational and responsible organisation based on the principles of co-operation, loyalty and honesty, without which such a Ministry cannot perform its sole function, which is to meet the requirements of the fighting Services.

Those were my considered opinions nearly twenty-five years ago. I have since had plenty of opportunity of thinking over my experience with M.A.P. and I have seen no reason to modify my views.

The Middle East

NOVEMBER 1940 – MAY 1943

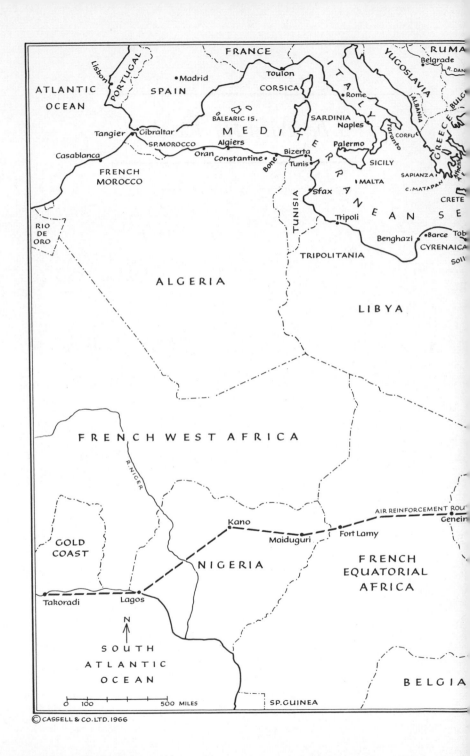

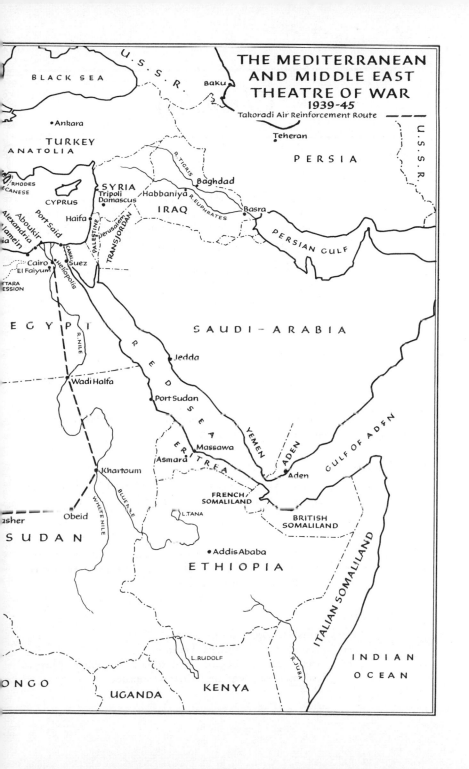

Chronology

1940

June:

3 Admiralty communiqué: 222 Naval ships and 665 other vessels had successfully evacuated 224,585 British and 112,546 French and Belgian troops from Dunkirk.

10 Italy declares war on France and breaks off relations with Poland.
All British and French forces withdrawn from Norway.

22 Signing of Franco–German Armistice.

24 Signing of Franco–Italian Armistice.

July:

4 Italians invade British Somaliland.

August:

15 Battle of Britain reaches climax.

20 Italy announces total blockade of British Mediterranean and African possessions.

September:

13 Italian Army under Marshal Graziani crosses the Egyptian border and occupies Sollum.

October:

28 Italian Ultimatum to Greece rejected. Italian troops cross frontier. Patras bombed and British help promised.

29 British troops land in Crete.

November:

3 British troops land in Greece.

11 Fleet Air Arm attacks Taranto.

14 Greek Army begins counter-attack which throws Italians back over the Albanian border.

1940
December:

9   First British Empire and Commonwealth offensive in Western Desert. O'Connor attacks across Egyptian border.

11   British capture Sidi Barrani.

12   British capture over 20,000 Italian prisoners.

1941
January:

5   British capture Bardia: over 30,000 Italian prisoners; 462 guns and 130 tanks captured or destroyed.

19   British troops advance into Eritrea.

21   Hitler orders armoured attack on Libya.

22   British capture Tobruk: over 25,000 Italian prisoners and 50 tanks taken.

30   British capture Derna.

February:

6   British capture Benghazi.

8   First German transports leave Naples for North Africa. British capture El Agheila.

12   General Rommel arrives in Tripoli.

22   Rommel attacks at El Agheila.

24   British Cabinet agree to send Expeditionary Force to Greece.

March:

9   Beginning of new Italian offensive against Greece from Albania.

24   British Somaliland cleared of Italians. Rommel occupies El Agheila.

April:

3   Pro–Axis coup by Rashid Ali in Iraq.

6   Germany invades Greece and Yugoslavia.

7   Rommel captures Derna.

9   Rommel captures Bardia.

13   Rommel encircles Tobruk.

14   Rommel's attack on Tobruk beaten off.

18   Indian and British troops arrive at Basra.

1941
April:

21 Greek Government inform British of inability to resist further and request withdrawal of British troops.
22 Withdrawal of British forces from Greece begins.
23 Signing of Capitulation of Greek Army in Salonika.
27 Rommel crosses Egyptian frontier and occupies Halfaya Pass.
28 Rommel captures Sollum.
30 Iraqi troops concentrate around R.A.F. aerodrome at Habbaniya.

May:

2 Completion of evacuation of British and Commonwealth forces from Greece.
    Iraqi forces attack Habbaniya.
3 R.A.F. bomb Iraqi forces around Habbaniya and aerodromes near Baghdad.
3 Iraqi troops occupy Rutbah and take over oil installations.
6 Iraqi troops defeated around Habbaniya.
12 German and Italian aircraft encountered in Iraq.
    Russia and Iraq establish diplomatic relations.
15 British recapture Sollum.
18 General Dentz announces French Army of the Levant will defend Syria against British.
20 Germany invades Crete.
22 R.A.F. withdraw from Crete airfields.
30 Iraq revolt collapses; Rashid Ali flees to Iran.

June:

1 Completion of evacuation of British and Commonwealth forces from Crete.
3 Mosul occupied by British.
8 Imperial and Free French Forces enter Syria supported by R.A.F. and Royal Navy.
13 Denial of tension between U.S.S.R. and Germany by *Tass* agency: 'There could be no misunderstanding between the two countries.'
15 'Battleaxe' launched by Eighth Army.
17 British withdraw in Desert after 'Battleaxe'
21 Free French occupy Damascus.

[22]

1941

June:

22   Germany invades U.S.S.R.

July:

1   General Wavell appointed C.-in-C. India; Gen. Auchinleck C.-in-C. Middle East.

9   General Dentz asks British for Armistice Terms in Syria.

25   Royal Naval convoy arrives in Malta after two-day battle.

August:

12   Atlantic Charter signed by Roosevelt and Churchill.

25   Iran invaded by Russian troops from the north and British from the south.

26   British take over Abadan and occupy oil installations.

31   British and Russian forces in Iran meet at Kazvin.

September:

12, 18, 28   Australians in Tobruk garrison relieved.

October:

19   Stalin announces state of siege in Moscow.

26   Last relief of Australian troops in Tobruk.

27   Russians counter-attack in Moscow area.

November:

9   Royal Naval Force annihilates two convoys (Italian) south of Taranto.

18   'Crusader' launched by Eighth Army in Western Desert under General Cunningham.
General Brooke appointed British C.I.G.S. in place of General Dill.

19   British reach Sidi Rezegh.

20   Fierce tank battles around Sidi Rezegh.

23   New Zealanders occupy Bardia.

24   General Auchinleck issues Order of the Day: 'Attack and pursue. All out everywhere.'

26   General Cunningham replaced by Major-General Ritchie in command of Eighth Army.
Tobruk garrison links up with Eighth Army.

[23]

1941
December:

4 General Wilson appointed C.-in-C. Ninth Army.
7 Japanese bomb Pearl Harbor and raid British Malaya, Manila, Shanghai and Hongkong.
Japan declares she is at war with Great Britain and U.S.A. since dawn.
Japanese landings in Thailand and north-east Malaya.
Japanese bomb Singapore.
8 All Allied countries, except Russia, declare war on Japan.
10 H.M.S. *Prince of Wales* and *Repulse* sunk by Japanese air attack.
11 Italy and Germany declare war on U.S.A.
U.S. Congress declares war on both and agrees on despatch of U.S. forces to any part of the world.
17 British advance to Gazala Line.
19 Italian frogmen damage H.M.S. *Valiant* and H.M.S. *Queen Elizabeth* in Alexandria Harbour.
British retake Derna and Mechili.
23 British retake Barce and Benina.
24 British retake Benghazi.
25 Hongkong surrenders.
29 Japanese bomb Singapore.

1942
January:

6 Rommel counter-attacks at Agedabia.
12 British take Sollum.
15 General Auchinleck assumes command of Iraq and Iran land forces in addition to those of Middle East Command.
23 Rommel retakes Agedabia.
28 Rommel retakes Benghazi.
29 Rommel advances on Barce.

February:

4 Japanese demand unconditional surrender of Singapore.
Rommel retakes Derna.
14 Rommel attacks again in desert.
15 Singapore surrenders to Japanese.

[24]

1942
April:

6   Axis raids on Alexandria and especially heavy raid on Malta.
7   Malta has 2,000th air-raid alert.
16 George Cross awarded to Malta.
29 Hitler and Mussolini meet at Salzburg, and decide on airborne invasion of Malta (Operation 'Hercules').

May:

7   Lord Gort appointed Governor of Malta.
11 Luftwaffe attack Royal Naval units in E. Mediterranean.
15 British forces retreat across Burmese–Indian frontier.
21 Hitler postpones Operation 'Hercules' (invasion of Malta) indefinitely.
26 Rommel resumes offensive in Western Desert by attack on Gazala Line.
28 Desert Air Force attacking Rommel's transport while tank battle rages around Bir Hachcim.
29 Fierce tank battle in the 'Cauldron'.

June:

3   Rommel attacks British near 'Knightsbridge'.
7   Rommel launches attacks on Free French at Bir Hacheim.
10 Free French withdraw from Bir Hacheim.
12 Fierce tank battle fought south-east of 'Knightsbridge'.
13 British tanks ambushed and destroyed at 'Knightsbridge'.
    British convoy leaves Gibraltar for Malta and another leaves Alexandria for Tobruk and Malta.
16 Gibraltar convoy reaches Malta.
    Alexandria convoy forced to turn back.
17 British withdraw from Sidi Rezegh, El Duda and El Adem towards Egyptian frontier leaving garrison in Tobruk.
18 Rommel sends armoured column towards Egyptian frontier.
21 Rommel takes Tobruk.
22 Hitler and Mussolini agree to continuation of North African offensive.

[25]

1942

June:

24 Rommel advances across Egyptian frontier towards Sidi Barrani.
British withdraw to Mersa Matruh.

25 General Auchinleck takes personal command in Desert.

28 Rommel takes Mersa Matruh.

30 Rommel reaches El Alamein.

July:

2 Rommel withdraws after First Battle of El Alamein.

24 Agreement reached between British and American Chiefs-of-Staff on 'Torch' landing in North Africa.

August:

11 Malta convoy; aircraft-carrier H.M.S. *Eagle* sunk.

12 First Moscow Conference.

18 General Alexander assumes command in Middle East in place of General Auchinleck.
Lieutenant-General Montgomery appointed to command Eighth Army.

23 General Wilson appointed G.O.C. Iran–Iraq.

31 Battle of Alam Halfa begins.

September:

30 Limited offensive by Eighth Army at El Alamein.

October:

23 Second Battle of Alamein opens.

November:

1 Eighth Army begins breakout at El Alamein.

3 Rommel's Afrika Korps begins to retreat.
Hitler commands Rommel to stand.

4 Axis forces in full retreat from El Alamein.

7 Allied 'Torch' landings in North Africa.

8 Eighth Army reaches Sollum and Sidi Barrani.

9 Admiral Cunningham appointed C.-in-C. Allied Naval Forces.

11 Eighth Army takes Sollum and Bardia.

12 British troops occupy Bône.
Eighth Army takes Tobruk.

1942

November:

14   Allied reinforcement land at Bône.

Eighth Army reaches Tmimi.

19   All French forces in North Africa join the Allies.

20   Eighth Army reaches Benghazi.

23   Russian Army breaking through German defences at Stalingrad.

December:

13   Rommel begins retreat from El Agheila.

1943
January:

14   Casablanca Conference.

23   Eighth Army enters Tripoli.

February:

23   Afrika Korps occupies defensive positions.

26   German forces in North Tunisia under von Arnim drive British back towards Medjez and Beja.

March:

9   General von Arnim replaces Rommel as Axis Commander-in-Chief, Africa.

May:

7   Allies capture Tunis and Bizerta.

9   Unconditional surrender of all Axis forces in north-east Tunisia.

12   Surrender of all Axis forces in North Africa. General von Arnim taken prisoner.

WHEN I got my orders to proceed to the Middle East, the opening scenes of the Mediterranean war had begun. In June 1940, when the Italians came into the war, the sphere of operations for the Air Officer Commanding-in-Chief Middle East was defined as follows: 'To command all Royal Air Force units stationed or operating in Egypt, Sudan, Palestine and Transjordan, East Africa, Aden, Somaliland, Iraq and adjacent territories, Cyprus, Turkey, Balkans, Jugoslavia, Greece, Mediterranean Sea, Red Sea, and Persian Gulf'—to which were to be added the 3,200 mile reinforcement route across Africa from Takoradi to Egypt.

The shortest route via Gibraltar was not usable by fighters except with the help of aircraft carriers to take them within flying distance of Malta. Alternatively, the route was by sea to Takoradi and thence by air on the Takoradi Route—that remarkable enterprise which was designed and destined to play a large part in the build-up of Air Force strength in Middle East. The third alternative route was round South Africa to Port Sudan. Whichever route was followed, at least two or three months must elapse between a decision to allocate to Middle East and the arrival of the aircraft, personnel, or stores, ready for operations in Egypt. Another factor was that Middle East was on the route to India and the Far East, with the result that in the event of an emergency and air reinforcements being required urgently (and in war, everything is urgent), the quickest way of getting air forces to Greece, Turkey, Russia, or the Far East, was simply to take from Middle East. In such circumstances, violent conflicts of priority were inevitable, especially when political factors came up against military practicabilities. The question of our policy towards Greece posed this dilemma in a most crucial and difficult manner. At the beginning of October 1940, when it became clear that the Italians were going to make inacceptable demands, the Greek Government begged our Minister in Athens to impress on the Foreign Secretary, Lord Halifax, the deplorable

[29]

consequences to us if, in spite of our guarantee, Greece were to be overrun; to which the Foreign Office told our Minister that he might assure the Greek Government we were prepared to give all assistance in our power immediately she was attacked, that such assistance must be confined mostly to naval action, and that we could not promise air assistance.

On 23 October, Air Marshal Longmore, A.O.C.-in-C. Middle East, in reply to various appeals from the Greeks for help, pointed out that the extent of existing commitments and slender resources meant that he was not in a position to provide any direct air assistance to Greece. With this Wavell, the Commander-in-Chief, had agreed. On the 28th, war between Greece and Italy began, and immediately there was much comment in Athens about the absence of British aircraft. On the 31st, Longmore signalled to the Prime Minister:

> It seems that it has become politically absolutely essential to send a token force to Greece, even at the expense of my Forces here. I have therefore arranged to despatch to Athens without delay one Blenheim Squadron.

to which Mr. Churchill replied:

> ... you have taken a very bold and wise decision. I hope to reinforce you as soon as possible.

On 1 November, Anthony Eden, now in Cairo, signalled after conversations with General Wavell, Admiral Sir Andrew Cunningham, Sir Miles Lampson (the British Ambassador) and Longmore, that it was clear we must expect further persistent calls for aid to the Royal Air Force and the Army for Greece, and it seemed essential that we should clear our minds on the main issue at once. His conclusion was that we could not from Middle East resources send sufficient air or land reinforcements to have any decisive influence on the course of fighting in Greece. To send such forces from the Middle East or to divert reinforcements now on their way to Middle East or approved, would imperil our whole position there. He thought it would be bad strategy to allow ourselves to be diverted from this task, and unwise to employ our forces in fragments in a theatre of war where they could not be decisive. To this, Churchill replied that the Greek situation must be held to dominate others now; and he followed this up on 3 November by saying that however unjust it might be, a collapse of Greece without any effort by us would have a deadly effect on Turkey and on the future of the war. 'Surely,' he wrote, 'effort must be made to aid Greece directly, even if only with token forces.'

The following day, Longmore signalled to Air Chief Marshal Portal, Chief of Air Staff, saying that if the political considerations overruled the recommendations of Eden, and if it was decided in London to order increased air assistance from Middle East, he would propose to send one Blenheim squadron, but he hoped he would not be called upon to provide further fighters from Middle East. Longmore referred to the time lag between the date of decision at home to despatch air reinforcements and the date on which such aircraft became operationally effective in the Middle East. On the same day the Chiefs-of-Staff telegraphed that it had been decided that it was necessary to give Greece the greatest possible material and moral support at the earliest moment. Since nothing from the United Kingdom could arrive in time, the only course was to draw upon resources in Egypt and to replace them from the United Kingdom as soon as possible. They therefore directed that three Blenheim squadrons, including the one already sent, and one Gladiator squadron, to be followed by a second the moment the strength in Hurricanes permitted, should go to Greece as soon as properly defended aerodromes were ready. All essential personnel, transport, equipment and ancillary services for these squadrons were to be provided from Middle East.

Whether the decision to send forces in to Greece was an act of courageous wisdom or one of tragic folly must remain a matter of opinion. It is easy enough to be wise after the event, and to point to the Greek campaign as yet another example of our attempting to honour a guarantee with inadequate military forces, a proceeding which involved expensive improvisation and entailed an aftermath of grim losses, the effects of which extended to the Desert campaign, and even at times endangered the security of the main base in Egypt. On the other hand, it is fair to point to the heavy losses the Germans suffered in Greece, and particularly to the Pyrrhic victory of Crete. It is also fair to quote the effect of the Greek campaign in delaying the launching of the German attack on Russia by some five weeks— a delay which resulted in the onset of the Russian winter before the Germans were able to achieve any decisive result.

*

When I joined Middle East Air Command, Longmore assigned to me, as his Deputy, particular responsibility for supervising the operations in the Western Desert and Egypt. I had consequently no direct personal dealings with the negotiations regarding Greece and the operations there. Nevertheless, I had ample grounds for realising the way in which diversions to Greece were sapping the strength of the Command as a whole, and in the Western Desert in particular. I had, therefore, very strong reasons for being closely concerned in the progress of events in Greece. I was under the impression that this was one of those cases of a politician (Eden), over-riding the military (Wavell). One can see now that nothing could be farther from the truth. The boot was on the other foot. It was the military commanders as much as the politicians who felt that the political considerations were overriding. My own feelings in the matter were, and have remained, firmly engraved in my mind. I was under no delusion as to the possibilities of success in Greece. I had very good reasons for seeing the dangers, and yet, illogical as it might seem, I was convinced that we had taken the right step as regards Greece. I know one factor was particularly strong in my mind, and that was the possible effect on the United States and their attitude towards us if we went back on our guarantee to Greece. I knew how important it was that nothing should endanger the programmes for the supply of munitions, and particularly aircraft, plans which were being very actively drawn up, and which might very well fall through if the United States lost their faith in us.

*

I was in Harrogate in late November 1940 when I had a phone call from Wilfrid Freeman, who had recently given up M.A.P. to become Vice Chief of Air Staff, saying that Arthur Longmore had asked that I should be sent out to help him as his Deputy. Would I be willing to undertake that job? The answer was only too easy. Would I not! It was fixed that I should go at the earliest possible moment that a passage could be arranged. Later that same day I had another call from Wilfrid Freeman. My posting to Middle East was off. Apparently the Prime Minister had stepped in and refused to agree. Owen Boyd was to go instead. So that was that!

A few days later I was up at Barrow to see the trial of a new 40-mm. aircraft gun which Rolls-Royce had designed and made. On my way back to London by train I had to change at Preston. Preston Station at one o'clock on a winter's morning, under wartime conditions of black-out, was no joy. Moreover, the London train was apparently subject to considerable but un-specified delay, owing to an equally unspecified 'incident' up the line. However, there was a restaurant open, in which after a struggle I managed to get a cup of hot coffee. While standing at the counter, my eye happened to catch the remains of an evening paper, and the big headlines—'AIR CHIEF CAP. . . .' Examination of the scrap of paper told me that Owen Boyd had forced landed in Sicily. I remarked to my colleague: 'That means me for Middle East within four days.' It did!

Noon, on 30 November, found me making a rough-sketch note of my final glimpse of England; a bit of golden coast and light seen as a distant gleam, framed by dark, lowering clouds and sullen seas. I was travelling in an Imperial Airways flying boat, booked through as passenger 'Mr.' Tedder to Lagos, via Lisbon and Freetown. I had decided, when I was planning my passage to Cairo, to go out via the Takoradi Route. I must admit that quite apart from the undoubted practical value to be derived from going over the reinforcement route oneself, there was the exciting prospect of girdling the greater part of the African Continent with all its infinite variety. It may well be that my escape from the intrigues that permeated the Ministry of Aircraft Production served as a supreme tonic and refreshed my powers of perception. Be that as it may, the fact is that far more than usual, many incidents and impressions during this journey engraved themselves in my memory; the dramatic contrast between the drab gloom of an English November and the sparkling clarity of Lisbon and Estoril with their many-coloured shuttered windows and beach tents; the chance meeting with an English bishop, last met in Borneo, who had just completed a six weeks' tour in the United States, and who remarked that many Americans he had been meeting were now more British than the British; then the fourteen-odd hours flight to Bathurst, including six hours without sight of land, until suddenly Venus blazed out as the morning star and confirmed that we were on the right course. Bathurst—a lonely little outpost on a small peninsula at the edge of the widespread swamps of the Gambia Estuary. The acting Governor and his wife—an American; cheerful and philosophic, despite the unpleasant proximity of a very hostile Vichy Governor at Dakar. The previous night, Dakar had broadcast a most virulent attack on Britain, to which they had added point by a number of Glenn Martin flights low over Bathurst, including two while we were taking off. It occurred to me that they might have ideas of being funny at our expense. If they had done so, they must have thought better of it, because there was no interference.

Freetown gave me a useful and interesting glimpse behind the scenes of the battle of the Atlantic. The naval C.-in-C. and his Chief of Staff, Raikes and Jackson, happened to be old friends of mine—fellow students at the Imperial Defence College and Naval Staff College respectively. Two convoy escort commanders added interest, especially about the French Navy, as they said that the French Navy had reverted to their traditional hatred of us. A submarine crew they had captured, quite apart from hating us, were quite convinced that we were already finished, and were amazed to see London picture papers of recent date; they thought all that had been finished months ago.

Spectacular lightning, dramatic thunder and sheets of rain, and, during the intervals between storms, the whole steamy scene looking and feeling as though someone had had much too hot a bath and hadn't opened the windows—probably a quite unfair generalisation about Freetown, but I must admit that I left it with no regrets.

The last leg of my flying-boat journey from Freetown to Lagos was uneventful, but since we were flying at a thousand feet most of the way to take advantage of a nice following breeze, one got a

[34]

remarkably good view of the country and the contrasts; Sierra Leone, Liberia, Gold Coast and, just at Lagos, Nigeria, mostly thin jungle country with patches of park-like land and farms, the Gold Coast by contrast giving the impression of being much more developed and prosperous. A good bird's-eye view of Takoradi anchorage and the aerodrome with its red runways, and then, finally, down to moor in the lagoon at Lagos.

When we arrived at Government House, His Excellency Sir Bernard Bourdillon (who had spent much of his time in Iraq and knew many of our Service people), was having tea on the lawn under a huge tree. We joined the party. His Excellency was very friendly and wanted my views on the military effect of the Vichy and Dakar affairs on defence in West Africa, warning me that the G.O.C., Giffard, whom I was going to see the following day, would certainly attack me strongly for our not having provided at least one fighter squadron for the defence of Takoradi and Lagos. I told Bourdillon that I saw no prospect whatever of any fighter defence being available. Moreover, I could not regard the threat as being in any way a serious one. H.E. appeared to be quite philosophic about it. Not so Giffard, whom I saw for an hour's interview at Accra on my way back to Takoradi. He appeared to think that we should have a complete fighter defence organisation covering the West Coast, from Gambia to Nigeria, complete with fighter squadrons. I had to disillusion him, and tried to explain the position as sympathetically as possible—not, I fear, with any notable success.

※

My natural wish to study the working of the Takoradi Route was sharpened by the fact that the establishment of such a route had been and was a subject of considerable controversy. It was alleged, justifiably, that the establishment three years earlier of a weekly civil air service from Lagos to Khartoum was not a firm foundation on which to base a military reinforcement route involving for each aircraft some four thousand miles of formation flying. Much of it would be over practically unmapped country under conditions varying from tropical humidity to desert sand, and it called for repair and maintenance facilities at intervals along the route. It was, indeed, a formidable task that faced Group Captain Thorold when he landed at Takoradi with an advance party in mid-July 1940. Not only had the port to be adapted for a special function and facilities provided on the aerodrome for the erection of aircraft, but the aerodrome itself had to be enlarged and adapted.

I went all round Takoradi pretty thoroughly, including the arrangements at the port, and was very impressed by what Thorold and his people had done. The whole show was a first-class piece of improvisation, from the devices for off-loading the extremely awkward Blenheim cases, to the excellent accommodation fixed up for the troops. The whole atmosphere struck me as being excellent, and they were all clearly imbued with the urgency of passing every aircraft up the line as quickly as possible. They had had many obstacles to overcome, particularly as regards shortages of tools, A.G.S. parts, and so on. In the meantime, pending the receipt of the necessary stores from the U.K., the workshops and garages of Sierra Leone, Gold Coast, and Nigeria had been thoroughly scoured to fill the gaps. The establishment and supervision of the staging posts at varying distances between Accra and Khartoum was an additional responsibility. They had a dual role to perform. First, to service the aircraft passing along the route, and secondly to provide wireless facilities to assist navigation. The object of the servicing parties was to keep the flow steady and avoid hold-ups. This was to prove easier said than done. When widespread engine unserviceability was experienced, due to the severe operating conditions, this was to provide easy meat for hostile or ignorant critics. The fact remained, however, that the aircraft did get through to Egypt.

Navigation also presented a serious problem. The maps over long stretches of the route were practically useless, and the key was efficient W.T. (Wireless Telegraphy) and D.F. (Direction Finder). One of the first convoys was lost (one Hurricane crashed and five scattered wide) due to failure on the part of an inexperienced wireless operator in the leading aircraft.

The flow of aircraft was organised in formations of six fighter aircraft, led by a twin-engined aircraft with a complete crew to serve as shepherd. We were very fortunate in the early stages to have the services of a number of very experienced Polish pilots, and they did grand work. I did, however, think it wise to warn the Air Ministry that many of the Poles would get restive if they were kept too long off operational flying.

Having completed my visit to Takoradi, I arranged to proceed along the route to Khartoum in an aircraft which was showing the route to some of the Poles. We did it in three stages: Kano, El Fasher, and Khartoum. At Kano, in the evening, we were greeted by the local policemen in long, blue cloaks and red cummerbunds; a very effective kit. The head man, or sergeant, at Kano was an especially fine-looking man—very black, with a fine profile and an air of dignity and character. Before we took off from Takoradi, our pilot had briefed me about the route and emphasised the necessary dependence on D.F., particularly on the stretch between Fort Lamy and El Fasher.

He said that without D.F. that particular leg was a gamble, and I was now able to see from the air how true that statement was. Nearly seven hundred miles of sheer nothingness; brown country, streaked with dry water-courses and dotted with bush; maps absolutely useless; nothing shown on them for the most part, for two hundred miles at a stretch, and where something was shown, it was obviously incorrect. I must say I would have hated to have to do that trip without wireless. The Polish navigator and I spent our time trying to keep a check on our position—good training for him. We made our landmark at Genelna accurately, and went on over a range of hills of up to 6,000 feet at El Fasher—glorious, rugged, and sparsely wooded country.

El Fasher was a different Africa; the first flavour of the Africa of Sudan and Egypt. The Acting Governor, with whom I stayed, seemed to be mainly concerned about his golf and his polo, which proved to be an unexpectedly interesting subject. One of the factors which had concerned me over the questions of the route had been that of the morale of officers and men isolated from the rest of their Service and from general civilised life— far from what are normally regarded as the essentials. In practice, so far as I was able to ascertain, the personnel of the staging posts were by and large extremely happy. They had in most cases used initiative to improvise various amenities. The most interesting case was the one which I came across at El Fasher. There it appeared that although none of the men concerned had ever ridden a horse before, they had taken to riding, and as a result were developing quite a passable polo team.

El Fasher was to me, with my arrival in Sudan, virtually the end of the Takoradi Route, and the beginning of my service in Middle East Command. I have never forgotten sleeping out that night on the roof with nothing but the stars above and around, stars such as I have never seen before or since. If I had not been so sleepy I would have lain awake for hours watching them swing slowly over. I awoke a few minutes before four to see the false dawn—the Zodiac light like a great streamer reaching almost to the zenith—and to hear all the cocks near and far announcing the new day. I awakened later to meet the real dawn, never having felt so fresh.

2

NO. 203 Group, commanded by Air Commodore Slatter with Headquarters at Khartoum, was to provide me with my first glimpse of that long list of responsibilities allocated to the A.O.C. and a foretaste of some of the problems which were facing, and were to face, R.A.F. commanders throughout Middle East.

In reporting to Freeman on my two days' visit to all the squadrons including South African and Rhodesian, I commented;

It is amazing what the fellows are getting out of the decrepit old aircraft with which they are equipped—Wellesleys, Harts, Blenheim Is, Gladiator Is and Gauntlets. Self-scaling tanks, armour and many other necessities of the European War are practically unknown here, except in the Wellingtons and Hurricanes. No twin guns for Blenheims yet. The Italians in the Sudan evidently have a few really tough airmen, but our chaps have got their measure all right. The thing which has impressed me most as a whole is the amount of successful improvisation. The way in which half a pat of butter is spread over a very large slice of bread, and the juggles which have to take place daily to filch a machine here, or wangle one there, to fill an immediate gap in the Front Line, are amusing but a trifle disturbing. Generally speaking, you can take it that everyone here is determined to make, and is in fact succeeding in making, the utmost of our limited resources. The spirit amongst all those I have met is quite first rate.

In writing to Longmore about this time, Harold Balfour, the Under-Secretary of State for Air, expressed the admiration felt at home for what the Royal Air Force was doing and had done in the Middle East and in Greece, and ended his remarks very aptly: 'I feel inclined to say; never has so much been done with so little equipment by such a small force.'

I completed my journey to Cairo as I had begun it—in one of

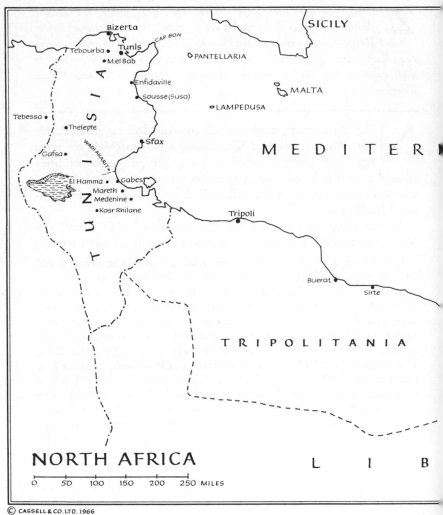

SICILY

Bizerta

CAP BON

Tebourba · Tunis

○ PANTELLARIA

· M.el Bab

Enfidaville

Sousse (Susa)

ꝏ MALTA

Tebessa ·

○ LAMPEDUSA

· Thelepte

Sfax

M E D I T E R

Gafsa ·

WADI AKARIT

El Hamma ·   · Gabes

Mareth

Medenine ·

· Kasr Rhilane

Tripoli ·

Buerat ·

Sirte

T R I P O L I T A N I A

NORTH AFRICA

L I B

0   50   100   150   200   250 MILES

GREECE

N

C. MATAPAN

Maleme · SUDA BAY
· Heraklion
Sphakia
CRETE

NEAN SEA

Derna
Marawa · Bomba
Barce · · Gazala
JEBEL EL AKHDAR Tmimi Tobruk
·Benina · Mechili El Adem · Sidi Rezegh
huzl · Gambut
olluch · Msus Bir Hacheim Bardia Sidi Barrani Mersa Matruh
· Beda Fomm Bir el Gubi Sollum Maaten Bagush
· Antelat Sidi Azzeiz HALFAYA PASS Sidi Hineish
· Agedabia Capuzzo El Daba
· Sidi Omar El Alamein Alexandria
· Mersa Brega · Bir Sheferzen ALAM HALFA RIDGE El Hammam
I Agheila · Fort Maddalena

Qarabub
CYRENAICA Siwa QATTARA DEPRESSION
SIWA

Y A EGYPT

the Imperial Airways flying-boats. In this case it was the *Corsair,* a boat which had recently spent two or three months on a river in the middle of the Congo jungle as the result of a forced landing. It certainly didn't appear any the worse for this. I arrived on the Nile at Cairo on the afternoon of 10 December to be greeted by Longmore and the news of the beginning of O'Connor's offensive in the Western Desert. Longmore's curt comment— 'Glad you've come'—blurted out in a pause in our general conversation about the Command, conveyed a more genuine sense of welcome than any number of formal speeches could have done. It was comforting, also, to feel that judging by his early conversation we should be able to find much common ground—an essential, if I was to be of value as his deputy. It was clear that if the appointment of a Deputy Commander-in-Chief was in practice really to afford any real relief to the C.-in-C., there would have to be some fairly definite delegation of duties, and Longmore's scheme, with which I agreed, was for me to take over responsibility for Libya and Egypt as soon as I had got into the general picture. Naturally, owing to the ever-changing course of events, no rigid line of demarcation was either possible, or indeed desirable, but by and large this system worked well.

When I left the Ministry of Aircraft Production, I thought that I was going to escape from the incessant series of conferences which plagued that Ministry, only to find that on my first two full days in Cairo I had no less than four conferences. The subject of two of them escapes me. The other two were to be regular events —first, the Commanders-in-Chief's Conference, or Meeting, attended by Wavell, Longmore, and Andrew Cunningham, the naval Commander-in-Chief, on which, as recorded in my daily journal[1], my first impressions are perhaps not without interest: 'Longmore was undoubtedly the pick of the three in that he had knowledge of all three—land, sea, and air—and appreciation of the relationship between the three.'

The second conference was my first experience of what was known as the 'weekly waffle'. It was held in the Embassy by the Ambassador, Sir Miles Lampson. He was a huge, affable, bear-like

---

[1] 'Journal' refers to extracts from private letters written almost nightly to my first wife.

man. I felt he would do very well as a dean of a college. His office was a lofty, crowded, Victorian study, cluttered with furniture, books, photographs and flowers, and bits and pieces of all sorts. A striking life-size portrait of Kitchener, with very blue eyes, presided from over the fireplace, and there were similar portraits of Plumer and Allenby on the side walls. Lampson presided and the rest of us sat round in big armchairs. Wavell, General Cornwall, Longmore, myself, and two civilians made up the party. At first sight most of the subjects for discussion appeared to be little local problems not really concerning us at all. Nevertheless, since it looked as if I would have to take an interest in Egyptian affairs in so far as they might affect us, I thought the 'weekly waffle' could well prove quite useful to me.

Having thus made my initial contacts with the military higher direction, and with the diplomatic and political side, it remained for me to be introduced into the social side of Cairo. This was provided early during the first week by a lunch at the Embassy, where I sat alongside Lady Lampson; a small, vivacious Italian, who talked very County English with all the underlining of words—'*Do* tell me *all*. How *terribly* interesting,' accompanied by the vaguely wandering eye of the professional hostess. There was quite a bevy of people at that lunch, most of whom I did not know even by sight, except, unexpectedly, the wife of a colonel whom my wife and I had known in the garrison at Singapore. He was now serving in Crete and had found it impossible to get anything done. He could not even obtain the most elementary tools such as spades and shovels. Delicate enquiries, and they had to be delicate, coming as they did from a very new boy, elicited the dismissal of this colonel as a 'bellyacher' and rather a nuisance; a sinister shadow of coming events!

During that first week I recorded: 'I'm afraid one is not terribly impressed by the Army Command,' and again: 'With one or two notable exceptions one's first impressions are not inspiring.'

In these early days, I made it my main task to get around and visit as many of the units as possible in the Delta, with a view not so much of inspecting as of meeting and talking to as many individuals as possible of all ranks—including the Egyptian Gladiator Home Defence squadron. The time I saw them they had one flight up on an interception exercise, and I watched them land their Gladiators quite well. I rather shocked them by having a close look at the guns and ammunition in one of their aircraft.

I was especially struck by the Wellington squadrons and their keen young squadron commanders. One of them was No. 70 Squadron—my old squadron from January to July 1917—with the C.O. a real tiger called Webb. My note at the end of the day was— 'A great tonic to me to meet them all'. Knowing the vital importance of repair and servicing generally, it was also encouraging to see the standard of workmanship and the pressure of work at the depot at Aboukir.

It was while on my way to Alexandria harbour to pick up a launch from 230 Flying Boat Squadron that I got hung up for some ten minutes by a long crocodile of Italian prisoners—the column some five or six deep, snaking over the sand towards the road and into a new prisoners' camp along the shores of Lake Mariut; very short, weedy little fellows, in their blue-grey, mostly with great-coats, but some with blankets over their shoulders, and they seemed neither depressed nor cheerful, just apathetic. They were all white. They were being escorted by Poles, a fine-looking lot.

On 21 December, Longmore, having come back from a visit to the Western Desert, asked me if I would be willing to take charge of 202 Group for a week or so. Air Commodore Collishaw, who commanded the Group, had had 'flu and was coming up to Cairo to convalesce. Actual command for a week or so would give me an insight into that part of the job which I could never have hoped to acquire in any other way. I noted—'It will be grand to be really amongst the chaps again for a bit!' My journal, written at the Headquarters, Maarten Bagush, Western Desert, on the next day, records:

Well, here I am, 'in the field'—damn all field about it! Just a flat, dusty plain, strewn with small rocks and big stones, but two miles on one side a sea which varies from dark grey when the dust is blowing to an incredible Reckitts Blue midday, and glowing violet as the sun sets. On the other side, about two miles away, a sharp rise in the ground of some 200 feet, called the escarpment. Beyond the crest of the escarpment the Desert runs away to the south as level and as featureless as the sea. The Desert horizon is a dead straight line, unbelievably straight and level. It was about an hour and three-quarters flight here in the Q.6 [a Percival] this morning, and now across the corner of the Delta and across the Desert, and then about forty minutes skirting the coast. Interesting along the coastal strip to see the marks of the old Greco-Roman farms which people insist on calling villas. There are a number of them all along here, the outline of their square stone walls visible from the air. It has been a glorious day, brilliant sun and cloudless sky and a gentle, cool wind, and, fortunately, no dust—except when an aircraft lands or takes off and a long plume of coffee-coloured dust streaks away across the country.

The odd huts, tents, and semi-dugouts which comprised the headquarters were scattered all over the place, fifty to a hundred yards from each other. It was quite an adventure to walk in the dark to one's own hut from the mess hut, and I personally found stars quite useful. It was also quite difficult initially to sort out in one's mind the various officers who were members of the head-quarters' mess—some twenty or thirty people, Operational staff, Intelligence, Signals, Cyphers, Met., Doctors, Admin., two soldiers, a sailor, plus a visitor or two. On the occasion of my first stay in the mess, one visitor was a U.S. Army Air Corps Colonel who had just come back from a week or two in Greece, during which he completed a sortie in a Wellington and, incidentally, got frost-bitten.

The headquarters had just had a change in that the previous Senior Air Staff Officer, Grigson, had been promoted to Air Commodore, and was being relieved by Freddy Guest, who had been in Egypt for two or three years training the Egyptians. Grigson was a very good staff officer, but rather lacking in any sense of humour, and therefore inclined to be rather fussy. He was, however, famed for possessing a unique faculty for sleeping on his feet at any time after 6 p.m. I felt that Guest, intelligent and obviously with ideas, would prove an asset to the Group. One temporary member of the mess was a squadron leader— very Irish—who had been Attorney-General in East Africa. I never quite found out what his job was except that he had just come back from Sidi Barrani, saying that something must be done to control the looting of the masses of Italian equipment

[45]

which was spread over some eighty to one hundred miles of country. The Group was also fortunate in having three first-class liaison officers in the two soldiers and the sailor, who were clearly invaluable in arguing our case with their senior Services.

I resumed in the Desert the policy I had been following in the Delta; visiting units, meeting and talking with individuals of all ranks; and once again I was tremendously impressed by our high morale. 'Getting acquainted' may mean different things to different people. For instance, one squadron commander, when I said I did not think I had met him, said—'You have not met me, but I have met you. I was the fellow who let off the Chinese crackers at the Mess Dinner at Singapore while you were making a speech to the visiting Indian squadrons!'

On Christmas Eve I spent a couple of hours at a typical troops' concert and sing-song. Almost every squadron at some time during the week or so had contrived to organise a concert, and so give me an opportunity of seeing and meeting the greater part of each squadron. By and large the concerts were mostly the sort of sing-song the troops normally like, but thanks to an infiltration of people known as Palestinians, many squadrons had one or two very talented performers. The so-called Palestinians were a strange mixture. They were enrolled in the R.A.F. and wore a uniform, but were polyglot—mostly refugees, Poles, Czechs, Germans, and pure Jews. Some of them could talk four or five languages fluently; some could scarcely speak English. I spoke to one who had just been interrogating an Italian shot down a day or two earlier. The first thing the Italian asked was whether the roof of the hut was bomb-proof, and when he heard it was not, he was very anxious to know where the nearest trench or shelter was, and was very puzzled and worried because our fellows said it was a matter of no importance.

Our American Colonel's comment on a Squadron concert (I think it was 208 Army Co-operation Squadron), was quite interesting. He said he had been tremendously impressed by the silence of the troops, and their consideration to the Pole who had given us about ten minutes of Grand Opera (I had not recognised it, nor did I know in what language he had sung) and then about

[46]

fifteen minutes of violin (beautifully played) in which there was not a single air or tune the troops could have followed. A pretty severe test for a packed house of very cheerful troops who probably wanted to sing the latest chorus. The American said he dreaded what would have happened to a similar party in America. He remarked—'It was real fine of your fellows—we are too crude.'

This, my first Christmas in the Western Desert, was marked by the fact that it was my first experience of the Desert in one of its more vicious moods. For most of the night it had been rustling around my hut, and when I looked out in the morning it was to be greeted, not by a white Christmas, but by the Desert's own special brand of 'pea-soup'—blowing hard, and the dust drifting like snow; visibility often only a few yards. Everything was covered with a fine, very soft, yellow powder—though it did not feel soft with a thirty or forty mile an hour wind behind it. Eyes blinked and teeth gritted with the sand. Outside one had to wear goggles, and some people occasionally even used their gas masks. On one occasion I had the front mud wings of my car literally sand-blasted down to the bare metal in the course of an hour's drive against the dust.

*

On 7 and 8 January 1941 at Alexandria I met two individuals who were to play a major role in the Middle East campaigns, individuals for whom I was to develop great admiration and real affection; Admiral Cunningham and General Sir Claude Auchinleck. It is not without interest to me to read my first impressions of these officers, written at that time:

Off in No. 201 Group's speed-launch to the *Warspite*—the Admiral's flagship; all the usual whistles and trumpets, with Willis, Chief-of-Staff, waiting on the quarter deck for me. I had met him at Greenwich some years ago—a dry little man without much humour, but very competent. We had a *tête-à-tête* in his cabin on Malta and Alex. defence, and then a full meeting on reconnaissance. Quite satisfactory in that I was able to get them to face facts and be reasonable. Then along to the C.-in-C's cabin for tea with him and Willis. Cunningham is no chicken, but there is a tremendous lot of kick in the old boy yet! I believe that when bombs as big as grand pianos were falling around his ship, he was hopping about on the deck like a schoolboy at a display.

[47]

We discussed Malta. I told him a few things about dive bombers and experience with them at home. I quoted the Squadron Commander's description of them as being 'the answer to the Hurricane's prayer', all of which, Cunningham said, cheered him up so much that he began talking about going out to sea to look for trouble and shoot down some more of the bombers. A very refreshing old bird!

The next morning I had meant to go up to the desert, but when we got to Amriyia it was blowing very hard from the south-west, and the sand was drifting fast and getting thick. I found two soldiers, one brass hat and one colonel, waiting to go up in the Q.6 with us. I did not know who they were. I was distinctly off-hand as to whether there would be room for them and whether it was fit to go. After a bit I discovered the brass hat was Auchinleck passing through *en route* to be C.-in-C. India. Decent bird. Honest-to-goodness, I think, and a good deal of force of character. I liked him. After a talk we came to the conclusion that the desert was out, and we separated—he to Alex. and I to Cairo.

*

By mid-December 1940 it had been clear that the Italians had no prospect whatever of being able either to close the British route from Gibraltar to Alex. or to ensure their own safe passage from Europe to North Africa, and Hitler successfully pressed Mussolini to accept Fliegerkorps 10 to operate from Sicily and to control a passage through the narrows. This move brought quick results, and on 10 January 1941 the convoy coming from Gibraltar was heavily attacked; in particular the aircraft-carrier *Illustrious* was very severely damaged, and just managed to make harbour in Malta. There, for about a fortnight, the carrier, the docks, the other shipping, and the airfields in Malta were subjected to a heavy pounding by some two hundred aircraft. To counter this, Malta had one Hurricane squadron and two Wellington bomber squadrons—the odds often about four to one. It was against such odds that Malta accounted for some twenty German aircraft while suffering a loss of twelve. This blitz, the *Illustrious* blitz, was but the first of many which Malta was to have to endure and from which she emerged triumphant. While the *Illustrious* blitz was at its height, Tobruk collapsed under the assault of O'Connor's 7th Armoured Division, and as a result the string of aerodromes in Cyrenaica gradually became available. It became possible to fly single-seater fighters direct by air from Cyrenaica to Malta, and in view of the losses of Hurricanes in the blitz it was decided to send six direct from Gazala, west of Tobruk, thus initiating what came to be the inevitable theme song for the next two years: 'Give us the airfields in Cyrenaica and we can look after Malta.'

Meantime, the political pendulum of priorities between Cyrenaica, Greece, and Turkey, was swinging violently most of the month. The capture of Bardia on 3 January had drawn hearty congratulations to Longmore for his 'brilliant support of Army operations'. The congratulations had, however, a sinister undertone. Four days later, Churchill wrote that we should soon, as usual, be torn between conflicting aims. Probably four or five squadrons would be required for Greece, and yet we would have to carry the Army forward in Libya. These were the directions when the Air Force, having been operating intensely for weeks on end, urgently required relief. For instance, two of the Blenheim squadrons could, at the end of the month, only muster seven serviceable aircraft between them. The Chiefs of Staff followed up Churchill's signal by informing the Middle East Commanders that a German move through Bulgaria appeared imminent. They directed that once Tobruk was taken, help to Greece must come before all other considerations in Middle East. It need not, however, prevent an advance to Benghazi if the going was good. Longmore ordered two squadrons over to Greece, both of them at half strength; but he resisted the proposal of Portal that two or three Hurricane squadrons should go as well. Churchill's reaction was quite clear and emphatic:

Nothing must hamper the capture of Tobruk, but thereafter all operations in Libya are subordinate to aiding Greece . . . we expect and require prompt and active compliance with our decisions, for which we bear full responsibility.

On 30 January, the day the Australians marched into Derna, Longmore received a further signal from London. It informed him of a proposal to infiltrate ten to thirteen R.A.F. squadrons into Turkey (to counter German penetration into Bulgaria); these squadrons would, of course, come wholly from Middle East. The transfer was not to take place until the situation in Cyrenaica had stabilised, but would be at the expense of the operations against Italian East Africa, and any further help to Greece.

Before I left London I had received a friendly tip that anything I could do to soften the acerbity of some signals from Middle East would be in the interest of all parties, and I did come to a gentlemen's agreement with Longmore that I would have a look at top-level signals on those lines. Longmore's reaction to this latest and most violent swing of the pendulum was very outspoken:

> Your message received. Quite frankly contents astound me . . . I cannot believe you fully appreciate present situation in Middle East, in which Libya drive in full career and Sudan offensive into Eritrea progressing satisfactorily. Neither show signs of immediate stabilisation. Arrival of aircraft in Middle East all routes now hardly keeping pace with casualties.

I do not remember having actually seen Longmore's signal, but even had I done so, I doubt whether I would have attempted to persuade him in any way to soften it, despite the fact that the proposal was clearly inspired by the Prime Minister himself. It was at this time that I received Wilfrid Freeman's acknowledgment of my first long semi-official letter (describing my trip out via Takoradi). He expressed the view that letters of that sort were more useful to him, enabling him to appreciate the situation in the Middle East, than all the telegrams that came by hundreds to his desk. My reaction to his similar letters was completely reciprocal. I found them intensely informative, constructive, interesting, and provocative. They brought life into our communications. After pointing out the impossibility of meeting all the applications for fighter defence, Freeman, in his first letter, proceeded:

> Some of our recent telegrams to you must make you feel inclined to say that 'people who live in glass houses etc. . .', but here we do feel that the Greek frontier is important. Turkey is going to think that we will leave her in the lurch, if by any chance she takes any action against German forces advancing through the Balkans, she will not in fact go into action. As you know, everyone is full of admiration for what has

been done in Libya, and I recognise that you must have been hard put to it to keep so many aircraft in the air. . . . I hope, with the aircraft that we have been able to send you, the position in this respect will be easier, but, of course, you will be short of spares of all sorts. You will only be able to keep going by living on parts filched from damaged machines. Eating into capital is the essential.

The 'admiration' referred to above led a lot of people to urge an immediate advance on Benghazi, and I had no doubt Wavell would be inclined to push ahead there. My own view was that an advance as far west as that would scarcely be worth while, and shades of Ctesiphon, Kut, and Townshend passed before me. The Germans, I think, would have liked to see us spread all over the world: threats of advances through Spain on to North-West Africa, through Italy and Sicily, through Hungary and the Balkans via Yugoslavia, Rumania, or Bulgaria, kept us guessing, and our diplomatists did not make it easier to select the probable course that the enemy would adopt because each and all of them cried 'Wolf, wolf!' whenever they had a conversation with any of their confrères. There were probably only two points that really mattered. One was to keep our base there secure, the other was to try and win the war in the Middle East.

On 21 January, the Chiefs of Staff swung the pendulum violently back to the west. They reviewed the Middle East policy in the light of the Greek refusal of immediate assistance by British land forces and of the arrival of German air forces from the Mediterranean. The capture of Benghazi they said, was now of the greatest importance, and it should become a strongly defended naval and air base. The importance of occupying Rhodes as soon as possible was also stressed. Middle East was told that a strategic reserve should be created with special reference to assistance for Turkey or Greece within the next few months, and that the first duty of the A.O.C.-in-C. was to maintain a sufficient air force in Malta to sustain its defence. The telegram did not say how any of these programmes was to be met. It took two or three days to digest, and on the 27th we replied that the equipment and reinforcements expected in Middle East in the next few months would go some way towards making it possible for the Army to meet the commitments laid down by the Chiefs of Staff, but this did not apply to the Navy and the Royal Air Force. Hitherto, the war had been conducted on an irreducible minimum force which had in fact been well below the danger line. These risks were less acceptable in the face of German involvement.

Towards the end of January the Chiefs of Staff arranged the despatch of three Glen (assault) ships and a mobile naval base organisation to Middle East via the Cape. Originally intended for an operation to seize Pantelleria, they were put at the disposal of the Commanders-in-Chief Middle East with the proviso that any action in the Ægean must be part of a combined plan dealing with the Dodecanese as a whole. The Commanders-in-Chief Middle East were firmly opposed to the idea of leaving the islands undisturbed until the middle of March when the assault shipping would be available. The Commanders-in-Chief's plan was to capture the island of Kasos (just east of Crete) and then Castelorizo. After the Glen ships arrived, they would capture Scarpanto as a preliminary to an assault on Rhodes.

An attempt to land on Kasos on 17 February failed owing to lack of information about the landing places and exits on the island. A week later, a force of Commandos landed at Castelorizo. One of the supporting ships was damaged by an air attack and withdrew. It had been intended to land a permanent garrison of troops from Cyprus, but after a series of misunderstandings and mishaps, they were now withdrawn to Alexandria. Another attempt was made. Meantime, the Italians had acted promptly and landed some three hundred men themselves. The resulting engagement cost the British about fifty casualties, and in the face of almost unopposed air attack it was decided to withdraw. The verdict on this inglorious affair has been pronounced in the Official War History with supreme tact: 'It was evident that there was much to be learned about the conduct of this sort of operation.'

How true!

*

During my brief stay at Maarten Bagush, commanding 202 Group, I had visits from General 'Jumbo' Wilson, commanding the British troops in Egypt, a huge, hearty man, whom I remembered as having met at Cambridge where he used to lecture on military subjects, and General Dick O'Connor, commanding the Western Desert Force, which in less than a fortnight had smashed the would-be Italian invaders and was now driving them back into Libya. I had formed the impression that G.H.Q. Cairo were regarding O'Connor's successes with mixed feelings. Naturally, everyone was delighted with the successes, but there was an element of nervousness. It all looked too good to be true: the Italian collapse was so utterly unexpected in the face of what was really intended to be only a reconnaissance in force. If that was the underlying intention, I suspect that from the very beginning Dick O'Connor was determined to achieve some positive results.

O'Connor had established his Advance Headquarters at Sollum, a good hour and a quarter's flight from Mersa Matruh where I went to see him. It was an interesting flight, though it is a feature-less country—flat, yellowish land, and all along to the north a line of electric blue Mediterranean. Sidi Barrani itself was nothing as a spectacle; one white-walled enclosure and a number of insig-nificant little buildings scattered around it. Nothing to indicate the fame which Kenneth Horne and the B.B.C. Light Programme were later to bestow upon it! To the west of Barrani, the roadways and tracks were more and more littered with abandoned vehicles, guns, and the like—all the varied jetsam which trailed behind a defeated army. To the landward side of Barrani, the escarpment begins to swing closer to the coast until at Sollum it comes direct to the sea, overhanging the tiny port of Sollum, and thence northward to the line of cliffs past Bardia. 'Both from the air and from the hill above it', I wrote at the time, 'Sollum is a beautiful little bay, tucked in under the escarpment at the end of a long, sweeping, curve of beach which fades away eastwards into the blue distance towards Barrani. Bare and barren, yes; but rocks and sand quite pink in the midday sun, and the sea in the bay almost emerald.'

The facility to land seaborne supplies at Sollum was of vital importance, affecting O'Connor's ability to keep up the momentum of his attack. It was this fact which led the Italian Air Force to make some attempts to interfere with his supply line, and in so doing provide our fighters, and in particular the Australian

Gladiator squadron, with some priceless opportunities of inflicting heavy losses on the Italians.

There were a number of abandoned Italian aircraft on the aerodrome above Sollum, but they had all been pretty well looted by the Australian soldiery, who had been rather like a swarm of locusts. I saw one C.R.42 in which the looter had been defeated by the metal skin until he had optimistically begun with a tin opener to cut out the rather nice heraldic design on the tail fin! I looked in on a bunch of Australian pilots who were brewing tea in a small mess tent. They were complaining that one of their aircraft had forced landed less than a mile away the night before (short of petrol but apart from that quite serviceable) and had been stripped by the soldiery. I remarked that this was what you had to expect from Aborigines—and beat a hasty retreat!

Then, on along the flat to Fort Capuzzo past the remains of what had been a very elaborate gateway across the frontier— 'the gateway of the Italian Army'. Capuzzo was nothing like as dramatic or ornamental as it may well sound in history, only the shattered remains of a Beau Geste fort; its outer walls were breached in many places, the buildings inside shattered, and great slabs of wall, washed with white and blue, thrown about in confusion . . . *sic transit!*

A day or so later I again went up to Sollum to take part in a conference with O'Connor. It was held in the most romantic setting imaginable, a huge Roman cistern cut out of solid rock; nothing visible on the flat, featureless surface of the Desert, except a small manhole. Through the manhole, down a vertical step ladder some thirty feet, and one found oneself in a huge cavern some thirty yards long and twenty yards across. Cool and still after the wind and dust above. Trestle tables dotted about on a yellow sand floor. Yellow light from the hurricane lamps on each table, and a narrow beam of yellow sunlight streaming down from the manhole above. Staff officers and others in all sorts of costumes from jerseys to sheep-skins—bending over maps and papers. Just like some pirate's lair. I told O'Connor he ought to get the War Office people to get a pictorial record of it. The movie people would have given anything for such a setting. I had no time or opportunity to make a note for a sketch myself.

On New Year's Eve, Raymond Collishaw came back to duty, and my time was up, and in the evening of New Year's Day I returned, very reluctantly, to the fleshpots of Cairo. 'I hate', I wrote, 'coming back to this place; still, it was grand having that opportunity of really getting inside the job out there, and being in direct touch with the squadrons. The best week I've had, from the Service point of view, for years.'

Collishaw, with his irrepressible 'gay aggressiveness', was the very epitome of the offensive spirit, and during those first months of the war in the Desert had by his widespread attacks succeeded in dispersing the Italian Air Forces and thus attained a considerable degree of air superiority. I classified him at that time as 'the village blacksmith in the village cricket match' with the warning that before long we looked like having to compete in a much more serious contest on a wider field than the village green. There is no doubt that Collishaw had his points, but on the other hand he was a 'bull in a china shop' with little of the administration without which operations cannot function properly. Moreover, he had a tendency to go off half-cock. To listen to Collishaw while plans were being drawn up for the next advance, one would think that the advance would be to Tripoli non-stop! I could not help feeling sorry for the Staff at 202 Group. Collishaw did not know how to use them, which left them feeling frustrated and miserable, and I wondered whether the change in methods which I had introduced had any chance of surviving. Guest, the new S.A.S.O., had just taken over, and I had made him and his Wing Commander Ops. draw up the operation orders for me. They managed to do the same for Collishaw—I only hoped that this would last.

There were some highly intelligent men on the Group's Staff; and I had been most struck by the quality and standard of the squadron commanders. I had made a point of seeing the three bomber squadrons' commanders at least once a day when I was with the Group, in order to explain and discuss our plans and the operations for the ensuing two or three days. They were a fine trio; young, keen, and intelligent, and needing a tight rein rather than a spur. I had to tell them that when we wanted bravery we would ask for it, but at the moment all we wanted was cunning. I think they saw the point: 'They were not used to having time to consider their tasks, or the opportunity to discuss them, and they did not mind showing how much they appreciated this.'

I had been interested, looking back, to see that Longmore had had twice to enjoin on Collishaw a greater economy in the employment of his limited forces; on the other hand, I also knew that he felt—quite rightly up to a point—that the man on the spot should be given as free a hand as possible. What I hoped was that instead of the lucky-dip sort of planning which had been customary up till then, the Group's Staff was now properly employed, and the A.O.C. would get put before him plans which were rational and economical. I also hoped that the squadron commanders would now have a much better understanding of the whole plan, and would adjust their operations in accordance with that plan.

On 4 January Bardia fell. A day or two later I took off from Bagush just behind a Bombay loaded up with six Italian Generals and a couple of dozen other officers, all exported from Bardia and bound for Heliopolis and prison camps. On the way back, above the clouds, we caught up with the Bombay and flew alongside it for a few minutes to give me an opportunity of making a sketch in my little book.

3

O'Connor's Headquarters–Beda Fomm–Rommel arrives in Libya–Rommel moves–Marooned in the desert–Midnight meeting with O'Connor –Priority to Cyrenaica–Eden and Dill visit Cairo–Reinforcements for the Desert–O'Connor and Neame captured–Germans attack Greece and Yugoslavia–Priority back to Greece–'The Army direction makes me shudder'–Tobruk besieged

IN the late autumn of 1940, Wavell's strategy had been to defeat the forces threatening Egypt and to knock out the Italian armies in East Africa, and with them the threat to the Red Sea. That accomplished, he proposed to build up forces which would help Greece, Turkey, and other Middle Eastern countries. The Cabinet and Defence Committee in London fully supported the Commander-in-Chief's desire to eliminate the Italian threat before German support reached North Africa, and the Prime Minister assured Wavell that the Government at home would sustain him in any well-considered, resolute action whatever its outcome. The Chiefs of Staff were at that time anxious at the prospect of a German occupation of Bulgaria and Greece and then of Turkish Thrace, a process which might end with an advance into Syria and even Northern Iraq. This would pose the threat to Egypt of a war on two fronts. We were not to know then that Hitler had rejected this operation as being unduly complicated. He was already thinking of Russia. The Cabinet decided that we in the Middle East must be prepared by the spring of 1941 to move north and meet a threat to Syria and Iraq, and to help Turkey, whose belligerency the Chiefs of Staff were most keen to secure. The rapid successes against the Italian Empire in East Africa, the breakthrough in the Western Desert, and the successes of the Greeks in holding off Mussolini's attack, did suggest for a time that there really was some hope that the strategy might be successful.

On 3 February 1941 I flew up to Tobruk, and thereon to Bomba where General O'Connor had pitched his headquarters. He and I had arranged that I would come up and be given an insight into his plans and timing, so that I could co-ordinate the operations of the heavy bombers with his own operations. He gave me an outline of the situation regarding supplies, which were inevitably a continual brake on his advance. He told me he had been in consultation with his 'Q' people very carefully, and as far as he could see it would be ten days before he could make a definite advance against Benghazi. I said I would adjust our air operations to fit in with his timetable. He then had to go on to Tobruk to sort out some supply headaches, but pressed me to stay the night at Bomba so that we could have a really good talk over the whole situation. I filled in the time by visiting an Australian squadron near Tmimi. When we joined up again at Bomba, I found that O'Connor was in a flaming rage—not in the least like his normal mood: 'Those bloody fools at Mechili have let the Italians slip through at night, although they could hear the tanks perfectly well. I am going down to Mechili at dawn tomorrow to drive them on!'—which is precisely what he did.

It was about a year before I had any first-hand account of what had happened at Mechili. Apparently, when O'Connor arrived there, he was quite brief and to the point: 'You are going to cut the coast-road south of Benghazi, and you are going *now*, repeat *now*!'

Remember, he had been told by his 'Q' people that it would take the best part of a fortnight before he could make a major move forward again. His 7th Armoured Division was in a very poor way mechanically, and could only raise fifty cruiser and eighty light tanks (two fresh armoured regiments were due in fact to come up as reinforcements). The stocks being built up at Mechili were still quite inadequate for a long march over rough country, followed by a battle. These were the odds which faced O'Connor, odds which he fully understood and accepted. He gave the order to 7th Armoured Division to move off at dawn on 4 February; it had only two days' rations and a bare sufficiency of petrol. On the evening of that day, O'Connor followed the armour in his staff car, determined to ensure that it operated with the utmost energy. His staff described him as like a terrier ratting. On the evening of the 4th, air reconnaissance showed the roads south of Benghazi crammed with Italian transport driving fast southward, and O'Connor decided to send a second cutting off force south-west to the coast road via Antelat, as well as due west through Solluch.

Early on the 5th, armoured-cars drove away from Msus towards Antelat. Later that morning the armoured-cars entered Antelat and found it deserted. They immediately drove on to Beda Fomm and had soon blocked the road. O'Connor's trap had closed with an hour to spare. The desperate Italian attempts to break through failed and early on 7 February the remainder surrendered. Graziani's army had been destroyed.

What next? O'Connor considered that further advance into Tripolitania was not merely possible, but should be done. He put his proposal to Wavell through Wilson, and Wavell immediately forwarded it to Whitehall—not, however, very enthusiastically: '. . . the extent of Italian defeat at Benghazi seems to me to make it possible that Tripoli might yield to a small force if despatched at once.' Three days later, Churchill banged the door on O'Connor's advance into Tripoli. Referring to Benghazi, he signalled: 'This does not alter, indeed, it rather confirms, our previous directive; namely, that your major effort must now be to aid Greece and/or Turkey.' In effect, the new directive, in closing the door to O'Connor and Tripolitania, opened the door to Rommel and Cyrenaica.

No time at all was lost in dismantling the hard-hitting force which O'Connor fashioned in the face of many difficulties during his six weeks' campaign from Sidi Barrani to Beda Fomm. The Western Desert Force (designated as 13 Corps since 1 January) was disbanded; 7th Armoured Division was back in the Delta with all its experienced personnel dispersed, being replaced by the inexperienced and understrength 2nd Armoured Division; O'Connor was in the Delta commanding British troops in Egypt, and in Cyrenaica a static command called Cyrenaica Command had been set up under General Wilson. I can well remember the atmosphere of unreality which surrounded the so-called Cyrenaica Command, and as far as I remember I don't think we could find a name for the Air Force Command in that area. Rommel landed at Tripoli on 12 February. His views regarding British opportunities are not without interest. On 8 February he wrote:

. . . leading units of the British army occupied El Agheila. . . . Graziani's army had virtually ceased to exist. All that remained of it was a few lorry columns and hordes of unarmed soldiers in full flight to the west. . . . If Wavell had now continued his advance into Tripolitania, no resistance worthy of the name could have been mounted against him. . . .[1]

But Rommel had no Balkan mirage to lead him astray. As early as February 1940, Anthony Eden, after a visit to Middle East, told the Cabinet that we were badly informed about the enemy's communications with North Africa which would be a serious handicap if German reinforcements were sent there. It is clear that Eden's report was near the mark, and the rate of German build-up at Tripoli took Wavell by surprise. Wavell did not consider that any substantial advance by the Germans was feasible, but Rommel was an unknown number. We can now realise from his own papers, that in making his advance he took a risk against his orders because the opportunity seemed favourable, and it soon became clear that we were facing a commander who thrived on a calculated gamble and on speedy strokes, a commander who possessed those qualities of leadership and drive which distinguished O'Connor, and it is one of the ironies of the War that the two were never opposed.

The Prime Minister presumed, wrongly, that Wavell was only waiting for the tortoise to stick its head out far enough before chopping it off. He telegraphed to the Commander-in-Chief with unconscious irony:

It seems extremely important to give them an early taste of our quality.[2]

In reply, Wavell pointed out that after the capture of Benghazi he had taken considerable risks in order to provide the maximum support for Greece. As for the Royal Air Force:

Longmore and his people give me magnificent support everywhere but there is never quite enough of them.[3]

The speed of the German build-up, and Rommel's high ability as a Desert Commander, provided completely new factors in

[1] Liddell Hart: *The Rommel Papers*, pp. 94-5. Details of all sources can be found in the Bibliography.
[2] Connell: *Wavell*, pp. 387-8.
[3] Ibid., p. 389.

our Middle Eastern theatre; but there was another factor, too. By the old standards, the successful naval engagement at Cape Matapan on 28 March, following the severe damage which Cunningham had inflicted on the Italian Navy at Taranto some months before, should have assured the Royal Navy command in the Mediterranean. We were to learn in the most painful manner that it did not.

The opening of Rommel's offensive could not have been better timed to exploit to the full the manifold weaknesses of the Allied powers' position in the Middle East. At the end of March we had to face, with meagre resources, actual or simmering threats in East Africa, Iraq, Greece, and the Desert. On Sunday 30 March I went up to Agedabia to see General Neame and Group Captain Brown, who were commanding in Cyrenaica. The former told me that if the Hun would give him another seven to ten days, he would feel much easier about the situation. He could not then know that he had but hours in which to prepare. The following morning I went by way of Derna to visit the heavy bomber squadrons at El Adem and Gambut and 73 Squadron (Hurricanes) near Tobruk, partly for the purpose of urging forward the attacks on Tripoli, some of which were being carried out by refuelling at Benina and some from airfields around El Adem. By then we knew that the coast-road from Agheila was packed with enemy transport which I forthwith ordered two or three Wellingtons to attack. Later that night, we received a garbled message to the effect that it was 'unsafe to use Benina for Heavies'. I decided to return to Barce to find out from Brown what was happening.

The journey turned out to be an eventful one. We were more than halfway on our journey when a bolt in our port engine gave way and the oil in the sump rapidly drained out. As the aircraft was fairly heavily loaded, we could not maintain height on one engine. We were just approaching unpleasant-looking country. The only thing to do was to land.

Our pilot, Flying Officer Holland, managed this operation admirably and came to rest on a faint track running along the crest of a narrow ridge which sloped upwards. I had been navigating and was fairly confident in deciding that our position was

22° 5' E, 32° N. There, sitting in the shade of one wing of the Q.6 at 4 p.m. on 2 April, I wrote in my journal:

My view is of a rather still, cloudless sky, miles and miles of bare, stony, yellowish country dotted with tiny clumps of dead silvery scrub, and in the distance a long line of bare hills, of which the only feature is one table top showing a little above the main horizon. . . .

Soon after we perched we heard, and saw, a couple of Hurricanes pass some distance away. Apart from that the only signs of life have been one or two pertinacious flies, two butterflies, a couple of ravens which looked a little sinister but on inspecting us decided we were not yet ripe, and a pretty little bird the size of a lark, which stood peering at us for nearly ten minutes and then went off in a vertical climb, showing a beautiful pale pink chest [a pipit *en route* to summer in England].

There were several choices. We could walk twenty miles southeast to Mechili, where we might, or might not, find a few troops; or walk some thirty-five miles west-north-west to a road where there should be some traffic; or sit and wait for air search to find us. Since our movements were somewhat uncertain, I doubted whether anyone would miss us until evening; but if we were missed in time for a search to be made that day, we might still reach Barce in the evening, whereas if we walked we could not hope to get in touch with our people until well on in into the following day. So we decided to stay put and to make some tea. We had seven Service water-bottles more or less full, rather part-worn but just 'potable'. Although we used a rag soaked in engine oil, the water took a long time to boil. After that, it was time to examine some of our emergency rations, biscuits, bully, Bovril, chocolate, chewing gum, and one or two pots of jam.

A Wellington passed some miles away and we fired a couple of Very lights. We tried unsuccessfully to make smoke with our fire, but the aircraft passed on its way. I had my camp kit with me, so I made up my bed and after a small drink of water and some of the emergency chocolate I turned in as the sun set, a glorious sunset at which I just lay and gazed. It was grand to sleep and to wake, as I did a number of times, under the stars, watching the constellations slowly swing round and recognising one old friend after another. It was cold just before dawn but I had plenty of blankets.

The day dawned cloudless and hot. A Lysander passed right over us during the morning but did not see us or our smoke smudge; nor did a Blenheim some distance away. We came to the conclusion that no one had missed us, for signal traffic was a trifle upset at that moment. Perhaps two of us had better start to walk, after all. I was very tempted, but since no one could hope to get to an aerodrome until late the following night, 4 April, I decided I would stay with the aircraft on the chance of being picked up. Our pilot, Holland, and Bray, a member of my staff, went tramping off to the north each with a water-bottle and some of the emergency rations. At that point things began to happen. A Blenheim came along some five miles away. We poured petrol on our smudge and fired a couple of Very lights, and to our joy the plane turned, came down very low, circled, put down its wheels and finally landed just on the edge of our landing ground. The aircraft turned out to contain a sergeant pilot named Dixon who was taking back for repair the Blenheim with a damaged sternpost. He was flying solo and had been smart to spot us. In landing he smashed his tail wheel and fittings and spoilt the bottom of his rudder. However, having handed over two of his three water-bottles, he made a fine take-off without doing any further damage. Three hours later Holland and Bray struggled back They had seen the Blenheim land and had just about come to the conclusion that the walk was beyond them and that air rescue was the thing!

After six o'clock that evening there was still no sign of anything coming to fetch us, and we resigned ourselves to another night in the desert. Three-quarters of an hour later, a Blenheim appeared and landed. It was our same Sergeant Dixon. He had collected another aircraft, spent over three hours vainly searching for us and in desperation had gone to his own aerodrome and had started to fly along the course from El Adem, knowing we were exactly on that course. We filled up all the water-bottles for Holland and the other member of our crew and left them some rations. Then Bray and I flew off with Dixon to Marawa, landing just after sunset.

I spent an hour or two talking to the aircrew of two squadrons there, and then set off by car to Barce to try to find General

O'Connor and, perhaps, Neame. It was not a pleasant drive down a very dark, steep, winding road from the hills to the plains. After about two hours, however, we arrived, and I was lucky to find the billet where O'Connor was. Although I did not know it until a few hours later, Wavell had signalled on his own return from Cyrenaica the previous day that while the situation was obscure he feared it was probable that a large part of 3rd Armoured Brigade and the Support Groups had been overrun and disorganised by superior German armoured force. This would uncover the left flank of the 9th Australian Division, two brigades of which were holding on to an escarpment east of and north-east of Benghazi. It might be necessary to withdraw them. In view of the apparent strength of the enemy and his intention to make a large-scale offensive towards Egypt, and with the continued report of German reinforcements to Libya, Wavell felt it necessary to re-establish a front in the Western Desert as soon as possible. A mobile force must be set up at El Adem with such armoured units as could be made available. It seemed still to be almost impossible for Rommel to maintain large forces far forward, but in view of our weakness in mobile and armoured forces, however, it would be most dangerous to leave our base in Egypt insufficiently defended. Wavell added:

In view of his greater experience of this type of warfare I yesterday sent for O'Connor with the intention of putting him in command, but on his arrival today the situation was so serious I considered change of command undesirable as Neame was doing well in a difficult situation; also found O'Connor had not been well lately and might become ill, so left Neame in command with O'Connor to help and advise him. This will work satisfactorily, and is agreeable to both.

By the time I had located O'Connor it was after midnight, and he had gone to bed to try to snatch an hour or two's sleep before moving off to the east before dawn. However, strict instructions had been left that if I turned up I was to be taken straight in to him at whatever time. I sat on the end of his bed while he told me all he knew about the situation, which was not much. It seemed probable that Benghazi had gone. O'Connor's position, sent out by Wavell 'to advise', was clearly a difficult one, and I think he felt it to be very unsatisfactory. As he remarked to me: 'Philip [Neame] has been landed with a very untidy and sticky affair; he is doing the best he can with it—what can I do? It won't improve the situation for us to have two commanders.'

I gave O'Connor an account of the general situation as seen from Middle East Headquarters and then made for Marawa to fly back to Cairo. The squadrons were all but ready to retreat again.

Reaching Cairo at midday on 4 April, I found that Longmore had left for the Sudan and at his request I signalled to the Chief of the Air Staff that the military situation in the Desert was somewhat dangerous owing largely to Rommel's armoured advance across the Desert towards Mechili. The only immediate means of checking it was air action. Though our squadrons were in grand form, they were very thin in numbers, both aircraft and crews. They had been withdrawn to Marawa and Derna. After discussion with Wavell I had given Cyrenaica priority for replacements since the casualties must be made good at once. 45 Squadron (Blenheims) would move there the following day and a further squadron would soon follow.

A few hours later came Portal's reply. He entirely agreed that absolute priority must be given to Cyrenaica. If necessary Blenheims should be operated from Greece but the squadrons should not be moved from there. Portal's message concluded:

> We all have fullest confidence that your squadrons will do as well in defence as in offence. No one could say more. We are sending you all we can. Best of luck.

The Foreign Secretary, Anthony Eden[1], and the C.I.G.S., Sir John Dill, were at this moment in Cairo after their prolonged efforts to succour the Greeks and to form the Balkan Front against the Axis. On 5 April, Eden and Dill discussed the situation fully with Wavell and myself. We agreed that the enemy's effort in Cyrenaica was a major diversion well timed to precede the German onslaught upon the Balkans. This judgment, as Eden telegraphed to Churchill, did not mean that the threat to Egypt

[1] He had gone to the Foreign Office from the War Office on 23 December 1940.

was in any way diminished, for the enemy must be expected to press any advantage he gained. Moreover, Rommel was attaining a greater measure of success than had been anticipated.[1]

The next morning I again attended a meeting with Wavell, Dill, and Eden, when we considered a telegram just received from the Chiefs of Staff. They agreed that the re-establishment of the front in the Western Desert was 'of first importance and must have priority over all other demands on your resources'. The Chiefs of Staff also pointed to the need for maintaining a heavy scale of air attack on Tripoli and for dominating the air in Cyrenaica. The despatch of thirty-eight more Wellingtons and of six Beauforts was promised. After our meeting we replied that we too fully appreciated the need to maintain attacks on Tripoli, and the Beaufort aircraft would be of great assistance. The air forces in Cyrenaica were being reinforced with a Blenheim squadron at once and a fighter squadron from the Delta area when the South African fighter squadron should arrive from the Sudan. Both squadrons would go to the Desert at the expense of Greece.

We met again that afternoon, being joined by Longmore, who had returned from Khartoum at lunch-time. It was agreed that we should withdraw gradually and hold the defences of Tobruk and Bardia.

No one could tell accurately what was happening in Libya, except that we were in an awkward position. Since Libya was my special responsibility in so far as I had one, it was decided that I should leave at dawn the following day with an Army staff officer to meet Neame and Brown, tell them of the decisions taken in Cairo, and get their end of the story, if they knew it. From a brief and very noisy telephone conversation with Brown that evening, 6 April, I gathered that in Tobruk they were hanging on by their teeth. No. 3 Squadron (Hurricanes) had shot down fourteen Huns on the previous day, with the possible loss of one pilot, but as usual the odds were heavy.

We set off in the early morning of 7 April to meet Brown and Neame at Gambut, some forty miles to the east of Tobruk. We arrived before ten to find that no one knew anything about our

[1] Churchill: *War Memoirs,* vol. III, p. 182.

rendezvous, or where anyone else was. The wind was blowing hard and the dust driving. We stayed for a couple of hours and then flew on to another landing ground near Tobruk. I borrowed a car and motored towards Tobruk, collecting Brown *en route*. We had some difficulty in finding the Army headquarters but succeeded at last, only to find that both Neame and O'Connor were missing. 'It looks very much,' I wrote, 'as though they have been ambushed driving back from Barce by one of a number of little raiding parties the enemy had got going. I am terribly sorry for them, particularly O'Connor.' Such was indeed the case. Wavell, with a fine sense of proportion, later offered to exchange any six Italian Generals for O'Connor, but without result.

Meanwhile the rest of the Army headquarters staff had arrived but a few hours earlier, an unshaven, sleepless, unfed lot, yellow with dust. Brigadier Harding, the B.G.S., was in charge. I thought him a grand little man. He looked like nothing on earth and had every excuse for being a trifle jittery, but showed not a sign of fuss or bother, though he was admittedly a little worried. We spent three hours with him going through the whole affair. I believed that the Germans and Italians were probably even more surprised than we were. At least, as it happened, the Australians had managed to get out of what appeared to be a most unpleasant position. Major-General Morshead, their divisional commander, seemed quite cheerful although he had been on the trek for the last two days.

I talked with Brown and we settled a plan for the time being. It was difficult to make long-range plans, for no one could tell how things would develop. Bray had efficiently collected four ration biscuits and a little cheese and bully which served for breakfast, lunch, and tea rolled into one. Shortly before six we got away, landing at Sollum to collect a soldier and taking off again just as the sun set behind the desert horizon, which seemed, absurdly enough, to be even straighter than the sea horizon. A comfortable and peaceful flight back in the moonlight took us along the coast where the sea looked almost blue, and then across the desert past the Wadi Natrun, and so to Cairo where the blackout was not impressive.

*

As we had foreseen in our meetings at Cairo on 5 April, the German onslaught now fell upon Greece and Yugoslavia. At once Portal reversed the order of priorities agreed in our exchange of signals three days before. He telegraphed that in the altered circumstances Longmore would realise the urgency of giving the maximum possible support to the ground forces in the Balkans and retaining in Egypt the minimum necessary to the security of the Western Flank. Information in London suggested that for the present the Germans were unable to reinforce their air strength in Libya. It seemed justifiable that Longmore should denude Aden of all except the obsolescent Vincent bombers, and Abyssinia, Kenya, and the Sudan of all except the minimum number of obsolescent types necessary to clear up the situation there.

Longmore replied that he fully realised the urgency of giving this support to the ground forces in the Balkans, and he was indeed sending some Wellingtons. The Libyan situation, however, seemed to him to be worse than was at present appreciated. The early success of the enemy's raids might lead him to exploit them to the full extent and continue. On account of the German Air Force's extreme mobility with transport aircraft, reinforcement of the Libyan Front must be anticipated from Sicily. Strong air support might well be required to save the situation for us, not because of the enemy air strength, but against fast moving and enterprising mechanised forces which we had not yet stopped and which had now denied to us the use of El Adem aerodrome. He was preparing to re-open aerodromes and satellite air-strips east of Mersa Matruh from which, in the event of a German advance beyond Sollum, he would operate all available aircraft in Egypt, including obsolete types.

Meanwhile I wrote at once to Group Captain Brown to assure him that it had been a grand tonic to see him and his men in such fine fighting form. We had by now further evidence of a considerable reduction in the numbers of German aircraft in Libya and of a refusal to reinforce them. I thought that this, coupled with the fact that we hoped to keep Brown fairly well supplied with aircraft, would more and more justify him in the next few days in making persistent machine-gun attacks on Rommel's transport columns in the Desert. Now the enemy had cleared us out of Western Cyrenaica and the Australian Division had escaped, the Desert advance no longer had any great value from his point of view. It seemed to me that the Germans and Italians would probably get their main transport lines off the desert on to the good communications over the high ground. Once there, these columns would be less vulnerable and it would be easier for the enemy to salvage damaged vehicles. Regular anti-aircraft defences would be established. If I was right in this, we might only have the opportunity of causing him very serious losses in transport in the Desert for a few more days.

I found that there had been in Cairo a good deal of unnecessary, but perhaps natural despondency, owing to the lack of news of the operations of our squadrons in the Desert. I told Brown:

> If people do not hear what is being done they are apt to think that nothing is being done, and deduce that the squadrons are out of action. Since nothing can be further from the truth I would urge you to try and let us have operational summaries as promptly as possible. In any case your chaps have been putting up a grand show, and it is only right that the world should know.

Like Longmore and myself, Wavell looked on the position in the Desert with grave anxiety, for it was essential to hold the enemy as far west as possible to reduce the air threat to the naval base at Alexandria and other places in Egypt, and because of the moral effect on Egypt of further enemy progress. While we could undoubtedly hold the enemy for some time at Tobruk, the position was not a good one to cling on to indefinitely. Wavell told the War Office on 10 April that he did not think the enemy could continue past Tobruk towards Egypt except with light raiding forces. He intended to hold Tobruk, to place a force in the Bardia-Sollum area with as much mobility as possible and to act against the flank or rear of the enemy attacking Tobruk, while building up our defences in the Mersa Matruh region. The distribution of forces so that we might gain time without risking defeat in detail would be a difficult calculation. His resources, he telegraphed, were very limited, especially in armoured and mobile troops and anti-tank and anti-aircraft weapons. It would be a race against time.

Although Wavell had little choice in making these dispositions, the reactions of our Army Command in Cairo seemed to me to be unduly sluggish.

'The Army direction here,' my journal for 11 April records, 'makes me shudder. We have got all our re-organisation to meet a new situation practically complete and working, but they are still dithering as to what their organisation is going to be, as to whether General So-and-so is not too junior to take Command because George So-and-so is in the offing. 'Orrible!'

The following day our forces were still retreating eastwards. I knew that they were desperately short of material, but there seemed to be a complete lack of leadership. On the night of 11 April, I tried vainly to persuade Arthur Smith, the Chief of the General Staff, to put one man in command at once. Early the next morning he came round to say that he had decided to put Lieutenant-General Evetts, the General Commanding British Troops in Egypt, in charge of the Western Desert and everything outside Tobruk. Later it was decided that this should take effect from 6 p.m. on 13 April, and should be a purely provisional arrangement until Wavell returned from Greece. I believed that Evetts was a good man, but nothing had been done in the meanwhile to get a grip on affairs in the Desert. By the evening of 12 April we heard that the Germans were in Bardia and the soldiers were talking about evacuating Sollum. I had to order No. 3 Squadron to fall back since they were getting dangerously exposed.

At a small meeting with the senior members of Air Headquarters, I arranged, in Longmore's absence, that we should throw all our aircraft into the breach if the soldiers retreated much farther. All available planes were to go to Collishaw in the Desert the next day, but I did not want to behave as if we were in the last ditch unless it were really necessary. A thick dust storm had shrouded the desert that day, which was the worse for us, since for the time being we enjoyed air superiority. I reported to Portal that the military situation was still obscure, and although the repeated moves of squadrons made it impossible to obtain a detailed picture of air action in the past ten days, it was already clear that heavy losses had been inflicted on the enemy in the air and on the ground. For the last five days, fighters and bombers had concentrated with good effect on columns of enemy transport. Air reconnaissance on 11 April had suggested that there was little behind the present thrust between Derna and Agheila. If the situation became critical, we should move up all aircraft irrespective of whether the squadrons were able to move as such. All our serviceable armoured-cars had already gone forward to assist the defence of aerodromes. That week we had received the heartening total of fifty-three new aircraft, and the move northwards of the South African squadrons had been accelerated.

Portal replied at once that my 'very clear' telegram was much appreciated and he had complete confidence in the dispositions I proposed. He thought I was right to leave two squadrons at Tobruk and to concentrate on hitting the enemy's rearward services, since his thrust must depend on the ability to use air transport and maintain a lengthening line of motor transport. I confided to my journal the thought that the signal was perhaps a little too friendly, in view of the rather acid messages Portal had recently been exchanging with Longmore.

On the next day, Easter Sunday, I went down to the river to meet Longmore and Wavell, who had returned from Greece in a Sunderland. The Commander-in-Chief was not looking too young or cheerful. I feared that he realised all had not been quite right with his organisation and choice of subordinates. Even Longmore had to make an effort to be cheerful. Wavell, in a gloomy signal sent that afternoon to the C.I.G.S., held out no hope of relieving Tobruk for several months, and questioned whether the garrison could hold out long enough. This would depend mainly on whether the port could be kept open. The enemy would not now be unenterprising and unready Italians, but largely Germans, and, moreover, under German control and direction. We should be much harder pressed on the ground and should not escape with the ineffective air attacks which the Italians had made in the previous year.

However, the activities at Tobruk provided some little comfort for us. The Australian and British garrison meted out most

[71]

severe punishment against Rommel's assaults. From Wing Commander Judge, an Australian whose job it was to select landing grounds, I learnt of the prodigious feats performed by our Hurricane pilots who had been shooting down the Hun, living and flying in an appalling dust—and all to an obbligato day and night of shells and bombs. That morning, 14 April, our forces had taken a lot of German prisoners at Tobruk. The enemy were in a poor state, many of them sobbing their hearts out. 'If only our soldiers would crack him one blow, I believe he'd bust!' I exclaimed in my journal.

Ironically enough we received at this critical moment the official congratulations of the House of Commons on the recent victories by sea, land, and air, in North Africa, Greece, and the Mediterranean. The Prime Minister telegraphed personally to Longmore on 15 April that all his vigorous reactions gave them in London the greatest pleasure. They had the feeling that the enemy in Libya was hard pressed after a bold effort:

Now is the time to strike. Compliment squadrons in Tobruk for clawing down dive bombers. We are crowding everything we can out to you, and stream is now beginning to flow. Whereas you have received only 370 from November until now, 528 more are on the way and a further 880 will start before the end of May.

4

Mr. Churchill puts 'Victory in Libya' first–Evacuation of Greece–Longmore's admirable philosophy–Air battle over Tobruk–Reorganisation of Air Command–Longmore recalled

WHILE we were thus deeply preoccupied with the Desert War, the German onrush in the Balkans forced us to turn our attention northwards.[1] Within a few days it was plain that our small air force in Greece had been swamped by overwhelming low-flying attacks on its virtually undefended aerodromes. In these circumstances it would have been visionary to expect our three fighter squadrons to hold their own against greatly superior numbers of Germans and Italians. By 16 April, Longmore expected an early collapse in Greece. He ordered two fighter squadrons to withdraw to Crete, a decision supported by Portal, who explained to the Prime Minister that it was obviously better to save what we could than to throw it away in a gesture. The most we could do was to put fighters into Crete and from there make every possible effort to cover any evacuation which might become necessary. Longmore had already reported that the heavy fighting in Libya absorbed all his available Hurricanes and Blenheims, and he now regarded this front as 'vital with highest priority'. Moreover, we had good reason to anticipate serious trouble in Iraq.

I felt deep sympathy for Longmore's predicament. He was still without a clear order of priority for air action in his sprawling command. He asked on 17 April whether fighter protection during the evacuation from Greece (in which he would probably lose more Hurricanes than he was getting) should have priority over fighter support in the Western Desert, such as protection to shipping entering Tobruk and the neutralisation of the enemy air force in that area. For the moment, the wastage rate in Hurricanes and Blenheims just balanced the flow of supply, but we knew that a temporary lean period in Hurricanes was approaching. The lately arrived Tomahawks were afflicted with many teething troubles in guns and engines, and were not yet operationally

---

[1] A map of Greece, Crete, and the Ægean area can be found later in the book, on page 468.

available. Longmore had just seen Churchill's signal to Wavell giving the decision to hold Crete. This, as the A.O.C.-in-C. told Portal, involved a heavy air commitment, if our action were to be effective enough to satisfy naval requirements for Suda Bay in Crete and to enable the Greek Government to continue to operate from the island.

In reply, Churchill ruled, on 18 April, that Crete would at first be a receptacle for whatever we could get there from Greece. Its fuller defence must be organised later, and in the meanwhile all forces must protect themselves from air bombing by dispersion, and must use their bayonets against parachutists or airborne intruders, if any:

> . . . Victory in Libya comes first. Evacuation of troops from Greece, second. Tobruk shipping, unless indispensable to victory, must be fitted in as convenient. Iraq can be ignored and Crete be worked up later.

But it was one thing to put victory in Libya first, from London, and quite another to secure it on the spot. Every meeting with the High Command in Cairo convinced me the more that we could not expect to win without a strengthening in its personnel. I wrote in my journal on the evening of 18 April:

> These soldiers of ours have really succeeded in making me depressed this evening, and I felt I must do something about it. The team at G.H.Q. really gives me the shudders. Wavell, I think, is a fine man, but the rest?!!!!! They swing daily from easy optimism to desperate defeatism and vice versa. It is really tragic that Wavell has not got a really solid right-hand man who can relieve him of some of the burden. He has got a terrific load, and he is damned badly served.
>
> The more one hears of this debacle, the worse it proves to have been. Practically no fighting at all. Just muddle, misdirection and lack of leadership. The whole utterly unnecessary. There is no doubt that our one and a half fighter squadrons saved them from what might have been a shambles—unfortunately, they could not save them from chasing themselves silly about the country until they literally fell into enemy hands. I hope to heaven they are not doing the same in Greece now. Oh, Hell!!

But it could only be a matter of days before the evacuation

from Greece, already foreshadowed, was ordered. Longmore had to tell the Chief of the Air Staff that on the previous evening the stock of Hurricanes available to d'Albiac, who was commanding our air forces in Greece, was less than a dozen and might well be less by the time the telegram went off. These few machines would be used to the last to provide such cover to re-embarkation as was possible. Six more Hurricanes were going to Crete at d'Albiac's disposal, but no more could be sent without denuding our slender fighting force now defending Tobruk and the Western Desert. Aircraft sent to Greece risked early destruction upon the ground. In Crete, we had but two aerodromes available, at Maleme and Heraklion. The former was not fit for heavily loaded Blenheims. The latter was extremely vulnerable to low attacks from Rhodes, which was now occupied by the Germans.

Since d'Albiac's few remaining Blenheims could now have no appreciable effect on the fighting, they were flown back to Egypt on 21 April. All the available Bombays and Sunderlands were being sent to Greece to help in evacuating key personnel, including R.A.F. pilots and air crews. Two B.O.A.C. Empire flying-boats had been pressed into service for ferry work between Suda Bay and Alexandria. Between 18 and 21 April, Longmore had lost sixteen Hurricanes in Greece and six in Libya. He flew to Crete on 22 April.

I still thought that we could not let the Greeks down. It was a known risk and had to be accepted, not least for its effect upon American opinion. It has to be remembered that our capacity to continue air warfare in the Middle East was going to depend to a large degree upon the flow of aircraft from the United States. I noted in my journal that the disaster in Greece was traceable to the 'Keep it on the island' policy of 'Beaverbrook and Company', which stopped material from coming out to the Middle East months earlier.

However, it is no use crying over spilt milk. It has certainly upset Adolf's plan, and has already cost him pretty dearly. It is true that so far as numbers and quantities of material [are concerned] he can afford to be reckless about the price—for a time, but things get more difficult for him the further he goes.

★

In response to the Chiefs of Staff's request, the Middle Eastern Commanders-in-Chief took stock of the whole situation on 23 April. We agreed with the Chiefs of Staff that the holding of Crete and the use of Suda Bay were of the greatest importance from the naval point of view, and its denial to the enemy was essential from naval and air aspects. Nevertheless, our resources did not permit immediate and adequate reinforcement. In the Western Desert the enemy forces operating in the forward area seemed temporarily to have outrun their communications, and the general plan was to check his further advance by holding defensive areas.

We estimated that the German Air Force's mobility was such that they could maintain at least four hundred operational aircraft working from aerodromes between Benghazi and Bardia, and the use of ports in Cyrenaica would enable them to increase this number. As against these increased potential dangers, we should be fighting on one major front only, and the ever-increasing air force, experienced in desert warfare, should be able to support effectively our land operations and by enterprising action neutralise any air offensive against Egypt.

As for naval action, it was not possible to keep permanent patrols off Benghazi, though destroyer patrols were carried out nightly along the coast as far as Tolmete. Our appreciation stressed that naval forces for this operation had to be 'on scale out of all proportion to tasks or naval risks entailed in order to try and meet air threat large superiority numbers enemy aircraft'.

On his return from Greece and Crete, Longmore brought depressing news. In agreement with him, Wavell signalled that day, 24 April, that the fighter situation was serious. All Hurricanes in Greece had been lost, and as a result of recent enemy air attacks on Tobruk a large proportion of the Hurricanes there had been destroyed or damaged. The A.O.C.-in-C. considered that any further attempt to maintain the fighter squadron inside Tobruk would only result in heavy future loss. This would mean that the enemy would have complete air superiority over Tobruk until a fresh fighter force could be built up. The difficulties of defence would be increased and the harbour probably rendered unusable, but it was inevitable.

Longmore managed, in all these dismal circumstances, to re main cheerful. He practised what I thought an admirable philosophy; if he felt that everything possible had been done to meet a situation, it was useless to worry about it, however menacing it might look. Certainly the state of affairs in Greece gave him ample opportunity to display these stoical qualities. Our air force had been completely blitzed out of the two landing grounds which remained. The enemy enjoyed overwhelming weight of numbers. There was nothing we could do. We had to stand impotently by and watch a convincing demonstration of the power of the air arm to neutralise and even obliterate ground and sea forces.

We all knew that this was but a prelude. In Crete, Iraq, Syria, the Desert, crises loomed. Everything would depend on the supply of aircraft. Arthur Longmore thought that there was a reasonable chance of keeping Suda Bay usable by the Navy if we employed one Hurricane squadron there, but it would be at the estimated cost of 100 per cent. reserve pilots at a replacement rate of 100 per cent. per month. Meanwhile, Blenheims and Gladiators were doing their best from Maleme and Heraklion to provide at least some air protection for our ships. As Wavell had already signalled, the exposed position of No. 73 Squadron inside Tobruk had caused losses so severe that Longmore had withdrawn the remaining machines and men to the Mersa area. In short, to defend our position in the Western Desert, upon which depended the security of Egypt, and therefore, probably, the whole outcome of the war, Longmore had twenty-one serviceable Hurricanes. To cover the canal and Alexandria he had fourteen Hurricanes. In sight, within seven days, were nineteen more, and beyond that a further thirty, twenty-three of which were at Takoradi. Twelve Tomahawks had arrived but could not yet be operated. Seventeen more were on the way and no fewer than 145 at Takoradi. Every thing possible was being done to remedy their teething troubles. 'We will keep going somehow,' Longmore signalled, 'whilst we build up with the reinforcements in sight and promised.'

*

In the press of all these events, I had been working at a new arrangement of our air strength in the Middle East. Longmore and

I both felt that the existing organisation was much too centralised, a fault which would be accentuated when the promised reinforcements arrived. The essence of the new plan was that an Air Command in the Western Desert should be set up under my direction, whilst Collishaw would run a Striking Force Group. There would be two other wings. The fighter defence of the Delta would be effected by 202 Group coming directly under the orders of Longmore's Headquarters. The objects of our reorganisation were three-fold; to reduce vulnerability to attack, to increase our mobility, and to facilitate the operation of sudden reinforcements in an emergency. To these ends we were organising refuelling landing grounds in the forward area (for example, in Tobruk and around Sidi Barrani), operational landing grounds in the central area around Mersa Matruh and Daba, and base aerodromes in the area of Daba and Bagush for servicing and inspection. Each squadron would thus have its main base in the rear and would operate from an operational landing ground. But all depended on getting the right aircraft in time. My knowledge of Thorold's work at Takoradi made me confident that an appeal for a supreme effort would be willingly met. I signalled to him on 24 April that we were at the beginning of an extremely critical phase and must make a further call upon him. Replacement with Hurricanes and Tomahawks was vital to make good the very heavy wastage in Greece and Libya:

Every day or hour which can be saved to expedite receipt of fighters in Egypt will be crucial. Know we can rely on you and your men to do all that is humanly possible, and more, towards this end during ensuing days and weeks.

Thorold's reply of the same day was characteristic of him:

You can rely on all ranks Takoradi to do their utmost to meet your urgent requirements during this critical phase.

Two days later I flew to the Group Headquarters in the Desert. This time the journey took only one and three-quarter hours; on the previous occasion it had been over three hours to Tobruk, and the time before, five hours to Barce. I found myself in the old underground Operations Room where we had been at Christmas. There I talked with Collishaw and explained the new organisation we were working out. I learnt of the terrible punishment which the Hurricanes of No. 73 Squadron had suffered at Tobruk, where they had been outnumbered on some occasions by more than ten to one. Later in the day, I met the men of 73 Squadron, or rather, I met those who were left. They had just flown out of Tobruk, and I do not think I have ever seen a tougher looking gang, bearded, with tousled hair and wild eyes. It was only too clear that the majority of their remaining pilots would have to be replaced at once. The squadron had had three commanders in a fortnight, and now boasted only four operationally serviceable aircraft.

Then I visited some of the other squadrons. When I had finished my business, I could not find my pilot, and finally got a strange message asking us to go along to a certain tent. I went there and found a little party of 39 Squadron sitting round on the floor listening to one fellow who was playing and singing to a ukelele. I sat down too, and we had a number of songs together.

In the middle of the afternoon we left for Cairo, on a very rough flight, though the dust was only bad in patches. Dozens of twirling dust devils were gliding along across the Desert. I was back at my office by 6 p.m. where I found Longmore, exceptionally for him, a little depressed and moody. I found that Portal had telegraphed to say that while appreciating fully Longmore's great difficulties, the Government were somewhat disturbed by the statement in Wavell's signal of 24 April that the enemy would have complete air superiority over Tobruk in the immediate future after the withdrawal of 73 Squadron from within the perimeter. According to the best available information in London, the operations of the Luftwaffe in Libya were as yet limited by supply difficulties and their serviceability rate was very low. The C.A.S. hoped that Longmore would manage, therefore, to give some support to the Tobruk garrison by maintaining offensive patrols, and that he should retain the ability to refuel and re-arm Hurricanes at Tobruk even though they could not stay there. I was able, from my visit to the Desert, to provide Longmore with some material for his reply, sent that evening. Longmore referred to the inevitability of the decision to withdraw 73 Squadron:

[79]

We are taking every possible step to re-establish the position, but I am sure you will agree when our Fighters do engage the enemy they must do it in reasonable strength, i.e., we must employ occasional strong patrols instead of trying to cover long periods with penny packets. When we have sufficient Hurricanes to maintain air cover of refuelling at Tobruk, we shall resume refuelling and re-arming there. Without such cover, aircraft on the ground at Tobruk are a hostage to fortune we cannot afford. This may mean a stiff period for the Tobruk garrison, and I have explained this to Wavell. We are doing all we can to lessen the scale of attack, by dusk and night attacks on enemy aerodromes at Gazala and Derna and on the sources of supply at Benghazi and Benina.

As we were entertaining guests for dinner that night, we all changed into dinner jackets. After the meal, we sat round the wireless to hear the Prime Minister explain the withdrawal from Greece. I thought his speech honest and accurate. The best part was the final, apt quotation:

> For while the tired waves, vainly breaking,
> Seem here no painful inch to gain,
> Far back, through creeks and inlets making,
> Comes silent, flooding in, the main.

> And not by eastern windows only,
> When daylight comes, comes in the light;
> In front the sun climbs slow, how slowly!
> But westward, look, the land is bright.

*

These days brought amazing stories of the evacuation from Greece, tales of almost unbelievable coolness, initiative, and bravery. Four Sunderland aircraft had managed to evacuate more than seven hundred people in about five days. They had landed and taken off in darkness in unknown bays, loaded up in quite incredible fashion. The top score for a single Sunderland was eighty-five people, and sixty was commonplace. There was also the news of a refuelling barge which made its way with a mixed bag of passengers from Athens round the coasts of the Pelepponese, hiding up by day covered with Service blankets, while Me. 110s were shooting up caiques and fishing boats. By rigging aerials with the help of an oar and a large pole, the barge maintained wireless touch with us and Crete all the time. The Navy's effort was magnificent and they brought away a far greater proportion of our troops than any one had ever thought possible. The Commonwealth troops, New Zealanders and Australians, had fought splendidly. It was heartening to hear from d'Albiac and others that the people of Greece remained warm-hearted and friendly to the very end, throwing flowers to our defeated troops as they departed. On the debit side, we estimated that we had lost in Greece 209 aircraft, although we had destroyed 244 enemy planes. Even worse, we had sacrificed 150 pilots, air gunners, and observers.

As we rose from breakfast on 1 May Longmore passed me a signal, observing: 'There's a bit of a shock.' It said that Churchill wished him to go home at once to discuss the changed situation in the Middle East. I was to be acting Air Commander-in-Chief, and Air Vice Marshal Drummond acting Deputy. I could not understand this new move which did not seem to be appropriately timed. I hoped it did not mean that the Prime Minister had lost his temper with Longmore and proposed to send someone else to relieve him. Later that morning, Longmore, in a rather shame-faced way, showed me a message he had sent to Portal on the previous day. He remarked, 'I do not know if that had anything to do with it.' This document explained that the A.O.C.-in-C. was being constantly pressed by his two fellow Commanders-in-Chief, on the subject of new types of aircraft and armament of which they had heard in recent optimistic broadcasts. Cunningham and Wavell wondered whether these were being sent to the Middle East. Longmore had explained the reasons for not sending Manchesters or Stirlings, but he was bound to admit that neither of the two Commanders seemed very convinced, and he had added: 'Undoubtedly we are not getting our fair share. The present period of extreme air weakness lends substance to this impression.' It would help him considerably if Portal could send a signal which could be shown to the other two Commanders, giving an outline of future policy with regard to new types and their allotment to the Middle East. He had been particularly asked about the Hurricane II, the Typhoon, the Beaufighter, the Blenheim V, and the Whirlwind, in addition to the Manchester and Stirling, and

[81]

whether it was the intention to send any of these to the Middle East even for trial. He wished to make it quite clear to his two colleagues that our deficiencies were not due to lack of energetic representation on his part.

I cast my mind back to the previous December when, at my final interview with Wilfrid Freeman, he had said: 'Tell Longmore that we fully appreciate all his difficulties, but we are becoming tired of moan, moan, moan.'

On my arrival in the Middle East I had duly warned Longmore that some of his signals were building up irritation and antagonism. He took the hint very well and, as I have said, agreed to let me see, before despatch, his signals to the Air Ministry. Only once or twice in the following four months had he sent off a message without showing it to me first. On these rare occasions he would tell me afterwards in a boyish way, 'I slipped that off when you weren't looking.'

Certainly I would never have let him send this latest signal. Now it was too late. The situation in Iraq was developing so ominously that the unhappy Longmore asked on 2 May whether, in view of this, he was still required to return to London. He received, as I fear he expected, a brief reply from Portal, saying that he should come back as arranged. Poor Longmore was very depressed. I think he felt he would probably not return, for two or three times he said to me, and I am sure he meant it: 'I hate leaving you such a mess to hold.'

I wrote in my journal:

It is a mess, and it is going to be pretty unpleasant for the next two or three months, but L. is certainly not to be blamed. If anyone is blameworthy it is the people at home who refused to send adequate forces out here many months ago. The Balkan affair was inevitable; we had to support Greece.

Longmore departed for London before lunch on 3 May. I felt very sorry for him, for I had come to like him and to appreciate his steadiness, honesty, decency, and thoughtfulness for others. As he was climbing into his aircraft, his grip on my elbow and his 'Good luck, Ted' were almost affectionate. I wondered whether he would come back. I had a feeling he would not.

5

Portal's advice–Iraqi rebellion–Habbaniya–Wavell reluctant to help–R.A.F. armoured-cars in action–Churchill approves my report to C.A.S.–Army misses opportunities

ON the morning of 5 May I received from Portal the first of a long series of heartening, straightforward, personal messages which we exchanged at short intervals for the rest of the war. He told me that 'on taking over command' I should feel free, in view of the ever-changing situation, to act as I saw fit despite any appreciation or directive issued before Longmore's departure. It seemed to the C.A.S. that the enemy were at full stretch and operating under difficult conditions. They were short of supplies, and yet managed to achieve results by concentrating all their forces, ground and air, on the achievement of some definite object. They appeared always ready to face risks. With a well-established base and shorter lines of communication, our operating conditions were far superior to the enemy's:

Yet there appears to be no co-ordinated plan for making the most of our opportunities at this juncture. Beyond holding Tobruk, have the Army a plan in which we could play our part now that the enemy is showing anxiety about his forward forces?

Portal expressed his belief that bold thrusts against the enemy's communications might make his position intolerable and bring about his defeat, or at least the retreat of all his forward forces. The risk of heavy casualties must be faced if big prizes were to be won. It did seem, however, that all three Services should make their big efforts in concert and not separately. The message ended on a note which could not have been more welcome to a Commander far from home and facing many conflicting demands:

I have complete faith in your judgment, determination, and ability to lead the Air Force in the Middle East, and you can rely on my not interfering but supporting you in any bold and well-conceived joint operation whatever its result may be. Best wishes to you and Drummond.

I replied at once that I would do my damnedest to justify Portal's confidence. I had already discussed with Wavell action for the Western Desert on the lines of Portal's message. I told

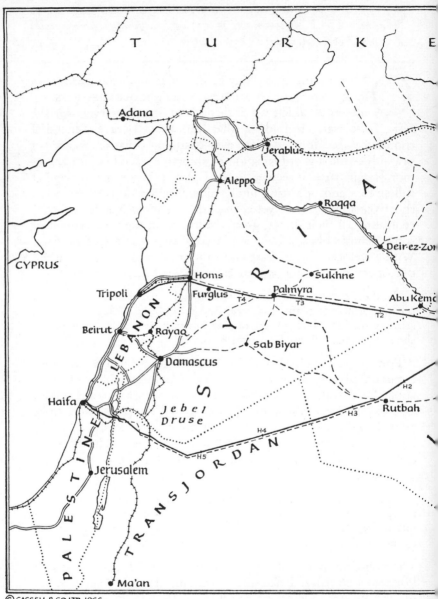

T U R K E

Adana

Jerablus

Aleppo

Raqqa

CYPRUS

Deir-ez-Zor

Homs   Sukhne

Tripoli   Furglus   Palmyra   Abu Kema
           T4   T3
                                 T2

Beirut   Rayaq

Damascus   Sab Biyar

Haifa

Jebel
Druse   H2

                    H3   Rutbah
              H4
PALESTINE   H5

Jerusalem

TRANSJORDAN

Ma'an

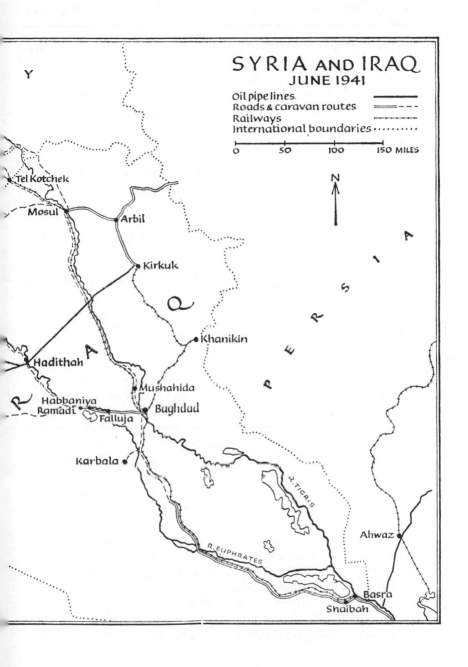

SYRIA AND IRAQ
JUNE 1941

Oil pipe lines
Roads & caravan routes
Railways
International boundaries

0   50   100   150 MILES

N

Y

Tel Kotchek

Mosul

Arbil

Kirkuk

Q

Khanikin

P E R S I A

Hadithah

A

Mushahida

Habbaniya
Ramadi
Falluja

Baghdad

R

Karbala

R. TIGRIS

R. EUPHRATES

Ahwaz

Basra

Shaibah

Wavell that by observing economy in the use of my force during the next ten days and by further efforts in the rear areas, I hoped to build up the existing units to full strength and possibly even to augment the squadrons. I was hopeful that with this support the Army would agree to stage a combined blitz. Relations with the Navy, I told the C.A.S., were good, although we did not give them all the reconnaissance cover they wished. I was doing my best to improve this situation but unfortunately Admiral Cunningham had been given by the Admiralty the total numbers of serviceable Blenheims and Marylands in the Middle Eastern Air Command as an indication of the reconnaissance force available. This was a misleading assessment, since only those Marylands fitted with long-range tanks could sweep the Ionian Sea. Trained crews were the other limiting factor.

Quite apart from the events in the Desert and our attempt to rebuild our strength in Crete, the situation in Iraq now claimed my immediate attention. In mid-April Longmore, deeply concerned at the growing unrest there, had wished to crush the rebels led by Rashid Ali before the Greek situation had time to influence the political atmosphere in Iraq to our disadvantage. Longmore was only too conscious of our weakness, for apart from obsolete aircraft and a training establishment, our force at Habbaniya where, as at Shaibah, we were allowed by treaty to maintain an air base, was negligible. Despite an order from London to the contrary, Longmore sent to Air Vice Marshal Smart, the A.O.C. at Habbaniya, six Gladiator fighters. When the crisis came, they were the only aircraft at Habbaniya which were not obsolete or trainers. Meantime, as far as it was possible, each and every training aircraft was modified with improvised fittings to carry guns and/or bombs. Towards the end of the month, Rashid Ali was building up a rebel army around our base at Habbaniya, and we wondered how much German support he would receive, especially as we already knew of the arrangements between Berlin and Vichy Syria to send a flow of arms to Iraq.

By the beginning of May some 9,000 men, with artillery support, were ringed around Habbaniya. Arming trainers, Smart decided on a surprise attack, which was launched on 2 May. The Iraqis replied by shelling the airfield. Smart's handling of the

attack, which failed, and his despatch of somewhat hysterical
messages, led me to think that his judgment might be affected. I
told Portal on 2 May that in view of the hour-to-hour changes in
the situation, control was still being left to Smart. We already had
unconfirmed reports that the Iraqis were in possession of Rutbah.
The British Embassy in Baghdad was surrounded and the
Ambassador appeared to have burnt the ciphers, but was still in
wireless communication *en clair*. It appeared that he would not
agree to the bombing of the Government Offices in Baghdad, and
that for this reason the major effort had been made against the
rebel Iraqi troops surrounding the air base. I was already moving
forward such air forces as could be spared, and d'Albiac was to
assume command of the R.A.F. in Palestine that night. By
arrangement with Wavell he also took charge of all operations
from Transjordan.

Portal, too, had been dissatisfied with the operations at Habbaniya on 2 May. He telegraphed to me that morning that from
reports received in London it seemed doubtful whether full
advantage had been taken of surprise and the period of our complete air superiority to press home the attack with all available
ground forces simultaneously with the start of bombing. The only
solution now seemed to be the speedy arrival of land reinforcements, coupled with energetic air action from outside Habbaniya
and determined resistance by the garrison, including the fullest
offensive use of armoured-cars[1] and infantry at every opportunity.
The C.A.S. hoped that the transfer of command to the Middle
East would result in the quickest possible relief of the Station.
This was a reference to the decision taken by the Chiefs of Staff
that day that Wavell must assume responsibility for operations in
Northern Iraq. Portal added, characteristically, that he very
much regretted the additional burden on my shoulders, and
appreciated the action I had already taken.

This signal arrived before Longmore left, and the two of us
discussed it with Wavell. We agreed that on the limited information
available in Cairo, the handling of the situation at Habbaniya did

[1] The armoured-cars were part of a force created by Trenchard in 1921
when the R.A.F. were, with Churchill's backing, made responsible for the
maintenance of peace and security in Mesopotamia.

not seem to have been good. The main need there was clearly armoured fighting vehicles and guns, but these could not be made available to meet the immediate situation. The bombing by Wellingtons from Shaibah of dispersed and entrenched rebel troops could not be expected to have a decisive effect. I was emphasising to Smart that the most effective measure was low-flying machine-gun attack against gun crews and aircraft. In view of my doubts about Smart's direction of his forces, I was now considering whether to place all air action from outside Habbaniya under d'Albiac.

The Defence Committee in London had already asked Wavell to send all possible help to Smart. The Commander-in-Chief showed himself reluctant, with his forces stretched everywhere to their limit. He protested that it would be necessary to send a brigade group with strong artillery and tank support, for the despatch of a weaker force would simply give further hostages to fortune. He and Longmore therefore suggested negotiation with the Iraqis under threat of air bombardment or blockade. Later that same day, 3 May, Wavell signalled again that by denuding Palestine he could send a mechanised brigade, one infantry battalion, and the greater part of a field artillery regiment. The Prime Minister reacted furiously, while the Chiefs of Staff told Wavell to stop talking about mediation and get on with the defence of Habbaniya. Preparations to send a force must be pressed on at once. Wavell replied brusquely on 5 May: 'You must face facts.'

The very earliest time at which the force could reach Habbaniya would be 12 May, and he feared it was not strong enough to retake the base, nor did he think that Habbaniya could hold out so long.

On the same day I ordered the armoured-cars back from the Desert to Amman for an immediate move forward by way of Rutbah. Immediate action on land was essential, and Wavell's force would not arrive at the frontier for a week, though if we could speed it up by using air transport, we would. To Portal I said:

At same time since Wavell feels this land relief is a forlorn hope he considers, and I agree, that if possible negotiations should be opened up. With the major threat of war with British Empire, there is no question of concessions by us. The essential value of negotiating is to give us time.

I felt no enthusiasm at the prospect of negotiating with Rashid Ali, and reflected in my journal that night that I feared Wavell was 'a tired old man. He is a big man, I think, but has got such an extremely weak team under him.'

Portal's reply firmly ruled out, rightly as I now think, any prospect of negotiation with the Iraqi rebels. Meanwhile, Smart had quite inexcusably misunderstood a direction from me, and was alleging that I was tying his hands and endangering Habbaniya.

Nevertheless, the garrison there fought magnificently, and the trainee pilots, in particular, did themselves the fullest justice in blasting out of their positions the rebels who were established in the hills overlooking the base. This meant for the moment that the immediate pressure on Habbaniya itself was relieved, although we still had every reason to fear future developments in Iraq and Syria. Wavell, indeed, still felt deep reluctance to become unduly involved there. He recommended to London on 8 May that in order to avoid a heavy military commitment in a non-vital area, a political solution should be sought by all available means. The Prime Minister replied that the Defence Committee believed Rashid Ali and his partisans to be in desperate straits. However this might be, Wavell was to fight hard against them. The mobile column being prepared in Palestine should advance and actively engage the enemy. There could be no question of negotiation with Rashid Ali unless he immediately accepted our terms. Moreover, the Government did not think that any ground forces Wavell might be able to divert to Iraq would affect his immediate problem in the Western Desert. The Air Force, Churchill telegraphed, must do its best to cover both situations:

Only in the event of your being actually engaged or about to engage in an offensive in the Western Desert should Tedder deny the necessary air support to the Iraq operations.

I noticed, on this and on many other occasions, how much easier it was in these matters of mobility, to convince Admirals than to convince Generals. The former were accustomed to think in terms of hundreds of miles; the latter in terms of the range of their guns. The R.A.F. armoured-car force set off for Iraq. In a signal to Wilfrid Freeman on 3 June I wrote:

As regards Iraq I hope this may be completely cleared up in the immediate future, but rather doubt if we are quite out of the wood. There is, incidentally, no doubt whatever that if it had not been for our armoured cars getting up there from the Western Desert, and for Brown taking some risks with the armoured cars and what few troops he had, the whole business would have been more leisurely. I believe his conduct of the operations leading to the capture of Rutbah quite horrified the soldiers.

*

I thought that the Army were most reluctant to take the excellent opportunity to attack the Germans in Libya. With a comparative stalemate on the Western Desert Front, and the immediate danger to Habbaniya passed, I tried to set out for Portal the principles which should govern our air action and the strategic situation in the Middle East as I saw it.

The main recurring problem in this Command [my signal began], is how to apportion the limited Air Forces immediately available to meet concurrent and often conflicting demands.

I pointed out that our prime responsibility, the security of lower Egypt as an effective base, could be secured only by the defeat of the Germans in the Middle East. Since they had superior numbers in material and personnel we must avoid dispersal of our forces and effort. Action in subsidiary theatres, for instance, East Africa and Iraq, would be unavoidable but must be liquidated as rapidly as possible.

As for the Western Desert, the area between Sollum and a line from Mechili to Derna offered almost unlimited sites for air bases, from which the enemy could develop a heavy scale of air attack against our communications in the Western Mediterranean, against the lines of communication of our armed forces in the Western Desert, and against Egypt itself. On the other hand, if this area were in our hands, our ability to maintain a sustained attack on the enemy's communications was greatly enhanced, and it should be possible to render Benghazi unusable. The area was, in fact one of the keys of the defence of Egypt:

At the moment the enemy has over-reached itself here, and for a brief period there has been, and is, a grand opportunity of relieving Tobruk and clearing the enemy from at least part of, and I hope the whole of, this area. I regard these operations as being of the utmost importance. They are our one immediate opportunity of regaining the initiative, and subject to meeting other unavoidable commitments am allocating all available forces to this theatre.

The method of providing air support for the defence of Crete against the attack which was clearly impending, depended upon the Army's plan of defence. There were at that time in Crete six Hurricanes and approximately fourteen very old Blenheim Is and Gladiators. My intention, in view of the need to minimise losses on the ground, was to maintain two Hurricane flights in Crete and to hold a reserve of aircraft and pilots in Egypt for immediate reinforcements. The most useful contribution towards the defence of Crete would be the attack on the aerodromes of the enemy, for which purpose we needed our maximum strength in Wellingtons. I was therefore withdrawing Wellingtons from Iraq and increasing the number of Blenheims there. Speedy liquidation of our commitments in Iraq seemed essential. The employment of Wellingtons there, although necessary and possibly decisive, had diverted more than half the heavy bomber effort from the Western Desert at a moment when sustained attack on Benghazi and Rommel's lines of communication was most needed. Now that we had to defend Crete as well, such a diversion of our main striking force was no longer acceptable.

The Indian High Command seemed to envisage a second Mesopotamian Campaign up the Tigris and Euphrates. A warning of what this would involve was given in a preliminary estimate by the General Officer Commanding Basra of a requirement of one bomber and two fighter squadrons for close support. The longer it was before a stable and friendly government was installed in Baghdad, the greater would be the probability of German intervention, possibly by way of Syria. I even thought it was possible that experience of the difficulties of operating and maintaining forces in the Western Desert, coupled with the new control of the Balkans and the Ægean, might lead the enemy to abandon the Libyan thrust except for its nuisance value, and to develop his main attack on Egypt via Cyprus, Syria, and Palestine.

I soon heard from Portal that after the Chiefs of Staff had expressed general agreement with my appreciation, the Prime Minister had discussed it fully with him. I learned that Mr. Churchill was much pleased with the general layout and felt glad that I had the handling of the important and complicated air operations impending. Portal added a few observations on the timetable and relative emphasis to be given to the various theatres without fettering my freedom of action and as always when he was acting upon the Prime Minister's instructions, he left in a few of the phrases, unmistakably Churchillian, so that I should understand the source of the message. The crucial sentences of this document were:

> Victory in Libya comes first in time and importance. Results would dominate Irak situation in German and Iraki minds. Our object in Irak is to get back a friendly Government in Baghdad and you should do all you can to help in this, but nothing must prejudice victory in the Western Desert . . . .
> One clear-cut result is worth a dozen wise precautions. Longer views about Irak, Syria and preparation in Palestine, can be taken later. Prime importance of Desert operations would justify accepting necessary risks elsewhere. . . .

*

By the middle of the month I had no doubt that Smart had broken down under the strain of events at Habbaniya. I replaced him by d'Albiac, who was to command all air operations in Syria and Iraq. He arrived at Habbaniya on 18 May. We were maintaining offensive reconnaissances over aerodromes in Syria and Iraq, and unidentified aircraft were being attacked on sight. I realised that this might involve damage to French aircraft but considered the risk must be taken. The shooting down in flames of two Me. 110s by Gladiators over the Rashid Aerodrome, Baghdad, should, I thought, have proved a useful stimulus to Iraqi thinking.

The following morning, 19 May, Wavell and I held a meeting

with General Catroux, leader of the Free French in Syria. Wavell took the general line that nothing but a large army would help us there. There was not one available at present and there was therefore nothing to be done. 'Personally,' I noted in my journal, 'I believe that two men and a boy could do *today* what it would require a division to do in a couple of months' time. Meantime, the Hun is digging himself in there and has become a real nuisance, to say the least.'

I signalled at once to Portal that while it was not for me to say what could or could not be done from the Army point of view, I felt it necessary to emphasise that the longer it was before action was taken the more dangerous did the situation become from the Air point of view. If the enemy was allowed to establish his forces in Syria, the threat to Egypt, particularly the canal and Suez, to Iraq, and to our vital oil supplies from Abadan, became gravely increased. Our land communications from Palestine to Baghdad would become precarious since it would be impossible to provide effective air cover. I had already taken such immediate air action as was possible with the improvised forces available, and would continue to use whatever reinforcing aircraft I could spare. This action had had some military effect and had apparently for the moment produced a favourable political reaction in Syria. Air action alone, however, could clearly not maintain this political effect, and since land action was not possible we had to face the probability of a considerable enemy air force operating from Syria.

Evidently Portal found no difficulty in interpreting this guarded message, for he replied at once that it would be helpful to him if I could, from time to time, send very private and personal telegrams giving with complete frankness my view of the Middle Eastern picture as it affected all three Services. Such messages would not be shown to anyone except possibly to the Prime Minister, and then only after reference back to me.

Again I feel whereas the Air Force and to a less extent the Navy have all their units in constant action which lash out in all directions whenever the chance occurs, the Army tends to proceed methodically and unimaginatively along approved text book lines, thereby missing opportunities which can only be seized if one is prepared to take chances.

To Portal it seemed that the Army regarded German infiltration into Syria and Iraq as an unpleasant subject to be ignored, and reference to it by the Chiefs of Staff was considered an attempt to thrust a puking infant into the unwilling arms of busy men concerned with Africa. The state of German supplies in Libya, the anxiety and uncertainty of Rashid Ali, the possibility of considerable French and Arab sympathy in Syria, indicated valuable prizes which might be won by bold and rapid action which could not be taken by one Service alone, but in which, he knew, I would co-operate fiercely if given the chance.

'Tell me frankly, if you think my impressions are wrong,' Portal added. 'No immediate reply expected. Best wishes.'

6

Controversy with the Admiral–Crete: too little too late–Our ships ringed by enemy shore air bases–Heavy naval losses–Priority to Crete–Fall of Crete–Fighter cover for the evacuation–A war for air bases–Recriminations–Arrival of Air Vice Marshal Dawson–Improvisation–Confirmed as C.-in-C.

THE German attack on Crete, which I described in my messages to Portal as impending, brought to the fore the question which caused at intervals throughout the war acrimonious discussion between the Services, a question, moreover, which I felt to be of prime importance for the effective employment of air force. In essence, the issue was whether our air forces, in the Middle East and elsewhere, should be split into separate components, so that the Army and the Royal Navy controlled directly their own air support, or whether all the air forces should be kept under a single direction and distributed as circumstances dictated from time to time.

To me, it seemed that the issue was between the feeble single stick and the bundle of faggots. Admiral Cunningham, however, was the redoubtable champion of different views. He was prone to send explosive messages to London about the alleged lack of air support to the Royal Navy. The first major instance which had come to my attention occurred after Cunningham had been obliged, against his will, to make a severe naval bombardment of Tripoli on 21 April, while Longmore was still A.O.C.-in-C. This operation caused much trouble and produced little result. Cunningham complained vigorously to the Admiralty that the haze caused by the aircraft attack had hampered the Navy's firing at Tripoli. He also apparently complained about the lack of air support and the absence of modern bombers, particularly Stirlings. He asked why Beauforts were withheld from Malta. Churchill replied at length to this message. He told Cunningham, on Portal's authority, that the same weight of bombs as the Navy had fired of shells into Tripoli in 42 minutes, that is, 530 tons, might have been dropped either by one Wellington squadron from Malta in 10½ weeks, or by one Stirling squadron from Egypt in 30 weeks. This latter figure was theoretical since the Stirling had not been operated at extreme range, nor was it suitable for operations under Middle East conditions. All the new class of heavy bombers, of which Cunningham spoke so confidently, were still suffering from the normal teething troubles common to all types when first brought into service. In fact, telegraphed Churchill, of the seventy new bombers on the strength of Bomber Command on the previous day, 23 April, sixty-eight were unserviceable from one cause or another. The Prime Minister said that Cunningham's remarks about withholding Beauforts from Malta showed that he did not appreciate the fact that the primary aim of the R.A.F. there was to defend the naval base against air attack in order that Cunningham's surface craft might operate against enemy convoys with their decisive power. The main disposition of forces between the various theatres rested with the Defence Committee over which he, Churchill, presided, and not with the Air Ministry, who executed their decisions. Ever since November, the Prime Minister claimed, he had tried by every method and every route to pump aircraft into the Middle East. Great risks had been run and sacrifices made, especially when two-thirds of one whole fighter squadron were drowned in trying to fly to Malta, and when the carrier *Furious* was taken off Atlantic duties to make three voyages with aircraft for Takoradi.

There the matter rested for a week or two. As soon as Longmore left for home, I re-examined the whole problem of co-operation in the Mediterranean with the Royal Navy, and wrote to Cunningham at length on 15 May to say that I had been trying to find a solution to what was actually a quite insoluble problem, the business of trying to provide him with the reconnaissance he needed for the impending operations in Crete:

The position is of course that you are now having to operate in waters quite literally surrounded by enemy air bases from which shore-based aircraft are operating. That in itself cuts out the employment of Sunderlands which have the range necessary for this role. The only bases we have from which to operate shore-based aircraft are those in the Western Desert, a precarious base in Malta . . . and the still more precarious one at Heraklion. . . .

I told the Admiral that I fully recognised the importance of reconnaissance to his operations, and that we would do our utmost with our depleted resources. It might appear a meagre provision, but I hoped that Admiral Cunningham would take it as the widow's mite it was.

He replied, thanking me for what the R.A.F. was doing. He quite saw the difficulties of this reconnaissance, but could not agree that the problem was insoluble. 'After all,' he wrote airily, 'at home they have precisely the same difficulties, and the Coastal Command solves them.'

It isn't only a question of the Crete operation, but we must have steady and reliable reconnaissance every day over the Ionian Sea.

I quite realise that your resources are meagre, but that seems to me only one more reason for pressing the Air Ministry to face up to facts and realise that the air situation out here calls for drastic measures.

There seemed little use in pointing out to the Admiral that the difficulties at home were not 'precisely the same'. In any case, there seemed every likelihood that we should learn this lesson the hard way within a very few days. In the fortnight since the evacuation of Greece we had tried desperately to send supplies to our forces in Crete. Of the 27,000 tons despatched by sea, some 21,000 tons were turned back to Egypt, 3,400 tons were lost at sea due to enemy air action and less than 3,000 actually arrived in Crete. This in itself was a sufficiently convincing demonstration of the importance of air-power, and no amount of reconnaissance would in itself have altered the situation.

The Middle East Commanders-in-Chief had signalled to London on 10 May that the main threat to Crete came from the air. The enemy had ample strength to maintain a very heavy scale of air attack, at the same time continuing operations in strength against Malta, Cyrenaica, and Egypt. We added that an adequate degree of fighter protection in Crete was not practical until further reinforcements arrived, and during this period the use of our naval and air bases there was liable to serious interruption. The heavy casualty rate in aircraft was inevitable. The landing of an enemy airborne division and of a seaborne expedition up to one division, supported by heavy air attack, was a possibility which we were preparing to counter. We considered, as Longmore had done, that there was a reasonable chance of keeping Suda Bay open for use by the Navy with one squadron of Hurricanes supplied with 100 per cent. reserve pilots and at a replacement rate in aircraft of 100 per cent. per month. If the enemy really concentrated on the problem, it seemed to us that there was little doubt the harbour could be rendered untenable. For the moment our defensive air garrison amounted to one fighter squadron of Gladiators, a few Hurricanes and Fleet Air Arm fighters.

On the island, we had three airfields and two more under construction. The defensive preparations had made little progress in the preceding four months, allegedly because there had always been some more urgent crisis which claimed our resources. Once again it was the old story of 'too little, too late'. Moreover, the German aircraft were now established in a crescent in Southern Greece and the islands close to Crete. Certainly we did what we could to apply the Germans' own formula, by attacking their squadrons on the ground. A dozen or so Ju. 52s were destroyed at Athens by Beaufighters from Malta. Wellingtons operating from Egypt assaulted airfields in the Dodecanese. Now that we were pushed back from Cyrenaica to bases in the Western Desert, the only aircraft with the necessary range were certain Marylands with long-range tanks. There had originally been seven. By 16 May we had two left, of which one was serviceable. The standard Maryland could only cover the required radius by refuelling at Heraklion, and with the repeated German air attacks now in progress there and at the other bases the maintenance of reconnaissance in this manner was precarious.

I told Portal it was not a question of priorities but of practicability. The Fleet was now having to operate in an area surrounded by enemy air bases, amply stocked with large numbers of aircraft including fighters, bombers, torpedo carriers, and reconnaissance. The Fleet was operating in the centre of the ring and as far as effective and secure air bases were concerned we were outside it. Once we could again operate from Cyrenaica reconnaissance cover could be given. Until then I found it difficult to see any satisfactory solution. The Germans' assault on Crete had begun in their usual manner with an attack on the three airfields. It made my blood curdle to think that we could provide from Egypt no fighter opposition whatever. All we could do was to get the heavy bombers to blast the enemy's aerodromes.

The German attack began in real earnest on 20 May with violent bombing and machine-gun attacks on and around Maleme airfield. These were followed immediately by paratroop, glider, and even troop transport landings, which were pressed home regardless of appalling loss. Similar attacks, on a smaller scale, were made on the airfields at Retino and Heraklion. The following morning, 21 May, Admiral Cunningham arrived in Cairo. Since he insisted on maintaining his Headquarters at Alexandria, some 125 miles away, he was not normally present at our daily Commanders-in-Chief's meetings. He came along to my office first and had half an hour's heated and at times violent argument. He had been, and was, asking for the impossible in the way of reconnaissance and was cursing the Air Ministry because he did not and could not get it. I managed to keep my temper, according to my journal, but told him some simple truths. We parted still friends. Conditions for air operations on the night of 20 May, with no moon and rough weather, had been unfavourable. On the following night they were so bad that friend and foe could not be distinguished. We had learned during that day that the Royal Navy had successfully attacked one enemy convoy trying to reach Crete. Captain Norman, Cunningham's representative in Cairo, then told me that the Navy had sailed gaily off into the Ægean to look for the other convoy. I spent a most uncomfortable day waiting to hear the almost inevitable result. There was nothing we could do.

At 6.30 that evening, Norman appeared in my office looking considerably more serious than usual. I guessed that the Navy had bought a packet. We did not then know what the damage was, but at least, as I wrote the next day, it had taught the lesson that it was not an operation of war to employ surface ships in an area surrounded by enemy shore air bases. This was what I had told Cunningham very bluntly only a few hours before. On the other hand, as I admitted, these convoys of small ships had to be prevented from reaching Crete. We could not stop them from the air since we could not reach that far and we could not operate from Crete, where our aerodromes were under overwhelming attack.

Wavell at least was beginning to appreciate these crucial facts. He rightly told the Prime Minister on 22 May that the whole position in the Middle East was at that time governed mainly by air-power and air bases: 'Enemy air bases in Greece make our hold of Crete precarious, and enemy air bases in Cyrenaica, Crete, Cyprus, and Syria would make our hold on Egypt difficult.'[1]

The morning of 23 May brought us yet more unpleasant news of the Royal Navy's losses. Cunningham was, as usual, at Alexandria, and General Blamey (in command of the Australians), Norman and I flew down there for a meeting with him. I thought Cunningham's reactions splendid. After our talk he said we had done wonders for his morale, and certainly he had done wonders for ours.[2]

The news later that day from Crete was depressing, the only good feature being a message that our attack by Blenheims from the Western Desert, just accomplished, had been most heartening to the troops. I had had to put all available aircraft on to this operation. That day I told Portal that the small scale of effective air support we were able to give to Crete had been, and was still, my main concern. In view of the critical situation at Maleme, the Western Desert Blenheims had operated there during the day and I had also sent six Hurricanes in the hope that they might be able to carry out a few sorties from Heraklion. This was a desperate gamble, but I felt that big risks had to be accepted. The two Beaufighters had been made nearly serviceable and were covering a disabled destroyer. The events of the last day and a half had shown that our ships could no longer operate in the Ægean or the vicinity of Crete during daylight. The enemy could therefore pass vessels to Crete from Greece or Melos. The convoys were escorted by Me. 110s and consisted mainly of small auxiliary vessels. There was little prospect that the Blenheims from the Western Desert could stop such movements.

Therefore, our main effort had to be against enemy forces landed or landing by air and sea. Regular operation from

---

[1] Churchill: *War Memoirs,* vol. III, p. 291.
[2] On 22 and 23 May, the Navy lost two cruisers and three destroyers sunk, one battleship (*Warspite*) was put out of action, and the battleship *Valiant* and many other units were badly damaged.

Heraklion would be precarious and expensive at the best. The bulk of our operations had necessarily to be based on Africa, near the operational limit of Blenheims and Marylands, and outside the range of Hurricanes and Tomahawks. All this meant diverting practically the whole of our effort from the Western Desert to Crete, but I felt that this was unavoidable at so critical a juncture.

It appeared to us that even now the situation was not fully understood in London. The Chiefs of Staff signalled on 25 May that it was essential that the Commanders-in-Chief in the Middle East should concert measures for 'clearing up the situation without delay. In so doing the Fleet and the Royal Air Force must accept whatever risk is entailed in preventing any considerable reinforcement of men and material from reaching the island either by night or by day.'[1]

Time, so we were told, was the dominating factor.

The Chiefs of Staff did not explain to us how we were to accomplish these desirable results. Cunningham replied sharply to this message, which arrived on the morning of 26 May. As I was getting up that day, an Army Staff Officer greeted me with a gloomy signal from Freyberg, who was in command of our ground forces in Crete.[2] I discussed this message with Wavell and Blamey and we decided that Mahomet must again go to the mountain, so we all set off for Alexandria to have a Commanders-in-Chief's meeting with Cunningham. Mr. Peter Fraser, Prime Minister of New Zealand, was also present. When we got there I found that Cunningham had again sent a signal to Mr. Churchill demanding more help from Britain, especially in the air. He had received a tart reply. This message had been discussed with the Army authorities but not with me. I told Cunningham bluntly what I thought about it, and signalled to Portal that Wavell had not consulted me.

'There are times,' I wrote in my journal, 'when I nearly lose my temper with the Army.'

We decided at our meeting to continue to push in reinforcements and supplies, though this could only be in small packets. As Cunningham records, the prospect of evacuation was in the air,

[1] Butler: *Grand Strategy,* vol. 2, p. 513.
[2] In Churchill: *War Memoirs,* vol. III, p. 261.

and Blamey and Fraser were full of anxiety as to the fate of Australian and New Zealand troops fighting desperately in Crete.[1]
Cunningham's own view was that it was impossible to abandon
our troops there. Our naval traditions, he thought, would never
survive such an action. Whatever the risks and losses, the remaining ships of the Fleet would make an all-out effort to bring
away the Army. Cunningham hoped that to take men off the
south coast would be less difficult than to operate ships in the
Ægean in the broad daylight. He told Wavell that with the enemy's
complete command in the air, the moment might come when,
with the terrible losses among the troops during their embarkation
and passage to Alexandria, lives might be saved if they surrendered
where they were.

Wavell's review of the situation was a gloomy one. Once or
twice I had to take him up on points of fact. Blamey, in his solid,
unimaginative way, was far less depressed. There was some
straight speaking between me and Cunningham. Our meeting
took an hour and a half in a small office on Alexandria aerodrome,
to which we had flown in an old Bombay full of bullet holes
collected at Habbaniya the previous week. It was all that there was
available in Cairo. By the time our meeting was over, the Bombay
was not functioning very well, so we returned to Cairo in two
Swordfish and a Roc. The situation there was gloomy, and after
a short talk with Wavell and Blamey I agreed that General
Evetts should be flown to Crete that night to help to relieve
Freyberg, the tone of whose messages indicated only too plainly
that he had endured more of a strain that he could bear. Late that
night we learnt that someone in the Army Headquarters had taken
it upon himself to cancel Evetts's move without reference to
anyone. By the time I heard of this it was too late to do anything
about it, since it would be light before a Sunderland could get to
Crete. I went to bed in a bad temper. It would not have been
improved if I had known that Churchill had cabled to Wavell:

Victory in Crete essential at this turning-point in the war. Keep
hurling in all aid you can.[2]

---

[1] Cunningham: *A Sailor's Odyssey,* p. 378.
[2] Churchill: *War Memoirs,* vol. III, p. 262.

Wavell explained on 27 May that an attempt to hold Crete longer would be useless and would be likely to exhaust the resources of all Services to such a degree as to compromise the Middle East position even more seriously than would the loss of Crete. He acknowledged that the enemy's overwhelming air superiority had made reinforcement impossible, while the R.A.F., having no bases within fighter range, had not been able to prevent the enemy from landing fresh troops by air.

So far as we could obtain a picture of what was happening at Crete, it appeared that heavy and continuous attacks by bombers and fighters, operating from the ring of enemy aerodromes, had completely knocked out our pitifully inadequate anti-aircraft defences, and consequently thinned down our troops and worn down their morale. Our squadrons had, I thought, and so told Portal, done all that was humanly possible, and sometimes more than one would have thought possible, to help. Now that the enemy was able to operate fighters from Crete itself our losses were heavy in proportion to our strength. Fighter protection for the Army against bombers and low-flying fighters had become impossible once the aerodromes in Crete were denied to us. I had no doubt it would be said that Crete was being lost for lack of air support, but the primary reason was lack of secure air bases and I warned Wavell that once the Hun was able to transfer his effort, a similar situation might arise in Tobruk unless eastern Cyrenaica was cleared in the immediate future.

The Chiefs of Staff told us, in a telegram of 26 May, that Crete should be evacuated forthwith, saving as many men as possible without regard to losses of material. A further telegram of the same day explained the reasons for the Chiefs of Staff's strategy in the Middle East. The possession of Crete would enable the enemy to set up a direct line of communication to Cyrenaica via the West coast of Greece and Crete. Unless we could establish our air forces in Cyrenaica, we could not interrupt this line, nor could we easily maintain Malta and continue interruption of the enemy's line of communications to Tripoli. They thought that the enemy attack through Turkey and perhaps through Syria could not develop in real strength for a good many weeks. Our first object must be to gain a decisive military success in the Western Desert and to destroy the enemy's armed forces in a battle fought with our whole available strength. Meanwhile, it was important to establish ourselves in Syria before the Germans had recovered from the immense drain on their air-power which the vigorous resistance of Freyberg's army had produced. Portal assured me that he knew our squadrons had done all that could be expected of them and Churchill had clearly endorsed at the time the decision to withdraw the remaining fighters from Crete on 19 May, while the War Cabinet fully understood the reasons which made it impossible for me to protect Crete against air attack and the German landings. The C.A.S. was confident that I would do all possible to help evacuation, particularly by protecting ships. The sinking of the *Bismarck* (27 May) meant the second and third instalments of Hurricanes would be with us in the Middle East earlier than he had dared to hope.

For the next few days the evacuation continued amidst scenes of indescribable chaos and to the accompaniment of a display of the utmost gallantry by all our forces. Cunningham strained every nerve to evacuate as many of our troops as possible, and we did our best to give him air cover. The geographical split between the centres of command, did not, however, help us in reaching our decisions. On the morning of 29 May, Cunningham sent up Evetts, who had been working at Alexandria on evacuation, to say that the naval losses were now becoming prohibitive. Wavell, Blamey and I discussed this, and decided that further efforts should be limited to a few destroyers going to Sphakia. Cunningham, of course, was still in Alexandria, and after no small delay we managed to contact him by telephone. He said that he had meantime decided he would continue on the full scale originally planned. I wrote in my journal:

It is, of course, sheer lunacy that vital decisions like this, where the three Services are deeply concerned, should have to be made at two places some 125 miles apart. Personally I cannot help feeling that Cunningham was wrong, since I feel that Naval losses are getting beyond what can be accepted. It is, however, his responsibility, and he knows the air risks from bitter experience now.

Absolved on 31 May by Wavell from any further responsibility,

Cunningham nevertheless said he was going in again that night with everything he had that would float. He succeeded in getting away another 4,000 men. All told, some 18,000 were evacuated from Crete, well over half the garrison. The first evacuation had been from Heraklion on the north side of the island, and subsequent evacuations from the south coast south of Canea. By careful timing, our forces made the best use of darkness for the embarkation of men, and for the perilous passage near Crete itself. The four convoys from southern Crete were successfully covered, though the one from Heraklion went badly awry. A cruiser and a destroyer were severely damaged as the convoy made its way there. Then, when the men and some stores had been embarked, a fault developed in one of our ships and held up the departure of the convoy. The meeting with the air escort was missed. All through the homeward passage the Heraklion convoy ploughed along under heavy air attack; two destroyers were sunk, and one cruiser very badly damaged. Yet a further cruiser was sunk north of Alexandria, no pre-arrangement having been made to notify our fighters.

There could be no doubt of the magnitude of our loss. I told Portal, after holding a stocktaking on 30 May, that our total aircraft losses in Crete up to that day had been forty-seven, of which thirty had occurred between the 20th and 27th. Of the soldiers, 1,800 had been killed and the better part of 12,000 taken prisoner. The Royal Navy had also lost more than 1,800 killed. Three cruisers and six destroyers had been sunk; a battleship, an aircraft-carrier, three cruisers, and a destroyer had been badly damaged; and another battleship, four cruisers, and six destroyers needed extensive repairs.

This, in itself, was a sufficiently melancholy reflection upon the consequences of weakness in the air. The operations at Scapa and Kiel in 1939, and even more those in Norway of 1940, had shown that sea-power could not henceforth be exercised independently of air-power. Crete had proved what was for me the central fact of the war. Air superiority was the pre-requisite to all winning operations, whether at sea, on land or in the air.

As Wavell acknowledged in his Despatch, we could have made Crete even harder for the enemy to seize had the defences been better developed during the early period of our occupation. The Despatch lays the blame for inadequate defences on the shortage of men and materials in Middle East. Moreover the enemy was able to launch far greater weight of attack on the ground and in the air than Wavell had considered likely. The Germans were prepared to accept very heavy casualties. Wavell's message to the survivors of Crete ended with these words:

> You are aware of the courage and skill with which the Navy brought you back from Crete; I have, on your behalf, sent them a message of gratitude. You saw little of the R.A.F. and may have thought your-selves deserted by them; I can assure you that, in circumstances of extreme difficulty, they did all they could to come to your assistance, and suffered heavy casualties in doing so.

We could not then know that the British and Commonwealth defenders of Crete had inflicted upon their invaders losses so severe that the enemy would never attempt again in the Second World War a major airborne landing. It has been well said that Freyberg and his troops, though they lost the battle of Crete, may have won the more important battle of Malta.

Certainly Wavell was right to tell the survivors that we had suffered severe losses in our efforts to help the island. The effect on our Blenheim squadrons in the Western Desert had been particularly severe. One of my staff, whose judgment I trusted, described two of our Wellington squadrons as being for the time being 'a broken remnant'. I kept on nagging at Wavell over Cyrenaica, and warning him that if we were still back at Mersa Matruh we could not prevent Tobruk from being blitzed as Crete had been. His retort was always, 'Well, how many more squadrons have you got?' I would reply that the Army had not been held up in Cyrenaica for lack of air support, and more than one German move had been stopped almost entirely by the air. It was only too easy to foresee the wounding recriminations which would soon follow. I wrote sadly:

> I am quite sure the Army will say we lost Crete because the R.A.F. let them down. Actually, we have been put out of commission because the Army have lost all our air bases for us, and without bases one cannot do much. I have been trying for the past three weeks to rub it in to

Wavell and Cunningham that this war is one for air bases. Wavell, who is a nice, solid, sound, honest old thing, is at last beginning to realise it, but it seems a pity that it should take three major defeats to bring the lesson home.

Our fellows have been doing some quite incredible things over Crete the last few days, but they will never get any credit for doing the impossible. Many of these soldiers give me the shudders. I like Wavell—he is intellectually—and in every other way—honest, but he does move so slowly. Even now I don't think he realises the need for speed, that (as Portal said in a signal to me) 'a stitch in time'. . . .

. . . Crete is going to be a very untidy affair. Afraid our soldiers are *pro tem* completely broken. Thank goodness the Swordfish—or beg, pardon, the Royal Navy—managed to get the *Bismarck*. Something to offset all the red ink entries!

A few days later, on 30 May, I told Portal that there was already, and there would undoubtedly be more, loose talk about the alleged lack of air support in Greece and Crete. I was taking the line that the root of the situation was secure air bases. We failed to clean up the Dodecanese and in Greece to secure our air bases in the Larissa Plain. As a result, enemy air operations were based on an ever-wider front, whereas ours were increasingly cramped, until finally the two remaining aerodromes were rendered untenable and out of range of effective support from Africa. My message ended: 'This campaign is primarily a battle for aerodromes.'

On the very next day Dickie Mountbatten, whose *Kelly* had been sunk under him off Crete a week before, pressed me hard on the subject of air support to the Navy and Army in Greece, the Ægean and Crete. I thought I had succeeded in getting him to realise the fundamental reason for lack of air support. He heckled me extensively on the ability of the Hun to move forward quickly and establish, and operate from, forward bases. I replied that of course one vital factor was the large number of transport aircraft which the Germans possessed. They also had large quantities of obsolete bombers which could be used to transport. A third line of attack, in which Mountbatten had been well primed by Wavell, the C.G.S. and company, was the fact that we had not got close support bombers and close support organisation for working with forward troops. Mountbatten's deduction was that the Army should have their own air force for close support and army co-operation. All the evidence on this point came from Greece and Crete. I challenged him as to whether he had any evidence of lack of close support in the Western Desert, and he replied that he had heard that our own troops had been bombed by our own aircraft on one occasion. It was as I had admitted to Portal, true that we had nothing like the highly refined organisation which the Germans had developed for communicating between close support aircraft and forward troops, but what he and many others completely overlooked was the fact that this highly specialised organisation depended utterly, as a prerequisite, on complete air superiority. It was noteworthy that the Stuka close support aircraft which the Germans had developed was known to our fighter squadrons as the answer to the Hurricane's prayer. Equally, the Lysander, specially designed for Army Co-operation, could not survive in the face of the Luftwaffe. I told Mountbatten that we could not conceivably afford the luxury of dividing our available air forces into penny packets, and so hopelessly prejudicing our fight to attain and maintain air superiority.

*

Amidst these disasters, however, came heartening signs of personal confidence and growing air strength in the Middle East. The celebrated 'Tiger' convoy had arrived in mid-May virtually intact, bearing 238 tanks and forty-three Hurricanes, all of which were rapidly erected and completed for service.[1] In the same month, I learned that Air Vice Marshal G. G. Dawson, whom I had known at the Ministry of Aircraft Production, was to come out to the Middle East as a result of Churchill's legitimate dissatisfaction with the rate of serviceability the R.A.F. was achieving there. Dawson arrived in June, and soon proposed drastic changes in organisation of which I wholeheartedly approved. He took the post of Chief Maintenance and Supply Officer, acting directly under me. A Maintenance Group was to superintend maintenance and repair work, vital to our existence, and to organise salvage units. I told the Air Ministry at once that I agreed with Dawson.

[1] See Churchill: *War Memoirs,* vol. III, p. 218.

They replied that the need for a Maintenance Group was admitted; but should it not, as usual, be placed under the Air Officer in charge of administration, who would be responsible for all the administrative services? I rejoined that there was no real analogy between home and Middle Eastern conditions. We had not the Air Ministry, the Ministry of Aircraft Production, an indigenous air industry and a Maintenance Command on which to rely. Finally, Whitehall relented. Dawson became Chief Maintenance and Supply Officer with the job of receiving, modifying, distributing, salvaging, and repairing the aircraft and spares in the Middle Eastern Air Command. His methods were frequently unorthodox to the point of brutality, but the results were startling.

On my arrival in the Middle East, I had thought that the Command was out of touch with the latest training and tactics. The arrival of the Luftwaffe and the increasing flow of modern aircraft to the Middle Eastern Command, had, I felt, remedied this deficiency; but the problems of maintenance, salvage, and repair in the Middle East were of a kind which were not met in the same degree in any other R.A.F. Command. Except in the direst emergency, shortage of crews and the likely losses made it unpractical to fly aircraft out to the Middle East. For lack of range, fighters could not in any case fly all the way. The choice was in practice between a journey round the Cape, taking ten to twelve weeks, or the Takoradi Route, which involved three weeks at sea and then an undefined period to transfer the aircraft across Africa. The distance from Takoradi to Abu Sueir was 3,697 miles, almost all of it over British territory. Thorold's men worked wonders there, and Dawson's men worked wonders in the Middle East. Without them I do not see how we could have mustered sufficient air strength to hold the Germans and Italians in 1941 and to defeat them in 1942 and 1943. I have sometimes reflected that it was an advantage to the Royal Air Force that we had no long Service tradition behind us, no set ways of tackling our job. Improvisation, which saved us in the Middle East, came the more easily to us, I think, than to our contemporaries in the Army and the Royal Navy.

I now knew from Portal that the Defence Committee in London had approved his proposal so to reinforce the Middle East that by

15 July we should have an effective strength of forty and a half squadrons of modern aircraft, and later more than fifty squadrons. But the aircraft mentioned in Portal's signal, except the Wellingtons, had a short radius of action, whereas we in the Middle East desperately needed aircraft with a long radius of action. All the same, the prospect of an increasing flow of modern aircraft, after the months of penury, was an attractive one.

By now, I knew at last, after nearly a month of uncertainty, that it would fall to me to employ this increased strength. On 14 May I had heard from Longmore that he expected to leave London for the Middle East a week later. Not until the end of the month did I receive from him a letter dated 19 May in which he said that I would already have heard that his return was indefinitely postponed. Churchill had decided that I was to be left in charge. Longmore would probably be offered a Governorship. In fact, this was the first definite information I had received, and even then I did not have any official confirmation from the Air Ministry of my appointment. I sympathised with Longmore, who had been kept waiting at home for over a fortnight, fully expecting to return to the Middle East. Nor did I admire the fashion in which he was told to join the ranks of those unfortunate British commanders who are called upon in the early months of war to face the situation foisted upon them by the neglect and fecklessness of others.

My journal records that I doubted whether I should last long as A.O.C.-in-C, as perhaps everyone who had anything to do with Crete would be fired. Moreover, I had sent one or two pretty blunt telegrams. All the same, the letters and signals I received from Portal and Freeman were uniformly sympathetic and helpful. To know that my many problems were understood at the nerve centre of the war was at once a solace and a spur. Often I would receive from Freeman helpful letters. In one, he told me that my 'stock' had been rising in the Air Ministry to where it had always stood with him. At much the same time I received another letter most characteristic of his wry humour:

I am afraid you are always getting telegrams from us saying you must attack ships, you must relieve Habbaniya, you must hold on to Crete, you must defend convoys, you must advance in Libya. All this must be maddening to you, and make it difficult to know what priorities really matter. I sometimes feel that we might end the next telegram by saying 'You must win the war'.

I hope it is unnecessary for me to tell you that I joined with the C.A.S.' handsome vote of confidence in you. We both know what you and Drummond have to put up with. . . .

Thus encouraged, I determined to accept Portal's invitation to send personal and private telegrams to him not only about the affairs of the R.A.F. in the Middle East, but about all three Services. I was fully aware that even private telegrams have a way of getting round and back. But our situation was by now so serious that such a consideration could not weigh heavily. My journal for Sunday 25 May concludes: 'I do not think this is a time to be mealy-mouthed. If Whitehall does not like what I say, then it is too bad.'

THE month of June 1941 opened for me with the official notification from the Secretary of State, Sir Archibald Sinclair, and from Portal, that I was now Air Officer Commanding-in-Chief, Middle East. Drummond was to be my Deputy.

My appointment, therefore, coincided exactly with the last stages of the evacuation from Crete. It was already clear enough that the disasters in Greece and Crete had not only cost us dearly in the short run, but might well cost us dearly in the long run, if we failed to apply to our Mediterranean strategy the lessons which seemed to me obvious. A new and disturbing element had intruded itself upon the scene. Naval power, upon which our whole Mediterranean and Far Eastern position had long rested, had shown itself to be incapable of sustaining without substantial help from the air our position in Egypt, upon which our capacity to continue the war largely depended.

We could now see that the Royal Navy could not proceed even as much as a hundred miles from Alexandria to the north or to the west, without having a fighter escort overhead. During the evacuation of Crete, I had been obliged to provide escorts for the convoys and therefore to divert our squadrons from their normal tasks. Nevertheless, there was no doubt that this method had been successful. No escorted ship had been seriously hit, although one loss had occurred on 1 June because Cunningham thought it would be a good idea to send the *Calcutta,* an anti-aircraft cruiser, to take part in the struggle and did not forewarn 204 Group; therefore, there were no fighters at hand and the cruiser was sunk. I hoped that at long last the Navy now realised the precise value of their anti-aircraft gun fire. Against high-level bombing, anti-aircraft fire was often effective, but against a converging attack by dive-bombers it was useless.

The result of these events was that the Royal Air Force, Middle East, now had to shoulder an additional and possibly heavy burden. I soon gathered that Cunningham was pitching his demands high, and indeed one report said that he was demanding no less than six squadrons of Beaufighters. I could give no support to such ideas, but I recognised at once that if and when the Royal Navy could usefully take to the sea again it would probably want more than one and a half squadrons of Beaufighters to provide continuous daylight cover for the two or three days that the ships would be at sea. We were doing everything possible to improvise long-range Hurricanes, but they were equally badly needed in the Western Desert and in Syria. Nevertheless, I gladly recognised the supreme effort which Cunningham had made. I signalled to him on 1 June:

> May I express on behalf of myself and the Royal Air Force, Middle East, our deep admiration of the way in which the Royal Navy has once again succeeded in doing what seemed almost impossible.

Cunningham thanked me for my signal and, much more, for the R.A.F's most valuable co-operation. It showed, he signalled, what could be done even with improvised long-range fighters; and he feared that the Navy would need a lot of fighter help in the future, especially on the route to Tobruk, but he well knew that the Royal Navy could count upon us.

In the Army, however, despite the message which Wavell had sent to the survivors from Crete, I was soon conscious of a 'first-class hate' working up against the R.A.F. for having 'let them down in Greece and Crete'. I told Freeman that Wavell was very worried by this and was doing his best to stamp it out, but I was not sure that even now the real reasons for the lack of air support were fully appreciated in the High Command. I had hardly written this to Freeman when I saw a signal of the same day from Wavell to Dill, which had been issued without discussion with me. I told Portal at once that in my opinion parts of this signal were misleading in that it omitted that our inability to provide fighter defence and other air action had been due to the loss of the essential air bases, also that the aerodromes on Crete, itself were deliberately limited in number so that the available ground defences could be concentrated. These proved to be utterly inadequate, not only to enable us to use the aerodromes, but even to prevent the enemy from seizing and using them himself. I was concerned, not so much with the inaccurate inquest on Crete, as with the grave danger that wrong conclusions might be drawn from these operations and one of the fundamental principles of air strategy be obscured, or forgotten. I showed my signal to Wavell before its despatch.

On the next day, 4 June, I attended one of the periodical meetings of the Commanders-in-Chief. So far I had found that though these gatherings had some value for the exchange of information, they were of little use for the discussion and decision of policy, and the talk tended to be amiable and vague. Being a newcomer, I had not until now attempted to force the pace, but on this occasion two issues of cardinal importance were raised. I thought that the times required some plain speaking. First of all, Admiral Cunningham, in connection with the fighter cover we had provided for the Fleet during the evacuation of Crete, raised the whole question of a special Group allocated solely for work with the Royal Navy. The admiral averred that he did not wish in any way to discuss the matter of operational control of such a Group, for he was quite prepared that no change should be made in that respect. He did insist, however, that this Group should have considerable forces of long-range reconnaissance and long-range fighter aircraft permanently allocated to it. The gist of Cunningham's argument was that our air forces in the Middle East were insufficient, that the air forces available to support the Fleet were quite inadequate, and that such forces must be occupied with that task and with nothing else.

I replied that the inadequacy of our forces to meet new commitments did not by any means apply only to the air forces. I entirely agreed that the main role of the Beaufighters in particular was to give cover to the Fleet in areas in which enemy single-seat fighters could not normally operate. However, I could not, and would not, tie my hands as to the use of these aircraft for other purposes should the situation demand it. Even with much larger forces than we yet possessed in the Middle East, I thought it would be foolish to tie up any large section to meet a commitment the scale of which would vary a great deal. The cover we had given to the evacuation from Crete had been effective only because of the concentration of fighters from the Western Desert. Similarly, I argued, it would be necessary to concentrate in the Western Desert for the forthcoming operation—'Battleaxe'—and naval commitments at that time would have to be correspondingly reduced. I told Freeman:

It was an out-spoken battle on both sides, but I do not think I penetrated the naval armour one inch, except in so far as I made my position quite clear.

The second part of the controversy arose when Wavell asked about the strength of the air force available for campaigning in the Western Desert. He and Cunningham joined in a demand that we three Commanders-in-Chief should at once signal home to demand much speedier and larger air reinforcements. I replied by saying what was being done, by telling them what I had asked for in addition, and by saying that I thought such a signal would not be useful, and I added that I knew there were also serious shortages of anti-aircraft guns, tanks, and motor transport, and of submarines and light naval craft. I was, of course, fully prepared to sign a joint signal stating the urgent requirements of all Services. At this point the matter was dropped.

I told Freeman that I did not want him to think from this account that I was spending my time squabbling with Wavell and Cunningham. On the contrary, our personal relations were very friendly, all the more so because there had been, for a change, some frank talking. All the same, we did have to face the fact that the naval situation in the Eastern Mediterranean had completely changed. It had now become what we had long prophesied and what the Royal Navy had refused to credit until they lost half their Mediterranean Fleet by deliberately putting their heads into a hornets' nest by day. Control of sea communications in that area had now to be exercised by air, or not at all. So far as I could gather, Cunningham envisaged putting to sea and staying there under a fighter umbrella, which would be a feasible, if extremely ineffective operation, so long as it was carried out within range of our Hurricanes or outside the range of the enemy aircraft. I did not see how we could provide cover for naval operations in the quadrilateral Malta–Tripoli–Benghazi–Patras. It was not going to be easy to cover even direct passages between Egypt and Malta. In accordance with my determination to express my full views on matters affecting all three Services, I told Freeman of the extreme difficulties of securing any effective combined control over operations. As far as the Army was concerned, it was largely a question of educating the soldiers in the realities of air-power. As for the Navy, we had an excellent Liaison Officer in Cairo in Captain Norman, but:

> He is often quite helpless, and until the Admiral can be persuaded to come away from his part-worn Flagship and leave the remains of his Fleet to be commanded by subordinate Flag Officers (as we do), I see no hope. What I am afraid of is that some all-seeing power at home may say—'Let there be an "issimo"—and since you have three Services incompatible, let there be a "civil issimo incomprehensible"'.

I suspect that as soon as our Commanders-in-Chief meeting was over Cunningham signalled to the Admiralty, for on 6 June I received from Portal a message saying that he thought I should take precisely the line I had taken at this meeting on the 4th at any similar future discussions. I imagine that Cunningham's signal had been an attempt to have my decision overruled, though we remained on excellent personal terms.

★

The successes of the Axis forces in the Ægean, and Rommel's advance across the desert, meant that the enemy might now launch upon us in Egypt heavy attacks from the west and from the north. The areas around Sollum provided more or less unlimited numbers of potential airfields. Our lines of communication were rendered much more vulnerable. Somehow, we had to supply the isolated garrison at Tobruk. Wavell was most keen to take advantage of Rommel's lull in activity to push him out of eastern Cyrenaica. While the German commander was trying to remove the thorn in his flesh at Tobruk, Wavell was planning an offensive, Operation 'Battleaxe'. Part of the cargo carried by the Tiger Convoy, the forty-three Hurricanes, had already proved their worth. The other 'Tiger Cubs' were in a less satisfactory condition. Of the twenty-one light tanks, Mark VIs, eight required complete overhaul. Of the Mark IVa cruiser tanks, the average mileage was 700, which was half their life expectation. While sixty-seven Mark VI cruiser tanks were in good order, many of the Infantry tanks needed as many as forty-eight man-hours apiece in the workshops before they were serviceable. Wavell told the Prime Minister that had the Cubs only required to be fitted with Desert equipment and camouflage, all would have been ready for operations by 31 May.[1]

Churchill, for his part, showed much impatience with our slow progress on land. On 3 June, he signalled to Wavell that he had 530,000 soldiers on his ration strength, together with 500 field guns, 350 anti-aircraft guns, 450 heavy tanks, and 350 anti-tank guns. In the five months since the beginning of the year, more than 7,000 mechanical vehicles had reached the Middle East, and yet:

The fighting in the south has for two months past enabled a north-ward movement to begin, yet you are evidently hard put to it to find a brigade or even a battalion, and in continual telegrams you complain of your shortage of transport which you declare limits all your operations.

Several days before this, on the afternoon of 29 May, we had decided to hold on to the Tobruk Line. It seemed deplorable to throw up western Cyrenaica so lightly, but there was nothing for it. While I thought that the Germans intended to make the Balkans their main theatre of operations in that year, I felt that if the Libyan offensive offered the enemy any scope he would exploit it for all his worth, since it gave the chance of striking at our main base. Rommel had probably succeeded already beyond his wildest hopes on account of our weakness in armoured vehicles and aircraft.

We could not, however, concentrate our gaze entirely on the west. I had to try to complete two squadrons for the advance into Syria. It seemed doubtful whether we could provide an adequate air force for this operation, though all indications were that a strong show of force at the beginning would cause a quick

[1] Connell: *Wavell*, p. 484.

collapse, whereas the despatch of a weak force would merely encourage opposition. As early as mid-May, our information left me in little doubt that the Germans intended to make a move on Iraq through Syria, with the help of the Iraqis. I also knew that the Turkish Government were most anxious for us to occupy Syria before the Germans got there. On 19 May, Wavell had told the Defence Committee that he must scrape together the strongest possible force to move there, without leaving the Western Desert too bare. The Commander-in-Chief grumbled a little, as in my opinion he was amply entitled to do, against some of the conditions imposed from London. Two days later, he had reached the point of telling the Defence Committee that they must either trust his judgment or relieve him of his command. They replied somewhat frostily that if Wavell was unwilling to meet their wishes, he would be relieved. All these events coincided with the final agony in Crete.

Such forces as Wavell was able to muster set out on 8 June under General Wilson with the help of four squadrons. A fortnight elapsed before Damascus was taken, and 'Battleaxe' was now due to be launched.

About a week before the target date, 15 June, I gave Wavell a note of our air strength and of the targets upon which we proposed to use it:

Now to 10th June: Ships in Benghazi. Now to 12th June: Convoys road Benghazi–Derna. 12th to 14th June: Transport between Tobruk and Frontier. Aerodromes.

Expect—up to 20th June: 2 Hurricane Squadrons, 2 Tomahawk, 2 Blenheim, 2 Glen[n] Martin, 1 Army Co-operation.[1]

Wavell, who was painfully conscious of the deficiencies of the Tiger Cubs and his other armoured strength, refused to adopt a confident attitude. Sir John Dill signalled to him on 7 June:

But Archie, your greatly superior air strength is surely your greatest asset, and you don't mention it. I hope that Tedder will see that his lads play their part in closest possible support.[1]

The Commander-in-Chief replied that he had not included a

[1] Connell: *Wavell,* p. 487.

report on air strength since he knew that I was cabling separately. My figures, however, showed no superiority, and at the moment we certainly had none. In fact, General Beresford-Peirse, commanding Western Desert Force, was very concerned about the air, though 'Tedder keeps assuring me he realises importance, and that it will be all right on the night.'

Although I had, indeed, every confidence that our squadrons would more than hold their own in the imminent battle, the situation in Cyrenaica did not look too healthy to me. If the Germans cared to stage it, Tobruk might be heavily blitzed from the air, and our insecure refuelling ground at Sidi Barrani did not enable us to provide an effective defence against such a blitz. The opportunity which, I was sure, had earlier existed for kicking the Germans out of the Sollum–El Adem area had gone. Rommel had been able to trickle forward reinforcements and supplies, and according to the Army view the prospects of pushing him back now were not particularly rosy. The Axis forces had moreover been reinforced through Benghazi, although even at the height of the crisis in Crete our attacks on that port had never ceased.

I was now the recipient of demands from the Army and Royal Navy which I could not carry out in full. The Army asked that all our heavy bombers should be employed against Benghazi and all the long-range Hurricanes on the lines of communication from there. Moreover, they pestered me to provide strategical reconnaissance and signalled in this sense to Beresford-Peirse in a cable which I did not see before despatch and of which I did not approve. I told Collishaw, commanding in the Western Desert, that I did not take the demands in this latter respect too seriously because I thought Beresford-Peirse should know what strategical reconnaissance he needed, and I pointed out to Wavell that any aircraft available for this work were under Collishaw's control. It would be for him to decide what reconnaissance could be done in the light of the other demands on his air strength. I wished to avoid, as far as possible, asking Collishaw to undertake specific tasks of reconnaissance, and told the Army Headquarters in Cairo that they must inform Beresford-Peirse of their needs, and then Collishaw and he must together decide what could be managed.

Meanwhile, I was being pressed very hard by the Navy to provide the usual fighter protection for their shipping between Alexandria and Tobruk and also for the Fleet itself in case they should decide to go to sea. On the same day that Beresford-Peirse was urging Collishaw to put every available Hurricane to the ground-strafing of motor transport and lines of communication, the General Officer Commanding Tobruk was signalling that he had only four days' supply of petrol left, while the Navy were saying that they could not send the petrol unless all the Hurricanes could protect the ship *en route* and while discharging at Tobruk.

I estimated that our maximum strength on 15 June would be sixty fighters, sixty-five medium bombers, twelve Army Co-operation fighters, and three and a half squadrons of heavy bombers. Against this, our estimate of the German Air Forces now in Libya was that they could call upon forty fighters, seventy bombers and some reconnaissance aircraft, which could probably be reinforced from a further forty fighters and 170 bombers at that time located in Sicily, the Dodecanese, and the Balkans. I thought the enemy would have no difficulty in maintaining these aircraft in Libya. Nor could we entirely ignore the Italian effort of some two hundred fighters and sixty bombers in Libya, and a proportion of about eighty fighters and a hundred bombers available for reinforcement from other adjacent Mediterranean theatres.

On the same day, Andrew Cunningham made his assessment for the Admiralty. He observed that at that moment there were only a dozen or so long-range fighters in the Middle East and they were vulnerable to enemy fighters based on either side of the line of approach. Experience showed that to cover the Fleet for a whole day required six sorties of five hours by six aircraft, and on this calculation a force of a hundred fighters would not be excessive to provide a reasonably strong umbrella to cover surface movements through the worst of the dive-bombing area, in addition to cover for essential supplies to the Western Desert. For the moment, our strength was so far from these figures that the sorely needed supply to Tobruk had perforce been stopped, so that the fighters might gather themselves to combat the enemy in the battle area. To attempt to interrupt the Benghazi traffic by surface forces could only cause heavy and recurrent damage and loss of ships, nor could such attempts be expected to be fruitful in the face of the far-flung and efficient enemy air reconnaissance which spied out every move. Cunningham acknowledged that there was little I could do to provide better protection, since the fundamental trouble was shortage of aircraft. He added ominously that improvement could, however, be made in the method of operating such fighter protection as we had and in the working and control of the aircraft allocated for Fleet duty. He signalled that he was having a 'certain amount of difficulty' in this matter, and would shortly have to raise it with London unless rapid changes took place.

*

Wishing to meet the squadron commanding officers before the battle, I flew to the Desert on 9 June. It was a glorious morning, the desert looking pink, the colour of mother-of-pearl. When we reached it after an hour, the sea shimmered electric blue. Below us, there floated over the desert little pink clouds, and over the sea blue clouds. I had never seen such colour.

It was grand to talk with the commanding officers, most of whom I knew. During the afternoon, Beresford-Peirse arrived to meet Wavell, who was spending the night with the Desert Force. He soon arrived in a Lockheed, and we adjourned to Collishaw's hut for a talk. On the whole, our conversation was amicable enough, though Wavell was somewhat peevish and I had to speak bluntly. I was becoming rather tired at hearing Generals say that we hadn't enough air strength. Wavell said he was worried because he was repeatedly told from home that we had strong numerical air superiority over the enemy, whereas this assessment was not borne out by the number of aircraft Collishaw had actually serviceable at any given time. I explained that it was misleading to compare our serviceability figures with the enemy's total strength. All the same, I was puzzled to know what was the basis for this alleged superiority. I told Wavell, and Collishaw agreed, that the fighter forces available for 'Battleaxe' should be able to secure and maintain a reasonable degree of air superiority. The main effort during the next few days would be against the enemy's lines of communication in the rear, followed during the two days preceding D-day by an attack upon his communications in the forward area. We also discussed aerodrome defence, which was very thin. Everyone agreed that it would be quite ineffective against determined air attack, but we considered that the risk must be accepted, for nothing more could be done at present. It was quite evident to me, however, and I so reported to Portal, that if 'Battleaxe' failed the reason would be 'insufficient air forces' and 'inadequate interruption of lines of communication'.

Wavell left for Mersa Matruh, and I for Cairo, flying along the coast and then across the desert. When I reached my office I discovered that Beresford-Peirse had signalled on the previous day that 204 Group had been unable to shoot up distant lines of communication since 4 June because the long-range Hurricanes were reserved for naval purposes, and would be unable to strafe forward lines of communication between 12 and 14 June owing to the lack of Blenheims. Moreover he reported that 204 Group (which under my reorganisation had become Air Headquarters Western Desert)[1] had no definite assurance yet of four complete fighter squadrons for 14 June, and four bomber squadrons were considered as very doubtful for the same date. He regarded the failure to strafe lines of communication as deplorable, and thought it essential to have fresh squadrons in time for 'Battleaxe'.

I signalled to him at once that I was surprised these matters had not been raised when we had discussed the situation that afternoon:

Must say frankly cannot feel your signal helpful. Neither I nor Collishaw have sent signals complaining of the deplorable shortage of the defence of our aerodromes. I had hoped both Services realised we have to do the best with what we have and had sufficient faith in each other.

Meanwhile the Prime Minister had telegraphed to Wavell his concern at the statement in an earlier message from Cairo that he could have only four fighter squadrons and four bomber squadrons by 15 June, whereas he was informed by Portal that on the latest information from me there should be available ten squadrons

[1] A chart of the organisation of Mediterranean Air Command at March 1943 faces page 403.

in the Western Desert and support from three and a half Wellington squadrons. The Prime Minister hoped that in addition, some
elements at least of the seven squadrons re-equipping and immobile might be used in this battle in view of its supreme importance. Churchill assumed that Wavell and I were working in the
closest concert, and would tell the Cabinet how it was proposed
to use the Air Force as one of the decisive and integral features
of the battle plan. He added:

> I venture once again to emphasise that the objective is not, repeat
> not, the reaching of particular positions but the destruction by
> fighting of the armed forces of the enemy wherever it may be found.
> As your Force diminishes so should his. He has a far longer line of
> communication than you and must be in greater difficulties about
> supplies, especially of ammunition.

Portal saw to it that I understood the R.A.F. to be fighting a
battle, not only in the Desert, but in London. He warned me
privately on 11 June that 'political circles' would be on the look-
out for any failure on the R.A.F's part to afford close support to
our troops in the forthcoming operations. It was being suggested
that we would pay too much attention to shooting up lines of
communication and aerodromes in the rear, and not enough to
dealing with anti-tank guns, tanks, and artillery that might be
firing on our own troops. The idea was current that when
German troops were in difficulties they immediately summoned
a pet aeroplane by radiotelephone to deal with the opposition.
The Chief of the Air Staff was being asked why we did not have the
same arrangement? He expressed his complete confidence in my
judgment as to the most effective way of helping our troops to
victory, but for the reason he mentioned, it was essential for
Collishaw and me to obtain in advance the complete agreement
of the Army to our tactical plans. If their requirements seemed to
us to be unsound, and if persuasion failed, we should do our
best to act as they wished, and should register our disagreement
to them and to him before the battle began. He hoped and believed
there would be no disagreement.

I thanked Portal at once for this thoughtful forewarning. There
did not seem to be any immediate danger of disagreement either

in the Desert or in Cairo, but if there were a failure it was quite clear that any opportunity to make the R.A.F. the scapegoat would be seized upon. I pointed out that it was sometimes forgotten that attacks on the rear lines of communication in the past two months, which had contributed largely to restricting enemy action, were a new development only made possible by improvisations with Hurricanes and other aircraft. I observed that having been given jam and cream the Army were now complaining that they did not always have both; but Wavell had returned from the Desert slightly more optimistic.

At the meeting of Commanders-in-Chief on 13 June (from which the Admiral was absent), two days before 'Battleaxe' was launched, I deliberately put the cat amongst the pigeons by stating flatly that the three Services were not really working together. An interesting and provocative argument ensued, but as I expected, we could carry the matter no farther because Admiral Cunningham insisted on staying 'at sea'. I remarked that I was getting rather tired of being between the devil and the deep sea, trying to meet conflicting requirements. The operations in Palestine and Syria, which had not been properly planned between the three Services, had obliged me to divert to the task of covering the Fleet almost all the fighter force originally allocated to cover the land operations.

Nevertheless, I was able to tell Portal that the reinforcements to Collishaw's force had been moving forward satisfactorily. Thirty-six Hurricanes had gone to the Desert on 11 and 12 June. The Chiefs of Staff had urged me to accept great risks elsewhere in order to give 'Battleaxe' the maximum air support. Everything should be hurled in at the outset so that the initiative might be gained. The Royal Air Force was now able to provide four squadrons of Hurricanes, two of Blenheim bombers, one of Tomahawks, one of Marylands and one Hurricane reconnaissance squadron. Many of the crews were newly arrived and unaccustomed to desert warfare. On 15 June we enjoyed effective though not numerical air superiority. In the whole of the day the enemy managed only six air attacks.

'Battleaxe' opened with an advance by three columns. Rommel countered the next day, moving additional armour swiftly from

Tobruk. Wavell, for his part, had no choice but to attack with a mixed force of cruiser and infantry tanks, many of which had a cross-country speed of five miles an hour. The plan was first to defeat Rommel on the frontier of Egypt, then to roll him back to Tobruk, from which the garrison would issue to meet the advancing force, and then to exploit the breakthrough in the direction of Derna and Mechili. I told Collishaw that I wanted him to exercise the closest supervision over the low-flying attacks being carried out by the R.A.F. in the Desert. Such attacks could be of great assistance to the Army, but it had to be remembered that conditions had changed since the campaign in Cyrenaica became static. The enemy had established strong fixed anti-aircraft defences at various points, low flying attack upon which was likely to involve casualties out of all proportion to the military results achieved. Moreover, such casualties were not offset by any corresponding weakening of the enemy's air strength and might therefore undermine the air superiority which it was Collishaw's first task to gain.

Our squadrons performed, as I knew they would, magnificently. All the same, I recorded in my journal on 16 June that I was far from happy about events in the Desert: 'Afraid I've got no more faith in the Army than they have themselves.'

That day, Wavell very naturally became worried about the unsatisfactory progress of the offensive and flew up to the Desert. On the morning of 17 June, he and Beresford-Peirse were foolish enough to go up in a Proctor and land in the forward area where 7th Armoured Division was on the move. No one quite knew where the two Generals were, and it was only thanks to much good luck and a very heavy fighter escort that Wavell escaped. That evening, when he got back to Cairo, I told him politely that this had been an act of criminal lunacy. It was not merely a question of his personal value, but the effect that the loss of the General Officer Commanding would have from the point of view of prestige. We had lost enough Generals already. My journal continues:

One thing is clear, and that is that the whole thing is a complete flop. The only bright spot is that our chaps have been simply grand and have done more than even the Army could have called for. There'll certainly be a hunt for scapegoats after this, and I know we were marked down as the prospective sacrifice—but I don't think that will come off this time! Now we'll have to see what we can do to help them to get a move on in Syria. What a life!

It's been cooler again in the last few days—a north wind, but the shine has gone out of the trees and grass, the flame trees have been glorious the past few weeks, but they are fading away now. The Nile begins to rise about the end of the month, and for a couple of months I think things get very heavy and sticky.

That morning, while Wavell was in the Desert, I had told Collishaw that in view of the enemy's fighter weakness, the air umbrella specially requested by the Army now appeared to be relatively unnecessary. He should concentrate his effort against land movements. News of the enemy 'right hook' breakthrough arrived after this, and our whole effort was then thrown against enemy columns, with considerable success. Wavell told me on his return that there had been some dive-bombing of our troops 'when the umbrella was not there'. Collishaw reported the demise of twelve Ju. 87s and three Me. 109s.

The next day, 18 June, it appeared that the position was now stabilised again, and I understood that there was no prospect of our being able to resume the land offensive in the immediate future. It was therefore essential to revert to a more economical use of my exiguous force. The low-flying attacks, which had helped very considerably, if not vitally, to extricate our land forces from a critical situation, had been expensive in personnel and material. I had built up fighter strength in the Western Desert by attaching half squadrons from units reforming and re-equipping in the Delta. Now that the Desert offensive had petered out, I felt it was most important to get these squadrons properly formed as trained fighter units. I had no doubt that more than half our casualties in the three days had been due to inexperience. Moreover, I wished to strengthen the force in Syria. Collishaw was accordingly told that his main aim from now onwards should again be the interruption of enemy lines of communication.

On the same day, Wavell reported to Sir John Dill that he did not expect to recover from the battle area more than the equivalent of one regiment of cruiser tanks and one regiment of infantry tanks. His judgment was that no offensive was possible in the Western Desert for at least three months.

Wavell had shown me the draft of his signal. In the first version he observed—'We never had air superiority'. I pointed out that this statement was utterly inaccurate, since the Army had had the complete cover for which they had asked. I also tried to explain that superiority 'to afford such protection' or 'to stop enemy movements' was unattainable unless the enemy air strength was completely eliminated. I quoted Greece, and Wavell replied by referring to Crete. It seemed to me pointless to continue the argument in the face of such apparent inability to understand the principles of air warfare.

Nevertheless, Wavell's signal as finally sent, which was admittedly unsatisfactory from the R.A.F. point of view, caused Portal to observe that in Greece the Germans with vast air superiority did not entirely protect their troops from bombing, and completely failed to stop the movement of our troops from north to south. He enquired whether the Army had in fact made any request for the bombing of enemy positions at Halfaya on the 16th. I replied that they had not done so. If we had been given the necessary information Blenheims could have carried out the attack within an hour and a half. A striking force was available on call but was not used at all on the Army's initiative. The Blenheims which protected the retirement of our troops on 18 June had been laid on to their targets as a result of air reconnaissance. The main difficulty throughout the operation, I told the C.A.S., had been the almost complete lack of information from the ground. Arrangements had been made for communication and recognition between our ground and air forces. Calls from the air for acknowledgment of the recognition signal were never answered. In such circumstances close-support bombing became impossible. Indeed, Army Headquarters had great difficulty even in giving a bombing line. Wavell's statement, 'we are not organised or trained', was correct. It appeared to me that the troops had been quite untrained, and apparently unable to keep their own commanders informed, much less to keep the air forces informed.

During this ill-fated offensive, we had lost about a third of our

strength in cruiser tanks, and nearer two-thirds of our infantry
tanks. The Royal Air Force was thirty-three fighters the worse
off.[1] In addition to the inadequacy of our training for desert
warfare, there was a cause of more permanent importance,
namely the dispersion of strength involved in the policy of
maintaining a fighter umbrella over the ground forces. Had this
continued, the enemy by defeating us in detail would have been
able to gain air superiority.

Although I thought that the handling of the offensive by our
soldiers had been deplorable, I nevertheless recognised that Wavell
had not been given the necessary materials. The much vaunted
Tiger Cubs were a very poor substitute in most cases for efficient
modern armour. Rommel, reflecting on the battle some time
later, observed justly that Wavell was placed at a great disadvantage by the slow speed of his heavy infantry tanks, which
prevented him from reacting quickly enough to the moves of the
faster German vehicles. Here was the soft spot, which he exploited
tactically.[2] Dill, in a signal to Wavell of 20 June, frankly acknowledged that the infantry tanks were not intended for desert warfare.

*

While all these events were unfolding in the Western Desert,
affairs in Iraq and Syria had come to a head. Under pressure from
London, the military force scraped together by Wavell had set
out from Palestine and reached Habbaniya on 18 May and Baghdad on 30 May. Wavell's apparent unwillingness to undertake
this operation had materially helped to undermine the Prime
Minister's confidence in him. Churchill had noted: 'He gives me
the impression of being tired out.'[3]

To secure the position in Syria was an operation which required
military strength and diplomatic tact in almost equal proportions.
Unfortunately, relations with the Free French and with General
de Gaulle personally were by no means easy. He had seen fit to
issue an instruction giving a list of certain French personnel who
had enlisted in the R.A.F.V.R. and who had refused to transfer

---

[1] Playfair: *The Mediterranean and Middle East,* vol. 2, p. 171.
[2] Liddell Hart: *The Rommel Papers,* p. 146.
[3] Churchill: *War Memoirs,* vol. III, p. 229.

to the Free French. It was announced that if these personnel did not join the Free French they would be classified as deserters and liable to arrest and trial for desertion if they should enter French territory. I had already told General Spears, who managed our liaison with the Free French, that in this matter de Gaulle would find me adamant. De Gaulle arrived in my office on the morning of Tuesday 3 June, accompanied by a young officer as interpreter. He asked if I spoke French. I replied that I did not, so the interpreter stayed. Actually, I understood perfectly well all that de Gaulle said, and I was pretty certain that he understood all I said. I am bound to confess that I was not impressed by him. Most of our talk was quite friendly, until I raised the matter of his proscription of Frenchmen who had joined the R.A.F.V.R. I did my best to put the case tactfully but de Gaulle became completely Calvinist. At length I felt obliged to say that if he pressed the point we should have to uphold our obligation to these men and guarantee their safety against him. I did not want to say this but saw no alternative. I found that de Gaulle could not be moved, and the last phases of our discussion consisted of a series of brief exchanges:

De Gaulle: 'C'est la loi.'

Myself: 'It is my honour.'

De Gaulle: 'C'est mon devoir.'

Myself: A shrug of the shoulders.

My recollection is that for good measure de Gaulle added: 'C'est la loi de France, et moi, moi je suis la France.' At the end of the interview we shook hands and wished each other luck!

My journal records that I thought him a 'dangerous menace'.

I told London of this encounter, and awaited reactions, which were not long in coming. They took the shape of a personal telegram from Churchill to de Gaulle on 7 June.

The Prime Minister pointed out courteously that in the agreement made between the Free French and the British Government in August 1940, it had been recognised that a number of Frenchmen would continue to serve in our forces, while we agreed that intending French recruits should preferably join de Gaulle. This part of the bargain we had carried out with complete loyalty, but we could not force those who had joined us to serve under de Gaulle. Churchill assured de Gaulle that he understood all the difficulties and strain to which he was exposed, and was certain that he would do everything to promote harmony and co-operation. De Gaulle seems to have been somewhat mollified by this, and the matter was settled soon afterwards by a compromise.

This meeting over, I set off for Lydda, where it was arranged that d'Albiac from Baghdad and Brown from Jerusalem should meet to discuss the Iraqi and Syrian operations. d'Albiac described to me the collapse of the Iraqi affair, where 90 per cent. of the work had been done on our side by the air forces, mostly by the Flying Training School, and half the remaining 10 per cent. by R.A.F. armoured-cars. d'Albiac proposed to send a flight of Gladiators to Palestine to operate against Syria, and from Mosul would assist with the attack on aerodromes in the north. Brown, who was to command the air side of the operation, would have available a Hurricane, a Tomahawk, an Army Co-operation Hurricane and a Blenheim squadron, together with one Gladiator flight and some help from Mosul. The Beaufighters would be fully occupied in going to cover the naval part of the operations. The limiting factor in Palestine was aerodromes. There were only three good ones and all were congested and vulnerable. The difficult conditions east of Haifa made our preparation of landing grounds there painfully slow. I understood at this meeting that the Army felt their force was inadequate, particularly in view of the French mechanised force they might be expected to meet. It was therefore anticipated that the R.A.F. would clear the way for them and stop the French tanks. I told Portal that I wished the Army had more faith in themselves and did less wishful thinking about air-power. If they had any difficulties in Syria I expected the explanation to be 'inadequate air support' and not lack of tanks.

The conduct of the operations in Syria was not eased by changes of plans. Admiral Cunningham had said at first that his naval operations were only in support of the land advance, and if proved to be unnecessary could and would be stopped. By 13 June, just before 'Battleaxe', he was saying that there were essential duties for the Navy to perform off Beirut. Wavell accepted this position. Our Tomahawks dealt successfully with an attack on the Fleet by Ju. 88s that day. Naturally, the unexpected need to give close support to the Fleet meant the diversion of most of the forces intended for the advance over land. I pointed out clearly to Cunningham and to Wavell at the time what this would mean. The whole episode provided another example of the three Services' failure to co-ordinate their plans.

As our forces moved forward, the situation to the north was transformed by Hitler's onslaught upon Russia, launched on 22 June. This made it unlikely that a threat from the north would develop against our position in the Middle East during 1941, and the Middle Eastern Commanders-in-Chiefs so informed the Chiefs of Staff on 2 July. Such a major land threat could still develop if the Germans began a move through Turkey in the near future, but success in Syria would greatly facilitate our ability to meet this threat should it develop. If Turkey gave the Germans facilities, air action from bases in Anatolia could be expected to follow within a very short time. Should the attack on Russia succeed rapidly and the Germans establish themselves in the Caucasus, it was difficult to see how Turkey could resist pressure for the granting of such facilities. At the same time, the Allies' influence in the contrary sense would be enhanced if we occupied Syria.

This we were soon able to do. On the evening of 11 July we heard officially of the request by General Dentz, the Vichy Commander-in-Chief, for an armistice. We decided to act on it at once. I stopped the Wellingtons, some of which were already on the way to Aleppo, while General Wilson called a halt on land. An appropriate reply was sent off to Dentz that night telling him to come to heel by nine o'clock the following morning. The French representatives in Syria displayed a most commendable eagerness to negotiate, and indeed turned up half an hour early bearing their flag of truce. I understood that the negotiations would be settled satisfactorily, although it was only too plain that we should have trouble with the Free French.

On 12 July I had two talks with General Spears—he had just come back from a tour through Syria. It was evidently going to be a very ticklish business to steer between the Free French, most of whom were violently anti-British, and the Arabs who hated and despised the French and were prepared, up to a point, to trust us. Brown told me from Jerusalem the following day that he had enjoyed a long talk with his Vichy opposite number during the negotiations. Their attitude had been very friendly, but what had shaken them more than anything else was the singling out and obliteration of the French Residency at Beirut on 29 June. I had noted in my journal on the 30th:

Went off suddenly to Palestine yesterday morning and got back this evening about 6.30. . . . Decided yesterday I must do something to try and get a move on up there. Saw one of the Squadron C.O.'s when I arrived, and one of them whom I put on to a special job made a first-class show of it later in the afternoon—Got the photos this morning, and it is a classic of accuracy.

The accuracy and implication of the blow, I gathered, had not escaped attention. Vichy French representatives thought that it had not been quite the gentlemanly thing to do, but were glad that they had been quarter of an hour late in arriving for a big conference due to be held in the building.

8   *Wavell to India–Verdict on Wavell–Lyttelton as Resident Minister–*
Auchinleck: 'I am quite ready to take a reasonable risk'–To London
with Auchinleck–India's plea for fighters–Discussion with the Air
Council on flexible organisation–Smuts: 'Air the architect of victory'–
'Mary' Coningham replaces Collishaw

ON the morning of 1 July, Wavell came into my office as he often did, to look round the Operations Room which showed everything that was going on—all the operations undertaken on the previous day and those ordered for the current day, together with the state of squadrons and the movement of reinforcements, the weather forecast, and so on. General Auchinleck was with him. After Auchinleck had gone, Wavell stayed behind and said simply: 'I'm going to India.'

I had felt that a change was coming and would probably be a good thing, but had not dreamt that Auchinleck would be Wavell's replacement. I now told Wavell how sorry I was personally, and the remark was true, for I liked him as a man. He replied with a quizzical smile: 'Well, it's probably a good thing to have a change of bowling—and I have had one or two sixes knocked off me lately!'

My journal shows that I felt some doubts about his replacement:

Don't know what Auchinleck will be like. He is a thinker, but I suspect lacks sense of humour. However, we'll see.

I did not then know that in early June, Wavell had intimated privately that he would like a month's rest. He had been told as far back as 21 June that he would be relieved and would change places with General Auchinleck from India. To the latter, Dill wrote a few days later from London:

The fact is that the Commander in the field will always be subject to great and often undue pressure from his Government. Wellington suffered from it: Haig suffered from it: Wavell suffered from it. Nothing will stop it. In fact, pressure from those who alone see the picture as a whole and carry the main responsibility may be necessary. It was, I think, right to press Wavell against his will to send a force to Baghdad, but in other directions he was, I feel, over-pressed.[1]

[1] Connell: *Auchinleck*, p. 247.

[133]

Wavell had himself written of Allenby that the great Commander is he who has both the courage to accept risks and the skill to minimise them, and in another place, 'think first, fight afterwards—the soldiers' art'.

Undue prudence, he recognised, had never yet won battles or campaigns or wars. Certainly I had not found Wavell unduly prudent, though I thought him very tired and consequently slow off the mark. I admired his fine brain and his courage in facing up to so many responsibilities, and to the mass of political and administrative business which fell upon him. Nor did I envy the Commander who had to put up with, and even worse, act upon, the imperious directives from the Prime Minister, whose imaginative powers, though strong, did not apparently enable him to make due allowance for the effect upon our Middle Eastern strategy of the particular conditions which prevailed in that sprawling theatre, and which distinguished it from any other in which our forces had so far fought during the war.

By June 1943 Wavell had waged no less than fourteen campaigns, nine of which—in the Western Desert, British Somaliland, Eritrea, Italian Somaliland, Abyssinia, Greece, Crete, Iraq, and Syria—were under way in my early months in the Middle East. The new Commander would at least be able to polarise his attention in a way which had been impossible for Wavell; and I hoped, too, that with judicious management the Army Command might be induced to learn the lessons of air-power and to establish that intimate working relationship with R.A.F. Headquarters which alone would enable our two Services to develop their full power.

This change in command was rapidly followed by a further alteration in our Middle Eastern machinery of war. The Cabinet had known for some time that Wavell was beset with the many political problems which inevitably arose in the length and breadth of his command. Several times the Middle East Commanders-in-Chief had urged on the Government the need for relief from dealing with these issues, which were outside their competence. Hence the appointment as Minister of State resident in the Middle East and representative of the War Cabinet, of Mr. Oliver Lyttelton, whom the Prime Minister sent, as he put it, to hold the gorgeous East in fee. The Lytteltons arrived on the morning of

5 July. My telephone rang at 2 a.m., 3 a.m., 6 a.m., and 6.30 a.m., telling me of their somewhat erratic progress in a Sunderland from Malta. The high spot of the saga was at 3 a.m. when I was told that the Sunderland reported it had been intercepted by a fighter somewhere off Derna, but not attacked. Later reports were more reassuring, and at 7.30 I was with Mr. Averell Harriman and the Ambassador, Sir Miles Lampson, when the Sunderland landed. That night I dined at the Embassy and recorded my first impressions of the new Minister:

Lyttelton a big man, heavy, but doesn't look it. Seems alive. Certainly has a sense of humour. I was alongside him at dinner. Mostly persiflage, but some deeper talk, and I think I like him. Harriman had a long *tête-à-tête* with him after dinner, and told me as we were coming back here in the car, that he thought he'd be good, that he was just out to help the job along, and not out for himself.

Meanwhile, Mr. Churchill and the new Commander-in-Chief were already exchanging telegrams. Auchinleck told the Prime Minister on 4 July that he fully realised the critical nature of the situation. Subject to closer investigation he felt that no further offensive in the Western Desert should be thought about till our bases were secure. His first concern was, therefore, the elimination of the Vichy French Forces from Syria. Once Syria and Iraq were secure, the Western Desert offensive could be considered, but at least two and preferably three armoured divisions, with a motor division, would be needed for success. Although the final objective would be the complete elimination of the enemy in North Africa, administrative considerations would enforce an advance by stages. Auchinleck said that it was quite clear to him that infantry divisions, no matter how well trained and equipped, were no good for offensive operations in the Middle Eastern terrain against enemy armoured forces. The second essential, he telegraphed, somewhat more ominously from my point of view, was an

. . . adequate and suitably trained air component at disposal Army for all its needs, including fighters, medium bombers, tactical reconnaissance and close support on the battlefield. This is non-existent at present.

The Prime Minister replied that he agreed that the Syrian affair must be polished off, but the Western Desert remained the decisive theatre in the autumn for the defence of the Nile Valley, and it was only by reconquering the lost airfields of eastern Cyrenaica that the Fleet and R.A.F. could resume effective action against the enemy's seaborne supplies.

The Prime Minister went on to state that he felt that for all major operational purposes Auchinleck's plans must govern the employment of the whole R.A.F. throughout the Middle East, bearing in mind that the Air Force had its own dominant strategical role to play and must not be frittered away in providing small umbrellas for the Army as it seemed to have been in the Sollum battle. The Prime Minister pointed out that the crucial question was to know the proportion in which the air strength was to be distributed, how much was to support the Army, how much was to support the Navy, and how much was to be employed on independent strategical tasks. He thought this would have to be arranged from time to time by the Commanders-in-Chief in consultation:

But nothing in these arrangements should mar the integrity of Air Force contribution to any major scheme you have in hand. One cannot help feeling in Sollum fight our air superiority was wasted and that our forces in Tobruk stood idle whilst all available enemy tanks were sent to defeat our Desert offensive.

Auchinleck, Cunningham and I discussed this signal together. The Prime Minister had stated that we should probably have decided air superiority in the Middle East during the next two and a half months, and I agreed, provided that no enemy offensive developed against Syria and perhaps Iraq. As for the principles enunciated by the Prime Minister for the use of the R.A.F., we agreed that they were correct. Cunningham suggested that the employment of the R.A.F. could not be subordinate exclusively to the implementation of the Army's plans since there might well be an urgent operational requirement for work with the Navy. This point applied with particular force while the Mediterranean Fleet was lacking an aircraft-carrier.

Churchill again replied in some detail, pressing Auchinleck to

use the lull accorded by the German attack on Russia to restore
the situation in Cyrenaica. Before replying, Auchinleck wrote to
Dill showing clearly that he intended to allow no undue interference from London. As for the Desert, it was unsound to take
an unreasonable risk:

> I am quite ready to take a reasonable risk as I think you know, but to
> attack with patently inadequate means is to take an unreasonable
> risk in the present circumstances, and it is almost certain to result in a
> much greater delay eventually than if we wait until the odds are reason-
> able. I am afraid I shall be quite firm on this point. . . . As to what
> constitutes a reasonable risk, I think that I alone can be the judge.
> You may be assured that no one is more anxious than I to get going.[1]

The timing of our next move in the Western Desert was
obviously the main problem facing the Commanders-in-Chief
now that Syria was no longer a source of anxiety. On 23 July
1941 we told the Chiefs of Staff in an important message that we
fully appreciated the importance of an early offensive to relieve
Tobruk which we had a reasonable chance of being able to hold
even after the end of September. We accepted that our relative air
strength would probably improve in September with the arrival
of fresh reinforcements, and perhaps thereafter. If, by maintaining
pressure on his ports and shipping, we could intensify the
enemy's difficulties of supply and replenishment, we might be
able, with air superiority, to undertake an offensive in Cyrenaica
with less than two armoured divisions; but by the end of
September we should not have even one armoured division
completely equipped and trained. Unless the situation should
change very greatly in our favour, therefore, no land offensive
was possible in September. We still thought two and preferably
three divisions were necessary to retake Cyrenaica, which would
mean that this operation could not be mounted until November
at the very earliest, and then only if we had received by mid-
September 150 cruiser tanks from home and 150 extra American
tanks.[2]

Immediately, Auchinleck was summoned to London. After

---

[1] This, and earlier Auchinleck–Churchill exchanges: Connell: *Auchinleck,*
pp. 250–63
[2] Connell: *Auchinleck,* pp. 264–5.

considering the matter carefully, I suggested that I should go with him, having discussed the matter with General Haining, the Intendant-General, and Lyttelton. Though realising that the main consultations in London would concern land strategy I felt it vital that these should not at any time be divorced from the parallel problems of air strategy in the Middle East. Experience of the last six months on land and sea, I told Portal, had shown decisively that the air was the vital factor. I appreciated that he could drive home this point with far more weight than I could command, and I was in many ways reluctant to be away from Cairo at this time. On the other hand, it was never likely that there would be a less inconvenient time, and I felt that quite apart from the value of discussing many questions directly there was a great deal to be said for Auchinleck and myself coming together and speaking with one voice.

I had every intention of pressing the Air Ministry to the utmost for all possible help. Our shortages in the Middle East were serious, but just as I left I had cause to realise that others were even worse off. Wavell signalled from India on 23 July, asking whether I could not possibly spare a few Gladiators to enable pilots to be trained on comparatively modern machines. He had visited Risalpur the day before and had found the R.A.F. squadron there training with Audax machines, the most modern fighting aircraft possessed by India: 'Does not this make your heart bleed?' he asked.

I replied: 'It does, but my heart's blood does not produce fighters. Do not think flight of our very part-worn Gladiators practicable from here to India. Am examining other possibility but prefer not to say more so as to avoid raising false hopes. Quite agree reality of need and will see if I can get help during my impending visit to U.K.'

We were in London by the end of the month, where we found the Defence Committee most anxious that some brisk action should be undertaken somewhere in the Middle East to show that Russia was not the only country fighting and to relieve the pressure on the Soviets. All the same, it was agreed that a further offensive should not be undertaken in the Desert until we had the resources to give a reasonable chance of decisive victory. The early despatch

of an armoured brigade was promised. In this and in other conversations, Auchinleck obliged Churchill, who was not more
than half convinced, to agree that the offensive should take place
on 1 November, all the conditions for which had been most
carefully laid down in our telegram of 23 July. Churchill records
that his military advisers were shaken by all the detailed argument
Auchinleck produced, and himself seems to have been impressed
with Auchinleck's dignified and commanding personality.[1]

Apart from these matters of high strategy, I held a number of
conversations at the Air Ministry. Throughout the summer, the
strength of our air forces in the Middle East was gradually
building up from $34\frac{1}{2}$ squadrons in the middle of June to fifty-two
squadrons in the middle of October. My problem was not so much
to expand the first line as to create the capacity to use it efficiently.
Aircraft by themselves were of little value, for unless they could
be properly used they merely crowded out the dispersal grounds
and presented agreeable targets to the enemy. The shortage of
trained personnel was desperate and it was not always easy to
convince those in authority in London that our conditions of
operation in the Middle East were so utterly different from theirs
that normal comparisons were invalid. At home, much of the
repair and maintenance work was undertaken in the usual way
by civilians. In the Middle East, we had to do the work ourselves.
Many new aircraft arriving from home had to be unloaded and
then erected, whereas at home they would be sent direct from
the factory to storage units or even to the squadrons. Our
aircraft in the Middle East were often operating hundreds of
miles from their repair depots under climatic and geographical
conditions which greatly increased the amount of necessary repair
and maintenance work. The fact that we were always expected
to be able to switch our strength from one end of the Command
to another at a moment's notice meant that we had no choice but
to maintain a basic ground organisation in each area. Our lines of
communication were extended and improvised. Outside the
Delta, telephone facilities were so poor that we had virtually to
rely upon wireless communication. The Command had on its

[1] Churchill: *War Memoirs*, vol. III, p. 361.

strength no fewer than 6,500 radio technicians and a further 3,700 men for observation purposes. Moreover, we had always to allow for the higher sickness rate inevitable in the tropics.

All this was in my mind when I attended a meeting on 4 August in the Air Council Room of the Air Ministry. The Secretary of State, Sir Archibald Sinclair, presided, and was accompanied by the Permanent Under Secretary and by Portal. Sinclair welcomed me kindly and he asked me to state my needs as fully as possible.

I replied that one of our fundamental problems in the Middle East was that of organisation. The R.A.F's peacetime organisation had not really been designed to meet wartime requirements there. The essential need was the ability to switch units and formations often from one continent to another and almost invariably over long distances. Only constant improvisation could keep pace with events. Flexibility of organisation was what we most needed. In reply to a question by Portal, I said, to general agreement, that a pool of additional personnel in the Middle East would not be satisfactory. It would lack the qualities of a living organisation and would suffer from the disadvantage that whenever a member was attached to a formation his function tended to become indispensable, and he could then be moved to another post only with difficulty. The meeting felt generally that the best solution lay in a more generous establishment. I said that I was satisfied with the flow of aircraft to the Middle East, and with our maintenance personnel, but that I felt there was still an insufficient appreciation in London of some of the practical difficulties in Middle Eastern requirements.

Auchinleck and I set out for the Middle East again on 10 August. After a reasonably fast run we landed at Gibraltar at about 4.30. There we found the weather quite fine except for a plume of cloud streaming away at the west of the Rock. I was most anxious that we should leave again that evening for Malta, but it was soon discovered that our engines needed some maintenance work and so we had to stay the night. Auchinleck and I were entertained for lunch the next day by Admiral Collins at his delightful house nine hundred feet up on the side of the Rock. There we overlooked a terraced garden full of flowering shrubs and creepers, especially plumbago, oleander and morning glory.

After lunch, Admiral Collins offered a deck chair in the garden which I accepted gratefully. There I spent an hour and a quarter looking out through the palms and trees upon the Bay, the Straits, the hills behind Algeciras, and, towering faintly beyond, the mountains of Africa. That evening we left for Malta, flying along the coast of Spain east of Gibraltar as the sun was setting. I noticed one of the mountains in the south still had a few streaks of snow glowing pink in the evening sun.

At Malta, the arrival of seven hundred maintenance personnel had transformed the position, and it was clear that we could now make greater use of its unique position astride the communications from Europe to North Africa. I proposed to operate two Wellington squadrons from Malta, telling the squadron commanders that they were to use Malta as an operational landing ground, and to maintain a minimum of ten operational aircraft in each squadron. I hoped to send half a squadron of Blenheims to Malta as soon as possible to learn the technique of anti-shipping operations. All this I discussed with Air Vice Marshal Lloyd whose work there I admired. The only limit would be the number of aircraft which Malta could service. I was impressed with the extraordinarily good dispersal facilities which had been arranged, and also with the extension of runways and the provision of satellite aerodromes.

We left the island just as the moon rose, for the final stage of our journey to Cairo. I slept only for an hour or so, and then went forward to look round from the transparent dome which projected from the top of our Sunderland behind the pilot's seat. In this way I had a perfect view all round. It was a glorious night with a half moon and Mars, Saturn, and Jupiter in a row slanting down across the sky ahead of us. Orion climbed in slow and stately fashion from the sea. Dozens of shooting stars radiated across the sky, some leaving long trails a deep red in colour. No Germans appeared. Towards dawn I flew the aircraft for an hour and a half, and the navigator landed us exactly on our mark. We reached the Nile at 7 a.m.

After a meeting of the Commanders-in-Chief that morning, we all went to greet General and Mrs. Smuts. They arrived at one o'clock, Smuts as keen, active and virile as ever. Mrs. Smuts, whom I did not know before, was a quaint little dowdy figure, tied up in a loose sort of black sack, with short curly grey hair which looked as if it had not been brushed or combed for years. I thought she was rather like a little old village school-marm to look at, though not to speak to. I sat next to her at the Embassy dinner that night and quite fell for her. In her way she was quite a match even for him, simple in the best sense, direct and quick. I found Smuts very conscious of the importance of the Middle East. He insisted again and again that it would be there that the final showdown would occur and that he expected a major campaign there the next spring. Strangely enough, Smuts expressed great surprise at the heavy losses of ships in the Ægean during the evacuation from Greece and Crete. I tried to explain that in the circumstances, and in view of the way in which the operations went, some such result was inevitable. The next day I attended the opening of a South African Club at which they both spoke. General and Mrs. Smuts were universally known, to themselves and everyone else, as 'Oubaas' and 'Ouma'. Both of them made wonderful speeches. General Smuts spoke about the war as a whole and about the Middle East in particular, referring to Armageddon of which we had talked earlier in the day. Both referred, naturally, to the South Africans, 'our boys' as they called them. I wished afterwards that I possessed the sort of memory which retained such speeches, for there was good stuff in them.

I went to see them off on 16 August. Before they left in their shining, silvery South African Lockheed, the General took me by the arm and said: 'The air, the architect of victory. My heart goes out to you.'

With Smuts, I had visited the Western Desert on the previous day. There I found that co-operation between the Army and the R.A.F. was now much closer. A week or two before, I had replaced Collishaw by Coningham, a New Zealander who had first been nicknamed 'Maori' and was now universally known as 'Mary'. I found that he was taking charge well. He and the General Officer Commanding proposed to share quarters, and I was hopeful of good results. The most disturbing fact was that the provision of cover for the seaborne supplies to Tobruk was using up so much of our fighting effort that only a spasmodic attack against the enemy air forces was possible. All the remaining force had been needed during the past ten days to cover sea supplies to Bardia. The enemy air forces were not being slow to take advantage of this situation, and were bombing our troops in the forward areas.

I was glad to have made the visit to London with Auchinleck, for the trip had done a great deal to bring us together. I had been impressed with the manner in which he refused to be rushed into premature decisions. So far I found that we thought alike on all the things that mattered, and I had every confidence that we would make a good team. I wished I could say the same about Cunningham. On a personal basis we remained on excellent terms, and I liked him, but as I told Portal:

On official matters, however satisfactorily things are arranged with his staff, one comes up against a case-hardened salt horse. I had another long letter from him on the subject of air operations over the sea and I am afraid one sees little prospect of a satisfactory solution under the present régime.

On my return from London, I had found a reply from Freeman to my letter of 11 June. Freeman surmised that Longmore had always been inclined to give way to the other Commanders-in-Chief, and therefore had a fairly easy passage with them. Now they might be beginning to feel the reaction. He assured me that he and Portal were quite certain that I was on the right lines, but in order to secure acceptance of my views he thought I must make a point of getting on well with Auchinleck. Certainly I had already done my best to establish good relations with the new Commander-in-Chief, whose quiet firmness and determination I came more and more to admire.

9

OPERATION 'Battleaxe' had ended in a complete stalemate and left the outcome of the Western Desert campaign poised on the future of Tobruk. 'Battleaxe' had shown that the enemy's land and air forces in Libya were not strong enough for a large scale attack against Tobruk; moreover, a major offensive against the Delta was not practicable so long as Tobruk remained in British hands threatening Rommel's flank. We reckoned that our occupation of Tobruk was likely to impose a delay, calculated at about two months, on enemy plans. This delay would be of the greatest value to us, for it would give time to clear up the situation in Syria and for the general reorganisation of our forces and the arrival of fresh material. On the other hand, we were forced to pay a high price. The area we held at Tobruk was not large enough to allow the stationing of squadrons on the spot—I have already referred to the gallant but ineffective attempt that had been made to maintain and operate a fighter squadron from within the perimeter. The Royal Navy was therefore faced with the necessity of running in seaborne supplies without direct protection from aircraft on the last part of the voyage or during unloading. As a corollary the Royal Air Force was committed to attempting to maintain standing patrols or 'umbrellas', the only consistent defensive which our air forces maintained during the war in the Western Desert.

I was compelled to employ three squadrons continuously in covering the maintenance of supply to Tobruk. This defensive cover suffered from all the inevitable weaknesses, and it was rarely that the supply convoys to Tobruk escaped damaging air attack.

HQ 202 Group, Western Desert, 31 December 1940

Air Headquarters, GHQ Tmimi, 27 January 1942

After O'Connor's offensive, in January 1941

At the end of June a further threat arose to complicate the problem of defence. The garrison of Tobruk consisted largely of Australians, and if it were lost serious political repercussions would be inevitable. The Australian Government were putting strong pressure on Churchill to relieve the garrison. Very reluctantly Auchinleck agreed that some of the troops in Tobruk, who were reported to be suffering from severe strain, should be replaced, and an infantry brigade group and an Indian cavalry regiment were accordingly brought out. This operation under-lined the risks involved, since almost all our ships were attacked by enemy aircraft and we had been obliged to use no less than five squadrons to escort the ships carrying out the relief. If further relief of the garrison were insisted upon it would have to be carried out during the moonless period, and it could not be completed until 26 October, precisely at the time when we planned to concentrate our efforts on securing air superiority in pre-paration for our next offensive. Moreover, it did not appear that the health and morale of the Tobruk garrison were much affected by the hardships endured. Admittedly, the senior officers were showing signs of tiredness, which was only too under-standable. All these considerations Auchinleck urged upon Churchill, and was well supported by Lyttelton, who told the Prime Minister that in his opinion the military arguments against relieving the garrison were unanswerable. If the troops were English, no commander would consider relief. The Minister of State had little doubt that the Australian Government was anxious to take out a political insurance policy, but the premium to be paid for it seemed to him to be too high. By all accounts, the Indian cavalry, recently brought out from Tobruk, were fit to fight as soon as they arrived in the Delta. The Australian Brigade had also been in good heart.

Mr. A. W. Fadden, the Prime Minister of Australia, supplied with arguments by Blamey, nevertheless pressed matters so far that Lyttelton had some difficulty in persuading Auchinleck not to resign his command. The Australians insisted, despite all our arguments, on further relief of the garrison. I told Portal on 17 September that from the Middle East's view the decision appeared to be most dangerous. What disturbed me most was the imposition of what I called 'the devastating diversion of our fighter effort just at the period when our air campaign should be working to the climax to ensure air superiority when the land operations begin.'

Not only did the extra burden mean that the continuity of our air operations was broken, but it also involved the grave risk of heavy losses to our fighter forces at a time when we could least afford them. The umbrella over the ships was no whit less dangerous and uneconomical than the air umbrella over ground troops. The decision left me in a cleft stick, since from one point of view I would have liked the land operations to be postponed so that our air operations to assert superiority could be fully resumed, and on the other hand, the longer the land offensive was postponed the greater the chance of an increase in the enemy's strength. I did not doubt that these points had been fully debated in London, but knowing how deeply concerned Churchill was about the success of the Desert operations, I wondered whether he really appreciated that the change of plan might seriously jeopardise the prospects.

A week or so later, Portal told me by telegraph that the home Government might try to persuade the Australians to discontinue the relief operations after the September moonless period. It depended on the difference which the discontinuance of reliefs would make to our air progress. Portal asked me for an appreciation on this point. I did my best to reinforce the arguments I had already put forward, but the Australian Government insisted that further efforts must be made during the October moonless period. With much effort, therefore, the programme of evacuation was carried out in September and October. The latter part of this operation caused some losses.

These Tobruk operations, and the campaign in Syria, gave extra point to the long battle which Admiral Cunningham and I waged on the subject of a Coastal Command. In his memoirs, Cunningham tells us that in the mid-summer of this year he was impressing upon me the crying need for something analogous to the Coastal Command. This organisation should have its headquarters at Alexandria. Moreover, Cunningham states that the Royal Navy's relations, and he thought those of the Army, with the R.A.F. in the Middle East were not easy, but since the Battle of Crete, on account of which the R.A.F. came in for much undeserved criticism, we had apparently become 'very touchy and difficult to approach'. What the Royal Navy wanted was aircraft definitely allocated for fleet co-operation, with specially trained personnel. He adds that although I accepted in principle the suggestion of a Coastal Command, I positively refused to allot aircraft for the sole duty of naval co-operation. It seemed to Cunningham that there was an unwillingness to admit that R.A.F. personnel working over the sea required special training, though the Royal Navy, with their long and hardly bought experience, knew otherwise. In retrospect, he thought that my reason for refusal was chiefly my lack of resources, though he charged that that was not the reason I gave. The result according to the Admiral was that the Navy still had to put up with in-sufficient and largely ineffective air reconnaissance and co-opera-tion.[1]

I have already recounted how Cunningham pressed his views on the Admiralty in his signal of 7 June. In a long letter to me, written four days later, he thought it necessary to develop along the Egyptian coast an air organisation providing a bombing and torpedo force, a reconnaissance force, and a fighter force to cover our lines of supply and the movements of our surface forces. A nucleus of such forces was being built up in Malta and in Egypt, and this he hoped to expand. The proposals I had made were, he argued, designed to deal with a far more local and passing phase of the situation. He thought the organisation he hoped to see set up — to his mind fundamentally analogous to the Coastal Command at home—should be commanded by the R.A.F; but if the officer commanding was to do his work effectively he must have a nucleus of aircraft belonging to him which would work first and foremost on the duties specified.

I replied on 27 June that I was, and always had been, in entire agreement with the principle that there should be a nucleus of specially trained air forces, whose primary role would be to co-operate with the Navy. As resources became available I was

[1] Cunningham: *A Sailor's Odyssey*, p. 406.

building up No. 201 Group to serve as that nucleus. I argued, however, that it was incorrect to apply the analogy of the Coastal Command at home to the eastern Mediterranean:

In my view the Naval air operations cannot be properly considered as a self-contained activity separate from the main land and air operations in the Middle East. With the shore bases he now possesses and with the air forces he can concentrate in this theatre, the enemy can bring such air forces into action either to attack our Surface vessels or to cover his own Surface movements as to compel us to concentrate all our available air forces by way of counter. Even the movement of individual supply ships to Tobruk may involve full-scale employment of all available fighter squadrons and consequently vitally affect the main land and air operations in the Western Desert. The air operations in support of the Navy must, in fact, continually be related to the general Air situation and to the air operations in support of the Army.

In my opinion, sea, land and air operations in the Middle East Theatre are now so closely inter-related that effective co-ordination will only be possible if the campaign is considered and controlled as a combined operation in the full sense of that term. The enemy has consistently gained his successes by concentration. Not only must we from the defence point of view be able to meet concentration with concentration, but also, if we are ever to regain the initiative, we must be able to concentrate on offence whenever the weak spot appears and opportunity arises.

The experience of the past few months had already convinced me that we should secure this effect not by attempting to segregate naval and air operations, but only by establishing a joint operational headquarters as would be provided for a combined operation. This headquarters would exercise co-ordinated direction of all the forces, at sea, on land and in the air, engaged in the Mediterranean theatre of operations. To segregate air forces for special duties, and thereby to preclude full concentration of our air effort, would be to play into German hands.

As I expected, Cunningham refused to accept this solution. He thought that we agreed on the fundamental point that an organisation was necessary for these special purposes, but disagreed as to its size. Important though the Army's requirements were, Admiral Cunningham was convinced that if we were to achieve success in the coming campaign, it was vital that we should be able to organise air forces to search out and strike at enemy warships and seaborne supplies, and which could protect our own surface forces to the best degree possible when they were operating at sea.

I could not help being quietly entertained at the reversal of attitude expressed in these letters. Whereas before the operations in Greece and Crete, the R.A.F's contribution had been regarded by the Naval authorities as being of a secondary nature, it now appeared that nothing at all could be done unless I could provide air forces for the Royal Navy on a scale far more considerable than my strength warranted. The controversy reverberated for months with the exchange of voluminous memoranda on both sides. I told Portal on 16 August that I feared I saw little prospect of a satisfactory solution under Cunningham's régime. So far as co-operation with the Navy was concerned, the Admiral had exactly the same position vis-à-vis 201 Group as had the Admiralty towards Coastal Command. I thought his only justifiable grounds of criticism were that we had no bomber squadrons in Egypt sufficiently trained or practised in attack on shipping. I had hoped that at least one of the squadrons in Palestine could be trained for this work, but a diversion to Persia had for the time being spoilt that prospect. Luckily, my arguments did not go unsupported. As Freeman had hoped, my relations with Auchinleck were excellent. We travelled about together as far as possible, particularly to conferences, and I was able to tell Freeman on 5 September that:

So far we have been able to speak with one voice without any difficult negotiations. We are very much of one view regarding the 'Old man of the sea'.

Certainly this combination of our strength was very necessary, for I had been having further arguments with Cunningham about the location of the Headquarters of 201 Group. The Admiral insisted that they should be close to a jetty to which his flagship was sometimes tied up. This site was in the middle of a target area surrounded by timber yards and oil tanks. Cunningham also refused to recognise that the soldiers had any place in this Headquarters, a point on which Auchinleck gave me complete support with Lyttelton. Deadlock was reached. After some careful talks, a solution was found: 201 Group would have a Combined Operations Room in a suitable site away from inflammable targets, and the Navy would there be represented, as was the case with Coastal Command. There would also be accommodation for soldiers, so that plans for such tasks as the supply of Tobruk, the affairs in Syria, the defence of Cyprus and so on, could be worked out by a proper Joint Staff. I also proposed to place on Cunningham's personal staff a good senior R.A.F. officer. The admiral averred that this arrangement met his requirements, but I had no doubt that he would in due course continue to complain. There was some evidence that he was working up to the point of making another gallant sortie into the Mediterranean with his Fleet. I could not imagine what useful function this might be expected to perform, and I knew Auchinleck was equally unable to see the point. I noted that there was no likelihood whatever that the Admiral would discuss the question with his fellow Commanders-in-Chief. I feared that he was incorrigible. Fortunately his staff, below flag rank, were excellent; our relationship with them was thoroughly good and succeeded in overcoming most obstacles.

In mid-September, the somewhat one-sided correspondence on the subject of air co-operation was still in full spate. I acknowledged that Cunningham had a legitimate grievance about the force available for oversea reconnaissance. His demands had been grossly excessive, but I admitted to Portal that our force for this purpose was not really adequate. I was doing my best to remedy the situation but the only aircraft with the necessary range and speed for much of the work was the long-range Maryland. We had so far managed to build up a total of seven Marylands of this type to meet the needs of all three Services in strategical reconnaissance. There was some hope that further supplies of long-range tanks would soon be forthcoming and thereafter the position would be improved. Once the R.A.F.–R.N. Headquarters in Alexandria was functioning I had every hope of efficient co-ordination.

As Lyttelton was about to go to London, he asked the Commanders-in-Chief whether there were any particular matters which they wished him to take up while he was at home. Cunningham at once pressed the question of the organisation and allocation of air forces for co-operation with the Navy. I thought that a statement of our case should accompany this request, and I pointed out that 201 Group was specifically charged with the operation of units for naval co-operation. Cunningham had in practice operational control of this Group's programme, and any alteration in it or diversion of the units was referred to him. The inability of surface ships with or without their own aircraft to maintain effective sea reconnaissance in the eastern Mediterranean, had thrown almost all the burden on to shore-based aircraft, while the loss of bases in Greece, Crete and Cyrenaica had greatly increased the range at which our reconnaissance aircraft had to operate. On the other hand, almost the whole area which we had to cover was within the range of high performance enemy fighters based on shore.

I felt bound to disagree entirely with Cunningham's view that the Naval Commander-in-Chief alone could hold the balance between the relative merits or needs of air and surface action in specific cases. I thought that the issue was a far wider one, and that Cunningham's own reference to a conference at which there should be an Air Force officer who knew what air forces were available and what could be made available, corroborated my point. It was not a balance merely between the merits and needs of air or surface action, but between the proper employment of the air forces within range of the target and available at a given time and between the air operations in support of the Army and those aimed at the main objective of air superiority. That balance could be established only by the Air Officer Commanding-in-Chief in close co-operation with his two colleagues. This principle had been most clearly confirmed by Churchill.

I put to Cunningham the difficulty, and occasional impossibility, of ensuring effective consultation and co-operation between the three Services in respect of air operations. The arrangement by which Cunningham's Headquarters at Alexandria were connected with Auchinleck and myself was subject to the gravest dangers which loomed only too large on occasions such as the evacuation of Crete, when vital decisions affecting all three Services had to be made over an unreliable public telephone. The

weekly meetings of Commanders-in-Chief were valuable, but
no more than an alleviation of the situation, which I thought
not merely inefficient but dangerous, and were certainly no
substitute for the close collaboration between the three staffs
which, in my view, was essential in the Middle East. All this
I had discussed fully with Lyttelton, and he appeared to be in full
agreement on the main questions of principle.

Towards the end of the month, I heard from Portal that he was
proposing to the Admiralty that the primary function of 201 Group
was to be the conduct of operations over the sea, and co-operation with the Mediterranean Fleet. The allocation of operational
units to the Group would be decided by the A.O.C.-in-C. after
consultation with his two colleagues, in accordance with the needs
of the general situation. As far as this allowed, as many units as
possible in the Middle East Command would be trained to operate
efficiently over the sea. The broad strategic plan for the employment of 201 Group would be agreed between the A.O.C.-in-C.
and the Commander-in-Chief, Mediterranean, who would
both approve the standing orders for the conduct of such
operations. The Admiralty had pressed for the Group to be
officially designated '201 (Coastal) Group', but Portal had resisted
this title as implying an unacceptable segregation. He asked
whether I agreed with these proposals, and I replied at once
that I did. It was finally directed, on 20 October, that 201 Group
should become 201 Naval Co-operation Group, and Cunningham
now had at Alexandria an R.A.F. officer whose main duty was
co-operation with the Fleet. R.A.F. liaison officers were also
appointed at lower levels to work with their opposite numbers of
the Royal Navy. I gladly agreed that the units of the newly
formed Group should not be diverted to other tasks without
consultation between the two Commanders-in-Chief. The increasing flow of aircraft also eased the situation, and the controversy
at last died down.

*

This wrangle with Cunningham was by no means my most
pressing preoccupation. In the second week of June our Military

Mission in Washington had telegraphed to the Chiefs of Staff disquieting information which was reaching the United States. Harry Hopkins had told our military attaché that the American Minister in Cairo, Mr. Kirk, had reported considerable dissatisfaction among Australians and New Zealanders in the Middle Eastern theatre. It appeared from these reports that they felt they had been let down and had not received adequate materials, and even that there was some talk on their part of a desire to return home. The United States Minister had also, apparently, continually reported low morale of the R.A.F. in the Middle East due, so he stated, to inferiority in the quantity and quality of aircraft; bad behaviour of aircraftsmen in Cairo and chaotic conditions at Takoradi were also alleged. If these reports were untrue, as the Military Mission suspected, and if they were also being exaggerated by the none too friendly State Department Division concerned, Sir Miles Lampson might perhaps have a word with the American Minister. Portal at once told me of this and suggested that I should call on the Minister and give him the opportunity, and perhaps the encouragement, to repeat such complaints, but without letting him know that these reports had come to my notice.

I acted upon this suggestion at once and saw the United States Minister on successive days, ostensibly on the subject of American observers in Egypt. Although I fished hard with a variety of bait I caught nothing. I had at first thought that his reports might perhaps be traceable to the receipt of half-baked stories from one or other of these American observers, although they talked very freely with members of my staff, and I had had no indication that such tales emanated from them. In fact the opinions they expressed about our morale were in the directly contrary sense. The only other explanation that I could think of was that Mr. Kirk thought that by sending such reports he could hasten and increase American help. I knew that there was a good deal of misdirected enthusiasm to that end in this and other quarters, and promised Portal I would do my best to direct such efforts on to saner and more productive lines. This was not easy to accomplish in view of the fact that I had to simulate ignorance of the Minister's reports.

Long before I heard of these rumours, I had told Portal in a letter of 15 June:

So far as our own fellows are concerned they are quite literally incredible. How they keep going, flung as they have been from one campaign to another, and then again to a third under foul conditions, I cannot imagine, but they do.

The matter was now thought serious enough to be taken up by the War Cabinet, to whom Portal reported that both Longmore and I had told him R.A.F. morale in the Middle East was excellent. Except for one small incident in Norway, the C.A.S. knew of no case where R.A.F. morale had been adversely reported upon during the whole war. He could well believe that the widely alleged failure of the R.A.F. to support the Army in Greece and Crete had aroused in the minds of officers and airmen a feeling of discouragement and resentment against conditions for which they were in no way responsible. But he was confident that as soon as they were given the chance of fighting on anything like fair terms it would be found that their morale was unimpaired. Inferiority in quantity, though not in quality, of aircraft, he admitted. He had heard no reports of serious misbehaviour in Cairo, and dismissed the allegedly chaotic conditions in Takoradi as being merely the fashionable explanation of our inferiority in numbers in the Mediterranean theatre. American observers in particular, Portal commented, seemed to expect the efficiency of a hastily developed route nearly 4,000 miles across the middle of Africa, to compare with that of a trans-American civil air line developed in peacetime through civilised territory. Of three competent senior officers who had recently inspected Takoradi, one had not reported fully as yet, and the other two were impressed with the efficiency of the Station.

This was not the end of the matter, however. On 16 July I felt compelled to speak seriously to Sir Miles Lampson who, I found, had sent a cable to Anthony Eden about the Takoradi Route, based on a report by one of our civil aviation specialists. This signal I had not seen, and I lost no time in telling the Ambassador what I thought of the individual in question and of the whole proceeding. He replied that I put him in a very awkward position. 'All very amicable,' says my journal, 'but it really is time the L. was stopped sending half-baked stories home. I think he'll be a trifle more tactful in future.'

I had every confidence in Thorold's ability to get the last ounce of effort out of his staff at Takoradi, and I knew that everything that was humanly possible was being done to surmount the many difficulties. It could not be denied, however, that for lack of effective co-ordination between the Royal Air Force and the Civil Transport organisation, we were not making the best use of the facilities.

I thought that as far as possible the air transport should be run by the civilian organisation, except in the actual area of war operations. Moreover, the organisation should be flexible so that in case of necessity the full weight of the transport's force could be concentrated to the best purpose. The need for air transport on a big scale throughout Africa and the Near East was becoming daily more evident, and was indeed becoming indispensable to the conduct of the war there. Yet, British Airways and the R.A.F. were each running separate systems, with the inevitable result that scanty resources were not put to the best advantage. I knew that British Airways were increasing the number of aircraft in the area, but were short of personnel and facilities to secure their fullest use. In due time the whole commitment of ferrying the aircraft from points of assembly to Cairo should be the responsibility of the Civil Air Transport Services, although it was quite clear that British Airways could not yet accept this duty. I thought it should be R.A.F. policy to hand over the commitment as soon as possible. Civil pilots might well become available from America, in which case British Airways would be better able to handle them than the R.A.F. Once Port Sudan and Basra came into full operation the monthly flow of aircraft into Egypt, including those arriving via the Takoradi Route, would be six hundred per month. It was not my intention to interfere with the British Airways services, but I thought there should be a Joint Board with Headquarters in Cairo and an independent chairman. This body would control the ferrying of Service aircraft, the return of ferry pilots, the operation of regular services and the necessary administration, maintenance and ground organisation. The matter was an urgent one, for the supply of aircraft from Takoradi increased every week.

In March we had received via this route 49 aircraft, in April 134, in May 105, and in June 151. In spite of the record effort in this last month, 82 aircraft were still awaiting collection at Takoradi on 9 July, mainly because we had not enough pilots, and the organisation needed to run a route nearly 4,000 miles in length, over some of the most difficult country in the world, had not yet been built up.

In August, I had some hopes that the arrival of Pan American Airways on the scene would ease our problems. Conversations in Cairo with their representative after I had returned from London in mid-August seemed to show that after military requirements had been met, any remaining pay load on the American services was to be offered for sale on a commercial basis, the revenue to accrue to the United States Government. I was told that this had been agreed between the British and U.S. Governments. When I asked about working with British Airways on the Trans-African route, I was told there would be no difficulty, particularly since Pan American were not operating the route commercially, and ordinary commercial competition would thus be eliminated. I noticed, however, that this crucial point was subsequently omitted from the note of the conversations. I pressed the Air Ministry to send me at once full details of the agreement, for I was most concerned that we might be handing our vital lifeline over completely to the mercy of a foreign commercial company. British Airways might thus be eliminated from the Trans-African route and our direct link between Cairo and the United Kingdom broken, which would entail a risk to our diplomatic and secret mail. The institution across Africa of a signal service which we should not control would provide an opportunity for the infiltration of enemy agents. I realised from my talks in London that we were irretrievably committed to an agreement with Pan American Airways but I insisted that we must safeguard our military interests and should, if possible, try to save what little was left of British Airways' birthright. The methods of Pan American Airways were well known to the

American administration and I thought it highly probable that if they were properly approached they would see that we got a square deal.

Sir Arthur Street, Permanent Under Secretary of State to the Air Ministry, replied on 22 August that final copies of the agreement with the United States Government had not yet been received. It appeared to the Air Ministry that the American offer to assist us with trans-Atlantic and trans-African ferrying would provide great relief and release British resources for service elsewhere. It had therefore been gratefully accepted on the spot by Air Marshal Arthur 'Bert' Harris, who was in Washington as Head of the R.A.F. Delegation. It was the United States Government which had nominated Pan American Airways as their instrument. The Air Ministry admitted that this concern certainly had an eye on their own interests, but the terms had been considerably modified to the British advantage during discussions. United States authorities and Pan American Airways were apparently becoming restive at continual harping on safeguards which they regarded as a reflection on their good faith, and I was told that signature could not be further delayed. The Air Ministry themselves had proposed that Pan American Airways should assume more responsibility for the efficiency of the route. This arrangement would 'Ensure that if P.A.A. fail to carry out their commitments according to plan, the blame can attach to nobody but themselves.'

My suggestion that an approach to the United States Government would get us more favourable terms was not, so I was told, borne out by facts. The ferrying route had not been handed over exclusively to P.A.A. British Airways would not retire from the route until the American company were in a position to carry all the traffic to our satisfaction, nor would the British Government be precluded from augmenting the Air Transport Service on a non-scheduled basis. No serious risk to our diplomatic and secret mail should arise, since it could always be entrusted to a responsible British official travelling on the aircraft. In any case it was hoped to arrange direct air transport between Britain and Egypt, a prospect which had been discussed with me in London. Sir Arthur Street felt sure that Pan American Airways would co-operate in allowing us to vet their Signal staff for security. His telegram concluded:

Importance of safeguarding B.O.A.C.'s birthright has been fully appreciated here from the outset, and agreement with P.A.A. is terminable at end of a year. American assistance on trans-African route will be substantial contribution to our war effort, and we must inevitably pay some price in return. . . .

I replied on the same day, 22 August, that this telegram did not appease me at all:

I am not interested in our ability to fix blame for failure on P.A.A. What does concern all of us is if they do fail for any reason we are left stranded for months until we can re-establish route ourselves. We must ensure effectively against possibility of P.A.A. failure, which, despite my unbounded faith in the amazing efficiency which is an inevitable feature of every American organization, is by no means impossible. We must keep the R.A.F. route in being.

I told Sir Arthur Street that I was unaware what 'facts' indicated that the U.S. Government was unlikely to procure for us more favourable terms. I suspected that these 'facts' were views expressed by Harris: 'Appears clear that Harris is "on the spot" in both senses.'

For good measure I added that it was indeed 'some price' that we were being called upon to pay, and was thoroughly in keeping with Pan American Airways' reputation.

I discussed the situation at once with Auchinleck, Lyttelton and Lampson, commenting in my journal that our American 'friends' were the toughest businessmen I had come across.

I still had some hope of securing more satisfactory conditions. Portal told me on 2 September that General Brett, Chief of the United States Army Air Corps, who was about to visit the Middle East, would work in the closest liaison in London with the Air Ministry. It was anticipated that in practice his activities would be largely determined by what I, and later the Air Ministry, represented to him as being our most urgent needs. The C.A.S. asked me to try to impress on General Brett as one of his principal concerns the implementation of major items on which American help had already been promised, such as depots and mechanics for the repair of American aircraft, and the construction of airfields.

I met Brett when he arrived in his Liberator on the afternoon of 10 September. I thought him a pleasant, quiet-spoken man, but so far as I could find out he was interested only in supply and maintenance. Someone aptly described him as 'super-Dawson'. A day or two later Brett and his bevy of experts were taken up to the Western Desert, where they found themselves in the middle of a battle. They returned much impressed, and I thought their outlook had changed very considerably. One of them remarked: 'Say, you babies don't need any teaching. Guess our boys need to come over and get some instruction!'

I gathered that they had seen the Tomahawk and Maryland squadrons during a battle, and also visited a Wellington squadron when the crews were being interrogated after a visit to Benghazi. The American party went to what remained of Abu Sueir and experienced an air raid in Cairo.

I thought Brett was anxious to help. His idea was to take over Massawa, Asmara and all the dock, rail and road facilities, and get American construction companies to bring in labour and material. On that foundation a complete Air Corps maintenance organisation would be set up at Asmara, with its mobile equipment manned by civilians. Later, when the permanent equipment for Asmara had arrived, the mobile equipment and organisation would move nearer the Delta as a forward American base. But before I had finished the letter in which I was reporting these developments to Portal, I learned that General Brett had somewhat antagonised the Minister of State by making some comments which were possibly too outspoken. By 23 September Sir Miles Lampson felt obliged to telegraph to Eden that he had seen Brett several times and that the General was so frankly critical that his comments ought to be passed on to the Foreign Office. Brett's first criticism, it appeared, was that a unified command should be set up. Harriman, who had visited us earlier in the summer, had been most insistent on the same point. Lampson, while admitting that this matter was hardly within his domain, thought that there was not much in the point. Brett bitterly criticised the confusion and lack of efficient organisation at Suez, where there were in his view too many separate authorities, and no proper co-ordination. He complained of perpetual change of plans at Port Sudan and of the failure to hit the enemy in Libya while he was held in Russia. He wanted to know why we did not bring out Liberators or Flying Fortresses to Egypt while the weather at home was too uncertain for their employment, so that they might be used in the Middle East to pulverise enemy bases in Libya before the full attack was switched on to Egypt (presumably after the Russian campaign had been won by the Germans). The Ambassador found Brett's attitude 'friendlily critical'. The General announced so openly what his report to Washington was going to say that Lampson was trying to arrange a meeting between him and the Service commanders.

I could not deny that by now the charms of General Brett's company were beginning to pall. After a talk with him on the afternoon of 25 September I wondered in my journal how he and all the American visitors could lay down the law about things of which they knew next to nothing. I did my best, with an effort, to appear duly interested and impressed. Two days afterwards, I was told in a signal from the Air Ministry that Bert Harris in Washington had reported a statement by Brett that my Chief Maintenance Officer, Dawson, was complaining bitterly of the lack of proportion in the allotment of spares between the various theatres of war, presumably by the Air Ministry. I was told that such a statement, besides being unfounded, tended to prejudice our relations with the United States authority, and was requested to ensure that discretion was used in giving information to prominent American visitors. The method of allocating spares among Commands was explained to me. I replied: 'What Bert says Brett says Dawson says, is not, repeat not, evidence.'

I asked my informant to believe that neither Dawson nor I was in the habit of throwing mud at the Air Ministry. If Brett and his cohort were to help, they had to be given the facts, but I feared that no discretion on our part could ensure discretion by Brett and Harris. I observed that loose statements by the former which were passed on and lost nothing in the telling by the latter, seemed more likely to prejudice relations between the Middle

East and the Air Ministry than those between the Air Ministry and the United States:

Have already experienced spate of well-meaning but half-baked criticism, and now treat it with detachment. Hope you will do same.

I hoped, but without undue confidence, that Brett was not going to make trouble. I feared that he suffered from the apparently not uncommon American complaint of going off at half-cock with sweeping criticisms and proposals, and gathered from various sources that he was a leading light in the controversy about the Army Air Corps as opposed to the independent Air Force in the United States. A few days before, one of the American party had remarked to me that the Middle East was regarded as a laboratory for this controversy. Each American appeared to send back cables with snippets of information and opinion which suited his own particular school of thought, and I told the Air Ministry that everything Brett said had to be viewed in this light. Apart from this aspect, I still thought his views generally sound and practical. Of course, he had never before seen squadrons operating under real war conditions, and was, I thought, horrified at the working conditions and improvisations which were necessary.

Until the last two or three days of his visit, General Brett had left strategic questions entirely alone. Then he gave me a long lecture about his views on the Middle East campaign. He clearly appreciated the importance of the enemy's communications across the Mediterranean, and had picked up bits of information about supplies getting into Benghazi. He also understood the importance of range, and said we ought to be hitting Benghazi harder and that we ought to have longer-range heavy bombers with which to do it. I was strongly of this opinion myself, and had often told the Air Ministry so, but I pleaded not guilty, on my behalf and on Dawson's, to having primed Brett on the subject. On the contrary, Dawson's relations with Brett had been excellent.

Naturally, I took the opportunity to discuss the Pan American situation with Brett, who was directly concerned from the point of view of the United States Government and Armed Forces. As a result, I had every hope that he would be able to safeguard our vital interests, for he was in a position to do so, and, what was more, he knew Pan American Airways. It appeared that the main agreement was between Pan American and the United States Army Air Corps, an arrangement which gave me some hopes that Brett would have far more power to keep a firm hand upon P.A.A. than we could ever hope to do.

*

Amidst all these preoccupations and the preparation for the coming campaign in the Desert, I felt confident that our air strength in the Middle East was increasing in every sense. I was most fortunate in the additions to my staff. Dawson had already performed miracles of improvisation, 'Mary' Coningham managed from the start in working closely with the soldiers, and I thought that with them we were in reasonable sight of obtaining really close co-operation. Coningham soon had the soldiers under his spell, and succeeded in rationalising the air operations in the Western Desert. Another new arrival, Lord Forbes, whom I irreverently nicknamed Little Lord Fauntleroy, I found to be quick-witted, observant and tough. He had for some time been attached to Lord Beaverbrook's entourage, and had been with him in America. Beaverbrook had personally trained him for journalism, had told him how to write, how to 'boil down' his stuff. I thought Forbes had a first-class brain and I attached him as my representative to the Minister of State. Occasionally I would go with him to dinner to the Mohamed Ali Club, the Pashas' Club—very much like one of those in Pall Mall. There we could enjoy a pleasant meal on the roof garden and talk of political scandal—of which Forbes, with his background, naturally knew more than a little—and philosophy and religion. One of the inducements which he held out to me to visit the Club was that there we could escape the soldiers, known to us as the 'brutal and licentious'. Perhaps we should have been more anxious to escape the Navy, for one evening after Forbes and I had left the Club, I was serenaded by a motley of sailors and marines, who chanted a little ditty:

> Roll out the *Nelson*, the *Rodney*, the *Hood*,
> Since the whole —— Air Force is no —— good!

As always, our Middle Eastern problems received the sympathy and prompt consideration of Portal and Freeman. At the end of August, we had an opportunity to establish those closer links between our Middle Eastern needs and the policy of the Air Ministry for which I often pleaded. The Inspector-General, Air Marshal Ludlow-Hewitt, visited me and travelled all over the Middle Eastern theatre. I was deeply impressed with his wide and detailed knowledge, his balanced criticisms and judgment and his desire to be of practical help. On almost all our problems we say eye to eye, except in the matter of the relative roles of the Air Force and the Army. His view was that the Army was the first line of defence, and that it was the R.A.F's main role to support it. He considered that the balance should therefore be adjusted so as to increase the proportion of fighters and fighter-bombers. With this I partially agreed, while feeling that the first line of defence in the Middle East and elsewhere was the air. With this view, Auchinleck agreed, even to the extent of telling a meeting of senior officers that the main role of the Army was to secure and maintain air bases as far forward as possible so that the R.A.F. could strike at the enemy's communications and bases, and at the same time deny to the enemy those air bases within effective range of our own main bases.

On 5 September we held a combined exercise with the Army in which all the senior commanders from the Western Desert and Syria took part. The main problem was to ensure effective co-operation between land and air, and we all felt most strongly that by far the most important contribution was that we should have good R.A.F. liaison officers living in each Army headquarters, at least down to the level of divisions and, I hoped, to the brigades of the armoured divisions. The difficulty would be to find suitable men for the posts. These exercises helped a good deal, and when Auchinleck and I summed up at the end of the day, we were in real, as well as apparent, agreement. The Commander-in-Chief spoke most highly of these exercises in a memorandum to the Minister of State. I commented to Portal that one could not in a few weeks remedy the result of over twenty years of neglect, or in that time hope effectively to educate the Army, which, generally speaking, had not troubled to study or even think about the air aspect seriously since flying began. None the less, I was hopeful, now that we had a C.-in-C. who understood the problem and was willing to help.

Perhaps I felt all this the more strongly since I had just been engaged in a minor tussle with Wavell who was on his way through the Middle East. At the Defence Committee Meeting on 4 September he had raised the question of India taking over control of the air force in Iraq. He started off the discussion in a most bitter manner, but I managed to get it back to a reasoned basis. It was very difficult to find any clear logical foundation for his demands, for his whole case was that he in India was responsible for the Army in Iraq and must therefore have complete control of the Air. Naturally, Wavell was very conscious of the fact that India had not an effective air force, and must have one. I did not dissent from this. He also said that the supply and maintenance of the air force in Iraq would have to come from India, but I objected that for as far ahead as we could reasonably see, the air force in Iraq must in fact draw upon the main pool of aircraft, equipment and personnel in the Middle East. This did not mean that India should not be built up so that she could in due course maintain some air force in Iraq. I also pointed out that the Indian Army in Iraq would suffer if the air force working with it were separated from the Middle East, and that air operations in support of the Army in Syria and Northern Iraq constituted one strategic problem. Indeed, squadrons operating from Syria would in all probability be supporting the Indian Army in Iraq. I explained how we were building up there the necessary organisation and material to enable us to switch a large air force into that area if the situation demanded it.

Lyttelton afterwards told me that he thought I was on the right side of the fence, and that Churchill would support my view. I hoped he was right, but felt certain that Wavell would fight his point tooth and nail. I gave him lunch, and we had a quiet talk afterwards, but I was sure that I had entirely failed to shake him.

*

My promotion to be Air Officer Commanding-in-Chief

necessarily increased my social activities, by no means all of which were an undiluted joy. Official dinners and parties at the Embassy were not notable for excitement. One such gathering ended appropriately enough with all of the guests gazing up at an enormous and fantastic oil painting by an Egyptian of Lady Lampson's race-horse. I comment in my journal that the animal looked like Tom Webster's 'Tishy' with its legs uncrossed.

Other diversions proved more entertaining. In mid-July I enjoyed a small dinner party given by the Egyptian Prime Minister, Hussein Sirry Pasha, a short, stubby man with a biggish head, a Turkish profile and a forceful character. The party was on board a river boat. Chairs and two big, low, Turkish tray-tables were set out under the awnings amidships. We arrived at about half-past nine, and were led along to a little saloon filled with a long table, groaning under a large variety of foods, from simple turkey to strange and elaborate Egyptian dishes. Each of the guests collected a large plate, a knife and a fork, and then filed round making selections. After that we went out on deck and sat round the tables and talked. We had just about finished our sweet, a very good mango ice, when Madame Sirry suddenly stood up, and we, not knowing why, followed suit. On looking round to see what it was all about, I saw a rather fat youth in dark blue suiting and a gaudy tie coming on board off the gangway. It was the Monarch, Farouk, who had arrived quite unrehearsed and unexpected:

A voluble young man, very self-possessed and very cheerful. Loud laughter at his own jokes (a royal prerogative, of course!) and at other people's. The hobby of the moment, apparently, the collection of fire arms of all sorts, ancient and modern. He certainly knew what he was talking about on the subject of modern revolvers, etc. While he was there (and he stayed till midnight) we all drank orange squash, he being a practising Moslem. He asked Sirry if he could see him at prayers this morning, and Sirry said, yes—rather like a schoolboy being told to go to church. He talked quite intelligently about the Air amongst other things. A rather flabby-looking youth, but struck me as being rather more of a character than he looks. We managed to make our getaway soon after the monarch.

A month later, I enjoyed an evening spent in the company of

a couple who lived in a flat just opposite my office, the Tabets. He was the proprietor of a newspaper, and I had met him at an official reception. I had also established the closest relations with their daughter. She was aged eighteen months. I asked him about the Egyptian attitude towards the British, and why we were so universally hated. He replied that we were not hated, on the whole, but there were three different outlooks; first, since the Egyptians had been ruled by us for some fifty years, there was a little of the malicious pleasure of a schoolboy seeing his master in trouble; second, there was the admiration of all Orientals for sheer power, whether good or evil, which aroused admiration for German success; and third, there was still a sprinkling of individual survivors of the old Turkish régime, who hated us for having displaced them. Tabet was most critical, and rightly so, of our propaganda news service, which he described as being always late. He gave me an interesting description of an interview with Hitler in 1933, which he'd achieved after a series of successful flatteries, up to and including Rudolph Hess. It appeared that the Führer had, in the manner of Mr. Gladstone, delivered himself of a series of public speeches to a one-man audience, until Tabet happened to get in a word to the effect that he had also met Mussolini. This fact seemed to impress Hitler. That was apparently still at the time when he was looking up to and following in the footsteps of the Duce. Early on in our conversation, my guest had remarked that the journalist's job was to show interest as a listener, and so to get people to talk, an observation which I recollected with wry interest some hours later, for throughout the evening I had only needed to drop in a word here and there. Perhaps this was not quite a fair comment, for I think he was particularly anxious to avoid any impression of trying to get news out of me. Of Wavell, Tabet said that he was extremely popular in Egypt, and inspired confidence, as did Jumbo Wilson.

Sometimes I was lucky enough to escape from the moist heat of Cairo. At the end of August, in company with Lyttelton, I went to Cyprus for two days. We threaded our way through the range of mountains which runs along the northern coast at heights of up to three thousand feet, to an old crusaders' castle called

Hilarion, the most romantic place I had ever seen. It was built out, and upon, a pinnacle, jutting over the narrow coastal plain fifteen hundred feet below. It had once been captured by Richard Cœur de Lion. We scrambled from the first gateway and the little court up to the main building, and then to the top of the pinnacle. The view was breathtaking. We stood in what must have been a lovely long room, with a line of windows looking due west along the coast and with a sheer drop below of a thousand feet or more. Later, Auchinleck joined us. We found the defences going ahead well and the R.A.F. squadron in good form. I thought the local General, Ramsden, a better specimen of the early Crimean school. We discovered that he had written to Lowe, whom I put in charge there, telling him that he, the General, was the senior commander on the island and was therefore in charge of all air operations. I showed the document to Auchinleck and we produced a joint directive putting it straight. I feared, however, that nothing would ever make General Ramsden understand the situation.

Egypt provided sights less spectacular than Cyprus and other parts of the Command, but no less attractive. One day in mid-September, driving down the Delta alongside a large canal, I watched the feluccas, one after another, driving up against the strong, reddish current, with big, curved sails bulging before the strong north wind, and pushing out a big coffee-chocolate coloured bow-wave ahead of them. The road traffic was the usual incongruous mixture of posh American limousines, paid for with our cotton subsidies, large and noisy motor buses, old taxis with a dozen or more bodies aboard, camels of which I could see only the legs and the head protruding from incredible bundles, the blue-black oxen, ugly brutes, and the inevitable moke.

When in Cairo, I could find quiet enjoyment at the Gezira Club. There I would often go for an hour or so at tea-time, to sip iced coffee in the shade of the flame trees, and watch the cricket. In this way I could find some relief from the immediate and ever-pressing business of the office. I believe that in some quarters I was adversely criticised for these petty relaxations—'fiddling while . . . .'

For all our difficulties, my reflections in that September of

1941 gave me grounds for confidence. Hitler had now engaged his main weight against Russia, and I knew the capacity of that country to swallow and digest its invaders. It seemed that the campaign there could not, at any rate, reach a conclusion that year. If this proved to be so, reinforcement of the Axis forces in the Mediterranean, though it would no doubt take place, would probably not be on the scale which would otherwise have been possible. Our supplies of aircraft were slowly but steadily increasing, and I knew that in quality they were quite a match for those of our enemy, and that our men were more than a match. So long as the Far East did not erupt, our prospects looked brighter than they had done since the previous December, especially since the vast capacity of the United States was now coming to our aid. I listened with deep satisfaction to the Prime Minister's broadcast on the night of 24 August, when he described his first wartime meeting with Roosevelt at Placentia Bay. Churchill described their meeting as symbolic of the deep underlying unities which stirred, and at decisive moments ruled, the English-speaking peoples. He spoke of the Atlantic Charter with its message of hope for oppressed people and the struggling Allies: 'Help is coming,' he said. 'Mighty forces are arming. . . . Have faith. Have hope. Deliverance is sure.'

10

Churchill's Directive–Anti-Aircraft improvisation–Timing of 'Crusader'–Lyttleton's defence of Auchinleck–Co-operation with the Navy–Axis shipping sunk–Equipment for Russia–Unified control of Air–Churchill demands air superiority–Auchinleck's support–Freeman's visit–'Crusader' Air plan–Unified control in action

I WAS heartily glad when the perennial controversy about the economical use of air-power was clarified by a directive from the Prime Minister early in September. Mr. Churchill's view amounted, in effect, to a corroboration of the line I had so often taken with Wavell and Admiral Cunningham. He ruled:

Never more must the ground troops expect, as a matter of course, to be protected against the air by aircraft. If this can be done, it must only be as a happy make-weight and a piece of good luck. Above all, the idea of keeping standing patrols of aircraft over moving columns should be abandoned. It is unsound to 'distribute' aircraft in this way, and no air superiority will stand any large application of such a mischievous practice. Upon the military Commander-in-Chief in the Middle East announcing that a battle is in prospect, the Air Officer Commanding-in-Chief will give him all possible aid irrespective of other targets, however attractive. Victory in the battle makes amends for all, and creates new favourable situations of a decisive character. The Army Commander-in-Chief will specify to the Air Officer Commanding-in-Chief the targets and tasks which he requires to be performed both in the preparatory attack on the rearward installations of the enemy and for air action during the progress of the battle. . . . As the interests of the two C.-in-Cs are identical it is not thought any difficulty should arise. The A.O.C.-in-C. would naturally lay aside all routine programmes and concentrate on bombing the rearward services of the enemy in the preparatory period. This he would do not only by night, but by day attacks with fighter protection. In this process he will bring about a trial of strength with the enemy fighters and has the best chance of obtaining local command of the air.

I found it most satisfying to be supported in this authoritative way by a ruling which recognised that we could not be so prodigal of our resources as to scatter them in driblets here and there, and which recognised also that apart from the essential aid which the air alone could render to the Army and Navy, there had emerged a new dimension in the Middle East struggle, air warfare in its own right.

The procedure which Mr. Churchill prescribed for the allocation of our air effort was very much in line with the arrangements already functioning in the Middle East. It was in any case a much easier proposition to convince Auchinleck than it had been to convince Wavell of the crucial importance of the closest co-operation between ground and air forces.

The next trial of strength in the Western Desert, which Auchinleck had conditionally promised for 1 November, was now only a few weeks away. In mid-September, it appeared that we might not be granted the privilege of choosing our own time for attack, for the Axis forces pushed forward suddenly from Sollum. (The first thrust was viewed by General Brett and his compatriots from rather closer quarters than they had anticipated.)

As it turned out, the move petered out south of Sidi Barrani, and it seemed to have been only a reconnaissance in force. The position might have been a great deal more serious for us, for we had no land forces of any strength whatever in that area, and had the enemy wished to do so he could certainly have occupied Sidi Barrani. We should then have been placed in a serious position and our capacity to maintain Tobruk would have been further weakened. 'Mary' Coningham, as usual, kept his head and distributed his strength coolly and sensibly. Our Marylands carried out some excellent bombing, and the enemy's reply was ineffective. Nevertheless, we lost three tactical reconnaissance aircraft in one day, and clearly still had to find the right answer to meet desert conditions.

What worried me most was our precarious hold on Sidi Barrani. With the full collaboration of the Army, Coningham had tried to establish the fighters there and the anti-aircraft defences at Mersa Matruh were stripped in order to build up really strong defences around Sidi Barrani aerodrome. We also installed radar, which was of limited value as far as low-flying aircraft were concerned, P.A.C. rocket (parachute and cable) and machine-gun defences. The Italians carried out one abortive attack, abortive largely because we intercepted it by luck, and then on

7 September two well-staged attacks were made on Sidi Barrani which cost us a number of aircraft on the ground. Even more disturbing was the reflection that with a little more skill and determination the enemy should have trebled his killings. Our fighters made no interceptions and no enemy aircraft was shot down by the ground defences. If we could not do better than this, I reflected, it would be impossible to push squadrons forward, as I urgently wished to do. I felt that our anti-aircraft defences in general and our aerodrome defences in particular, were our weakest spot, and a vital one.

As for the forthcoming campaign in the Western Desert, we were given from home an estimate of 600 enemy aircraft in Cyrenaica, excluding those based in Greece and Crete. Our own first estimate of available strength was only 450 aircraft, but after re-examination we increased this figure to 540. I pointed out that the 600 was a purely hypothetical figure and was certainly not on the optimistic side, whereas our 540 was a firm figure. I told my colleagues that with those relative strengths we could not attain absolute air superiority, but we could reasonably guarantee that the enemy would not have absolute air superiority either, and consequently that his bombers would not be free to act as they had been free in so many other campaigns. I could see, however, and so informed Portal, that Coningham would have to be firm and stimulating towards his opposite number, for General Cunningham, who had recently joined us from East Africa and was the brother of Andrew Cunningham, and his C.G.S., Major-General Galloway, had shown a certain amount of alarm at being given these figures. I had a feeling that on Galloway's mind and morale the experiences of Greece and Crete were indelibly marked. As for Cunningham, who was now to command in the Western Desert, I found him agreeable and a great deal more receptive to fresh ideas than was his brother.

The Prime Minister, eager as ever for the operation to start, entertained far-reaching ideas about its exploitation. If 'Crusader' were successful, he hoped to launch 'Acrobat', an advance from Cyrenaica into Tripolitania. Churchill believed that if the enemy lost too many bases in North Africa, they might arouse the indignation of the Vichy French authorities by demanding the facilities of Bizerta or Tunis. General Weygand would then be offered British help, with the possibility of American intervention.

Apart from these political considerations, we in the Middle East found ourselves in something of a dilemma. Auchinleck and I knew that our forces were in urgent need of time, so that re-equipment and necessary training could be accomplished before battle began. On the other hand, the longer 'Crusader' was postponed, the better chance Rommel had of receiving substantial reinforcements. I felt no doubt that Auchinleck was right in judging armour to be the deciding factor in the land battle. Sheer weight of numbers counted for comparatively little, and elaborate calculations of the exact balance of numerical strength were to this degree out of place. When Auchinleck had taken over from Wavell in July, only one complete armoured formation was available. We had always known that re-equipment with cruiser tanks could not be complete before October. The rapid progress of Hitler's assault upon Russia had caused us to become more sensitive than ever in the Middle East to the threat from the north, a threat which in view of his Indian training, Auchinleck took most seriously. Working in the closest contact with him, I had no doubt of his eagerness to take the offensive in Libya at the earliest moment; but I had wholly sympathised with his view that to launch an offensive with inadequate means was not a justifiable operation of war.

While the Minister of State, Oliver Lyttelton, was at home in London for consultations at the end of September, Churchill urged upon him the need for a rapid move forward in the Desert. Lyttelton tried, not with complete success, to convince the Prime Minister that Auchinleck was neither obstinate nor lethargic. Auchinleck had already signalled that he was determined to launch an offensive at the earliest possible moment, but that the first requisite for success was the establishment of reasonable air superiority: 'And this, unless we are relatively in overwhelming strength in the air, can be achieved only by wearing down the enemy's air forces over a considerable period prior to the launching of the main land offensive.'[1]

[1] Connell: *Auchinleck,* p. 310.

Auchinleck pointed out that this period coincided with the operations for the relief of the Tobruk garrison which had been undertaken on purely political grounds and against the united opinion of the Middle Eastern Commanders-in-Chief and the Minister of State. He hoped that the effect of the Tobruk operations would not seriously prejudice the gaining of air superiority.

As a counter to the Tobruk operations, we could at least congratulate ourselves that at this stage we were making the Mediterranean too hot to hold the German and Italian supply ships. The enemy's convoys from Naples generally sailed either through the Straits of Messina, or, more often, to the west of Sicily. Whichever route they took, we could strike at them from Malta. In the six months from the beginning of May 1941, we contrived to sink 270,000 tons of Axis shipping on the routes to Africa, 44 per cent. of this total being accounted for by submarines, 47 per cent. by aircraft, and the rest by surface craft. Early in November, when for the first time for six months we had a surface force at Malta, a complete convoy from Naples, with two of its accompanying destroyers, was sunk. The supply of Malta, however, constituted one of our gravest problems. Unless we could continue to hold the island and to use it against Axis shipping, we had no hope of cutting Rommel's lifeline. At the same time, until we could turn Rommel out of Cyrenaica, we lacked the essential air bases. Supreme efforts were made to overcome these disadvantages, and I was much heartened at the close co-operation between the R.A.F. and the Royal Navy which enabled the 'Halberd' convoy to reach Malta at the end of September 1941. Admiral Somerville, commander of Force H from Gibraltar, paid tribute to the R.A.F. for its reconnaissance and fighter cover and for its low level attacks on Italian airfields in Sardinia and Sicily, to which the absence of enemy bombing was attributed. He told the Admiralty that the excellent co-operation of our fighters had given the Fleet a greater sense of security.

We continued to attack the enemy-held ports, particularly Benghazi, with all our might. Towards the end of September, I reduced the scale of effort by the Wellington bombers against Benghazi, and Freeman telegraphed to ask me why. I replied that we were at this time attempting to dislocate enemy sea communications and other vulnerable points. For instance, we were undertaking attacks on the Corinth Canal at Admiral Cunningham's request. We also wished to reduce the scale of enemy action against our bases, and I felt that our crews' efficiency and morale would suffer if they were not given some variation from an unrelieved diet of the Benghazi raids.

Freeman answered:

Can understand the need for a balanced diet. However, the African date is better food than the Grecian grape.

I retorted:

Quote noted. English raspberry good appetizer in balanced diet.

*

In preparing to throw all our forces into the Desert offensive, I had to take serious account of the heavy wastage in aircraft which would inevitably result. When Lyttelton had returned from London, we discussed at the Middle East Defence Committee on 11 October the probable effects on our Middle Eastern strength of the promises made by the British and American Governments to Russia, and by the British Government to Turkey. I asked whether we were going to pour large quantities of equipment into Russia. The Minister of State replied that we had certainly made large promises, but their fulfilment depended on the development of the situation. I observed that deliveries of aircraft to Russia were already affecting our fighter strength, and I was very worried at the outlook. The promised fighter reinforcements had been whittled down, and I was considering whether I should telegraph the Air Ministry pointing out that our offer of help to Turkey might have to be reduced. Auchinleck said the tank deliveries to the Middle East had also been cut down. When Lyttelton pointed out that much of the equipment for Russia would pass through the Middle East and might be available there if it could not go to Russia, Andrew Cunningham objected that the supplies might not be available at the time and place required. He said, with much truth, that the situation in the Middle East held out great possibilities but the margin was very narrow and the diversion of equipment might just rob us of the great successes within our grasp.

On 3 October, Auchinleck and I had held a meeting at G.H.Q., Cairo, in order to co-ordinate the efforts of our land and air forces. 'Mary' Coningham told us on that occasion that he had considered putting some air forces under the command of corps commanders, but had decided that he should control all the air forces except Army Co-operation squadrons. It would probably be necessary to give fighter support to bomber and Army Co-operation aircraft, and it was therefore essential for fighters and bombers to come under one command. The A.O.C. would be receiving information both from the air and from the ground, and his headquarters would be in the main aerodrome area.

General Alan Cunningham was not altogether satisfied with this arrangement, and expressed his anxiety lest there be delays in giving support to forward formations on account of the extra link imposed by the A.O.C. remaining in control. I said that the R.A.F. were concerned only to give the Army the greatest possible assistance in the most effective way. In order to do this our forces had to be concentrated under a single control, for we could not enjoy sufficient superiority to enable our aircraft to operate freely over the battle area. The burden of Cunningham's argument was that his corps commanders would feel lonely and unsupported unless they had a fighter and a bomber squadron at their own personal beck and call.

I pointed out that if they really did need air support, one fighter and one bomber squadron would probably prove quite inadequate. I tried to make it clear that to divide up our forces into penny packets would be to fritter away our strength without giving the troops any effective support. Cunningham saw the point in theory, but felt that in practice it depended upon communications, and he did not think that communications between the corps and headquarters could be relied on. I retorted that we could not sit back and accept the proposition that good communications were impossible. I also pointed out that in each of the last two main operations in the Western Desert, where air action had been successful on both occasions, it had been taken as a result of direct air reconnaissance and on the initiative of the A.O.C., after squadrons had been standing by for hours on call without receiving any such call from the Army.

General Blamey, who had political axes to grind, made some sweeping and inaccurate statements about what the Germans could do. I declined to argue about facts, but emphasised that if one obtained complete air superiority first to the extent of wiping out the opposing air, one could afford to do all kinds of things. I finally told the meeting that I was determined to make sure that we had the organisation and material to give the Army every possible support, but I was equally determined that it should be done in an effective way.

Auchinleck followed by saying that he appreciated the arguments in favour of decentralising the control of some of the air forces, but given the circumstances that were likely to prevail, he was quite convinced that the line I was taking was the right one.

A day or two later, I heard from Portal that after a series of most exhausting and prolonged discussions with the Admiralty, agreement had at length been reached on Cunningham's request for a Coastal Command. Although 201 Group was now known as 201 (Naval Co-operation) Group, operational control would in practice be exercised by the R.A.F., and I was recognised as the Service authority ultimately responsible for the employment of all the air forces under my command. At least, therefore, I felt reassured that the principle of unified control of our air strength, vital, as I was convinced, to our success in the coming battle, had emerged more or less unscathed. These issues were no sooner settled than there arose a crisis between London and the Middle East more serious than any I had so far faced.

On 13 October Churchill received from Mr. Peter Fraser, the Prime Minister of New Zealand, a telegram pressing for some reassurance that after experience in Greece, and particularly in Crete, New Zealand troops should not for the third time be committed to go into battle without adequate air support, and in circumstances in which they could not defend themselves against unrestricted air attack. Mr. Fraser said that he and his colleagues fully realised the exigencies of the situation and the need to strike an early blow in the Desert to improve our own position while the enemy was heavily engaged elsewhere, and to ease the pressure on Russia. They would, however, be glad to know the best appreciation possible of the air, tank and armoured fighting vehicle

At a Middle East Defence Committee Meeting in early 1941. On my right is Wigglesworth, and to my left, Longmore (A.O.C.-in-C.), Admiral Cunningham, Dick (the Naval Staff Captain to the C.-in-C.) and Captain Norman, the Naval liaison officer in Cairo. On Eden's left is Pierson Dixon of the Foreign Office, and on his right, Wavell, Dill, and Arthur Smith, Wavell's Chief of Staff

'Morning Prayers' in 1942, with Pirie, Wigglesworth and Boswell (standing), and Drummond seated on my left

The Auk

Constantine from 'Mary's'
office window during
'Morning Prayers'

strengths of the enemy and ourselves in the Middle East and would welcome an assurance that the question of air support which they regarded as the vital factor had been fully considered and appreciated by those responsible.

Churchill answered confidently that ample air and tank strength would be available, and he would send Mr. Fraser the detailed figures shortly. On the same day, Portal received from me the signal giving our estimate of relative strengths for the 'Crusader' offensive. On the basis of our Intelligence in the Middle East, we had concluded that we should be definitely superior in mechanised forces but numerically inferior in the air. Nevertheless, we anticipated being able to gain air superiority and to use it to support the Army. Operations to this end were already in full blast so that the enemy's land and air forces might be weakened by the interruption of their supplies. Until the active land operations began, our plan was to strike at enemy supplies on the sea, at the ports of loading and unloading, on the roads, and at the dumps where these offered a reasonable target. For the attack on seaborne supplies and lines of communication in Tripolitania, Malta was the strategic centre. I intended to maintain there the greatest striking force which could be operated. Sustained light attacks, interspersed with heavy onslaughts, would be continued against Benghazi, and in Cyrenaica the use at night of Swordfish to identify and illuminate targets, followed up by Blenheims, promised to be effective. In daylight, the Maryland squadrons with fighter escort were showing good results against dumps and motor transport concentrations, and had already attracted enemy fighter action. I told Portal that the fighter commitment to cover supplies to Tobruk had been a continual drag on fighter operations, but the enemy rarely accepted battle with our fighter sweeps and had confined himself largely to tip-and-run attacks on our reconnaissance aircraft. I hoped that the combined bomber and fighter action would force him to accept battle under our conditions. Immediately before the beginning of 'Crusader' we intended to intensify action against aerodromes.

I summarised the situation thus:

Exact nature of action once land battle is joined must depend on air and land situation but principle clearly established that main

Army requirement is the freedom from air interference which can only be given by air superiority. Complete immunity from air impossible until enemy air knocked out, but reasonable degree of freedom from air attack should be attainable provided enemy does not send substantial air reinforcements during next three weeks. Organisation being built up and training proceeding to provide close support for Army should it be required.

We hoped that threats of land raids would force the enemy to evacuate his forward aerodromes, and would cause him to withdraw into Western Cyrenaica where the number of aerodromes was limited and where he would be, therefore, more vulnerable. Once air superiority had been obtained, we looked forward to attacking the enemy's supplies, especially of petrol. In this way we hoped to immobilise Rommel.

Of course, when I sent this appreciation I did not know that its arrival in London would coincide with that of the telegram from New Zealand. On the evening of 14 October, Portal read out to the Prime Minister my signal. Churchill indicated disapproval. The C.A.S. then told him the terms of his answer, which was better received. Portal's reply was that my appreciation had caused him considerable disappointment. No commander, I was told, could expect to go into battle with all units up to their full establishment, and no squadron should be left out merely because of a shortage of M.T. In a battle of such far-reaching importance every unit in my Command, which by improvisation could be made fit to fight, should be used, and other units should be denuded if necessary. My comparison of strength was dubbed 'most depressing', and, in the C.A.S's opinion, most unjustifiably depressing. He thought that I was counting in my estimates many German and Italian aircraft which were not likely to be able to intervene in the battle area. The total serviceable strength of German Air forces in Libya was about 100, including 30 fighters. Supply and maintenance difficulties of the enemy air forces were well known to me and should heavily discount his paper strength. Reinforcements of fighter pilots were on the way via Takoradi, and some at least should reach Egypt in time to take part in the battle:

The Royal Air Force, Middle East, must go into this battle with one thought only, and that is to win it at all costs. Nothing must be held back for insurance in Syria, Iraq and Persia, or to enable our promises to Turkey to be kept. It is the responsibility of the Air Ministry to ensure that your losses are replaced to enable you to meet these later commitments.

This signal arrived on the morning of 16 October. It was shortly followed by another, asking me to tell London as soon as possible for the information of the Defence Committee, what extra strength I could make available for the battle by the means Portal had suggested. I was asked if I proposed to leave operational units in Iraq, Cyprus and Palestine. Did I agree that when the battle began all possible bomber effect, including the Wellingtons from Egypt, should be applied to the battle area, the aerodromes and forward lines of communication? Did I intend to use any Blenheims by day? What were our probable objectives in the battle, the weight of our attack, the proportion of fighters to be used in defensive and offensive operations and in the attack on ground targets? Had I considered the possibility of using Wellingtons by day with or without fighter escort? What arrangements had been made for seizing and defending additional aerodromes as the advance across the Desert proceeded, and for the concentration and use of every available transport aircraft to help supplies and maintenance? Portal said he was sure that I would already have thought over most of these points, but I must understand the need for him to have early answers. Feeling sure that the telegram owed its inspiration, if not its language, to the Prime Minister, I had no difficulty in reading between the lines:

The stakes are so high [Portal's message concluded] that we must both try to ensure by every means that nothing likely to contribute to success has been overlooked either here or in the Middle East.

I felt sure that my telegram had given in London an impression more pessimistic than was intended. I replied at once, promising Portal a detailed answer after Coningham and I had discussed the matter. On the merits of the issue, I refused to recant:

I set little store by numerical comparisons of strength. Serviceability, reserves, supply, morale, are vital factors in any real comparison.

Have repeatedly emphasised this here, and realise I should have made this clear in my signal to you.

I assured the C.A.S. that we were not in the least depressed by the comparison we had sent, and the promised help with pilots relieved me of my only real anxiety. I told him that I was ruthlessly stripping other theatres and formations to give everything to the Western Desert:

I am not satisfied I cannot do more, but I will not, repeat will not, promise until I am sure I can effectively keep promise. I will not put dummies in shop window for D Day. Our battle is joined now, repeat now, and my object is to maintain and increase the pressure to attain air superiority before the Army move.

Later in the day, I was able to assure Portal with detailed factual corroboration, that everything possible was being done to reinforce the Desert. Iraq, Cyprus, Palestine, and the Delta were being left with the barest minimum of air forces. We had already planned to use the whole bomber effort as he suggested, and to employ our Blenheims by day. Auchinleck and I were agreed that it was not possible at this stage to specify the objectives and relative weight of attack. This had to be decided at the time by the Army and Air commanders in the Western Desert. The immediate aim must be to knock out the German fighter force, and all our detailed planning to this end was in hand. The use of Wellingtons by day must depend on the degree of air superiority we were able to secure. As for the seizure of landing grounds, our plans were already laid with the Army command for the use of armoured-cars. Requirements for air transport for ourselves and for the Army were being carefully studied and all necessary arrangements made.

By the time this signal was ready for despatch, a further message, marked 'Most Secret and Strictly Private' had arrived from Portal. I now learnt for the first time that my signal and an earlier appreciation by the Middle East Commanders-in-Chief had unfortunately raised acute political difficulties, because the New Zealand Government had just asked for the assurance that we should have air superiority. Churchill felt unable to give this in the light of my unqualified figures. The Prime Minister had

decided that 'no mere process of discounting strength by telegram' between Portal and me would enable him to give Mr.
Fraser the necessary assurance. It was deemed to be politically
essential that some very senior officer should come at once to
Egypt, to investigate thoroughly the comparison of forces and
report to the C.A.S. Wilfrid Freeman would, therefore, leave
almost at once to spend three or four days in Cairo. I was much
encouraged by the final paragraph of Portal's telegram, thoughtful
and kindly as ever:

Greatly regret this intrusion when you are so much occupied with
your preparations, but you can picture situation here and understand
my difficulties. Assure you that this unfortunate development in no
way affects my absolute confidence in your ability and determination
to win.

I more than suspected at the time, although I did not then
know it, that the Prime Minister had prejudged the issue. In
a letter to Auchinleck, dated 16 October, he observed that
my estimate of strength was 'so misleading and militarily untrue'
that he had found it necessary to send Freeman at once to Cairo.
The Air Staff, the Prime Minister wrote, knew just as much and
in some ways more than the Air Intelligence in Egypt. They
were convinced that Auchinleck would have a substantial numerical superiority in the battle zone. Moreover, my telegram had
assumed that the Russian Front would be stabilised by 15 October,
whereas it certainly would not be stabilised for some weeks, if
then, and several more weeks must elapse before any effective
transference could be made of German air units already battered
and worn. Churchill's letter went on:

I thought it very wrong that such mis-statements should be made
by the Air authorities in Cairo on the eve of a decisive battle, and I
shall not conceal from you that such conduct has affected my confidence
in their quality and judgment.

You will find Freeman an officer of altogether larger calibre, and if
you feel he would be a greater help to you and that you would have
more confidence in the Air Command if he assumed it, you should not
hesitate to tell me so. The time has now come when for the purposes
of the major operation impending, the Air is subordinated to you. Do
not let any thought of Tedder's personal feelings influence you. This

is no time for such considerations. On the other hand I am very glad to see that you and Tedder are in accord upon the tactical employment of the Air Force and that there is no danger of its being parcelled out among the various divisions, thus losing its power to make the characteristic contribution of its arm.[1]

Before this letter had been received in the Middle East, a further squall had blown up, this time between Auchinleck and the Prime Minister. As Churchill was writing his letter, which Freeman must bring to Cairo, the Commander-in-Chief warned him that the date of 'Crusader' might have to be put back. A tart exchange of signals followed. I thought Auchinleck quite justified in pointing out that the telegram of 23 July had laid down strict conditions on which alone the date of 1 November would be feasible for the opening of the 'Crusader' offensive. These conditions had not been fulfilled, not through any fault of the Prime Minister, nor through any fault of the Middle East Commanders-in-Chief. Not only had the necessary tanks and personnel arrived late, but they had arrived in insufficient quantities. In July we had said that two armoured divisions were essential and three desirable, for an offensive which we were now about to undertake with one and a half armoured divisions. Churchill replied that it seemed misleading to calculate in divisions when ours were 'wholly different from those of the enemy'. This remark, though doubtless true, was scarcely relevant, since we had been fully aware of this factor when making our forecast in July. In the end, Churchill had no alternative but to submit with reluctance to the delay.

*

On the morning of 20 October I was woken at six o'clock by the telephone with a message that Freeman was due at 7.15. My journal records:

Got down to the river in plenty of time, and after a wait saw the lovely grey and green Sunderland do a beautiful, graceful perch on the Nile just in front of the riverboat I was in. Wilfrid very cheerful. . . . Since then things have been pretty lively. I am very glad he's come out. He really can tell us what they are thinking at home—and that is a

---

[1] Connell: *Auchinleck*, p. 316.

great help. But everything is a bit complicated, and heaven knows what's going to come out of it all.

Freeman and I plunged at once into a discussion of air strengths. I had noticed that the Prime Minister, in his signal to Auchinleck, announcing that Freeman was coming, had accused me of saying that we would not have air superiority. What I had actually said was that so far as I could see we should not have numerical superiority —a quite different thing. After full discussion, Freeman and I agreed the probable relative strengths at the time of 'Crusader'. An increase in our own figures had been achieved by stripping Iraq, Palestine, Aden, and the Delta of all except negligible units of no operational value. I had not then told Wavell, though I had warned him, of the possible fleecing of Iraq.

Freeman felt that the alarm caused by my signal was mainly a question of presenting the figures. We discussed them fully that day with Auchinleck, who said firmly that he did not doubt we should gain air superiority even if we did not have actual superiority in numbers. The V.C.A.S. assured me of Portal's confidence, while Auchinleck, though I did not then know it, also told Churchill of his full confidence in me and earnestly asked that no change in the Air Command in the Middle East should be considered at the present time. A day or two later, on 23 October he again assured the Prime Minister that he was not, and had not been, unduly anxious about the air situation. It did not seem likely that there would be a tremendous disparity one way or the other, in which event the gaining of a reasonable degree of air superiority was more a matter of leadership, skill, and general efficiency than of general numbers:

I have confidence in the ability of Tedder and his subordinate commanders to do what we require of them and I am glad to be able to think that the confidence of the Army generally in the R.A.F. in this theatre, which was somewhat shaken after the campaigns in Greece and Crete, is now restored. The co-operation between the two Services is very good, and I hope that they understand each other's capabilities and limitations much better than has sometimes been the case in the past.[1]

---

[1] Connell: *Auchinleck*, p. 322.

Auchinleck said that he felt that the worst possible case must always be considered and stated, though one need not necessarily be over-awed by it when making plans for future operations: 'Figures can be made to prove anything, but I do not think we have allowed ourselves to be governed by them. . . .'[1]

I was heartily glad that this troublesome business had now been cleared up. Quite apart from the actual figures, we had to remember that the Me. 109F, which was now being used by the Germans to good effect, was a better aircraft than any fighter available to us, a fact of which Coningham had already received unpleasant evidence in the Desert. Moreover, the enemy's total number of aircraft in Tripolitania, Sicily, Sardinia, Greece, and Crete, amounted to about 750. Whether he would be able to use them depended on our activities at sea and in the air. When it was pointed out later to the Prime Minister that the two estimates were very close, he minuted:

The only difference was that the first version stated that we should be inferior, and the revised version that we should be superior. It is only the kind of difference between plus and minus, or black and white.

*

Now that this immediate crisis was over, Freeman returned to London, having told me that he had no intention of 'doing a Brutus' on me. Operations in the Desert were in full blast, and towards the end of the month I went by Lockheed to 'Mary' Coningham's headquarters. Air Commodore Basil Embry, an outstanding fighter leader for whose services I had asked, and who had come out with Freeman, greeted me. During the afternoon we visited three South African fighter squadrons, and then travelled back in the moonlight with a guide until we reached the road. I dined in the Mess shared by the Army and R.A.F. Staffs. General Cunningham and his two senior officers, 'Mary' Coningham and his, a sailor, and two or three of their personal staff were our hosts. My quarters were quite luxurious, in a large tent with a real bed, rugs, a wash-stand, chest of drawers, and electric light. The air was strong:

A glorious night; a brilliant half moon, stars overhead, Sirius in the

---

[1] Connell: *Auchinleck,* p. 323.

east and Orion rising—sand soft and white like snow, and an indigo sea. Not a sound except the chug of a lighting plant in the distance.

The next day, Coningham and I went to visit 274 Squadron, who had asked me to lunch. All the pilots, officers, and N.C.Os ate in one Mess. I thought them a fine lot. They had only arrived three days before, but turned out a sumptuous lunch. Coningham, who had not met this fighter squadron before, gave them information on their new duties. In the afternoon, he and I sat on the rocks on a brown headland watching the waves and the squadrons of Hurricanes practising the new tactics. Later, all the squadron commanding officers came in for beer and food. I passed four pleasant, inspiring hours, standing in the crowded mess tent talking to British, Australians, many South Africans, New Zealanders and Rhodesians. Towards the end we had some songs, South African, English and even an Irish folk-song. Then I went to bed to the sound of the breaking waves and the occasional drone of a Hurricane looking for the Hun.

Seven more squadrons welcomed me the following day on their aerodromes. Thick dust storms hampered our progress, and we had to leave our Proctor at one aerodrome and do the rest of the journey by car. In the evening I went to a party for all the squadrons within reach. We had some job in finding them, despite the full moon. They all seemed to be very cheery. The dust storms intensified later in the evening, and when we left at about eleven o'clock, it was blowing hard and the dust was very thick. Fortunately we could see the moon and some of the stars. The driver asserted that he knew his way, so I let him wander around for some time. After we had completed a circle round the aerodrome I got out, and led him with the help of the stars. It took an hour and a half to cover the four miles of road.

The following day, I went up with Coningham in a Blenheim to the forward area. An escort of six Tomahawks was insisted upon:

They were a pretty sight, two of them weaving across, above and ahead of us, and two other pairs weaving behind and below.

It's a bare, stony country, practically featureless but not quite flat—just vague waves of country. One doesn't realise it isn't flat until one sees cars disappear behind a fold of country. Lunch with the corps commander in a lonely tent, half dug into the sand and stones. The General a cheerful soul—a 'good fellow!' When we got back this afternoon, I went down to the beach and sat on that headland for nearly an hour watching the fighters practising their weaving.

More visits and conferences on plans filled the next two days. I talked to our pilots and crews, many of whom were inexperienced. I was amused by the reactions of a new Australian fighter pilot to his equipment:

I asked him about the Tomahawk which was new to him—his reply, a little off-hand. I then asked him if he'd fired the guns, and his face lit up and completely altered when he said 'Yes', and when I asked him if they were all right, he said 'Too right', with a broad grin.

I was back in Cairo by the evening of 2 November and reported to London that the concentration of units was complete except for one or two squadrons from Aden and Syria which would go forward as soon as the aerodromes were ready. Our strength in fighter aircraft was good, our morale high, and our pilots first-rate fighting material. Their fighting efficiency varied, however. Certain squadrons were excellent, while others lacked experience and leadership. Most of them had suffered from the long series of defensive patrols over shipping, which had made the supply of Tobruk possible, but had inevitably reduced their offensive efficiency. All were intensively practising more flexible and offensive tactics recently evolved at home. I looked for good results from the arrival of experienced pilots whom Portal was sending at my request. 'In another four days,' I telegraphed, 'all should be at concert pitch.'

Similar variations were visible in the medium bomber squadrons. The two Army Co-operation squadrons were up to strength and working well, but tactical reconnaissance by the Hurricane Is was, for the moment, difficult and expensive. The South Africans were doing excellent work in strategic reconnaissance flights with their Marylands, and General Cunningham now expressed himself satisfied with reconnaissance and photography. I had discussed the whole air plan with him and with Coningham and his fighter and bomber commanders. Their original plan had been to attack supplies before D Day, but to conserve their forces for a maximum effort on D Day itself and the previous night, and on the following day. I thought this wrong, for D Day would fall in a moonless period, and the weather, now very treacherous, might be bad. Moreover, air superiority could not be achieved in one day over a prepared enemy, and loss of surprise was not a real factor, since the concentration of our armies would, in any case, destroy strategic surprise. I had ruled, therefore, that heavy bombers should operate at their maximum effort at once against supplies, and especially against Benghazi. The concentrated attack on the enemy's air strength, with all our forces at maximum effort, was to begin as soon as the fighters were ready, probably at the end of that week. These dispositions would not affect the plans already made for combined attacks by land and air on enemy fighter and dive-bomber aerodromes on the night before the offensive, and on D Day itself. I was satisfied, and so informed Portal, that the Air plan was being closely co-ordinated with the Army's plans.

Our Air plan was in three phases. The first was the interruption and destruction of supplies; the second, the destruction of enemy air forces on the ground and in the air; the third, to support the Army's advance. The nature of the targets to be attacked in this third phase would depend on events, and the extent of the support which we could render would depend on the degree of success we might already have achieved in knocking out the enemy's air forces. As I explained to Portal:

The key to air superiority is the comparatively small number of German fighters, and apart from the maintenance of pressure on enemy supplies, every effort is being directed towards ensuring an effective knock-out of the Hun in the air.

I was determined that we should use to the full the extra time granted by the postponement of 'Crusader'. Every day was occupied with intensive practice of new fighter tactics, and with attacks upon the enemy's supplies. One of our main difficulties was to find worthwhile targets in Cyrenaica. The relatively small ships which the enemy sent into Benghazi made poor targets, although the heavy bombers did some damage. Early in November one petrol and one ammunition ship were blown up, leaving a gap in the outer mole of the harbour which must have caused the enemy some difficulties now that the winds were fresh. The enemy's method was to bring the ships into the harbour at dawn and to leave them outside the harbour at night. So far as possible, cargo was cleared from the wharves during daylight. All the same, the Marylands were able to do some excellent raiding in daylight, and their accuracy from 15,000 to 18,000 feet, as I was able to see for myself from the photographs, was excellent. Extra Wellingtons had now arrived at Malta, to my great relief. I thought it justifiable to maintain there, despite the obvious risks, the largest serviceable Wellington force, since Malta provided unique opportunities of striking at the most tender spots on the enemy's lines of communication. Undeniably, this policy had meant a drain on our force in Egypt.

As for the air battle proper, the immediate problem was to induce the enemy to fight or to force him to be shot up and bombed on the ground. The German tactics, which depended on their possession of aircraft with higher speed and a better rate of climb than ours, were to hold back until it was possible to pick off a straggler or two. German squadrons were based at Gazala and would sometimes come forward to refuel at Gambut. We could not find very many appetizing targets to bomb in the desert, and the scale of the enemy's A.A. defence around such targets was heavy. I thought that with an effort we could find enough tender spots, an attack on which would sting the enemy sufficiently for him to come up and fight. We had laid out dummies on the Gazala landing grounds so that our pilots might practise low-flying attack, and for the very beginning of the offensive we prepared an agreeable variety of surprises in the shape of parachute parties, armoured-cars, spikes, and low-flying bombing and machine-gun attacks.

I felt confident that when the battle came our men would co-operate to the full with the Army. Each of the two corps, 13 and 30, was allotted one squadron, the commander of which shared headquarters with the corps commander. A third squadron was in reserve to reinforce either corps as necessary. Joint exercises were constantly going forward to perfect the plans. The main risk was a breakdown in communications, for in previous offensives the Army commander had always seemed to be completely out of touch with events on his own front. I was satisfied that the Army had genuinely done their best to provide for defence of forward aerodromes, and I had myself denuded our aerodromes in the Delta most drastically of machine-guns. The armoured-cars had been brought back all the way from Habbaniya and would go forward to support the anti-aircraft defences. Nevertheless, I had to recognise that a really enterprising enemy might well prove troublesome.

The work of Dawson and his team had much improved our rate of serviceability and the erection and repair of aircraft. Although the intake of aircraft had been well below the promised programme, we had by now just over a thousand serviceable operational types in my Command.

This prelude to 'Crusader' gave me the opportunity to show what air-power could do when directed from one centre in accordance with a coherent plan. With the aid of my force in Malta, we attacked the enemy's ports of departure and arrival, Naples and Palermo, and Tripoli and Benghazi. The enemy's shipping was attacked, not only in port but on its way across the high seas; we repeatedly hammered away at his dumps and transport on the lines of communication between the ports of intake and the front. Our aircraft were carrying out reconnaissance over the sea for the Royal Navy, and our activities, quite apart from the immediate damage they caused to the enemy's supplies, obliged him to divert his fighter strength to the defence of rearward areas, and therefore weakened his effort in the forward area and minimised his bombing. I had no doubt at all that we should give a very good account of ourselves. How long I should remain in Cairo was another matter. Just at this time, my wife was considering whether to join me. I told her on 3 November that I did not feel she ought to come until matters had cleared a little:

If this next show goes well and the soldiers do their stuff, then one should be fairly secure for some months, but if they make a mess of it again there is no question at all but that I shall be made a scapegoat, and that might mean your arriving out to find I was just going, or had even gone! I hate leaving you in this quandary. As far as I am personally concerned, I don't give a damn about all this political business. I think I have the confidence of the people here and of our own chaps, and that is all that matters. But I think we must wait and see how this party goes. Don't worry about me. These flaps don't disturb me in the least.

Soon afterwards there arrived a cheerful signal from the Prime Minister which was most welcome. I asked Portal to let him know that we were all fit and keen, and determined to make a job of it. In the five weeks of preparatory air action from 14 October to 17 November, the Allied Air Forces in the Middle East flew about three thousand sorties. Our reserves had now increased to such a degree that we replaced over 230 aircraft in the month beginning the middle of October. This was already a far cry from the situation Longmore had faced only a few months earlier. I reported to the C.A.S. on 17 November: 'Squadrons are at full strength, aircraft and crews, with reserve aircraft, and the whole force is on its toes.'

11

'Crusader' opens–Air's part in offensive–Auchinleck 'a fighter'–General Cunningham relieved–Army and airfield protection–Rommel turns west–Facing the Me. 109F–Gazala– A lost opportunity–Reports from home–Naval controversy– Outbreak of Japanese War–'Crusader' summing up–Strategy in a world war

THE 'Crusader' offensive proper opened on 18 November with the advance of the three armoured brigades of 30 Corps, 4th, 7th, and 22nd, through the frontier wire between Bir Sheferzen and Fort Maddalena, followed by a north-westerly wheel towards Tobruk.[1]

On the eve of battle, the Prime Minister telegraphed to Auchinleck at the King's command, to express His Majesty's confidence that all our forces in the Middle East would do their duty with exemplary devotion in the supremely important battle lying before them. For the first time, the message ran, British and Empire troops would meet the Germans with an ample equipment in modern weapons of all kinds. The battle would affect the whole course of the war:

Now is the time to strike the hardest blow yet for final Victory, Home and Freedom. The Desert Army may add a page to history which will rank with Blenheim and with Waterloo.

The eyes of all Nations are upon you. All our hearts are with you. May God uphold the right.

To my forces I signalled: 'Good hunting.'

At first, the air operations went almost too well. Alan Cunningham's forces moved forward on 15 November. The next evening, when I spoke by telephone to 'Mary' Coningham he sounded very cheerful. The weather was poor, with frequent dust storms, and the Germans and Italians extremely shy. Repeated efforts by our forces to flush them produced no results at all. I could only suppose that the enemy was reserving his strength, but even if this was so our Army was able to benefit by moving forward entirely unmolested from the air. Even by mid-day on 18 November, no enemy air forces had put in an appearance. It began to look as if they had

[1] For a full account of the ground forces' battle during 'Crusader', see Liddell Hart: *The Tanks,* vol. II, Chapter IV.

been surprised, or perhaps Rommel was merely playing some crafty game. Meanwhile, the Army rolled forward. The weather was foul. When I complained bitterly that day that it had taken some fifteen hours to get a signal through, I was told that in the Desert they had been flooded with torrents of rain for hours during the night. Violent thunderstorms broke out, and the wireless station itself had been struck by lightning. It was strange to have to sit in Cairo waiting for news not even knowing whether the tank battle had begun or not. Auchinleck and I reported to Churchill that although our ground forces had made little contact with the enemy, the armoured troops were now well positioned on Rommel's southern flank. The heavy rain might have impeded our advance slightly, and it certainly limited air action on both sides, but we thought the probability was that the enemy were suffering more from the bad weather than we were. Despite the area now covered by our mechanised forces it still seemed that Rommel might not have appreciated the scale of our operations in the air and on land, and for this reason we were most anxious not to disclose the fact in our communiqués or by any other means.

I was with Auchinleck when he was composing the draft of his first such signal. He said to me: 'What about the Air?' I suggested one or two suitable phrases.

Then he exclaimed: 'Not a word about the Air unless this goes "from Tedder and Auchinleck".' I reflected that this was a very different attitude from that which had prevailed in Wavell's time.

Meanwhile, during that day our forces were moving forward to such good effect that I hoped we might even clear Tobruk in two or three days' time. I found it most frustrating to have to sit in Cairo waiting for news which came through intermittently on a bad telephone line, but it was grand to be told on all sides that co-operation between the Army and the R.A.F. was paying dividends after all the attention that we had given to it. The Minister of State, Lyttelton, told me how pleased he was to hear that the Army were well satisfied with the help they were getting from us. General Ritchie, one of Auchinleck's senior staff, returned from the front on the evening of 21 November. It appeared, from his account, that so far about four tank battles had taken place and what might prove to be the decisive battle was probably occurring that afternoon. In my journal I wrote:

With any luck at all they should clear up the Hun, but there's always a chance they may get away. Our chaps have for the time being knocked the enemy right out of the air. I had a few seconds talk on a fairly bad 'phone with Basil Embry this evening. Said things were very satisfactory, but 'the Hun won't fly—they can't take it'. He seemed rather annoyed about it. Ritchie said the air situation was marvellous— 'like France, only the other way round'.

General Ritchie brought me a very cheering note from 'Mary' Coningham. He said they would welcome me at any time in the Desert, and I promised I would go up there in a day or two to discuss the next phase with him. Ritchie was loud in his praises of the co-operation between our two forces, quoting as an example a distress call for ammunition made at 12.30 and the delivery by air from Matruh made at 16.45. From Cunningham's account and from Ritchie, it was clear that the Army, for once, was pleased with the R.A.F.

On the first day of battle our bomber efforts had been concentrated according to plan against the enemy landing grounds. Fighter sweeps had been maintained over Tobruk, Bardia, and the Maddalena area throughout the day, and a concentration of enemy armour and transport at Gobi was successfully attacked. Our long-range fighters concentrated on knocking out road tankers and aircraft on the ground and in the air in the rearward areas. The results were excellent. Night bombers hammered the landing grounds. The combined result of these operations was that during the first three days of the land battle the enemy's offensive air action was almost negligible. Air reconnaissance located some choice targets in the shape of armour and transport concentrations, upon which we launched escorted bomber attacks. By 20 November it was clear that for the time being we had attained air superiority. The whole bomber force was therefore put at the disposal of the Army commanders. Great difficulty was found in allotting targets for this force, partly because of rapid changes in the battle situation, and partly for lack of information. When we came to consider the exercise of our air-power in this phase, it was only too plain that the bomber force had not been used to anything like its full capacity.

On the evening of 21 November Auchinleck came into my office to say that he was sending a report direct to Churchill, and he urged that I should do likewise. After some hesitation I said I would. I told the Prime Minister that the present phase in the air battle appeared to be going satisfactorily. The exceptional storms on the 17th and 18th had upset our plans and the enemy's, but our low flying attacks on enemy aerodromes had been effective and had reduced the enemy's bomber effort. Fourteen more Ju. 87s had been burnt on the ground on 20 November. I described how we had attained air superiority and how the bomber force had been put on to the targets indicated by General Cunningham. We already knew that our fighter sweeps had collected on the previous day four Me. 110s, a Ju. 88, three Me. 109s, and at least two more Ju. 87s. All this was apparently at the cost of four of our fighters.

To Coningham and his squadrons I expressed my warm congratulations. Even now I thought it was necessary for him to continue the good work of educating the Army. One senior officer had just told me how splendid everything in the Desert was, quoting as an example that he had seen forty of our fighters over headquarters at the same time. Our soldiers' attitude seemed to me illogical. They were delighted if our fighters managed to protect them from interference, and yet they disliked being bombed themselves so much that they completely ignored the effect on the enemy of our bombing. I wanted our soldiers to be brought to realise that our bombing on the enemy was as unpleasant and as important as enemy bombing was against our land forces.

The following day, 23 November, I received a message from Coningham asking me to go up to the Desert as soon as possible. Shortly afterwards, Auchinleck received a similar message from Alan Cunningham, saying that vital decisions might be called for, and we decided to fly to the Desert together. I had just enough time to change into khaki and collect my camp kit:

A longish, bumpy trip under broken clouds, and through some heavy rain squalls. Strange to see the Desert running in water; ponds and almost small lakes of water shining in the patches of sun, and dots of green appearing in beds of water-courses, and in pans where water had collected. Stopped to refuel at Collishaw's old haunt, and had a word or two with some of our pilots back to collect new aircraft. All full of beans.

We flew on through some heavy rain at about a hundred feet over the Desert until we reached the frontier. General Auchinleck and I, Alan Cunningham and 'Mary' reviewed the situation carefully, then I went off to confer with our Air commanders. It was already clear the situation on land was far from satisfactory. The heavy air fighting in the last day or two, however, had given our crews full confidence, and any tendency to make a bogey of the Me. 109F had disappeared, despite that aircraft's superior performance. Interrogation of a captured German pilot showed that he had a healthy respect for our fighters. The bombing attacks continued to be successful, and I found Coningham and his team working with zest, full of fight and not worrying about the details.

Meanwhile, Auchinleck was assessing the land situation. Alan Cunningham told him that on account of recent losses we were now probably inferior to the enemy in fast tanks. Our southern flank, towards Sidi Rezegh, might be turned, and our forces there isolated. There might then be nothing solid to stop an enemy advance into Egypt. Should the battle be broken off? Auchinleck replied instantly that the offensive must go forward at once to recapture Sidi Rezegh. It appeared to him that the enemy was probably stretched to the limit and that the strategic initiative was still with us. We must retain it. I noted in my journal:

The A. is first-rate, cool, cheerful and a fighter. His visit did a tremendous lot of good.

It was a bitterly cold, brilliant star-lit night. I was glad to put my great-coat on top of the blankets. The only light in the tent was provided by a flickering torch, and so I did not write up my journal that night. I was awake at dawn:

First sound that of a number of short bursts of machine-gun fire—

the A.A. clearing their lungs. Shave outside my tent with hot water brought in a Thermos by 'Mary's' P.A., while the sun came up over the edge of the Desert. It was a fine sight twice during the morning to see formations of Marylands and Blenheims come over. . . .

After breakfast on 25 November, I had a quiet talk with Auchinleck. I had felt very uneasy about Alan Cunningham for some time. Again and again he had struck me as taking counsel of his fears. He seemed to be obsessed by the counting of heads, and gave me the impression of feeling completely at sea in matters of armoured warfare. General Cunningham himself remarked to me: 'I wish I knew what Rommel means to do.' This impressed me as being a strange outlook for the commander of a superior attacking force. Once the battle had begun, he fluctuated between wishful optimism and the depths of pessimism until after a day or two 'Mary' Coningham had become so worried that he signalled asking me to come. Although Auchinleck's arrival had produced an immediate tonic effect, and although matters now seemed to be working satisfactorily again, I urged that the Commander-in-Chief should stay there in the Desert a while longer. I felt that Alan Cunningham would inevitably relapse. I think that Auchinleck had probably made up his mind already that he would stay; at all events he agreed. I made no secret of my grave misgivings about the direction of the Eighth Army.

After lunch, I returned to Cairo in the Lockheed, landing as the sun sank low behind a lovely golden blaze over the Nile. I wondered what was happening in the Desert. The next day, Auchinleck returned to Cairo. Alan Cunningham had again relapsed. I learnt that Auchinleck had discussed the affair with 'Mary' Coningham, whom I had told to speak frankly, and with the B.G.S., General Galloway, who was level-headed and sound but felt that he must be loyal to General Cunningham. Auchinleck and I discussed the situation. He told me that he had decided that an immediate change in command was needed. I assured him of my whole-hearted support. That night I met Oliver Lyttelton in the corridor leading to the Map Room. I told him that it was a great mistake for Auchinleck to have come back to Cairo. He asked: 'You mean that Cunningham is not confident of winning the battle?'

'Yes,' I replied.

'Then he must be relieved tonight,' said the Minister of State. He urged this course on Auchinleck, offering to support him fully in London.

Auchinleck had already received that night a telegram from Churchill warmly endorsing his determination to fight it out to the last inch whatever the result. The Prime Minister said that he was sure that we were the stronger and would win:

Am immensely heartened by your magnificent spirit and willpower. Say bravo to Tedder and R.A.F. on air mastery. . . .

Auchinleck acted at once on his conclusion that Cunningham was no longer fit to conduct the intensive attacking action we needed. He wrote at once to relieve Cunningham of his command, and signalled that night to the C.I.G.S., while Lyttelton, as he had promised, sent a supporting cable to the Prime Minister. Churchill replied at once that Auchinleck could, of course, count upon his approval for what he had done. To Lyttelton, Churchill telegraphed: 'Your action and attitude highly approved.'

I think that Auchinleck was glad to have my support, and certainly I admired the unselfish and courageous way in which he had taken a grip on the battle at a critical stage and had not hesitated to face the unpleasantness of dismissing a colleague.

*

With the change in command on 26 November, in which General Ritchie had replaced Cunningham, I looked for still closer co-operation between the two forces. 'Mary' Coningham wrote the next day that the whole atmosphere had altered: 'The position was really becoming most serious, and it was beginning to react down to units.'

He told me how our units had been moved during the nights of 24/25 and 25/26 November. On the first of these, it was reported that enemy forces were moving south, and that two or three unidentified columns were approaching Coningham's headquarters from the north-west. Realising the value of the fighter force as a potential target for such raids, and its defencelessness in the dark, Coningham had moved the Hurricanes back from two forward landing grounds. This difficult task had been successfully accomplished in the dust and failing light. A very worrying night was spent, for the air was thick with rumours and the Army could give no reliable information. All the A.A. guns and some tanks were set to defend the perimeter of the aerodrome, and everyone stood to near his aircraft. The whole camp was at a half an hour's notice to move. During the day of 25 November, General Cunningham had asked the A.O.C. to evacuate two of the forward landing grounds, and advised him to send the aircraft back from Air Headquarters. All Hurricanes had accordingly been despatched to Bagush for a night's rest, and the ground personnel from the two evacuated landing grounds spent the night ten miles south of them. Another anxious night was spent at the Air headquarters. During the course of the next day, 26 November, affairs became more normal, and fighter protection was maintained as usual. Coningham had been loath to make any of these moves at all, but felt the force to be so valuable that it could not be risked. One of the results had been that sweeps could not be continued all day on 25 November, and the enemy was therefore able to make two attacks on the New Zealanders who nevertheless recovered enough to effect a junction with the Tobruk garrison on the 26th. Coningham told me that he had explained the circumstances to the Army, and had left them in no doubt about their obligation to give the R.A.F. security. They realised the position but lacking vital information could do little about it in the prevailing confusion.

Often our aircraft had to land away from their own bases. One night, in a severe dust storm, only two aircraft out of twenty-four returned from one operation. The remainder, apart from the casualties, had drifted in the following morning. I was satisfied that every possible effort, and more, was being made to produce and maintain the maximum scale of bomber attack. Indeed, I told Portal that we had heavily mortgaged the future—which did not worry me since he had promised to pay off the mortgage!

You have given me a good team, and I am satisfied that from the fighting units and commanders, back to the supply units and organisation, R.A.F. Middle East is pulling its fullest possible weight. The horses are willing and are neither being spared nor sparing themselves.

'Mary' Coningham was most eager to make a combined ground/air attack on Benghazi which he thought would be fatal for Rommel. According to our Intelligence, the defences there were very thin, and there were no ground forces which could stand up to a mobile column containing armour. Certainly we had sufficient air superiority to spare a fighter force which would ensure protection of the column and would give us air superiority over Benghazi itself. If this operation were successful it would lead to success at Derna, and would effectively stop reinforcement from Tripoli. The new Army Commander, Ritchie, was keen. The Army's plan would be to send a brigade group with fifty or sixty American tanks and sufficient forces to take over and hold Benghazi. I was wholeheartedly in favour of any bold plan which would exploit our success speedily; but for the moment the Eighth Army seemed to be fully occupied with more immediate affairs.

A day or two later Auchinleck decided that he would like to go up to the Desert again, so we made the journey together. It was a bumpy trip through a number of rain squalls. 'Mary' Coningham was surprised when we arrived but was glad to see me, I think. He had lost two of the most valuable members of his staff the day before, shot down by our own anti-aircraft in the south. Despite this inexcusable tragedy, his people were in good cheer and everything was running very smoothly. Auchinleck and Neil Ritchie were refreshingly calm and determined, and I heard from the soldiers on all sides how enthusiastic they were at our air support. Shortly before I left, General Freyberg, who had said many quite unpardonable things about us after Crete, came up to me and said: 'I want to tell you I think your fellows are simply magnificent, and all my men are saying the same.'

This was generous of him, for the New Zealanders whom he was commanding had just taken a severe battering. I thought it striking that Freyberg should have made a point of seeking me out in this way.

I was forcibly struck by the change in atmosphere at Eighth Army headquarters. In view of the sharp knocks taken by the South African and the New Zealand divisions there might have been some excuse, at least, for worry. It appeared that

Rommel had pulled off another of his escapes. Ritchie, however, was quite level-headed and determined, and clearly knew what he meant to do. Coningham told me that under the new regime co-operation was close, whereas under the old one it was becoming almost impossible since General Alan Cunningham would not discuss the plans or even disclose them except under extreme pressure. All this was now altered, and 'Mary' Coningham and Ritchie were hand in glove. I told Portal that I thought Auchinleck had shown up extraordinarily well:

He does not fuss, and is a fighter. . . . One can only be thankful that it is he and not his predecessor who is at the head of the Army. I shudder to think what would have happened under W.

I was glad to have strengthened my intimate personal relations with Auchinleck during the crisis over Cunningham's dismissal. I thought that I had been able to help him, and that we both felt we could talk quite freely to each other.

I think he has been first-class [says my journal]. Calm, determined and confident, without indulging in the wishful thinking which has been so much a weakness of some of the senior soldiers (when they are not in the depths of equally unjustifiable pessimism!) A. is balanced —which is worth anything!

During the day, Embry and I visited the fighter squadrons. The atmosphere among them was splendid. Of course, I knew the wing and squadron commanding officers, and that they were good, but the whole tone amongst pilots and men was grand. I felt that they were a much finer body of men than those of the First War. I saw two squadrons set out and one come back. Each squadron of twelve aircraft took off in sections of four, each one leaving in its wake a streaming cloud of dust. In one squadron mess I had a cup of tea, in another, more tea with the South Africans, and in yet another, a can of American beer. It was a grand sight to see and hear the formations of Marylands and Blenheims come over and circle in formation while the fighters went streaming up, one after another, in a widening spiral above and around the bombers. Still better was it to see the bombers come back in equally good formation, and with no empty places.

I slept in a little ridge tent tucked alongside the luxurious caravan inhabitated by 'Mary' Coningham. I refused his pink upholstered settee in favour of a camp bed. The night was bitterly cold, and I was glad of my greatcoat. Just before dawn the patter of rain on the tent roof awakened me. It was only a shower, but all day the rain-clouds piled up and squalls drifted across the Desert. Over Tobruk it was heavy and the clouds were down to two or three hundred feet.

It is difficult to express how exhilarating it was in the Desert. It was partly the air, keen and sparkling, and partly the magnificent feeling among our men. The terrain seemed to be flat and featureless:

... and yet in a mile or so you can completely lose sight of the place you have just left. It's just sand and small stones in a crust, through which vehicles break at once and raise a dust trail behind them, folds of ground without any definite pattern, and in many places shallow saucers of very smooth, hard-caked mud, which gets slippery at the least rain. Some of these we use as landing grounds.

The reverse at Sidi Rezegh had come as a nasty blow to the Army, and a bitter disappointment to our squadrons who were aching to get ahead. Our great need was to get fighter aerodromes farther forward. Tobruk, although we were using it for a limited number of special operations, was not at that time suitable for regular fighter operations. I could not help feeling that we had once again been baulked of the speedy victory which greater boldness and expertise should have secured. I telegraphed to Portal:

My reading of the land situation is that we have been repeatedly out-manœuvred by an enemy, who, though practically blinded in the air, and despite jamming interference, nearly always manages to have his mobile forces under full control. A senior soldier in the 8th Army aptly summed up the armoured battles to me as professional versus amateur.

All the evidence suggested that the fine fight the enemy was making depended greatly on the personal leadership of Rommel, by whose importance some sections of the Army had become almost obsessed. While we were in the Desert we actually laid plans for hunting down and capturing him, or at least breaking down his controls. But even if these came to nothing I was confident that our attacks on enemy supplies in the battle area, and on his lines of communication, were likely to prove decisive. However well Rommel controlled his armour, it would be helpless without its vulnerable tail of transport and supply.

I discussed also with Auchinleck, Ritchie, and 'Mary' Coningham, the possibilities of improving our direct aid to the ground forces. This depended largely on better Army communications and control of the armour.

It was possible to lay plans of this kind, since we still enjoyed air superiority. The Germans, even with their Me. 109Fs, were still refusing to fight except on very rare occasions. Their game was that of jumping on the occasional straggler, or of making a single stab at an outside aircraft in a formation. This despite the fact that both the Tomahawk and the Hurricane II were outclassed in speed and climb by the enemy aircraft. One squadron of Spitfire Vs would have been worth a lot.

The journey back to Cairo on 25 November was not a comfortable one. It was raining a little when we left, and we flew about 150 miles at three hundred feet above the track. The whole Desert was literally awash:

As a result of all this recent rain, mud patches are beginning to mottle the desert, and some of them are getting quite green. The last part of the trip was pretty sticky too. After passing through a relatively clear patch, where there were some streaks of sunlight making vivid emerald patches on an otherwise purple-black sea, and also a strip of brilliant rainbow, we suddenly ran into a weird, shapeless, vague, dusty mist, and for over an hour—until we were well over the Delta— we were flying in a strange sort of nothingness; no ground, no sky, not even visible mist.

The events of the next few days confirmed the number of the impressions I had received in this latest visit to the Desert. On the ground, the enemy, under Rommel's inspiriting direction, was evidently prepared to fight to the last tank. His control of his armoured forces and organisation for the recovery of unserviceable tanks were clearly superior to ours. The lack of adequate contact between our armoured forces and the corps or even the divisional headquarters had certainly limited our ability to give really close support, although that situation was improving. Tactical reconnaissance to the divisions had been good, quick and direct, but there had been instances of our armour being in doubt for over two hours as to the identity of enemy armoured units less than two miles distant. This fog had not been dissipated by the known fact that the enemy had some of our tanks and a great deal of our motor transport in use.

Nevertheless, all my information, as I told Portal on 7 December, was that the Army were still more than satisfied that they were getting the fullest air support in the circumstances. The indications were that the enemy had now concentrated practically all his strength in the El Adem area. An excursion to the east which threatened on the 5th and 6th petered out, perhaps because of low-flying attacks by Hurricane bombers, coupled with raids by 'Jock columns' of mixed arms. We had struck repeatedly at the El Adem concentrations, and on the night of the 6th the Wellingtons did two sorties apiece and kept up the attack without intermission. In view of the fact that Rommel was prepared to fight to the end and that his control of his forces was so close, I still felt that the determining factor of the battle was motor transport and supply: 'If we can throttle that he will break and break completely and suddenly.'

In the air we still had local air superiority in general, but it was hard fighting all the way. Occasionally the enemy would stage a large combined formation, and fighter sweeps of Me. 109s and Me. 202s. Both types were considerably better in performance than anything we had. With these aircraft the enemy held the tactical initiative in combat, and even if it were temporarily lost could readily regain it. For nearly three weeks now, almost all my forces had been concentrated on targets in direct support of the land battle. The continued bad weather had prevented Malta from maintaining attacks on Benghazi, and therefore except for the Beaufighter attacks on road traffic, the flow of enemy supplies into Cyrenaica had been relatively uninterrupted. His aerodromes had also gone largely unattacked. Rommel was now making intensive efforts to take in supplies. He was also receiving substantial air reinforcements of Me. 109s and other types, and the time was coming when I would have to reconsider the allocation of our air effort. Just as I was writing this report to Portal I learnt from a liaison officer that the enemy was moving west, and that the whole of Coningham's force was attacking his retreating columns with good effect. Perhaps we might now threaten the aerodromes between Gazala and Derna.

I flew up to the Desert the next morning, 8 December. Auchinleck was there, and we discussed the disposition of our air effort. The situation was still very confused, partly because of the nature of the country and the wide area over which operations were taking place. There were thousands of square miles over which the armoured forces and motor transport could wander at will, and often wander unwillingly because completely lost. Conditions for the control and recognition of forces were evidently far more difficult than in normal country. I hoped that as the Army moved further west this situation would be improved. Meanwhile it was most difficult to make the best use of our medium bomber forces. During the afternoon of 7 December, for instance, most of these forces were detailed to meet a request from the Army for close support. This operation had to be called off at the last moment because the Army thought that some of our own raiding columns *might* perhaps be in the area we were about to bomb. By the time the decision was confirmed, it was too late for the force to operate against any alternative target before dark. The Army Command fully realised the problem, but the solution depended upon better control of land forces. This in its turn depended upon better communications, training, and recognition methods.

I found that the air situation had not altered much, although the increased use of Tobruk, of other landing grounds in the area between there and Sollum, and the early denial to the enemy of aerodromes round Gazala, would materially assist us. As the enemy was pushed back to the west his available aerodromes decreased in number, and the resulting congestion should make him, I hoped, more vulnerable.

I watched a low-flying attack by Me. 110s, supported by Me. 109s, which shot down one of our de Havilland 86 ambulances. However, the pilot managed to get the aircraft down in time, though it was on fire. After this I returned to Cairo. The next day was not a very good one in the Desert. The Me. 109Fs had been picking off our aircraft, and since they enjoyed better performance than anything we had, it was difficult to devise countermeasures. Nonetheless, 'Mary' Coningham sounded quite cheerful when I spoke to him on the telephone, although he was naturally worried by the success of the Me. 109s, which he attributed in part to the lower standard of experience of our pilots, coupled with unjustified over-confidence engendered by the weak opposition we had met since the air offensive began. We badly needed better aircraft and intensive fighting practice. He wrote urging on me that Middle East must be given a higher priority in the supply of the latest machines :

We must stop England thinking that second-class aircraft will do us out here. This has become part of the European Front, and the German has appreciated it to the extent of sending his best aircraft and units. The climate allows more intensive action than both England and Russia for the next four to five months. I think that air operations in the Middle East will take priority, owing to the probable stabilisation of the Russian Front and to the reduced threat to England owing to the fighter strength there. Air Ministry must reply to the German reinforcement of the African Front with equal reinforcements of the best aircraft and personnel from England.

Preliminary experience of the Kittyhawk, the first examples of which had just arrived, showed little improvement on the Tomahawk except in hitting power. I had been so concerned at the loss of opportunities and the relative waste of available bomber effort that I had again pressed 'Mary' Coningham to emphasise this aspect to Ritchie, and to urge that we must accept the risk of mistake. Auchinleck had agreed with this view, and was pressing it upon Ritchie too. The crux of both the land and air battles was more than ever one of supply. For the moment we were concentrating against enemy petrol supplies from the west by road, from the north by air and sea, and against movements in Cyrenaica and the dumps at aerodromes. For the next three days I intended to concentrate our forces against the enemy's sea supply. If we could ground his air forces and starve his motor transport I thought we should be well on the way to success.

I was somewhat concerned to learn from the signals that a number of Coningham's attacks appeared to be against targets which were not of immediate importance. He had told me ruefully that the most intensive fighting on 10 December had been in the Advanced Air Headquarters, Western Desert—his fighting for targets. This had taken three and a half hours. While the battle raged round Gazala it appeared that we had a good chance of encircling and completely defeating the enemy. The whole of the enemy land forces were located in a comparatively small area south-west of Gazala, and yet for nearly three days they had not been bombed at all, although our forces had enjoyed absolute superiority without any interference for most of that time. Squadrons of bombers had been at call, but always their operations had to be postponed because of the lack of identification and the close contact of the enemy forces with our own. Outside the battle area, Coningham told me, there had not been any targets suitable for bomber formations which justified the weakening of fighter patrols for escort duty. He appreciated that the enemy would make every possible effort to escape into Derna, and did his best to block Rommel's route. Although Neil Ritchie was a convinced protagonist of close support bombing, and although Coningham himself was most anxious to exploit our air superiority to the full, the poor dispersal of our forces and unreliable communications showed only too clearly that we had not yet learnt the secrets of bombing in the battle area. Coningham wrote on 17 December:

I think that one can say definitely that German air superiority or real effective bombing would have ended this offensive weeks ago.

He told me that he regarded fighter operations over the battle area not as a matter of protection for the ground forces, which was merely an additional and welcome advantage, but as an offensive operation in its own right. Ground forces at battle, from the air aspect, provided a focal point where fighters had more chances of finding and destroying the enemy than they did elsewhere :

In point of fact we use the ground forces purely as ground bait for enemy bombers and fighters. If the effect on our forces is one of protection, then all concerned, except perhaps the enemy, are happy, but I do not want our own tactical thinkers to be led astray into considering the operation as any more defensive than an ordinary O.P. [offensive patrol].

The M.E. 109F4s we have examined are the newest and latest from Germany, and we have undoubtedly been saved hard fighting by their lack of fuel over the way. Such luck will not continue. . . .

A distressing and to me infuriating feature of these days was the appearance in the London Press of reports which were discouraging to our men who were, in my view and in the Army's, magnificent. For instance, our original air superiority was being discounted on the grounds that the enemy were earth-bound by waterlogged aerodromes. This was only true to a very limited extent and temporarily. It was stated that on 5 December we had numerical as well as tactical superiority. This had never been true, and was less true than ever in view of enemy reinforcements. On 7 December there appeared an article by Scrutator in the *Sunday Times*, which was inaccurate and poisonous even by the somewhat flexible standards of the British Press. I told Portal at once that to my men in the Desert it would appear rather like a stab in the back. I was sure it would receive no support from Auchinleck. I showed the article to Lyttelton, who was outraged.

Meanwhile, Admiral Cunningham was expressing his dissatisfaction at the decision of the Chiefs of Staff that he must attack the enemy's ships in convoy rather than the Battle Fleet. This he regarded as a serious strategic blunder, and he protested accordingly to the First Sea Lord. Cunningham's argument was that an attack on the enemy Battle Fleet might enable him to strike a blow so telling that the supplies to Libya might be brought to a standstill. It seemed to him that the course of operations had proved the validity of this argument, for the enemy Fleet was for the first time within reasonable range of our air forces. Had the blow been struck, he thought that the Libyan supplies would have ceased, and that other far-reaching repercussions would have followed. He telegraphed to London:

Sea operations must be coordinated by one Command, and that

Command must have adequate air forces for its purposes. It is noted that this principle has, to a large extent been accepted in the Western Desert. So long as the decision on the amount of reconnaissance to be sent out and the targets and the weight of attack to be launched, rest with anyone not directly responsible for the sea operations, failures of this sort will occur. We cannot afford this fatal weakness in our naval operations.

These issues were discussed under Lyttelton's chairmanship in the Defence Committee shortly before Christmas. Cunningham admitted that with his agreement nearly all the aircraft normally available for naval operations had been placed in the pool for the battle in the Western Desert. He now wanted to see a sufficient number revert to the control of the Naval Co-operation Group at Alexandria. He was not in any way raising the issue of their being placed under naval control, and was in fact quite satisfied with the arrangements by which they were controlled by A.O.C. 201 Group. There the matter rested for the moment.

*

In assessing our prospects for exploiting the success in the Desert and for controlling the Central Mediterranean, we had now to take account of a new and most serious diversion. As I had been writing my journal on the night of 7 December, a signal arrived, repeated from the Admiralty, saying: 'Commence hostilities against Japan at once, repeat at once.'

I had feared all through the autumn the temptation to make capital from British weakness and American blindness would prove too much for the Japanese military. My experience as Air Officer Commanding-in-Chief of our exiguous forces in the Far East between 1936 and 1938 had shown me how long a start the Japanese had. I reflected in my journal:

One had hoped they might have been warned off, but I suppose they had gone so far that they couldn't withdraw without loss of 'face', which of course they couldn't bear. A pity. I suppose the Yanks will give us full help—as advisers. I wonder if the little beasts have gone for the northern neck of Malaya or whether to Siam?

It was not until a few hours later that we knew of the assault upon Pearl Harbor, and a few days later of the sinking of our battleships *Repulse* and *Prince of Wales*, whose departure to the Far East without adequate cover had caused Smuts to warn Churchill in November that there were here the makings of a first-class disaster. Admiral Tom Phillips, who was in command, had always been sceptical of the ability of air-power to cripple or sink capital ships. For this misapprehension, he and many others now paid with their lives. Some weeks later, Tennant, Captain of the *Repulse,* who was passing back to the U.K., told us the whole story. It appeared that Phillips had not told headquarters at Singapore where he was, even when he was being attacked. When the A.O.C. was informed from *Repulse* that an attack was in progress, he sent out his fighters, which left within six minutes. Of course, it was too late. Tennant saw them come over while he and some of his men were struggling in the water.

We had already been warned of serious losses in the supplies of American aircraft to the Middle East in order to help Russia. It was now only a matter of time before the Far East claimed some of our painfully acquired strength. Even before Christmas, several signals confirmed that I should either fail to receive aircraft promised, or must divert to the Far East aircraft already in my possession. Indeed, the only bright patch in the clouds was that the Americans openly said that they would no longer go about telling us how to do our job. On 11 December, General Brett turned up in Cairo again. He appeared to me to be a chastened man now that his country was involved in the real war. When he came to my office, he said: 'You look very cheerful.'

I am sorry to say that I replied, 'Why not?'

Later in our conversation, Brett said, 'I guess you are an Independent Air Force man.' I pretended not to know what he meant, and merely replied, 'Of course, I am Royal Air Force.'

Brett observed, 'Well, I guess the newspapers in the United States are going to be full of Independent Air Force after this affair at Hawaii.'

It appeared from his account that it was the job of the Naval Air Service to cover Hawaii, which they didn't seem to have done very well. The whole question of the Air Force's independence seemed to be a very fruity political and inter-Service controversy over there. I gathered that all our Americans were not quite so convinced now that they knew all about everything. This, at least, was a relief.

Certainly some cheering news was needed, for I heard that four fighter squadrons in transit to Iraq were to be diverted at once to India, and three others destined for Malta and Gibraltar were redirected via the Cape. Some thirty-two Kittyhawks, still packed in their crates and forming part of our unassembled reserves, had just arrived in the Middle East. I was told that these must be held in readiness for immediate despatch to the Far East. Such diversions must evidently affect our ability to exploit our success in the Western Desert.

On Christmas Eve, 7th Armoured Division at long last took Benghazi. Early in the New Year, Rommel withdrew to El Agheila, and we took Sollum soon afterwards. The garrison at Tobruk had now been relieved. Its maintenance had been an expensive business, for the Royal Navy had lost no fewer than twenty-five ships sunk and nine seriously damaged.[1]

'Crusader' had succeeded, but not so rapidly as we had hoped. Whether the success had been speedy or slow, our difficulties were bound to multiply as the lines of communication and supply lengthened. The Axis casualties were not far short of 40,000, about a third of their total strength, whereas ours had been about 17,500, perhaps 15 per cent. of our force.[2] Auchinleck fully realised that to consolidate this position we needed to get west of Agheila. But there lay Rommel's Army, and our troops were for the moment in no position to turn him out. We could not at this stage tell what might happen on the Russian front, nor what would transpire in the Far East. India might even be lost; and nearer home the scale of enemy reinforcement in the Mediterranean not only made it doubtful whether we could turn Rommel out of North Africa, but even whether we could maintain our own position. By the end of the year we were again losing control of the Central Mediterranean because Hitler had decided to put extra strength into that theatre. The loss of *Ark Royal* in mid-November and the torpedo attack by Italian frogmen on Cunningham's ships in Alexandria Harbour itself, were symptomatic. The

[1] Roskill: *The War at Sea,* vol. 1, pp. 519–20.
[2] Playfair: *The Mediterranean and Middle East,* vol. 3, p. 97.

Mediterranean Fleet was most seriously depleted, while heavy air reinforcement had almost doubled the Luftwaffe's strength. In short, the balance in the battle of supply had tilted against us, for the moment at least. Early in December I told Portal that the essential sea supply routes to Benghazi and to the westward were likely to become very expensive unless we could deal drastically both with the submarine and aircraft. If the Germans made up their minds to allocate the necessary forces, both air and submarine, he could from Greece and Crete make life hot for us. I always had to remember the inevitable time lag between decision in London and receipt of the results in Cairo and I used every opportunity to press upon the Air Ministry the need for adequate supplies of the most up-to-date equipment if we were to hold our own and more.

The bravery of our air crews and the energy displayed by Dawson and his staff, together with Auchinleck's refusal to accept defeatist counsel, had enabled us to score a limited but highly valuable success. Although I did not then know it, there was more than a chance that I might soon leave the Middle East. On 25 November, Portal wrote to Auchinleck asking whether I should not be replaced in the Middle East after 'Crusader', in order to take up a responsible post in the United Kingdom. Portal apparently added that Auchinleck's attitude had been helpful in October, when my fate was in the balance on account of the supposed crisis about air strengths. This letter Auchinleck received on 10 December. He replied at once that he would be very sorry indeed to see me go, and spoke in flattering terms of my part in the battle:

The co-operation has, I think, been almost perfect. Anyway, the Army thinks it has been wonderful and so do I.[1]

On the day after this letter was sent, General Norrie, commanding 30 Corps, forwarded to Neil Ritchie a message from him to 'Mary' Coningham, recording his deep gratitude for the R.A.F.'s co-operation. Not only had the fighter force, General Norrie wrote, provided almost complete protection, but time and again

[1] Connell: *Auchinleck,* p. 402.

the Bomber Striking Force had seriously disorganised the enemy, often in answer to calls from his troops:

> I want you to know how fully 30 Corps have appreciated the work of your air crews, which has been remarked upon by all under my Command with great admiration and gratitude. . . . . It is quite apparent that we are on the way to a new standard of inter-Service co-operation which will surpass anything yet seen in the war.

A few days later Auchinleck told the Prime Minister that the way in which Coningham had moved his fighter landing grounds on the heels of the forward troops was 'most striking and exhilarating'.[1]

The entry of Japan and the United States into the war was bound to transform the situation in the Middle East. At this stage, none of us knew what the American reaction might be. There were obvious arguments for placing the overwhelming preponderance of American effort in the Pacific. It was this problem that I set out to consider in a memorandum for the Middle Eastern Commanders-in-Chief of 23 December. The question was where American effort could best be applied in order to bring about the speediest victory. I argued that Germany was the heart of the forces and ideas against which the Allies were fighting, and it was in Europe that the decision must be won. Of the four theatres in the world, the British Isles, the Mediterranean, Russia, and the Far East, it was in one or other of the European theatres that the American effort could best be applied. The limitations of the supply routes into Russia from whichever direction were so great as to preclude the sending into Russia and the maintenance there of really large forces from America. Presumably American forces could be sent to, and maintained through, the British Isles, with a view to operations in North-West Europe. To strike anywhere from Northern France to Denmark, however, would be to strike where the enemy was strongest, where he could most readily reinforce and where his lines of supply would be shortest. It was in the Mediterranean that Germany was weakest. Should the enemy during the next few months thrust downwards through Spain to North Africa, he

[1] Connell: *Auchinleck,* p. 411.

would have to maintain a long and expensive land line of communication and also to keep up sea communications across the Mediterranean. Italy was becoming more and more of a commitment and less and less of an asset to Germany. In the Balkans the Germans were occupying two countries, Greece and Yugoslavia, whose hostility only awaited the opportunity to become active, and which had not been subjugated as thoroughly as Northern France. Farther inland, Hungary, Austria, and Czechoslovakia were weaker links in the Nazi chain. I concluded, therefore, that Allied policy should be defensive in the Far East and offensive in Europe. It was in the Mediterranean that the offensive should be developed, and to which the striking force of the United States should be directed. In the Mediterranean theatre, the Caucasus front should be regarded as purely defensive, though with the proviso that we must at least deny the trans-Caucasian oilfields to the enemy. Detailed examination of the lines of communication through Anatolia showed that it was impossible to operate or maintain large forces there, though the exits from Anatolia must be secured. As for North Africa, control of sea communications in the Mediterranean was passing in ever-increasing degree into the hands of air forces. Enemy air action had already virtually closed the sea route to Egypt from the west. Our own air action, in close collaboration with that of submarines, had been largely responsible for crippling the enemy's supplies to North Africa. The most potent guarantee for the security of Egypt from the west would be air superiority over the Mediterranean, and in particular over the Sicilian Channel. This would also be an essential prelude to any offensive action from North Africa into Europe.

Probably it would be many months before the Americans were in a position to organise and despatch a large seaborne expedition. Should such an expedition enter the Mediterranean theatre from the west, the demands on shipping would be much less both for the expedition itself and for its subsequent maintenance, than they would be if the expedition entered via Egypt. Very considerable air forces could be transferred to the Mediterranean theatre by the established Takoradi Route at a much earlier date than could land forces. The addition to the Middle

Eastern theatre of a substantial American air force should make it possible, with the air forces already earmarked for despatch there, to undertake a campaign to secure air superiority over the Central Mediterranean, especially if Tunisia could be occupied by land. This latter operation would be greatly eased by such an increase in the available air forces. The re-opening of the Mediterranean route would not only facilitate the supply of the Middle East but would also provide the essential foundation for a direct offensive against the enemy on European soil. These views were discussed by the Middle East Defence Committee on 27 December.

The following day brought news that I had been awarded the K.C.B., Lloyd a C.B., and Dawson and Air Vice Marshal Pirie, who dealt with organisation and administration in the Command, C.B.Es. It was a shock to see letters and messages addressed to Sir Arthur Tedder, for I knew only one person of that name, my father. I received among others a telegram from Walter Monckton: GOOD KNIGHT, GOOD LUCK IN 1942, AND ALWAYS YOURS. WALTER.

12

THE year 1942 opened somewhat gloomily in the Western Desert. My journal for New Year's Day records:

Our soldiers haven't been very clever up in the Desert, and I fancy it is going to take a bit longer to clear up. Of course, it isn't easy. The distances are enormous, and the supply problems terrific. Moreover, the weather hasn't been helpful. I hear it has rained almost continuously at Benghazi for the past ten days, and many places are bogged. Meantime we have our other preoccupations at Malta and the Far East.

The weather in Cyrenaica remained foul, causing many of our aircraft to sink down into the makeshift runways. As a result of reports that an Italian convoy was making for Tripoli, two formations were sent out on 4 January to intercept the enemy's shipping, in spite of the bad weather conditions. A Blenheim of 203 Squadron, operating from Tobruk, signalled that it had sighted a battleship, nine destroyers and three cruisers of the Italian Fleet some three hundred miles east of Malta heading south. In spite of determined efforts to drive them away, the crew shadowed the force for two hours, during which time they were able to signal accurate information about the types of ships, their course and speed. They also obtained photographs from which the 201 Group interpreters were later able to confirm that they had made only one small error in their ship identification. Admiral Cunningham was sufficiently impressed to signal his congratulations to the crew on 'their excellent sighting and position reports'—a welcome indication that he had revised his earlier opinion regarding the ability of the R.A.F. to carry out the 'highly specialised function' of maritime operations. Auchinleck came round to see me that evening to hear of our efforts, and I showed him what was being done. My journal records:

He is very charming and full of support for anything I have in hand. Very inclined to say—'That's grand, but what's the Navy doing about it all?' I am having to try and curb him a bit on the subject.

[215]

At the same time the old man of the sea is rather a trial. I don't know how much longer we can carry on with him. He is a grand old man, but has had a devil of a racket the past year . . . he would be an anachronism any way, but now is, I think, a real menace.

For the moment our offensive in the Desert had petered out and Rommel was licking his wounds. Early in January I heard from 'Mary' Coningham about the recent developments in the air warfare. He showed that as Rommel's forces had fallen back towards Agedabia they came under the protection of their own aircraft based in Tripolitania, while our own columns were rapidly moving beyond the range of our aircraft based at Tobruk. We were doing our best to push our squadrons and their supplies forward behind the advancing army as quickly as possible. From Maddalena, our formations and headquarters had been moved first to the Gazalas and then to Mechili, and finally to an area twenty or thirty miles short of Msus. The principal problem had been the lack of transport to carry fuel to the forward landing grounds, a shortage so acute that Coningham's own headquarters were immobilised in order that motor transport might be used for other purposes. The second obstacle was the lack of sites for landing grounds, but Coningham reported that each push forward was dependent on the co-operation of anti-aircraft and engineer units and personnel:

Improvisation, quick decisions and reasonable risk are necessary ingredients of any success achieved.

In the result, however, good airmanship takes first place. With all these moves, plus the landing ground needs of the Tomahawk and the simultaneous operations of Wing formations the wastage rate should be greatly increased. It says much for our fighters that during these days of rapid change, with rain and dust storms alternating in different parts of the area, operations were uninterrupted, and only two landing ground accidents occurred. Though operating over 200 miles of new desert country, on only two occasions did formations lose their way, and in each case they returned safely to other bases. It is a great tribute to our fighter control and units, that a short-range interceptor like the Hurricane II should be used successfully and without loss in such unsuitable conditions.

It was a great asset for me to have at the head of the Desert

Air Force a commander so able and enterprising and so determined to work closely with the Army Command.

I was content to leave Coningham a large measure of latitude, and tried so to arrange matters in Cairo that decisions were promptly made and properly co-ordinated. On a normal day, I would arrive at my office by 8.45 a.m., in time to look through special signals and a bunch of operation reports before attending 'morning prayers' at 9 o'clock. 'Morning prayers' consisted of a small gathering conducted by Drummond, my Deputy C.-in-C., and attended by the senior members of my staff. Whenever possible I myself attended in a listening capacity. At these meetings the immediate problems were thrashed out between my senior air staff officer, Air Vice Marshal Wigglesworth, and Air Vice Marshals Pirie (organisation and administration) and Dawson (maintenance and supply). We would decide there and then on the movement or re-equipment of squadrons, the organisation of groups or commands, or questions of reinforcement from the United Kingdom or to the Far East. In this way the varied and ever-changing problems of the far-flung Middle Eastern Command could be met.

There was a limit, however, to what the Royal Air Force could do. I always felt complete confidence that our men would achieve more than any reasonable outsider could have expected from them; moreover, I knew that they were receptive to new ideas and techniques, and eager to practise them. I felt less confident that these characteristics were found in equal measure in the other two Services. I did not underrate their enormous difficulties, but the desert warfare and our repeated failure to round off a successful offensive left me with the impression that we still did not understand as fully as our opponents the methods of employing armoured mobility to the best advantage. By the middle of the month, it was indeed being suggested in signals that the further advance, 'Acrobat', to which 'Crusader' had been intended as the prelude, should be abandoned, and it was clear that there must be a delay of some weeks at the least. I told Wilfrid Freeman on 13 January:

The Cyrenaica affair is dragging a bit. There is no doubt that one or two opportunities of putting the Hun in the bag have been lost, mostly, I think, through an excess of bravery and a shortage of brains.

There is no doubt that the Hun has tactically beaten us again and again on the ground. As the Army have themselves remarked to me two or three times, 'We are still amateurs'—strange for a professional Army but true. Now, unfortunately, the 22nd Armoured Brigade who might have been expected to have lost their amateur status, are being relieved by a new Armoured Division who are new to real war, so I am afraid we shall have to expect some more bloody noses. The other limiting factor is, of course, supply, especially since the chance of a snap decision appears once again to have gone. I am afraid it will be three or four weeks before they are able to undertake a real push forward; nevertheless I do hope that the sinister suggestions about stopping 'Acrobat' which I have seen in one or two recent signals, will not be allowed to take effect. Out here we all feel most strongly that it is vital that 'Acrobat' should be pushed right home; if it is not, Libya will remain a running sore, seriously weakening our power to deal with the northern threat.

*

The comparative lull in the Desert battle gave me a chance to take up other matters, foremost among which was my continuing anxiety about air transport and civil aviation to, and through, the Middle Eastern Command. During the summer of 1941, I had emphasised the need for a co-ordinating body in the Middle East, with a chairman of suitable standing, which would bring together the operations of the Royal Air Force Transport Command and those of the various civil air lines. This suggestion had been agreed in principle but had not been followed with any action. Meanwhile, the fears I had already expressed forcibly about Pan American Airways were proving to be only too well justified. They were doing much as they pleased about the routes across Africa and through the Middle East. As a result of one of their manœuvres, Qantas were already calling on British Airways to divert to the Far East flying-boats which were on the service to the United Kingdom. I signalled on 15 January to London:

We sold our birthright to America, and now we are getting well in the mess. I must press most strongly for the immediate appointment of the chairman for whom I have been asking. He must be a bigger and tougher man than would have sufficed last year.

Pan American Airways showed themselves by no means backward in advancing their own interests, and I sent word to

Sir Arthur Street that I intended to make a stand for British interests:

The cloven hoof of Pan American now well to fore. They are about to open a booking office in Cairo for passenger services, and they are advertising postal services from Cairo. I expect to see similar announcements for services to East any day. Must make it clear that in so far as I have any authority as A.O.C.-in-C. M.E., I will not, repeat not, agree any further extension Pan American activities unless and until they have met their bond to maintain twice-daily service West Coast to Khartoum. This is of vital importance to our war effort. At present they only operate five services weekly instead of fourteen.

A meeting was duly held on 1 February at which Air Vice Marshal Pirie represented me. Mr. Gledhill, the Pan American Airways representative, proclaimed openly that it was his company's intention to operate commercially east of Cairo on the grounds that 'naturally Uncle Sam must try to get some return on the expenditure he is incurring in operating an air service to the Far East for military purposes'. Informed that his company ought first to fulfil their obligation to run services twice a day between Takoradi and Khartoum, Gledhill hedged by saying that all that was required of his company had been done. It was pointed out to him that by arrangement with London no loads in excess of available capacity had been sent to West Africa by us; but we had expected by now to have available more than twice the capacity which Pan American Airways had provided. Eventually, a somewhat tenuous guarantee was obtained from Gledhill that his company would eventually operate two services a day for us from West Africa to Khartoum or Cairo. He also said that P.A.A. would probably be required to operate two or three services a day for the U.S. Air Corps from Liberia to the Far East.

It appeared to us, therefore, that we should have difficulty in preventing the extension of Pan American Airways' activities to the Far East, and that there was apparently no intention of making the service a military one, as we had been led to believe. On the contrary, many of the passengers would be civilians, most of them connected only indirectly with the war effort. Pressed for his views about the pooling of resources, and a Joint Priorities Board,

Gledhill reluctantly agreed that this might be arranged both in West Africa and Cairo.

This was a most unsatisfactory position. On 11 February I told Street that if he agreed, I would inform P.A.A. that I would not allow any extension of their services beyond Khartoum except on a purely military basis, with no commercial rights whatever, and then only as far as Cairo. This would prevent them from carrying non-official passengers, commercial freight, or mail. Street replied that the agreement with Pan American Airways did not allow such action to come from me, but assured me that the situation was under control. Mr. Eden, the Foreign Secretary, had lodged a strong protest with the American Ambassador in London, and any further complaints should be taken up with the British Embassy in Cairo. The Minister of State, Lyttelton, also signalled in stiff terms to Sir Archibald Sinclair, reiterating our dissatisfaction with Pan American's performance. He received a similar assurance that the Foreign Office had matters in hand.

Here the matter rested for some weeks. Early in March I told Street that there should be an allocation of responsibility between P.A.A. and B.O.A.C., and that they should each be given certain routes, for it should not be a case of the former forcing the latter from any particular route:

The R.A.F. and B.A. have well-established routes. It is ludicrous to think that P.A.A., who have no experience of this area, and whose requirements are different from ours as regards facilities, can hope to provide fresh services as quickly or as efficiently as B.A., with our help, can increase the present services.

The Permanent Under Secretary replied that while the Air Ministry fully shared my desire to halt Pan American's commercial expansion, he did not think that the proposal to stop American services beyond Khartoum was practical, for if, as was possible, American forces were built up in India, they would certainly expect their own countrymen to provide the transportation. Street further maintained that Pan American Airways had changed their policy and were now militarising their African services. The only possible course was to concentrate on Anglo–American development and direction of the route to India.

Our experience in the Middle East inclined us to form a less trusting opinion of Pan American's activities. I replied on 16 March:

Fear your view that situation has radically changed will probably be falsified. Maximum change likely is temporary one of dress. Sheep's clothing of U.S.A.A.C. will not change habits or diets of the wolf.
Americans are already developing their routes quite regardless of our interests, despite the fact that they are only able to do so with our active assistance.

With the best will in the world to establish close relations with the Americans, I could only be very sceptical of Pan American's promises to operate large numbers of aircraft on many routes between India and Burma, Khartoum and Karachi, Takoradi and Khartoum, and across the South Atlantic. The airline's technique was to get a foot in the door by making promises to fulfil commitments regardless of their ability to do so satisfactorily. I told Street that I was still convinced the only sound and economical method was to operate the African route in sections, as I had suggested:

I fail to see force of argument that Americans have right to insist on their supplies being carried by American aircraft when one of the main conditions of their African Agreement was that scheduled British runs should cease. What is sauce for the goose (which I fear we are) is not, apparently. . . .

Once again I urged that we must have a policy. The constitution of a proper co-ordinating board would not safeguard our interests unless we had such a policy. The Americans knew what they wanted to do, which was to establish and control the whole route in their own interests regardless of ours. If we continued to let them think that we could not operate unless they were kind enough to allow us some of their transport aircraft, we were putting ourselves in a most dangerous position. The provision of certain aircraft and a definite assumption of responsibility for a given section of the route was the only method of ensuring that our rights were not overridden:

We must establish our right to be a partner and not a subordinate recipient of charity. We can only do this by pushing a positive policy backed by aircraft. We need not be too squeamish in overstating the aircraft we intend to put on the route.

Three days afterwards I met the leader of the American Military Mission in North Africa, General R. L. Maxwell. After some discussion of Pan American Airways' behaviour, I handed him a letter of complaint. It drew particular attention to the fact that I knew Pan American Airways to be operating a series of special services from Cairo to Basra which amounted to more than a twice-weekly airline service. Between 1 March and 16 March P.A.A. had operated five services from Cairo to Basra and back. The British Government had only given authority for a service between Cairo and Khartoum on condition that such services were strictly military, carrying only official passengers and freight. A diversion of Pan American aircraft from the Takoradi Route to Basra meant a reduction of the load carried on the Trans-African route, which was of vital importance both to General Maxwell and to me. It was especially undesirable, in view of the fact that a large amount of freight was awaiting onward transport at Lagos and Takoradi. Moreover, B.O.A.C. had ample capacity to deal with all high priority traffic on offer between Cairo and Basra. I told General Maxwell that I was relying on him to impress on P.A.A. that there was a risk of their aircraft being inadvertently shot down by our fighters unless the Commands in question were properly notified of all air activity other than R.A.F. flights. I asked him to ensure that no U.S. aircraft should fly east of Cairo or Khartoum without the knowledge and authority of my headquarters. The question of P.A.A. running services beyond Cairo and Khartoum to India and elsewhere, which entailed flying over British and Allied territories, was a matter for discussion between the British and United States Governments, in view of the fact that P.A.A. was a commercial concern carrying passengers and freight for hire and reward.

The threat of an American annexation of our airline routes was not due solely to the drive of P.A.A. The British air lines could certainly have put up a stouter defence of their interests. A few days after my meeting with General Maxwell, I heard that the Chairman of B.O.A.C. was doubtful about his company's ability to assume, as I had suggested, the responsibility for running a Wellington service between Cairo and Malta. It was claimed, no doubt rightly, that B.O.A.C. suffered from a lack of expert operational personnel, and that it would be unsound to extend the company's commitments until this shortage could be overcome. In reply, I told Balfour, our Under Secretary of State, of my concern at the hopelessly defeatist attitude of the B.O.A.C. management. They did not appear to realise the vital importance to our military effort in the Middle East and beyond of air transport, or the extent to which their present efforts depended on the support I had given them. I had already explained in the summer of 1941 that the increasing need for air transport would best be met by expansion of the civil organisations rather than by operating R.A.F. transport squadrons where civil routes could run. During special military operations and emergencies, normal services could be diverted to meet immediate military needs. as in the recent offensive, for instance, when B.O.A.C. had run services up to the advanced aerodromes in the battle zones. This was by far the most economical way of employing our limited number of transport aircraft. It was for this reason that I had helped B.O.A.C. with the loan of aircraft, pilots, engineers, and ground personnel. They had been given the use of a well-equipped base, and R.A.F. Middle East had assisted in the recruitment of more than four hundred technical personnel.

The Chairman's attitude towards the proposed Malta service was only explicable to me on the assumption that he had been completely misinformed. The total effect of running this vital and urgent service would be simply to employ aircraft and crews which I had already loaned to B.O.A.C. The alternative was that I should withdraw the necessary aircraft and crews so that the R.A.F. might run the service themselves. I submitted to the Air Ministry that the Middle East Defence Committee, though not the only judges, were at least competent judges as to the vital tasks of air transport in Africa, the Levant, and Iraq. I asked whether the reluctance of the B.O.A.C. management to undertake additional tasks with R.A.F. assistance was endorsed by the Air Ministry. I could not believe this to be so, but if it were so I must reconsider my policy and form my own transport organisation. I thought it well to end this signal with a judgment of the real issue:

Future of British Civil Aviation is not my concern, but I suggest that its prospects of winning the peace are in direct proportion to the volume of its contribution towards winning the war.

Balfour agreed that it was better in the short term to employ all available resources, using unorthodox methods of improvisation and without waiting to build up strength as we should have done in peacetime. On that basis, B.O.A.C. agreed to undertake the new Malta service with 'great goodwill'.

The situation between B.O.A.C. and Pan American Airways remained unsatisfactory, however. Evidence of encroachment continued to reach me. Meanwhile, as a result of the Foreign Office's intervention, the United States Government was forced to recognise certain limits to the activities of the new American interest in the Middle East. On 30 April the Air Ministry notified me that the American Embassy in London had confirmed that the services between Khartoum and Cairo would be for official purposes only, and that Pan American Airways would promise not to establish facilities on routes where adequate facilities already existed. Furthermore, the President of Pan American had been told by the State Department that if there was a need for commercial operations in Egypt, he should approach the U.S. Government so that action might be taken through diplomatic channels.

*

The prolonged 'Crusader' offensive had naturally caused heavy wastage to the Royal Air Force in the Middle East. At the same time, the drain of aircraft to Russia and Far East was causing serious deficiencies. Moreover, on political grounds, with which I generally sympathised, we were often being urged to equip squadrons for an assortment of European allies. Wilfrid Freeman was anxious that the R.A.F. Middle East should equip one or two Yugoslav squadrons. I had to reply that we had insufficient aircraft and equipment even for our own squadrons. In any event, the Command could not afford to carry passengers until more aircraft became available for training and operations.

At a time when our forces were fully engaged, it was particularly disturbing to discover that delivery figures consistently fell well below promises. I was most anxious to have confirmation that deliveries would be maintained. The American consignment was vital to me now because I had had to send squadrons and aircraft to the Far East and Burma.

In the Desert, the shortage of aircraft was beginning to affect individual units seriously, while the prolonged offensive had reacted on the fitness and freshness of our crews. Nor could we flatter ourselves that Rommel would be inclined to accept defeat tamely. Coningham wrote on 14 January pleading for fighters to bring his units up to strength. The shortage of fighters, caused by wholesale diversion to the Far East, had coincided with much increased air activity on the part of the enemy, temporarily freed from fuel restrictions, and now superior in numbers. According to Coningham's report, the enemy's shortage of bombs had forced him to rely on the more effective use of fighters, especially the Me. 109, for ground straffing. Our two Kittyhawk squadrons were the only forces available which could use similar tactics in small numbers, the remainder of our fighters being outclassed in performance, having to go about at least in squadron strength. The enemy air forces did considerable damage to our columns and advanced forces. This development impelled Coningham to warn General Ritchie that the Army should rely to a greater extent on their dispersion and fire-power. The A.O.C. had to fight two separate battles—the war against the enemy in the air, and the war in protection and support of ground forces. As he wrote to me:

The vital difference between fighter action in England, Malta and here, is that there is no water barrier between the enemy and us, and that we are linked to a second service that can be defeated if our support is withdrawn. It is the difference between static warfare on an island and mobile warfare on a land front. The same conditions exist in Malaya, and already there are murmurings of the ground forces being penalised by lack of air support, i.e. fighters. We must keep the flag flying here.

There was never any question of my having a reserve of aircraft and crews from which I could despatch reinforcements to the Far East without materially weakening the Command. On 10 February, Portal asked whether some forty-six Gladiator fighters which were still in the Command and which the Air Ministry supposed to be serviceable, could be sent to the East. We replied that nearly half of these aircraft were unserviceable, and that they could not be restored to operational fitness until certain spares and equipment were manufactured locally. Moreover, some of the serviceable remnants were already in service with the Free French fighter squadron, while others, on account of their age, were none too reliable on long-range flights in any case. The A.O.C. in India, Air Chief Marshal Sir Richard Peirse, told the C.A.S. that while he was grateful for the proposal, he considered the Gladiators, even if available, to be completely outclassed by enemy fighters, which were already meeting Hurricanes and the American P.40s on equal terms.

The Chiefs of Staff then promptly called for two Hurricane squadrons, with thirty-six aircraft and ground personnel, to be sent to Burma from the Middle East. They presumed that the aircraft would be Hurricane IIBs. We replied that we should have to send Hurricane Is, since we did not possess enough Hurricane IIBs.

The low ebb of the Middle East Air Force at the beginning of 1942 showed no sign of turning for the moment. When the material promised to my Command was despatched, it took a long time to arrive, and when it did so, technical faults delayed the introduction of the aircraft to operational service. The Baltimore, especially, was beset by numerous faults, some of which should have been ironed out at the factory inspection stage. Moreover, our ground personnel were seriously handicapped by the lack of detailed technical information which should have been sent out with American equipment. Aircraft inspectors at home preferred to replace the American manuals with Air Ministry publications, which invariably seemed to arrive separately after a long delay. Meanwhile we fumbled about, wasting aircraft and equipment. I signalled to the Air Ministry on 13 March:

Most grateful you arrange for contractors to pack appropriate handbooks etc. with relevant equipment. We can now understand American language, and need not wait Air Ministry interpretation.

*

The recapture of Cyrenaica and its aerodromes caused the Royal Navy to request closer air support for supply convoys. Such support could be given only by neglecting to some degree our land lines of communications and the protection of our bases. 'Mary' Coningham was concerned at a proposed change in the method of deploying our fighter strength, feeling that convoy work was periodic, while land coverage was necessary at all times.

He feared, too, that the new demands would subordinate air defences to naval requirements and bring them under naval control. Admittedly, we had to provide air protection for shipping; but how should this be achieved? Coningham thought that we should use the method practised at home, whereby a fighter sector organisation was set up, and each sector commander became responsible for the protection of any convoy on his front. The A.O.C. insisted that fighter organisation and operational control should be divorced entirely from naval control and operations. This was not on personal grounds or because of inter-Service rivalry, but rather because experience had shown that naval control of air operations resulted in serious inefficiency except in certain specialised functions suitable for the R.N.A.S. Coningham quoted a message from Admiral Cunningham to Air Vice Marshal Slatter, the officer commanding 201 Group, which ran as follows:

It is intended to form a combined Naval and R.A.F. Operations Room at Benghazi for sea port and No. 201 Group Advanced Head-quarters. Request you will ear-mark a suitable place in co-operation with Air Commodore Cole.

Coningham commented that the whole trend of present action was to give the Navy virtual control of our air defences, which, at this stage of reduced naval resources and increased reliance on the air, would prejudice air action and provide a dangerous precedent. His own alternative was to leave 201 Group to its restricted role of naval co-operation and to form a new group which would control air forces along the Egyptian and Cyrenaican coasts as a prelude to an eventual expansion into an Air Headquarters for the Mediterranean.

Coningham's last remarks met with my full approval:

The virtual control of the Mediterranean is passing to air forces, and these early decisions will probably govern the future. There is a lot at stake.

The vital commitments at sea were two-fold and interconnected. We had to supply Malta and we had to interrupt the flow of enemy reinforcements, fuel, and equipment, to North Africa. Signalling to the Admiralty on 10 January, Admiral Cunningham complained of insufficient air reconnaissance, with particular reference to the safe passage of a large Italian convoy to Tripoli a few days earlier. Cunningham admitted that his surface forces were powerless to intervene in the face of the enemy's strength, but he thought that air forces trained for operations over the sea were not adequate even to maintain sufficient reconnaissance, let alone to provide the necessary striking force.

Unless some naval and strong air reinforcements are shortly forthcoming, I cannot see how Malta can be maintained, far less the enemy's supplies to Tripoli stopped. Nor can sea-borne attack on Malta be ruled out, particularly observing the increased scale of air attack to which they are now being exposed and appear unable to defeat.

Two days later, Peter Drummond, who was in London, told me by telegram that the whole question of the control of air operations over the sea was in the balance, and that Freeman had asked him to stay for the contest. Drummond asked that I should send full information about certain air/sea operations, which we thought Cunningham had misreported to the Admiralty.

I pointed out to the Defence Committee in Cairo on 14 January that in his account of the passage of the Italian convoy to Tripoli, Cunningham had omitted certain essential facts. Auchinleck expressed his serious concern at the situation described in Cunningham's message, and asked that it should be examined on an inter-Service basis. We discussed the whole question of presenting the views of Middle Eastern Commanders to London. It was generally

[228]

felt that where matters of policy affecting more than one Service were concerned, the presentation of views should be done through the machinery of the Commanders-in-Chief or the Defence Committee, and not on the basis of a report by a single Service.

Accordingly, Cunningham's signal to the Admiralty the next day stated that he had no desire to criticise the co-operation afforded by the Royal Air Force in the Mediterranean. In fact, Malta had placed every available reconnaissance aircraft at the disposal of the Royal Navy, who had made admitted errors in placing the reconnaissance forces. Cunningham thought, and I did not disagree, that the naval authoritities had been presented with an almost impossible problem owing to the lack of aircraft. The further trouble, according to his account, was that neither he nor the Fleet had been informed of this.

Meanwhile I had reported to Freeman that various naval reports had gone to London without reference to myself or to the Air Officer Commanding 201 Group, and that they were, as a result, misleading, in particular as regards the coverage afforded to the merchant ship *Breconshire,* carrying petrol and munitions, on 17 December. Admiral Cunningham reported that he had been in doubt as to what enemy forces were at sea and uncertain of their position until the late afternoon of the 17th, and that the *Breconshire* and her escort had been completely surprised by them and only just got away. I told Freeman:

It is quite incomprehensible to me how the *Breconshire* and escort came to be surprised. It was clear to A.O.C. 201 Group in Alex. and to me in Cairo on the morning of the 17th, that the *Breconshire* was in grave danger of being intercepted unless some drastic change was made in her movements. When no such change was made, I could only assume C.-in-C. Med. was prepared to take the risk.

It would appear that the Admiral was not fully informed about weather conditions in the central Mediterranean on the 17th. Coningham himself described them in non-technical language as 'horrible' and the bombers were bogged down as a result of heavy rain. The following day, only the reconnaissance aircraft were able to leave the ground, and electrical storms ruined even the fruits of that effort. On the 19th it rained all day, and Takali and Halfar aerodromes on Malta were completely unserviceable.

Every serviceable aeroplane on the island that could be moved was transferred to Luqa aerodrome.

On the general question of the future control of sea communications in the Mediterranean, it was clear that as the Army advanced into Tripolitania, the scale of our supporting air effort would decrease. The defence of land and sea communications over the 1,200 miles between Tripoli and Egypt would clearly demand a major effort, however. We should have to attend to the fighter defence of the main ports, Tripoli, Benghazi, Tobruk, Mersa Matruh, and possibly Derna. Nor could we neglect the defence of railheads and aerodromes and the provision of cover for our shipping along the coast and between Malta and Egypt; but the defence of coastal shipping and the defence of ports were inseparable, for it was improbable that we should have enough forces to earmark units solely for shipping protection and the defence of ports respectively. Nor could the defence of shipping of any kind be separated from action against enemy shipping, since both reconnaissance and striking forces had a dual offensive and defensive role. From the operational point of view, therefore, all our units dealing with the control of sea communications should come under one operational control, and the ultimate requirement would seem to be an Air Headquarters, Mediterranean, responsible for the control of sea communications in the Eastern Mediterranean. Logically, this organisation should grow out of 201 Group.

One interpretation of the Directive issued by the Air Ministry and the Admiralty in the previous autumn[1] might well be that all such operations should come under 201 Group and virtually under the immediate control of the Commander-in-Chief, Mediterranean. I thought that any such system would be absolutely unsound, since with the present and prospective naval forces available in the Eastern Mediterranean, the contribution made by the Royal Navy to the control of sea communications was likely to be extremely small compared with the air effort involved:

The main responsibility would in fact rest with the Royal Air Force,

---

[1] See page 176.

and operation of surface ships must more and more conform to air operations.

Portal agreed with me in general, though there were some obvious difficulties. The situation in the Middle East was not the same as it had been in the previous autumn, when he had agreed with the Admiralty on the functions of 201 Group. Naval control of the Eastern Mediterranean had now virtually ceased to exist, and would have to be replaced by air control. In the exchange of the previous October, a distinction had deliberately been drawn between operations over the sea and the co-operation with the Mediterranean Fleet required by the C.-in-C. Mediterranean. Portal's interpretation of this Directive was that Admiral Cunningham was concerned with the latter part but only indirectly with the former. As Portal signalled: 'The acid test is whether there is mutual co-operation between the aircraft and a naval force at sea.'

Thus, fighter aircraft detailed for the protection of convoys moving along the coast, and aircraft on reconnaissance duties over the sea on behalf of our bomber forces ashore, would not operate under the instructions of the C.-in-C. Mediterranean. If Cunningham was determined to issue all orders to 201 Group, it might be necessary to limit 201 Group to those units which would co-operate with our surface vessels. In this event, a new formation would be required for the purposes of convoy protection and reconnaissance, and for use as a striking force over the sea.

I 3

*Fourfold weakness in Desert Air Force–Rommel's riposte–
Fighter leapfrog withdrawal–Fifty more fighters for Far East–
Chaos in the Desert–Timing of possible offensive–To hold
Tobruk or not?–Benghazi falls–Airmen take on German
tanks–Interdependence of the three Services–Malta–Reduction in land strength
to Far East–Probable postponement of offensive until July 1942–Churchill
gets out whip–British and U.S. division of responsibilities–Review of Air
situation in the Desert–Urgent calls from Far East–'Bomber' Harris: 'I
appeal to you personally'–Controversy over aircraft and crews–Gossip–Sir
Stafford Cripps–'Twenty Questions'*

ATTENTION was quickly diverted from my exchanges with
Cunningham and Portal to events more serious and immediate in the Western Desert. Although our move forward
had been halted, and we realised that it would not be resumed for
some weeks, we had as yet no real reason to anticipate that we
might have to go through the events of 1941 again. On 19 January
I set out on a bitterly cold morning to visit the battlefield and
forward aerodromes. A Blenheim of 45 Squadron was waiting at
Heliopolis Aerodrome to take me forward. I sat up alongside the
pilot, as we battled into a head wind of some forty miles an hour.
The sky was cold and grey, though we could see a little blue to the
west. After we crossed the line south of Halfaya, we swooped
down low to have a look at the so-called battlefield:

Just hundreds of square miles of this stony, sandy desert, fretted
all over with twisting track marks and dotted here and there with
derelict vehicles or the odd tank.

Soon afterwards we saw Tobruk in the distance with its
inevitable dust cloud above. Then we flew on over the Gazalas,
and landed a few minutes later. After lunch I went off in a car to
visit Derna. The road was still in good condition, although there
was ample sign of the enemy's retreat on either side. At one place
there was clear evidence of the devastation wrought on motor
transport and ammunition lorries by the Hurricane bombers of
80 Squadron. As for Derna:

An extraordinary sight, littered with aircraft, mostly Hun, in all

[232]

stages of repair and disrepair! Some, obviously deliberately 'demolished'. Others equally obviously knocked out by our bombing and low
shoot-ups. A few in good repair, and behind the remains of a hanger I
found a group of S. Africans hard at work getting an Me. 109 serviceable. The whole place a sea of bright red mud. Then down the hill
for a few minutes look at Derna, still a pretty little place, despite a good
many scars. A heavy sea running, with breakers smashing high up
all along the coast—very refreshing to see and hear, but not so good
from a military point of view!

I got back to the Advanced Headquarters just before dark,
arriving at almost the same time as 'Mary' Coningham. I talked
with him and Neil Ritchie, and thought they made a good pair.
The next morning Coningham and I went off in a Blenheim to
visit the fighters, and to have a look at Benghazi. We flew along
the coast over Derna and Barce. The country was looking lovely,
with green appearing everywhere, and splashes of yellow wattle
among the scrub. The weather was less attractive. We fought
our way through squall after squall of heavy cold rain, with very
few glimpses of sun or sky in between. Benina provided an even
more extraordinary sight than Derna. Ruined German aircraft
lay everywhere. A whole row of Ju. 52s had been burnt out where a
string of bombs had caught them as they were off-loading petrol.
Beside one of the remains was the remnant of a big petrol lorry
caught in the act.

Here on the coast, flowers were beginning to push up through
the mud, some little yellow ones rather like celandines, and some
white ones like narcissi. When we flew south after lunch, however,
the greenery gave place to desert, though even the desert itself
was beginning to be streaked with dark patches where scrub
and thorn were turning green.

Although I still had no reason to anticipate an immediate
riposte by Rommel to 'Crusader', I had been concerned at the
relative weakness of our air forces. My visit showed that the causes
were fourfold. First, it was difficult to provide regular supplies,
especially of fuel, to our aircraft in the forward areas. The opening
of the port at Benghazi was easing the problem as far as fighters
and light bombers were concerned, but it would take some time
before a large medium bomber force could operate from that

area. The exceptionally bad weather had caused aircraft to bog down, not only along the coast at Derna, Barce, and Benghazi, but also in the south. The drain of aircraft to the new theatre of war in the Far East provided a third cause of weakness, especially in our bomber strength, after the diversion of four out of the six Blenheim squadrons which had been supporting land operations. The final factor, the discovery of many technical faults in the newly delivered Bostons, and the delay in the availability of Baltimores, had made it difficult for us to replace the ageing Maryland aircraft. I told Portal that we were making:

. . . neither complaint nor alibi. Necessity for diversions to Far East fully appreciated by all ranks, and supreme effort being made to meet both conflicting requirements. Consider it urgently necessary to build up numerical strength in Cyrenaica again as quickly as possible. but in meantime saw no signs of slackening off. Morale as high as ever.

By the time this signal was sent, Rommel's counter-offensive was under way. He had the advantage of a vastly improved position in the Central Mediterranean, which meant that for the moment he was receiving supplies fairly freely, and had been heartened by the arrival of armoured reinforcements. No man knew better how to exploit our fatal tendency to disperse strength. As soon as I heard the first news of enemy movements, I knew enough to be deeply apprehensive. We had been through all this before. On 24 January, 'Mary' Coningham told me of his fears of what might happen in any sudden retreat:

I hope you will agree in my taking the worst case as a basis for action. The penalty of over-insurance is far less in the circumstances than optimism and under-insurance, because retirement based on one long road could, in the latter case, lead to disaster which early movement avoids.

He had therefore ordered the withdrawal of all maintenance and heavy units to the Egyptian side of the wire, and was allotting to them their former bases. Coningham had been told that the Army intended to fight successive delaying actions on the axis Msus–Mechili–Gazala–Tobruk–Omar, the main stand being at Gazala. This plan might be altered if it were decided in Cairo that we must try to hold Tobruk. As the Army fell back, so fighter forces would leapfrog behind it, covering the withdrawal of huge quantities of our motor transport. As a preparation, our main force had retired to Mechili, while a secondary force from Benghazi covered the traffic in the Jebel. Our bomber forces would retire from Tobruk eventually to the Bagush area, and Coningham asked that our ground forces should concentrate so that the day bombers could safely be used against enemy targets. Air strikes would continue against the bottleneck at Agedabia, but the A.O.C. feared that the loss of Benghazi would prevent effective air action against Tripoli. He commented, truly enough:

The foregoing may sound very depressing but it is the worst case, and I can at any time about-turn any essential services that may be moving. . . .

The next day I received from Portal yet another request for the despatch of reinforcements to the East. This time, I was to provide a further fifty Hurricanes and pilots in a fortnight or so. The C.A.S. expressed his warm appreciation of R.A.F. Middle East's achievements in helping the Far East, and promised that he would do his best to compensate for this further withdrawal by a carrier operation to Malta.

Before this signal was received Auchinleck and I, thinking that we had better investigate for ourselves, had left for the Desert. When we arrived at the advanced headquarters at T'mimi we could not discover the full facts about Rommel's offensive. It was clear already that the original thrust through Agedabia or Antelat came as a complete surprise, and for some reason which was not at that moment explicable, seemed to have been practically unopposed. Our main fighter force at Antelat received no warning of withdrawal, and had only been extricated by a frantic effort at the last minute. The aircraft had to be manhandled on to a small flying-off strip which was under artillery fire by the time the last aircraft got away. Only six unserviceable aircraft from six squadrons had to be left for destruction. If Rommel had moved a day earlier we should have lost the whole lot, since they were bogged down. Some of our armoured-cars which covered the withdrawal had been lost. The fighters had meanwhile withdrawn to Mechili and had used Msus as an advance landing ground until the morning of 25 January, when it was occupied by the enemy.

Here, for the moment, Rommel's vigorous thrust seemed to stop short. This was the situation which Auchinleck and I discussed with Coningham and Ritchie at the latter's headquarters that afternoon, when it seemed to us that Rommel's move was a characteristically daring and bellicose exploitation of an unexpected early success. We thought we had time to stop him, and the withdrawal of our forces was countermanded by Ritchie that afternoon. I found that Auchinleck fully appreciated the importance of retaining Cyrenaica, not least in order to hold the aerodromes, and agreed with me that the Army should counter-attack forcefully rather than retreat and consolidate. I told Portal on 26 January that I hoped some offensive counter-action on land might now begin. I felt sure that the only way of stopping this nonsense was to hit back. Our fighter pilots were in an angry mood and had concentrated against the Germans on the ground. I felt sure that Auchinleck would not let Cyrenaica go lightly. He and I decided to stay in the Desert for a day or two.

By 28 January I was becoming rather restless, for there was really nothing for me to do. 'Mary' Coningham was quite capable of dealing not only with the Germans but also with our soldiers. I was mainly there in order to lend Auchinleck moral support in a situation none too easy. That day we had a long talk in Neil Ritchie's operations room, where Auchinleck, Ritchie, 'Mary' and I sat on little stools in a well-lit room, the walls of which were covered with maps of the country. Each map had a transparent talc shroud on which the latest positions and reports were recorded in coloured pencils:

A very graphic and effective way of giving the whole situation at a glance—if it is true! Have a horrid feeling (based on some little experience) that many of our air reports of *enemy* positions are more accurate than the alleged positions of our own troops—we seem to have lost complete control of our forces in various areas. It's beginning to clear up—but it's been untidy.

It soon became clear enough that events of 1941 had still not enabled us to master the problem of proper control of our forces in battle. An example of muddle on this occasion was the premature withdrawal of our fighter wing from Mechili under the orders of 13 Corps. I complained to Auchinleck, calling for the re-establishment of that force at Mechili, and he replied that he was infuriated to hear of this avoidable mistake. The blame rested entirely with 13 Corps Staff which ordered the move, because they were rightly moving themselves but apparently did not ascertain the conditions under which the fighters were working. They were much influenced by what happened at Antelat, and feared a recurrence, but he could see no excuse for a blunder.

'Mary' Coningham and his team were keeping their heads as usual, but were incensed at the Army's defeatist attitude. I wrote in my diary on 26 January:

> Our Fighter chaps have been doing some grand work—they are feeling rather angry about it all. Been talking this evening to see if we cannot pass on some of their anger—and spirit—to the Land Forces. A. is first-rate. He has got fight and leadership, so have a lot of our chaps.

While I was in the Desert yet another plea for help had been received in Cairo. This time it was from Wavell. He asked that a further twenty-four Hurricanes should be flown to Burma, where one fighter squadron now possessed but four aircraft. Such requests, however well justified, were becoming monotonous by repetition. I quite understood and sympathised with Portal in his agonising dilemma. If he tilted the balance too far in either direction, he might cause us to lose the Far East or the Middle East. It was my duty to see that we did not lose the air war, and therefore in due course the whole campaign, in the Middle East, and I signalled to the C.A.S. on 29 January telling him that within my command we needed twenty-five Hurricane IIBs in Cyrenaica and at least fifteen more for Malta. This did not allow for wastage during February. Takoradi had fifty-two Hurricane IIBs, but we were short of air crews to ferry them to the Middle East. Earlier diversions to Burma were still being completed, but I simply could not send fifty more Hurricane IIBs to the Far East, as Portal had asked on 25 January, without endangering the whole position in the Desert. Our fighter force there had been, and was likely to be, the vital stabilising forces in Cyrenaica:

> I do not wish to overstate the case, but that force is already weak,

and I feel strongly that if it is further weakened, as it would be by the proposed diversions during the next few weeks, the situation would be dangerous. I have discussed with Auchinleck, and he strongly agrees with this view. To add to this there is the question of Malta which needs no elaboration. It is probable that reinforcements by carrier via Malta would merely suffice to bring Malta up to strength. Fully appreciate Far East needs, and have done best possible to assist, but it is my considered opinion that it is not, repeat not, possible to do more from here in the immediate future without endangering the whole situation in Middle East.

Portal, unrelenting, replied that he must ask me, if it were possible, to ship the fifty Hurricanes to the Far East in the carrier *Indomitable*, which was to arrive at Port Sudan about 10 February. He was sure I should do my best to have these fifty aircraft ready for shipment by this date. I could, however, send Hurricane Is instead of Hurricane IIBs. Portal explained his decision as being based

. . . on the fact that the more urgent need at the moment as we see it is the Far East. The aircraft may never reach Singapore, but they will probably be equally urgently needed in Burma or East Indies. You have a steady pipe line feeding your Command and great resources which enable you to make special efforts in your repair organisation which meet a temporary shortage of this nature whereas there is no adequate repair organisation in the Far East.

The C.A.S. made promises of large reinforcements which should arrive in the Middle East by the end of April. These reinforcements would, indeed, amount to about 590 aircraft in all, including 300 Hurricanes and 90 Spitfires. Previous experience indicated, however, that these deliveries were unlikely to be made in full. In any case, they could not affect our effort in the existing critical circumstances.

When the Middle East Defence Committee reviewed the strategic situation at the end of January the prospect was bleak. The two strategic aims of the Command were to secure the Egyptian and Persian Gulf bases, keeping the enemy as far away from them as possible, and to support Turkey if she were attacked. However, our resources did not allow us to prepare for any German offensive against Turkey, and even if the enemy were to delay such an attack until the middle of May our only course would be to fall back on Persia, Central Iraq, and Southern Syria, thereby exposing our main base area to a serious scale of air attack. Everything depended upon the speed with which the known deficiencies could be made good. About four months would elapse between the time of decision in London to send reinforcements and their deployment in the Middle Eastern theatre.

Nor could we take much more comfort from the situation in the Western Desert. As Auchinleck wrote early in February, the campaign in Cyrenaica had shown that generally the German tanks were superior to ours in mechanical reliability and in gun-power, while the latest Italian tank was only slightly inferior to our better machines and superior to our older ones. After consultation, Auchinleck had concluded that the Allied Forces would need 50 per cent. numerical superiority in tanks, if we were to have a reasonable chance of beating the enemy's armoured forces on a ground of his own choosing. Auchinleck made an assessment of our future monthly strength as compared with the enemy's, omitting a 50 per cent. reserve force on our side, and assuming that Rommel would receive no tank reinforcements after the end of March. On this basis the Commander-in-Chief showed that we should by 1 June have the necessary margin. He thought that the end of that month or the beginning of July would be the opportune time for an offensive. Even then, it could only be undertaken if we were in a position to neglect the northern front. The earliest possible timing of an offensive would be in March, but this would allow only for a 25 per cent. reserve. Admittedly, the newly arrived American tanks gave the promise of improved mechanical reliability, and Auchinleck did not at this stage claim finality for his analysis.

He had already decided to confirm instructions given to General Ritchie that he should hold the line covering Tobruk in the north and Giarabub in the south, while defences should be prepared around Sollum and Maddalena. However, since the recapture of Benghazi was vital for the supply and equipment of his armoured forces, artillery and infantry, a striking force should be built up as quickly as possible so that we might make an offensive to regain the port. These proposals were discussed at the

Defence Committee on 4 February. Auchinleck said he did not regard them as permanent, and if, for instance, a sudden thrust were to develop on the northern front, it would still be possible to call off the offensive and concentrate our forces elsewhere. He had to confess that the necessary superiority for an offensive might not be ready before 1 May or even then. Both the Minister of State and Admiral Cunningham pressed for an earlier date. The Admiral, now zealous for air protection, wanted the early recapture of airfields in Western Cyrenaica so that fighter cover might be assured for the convoys to Malta, and the harassment of enemy shipping at Benghazi. Drummond, who represented me at this meeting, weighed in to point out that until we could get forward beyond Derna, the air effort against Benghazi must be hampered by our inability to provide fighter escort. Auchinleck fully appreciated how desirable it was to resume the offensive as soon as possible, but held to his ground that our limited resources should not be frittered away on minor land actions, thus prejudicing the main offensive later on. The Committee accepted the policy which he had outlined.

The meeting also discussed policy in the Western Desert. The Joint Planning Staff had recommended that the defence of Egypt against the major threat should be based on holding defended areas well forward of the Egyptian frontier, including Tobruk. In view of all that happened a few months later, it is of some interest to record that we were aware as early as 4 February that Tobruk might become more of a liability than an asset. Auchinleck said that while he fully realised the importance of Tobruk to ourselves and to the enemy, the configuration of the coast at that point invited investment, and with his present resources of infantry and armour he did not think he could afford the risk of having one and a quarter divisions cooped up. This disadvantage did not apply in nearly the same degree to the Sollum–Maddalena position, which it would be far harder for the enemy to penetrate. Moreover, a line held farther forward and including Tobruk would be some forty miles longer, a disadvantage that could not be disregarded when the circuit of action of motorised forces would play an important part in the general scheme of defence. General Ritchie agreed with him that we should not attempt to hold Tobruk if we were forced to defend Egypt against a major enemy offensive. This did not mean that we should not fight for Tobruk, but the essential was to avoid the risk of investment.

I was much interested to notice, when reading the minutes of this meeting, and hearing about it from Drummond, that the rest of the Committee had agreed with Auchinleck's view with comparatively little discussion. Admiral Cunningham said he was inclined to agree that we should not attempt to hold Tobruk, the cost of maintaining which, when isolated in 1941, had been very heavy, including the loss of no fewer than fifty-two ships. Drummond thought that we might very well be unable to hold the port, particularly as it would be impossible to provide fighter cover over the area. The Committee were, therefore, in general agreement that in the event of our being forced to defend Egypt against a major enemy offensive, it would be unsound to risk investment in an attempt to hold Tobruk, and they endorsed their previous decision that the ultimate defence of Egypt should be based on the general line Sollum to Giarabub.

I had not been at this meeting because I was confined to bed with influenza. I had been plagued with a series of minor attacks during January, and the two visits to the Desert had not helped. Finally I was persuaded to go to hospital for special treatment:

They threatened me with pneumonia and all sorts of things, so I had to give way, subject to the proviso that I could hold special meetings in my room, had a telephone, and was accessible to three of my people, the A. and the Commissar [the friendly title I used for Lyttelton]. They accepted my terms, so here I am, now feeling quite sane and well. The special dope they gave me (M. and B.) leaves one feeling like a month of Sundays of 'mornings after', and Wednesday evening and yesterday, though my temperature was down and everything in the garden was lovely, I felt like a sermon by St. Paul.

I was nevertheless able to supervise the provision of air cover during the retreat in Cyrenaica, signalling to 'Mary' Coningham that in view of the enemy's known weakness in the air and on land it should be possible, with the Army's help, to discourage him from venturing to Derna. Certainly we should be able to keep Rommel from the Martubas or Mechili without paying a price in air strength which we could ill afford. In this respect, the gap between Msus to Marawa, and Mechili to Derna, was as important to the defence of the Egyptian border area as the English Channel was to Great Britain:

On major issues what we all need and what I am sure you out there have, is a cold-blooded determination free from pessimism or optimism and free from wishful thinking or excessive head counting, to remove this gambler from Cyrenaica as soon as possible, and then get on with the main job.

By the end of the first week in February we were back on the Gazala–Bir Hacheim Line. Rommel had retaken Benghazi on 29 January, the very day when Churchill had felt it necessary to ask for a vote of confidence from the House of Commons. Although the bad weather had continued to hamper our operations, the air forces had flown about two thousand sorties in a fortnight. Lloyd joined in from Malta with all his might, despite trying elemental conditions. Auchinleck freely acknowledged that Coningham's support had been magnificent; but nothing could conceal the fact that our handling of armour was inexpert. Against a motorised and armoured enemy, wrote Rommel, non-motorised infantry divisions are of use only in prepared positions. Rommel himself had been severely hampered in his retreat from Cyrenaica because all the Italian and most of the German infantry had no motor transport. Now, for the moment at any rate, the boot was on the other foot. General Bayerlein has commented on our Army's failure to mass their armour at the crucial point. Rather we tended to scatter our strength.[1]

I was deeply disappointed at the suddenness and scale of this reverse, but I fully realised how great were Auchinleck's difficulties, and was furious to learn in cables from home of more half-baked criticism of the R.A.F. in newspaper leading articles and in contributions by retired officers, who attempted to pin every failure of the Army and Navy on the lack of air support, and advocated an Army Air Force. So seriously did I regard these recriminations that I telegraphed, with Auchinleck's consent,

[1] Liddell Hart: *The Rommel Papers,* p. 184.

to Sir Archibald Sinclair on 12 February, asking that he should administer a sharp rebuke to such writers, since Auchinleck and I were gravely concerned of the dangerous effect that such loose and ill-informed talk might have on the morale of R.A.F. air crews in the Desert at so critical a time :

You should know that the R.A.F. in the desert realise that they have saved the Army, both in the recent advance and in the withdrawal, and naturally resent any suggestion that the Army should control them.

The R.A.F. have on this occasion given the Army, at great sacrifice, all the air support and protection they required. The German Air Force has interfered little with Army operations. Yet the Army continues to withdraw; therefore, the R.A.F. crews are perplexed and feel that their efforts have been wasted.

I told the Secretary of State that during the withdrawal some R.A.F. armoured-car crews had driven back nine serviceable tanks abandoned by the Army. This, and similar stories, had naturally circulated, and whether rightly or wrongly, the R.A.F. in the Desert felt that the Army did not know how to use their weapons and were not willing fighters. This impression had been further strengthened by the aggressive action of some R.A.F. armoured-cars who took on some German tanks. The spirit of the R.A.F's personnel in the Desert was: 'Give us some tanks and we will stop this retreating if the Army does not wish to fight.' There was therefore real danger that incessant Press correspondence on the failure to exploit air superiority might lead to strained relations between the Army and R.A.F.

Many years later, when I was Chief of the Air Staff, I was much interested to read an account of these events written by Field Marshal Kesselring. He claimed that Rommel's counter-offensive of 21 January and after had been carried out by very weak forces with wonderful enthusiasm and supported in model fashion by the Luftwaffe. Kesselring thought that Rommel deserved all the credit for the success of his counter-offensive, and described him as being unsurpassed in leading armoured formations and such-like raids, provided his nerve did not desert him.

It was also clear from Kesselring's account that he was aware of our weakness in the air. He had no doubt that at this time the German and Italian Air Forces in Africa, although weak, were superior to the R.A.F. Shortage of fuel on the German side was not enough to balance things up. The German fighters were better, he thought, but the bombing activities of the British, with their nightly firework display at Benghazi, led the Germans to assume greater bomber strength.

*

The campaigns in North Africa provide a prime example of the complementary roles played in the Second World War by all three Services. The brunt of the Desert battles fell upon the Army and the Royal Air Force; the eventual intention was to turn out of North Africa, bag and baggage, the Italian and German forces. By seeming paradox, this object could not be achieved without success at sea. Whichever side secured mastery there was likely to win, for without seaborne supplies the Axis armies would wither and starve away, while without Malta we could not interrupt Rommel's lines of supply. By a further paradox, such superiority at sea could after 1941 be secured only by the exercise of air-power, and could certainly not be secured by surface forces alone. Airpower could not supply Malta; but without air-power Malta could not be supplied. At all costs we had to keep open the route from Gibraltar through Malta to Egypt. The enemy's problem was a good deal simpler than ours, since the sea routes to Tripoli and Benghazi from Italy were far shorter and far less exposed to attack, except from Malta. Here was the key to our whole position in the Central Mediterranean. Thanks to the Cape and Takoradi routes, forces in Egypt could, at a pinch, manage reasonably well without the use of the Mediterranean route; but the retention of Malta was literally vital, not only to any possibility of denying the cross-sea route to the enemy, but also to any prospect of re-opening our own through route

As a base from which to operate naval and air forces against the enemy's supply routes, Malta's position was ideal. It lay in the path of enemy reinforcements and all the main enemy ports of arrival and departure were within range of its air reconnaissance. The island was, however, vulnerable on two counts; the base itself might be destroyed beyond repair by air attack or starved out by the sinking of supply convoys. Three times when the use of Malta as an offensive base seriously prejudiced the maintenance of the Axis effort in Africa, did the Germans try to neutralise it by air attack. In the third quarter of 1941, air action from Malta had destroyed about 350,000 tons, and had severely damaged a further 186,000 tons of enemy shipping. Count Ciano recorded in his diary on 6 October that only 20 per cent. of the September supplies to North Africa had been successfully shipped and delivered. The forces of Air Vice Marshal Lloyd, A.O.C. in Malta, were hopelessly outnumbered, sometimes by as much as six or even eight to one. Moreover, the dreadful weather of the winter had ruined the makeshift tracks to the dispersal points which alone enabled Lloyd to preserve a percentage of his aircraft against the incessant attacks of the Luftwaffe. Aircraft taxi-ing to the runways were frequently bogged down. In mid-November, Kesselring had made particularly severe attacks on the aerodromes, but had called them off. In December the battle began again, and was waged with redoubled fury from the beginning of January, mainly by night. The aerodromes were reduced again and again to a shambles of water-logged craters.

Our advances in the Western Desert during November and December lent extra urgency to the Axis Powers' decision to neutralise the island in order that Rommel might be sustained. Had Kesselring concentrated in blotting out our radar installations in Malta, I think he might have succeeded. The success of Rommel's counter-attack at the end of January and the loss of the airfields in the Cyrenaican bulge meant that our Malta convoys could no longer be properly protected. We did not have the naval strength to send them in from the west. Grand Admiral Raeder reported to Hitler on 13 February that the Axis ruled the air and sea in the Central Mediterranean. This was not quite true, for Malta had still not been knocked out although it could certainly not undertake any sustained offensive for the moment. The rate of wastage was so high that Lloyd was driven to use any expedient in order to keep his force alive. It would occasionally happen that by an understandable administrative error a new Wellington being sent to the Middle East or Far East would stop to refuel at Malta and an older machine would actually arrive at the intended destination. Then again, air crew would often be so charmed with the scenic beauties and the peaceful way of life they found in Malta that they would decide to stay.

The orders of Hitler and Mussolini to neutralise Malta had been given in October 1941. The renewed air offensive and the inclement weather caused the withdrawal of some of our bomber squadrons early in January. A month or so later, the Air Ministry proposed that we should increase our fighter strength in Malta to six squadrons, five of which would be Spitfires, so as to provide some night defence for the island. Since the aerodrome accommodation was desperately short, this proposal would mean that our air striking force would have to be reduced. The only alternative was to increase largely the aerodrome accommodation and the amount of dispersal, which could obviously not be done immediately. Our opinion in Cairo was that even if we were able to put into Malta the proposed six fighter squadrons, the enemy would still be able to produce a superior single-seater fighter force over the island, assuming that he was willing to maintain such a force in the area of Sicily. Moreover, our strength had been so much sapped by the demands from the Far East that a further despatch of aircraft to Malta would jeopardise the situation in the Delta and the Western Desert. We had by now diverted or sent on to the East no fewer than 320 fighter aircraft.

Admiral Cunningham, too, was much preoccupied by the serious naval situation in the Central Mediterranean, which was discussed by the Defence Committee on 18 February. The Committee recorded the need for increased fighter strength in Malta at the earliest possible moment. Drummond, who again deputised for me, said that we did propose to build up to a strength of six fighter squadrons, but this would take some time. In the immediate future it was hoped to fly in from carriers some fifteen or sixteen Spitfires.

At the same meeting, Auchinleck reported that he had just received a warning order that it was proposed to divert for the Far East two more infantry divisions. He took this so seriously that he was led to think that the time had come when he could no longer accept the responsibility for the defence of his Command.

He would shortly be three divisions short of the minimum number required for a close-in defence of our essential bases in Egypt and the Persian Gulf. Three days later he suggested to the Defence Committee that if it was the shortage of shipping which ruled out the despatch of further land forces to the Middle East, then large air forces might be sent. These, he thought, would almost certainly halt any enemy advance in the north. In taking this view Auchinleck was being more royalist than the king. His explicit compliment to the R.A.F. provided no solution to our problems because the despatch of air forces on this scale would take up as much shipping as the despatch of large land reinforcements, and in any case it was a mistake to think that the Air Force alone could hold up the enemy, even in the ideal conditions of the Northern Front. However, everyone agreed with me that there should be a general strengthening of the Middle East Air Forces as a measure of compensation for the recent drastic reduction in our land strength.

In this latter connection, Auchinleck had already been told that he would in the end almost certainly lose three or four divisions and would not get more than one replacement division from the United Kingdom during the next six months. Brooke let him know on 17 February that he realised the plans for regaining Cyrenaica might have to be abandoned in favour of the defence of the Egyptian frontier.[1]

Ten days later the Chiefs of Staff signalled that they agreed that the prevention of enemy reinforcement to Libya, and probably also the ultimate fate of Malta, depended on the recapture of air bases in Western Cyrenaica:

We appreciate that the timing of another offensive will depend on building up adequate tank superiority, and that its launching may necessitate taking considerable risks in other parts of the Middle East Command. Nevertheless, we feel that we must aim to be so placed in Cyrenaica by April dark period that we can pass a substantial convoy to Malta.

All this bore little relation to Auchinleck's earlier calculations that the right time for the offensive would be certainly no earlier

[1] Connell: *Auchinleck,* p. 454.

than May, and probably the end of June or the beginning of July. This message was the signal for a sharp exchange of views between the Middle East and London.

The Chiefs of Staff cabled on 3 March that they were much disturbed by the Middle East Commanders-in-Chief's review of the situation. The dominant fact was Malta, and if we did not succeed in running a substantial convoy into Malta by May the island's position would be critical.

The loss of Malta, or even its effective neutralisation, would mean that the Axis could reinforce Libya much faster than we could. Supplies of aircraft to the Middle East could be seriously affected, and a convoy could only be run into Malta if we had the use of the landing grounds in Western Cyrenaica. The recapture of these landing grounds in the near future was, therefore, vital. The Chiefs of Staff went on to accuse us of giving a picture heavily biased in favour of the enemy:

Every tank he has in the country is counted as effective, whereas on our side on the 23rd of February you could only produce 298 serviceable in the Western Desert out of a total in your Command of 1,271. How is it that he can land his tanks at Tripoli and have them all with very short delay effective in Cyrenaica, whereas many of our tanks which arrived in January have still not even been issued to units?

Your review takes no account whatever of the Air situation. The figures show that although our reserves are lower, our serviceable strength does not differ much from that with which you started the offensive.

On the other hand, the Axis Air Force is at a considerably lower strength, and he is at present very short of fuel in the forward areas.

It was clear enough that much of this message owed its inspiration, if not its actual words, to the Prime Minister. It pointed out that in a few weeks time the enemy would have large fuel stocks in the forward areas and would be able to transfer to Libya a large proportion of the air forces now in Sicily:

Our present superiority will have disappeared, possibly for ever. From the air point of view is it not, repeat not, now or never?

We realise that the Germans have a definite advantage in the armament of their tanks.

Nevertheless, we cannot understand how his 15th and 21st Panzer

Divisions and the Italian Ariete Division can have become so formidable in so short a time after the hammering they received at your hands.

The Chiefs of Staff asked us, too, to consider not only the situation in North Africa and the Mediterranean, but the future situation on the Levant–Caspian Front. What would happen there if we had allowed the enemy to build up in Africa a force which would pin down our remaining strength to the defence of Egypt's western flank? We could not afford to stand idle at a time when the Russians were straining every nerve to give the enemy no rest, and when it was so important to increase by every possible means the drain on the German armed forces:

If our view of the situation is correct, you must either grasp the opportunity which is held out in the immediate future or else we must face the loss of Malta and a precarious defensive.

All this was somewhat reminiscent of my brush with Churchill before 'Crusader'. Once again, London was counting heads instead of effective strength, and failing to take into account the many and various calls on the Command or the extraordinary conditions in which our Middle Eastern strength had to be deployed and exercised. Nor was sufficient allowance made for the dislocation caused by wholesale diversions to the Far East. As far as the R.A.F. was concerned, ideas of our superior strength in the Desert were quite false. On 4 March, Drummond told Portal of the factors which governed our operations there. Our operational strength in fighters had been drastically reduced, and in fact the greatly superior Me. 109Fs were now appearing in considerable numbers. Our forward aerodromes, lacking good anti-aircraft defences, had been bombed and shot up with impunity by the 109s with heavy losses to ourselves. We could only reply by night bombing raids. Furthermore, our squadrons had been operating at high pressure for several months, and it was essential to bring some back to the Delta for a rest and for re-equipment. Drummond had no doubt that the morale of our crews was still high, but if it were to remain so we must recapture the initiative by a resolute attack on objectives which the enemy was bound to defend. He wrote:

In no other way can we hope to take advantage of our superior

[249]

numbers compared with the Germans and to prevent a dangerous retrogression of morale among our own units.

The Prime Minister was sufficiently impressed with the signals from the Middle East to cable President Roosevelt on 5 March asking whether the United States could not offer Australia and New Zealand a division apiece, as an alternative to recall by those Governments of the divisions now in the Middle East. This would also save extremely heavy demands on shipping. Roosevelt replied in the affirmative. In addition, two more divisions would be ferried from the United Kingdom to the Middle East and India, on the understanding that 'Gymnast'—the proposed landings in North-West Africa—should not be undertaken during this period, and that the troops would be those originally destined for the British Isles.

A further signal from Roosevelt on 10 March suggested the allocation of operational responsibility in the various theatres of war. Britain would assume direct responsibility for the middle area, from Singapore to Libya and the Mediterranean, and all operating matters would be decided by the British with the understanding that as much assistance as possible would be given to India or the Near East by Australia and New Zealand, while the United States continued to help with munitions and vessels. The United States would undertake operational responsibility for the Pacific, and the two Governments would together look after the North and South Atlantic, laying plans for a new Front in Europe.

Churchill replied that the British Government saw much merit in the simplification of Command proposed by Roosevelt. They made proposals to ensure that British–American forces should be properly co-ordinated, and on this basis welcomed the proposal that an American should be Commander-in-Chief of all the Allied forces and of all three Services in the Pacific area.

★

On 10 March I reviewed for Portal the air situation. The last two months or so had been a trying and uneasy time. The despatch of aircraft and spares to the Far East had strained us to the limit, and we should have been completely lost if Dawson and his staff had not already paid good dividends from his repair organisation. For the last five weeks Coningham's fighter force in the forward area had been reduced to four squadrons, and of these, the newly arrived Kittyhawks had suffered from the usual teething troubles. The Army seemed to be quite incapable of providing anti-aircraft defence in any way comparable with that available to the enemy.

There was no doubt that our weakness since the end of January had allowed the enemy to get his tail up. His tip-and-run tactics with the Me. 109s had been a nuisance, and we had lost a number of aircraft shot up on the ground in this way. Coningham was now getting three more fighter squadrons back into the forward area, and was beginning to return to the offensive. Our bomber forces were strengthened by the newly operational Bostons, but now that the enemy had learnt the art of dispersion, worthwhile targets were seldom found.

I felt that the setback in Cyrenaica must seriously affect our plans for the northern front. We had said that it would be unwise to go into Turkey with less than twenty-six squadrons, and such a force seemed for the moment to be beyond our limits. Certainly, in order to send any substantial air force to Turkey we should have to strip Libya to the bare minimum, despite Auchinleck's view that the ground forces we must retain for the defence of Egypt would be only a little smaller than those required for an offensive. Thus, if the Army wished to take the offensive while we were also committed in the north, it would have to do so virtually without air support. I pressed for the urgent despatch of Spitfire Vs, which could meet the Me. 109s on equal terms, and for a flight of Mosquitoes, so that we might provide the Army with an efficient service of strategical reconnaissance.

The fall of Singapore, and the rapid Japanese onrush in the Far East, inclined the authorities at home to think more of reinforcing India than of providing me with Spitfires. Portal told me on 15 March that as India's weakness in aircraft would be critical during the next two months, new demands must be made on the Middle East, even down to individual aircraft and equipment, this being the only source of reinforcements beyond those already *en route*. I was therefore to make an immediate survey of all my resources, bearing in mind the prospect of a new offensive in Cyrenaica and earmarking for India whatever I could spare. If this weakened me dangerously or prejudiced operations in prospect I was to refer home so that the issue could be decided by the Chiefs of Staff. The next day I received from Peirse information about his dire need of a minimum of two fighter and two light bomber squadrons to defend Burma and Calcutta. As there was little likelihood that fresh units could reach India in the near future, reinforcement was urgently needed to keep the few existing units up to strength. I sent twenty more Hurricanes and twenty Blenheims.

At the same time, I wanted Peirse to be aware of the effect of such demands. I reminded him of the fact that since he passed through Cairo on his way to India we had despatched 139 Blenheims, reducing our effective light bomber force for the Mediterranean and the Western Desert to a mere three squadrons. The despatch of three hundred fighters had so undermined our strength that we had lost air superiority and were only just beginning to attempt its recovery. On this I commented:

We must recover it and maintain it, quite irrespective of offensive land operations, in order to secure our essential communications. Malta has become an increasingly heavy commitment. Syria and Iraq have been stripped of operational units. We are still gravely short of mobile technical equipment without which our squadrons will lack the mobility essential to meet the threat to Iraq from the North.

This latest despatch of forces to the East meant that I would have nothing with which to replace the wastage in Hurricane II and Blenheim squadrons for at least three weeks. On 17 March I promised a further twenty Hurricanes and twenty Blenheims to Peirse, and then notified Portal of the basis on which I had made these decisions. Thanks to the efforts of our maintenance staff, who would stop at nothing, our front line squadrons had been built up again, and since there was a lull in the Desert war, I thought that to send forty aircraft to the Far East during the next two weeks involved risks which could and must be accepted. I told the C.A.S. that we were being strained to the limit for the second time. He replied on 19 March:

I much appreciate all the efforts you have made and are making to help India, and fully realise how much your sacrifice adds to your anxieties and to the strain on your units.

Peirse, too, thanked me for the help the Middle East was giving. He assured me that the position in India was most critical. There was virtually nothing to stop the Japanese sea approach to Calcutta and East India. If only they could tide over the next two months they would be in a much better position to meet the threat.

*

It was not only in matters of high strategy that we sometimes found it impossible to agree with the home authorities. On 17 March I received from Air Marshal 'Bomber' Harris a signal which my journal describes as 'three pages of hysterical verbosity'. It began in his characteristic style:

I appeal to you personally on the subject of aircraft crews, in the light of the continued failure of Middle East to return to us any reasonable proportion of the vast numbers of crews we have trained and sent out. The best part of a thousand crews, all trained at immense cost in labour and material in our O.T.Us, have been sent to you in the last twelve months alone. So far as I can trace, approximately 30 crews and a few driblets of individuals only have been returned in spite of repeated appeals and orders. No conceivable organisation can stand this strain, and it is simply impossible for it to continue.

I was informed that officer after officer, returning from the Middle East, spoke not only of over-established crews kicking their heels in units, but of apparently large numbers of individuals who had received operational training and were now misemployed within my Command. The situation had now reached the point, Harris's telegram continued, where it would be impossible for the home authorities to continue sending me aircraft for lack of crews to fly them. Bomber Command was now down to a daily average of operational crews approximating to about half its establishment, and that at this rate would within a few weeks be back to its 1939 strength. Harris asked for my personal and most energetic intervention. He went on to give at considerable length details of the demands on his resources:

> If some of my facts are incorrect, let us not waste time in argument. The bare fact, that of the vast numbers of crews sent out to you practically none return here, speaks for itself.
>
> We either alter this hopeless state of affairs, and at once, or we perish.

I retorted:

> Your information is fantastically incorrect.
>
> Fully appreciate we live on your output and must do all possible to keep goose alive and healthy. Your eggs saved our bacon for November offensive.
>
> Agree no time for argument, but clearly difficult even for A.M.P. [Air Member for Personnel, Air Marshal Sir Phillip Babington] fully to appreciate situation here, and am trying again to clarify.
>
> For months now this has been under constant review, and further comb-out now on, but don't expect white rabbits out of a hat. Remember:
>> A. time and distance,
>> B. delays in transport,
>> C. our own expansion,
>> D. the East has been, and still is, living on us.

The following day, 19 March, I received another appeal from Harris which included the words:

> Forgive me saying, spate of first-hand information here is that previous comb-outs have been conducted with tongue in cheek by bad boys beyond the sand-dunes, and expressing hope that this time you employ trustiest ferrets and biggest stick.

I thought it was time to signal to Portal showing how we had employed the 280 Wellington crews which had reached the Middle East in the previous twelve months. During that period we had lost seventy-seven complete crews through casualties, thirty-four operationally tired crews had been returned home, thirty more had formed a Liberator squadron in the United Kingdom, whilst others were waiting to go to India or had been seconded to British Overseas Airways. Only eighty-two crews had been absorbed into the Middle Eastern Command in the course of a year's expansion of our force to its established strength. The rate at which Wellington crews could be returned home would be the rate at which they were despatched to the Middle East, less the losses *en route*, the diversions to India, operational and other casualties, and the number required to complete the full establishment of nine squadrons.

The Air Ministry replied a day or two later that in their opinion we were employing certain highly trained air crew on tasks which were not really commensurate with their ability, and that we were using, for instance, too many Wellington pilots for operational staff duties. We were also said to be allotting too many such air crew for training with Liberators, particularly since the second Liberator squadron could not start to form in the Middle East until June. It was suggested that 200 Wellington crews in the Middle East should be sufficient for present requirements, and I was asked therefore to return approximately sixty.

I happily agreed that about 200 Wellington crews should meet our requirements and promised to withdraw the surplus and return them to the United Kingdom. That settled the Wellington dispute. But I was able to make certain economies in air crew, and ten Liberator crews were returned to the United Kingdom. Four more crews would shortly follow, which meant that the Middle East would then have despatched enough Liberator crews for two squadrons plus one to two months' wastage. I had also heard from Air Marshal Sholto Douglas that he was sending me 400 fighter pilots during March and April, but he wanted an assurance that these men were really required in my Command, since he had heard 'rumours of Fighter Pilots kicking their heels for months at a time with no aircraft to fly'.

I replied at once, telling him not to listen to gossip. I added that thanks to his help during the past three months we had had at most times a reserve of fighter pilots without which we would have been sunk.

We had to hold a reasonable reserve because of the low output of our Operational Training Units, the uncertainty and length of time taken before pilots arrived in the Middle East, the need for refresher training and conversion to the use of the new aircraft, not to mention sudden unforeseen commitments. I said I would be

[255]

willing to receive the 400 pilots over a period of three months instead of two, or even to forego a few of them in case of necessity. Much more important in the long run was the clear evidence contained in these signals of mischief-making chatter at home. I wrote to Freeman on 25 March:

> To judge by signals I have had from Harris and Douglas it appears that some poison tongues are active at home, and spreading half-baked stories. I appreciate that other Commands, both at home and overseas, have their problems, and have done, and will do, everything I can to help them as they have helped me. Mutual confidence between A.O.C.'s-in-C. is vitally important. There is grave risk that the loose talk now evidently going about at home may sap that confidence. It would be a great service to all concerned if it could be scotched.

*

We were meanwhile engaged on ironing out other misunderstandings at a higher level. The exchanges of telegrams between the Middle Eastern Commanders-in-Chief and the Chiefs of Staff in early March had, as usual, led to no very satisfactory conclusion. Soon we were told that Sir Stafford Cripps, the Lord Privy Seal, would look into the matter on the spot. He arrived on 19 March. I liked the look of him:

> His dress scarcely that of a Cabinet Minister—a dilapidated blue blazer, a pair of rather tired flannel bags, a flannel shirt and flannel tie. He is alive—but not aggressively so—and he reacts quickly and has a quick sense of humour. A good listener. I thought he handled the A. very well. One feels that he is an honest man and an idealist— so refreshing. Apparently not in the least tired, though he admitted to having only $3\frac{1}{2}$ hours sleep in three days.

Cripps was accompanied by Lieutenant-General Nye, Vice-Chief of the Imperial General Staff. The Prime Minister had evidently found it hard, if not impossible, to believe that Auchinleck was working keenly to resume the offensive. To Churchill, Auchinleck's insistence on a delay no doubt indicated a lack of belligerent spirit, whereas it really meant that Auchinleck intended to secure Rommel's final defeat rather than fight another 'Battle-axe' campaign. Nor did London seem to have appreciated fully how apprehensive we were bound to feel about the northern front, and about the Pacific, now that the Germans were resuming the offensive against Russia, and the Japanese were apparently carrying all before them. On the morning of 20 March, Cripps presided over a meeting of the Middle East Defence Committee. Nye, who had brought with him from London a questionnaire consisting of two foolscap pages containing twenty questions, said that everyone agreed on the urgency of resuming the offensive in the Desert. However, the Chiefs of Staff were not quite clear why it might be necessary to postpone the offensive to the dates mentioned in the appreciation they had received.

Auchinleck explained that all three Commanders-in-Chief had constantly to bear in mind the possiblity of developments on the Northern Front later in the summer. While it was now thought that a threat to the Caucasus could not develop before August, an enemy attack through Turkey might come in June or before. Some warning might be expected, but as soon as the threat appeared the bulk of our air forces would have to be transferred from the Western Desert to the north. The Commander-in-Chief explained that in order to hold Cyrenaica we had to get forward as far as the general line Agheila–Marada. Intermediate positions were open to serious objection since their southern flanks were exposed to envelopment. Even the Gazala position, on which we were at present established, was not entirely satisfactory. The only really strong position, apart from Agheila–Marada, was the Egyptian frontier. Operations to secure this Agheila line could not be in the nature of a lightning campaign and might easily take two months. The real question which the Commanders-in-Chief had to face, therefore, was to decide whether in the time available there was a reasonable chance of reaching that line before the threat developed on the northern front. It was obviously a matter on which unduly great risks could not be taken. The battle would be primarily one of armoured forces. If we were to lose our armour in a premature attempt, prepared positions in the rear which depended for effectiveness on the presence of mobile armoured forces would be useless. Auchinleck insisted on having a reasonable superiority in numbers before an offensive began, but especially if we had to take on the enemy on ground of his own choice. For the moment, we had 150 cruiser tanks in good shape and ready for battle. There was also a brigade of 150 infantry tanks, but they were not fast enough to manœuvre against the enemy's medium tanks, and could not therefore be counted for an armoured battle. With this force it was obviously quite out of the question to start the offensive. However, by the middle of May we should have 450 medium tanks, and with these, if the enemy had not succeeded in getting further supplies of tanks, he would probably be prepared to take the risk—but even then it would be a risk.

The Commander-in-Chief expressly asked that this date, 15 May, should be used with the greatest caution. It was not possible to make an accurate forecast, since so many factors were liable to change in the intervening two months, and he particularly wanted it to be understood that he was not committing himself to the middle of May.

Sir Stafford Cripps said that he clearly understood the position. On the other hand, for the purposes of planning, it seemed that an approximate date would be to the general advantage. He asked me whether I had anything to add to Auchinleck's description? I replied that the R.A.F. was just beginning to recover from the effects of three months' intensive operations and of the recent heavy diversions. I explained how thin Coningham's force had been for five weeks, and our consequent loss of air superiority. Now replacements were coming in fairly well, and the arrangements for recovery and repair were working satisfactorily. I thought that if there were no further changes the situation should be reasonably restored in three weeks' time. The essence of the situation was that a defensive policy in the air meant the loss of air superiority and a progressive deterioration of the whole situation.

Cripps then helpfully asked that we should discuss the ways in which the British Government might assist. On our suggestion, he telegraphed to Churchill the same night that the despatch of heavy bombers, which had a sufficiently long range to attack Tripoli, and of medium bombers for the attack on Benghazi, would make a material difference to the Middle Eastern air situation. I was impressed with the way in which Cripps produced an excellent draft signal as the result of careful listening and without taking a single note.

The next morning, 21 March, Cripps left for the East. Egypt looked at its best, fresh, bright, and sparkling, and the Nile like mother-of-pearl. I was sorry to see him go, but glad that Auchinleck had been able to impress on him the real facts of our situation.

Shortly afterwards, I received from Auchinleck a long memorandum in which he described the way in which he proposed to take the offensive. The first stage would be to secure Cyrenaica, and the second to build up our striking forces there and in Malta with a view to taking control of the Central Mediterranean. The last stage would be the occupation of Tripolitania, and, if necessary, of Tunisia.

Perhaps because of his long career in the Indian Army, the Auk was particularly sensitive to the threat from the north. He felt that taking the war as a whole the enemy would have the initiative during the summer of 1942. This factor would influence operations in North Africa in the sense that we should not become so involved in Libya that we could not break off the engagement at short notice. We must aim at being able to pass quickly to the defensive and to consolidate our gains speedily, so that if necessary, forces might be released to meet the enemy elsewhere. Auchinleck's paper showed that he realised clearly that it was more difficult to hold than to capture Cyrenaica. Everything, he wrote, turned on the destruction of the enemy's armoured divisions. He was only too well aware, as were all of us, that the supply situation in Malta was desperate, and was likely to become worse after May. Moreover, Malta's effort was inevitably waning, so that enemy convoys were passing more easily to North Africa. Auchinleck now thought that we needed about 50 per cent. numerical superiority over the German armoured forces, though we could accept equality in numbers with the Italians. Our infantry formations, supported by Valentine tanks, were superior in quality and, for the moment, in quantity, to the enemy's infantry formations. He thought that 1 June was a more likely date for the attack than 15 May.

All these questions were being carefully investigated by General

Nye. The replies to his twenty questions took up twenty printed pages of foolscap, conveyed to London in no less than ten separate telegrams. Some of the questions verged, in my opinion, on the insulting; for instance:

Is it fully appreciated that failure to act quickly may allow the enemy, who is almost certain to be contemplating offensive action, to mass superior forces of both tanks and aircraft, so that our situation becomes relatively worse as time goes on?

And again:

Is it agreed that the air situation is as favourable for us now as it is likely to be, and that it will deteriorate month by month?

General Nye's answers to these questions constituted in effect firm support for our position. He explained to the Chiefs of Staff, in answer to the first question quoted above, that our situation in armour might deteriorate for a time if the enemy succeeded in shipping to Libya enough tanks to bring his armoured formations up to establishment. This might be done by 1 May, and in that case we should not be in a position to match his strength up to that time or indeed before August. If such enemy reinforcements did not arrive, it was calculated that we might have

. . . the necessary superiority about the end of May. It is, therefore, incorrect to say that our situation in armour must in all circumstances become relatively worse as time goes on.

As for the air situation, which Nye had discussed with me, he judged that it was for the moment becoming favourable to us. Our air strength was not likely to be materially improved in the next two or three months, but future relative strengths in the Mediterranean could not possibly be assessed and must depend on developments in Europe, Russia, and the Far East.

Auchinleck was reported as being well aware of every detail of the problem, and Nye telegraphed:

No one could be more determined to expedite readiness of formations for battle.

At the end of the month we heard that the Defence Committee in London had again considered Auchinleck's telegrams and the

reports of Cripps and Nye. They decided to accept the date of
15 May on the understanding that any favourable opportunity for
action which occurred before then would be taken. The Committee, we were told

. . . recorded this decision with reluctance on account of the increasing
danger to Malta, and the probability of the enemy receiving reinforcements at least as fast as you will during the interval. They consider
these are two very great dangers.

In spite of a private telegram from Alanbrooke saying that he
clearly appreciated the position, Auchinleck felt it would be a
mistake to leave on record this supposed expression of the Middle
East Defence Committee's views. We telegraphed accordingly
that the date 15 May had been mentioned under conditions.
There could not be any question of the acceptance of 15 May as a
firm date on which an offensive would be launched whatever the
circumstances might be.

14

Malta convoy–Breconshire–Dobbie v. Lloyd–Visit to Malta with Monckton–'Spirit of Malta'–Malta and Cyrenaica–More convoy talk–Aircraft diversions to India–India and Ceylon or the Middle East?–Where must the war be won?

ON the morning of 20 March a small convoy of merchant-men under Admiral Vian left Alexandria under heavy escort for Malta. A supreme effort to assist this convoy was planned. Action on land, in the air, and at sea was set on foot. One of the ships, the *Clan Campbell,* was sunk only eight miles from Malta. The other three, the *Breconshire,* the *Talabot,* and the *Pampas,* were still afloat, and Lloyd strained every nerve and re-source to help them. Air-sea co-operation did its work successfully and Admiral Cunningham signalled the Royal Navy's gratitude for the prodigious effort put out by the 201 Naval Co-operation Group. Kesselring, of course, flew every available aircraft from Sicily to sink the ships. The *Breconshire* was hit, and because of the high sea then running, could not be towed. She had to be anchored in an inlet, but the *Talabot* and *Pampas* arrived safely in the Grand Harbour at Valetta on the morning of 23 March. More than sixty Ju. 88s, escorted by over a hundred fighters, attacked them. Lloyd started that day with eleven fighters serviceable, and ended it with five. The Germans did not succeed in sinking either of the ships, from which some of our airmen that night unloaded vital spares, including engines. Against Lloyd's advice, the ships were left in mid-stream instead of being brought up alongside one of the many quays. By dawn on the following day, Lloyd had eighteen Hurricanes and Spitfires serviceable to meet the attack which the Axis forces launched with redoubled fury at the two ships in harbour and the three aerodromes. There was little or no bombing that night of 24/25 March. The next day, the *Breconshire* was also attacked but was not sunk. There was little bombing again that night, 25/26 March. Lloyd had urged before the convoy arrived, that regardless of bombing, every soldier, airman, and civilian must unload the ships every minute of every twenty-four hours. On the morning of 26 March, the ships had still not been sunk; nor, unfortunately, had they been unloaded. The *Talabot* and *Pampas* were hit and set on fire that day at about 1 p.m. and the *Breconshire* received like treatment three hours later. The only substantial portion of the cargo which had been unloaded was that taken off by our airmen nearly three days before. We had eight serviceable fighters left.

In his signal to me, Lloyd described the efforts at removing cargo as pathetic:

Too many old and worn-out men, some far too bomb-shy. Civilian stevedores did practically no work. They must be conscripted and worked under guard. Suggest need impartial investigation to wake this place up. People want a leader and someone with energy. Excuses are given for failure to take off cargo but I accept none.

I have listened at a conference concerning it, but what we want is active energy, guts and ruthless sacking of useless commanders and civil servants. Ships must be unloaded at all costs. Regarding convoy, *Breconshire, Pampas, Talabot,* all fast ships could have made mouth harbour in dark, but had to wait for slow ship *Clan Campbell.* In any event, first three should have been sent ahead at speed; escort could then have returned for *Clan Campbell. Clan Campbell* was sunk and mined arrival here, same old mistake—fast and slow in same convoy.

Lloyd also signalled that the tragic results of 26 March showed the need for more and more Spitfires. He had been able to put up six Spitfires and six Hurricanes, and this at great effort. In each sortie our men were outnumbered, and yet in spite of every effort by Me. 109s to prevent interference with enemy bombers, we had taken heavy toll without loss. But there were so many bombers that fighters could not kill or disable them all. The spirit Lloyd described as magnificent:

Battle of last three days has shown that Battle of Britain is nothing compared with it, certainly as regards being outnumbered and in having no reserves whatsoever.

He pleaded that the R.A.F. in Malta could do the job, and do it well, if only they were given the tools. He must have thirty-two more Spitfires and a monthly instalment of sixteen aircraft, and there was no middle course. On the same day, 27 March, the Governor of Malta, General Dobbie, signalled to Portal in similar terms. Meantime, Drummond telegraphed directly to

Portal that the decision to put the March convoy into Malta had been taken, although we had made it clear from the Middle East that Malta's fighter strength could not be increased before April, except in so far as Spitfires could be brought in from the west. We proposed to send Malta twenty Hurricane IICs each month, but the first ten had only been despatched on 27 March, and ten more were following the next day. It would probably be three weeks before we could despatch another twenty. As for the Spitfires, Drummond pointed out that we did not possess any!

Portal replied to General Dobbie telling him what was being done to try to put extra Spitfires into Malta, and pointing out that I was hard pressed to respond to all the calls on my resources. The C.A.S. said he knew I would do everything possible to meet Malta's requirements. This was certainly true, and all that I heard from Lloyd inclined me to the view that an early visit to Malta was essential. He wrote to me to say that he hoped I would pardon the signal he had sent about the sinking of the three ships. Those in the know, he wrote, were so bitter about it all that he was wondering if his signal was sufficiently strong!

I was not altogether surprised to learn that Lloyd's outspoken approach had not been wholly welcome. A day or two later I received from General Dobbie a private letter to the effect that he thought Lloyd should be relieved. Lloyd was described as being 'a difficult person to absorb into a team'. The Governor also referred to the 'lack of the best harmonious atmosphere in our team'. I had the highest admiration for Lloyd's fighting determination, and signalled to Portal that on all my present information, Lloyd was the main driving force and inspiration of the defence of Malta. I suspected that he had been outspoken, rightly in my opinion, regarding questions such as the control of labour and the failure to ensure the rapid unloading of the convoy:

Lloyd feels, and I agree, that this is no time for mincing words. What is needed is more leadership and less talk of harmony.

To General Dobbie I replied that I could not consider replacing Lloyd.

Oliver Lyttelton, to my sorrow, had now been recalled to the Cabinet in London. The British Government were represented for the moment in the Middle East by Sir Walter Monckton, who expressed the wish to visit Malta. He and I arrived there on 12 April. I was given a memorandum by General Dobbie which showed that the minimum monthly requirement of the island was 20,000 tons of supplies, which must be brought by heavy service ships, and which could not be unloaded unless we possessed something approaching complete air supremacy. A really strong force of fighters must be maintained in Malta. Driblet reinforcements were useless. Everything was moving in a vicious circle because of the lack of air supremacy. This lack threw a great strain on the anti-aircraft artillery. The result was that Malta was running out of ammunition. Lack of air superiority had a depressing effect on civilian morale which meant that it was not possible to get civilian labour to turn out in the right numbers to work in target areas, in the extremely dangerous conditions created by Kesselring's scale of attack. It was already known that no convoy was to be run to Malta in April. The supplies in the island might perhaps last until early July.

I learnt that daily rations for the population consisted of one and a half slices of poor bread with jam for breakfast, bully beef with one slice of bread for lunch, and the same with two slices of bread for dinner. Fuel for lighting and cooking was desperately short. The daily requirement of flour was a hundred tons, and only one mill was working, producing a maximum of twenty tons a day. If no further damage was sustained, the mills could probably be repaired in time. The number of ships which could be accommodated was seriously reduced by the lack of lighters, and so many vessels had been sunk in Valetta Harbour that the number of berths available was quite inadequate.

The next afternoon, Monckton and I met the Malta Defence Committee. The Officers Commanding there were in turn invited to give their appreciation. Of these the fullest and most interesting was given by Lloyd, who told us that the enemy had now for some time been operating about 160 fighters from three aerodromes in Sicily and some 250 bombers from three more aerodromes. The attacks had been directed at the three airfields on Malta and forced Lloyd to send away his Wellingtons and Blenheims and had gradually worn down his fighter force.

The small fighter reinforcements he had received had again been worn down, the enemy having little difficulty in sustaining an effort of some seventy fighters in the air. Further fighter reinforcements were expected, and to cover their arrival he must be able to put up an umbrella for forty-eight hours while they were being refitted. Much against his will, he was therefore obliged for the moment to conserve his few remaining fighters and to allow the present enemy air attacks to continue without any appreciable opposition from us. As soon as the reinforcements were fit for battle he proposed to go all out to regain air superiority. His plan was to attack the German fighter aerodromes three times each night and thus force the enemy at least to call off his daylight attacks.

I asked Lloyd under what circumstances he could accept the Wellingtons. He replied that he could only accept them when he was in a position to put up a fighter umbrella. As soon as this stage had been reached he would call for the Wellingtons. I then asked whether Lloyd thought that the enemy knew how many fighters we could put in the air? He replied that he thought the enemy were in some doubt, and probably for this reason had adopted the policy of a limited number of concentrated daylight attacks. The enemy was probably unwilling to spread his fighter effort and risk sudden attack and defeat in detail. It could fairly be said that this was some achievement, for the concentrated attacks caused far less dislocation than had been the case when the island was under warning the whole day.

The General Officer Commanding, General Beak, then described to us the many calls on his available manpower. His three brigades all needed training, and he had to provide some degree of vigilance along eighty miles of coastline. His policy was to give Lloyd approximately 400 men a day to work on each aerodrome. Lloyd expressed his satisfaction at this state of affairs. The Naval Officer Commanding, Vice-Admiral Leatham, said that it appeared that the next convoys would be run simultaneously from east and west. The enemy were bound to spot such convoys and to act accordingly. Unless we had achieved air superiority by that time, he thought we could not expect to get much through. General Beak intervened to say that he hoped the convoy would not be delayed too long, for he had to face the critical situation of his anti-aircraft ammunition.

General Dobbie referred to the need to use every possible means besides ships to replenish supplies. He had represented this to the Chiefs of Staff and asked whether anything was likely to come of such representations. I replied that transport aircraft did not exist. It was possible to send in by air very limited supplies of small but vital items, and this we were doing.

This visit to the beleaguered Malta was for me one of the most inspiriting experiences of the war. Very shortly after Monckton and I arrived, Kesselring's forces began a raid on Takali aerodrome. I watched from the veranda of the officers' mess. Some of the enemy so far forgot their manners as to fire at me as I stood there, but no damage was done, although a keen officer who was trying to take my photograph thought it best to retreat smartly. When, a little later, I reached the airfield at Luqa, I found that the enemy had beaten me to it by a few minutes. The whole place was swarming with British and Maltese, without distinction of rank and occupation, who were filling in the craters with stones. I was thrilled. Lloyd records that I said to him: 'That — is the spirit of Malta.'[1]

During that month, Kesselring's forces dropped more than six thousand tons of bombs on Malta. A week or so after my visit, forty-six Spitfires were flown in. The Germans gave them a warm welcome. Within three days seventeen fighters had been destroyed on the ground and twenty-nine more damaged. This was quite apart from those lost in combat. On 23 April I heard from Dobbie that once more Lloyd had only six serviceable fighters left. In these circumstances, Malta had become virtually useless as a sally point against enemy shipping, though we continued to use it freely as a staging post for aircraft.

The account written by Kesselring after the war shows that he had personally ensured that a certain number of Luftwaffe bomber crews, fighter pilots and air sea rescue crews had been specially trained for their tasks, and that stocks of all the necessary supplies were adequate. He was satisfied that the orders for the offensive

---

[1] Lloyd: *Briefed to Attack*, p. 170.

against Malta were thoroughly understood by the commanders. The essential point of Luftflotte II's orders was to eliminate our fighters by surprise attack, or at least so to reduce them that they could no longer be a serious menace to the bomber raids. Everything possible was to be done to smash aircraft on the ground and to make the runways at least temporarily unserviceable. Kesselring acknowledged that the attack on Malta was made difficult for him by the natural and artificial installations of every type in the rock, on the outskirts of airfields and in the harbour. Against such installations even one-ton bombs had no penetrating effect. The concentration of our anti-aircraft artillery and ships' anti-aircraft guns protecting the harbour made an effective barrage requiring a great deal of courage to penetrate. He also paid to our men the tribute amply merited:

The British fighter units deserve admiring recognition for their bravery, their manœuvrability in action, and especially for their perfectly executed tactics of diving from a great height (10 to 12,000 metres) through the close-flying formations of bombers. The same recognition must be extended to the British unloading organisation. Tankers and ships which arrived were unloaded in an unbelievably short time.

In Malta the Luftwaffe had met a worthy opponent.

Back in Cairo, Monckton and I told Cripps, who was now on his way home, about all that we had heard and seen in Malta. I also signalled privately to Portal that the enemy's object was clearly to neutralise the aerodromes and dockyards of Malta. I described the difficulties of maintenance, the effect of losses and damage to aerodrome equipment, the cratering of runways, the shortage of labour, and ruin of many facilities in the dockyard, the tiny serviceable fighter force, reduced during my visit to four Hurricanes, a Spitfire and a Beaufighter. As agreed with Lloyd, I soon sent eight Wellingtons with a double allocation of crews to operate two or three sorties a night against the enemy's three aerodromes in Sicily.

I told Portal that according to what we had heard in Malta, supplies must be got in by convoy during the next six weeks if the island was to be held. Our naval inferiority was such that an air striking force to support the convoy and escort was necessary. This striking force in turn must have fighter cover at Malta. I considered that the berthing and unloading of the last convoy had been gravely mismanaged, but even if these errors were not repeated the next time it would be far more difficult to unload the convoy because of recent damage to the dockyard.

Monckton and I both felt that General Dobbie was exhausted and should be replaced as Governor forthwith. Lloyd's position I thought outstanding:

His personal bravery and dynamic energy have widespread effect, and more than anyone he is personification of Malta's resistance. To see the morale of R.A.F. personnel is one of the most stimulating experiences I have ever met. Beak impressed me as being a determined leader on excellent terms with Lloyd.

The Governor had urged that both Lloyd and Beak should be relieved at once. The Naval Commander, Admiral Leatham, got on well with the other Services, but did not strike me as having the drive so badly needed, and Monckton and I thought his staff and the staff at the dockyard deplorably weak. Auchinleck had recommended the appointment of Lloyd as Governor and Commander-in-Chief, but I felt obliged to advise against it. Lloyd already had a twenty-four hour job; a new Governor must be concerned with civil administration which would mean that Lloyd, if he became that Governor, would be obliged to leave much of the air operations to subordinates. The air was the key to Malta. All Lloyd's attention was needed for the battle. I did think, too, that he should be relieved as soon as the present battle was over, say, within two months. He had been under terrific strain for nearly a year, and indefinite continuance of it would, I thought, break him. Lloyd himself felt the need for relief within a reasonable time.

At the Middle East Defence Committee's Meeting in Cairo on 22 April we had before us a telegram from the Chiefs of Staff announcing that there would be no convoy from Gibraltar to Malta in May, and another message from the Governor of Malta emphasising the critical nature of the situation. This was followed by another telegram from London giving the Defence Committee's

views on a Malta convoy, which question, of course, was inseparable from that of the offensive in the Western Desert. It seemed
that London still did not realise that the date on which it might
be possible to launch an offensive was dependent on factors
beyond our control and could not therefore be guaranteed. The
Chiefs of Staff were thinking of running the convoy to Malta
from the east, covered by heavy ships and aircraft-carriers, but
it was not clear to us how such ships and carriers could be made
available.

I told Portal of my concern:

I had hoped that we had by now learnt that it is sheer folly to attempt
to operate aircraft carriers within close range of a heavy scale of shore-
based air attack. The lucky escape of the remains of the *Illustrious* took
place when the scale of the attack in the Mediterranean was considerably
less than that now to be expected. Under such conditions an aircraft
carrier in these waters is a commitment and not an asset. I appreciate
the arguments for having battleships as cover against enemy heavy
naval forces in view our shortage of air striking force for this purpose.
Feel however that battleships and convoy should depend for air protection on the very limited long range fighter force available here
rather than risk the almost certain loss of carriers.

Auchinleck thought the tenor of the Chiefs of Staff's proposals was altogether too optimistic. He doubted whether it
would be possible to bring heavy ships and carriers from the
Indian Ocean, or to achieve the necessary air superiority over
Malta for the running in and unloading of the convoys. I was
not so sure about that, and said I thought that because of the
Russian situation or by developments in Libya there were fair
grounds for the suggestion that the Germans might in the next
few weeks have to withdraw some of their air forces from Sicily.
We agreed to telegraph to the Governor of Malta stressing the
need for assessing and controlling all stocks of food, and of
putting the garrison and population on the lowest possible scale
of rations. With this cold comfort Malta had to be content for
the moment.

★

The events of April soon confirmed what we had told Cripps and
Nye, that our air strength in the Middle East was unlikely to

increase substantially for eight or twelve weeks. It was clear that we depended heavily on American aircraft, but the rate of delivery often proved to be disappointing. Early in April, I was advised that only thirty-one Kittyhawk aircraft were at sea, destined for the Middle East, including twelve from the February shipment. I asked that something be done to accelerate the rate of shipment at once, otherwise my position in May and June would be most critical.

The very next day we received from the Chiefs of Staff a telegram saying that Japanese heavy ships and aircraft-carriers were producing a situation in which the security of Ceylon was gravely menaced. If Ceylon were occupied by Japanese, the effect on India's line of communication with Britain and with Abadan would be incalculable and might be disastrous. The first need in Ceylon was an air striking force capable of damaging the aircraft-carriers which alone could give air cover to an attempted invasion. The second requirement was for fighter cover strong enough to enable the Eastern Fleet to use Colombo. Only the Middle East could meet these requirements without dangerous delay. I was therefore asked to transfer to Ceylon thirty Hurricane IIs, twenty Blenheim IVs and a Beaufort torpedo bomber squadron. Every effort would be made to compensate me for these withdrawals. The Chiefs of Staff deplored the necessity which compelled them to weaken my forces at this time, but felt certain that Ceylon's dire need would be realised.

I signalled at once to Peirse that most of these aircraft would leave for India within four days, and the rest within ten days. This was on condition that some of the pilots from his Command would help in the ferrying. The Middle Eastern Commanders-in-Chief telegraphed home to say that the loss of thirty Hurricanes would mean a further serious reduction in the aircraft available to replace wastage and so sustain the air effort for the offensive in the Western Desert. This deficiency would be the more serious owing to the gap in the flow of Kittyhawks. The departure of the twenty Blenheims would have a similar effect on our ability to sustain intensive operations, while the loss of the Beaufort squadron meant that we could not increase our air striking force and so cause some further interruption in the enemy's supply lines to Libya. We thought therefore that the diversions, while unlikely to affect the date by which we might resume the offensive, would very seriously affect our ability to sustain the air effort once battle was joined, and might make it somewhat easier for the enemy to build up his strength in Libya:

We must emphasise that our maintenance of air superiority during Crusader was only made possible by our possession at that time of adequate reserves of aircraft and air crews. As a measure of compensation for the heavy diversions which have been made from this theatre we would press most strongly our request for earliest possible despatch of heavy bombers from either U.K. or U.S.A.

Although the Kittyhawk situation gave promise of improvement with an assurance from the Air Ministry that a further eighty aircraft would be shipped during April, we were now rapidly approaching the crucial question of relative priorities. Sir Stafford Cripps presided over two more meetings of the Defence Committee on 14 and 15 April, when he was passing through Cairo on his way back to London. On the first occasion we discussed changes in the situation since his visit in the previous month. Auchinleck said that in the Desert things remained much the same, with both sides busy building up their armour. Two new factors had, however, emerged; further diversions of aircraft to Ceylon and the fact that the Admiralty were now considering whether they should withdraw one flotilla of submarines from Malta to Alexandria. Neither of these factors improved the prospect of an offensive. He thought the Chiefs of Staff must make up their minds very soon whether they were going to throw everything into stabilising the situation in Burma, India, and Ceylon at the expense of the Middle East, or whether they really meant to pursue the idea of an offensive in the Desert. It looked as if they could not have both.

Cripps said how grave the situation in the Indian Ocean was, to which Auchinleck replied, and I agreed, that if the situation there really was that serious, the sooner we in the Middle East were told the better. If a serious threat developed against the line of sea communications around the Cape, any idea of an offensive in the Desert must certainly be given up.

Winston, 9 August
1942

Smuts

In the Embassy Gardens, Cairo, on 4 August 1942. Left to right, Mr. Churchill, Wavell, Harwood, Alan Brooke and myself, with Peirse standing behind the P.M.

With Mrs. Smuts ('Ouma') and, in the background, Smuts, in Cairo, August 1941

The next day we discussed the whole war situation and the broad strategic policy we should follow in the coming months, while the Americans and ourselves were still developing our strength. Our general feeling in the Committee was that we were not taking a long enough view. For instance, given the progress made by the Japanese and our own recent heavy losses and still attenuated forces, was it strategically sound that we should still attempt to plug holes everywhere? Were we right in risking our available armour in an offensive in the Western Desert? Were we right to risk our few ships in an attempt to get a convoy into Malta? Were we right to try and pass in fighter reinforcements to Malta in order to bolster up its defences, perhaps only for a short time? Should we not rather take a broader view and decide once and for all, in the light of available resources, what we must hold and, however unpleasant it might be, face up to the prospect of abandoning the rest? Such decisions would have to be agreed in Washington and London on the highest level. Cripps said he was convinced that some such facing up to the facts was urgently required, and he hoped to tackle the problem with Churchill immediately on his arrival in London. He went so far as to ask whether one of us would be prepared to go home with him and help him fight the case for a more realistic strategic policy. But we took the view that the real need was for one of the Chiefs of Staff, or someone who knew their mind, to come and see the situation overseas.

As further disquietening news of Japanese successes flooded in during the last fortnight in April, I reflected on these broad issues. We were told by the Chiefs of Staff that India itself was in grave danger if the Japanese were prepared to take certain risks, which they seemed to be willing to do. From this it was clear that for the next two or three months it was in India, not in the Middle East, that the real danger threatened, for India was weak in all armed forces. Further help could only come from the Middle East, and if it did so, it could only be given at the expense of offensive action there. But we ought to be clear about the price which would have to be paid. The suspension of the projected offensive in Libya would almost certainly seal the fate of Malta. If we definitely adopted the defensive position in the Desert, the enemy would be able to build up his strength in Libya, especially if Malta fell, and perhaps build up concurrently a striking force against our northern front. Such a policy would also remove all chance of recovering control of the Mediterranean in 1942 to such a degree that we could not pass convoys through from the west.

Nor was it certain that the withdrawal of forces to India would enable us merely to remain on the defensive in the Middle East. Such withdrawal might cause us to lose Egypt. I recognised that the Chiefs of Staff knew far more of the wide strategic picture, especially in relation to the naval situation throughout the world, than we did. It seemed reasonable to assume that since they had not ordered further diversions to India from the Middle East they were satisfied that action being taken by us and the Americans should suffice to avert the immediate threat to the Indian Empire. A further signal, however, as we have already seen, proposed the diversion of three aircraft-carriers and a battleship from the Indian Ocean in order to run a convoy into Malta. This suggested either that the Indian situation was not as grave as we had been told, or that the Chiefs of Staff considered Malta to be as important as India and were, therefore, prepared to risk the latter for the sake of a gamble on Malta. I thought that we should try to obtain from London a clear definition of their view of the relative importance of India and the Middle East. Pending such a review, I gave it as my own opinion that provided we and the Americans did not further fritter away our naval forces in penny packets, I doubted the Japanese ability to develop any serious threat to Western India or the West Indian Ocean for many months. If they could not do it soon, I doubted their ability to do it at all. If a defensive in the Middle East was to be effective, I doubted our ability to send any more forces to India. Indeed, I thought that if we stayed on the defensive and allowed the enemy to build up on the west, and in due course to attack from the north-west and north, we should have adequate forces to defend Egypt and the oil of southern Persia.

To put the matter shortly, I saw no real alternative between resuming the offensive in Libya and abandoning the Middle East. I did not think that the importance of the Libyan theatre could be judged merely by counting heads and making comparisons with the Russian theatre. The German air forces now employed in the Mediterranean, even on a similar basis, constituted a very considerable diversion from the main theatres in Russia and Great Britain, and from the point of view of supply and maintenance they certainly involved a far greater effort by the Axis than corresponding numbers in other theatres. I thought this was far more true of the land forces, which had to be specially trained and equipped for operations in Africa, and to be supplied by a somewhat precarious sea route. The problem was not a simple choice between securing India and relieving Malta, or even between India and the Middle East. The war was going to be won in Europe. The goal was in Berlin. We knew that the failures over England, the Russian and Libyan campaigns, had stretched the Germans very severely. If we withdrew from the Middle East, not only would the enemy be relieved of one of the three theatres at present draining his resources, but his security problems throughout the occupied countries would be enormously eased and the moral effect throughout the world incalculable. It would free Italy, for the moment by far the weakest spot in the Axis. It would certainly affect the situation in the French Colonies, jeopardise our supply route through Africa, and might even jeopardise our position in South Africa itself. As for the future:

There is every reason to think that Germany intends to try and force a decision this year before American power can really be felt. In my opinion it is of critical importance that we keep up the maximum pressure on the Germans throughout this summer. His resources are not unlimited. We know that the last Cyrenaica offensive forced the enemy to divert air forces from Russia. Similar diversions this year would be invaluable. We must keep him stretched, and can only do that by offensives. I realise that the offensive involves considerable risks, but I consider that a defensive policy involves greater risks in that it allows the enemy to build up his forces and employ them when and where he likes. I consider that a policy of withdrawal in the Middle East would serve to provide little for India, and might well jeopardise the whole situation in Europe—where, as I have said, I feel this war must be won.

15

Renewed wrangle with Whitehall–Delay in U.S. supplies–
P.A.A. empire-building again–Smuts's views on Russian
situation–Malta convoys–Smuts: 'the greatest man I ever met'–
The closing of my 'journal'

TOWARDS the end of April 1942 the Chiefs of Staff had
told the Middle East Commanders-in-Chief that India was
in grave danger if the Japanese continued to press westwards. The eventual security of the Middle East and its supply lines
might well be threatened. Auchinleck took the view that if this
were true, an offensive in Libya meant a tremendous risk. All
our efforts should rather be applied to strengthening the defences
in the Middle East, and sparing everything possible in order
to hold India. It must be remembered that the Middle Eastern
Commanders-in-Chief were by no means fully informed of the
Government's conclusions, or of the grounds on which they had
been reached. In my memorandum of 30 April, I had pointed
out that the views of the Chiefs of Staff in certain important
respects seemed, indeed, to be contradictory. I fully agreed with
Auchinleck that the safety of India and the Indian Ocean were
vital to our effort, though I disagreed with him somewhat in
thinking that no conceivable diversion of force from the
Middle East could make the difference between losing and holding
the Indian sub-continent. Nevertheless, I agreed with the action
of the Middle Eastern Defence Committee in telegraphing to
London on 3 May that if the situation in the East was really as
serious as we were led to believe, every resource must be concentrated on the defence of India, so that the Japanese advance
might be arrested before it was too late.

Auchinleck explained to the C.I.G.S. how the success of an
offensive in Libya depended on our being able to collect sufficient
tanks to produce a reasonable superiority over the enemy's
strength, and on our being able to keep sufficient air forces in
the Middle East to give us a reasonable measure of air superiority.
If these two conditions were not fulfilled, he warned that the
launching of an offensive would become an extremely hazardous
operation of war. It was even more hazardous because of the

possibility, which Auchinleck thought almost a probability, of our having to call a halt to the offensive while it was still uncompleted, in order to meet a threat on the northern front. He did not think that we could expect our advance through Cyrenaica to El Agheila to take less than three months.

There now ensued a brisk controversy with London. I think that we were all conscious of the dangers of allowing ourselves to be rushed into the launching of a premature offensive by undue pressure from the Prime Minister and Chiefs of Staff. We could hardly forget the fate of Wavell's 'Battleaxe' offensive of the previous year. On the basis of the latest figures of enemy tank strength, Auchinleck did not see how we could have a sufficient number of cruiser tanks with the trained armoured brigades before 15 June. He would be prepared to accept the risk of launching an offensive on that date.[1] On 6 May, he signalled to London the suggestion that in view of the need for the further training of the armoured brigades, the offensive should be postponed until then. An earlier start would incur the risk of tank losses and only partial success, and might lead to a serious reverse with extremely dangerous consequences. The day before, Churchill had urged on Auchinleck that an offensive should begin in the Western Desert, if possible on 15 May. Here was a clash of views of a familiar kind.

In London it was felt that Auchinleck's signal gave insufficient weight to the fate of Malta. The Prime Minister telegraphed on behalf of the Chiefs of Staff and War Cabinet that the loss of Malta would be a disaster of the first magnitude to the British Empire, and would probably be fatal in the long run to the defence of the Nile Valley:

We are agreed that in spite of the risks you mention you would be right to attack the enemy and fight a major battle, if possible during May, and the sooner the better. We are prepared to take full responsibility for these general directions leaving you the necessary latitude for their execution.

Churchill added that the enemy might himself be intending to attack early in June.[2]

[1] Connell: *Auchinleck,* pp. 489–93.
[2] Connell: *Auchinleck,* p. 495.

The Prime Minister did not go to the length of ordering Auchinleck to take the offensive at the earlier date. Nevertheless, the impression seems to have prevailed in London that Auchinleck was unduly cautious. Alan Brooke noted in his diary that Auchinleck's message, which he disliked, was purely based on the number of tanks available, and not on the strategical situation: 'He never takes into account the danger that Malta is exposed to through his proposed delays. . . .'[1]

The Middle East Commanders-in-Chief, however, refused to accept the Government's view of the Mediterranean situation. We replied on 9 May that the fall of Malta would not necessarily be fatal to the security of Egypt for a very long time, if at all, so long as the supply lines through the Indian Ocean could be maintained:

We feel that to launch an offensive with inadequate armoured forces, may well result in the almost complete destruction of these troops, in view of our experience in the last Cyrenaican Campaign. We cannot hope to hold the defensive positions we have prepared covering Egypt, however strong we may be in infantry, against a serious enemy offensive, unless we can dispose of a reasonably strong armoured force in reserve, which we should not then have. This also was proved last December, and will also be so in terrain such as the Western Desert where the southern flank of any defensive position west of the El Alamein–Qattara Depression must be open to attack and encirclement. . . . We still feel that the risk to Egypt incurred by the piecemeal destruction of our armoured forces which may result from a premature offensive, may be more serious and more immediate than that involved in the possible loss of Malta, serious though this would be.

We agreed that there were signs that the enemy might be preparing to attack our fortified positions at Gazala. This might so weaken his armour that it could be destroyed.

This telegram, which amounted in substance to a reinforcement of Auchinleck's long-held view of the Desert situation, was not well received in London. Churchill replied on 10 May, in the name of the War Cabinet, the Defence Committee and the Chiefs of Staff:

[1] Bryant: *The Turn of the Tide,* p. 381.

We are determined that Malta shall not be allowed to fall without a battle being fought by your whole Army for its retention. The starving-out of this fortress will involve the surrender of over 30,000 men, Army and Air, together with several hundred guns. Its possession would give the enemy a clear and sure bridge to Africa with all the consequences flowing from that. Its loss would sever the air route upon which both you and India must depend for a substantial part of your air reinforcements. Besides this, it would compromise any offensive against Italy, and future plans such as 'Acrobat' and 'Gymnast'[1]. Compared with the certainty of these disasters, we consider the risks you have set out to the safety of Egypt are definitely less, and we accept them. The very latest date which the Defence Committee could approve, would be one which would provide a distraction in time to help the passage of a convoy to Malta in the June dark-period.

The message ended:

This telegram, like that of 8 May, is addressed to you as Military Commander-in-Chief, the Air having been placed under your general direction for the purposes of all major operations.

Auchinleck showed this paragraph to the Minister of State only, and then replied on 12 May that he did not propose to act on it:

My relations with Tedder are excellent as they have always been and his support and co-operation could not be bettered. I do not wish to run any risk of disturbing present good relations between three Services, and your proposal must inevitably react on naval staff as well.[2]

Apart from this disagreement, of which I knew nothing at the time, Auchinleck undertook to carry out a major offensive, timed to help the sailing of the Malta convoy in June. He warned the Prime Minister that on account of the narrowness of our margin on land and in the air, success was by no means certain. In any event, it was not likely to be rapid or spectacular. I was shown, and agreed with, this signal before its despatch. In a later message, Churchill asked whether Auchinleck might not perhaps take command himself. Auchinleck replied that he felt it would

[1] 'Gymnast' was the codename for the operation which eventually became 'Torch', the landings in North-West Africa.
[2] Connell: *Auchinleck*, pp. 497–8.

be most difficult for him to keep a right sense of proportion if he became immersed in tactical problems in Libya. It was understood that the offensive would be not merely a distraction to help the convoy, but would be designed to destroy the enemy's forces in Cyrenaica, and ultimately to expel Rommel from Libya. There were by now strong signs of an impending enemy attack. But if Rommel did not move, Ritchie would do so at the agreed moment.

*

Meanwhile I was doing everything possible to build up our air strength in the Desert, a task rendered no easier by our dependence upon American supplies and the apparent inability of the Americans to deliver anything like the promised quantity of goods anywhere near the promised time. The early months of 1942 had brought so many delays and postponements in the despatch of Kittyhawks that I had long since ceased to be surprised or annoyed at receiving news of further interruptions. While the ground fighting in the Desert was only fitful, our wastage in aircraft and crews was limited, and we could manage with the aid of Dawson's admirable repair and salvage organisation. Once battle was joined, however, we must expect a very different wastage rate. Early in May I heard of a further substantial delay in the flow of Kittyhawks to Takoradi. I urged most strongly to Washington that the largest possible number should be despatched rapidly to Takoradi and as many more as possible to Port Sudan. The anticipated deliveries were by now so far behind schedule that I was faced with the task of cannibalizing a Kittyhawk and a Hurricane squadron. In certain respects we were weaker than before 'Crusader'. For instance, the neutralisation of Malta had weakened our striking power against enemy seaborne supplies. My striking force of day bombers was considerably less than it had been in the previous year and my reserve of operational aircraft available behind the first line was less than it had been for 'Crusader' and might, in the event of a prolonged battle, lead to a reduced effort. So far as we could judge, we should have available on the day of the projected offensive, 15 June, forty-nine squadrons, numbering 806 aircraft. Against this the Germans and

Italians would have about 1,200 aircraft. I emphasised to Portal that I thought these figures to be of very limited value for the assessment of relative strengths in the Western Desert at any particular time. For this reason I had always discouraged any arguments on the basis of counting heads. The vital factors were not reducible to figures:

Leadership, training, serviceability, reserves of aircraft and of air crews, relative performances of aircraft, relative location of units, possibility of reinforcement or withdrawal, these are some of the main factors on which I have based my opinion. . . . I do not consider we have any margin to allow for the diversion of units to another front unless the enemy makes corresponding diversions. Nevertheless, taking all the factors into account I consider my forces should be sufficient to provide adequate support for a land offensive.

With Malta hanging on by a thread and the Central Mediterranean almost barred to us, extra importance attached to the alternative routes of supply. Of these, the most important was the route from Takoradi. We were by now beginning to reap the fruits of the mistaken policy which had allowed Pan American Airways to establish themselves by the distribution of promises which they proved unable to fulfil. On 8 May I heard from Sir Arthur Street that Balfour, who was then visiting West Africa as Under-Secretary of State, had reported serious congestion of passengers and freight awaiting forward air transport to the Middle East. Sir Arthur proposed one or two minor palliatives. More substantially, he suggested that my recent proposals for a number of new B.O.A.C. services to Aden, Addis Ababa, Jedda, Teheran, and Karachi, should be shelved so that the service from Takoradi to Cairo might have prior claim on the available equipment. The Air Ministry was suggesting that the whole question of the accumulation in West Africa should be referred to a committee sitting in Washington. Sir Arthur remarked that we were already making large demands on the United States authority for transport aircraft, and it was doubtful if they would be able to spare many for operation on the trans-African route. Anything I could do from Middle Eastern resources to keep traffic moving would be of great assistance.

[281]

I replied that Balfour's alarm was not shared by me. I feared that it was based on incomplete knowledge. Had he been in West Africa in mid-April he would have found no accumulation, and the Pan American services not loaded to capacity. The congestion in early May was the most severe on record, and was the result of shipping to West Africa personnel and freight in excess of the known capacity of the services to carry them forward to the Middle East. I recognised that the difficulties of shipping might make spasmodic large shipments unavoidable. I told Sir Arthur that he would no doubt realise that it was not easy to restart B.O.A.C. services on this route since we had practically forced them off when Pan American took over. As for his detailed suggestions:

Really must ask you have some faith in my judgment. We here have got knowledge of day -to-day conditions, requirements and capacities as regards, not only the Middle East, but also as regards India and the Americans, which Air Ministry cannot have. Recognise that Air Ministry is omnipotent, but it is not, and cannot be, omniscient.

I pointed out that the United States Ferry Command had started off with the idea that they could run everything from Washington, but were rapidly learning as a result of bitter experience that any such attempt was hopeless. What was needed was the co-ordinating board for which I had asked in August 1941. The Minister of State was now, at last, forming such a board. It would, meanwhile, be most undesirable that Balfour should raise the whole question of accumulation in West Africa with Washington. Balfour replied that he would certainly hold his hand in this matter. He realised that I had to carry the responsibility, and his only wish was to help.

Since Pan American Airways proved incapable of clearing the accumulation of passengers and freight rapidly, I put B.O.A.C. back on to this route, at first with two services a week, then with three, then with four. With the entry of the United States into the war, American commitments had far exceeded those foreseen in 1941 and had caused a heavy drain on the supply of transport machines. Nevertheless the situation was more than a little ludicrous. The route across Africa had been pioneered by the

R.A.F. and operated by B.O.A.C. on regular schedules since 1936. Almost all the existing facilities used by the Americans had been installed by B.O.A.C. or the British Government.

I knew from the new Minister of State in the Middle East, Richard Casey, that this whole question had been under discussion in London and that the Treasury were aware of the gross attempts of P.A.A. to reap benefits from the war situation. Casey cabled to London on 12 June that this judgment was only too well borne out by the activities of P.A.A's representatives in the Middle East. He reinforced the enquiry I had already made at the Air Ministry as to whether P.A.A., as such, had any real right to operate in Africa and the Middle East, or whether it was only P.A.A's subsidiary companies which had this right. P.A.A., using the name P.A.A. Africa Limited, had by early June, without authorisation and without consulting any of the authorities in Cairo, instituted a weekly scheduled air service between Cairo and Teheran, via Baghdad and Basra, on the pretext of returning United States ferry crews from Teheran to Abadan and Basra. P.A.A. Africa Limited were also attempting to engage in direct negotiations with the Iraqi Government for the erection of their own wireless station and other facilities at Baghdad and Basra.

Casey drew the conclusion from this and other reports that Pan American Airways as such were attempting to leave no stone unturned in infiltrating to the maximum extent, legally or illegally. This process he thought would continue until Washington were able to put a damper on the company by militarisation of its subsidiaries or even of P.A.A. itself. He asked whether we were simply to swallow such behaviour and say nothing about it, or whether we were to make active efforts to try to prevent this kind of activity. Eventually the Air Ministry replied, to the effect that our policy was to resist P.A.A's efforts to infiltrate into Africa and the Middle East.

*

Now that the differences of view between the War Cabinet and the Middle East Defence Committee had been, for the moment, settled, we were able to proceed along the lines of an agreed strategy. Whether it was Rommel or Ritchie who attacked first, the trial of strength could not be long delayed. When the Middle East Defence Committee met on 19 May to review the whole situation, we were joined by Field-Marshal Smuts and Major-General Davidson, Director of Military Intelligence at the War Office. Everyone recognised how much turned on the Russians' ability to meet the German offensive. The Intelligence Services in London and Cairo had agreed that the major enemy offensive in 1942 would probably be directed against the Russians in the south-east. During the previous winter, only the weather had defeated the German attempt to reach Moscow. No one could yet tell how far the Russians would be able to meet the renewed attack. Despite the Russian counter-offensive, the Germans had clung on to all the main strategic key points, and it appeared that they had managed to extricate some nine armoured divisons which were being re-equipped and rested for the coming campaign. The best estimate we could get was that the Germans would probably be able to muster a total force of at least thirty divisions, to be ready about the end of May. Meanwhile the Russians refused to give us any worthwhile information, and we had no idea what reserves they had built up or what their plans might be. At least it seemed clear that they would not be taken again by surprise, and it was a fact that during the winter they had succeeded in maintaining air superiority, although it seemed unlikely that they would be able to prevent the Germans from gaining at least an initial success.

Field-Marshal Smuts asked where, if the Germans did gain this initial success, the Russians would be likely to try and stop them. If the thrust were towards the Caucasus, would the Russian Army retire in that direction, or would they draw off towards the Volga? Davidson replied that we were completely ignorant of the Russian intentions in this respect. It was likely that the main Russian Army would withdraw to the north. Smuts commented that the situation looked somewhat gloomy for the Middle East and Africa if the Russians did leave their troops in the Caucasus area to fight it out. He wanted to know how long it would be before the threat could develop against our northern front. Davidson said that this depended on the unkown degree of resistance which the Russians might put up, and that once the

Germans were across the Don, they might reach the Caucasus Mountains in about eight weeks. It was unlikely, however, that any threat could develop on our northern front before the autumn.

In the Far East, he thought the Japanese strategic policy had three objects; to settle the 'China incident', to consolidate in the Pacific, and to remove the Soviet menace from the north. She might, of course, undertake the invasion of India, and it was estimated that she had sufficient shipping for ten to fifteen divisions. In London it was felt that the invasion of India would be an immense undertaking which Japan was unlikely to attempt and it would pay her better to make India a British commitment than to mount the invasion herself. The recent operations in the Coral Sea seemed to indicate that Japan wanted to cut the direct lines of communication in the Pacific between America and Australia. Smuts at once questioned this estimate. He thought it quite possible the Japanese would push on to the vital areas of India.

As for Germany, Davidson said that while the German people were no doubt disillusioned, their discipline and patriotism would carry them through at least to the stage when they realised that military victory was out of the question, and until then we could not look for a break in their morale.

Smuts then summed up this part of the discussion in his habitual masterly fashion. He thought the situation described by Davidson a gloomy one, seeing the possibility of a Russian defeat and the threat developing against the Middle East's northern front, and on the other hand the Japanese knocking at the door of India. Everything would depend, Smuts said, for Africa and the Middle East, on our ability to hold Ceylon and bring the Japanese Fleet to action. It seemed deplorable to him that we could find no way of concentrating the available British and American naval strength instead of dispersing it in the Pacific and Indian Oceans.

We discussed Malta. The new Governor, Lord Gort, who had replaced Dobbie when the latter had been removed in early May on the recommendation of Monckton and myself, had asked for more fighters. Sixteen had already been flown in and the Chiefs of Staff proposed to send a further thirty-two in June.

The Royal Navy had been told to prepare a plan for a convoy from the east, based on the assumption that certain naval reinforcements would be needed to give the convoy a reasonable chance of success. The most critical stage of its passage would be between Cyrenaica and Crete, a region known to us as 'Bomb Alley', and no amount of air reinforcement which the Chiefs-of-Staff could hope to send out would be enough to neutralise the scale of attack which the enemy could, and in my view certainly would, develop against so large a convoy. It was not clear from the information the Government had sent us whether it was intended that a proposed convoy into Malta from the west should be an alternative to, or simultaneous with, a convoy from the east. I thought that a convoy from the east alone was not a practicable operation of war, and we all felt that an operation from both ends of the Mediterranean would at best be a desperate venture.

The running of a convoy from the east, and the Western Desert situation, were inseparable operations. In Smuts's presence, Auchinleck told us that according to his latest information it seemed highly probable that the enemy was about to launch an offensive. We could not yet assess the effect which this might have on the convoy, but he agreed with me that if the enemy succeeded in preventing or restricting our use of the landing grounds and facilities to the west of Sollum, the ability of our air forces to protect the convoy through 'Bomb Alley' would be drastically limited.

I was deeply impressed by the speed and thoroughness with which Smuts's agile, comprehending mind grasped the essentials of the situation, and by his capacity to get to the root of the matter by short, well-directed questions. He was always kindness itself to me, and I thought him then, and still think him, incomparably the greatest man I have ever met, possessing Churchill's versatility and vision without his vices. To those whom he deemed to have failed in their work or their duty, he could be ruthless and hard. A steely glint would come into his eyes as he probed each problem to the bottom. But generally he wore an aspect of wisdom and understanding. My wife, who had now joined me in Cairo, said after this meeting with Smuts: 'There is something Christ-like about that man.'

[286]

Smuts was one of the very few to whom Churchill would listen, and was for that reason of the greatest value to us in the Middle East. Once I said to him, when he passed through Cairo on his way to London: 'Do stay as long as you can. When you are there we get fewer tiresome telegrams from the old man. Stay and hold his hand for a while since you are such a friend of his and he will listen to you.'

Smuts replied with a twinkle: 'There is an empty seat waiting for me at the Cape, and if I don't get back there soon I shall find someone else sitting in it and that would never do.'

*

I would like to include a personal note here, to say that my 'journal' came to an end with my wife's arrival in Egypt. She at once set about finding out the welfare needs of the airmen and how they could be met, and it was on returning from a visit to an R.A.F. hospital and welfare centres in Cyrenaica that her aircraft crashed near Heliopolis and she was killed.

16

Rommel attacks, 26 May–'Cauldron' and 'Knightsbridge'–Sidi Rezegh, a battle lost–Coningham's mastery–Malta blitz eases Rommel's supply–Kesselring and Rommel differ over priorities–The Malta convoys run–Collapse of Tobruk–The Auk takes command–Round-the-clock bombing and round-the-clock salvage–Freyburg's testimony–Axis Command's views–'. . . the friend that endureth. . .'–Priorities again–Plain speaking to the Generals–Weak Army team–My opinion of the Auk

THE information Auchinleck had given us about Rommel's intentions soon proved to be correct. Before 15 June, about which date we had argued so much, arrived, the battle was joined. Rommel opened his assault on our prepared lines, which extended from Gazala to Bir Hacheim. The attack began on the night of 26/27 May with the initial object, no doubt, of turning our left flank and seizing Tobruk. The first tank battles caused both sides heavy casualties. For a time, enemy shortages of ammunition and fuel gave the Eighth Army an opportunity to retake the initiative. Our night bombers hammered the enemy's forward aerodromes and communications, but when our counter-attack went forward on 5 June, in the area to the south-east of Gazala known as 'the Cauldron', it was too late, for Rommel had been able to consolidate his supply columns through the gaps torn in the minefields by the earlier battles. Our losses in armour, as a result, were most severe, especially on 12 and 13 June which saw the decisive defeat of the British armoured units in the area known as 'Knightsbridge' to the north of the Cauldron. I think that if Auchinleck had fully realised in time what had happened, he would himself have taken over from Ritchie. Rommel, in a pregnant sentence, wrote of the Guards Brigade which had fought its heart out at Knightsbridge: 'This Brigade was almost a living embodiment of the virtues and faults of the British soldier—tremendous courage and tenacity combined with a rigid lack of mobility.'[1]

[1] Liddell Hart: *The Rommel Papers*, p. 222.

It was now a question whether our Army should retire on the Egyptian frontier or attempt to hold a line including Tobruk.

On 15 June Auchinleck assured the Prime Minister that he had ordered that Rommel was not to be allowed to establish himself east of the line Acroma–El Adem–El Gubi. There was no intention of giving up Tobruk. This the Cabinet and the Prime Minister interpreted to mean that if the need arose Ritchie would leave as many troops in Tobruk as were necessary to hold the place for certain. Lieutenant-General T. W. Corbett, Chief of Staff, Cairo, bearing Auchinleck's instructions to the Desert, found Ritchie unwilling, or unable, to carry them out. The Commander-in-Chief assured Churchill on 16 June that Ritchie was putting into Tobruk what he considered an adequate force to hold the fortress even if it were temporarily isolated by the enemy. The basis of the garrison was four brigade groups; the Eighth Army would hold the El Adem fortified area as a pivot of manœuvre, and use all available mobile forces to prevent the enemy from establishing himself east of El Adem or Tobruk. Auchinleck's telegram was sent after a meeting of the Middle East Defence Committee. It continued:

> Position is quite different from last year as *we* and *not* enemy now hold fortified positions on Frontier and can operate fighter aircraft over Tobruk even if use of Gambut landing grounds should be temporarily denied to us. It seems to me that to invest Tobruk *and* to mask our forces in the frontier positions, the enemy would need more troops than our information shows him to have. This being so we should be able to prevent area between the Frontier and Tobruk passing under enemy control.[1]

It was clear to me that Auchinleck appreciated the vital importance to everyone of the Gambut area and had no intention of letting the enemy obtain the use of it. My liaison officer, who flew from Gambut to Cairo on the afternoon of 16 June, confirmed all I had heard and seen of the intense activity and enthusiasm on the part of our squadrons. In the battle around Sidi Rezegh, which was now raging, escorted Boston sorties were going over each hour,

---

[1] Connell: *Auchinleck*, p. 578.

and the Kittyhawks were in action almost continuously. Since organisations in the forward area had been reduced to the barest minimum, it was hard to get accurate information promptly, for everyone was wholly preoccupied with the servicing and arming of aircraft, and with hitting the enemy. Coningham had signalled to me that morning:

Have thinned out all units, the guiding principle being that all wings must be able to work full pressure. We are all at one hour's notice to move, and owing to proved value of force. Army has given one brigade for close defence which helps my judgment of night security. I have prepared landing grounds all the way back to the frontier and plan is steady withdrawal of squadrons keeping about 20 miles away from enemy. See our own bombs bursting is rough deadline. As units move the R.S.U. [Rear Servicing Unit] Squadrons are fearful of being taken too far from enemy as they like present form of warfare. Squadron commanders explain situation to voluntary parade of men daily and point of honour that there are no flaps and nothing left for enemy. Am content that whole machinery working very smoothly. Work of both bombers and fighters has been brilliant. The work, keenness of atmosphere of the Air Force here would, I am sure, give you the greatest satisfaction.

The air activity in the Desert was, indeed, intense. On 17 June our squadrons hung on until the very last minute at Gambut, putting the maximum effort against the enemy in the battle of Sidi Rezegh in the face of vigorous defence by Me. 109s. Two of our best fighter squadron commanders were lost. The scale of the enemy's fighter effort indicated to Coningham that they were operating from Gazala, which was proved by reconnaissance to be the fact. A low-flying fighter-bomber attack by about thirty Kittyhawks was at once mounted, and proved successful. The 109s gave no further bother. Only when it was beyond doubt that the Sidi Rezegh battle had gone against us did the squadrons leave Gambut. Enemy tanks were on the airfields at Gambut within the hour. So far as I could discover we lost no aircraft on the ground, nor any transport. In view of the serious land situation the squadrons moved to Baheira, and then, on the morning of 18 June, to landing grounds south of Sidi Barrani. Coningham's intention was to use Sidi Azzeiz as a refuelling landing ground only. I thought he was right to do this, since we could not afford to lose one single damaged aircraft. As for the effect of air-power during the retreat, I told Portal:

Enemy's air effort against our retiring forces has been practically nil, his sole pre-occupation being fighter protection of his forward troops and L.Gs [landing grounds]. I hope his experience at Gazala will encourage him to adhere to this policy until our land forces are reorganised.

These operations were carried on simultaneously with the attempted running of the convoys into Malta with a consequent air cover commitment. All the same, our aircraft managed to protect the troops retreating from Gazala so successfully that the land forces suffered only six casualties from air attacks. Yet for nearly three days one road was packed solid with traffic and there was an enemy fighter base only forty miles away. At the same time, our fighters were carrying on the battle around El Adem. The whole fighter force waited at advance aerodromes continuously attacking the enemy's tanks and other vehicles until Rommel's rolling line came within twelve miles of the landing ground. The fighter wings then gradually withdrew, keeping approximately that distance from the advancing enemy. The advanced fighter squadrons were among the last to retire within the Egyptian Frontier. At no time during this battle in the Western Desert had we enjoyed numerical superiority. The fact that we established ascendancy over the enemy's forces in the battle area was due entirely to the fine fighting spirit of our pilots, and the magnificent work of the maintenance crews and personnel of the repair and salvage units. Between 26 May and 17 June, twelve squadrons of fighters maintained an average serviceability of ten to twelve aircraft, and made between them 4,882 sorties. Two squadrons of light bombers with an average serviceability of fifteen aircraft did 404 sorties. The medium bombers did 446 night sorties.

Even so, telegrams from home showed that there were still some who scarcely appreciated what air-power had achieved. On 20 June, Auchinleck took it upon himself to signal personally to the Prime Minister about his alarm at reports from London of a Press campaign attributing the reverses in Libya to the failure of the R.A.F. to provide adequate support for the Army:

So far as Army is concerned NOTHING could be further from the truth. So far as my knowledge goes, air support throughout has been continuous and most effective, great damage having been caused to enemy. This lying campaign, if allowed to continue, can NOT fail to prejudice efficiency of both Army and Air Force at this very critical juncture. We are NOT strong enough to fight our own people as well as the enemy, and I beg your personal intervention to put matters right.

There was now a total of fifty-one operational squadrons in the Middle East, forty-two of which were in the Western Desert and Egypt and four and a half in Malta. Our reserves of aircraft had been so far consumed, and so many promises of further deliveries unfulfilled, that I had enough trained personnel to form a further eighteen and a half squadrons. For the moment, I was not in a position even to meet current wastage, for the reserves of aircraft had been used up and the prospects of replacement of single-engined fighters were appreciably below the rate at which they were being lost in the Desert. If this continued, fighter strength must progressively decline. So far as could be foreseen, the situation would not improve before the end of July. Unfortunately, Rommel was not likely to wait upon our convenience in this matter. Indeed, his triumphant forces were already on the borders of Egypt.

*

While the Desert battle raged, serious events were taking place in the Mediterranean. The onslaught on Malta in the spring had certainly improved Rommel's supply position. In April and May the enemy moved more freely in the Central Mediterranean than at any time in the war. We were no longer in a position to bomb airfields in Sicily, nor had we aircraft with sufficient range to shadow enemy convoys long enough to direct submarines accurately to them. Kesselring wrote that by 10 May he considered it would have been a simple task to capture Malta after the bombing raids. That this was not attempted was the fault of the German and Italian High Commands, which were later to pay for this omission. Subsequently, most of the German air forces were withdrawn from the Mediterranean theatre for use in the east. Kesselring felt that Malta was too well protected by underground installations to be kept down indefinitely with such weak forces, and that once refreshed and ready to do battle Malta would be bound to endanger the supply route to Africa as it had done in the summer and autumn of 1941. It was this reasoning which had decided him quite early to try to win over his superiors to the idea of capturing the island. Permission was apparently obtained in February 1942. The German and Italian air forces enjoyed air supremacy until July, and the attack was scheduled for the beginning of that month. Kesselring wrote:

> What with the resurgence of British sea and air activity against Axis convoys and the restrengthening of Malta, particularly since the attack had to be abandoned, coupled with the ever-increasing demands on the Luftwaffe, German supremacy in the Mediterranean was gradually crumbling away.

At first, Rommel supported the plan for an attack on Malta, but in the end proposed instead to launch an offensive in Africa beforehand. Kesselring thought this a mistake, believing that a tactical success could only be exploited and sustained if the supply services were functioning faultlessly. He claimed that in his reports to Hitler he never left any doubt that North Africa could only be held for any length of time if the Axis possessed Malta, and that the misgivings of Göring, who feared high casualties as in the Crete operations, were not plausible, since the conditions on Crete were different in every respect from those on Malta. Luckily for us, however, other events distracted the attention of the German High Command.

Officially, Gort had been appointed as 'Supreme Commander of the Fighting Services and of the Civil Administration' in Malta. This designation gave rise to a good deal of correspondence by telegram, but to no avail. To the Defence Committee I observed on 19 May that if Gort's instructions were observed literally, the position from my point of view would be quite impossible. However, we had to do our best to make the system work.

I proposed to repeat to the Governor any instructions I had to send to the A.O.C. Malta. On 27 May Air Chief Marshal Ludlow-Hewitt, the Inspector-General, who had just been in Malta, attended the Defence Committee. It appeared from his account that Gort's interpretation of the powers conferred on him by Churchill was reasonable and workable for the moment. Ludlow-Hewitt described the intense concentration of everyone in Malta on the supreme importance of getting the next convoy through. He remarked, for example, that the administration in Malta would resent aircraft being used to attack objectives which did not directly contribute to the safe passage of the convoy, on the grounds that such operations would use up Malta's resources and so affect its security. Later, he thought, when the island had been replenished, the Governor and administration would do everything they could to restore Malta to its position as a base for offensive operations, and would not dispute the right of the Commanders-in-Chief to control such operations.

I said that sooner or later the question of control of strategical operations from Malta would have to be faced. As for the suggestion that air operations would use up the resources available for Malta's defence, I pointed out that the real limiting factor in Malta's ability to hold out was the food supply. The fuel position was much more satisfactory. Ludlow-Hewitt's description of the situation raised an important issue:

> Could I continue to use the bomber effort based on Malta in operations to help the land battle in Cyrenaica which had just begun, or must we now confine air operations to those which would contribute to the safe passage of the convoy in June?

Auchinleck said that it was for the moment too early for him to say how the land battle would develop. Nor could he yet give an opinion on the extent to which it would be desirable for the air forces in Malta to assist.

Richard Casey said that he was greatly impressed with the need for heavy bombers. It seemed to him that they were the only possible deterrent to the Italian Fleet, and he said that he would telegraph further to Churchill on this subject.

We still did not know for certain whether the authorities in

London intended that a convoy should be run to Malta from the east. I suggested that the point be taken up immediately with the Chiefs of Staff in London, for I still thought that the convoy from the east was not a practical operation of war under present conditions. If we waited and were subsequently ordered to attempt the passage of such a convoy, we should be too late to get the essential air reinforcements which had been asked for.

Admiral Sir Henry Harwood[1] felt that the situation might mature favourably in Cyrenaica and so make the passage of the convoy a more practicable proposition. Even then, the risk could be great, particularly from attack by surface forces. I agreed, but suggested that steps be taken to hold up the Liberators destined for India and use them for operations to assist the convoy. At my request, we signalled to Churchill in this sense.

It did not take long for us to realise that whatever else might be said about the operations in Cyrenaica, they were certainly not going to assist us in passing a convoy to Malta. At the same time, it was felt in London that there was no choice but to make the attempt. From the beginning of June, preparations went forward for the passage of two convoys to Malta, Operation 'Vigorous' from the east and Operation 'Harpoon' from the west. Admiral Harwood showed himself fully seized of the crucial role which air-power must play in this operation. In agreement with him, I instructed Lloyd at Malta that he must at once find the Italian Fleet and strike at it with his Wellington bomber force for two or three nights before the Wellington bombers had to be withdrawn to make room for Wellington torpedo bombers. I hoped to supplement Malta's effort with some Liberators. If the Italian Fleet were discovered in Taranto, it might be possible to carry out one attack by daylight, just after sunset, with the Liberators. They might also be used to attack the Fleet in the Mediterranean Central Basin by day. Farther east, the bulk of the Wellington force in the Western Desert was being switched to use against the aerodromes on Crete, up to the night on which

---

[1] He had recently been appointed Naval Commander-in-Chief, Mediterranean, in place of Sir Andrew Cunningham, who had gone to Washington as the head of the British Naval delegation. Cunningham returned to the Mediterranean shortly before 'Torch'.

the convoy was to sail. The need for this operation to take place in the dark period handicapped the supporting air operations, and I hoped that some Albacores would be available to help the Wellingtons in Cyrenaica.

'Vigorous' was controlled from 201 Group operations room with the combined staff. Harwood and I were there throughout from the 13th, except for a few hours when I returned to Cairo to consult with Auchinleck about the Desert retreat. The main events of Operations 'Vigorous' and 'Harpoon' were unfortunately rather what we had anticipated. One of the principal difficulties during and after the operation was to obtain enough detailed information to form firm conclusions. When I made my report to Portal on 16 June, we had had practically no information from the commanders of the naval forces, and there was, I thought, no doubt not only that air action had been handicapped by the complete lack of information from our own ships, but that Harwood himself had been gravely handicapped and blindfolded:

> Our fighters were completely ignorant of the position or movement of the convoy once it departed from original programme, and no one had any information as to nature or scale of enemy attacks. I hope we may be able to get some improvement in this respect in future but the tradition of silence dies hard.

The air plan which had been worked out in advance and agreed with the naval staff proved to be sound. The searches and the plan for striking fitted the actual events with almost mathematical precision. The Italian naval forces were located and identified in harbour and their movements out of port were shadowed. The main Fleet was followed on the night of 14 June as it moved south and the torpedo Wellingtons successfully homed on to it although their attack proved abortive because of the effective smoke screen. An A.S.V. [Anti Submarine Vessel] sweep in the latter part of the night, however, failed to locate the Italian Fleet.

The Beauforts in Malta and the Western Desert and the four-engined Liberators from the Delta had been given an approximate area for the target which proved correct and a time for carrying out an attack with the intention that attacks should be as nearly synchronised as possible. The Liberators left before dawn on the 15th and rendezvoused over the Western Desert. The Beauforts left at first light. The estimated position of the target was passed to them *en route*. A Maryland reconnaissance at first light located the Italian Fleet and successfully directed the striking forces towards it. The attack was made by the two forces simultaneously. A number of hits were scored and there was no doubt that both the bomb and the torpedo attacks were well executed. One of our submarines observed numbers of hits on the battleship *Littorio,* while one 'Trento' class cruiser was set on fire by bombs and another sunk by a torpedo. Naval observers in the Liberators saw a cruiser and a destroyer hit by torpedoes. The results would have been better had the Liberators been able to carry an S.A.P. [Semi-Armour Piercing] or A.P. bomb larger than 500 lbs., which was not enough for a capital ship. This part of the operation had a wider significance:

Suggest that the main lesson from this strike is that given the right aircraft carrying the right bombs we can restore the situation in the Mediterranean, deny the sea to enemy capital ships and so free our own sea communications, and at the same time deal piecemeal with his own supply ships.

As for subsequent shadowing, some excellent work was done, but the shortage of aircraft meant that there were periods of ignorance, made doubly disturbing by our complete lack of information about the position and state of our own ships. A second strike proved impossible, since there was insufficient time to get a second sortie from the same aircraft, and we had no others. The difficulties of giving good fighter cover were increased by the fact that our naval anti-aircraft guns repeatedly and accurately fired at our own fighters. A number of our Beau-fighter losses were undoubtedly due to this, despite the fact that careful arrangements had been made in advance with the naval gunnery controller.

The result of all this effort was deeply disappointing. From the Gibraltar convoy, two ships did get through, but although the Italian Fleet soon made off to the north after our attacks, the convoy from the east returned to Alexandria. In these operations we lost two cruisers and five destroyers. The events of these few days, all the same, had provided an admirable example of the flexibility and concentration which are the especial character-istics of air-power. The strongest enemy air attack on convoy 'Vigorous' came one morning when the ships were north of Tobruk. It was mounted by more than forty Stukas and Ju. 88s escorted by twenty or more Me. 109s. Coningham was able to put into the air three fighter squadrons, which forced the Stukas and most of the Ju. 88s to jettison their bombs and destroyed or damaged a number of enemy aircraft. This successful interception, when the convoy was at its most dangerous position, produced a marked effect, for our shipping losses must have been extremely heavy without Coningham's intervention.

*

The series of reverses in the Desert continued without inter-mission. On the morning of Sunday, 21 June, Casey, Harwood, Auchinleck and I met to 'appreciate' the situation in the light of the reports we had just received about the imminent fall of Tobruk. Auchinleck read out telegrams reporting that the enemy, having penetrated the perimeter, had apparently succeeded in putting out of action the bulk of our tanks and a large proportion of artillery. It was apparent to us all that Tobruk was about to fall, if it had not already done so. General Ritchie had authorised General Klopper, in command of the garrison, to try and fight his way out, and had telegraphed his own appreciation of the general situation. He thought that owing to his lack of armoured strength it would be impossible to hold the frontier position from Sollum to Hamar for any long period against a determined enemy attack, so he recommended that the frontier position should be held with mobile troops and by air attack as long as possible, while the main body of the Eighth Army withdrew to the vicinity of Matruh in order to gain time and reorganise for an offensive. The General Staff appeared to be in agreement with Ritchie.

To Auchinleck, the fall of Tobruk came as a surprise which was very difficult to understand. The main essential now was that the garrison should destroy all the stocks in reserve, particularly petrol. Meanwhile we had to consider the broader question raised by Ritchie and decide on the general disposition our forces in the Desert should take up. I said I would telegraph instructions to Lord Gort in Malta to return twenty Spitfires, and Casey said that in view of the seriousness of the situation he intended once again to telegraph to Churchill asking for more heavy bombers.

The Prime Minister was at this time in Washington. The fall of Tobruk, to which he attached even more importance than the Middle East Commanders-in-Chief, came as a body blow to him. Roosevelt at once offered practical comfort by saying that he would send a substantial number of tanks forthwith to the Middle East. Churchill telegraphed on 22 June that he, Brooke, and Field-Marshal Dill all hoped that stern resistance would be offered on the Sollum frontier line. Large reinforcements were approaching. Attlee and the War Cabinet telegraphed in the same sense from London. Casey had already cabled to Churchill in Washington that the forces at our command in the Middle East theatre were inadequate to enable us to cope with the enemy. The day before, when we did not know that Tobruk was about to fall, Casey, reflecting on his repeated requests for heavy bombers with which we could scour the Mediterranean, noted in his diary:

The impression grows that this Middle East theatre, in spite of lip service to the contrary, is low on the list of priorities in the minds of London and Washington. Difficulty in getting heavy bombing aircraft is evidence of this. . . .[1]

We replied to Churchill on 23 June that we had not the minimum armoured forces needed to hold the frontier defences. Only by increasing the distances which the enemy had to travel before engaging our main forces could we buy the time needed to regroup and reorganise. If we built up our strength around Matruh, Rommel would be obliged to traverse an extra 120 miles of waterless desert. Auchinleck, accepting the fullest responsibility for the recent setbacks, pointed out to the Prime Minister that we were trying to train an Army and fight with it at the same time:

We are catching up but have NOT caught up yet. As to using all my manpower, I hope I am doing this, BUT infantry can NOT win

[1] Casey: *Personal Experience,* p. 122.

battles in the desert so long as the enemy has superiority in armour, and nothing can be said or done to change that fact.

Of course, I had already telegraphed fully to Portal about the air aspect. Our ability to assist Tobruk was completely hamstrung once the landing grounds north and west of the Sollum position were lost. I had discussed the problem with Coningham only two days before Tobruk fell, and the limit of what could be done was a raid by twin-engined Boston bombers escorted by long-range Kittyhawks, and a fleeting visit by a long-range Kittyhawk patrol. Night attacks on Tmimi had been directed against the Stuka force based there. It was clear that the loss of Tobruk and the larger part of our trained armoured force, bringing with it the unavoidable decision to fight only a delaying action at Sollum, would necessitate the maximum air effort on our part. We had not only to cover our retiring forces, but also at all costs to delay Rommel's advance. As well as asking Malta to send twenty Spitfires, I was robbing my already starving training units in order to retain in the field one Hurricane II squadron which would otherwise have to be withdrawn, and also to complete an additional Hurricane II squadron. The day defence of the Delta now had to rely on the night Beaufighters and the one or two Spitfires which might be waiting their turn for modification at Aboukir.

Coningham was continuing to operate the squadrons on the same basis as before. The purely operational part of the squadrons, with skeleton ground crews, were in the forward area, with the remainder around Maarten Bagush. We intended to organise additional refuelling landing grounds in the intermediate areas. If it were necessary to fall back yet farther, groups of landing grounds in the Daba and Amriya–Natrun areas would come successively into use. Auchinleck promised any assistance I needed in the way of transport. I had no doubt that we could give the Germans a very rough passage, but our ability to do this continuously would depend upon the Army securing our advanced landing grounds to the last possible moment. I reported to Portal:

This has not been adequately done in past, but Auchinleck fully realises its vital importance and has impressed it on Army Commander. Given Army support all we need is more and more aircraft. I think we have been getting as much as is humanly possible out of what we have and what we can salve and repair.

Portal replied in his characteristic way, confident, and heartening. He telegraphed on the night of 22 June that during the full and free discussion at that evening's War Cabinet, which he had attended, there was no suggestion that my forces could have done more. He was sure that it was right to put everything we had into battle, regardless of the future, though the possibility of at least a feint by the Germans on Cyprus could not be ruled out. We might be sure that the Government would do everything possible to provide more aircraft by diversion of Hurricanes, Beauforts, and Blenheims on their way to India, and by speeding the flow via Gibraltar. Portal presumed (rightly) that I was pressing Takoradi. It had now been agreed that two squadrons of four-engined Halifaxes should come to the Middle East, and the C.A.S. told me that work on tropicalising them was proceeding by day and night:

We all realise and appreciate magnificent effort your Squadrons are putting forth in this crisis and we fully share your conviction that the enemy is in for a rough passage. Best wishes to you all.

Rommel's advance was so rapid that it seemed we might have to face escorted bomber attacks on the Fleet base at Alexandria within about three days of his obtaining the use of the aerodromes around Matruh. By 25 June, Admiral Harwood was discussing with the Middle East Defence Committee whether the Fleet should be withdrawn in such circumstances, bearing in mind the political implications of such a move. But it seemed to us that Rommel's first object would remain the land battle, and it was debatable whether he would divert sufficient aircraft to make it necessary for the Fleet to leave. We thought we would be better advised to wait and see what policy the enemy might decide to adopt. We did not think that the battle would be fought from the fixed defences of the Matruh position. On the contrary, it would be a mobile operation which might well sway backwards and forwards in the area between Matruh and El Alamein. The decision whether or when to withdraw the Fleet would have to be closely related to this situation.

On the same day, we sent to the Chiefs of Staff our appreciation of the Desert battle. It was thought by my fellow Commanders-in-Chief, and needless to say by me, that air co-operation throughout the action had been admirable. We knew that the enemy had suffered heavy casualties through our air action although troops moving dispersed in the open desert did not present decisive targets, and were unlikely ever to do so.

Until 13 June our recovery of disabled or immobilised tanks was very satisfactory. After this date, because we lost possession of the battlefield, recovery was in most cases impossible. Since the beginning of the battle, 153 tanks had been written off as destroyed. No spares and assemblies for the Grant tanks had been received before the battle, and only a few engines and cases of spare parts were received during it. The organisation of the armoured regiments had included one Grant squadron to two squadrons of the Crusader type. It had been hoped that this mixture would strengthen the fighting power of all the armoured units engaged, but the Crusader tanks, mounting only a 2-pounder gun, were no longer fit to face the latest German tanks. The result was that the burden of the battle in all units had to be carried by the Grants, and to that extent, therefore, they were not used *en masse*. The enemy had been superior in anti-tank weapons. We did not think that the tactical reconnaissance had been inadequate, particularly under the abnormal conditions of fighting in a barren and very dusty area, where all objects looked very much alike even at a thousand yards and it was practically impossible to distinguish friend from foe. While the staff work had been very satisfactory, it was not possible to train junior commanders very quickly, and a tactical sense was something of long development. Although the training of commanders had been continuous, even in the foremost area, it was acknowledged that we were 'still largely an amateur army fighting professionals'.

We found no indication of culpable indecision on the part of the highest command, and our men had fought to the end and continued to attack, fully realising the disparity in equipment between ourselves and the enemy. On the first day of the battle the Eighth Army had checked and thrown back Rommel's massed armoured assault, but suffered so seriously as to make it impossible for Ritchie both to contain the enemy in the area to which he had recoiled, and to develop a counter-offensive against his rear. The exhaustion was largely one of material, for it was clearly evident that the greater part of our tanks had very low fighting value. The battle had been won by a small but very well armed and highly organised body of German troops, the equivalent of two armoured and one mechanised division. Their victory we reported to be due to better equipment in the hands of highly trained troops:

Undoubtedly the day of large infantry formations in the Western Desert is past. It is perfectly possible to reorganise our forces on an armoured and mobile basis which should be at least as effective as the Germans. This we are engaged in now. . . .

Once we are reorganised and rearmed we do not doubt our ability to avenge this reverse. All efforts are being devoted to this object now. It must always be realised that all three fighting services in the Middle East suffer from a chronic shortage of material and personnel. In fact we live from hand to mouth, and at critical periods are expected to reinforce other theatres.

It appeared from the reports reaching us in Cairo that Ritchie and Brigadier-General Whiteley, his B.G.S., were exhausted. By the evening of 24 June Auchinleck and I had agreed that I should fly to Maarten Bagush the next day. Auchinleck would follow soon afterwards. He had decided that he must take command in the Desert himself, and signalled accordingly to London the next morning. At the same time, I flew to the Desert, where I talked over the situation at length with Ritchie and Coningham. Ritchie did not then know that Auchinleck was coming to take over. At the end of our conversation I felt more than ever relieved that the change was being made, and at once. I felt sure that Ritchie and his B.G.S. were, as I wrote to Portal, completely whacked. Ritchie's main preoccupation was to know how many tanks of various types he had and would have on various dates. It seemed to have become an obsession. I felt that he had been a good stop-gap after Cunningham's dismissal, but had been allowed to remain in command too long.

Later, Auchinleck arrived and told Ritchie of his decision that he must go. Ritchie left at once. The same day, Churchill assured Auchinleck of the War Cabinet's full confidence.

At about 7 o'clock that evening, Auchinleck called me to the Operations Room. There he had been taking stock of the situation as best he could, battling with the very poor communications system, which appeared to consist of intermittently effective wireless from the command car to the armoured-cars. I was much impressed by the contrast between his calm authority and Ritchie's fumbling. Auchinleck had grasped the essentials of a most confused situation in about two hours. He had decided at once not to be bottled up in Matruh, but to halt Rommel between Matruh, El Alamein, and the Qattara Depression. The idea, as we had already agreed in principle at the Middle East Defence Committee, was a sound one, although for a few days the battle went badly, since Rommel, this time by a lucky chance, hit the weakly defended gap between the main bodies of our 10 and 13 Corps.

Throughout the whole of our discussions that evening Auchinleck did not once mention numbers of tanks. I felt that passive bewilderment was being replaced by active command. At that moment, the Germans were reported to be massing to the west of the Matruh defences. Theirs was said to be a concentration of five thousand vehicles and so we did everything possible to produce the heaviest scale of effort by day and night. From dusk till dawn, the Wellingtons, assisted by Albacores, hammered away, and at seven o'clock in the morning the Bostons started an hourly service which went on throughout the hours of daylight. This treatment was continued the following night at the maximum intensity. Being on the spot I was able to gather at first hand the squadrons' accounts of these operations. There was no doubt that quite impossible things were being done. I even knew of well authenticated instances in which fighter squadrons and fighter aircraft had done as many as seven sorties in the day, and individual pilots had done as many as five. One of the fighter squadron commanders who had been in the Battle of Britain told me that the intensity of operations was far greater than anything he had

'Morning Prayers', North Africa Tactical Air
Force, 10 May 1943

La Marsa. My 'requisitioned' Air Command Post,
July 1943

On the road to Tripoli, 31 December 1942

What air superiority means! The Army moving into Tunis on 9 May 1943. From the traces of smoke, there is a small battle going on to the left of the hills

yet seen. The credit for this lay not only with the pilots and air crews, but even more with ground crews, reduced as they were to the minimum in order to effect rapid moves without stopping operations, and handicapped as they were by bad conditions and minor nuisances such as bombs and flares at night.

It certainly appeared that these continuous attacks on the enemy transport columns and concentrations were being effective. An entirely unsolicited testimonial came from General Freyberg when I went to see him in his ambulance fresh from the battle. He had seen the Bostons carry out their bombing attacks, and was most enthusiastic. It was unfortunate that some of our best results seemed to have been achieved at the expense of the Italians rather than the Germans. Thereafter we made efforts to give the Germans a special degree of attention despite their skill in dispersal, and I hoped that if only our mobile columns on the ground could keep active during the hours of darkness, the Hun would be forced to concentrate at night for his own protection from ground attack, and that would give us our opportunity.

On the evening of Friday, 26 June, we had the shock of the report that a large enemy column had passed through the gap south of the main Matruh defences held by 10 Corps, and that in consequence the enemy were within twenty miles of the aerodromes on which our whole fighter force was based. Coningham had made his preparations for a sudden move, but as the dark was coming on there was no time to get the squadrons off and down again at their next landing grounds before dark. The Bagush–Sidi Hinaish landing ground had no defence except for anti aircraft guns. All that Coningham could do was to send out a screen of our own armoured-cars to the westward so that we could get warning and fly off, and so save at least some of the fighter force. It was decided to move the advanced headquarters back at once but to stay on with the mobile operations room until the morning, so that operational control might be retained should a night move prove unnecessary. It was an uneasy, noisy night, but happily Rommel did not for once push straight on and at dawn the fighters began to move back to the landing grounds made ready for them in the Daba area. Meanwhile, operations went on, though at a reduced pitch of intensity.

The losses due to the evacuation of the landing grounds were not numerous, and the efforts at salvage remarkable. Despite the series of rapid backward moves the spirit of all ranks was excellent, and although it was hard to see the light in these continual retreats, I had confidence that our efforts were not being wasted. 'Though dividends may not be immediately payable,' I signalled to Portal, 'one feels they will be paid in full.'

To a kindly message of congratulation from the War Cabinet, I replied that the effort which Coningham's force had put forth in the last thirty-six hours was unique. Years afterwards I was interested to read about Rommel's recognition of the effect of the R.A.F's 'continuous round-the-clock bombing'.[1]

Arriving at the new site for the combined advanced headquarters at Daba I was infuriated to find that it was about half an hour's drive from the nearest aerodrome. Such a complete failure on the part of the Army, even at this stage, to understand some of the most elementary principles of modern warfare defeated me. At least I felt confident that such an error would not be repeated under Auchinleck's régime. He had modified Ritchie's plans and had emphasised to his corps commanders the importance of not being shut up behind static defences. He then gave instructions for a second delaying action to be fought roughly on the Fuka line. I felt that if these orders were really put into effect, and if people fought as they were told to do, the whole outlook would become more healthy.

One of the most remarkable achievements in these frenzied days was the salvage operations of the squadrons. They had managed to clean up behind them, and had left practically nothing which could be of any use to us, and literally nothing which could be of any use to the enemy. In the last stages, this became progressively more difficult, since there had not been sufficient time between moves to allow accumulations to be cleared. At one fighter aerodrome on 28 June I watched a hundred men lift a Spitfire bodily so as to get the articulator beneath it. There was no crane available, but they were determined not to lose the Spitfire. That was the spirit that I had seen throughout the R.A.F. in the Western Desert.

[1] Liddell Hart: *The Rommel Papers,* p. 245.

On no occasion during this long retreat did the German Air Force seriously attack our retiring columns, although again and again there were horrifying congestions and blocks involving thousands of vehicles: 'Thank God you didn't let the Huns Stuka us,' said Freyberg to me, 'because we were an appalling target.'

I knew that insinuations that the R.A.F. had failed to provide the right degree of support were bitterly resented. Unthinking comments about the loss of Bir Hacheim and Tobruk found their mark, and I told Portal that I wished the B.B.C. would realise that our troops listened to the news and reacted very quickly indeed to any implications of this kind. I added that if I were a fifth columnist my most productive line so far as this battle was concerned would be to drop a few words in bulletins and commentaries suggesting that the Air Force was not helping the Army. As for the immediate future, I felt that our continuous attacks on the enemy's supplies must ultimately produce a decisive effect if the Army could take advantage of it. I did not then know, on 29 June, how far it had been possible to complete the preparation of the El Alamein line. Neither I nor Auchinleck had much belief in lines of trenches. As I understood it, his plan was to use the line of defended positions in order to canalize any enemy attack, and enable us to meet it with a mixed mobile force of tanks, guns, and infantry. It seemed to me that the main failures in the past had been attributable to the loss of effective control. I knew that Auchinleck intended to exercise direct control over the battle now, and on this restricted front I felt he could do so:

If he can give them a good smack here I feel that we ought to be able together to clean up the whole party. I have told all my people that the move back which they are now making today is to be made in such a way as not to prejudice an immediate move forward. The campaigns out here have been starred with a number of lost opportunities; each one lost through the inability of the Army to strike back hard and follow up. I know Auchinleck fully appreciates this and has determined to follow up any successes quickly and ruthlessly. We intend to be ready.

For his part, Auchinleck had already advised the C.I.G.S. that

we could not resume the offensive on land until we had rebuilt
our armoured forces to the required strength. Meanwhile, our
only offensive weapon was our air striking force, which had to be
maintained at the maximum strength

. . . as it alone enables us to retain any semblance of the initiative.
My intention, with which A.O.C.-in-C. is in full agreement, is to
keep Eighth Army in being as a mobile field force and resist by every
possible means any further attempt by the enemy to advance eastwards.[1]

Recollecting these events after the war, Kesselring wrote that
at the time of the assault on Tobruk the preparations for the
attack on Malta were well advanced.

At about this time, he attended a conference at Gambut, at
which Marshal Cavallero took the chair. The other Commanders-
in-Chief were present. Rommel, according to Kesselring,
reported that there was practically no opposition of any importance left, and that he could promise that the Army would
be in Cairo in ten days. Kesselring apparently thought otherwise. He said that casualties must be expected during the new
advance; that the supplies necessary could not be maintained
for any length of time; that even if there were no British troops
worth mentioning in Egypt, there would certainly be some on
their way from elsewhere. The Luftwaffe would be completely
exhausted. Their aircraft needed overhauling, supplies were
lacking, and there would be opposition by formations at full
strength with serviceable aircraft which could be reinforced in a
very short time. As an airman he thought it was madness to rush
in against intact air bases. Bastico and Cavallero agreed with
Rommel—the Duce himself was about to arrive at Derna complete with white charger for the ceremonial entry into Cairo.

Kesselring received a curt order from Hitler by wireless not to
obstruct Rommel but to support him in every way. The Italian
commanders, it appears, were so entranced at the certain success
of the move on Cairo that they were already consulting their
guide-books to find the best hotels. Kesselring told them to stop
indulging in fantasies; it was more important to take steps to
overcome practical obstacles lying on the route to Cairo.

[1] Connell: *Auchinleck,* p. 622.

For a few more days, Rommel's predictions seemed to be correct. Then the resistance of the British and Commonwealth forces stiffened up so markedly that the state of the battle became critical. The situation was only restored by committing armoured reconnaissance units and the Luftwaffe, regardless of losses. In order to guarantee supplies, the capture of Malta was essential; and now it was no longer possible. 'The abandonment of this project', Kesselring wrote, 'was the first death blow to the whole undertaking in North Africa.'

*

Churchill, back from his visit to Washington, sent me a message of encouragement on 4 July:

Here at home we are watching with enthusiasm the brilliant supreme exertions of the Royal Air Force in the battle now proceeding in Egypt.

From every quarter the reports come in of the effect of the vital part which your officers and men are playing in this Homeric struggle for the Nile Valley. The days of the Battle of Britain are being repeated far from home. We are sure you will be to our glorious Army the friend that endureth to the end.

Though we did not then know it, Rommel's push had met its real breaking point on 2 July. I was at this time again in the Desert and returned on the 6th having had a most stimulating stay with 'Mary' Coningham's force. I described my visit in a letter to Portal on the 12th:

I saw all the squadrons at least once. They have all been at full stretch for six weeks and more, and the squadrons as a whole would be tired if they would admit it, which they won't. The strain, particularly of the past three weeks, has been pretty intense, but the question I was most frequently asked in the squadrons was 'when are we going to start getting the Hun on the run so that we can really get at him?' Fighter squadrons in particular are stretched to the barest necessities so that they can move forward with the minimum delay. One Wing asserted their ability to get their whole organisation on the road within 15 minutes of the word 'go'—from what I saw this was no idle boast.

The Squadron and Wing organisation which has been developing here during the past twelve months is now really crystallising. The fighter wings have acquired an *esprit de corps* of their own, i.e. the wings have now the corporate entity. This does not in any way weaken the intense squadron spirit of the squadrons at the operational landing ground, but it does allow the pooling of the squadron base maintenance parties at the Wing base. Squadron base parties have in fact now amalgamated into a Wing R.S.U. The squadrons at the operational landing ground are divided into two parties, an 'A' and 'B' party. They can operate for a day or two with either party only. In other words, in the event of a move the 'A' party goes on by road, the squadron continuing to operate from its existing base with the 'B' party until the 'A' party has reached the new landing ground and is ready to service the squadron. It was this organisation which made it possible for the squadrons to maintain their operational effort throughout the retreat and should make it equally possible for them to maintain it in an advance.

Of course, the crux of the whole matter as regards maintaining the fighter effort both in retreat and in advance is security of advanced landing grounds. Recently the Army have paid lip service to the paramount importance of this point, but in fact have done nothing except as regards A.A. As I think I told you, on two occasions at least it was only our own Armoured Car screen that saved the fighter force from being wiped out on the ground by enemy land forces. Our armoured cars have done yeoman service, and under present conditions it would be quite impossible to accept the risks of operating fighters from really advanced landing grounds if we had not got our own armoured car screen. There is no doubt that under conditions of mobile warfare armoured cars are essential a part of the R.A.F. in the field as are the wireless observation units.

I felt from these experiences that the working of what was known as air support was still far from satisfactory. Army support and co-operation were still lacking to a deplorable extent. Coningham had been obliged to r ly almost entirely on his own sources of information in order to give effective support. The Army still seemed to be incapable of knowing the positions and movements of their own forces. The 'bomb line' given by Corps, if adhered to, would again and again have hamstrung our ability to give effective help in the battle:

The complacency with which the Army Staff have frequently said that they really did not have any idea where our advanced forces were, has been at times quite infuriating.

Coningham had to arrange his own tactical reconnaissance in order to be able to direct his fighter bombers and bombers. Auchinleck fully appreciated the position, but I feared it would take some time to clean out the Army stable.

Interrogations of prisoners-of-war left no doubt of the effect of our air operations. A British officer who had escaped after capture by the enemy, and who had gone through a good deal of experience of the Stukas during the siege of Tobruk in 1941, had been with enemy forces which had twice received the attention of our Bostons at Matruh. He remarked that he did not mind Stukas but would never attend another Boston tea party if he could help it.

Our problem now was to stop supplies getting in at Benghazi and Tobruk. It was infinitely more difficult once we were right back at the Delta. For the better part of six weeks, Rommel had driven victoriously to the east. As Tobruk, then Sollum, then Matruh, fell in succession, the apprehension in Cairo, afterwards known as the 'Flap', became more intense. The Eighth Army and the Desert Air Force had withdrawn to the lines at El Alamein, holding the Ruweisat Ridge. We were hastily plugging up as best we might the gap between our effective left flank and the anchor of the Qattara Depression. The task was now to parry the inevitable assault on our prepared position. When Rommel's assault was held during the opening days of July in the first Battle of Alamein, he ordered his troops to dig in. He was only fifty miles or so from Alexandria.

*

Still the crucial question of priorities engaged our deep attention. On 9 July the Middle Eastern Defence Committee asked the Chiefs of Staff for strategical guidance on the main issue. The large diversions to the Far East had given us no choice but to denude the northern front, where we were now really dependent on the Russians. Nor was it easy to see how the situation there could be much improved. If we lost the battle in the Desert there would be no spare forces to go to the northern front. If we won the battle, we should try to exploit success by thrusting westward and taking the whole of Cyrenaica. If the Russians' resistance were to crack, and more troops could not get to the

Middle East in time, we should have to decide between the transfer of forces from Egypt to secure the Persian oilfields, the source of our energy, and defending Egypt. In the first case we should lose Egypt and in the second Persia.

Three days later, the Prime Minister told Auchinleck that he realised that the diversions to India had stripped bare the northern front. It was impossible for six or even four divisions from home to make up the deficiencies by the end of October. The only solution was the defeat of Rommel. If this could not be achieved, all would depend on the Russian front. Auchinleck replied that he would do his utmost to defeat the enemy in the west, or to drive him back sufficiently far to lessen the threat to Egypt. His aim was to destroy Rommel as far east as possible, but even if the enemy were driven back substantial forces must remain in the Desert. The implications of Churchill's telegram appeared to him to be that unless the German forces could be destroyed in the Desert, we could not transfer troops to Persia. In this event we stood to lose Iraq and the oil, should the Russian front break. Whether this was a justifiable risk it was not within his competence to say, but he understood that it had been accepted by the Prime Minister, and that he was therefore to continue to apply all available resources to the destruction of the German forces.

Auchinleck remained in command in the Desert, while I attended the monthly meeting of the Army Commanders on 16 July. After Major-General Thomas Corbett, recently appointed C.G.S. in place of Arthur Smith, had pointed to some lessons of the recent debacle, I indulged in some plain speaking on the air aspect. I told them that on three occasions our fighter force, without which their retreat would have become a shambles, had only been saved by the R.A.F. armoured-cars from being overrun. I complained of the inadequate bomb lines, and explained how Coningham was only able to give effective help by collecting his own information. What we needed was Army support and Army co-operation, and so far we had received far too little of either. Two or three of them came up to me afterwards and said it was about time there was some plain speaking on the subject, but I noted that to try and make an impression on the Army was rather like hitting a wall of cotton wool.

Reports from the battle suggested that the Army were at long last beginning to pass worthwhile information to the Air Forces, and as a result air action was approaching more closely to the actual front line. I looked forward to observing the Army's reactions when the air forces moved again out of sight in order to turn the enemy's retreat into a rout. This day still appeared to be somewhat distant, for although Rommel's advance had been checked, we seemed unable to launch a successful counter-blast. I told Portal on 25 July that the golden opportunity had been slipping away day by day. For some reasons which I could not establish, the Army had not been able to build up their tank strength in Grants. Therefore they felt unable to try for a real decision until the new 23rd Armoured Brigade was available. I had repeatedly urged the vital importance of the time factor and the gradual passing of the chance was an intense worry.

As events turned out, the new brigade proved a broken reed. No doubt their inexperience turned a failure into a fiasco, but I felt that the primary cause was mishandling by 30 Corps, now under General Ramsden, who was himself new to mobile desert war. It seemed to be impossible to get the facts. Eight hours after the battle opened, the corps were telling the Eighth Army that things were going very well and our armour had not yet been engaged. Twenty hours after the start Auchinleck was still in the dark. I left Ramsden the next day feeling very worried. Auchinleck was no less concerned. It was clear that if he had insisted, as I knew he wanted to do, on an attack being made the following day, it would have been predestined to failure. I signalled home that the position was now so static that thorough preparation was essential. On the other hand, we still faced only a comparatively thin crust, and if the Army could break it and exploit the opportunity it was still there for the grasping.

It was the weakness of the team that really disturbed me, and I felt justified in telling Portal privately of all my misgivings:

The difference between those Army meetings and 'Mary's' meetings is the difference between a funeral breakfast and a wedding breakfast. There's no life about them. Too many old men and 'nice chaps'. As Auck. remarked to me, the Army is suffering from 'good fellows'. It's too true.

I had a feeling that people at home might be losing confidence in Auchinleck. I had got to know him well and found him honest, clear thinking and full of guts, head and shoulders above any other senior soldier in the Middle East. He was badly served. With a few exceptions his senior staff and commanders were useless 'good fellows'. No one could expect to win a war against professionals in these circumstances. Auchinleck had admittedly sacked some, but his weakness had been that he had sacked too few too late:

Some commander should have been shot after the bolt from Agedabia. I wish he was a better judge of character and more ruthless in judging people solely by results. I also wish he had the ability to inspire the Army here. I am afraid he hasn't. I believe it is what is needed by the Army more than anything else—not only in M.E.—inspiration—fire. To write like this of a man who has so loyally and whole-heartedly supported me may seem pretty foul, but I feel that personal feelings should not come into this sort of question. Give Auck. some commanders and staff who are alive and young, who can think and act, and can infuse some life into this fine Army of ours, which is dying for lack of it—do that, and all would be well. But what I am afraid of is that if the present business fails there will be a demand for the Auck. to be sacked and for him to be replaced by someone who has a 'name'. I can see that his going would be a shock to public confidence, and that the Government would feel he must be replaced by someone whom the public know well—and that would be tragic. The public knows the Gorts and Wavells—! If ever a change at the top becomes unavoidable, for heaven's sake let them choose someone who is alive and young, someone with fire. Surely the Army has men like that amongst its galaxy of Generals?

You may feel that most of this is quite outside my province. It is. I only write it because I feel the whole situation is grave, and so far I see no move towards improvement.

The air situation in the desert remained satisfactory in general but needed careful watching. The balance between fighter-bomber and bomber action in direct support of the land battle, fighter and bomber action against the enemy air forces, and action against enemy seaborne and airborne supplies, was a delicate one, changing daily. It was affected not only by alterations in the land and air situation, but also by relative air strength. Coningham handled his force with flexibility and skill, and maintained ascendancy over an enemy whose air effort had so far proved remarkably ineffective despite the superior performance of his aircraft. On 24 July two German Stuka pilots were so frightened that without a shot being fired they landed far behind their lines and ran for it. Their aircraft were located the following morning and destroyed by shooting up. The enemy in the battle area had been forced to adopt a degree of dispersal so extreme that this of itself severely handicapped his operations. The main concern was the numerical weakness of our fighter squadrons, despite their high rate of serviceability. The wastage in battle was high and the strength of nearly all squadrons was now below 50 per cent. Kittyhawk squadrons were particularly badly affected, partly because deliveries of the aircraft bore little relation to the promises made, and partly because of mechanical failures. This shortage of aircraft naturally affected training and tended to throw an undue burden on the most experienced pilots.

Auchinleck assessed the situation in the Desert on 27 July, in his report to Churchill, a report that is of great interest. He said that he believed Rommel would hardly be able to secure a decisive superiority in the first two weeks of August, though he was strong enough for defensive action. An attempt at the conquest of the Delta could only be a gamble and then only under very strong air cover. The Eighth Army would receive sixty more Grant tanks early in August, but no further supplies until September. Auchinleck deduced that it was necessary to husband our armour carefully in view of the fact that during August the enemy might build up to between 150 and 200 German tanks. The Eighth Army's deficiencies in transport were mounting, and its resources of ammunition were far from adequate. Rommel, too, suffered from similar deficiencies. Auchinleck judged that none of the formations in the Eighth Army was sufficiently well trained for offensive operations, and a reinforcement of well-trained formations, or a quiet period in which to train, was urgently needed. For the moment we had such a degree of air superiority that while our troops were relatively free from molestation, the enemy was continually attacked by night and day. Our land forces were considerably heartened by this state of affairs, from which a large measure of tactical freedom and security accrued. Unless the enemy should be strongly reinforced and our own air forces correspondingly reduced, this superiority would assist our operations, whether offensive or defensive, and gravely impede the enemy.

Our two vulnerable points were Cairo and Alexandria. The position of the Eighth Army at El Alamein denied direct access to either place by road and flanked any attempt to by-pass. The defences of the area would be well forward by the middle of August, and, so far as possible, complete by the end of that month. Rommel, in turn, had few really vulnerable points. There were bottlenecks at Sollum, and around Matruh and Bagush, and the long lines of communication were vulnerable to attack by raids from the air or from the sea, but otherwise he was not physically vulnerable except to direct assault. His weakness was in the maintenance of his present forces at El Alamein, whereas our own presented no real difficulties. We could certainly maintain forces twice the present size of the Eighth Army in the battle area, if they existed, but even so, Rommel's positions were too strongly held to be attacked successfully with our available resources.

Two attempts to break the German front had failed. An attack in the south, intended largely as a diversion, had failed also, but had shown that the enemy was not numerous in this region, and that this front might give way if suddenly attacked. If this happened, it would offer access for our mobile troops to the enemy's flanks and rear. The alternative was to adopt the tactical defensive until we were strong enough, but unless the enemy's position worsened, this would not be until mid-September.

Auchinleck believed Rommel would certainly try to attack before the end of August, probably by manœuvre rather than a frontal onslaught on our prepared defences. Our own best course, he thought, would be a defensive combined with offensive gestures from time to time. The cover plan should be such as would induce the enemy to strike prematurely, and we had to be prepared to fight a modern defensive battle in the area El Alamein–El Hammam. Eventually we would have to renew the offensive, which would probably mean a break through the enemy position around El Alamein. The newly arrived infantry divisions and the armoured divisions must be trained for this and for pursuit. Auchinleck hoped that this counter-offensive might begin in the latter part of September, when the newly arrived divisions were trained.

This, then, was the situation at the end of July. Neither side was able to deliver a knock-out blow. Rommel's swift onrush had made us desperately short of aerodromes, and had given him advanced landing grounds only eighty miles or so from Alexandria and 185 miles from Cairo. Between 1 July and 27 July the R.A.F. in Egypt and the Levant had flown nearly 15,400 sorties, excluding those against ships. Auchinleck declared that the air forces could not have done more than they did to help and sustain the Eighth Army in its struggle. Their effort was continuous by day and night, and the effect on the enemy tremendous. He was certain that without them we should not have been able to stop the enemy on the El Alamein position. As for Auchinleck himself, although attacks made on 21–22 July, and again on 26–27 July, failed, he had, as Rommel later observed, achieved the one thing that mattered to him. The advance of the Axis forces had been halted.[1]

[1] Liddell Hart: *The Rommel Papers,* p. 260.

FOR some time the C.I.G.S., General Brooke, had sought an opportunity to visit the Middle East. It was clear to him that something was radically wrong, but it was not easy at a distance to judge where the fault lay.

Originally, Brooke had received Churchill's permission to make the trip alone, but on 30 July, to the C.I.G.S's dismay, Churchill insisted that he too would visit Cairo. Impatient with the Eighth Army's lack of progress, the Prime Minister was intent on seeing for himself. As he later wrote, it was during this month of July when he was politically at his weakest and without a gleam of military success, that he had to obtain from the United States Government the crucial decision to abandon all plans for a Channel crossing in 1942. It was a decision which was bound to come as a severe blow to Stalin, and Churchill courageously determined to convey the news to Moscow in person.

It was a very grey dawn on 3 August as we assembled our little reception party at the piece of desert glorified by the name of Cairo West, some twenty miles north-west of Cairo on the Alexandria–Cairo road. Our party included Miles Lampson the Ambassador, Dick Casey the Minister of State, General Corbett, my deputy Air Marshal Drummond, and a number of staff officers. Our two principal guests were the C.I.G.S. who, having stopped off a day at Malta, was coming in to us from the north, and Churchill who had come round from Gibraltar in a wide sweep to El Faiyum, and consequently came in to Cairo from the south. It was an immense relief to hear that both these aircraft were already over Egypt; after all, both of them had had to cross the Bay of Biscay where more than one V.I.P. aircraft had disappeared without trace. The C.I.G.S. had flown practically the whole length of the Mediterranean and stayed two nights in Malta, which was still under regular air bombardment. The Prime Minister, on the other hand, had flown over semi-hostile Vichy territory, and over hundreds of miles of trackless desert. Brooke was the first to arrive, and by that time the fleecy low clouds had begun to break and through the gaps we could see that clear, yellow, first light of dawn, which is so typical of Egypt.

Meantime, up from the south came the other aircraft. Churchill records:

It was my practice on these journeys to sit in the co-pilot's seat before sunrise, and when I reached it on this morning of August 3 there in the pale, glimmering dawn the endless winding silver ribbon of the Nile stretched joyously before us. . . . Never had the glint of daylight on its waters been so welcome to me.[1]

His pilot made a copy-book landing, and came round, taxi-ing so as to stop with the side of the aircraft from which the passengers would come facing our little reception party. No one, I think, can call the Liberator a thing of beauty—fine aircraft though it was—but its slabsided flanks made it look rather whale-like, and there for some minutes—it seemed a very long time—nothing happened, no sign from the aircraft, no movement at all, until from the bottom of its belly came floating bits of paper drifting away in the wind. I suppose we were rather tense, and reaction may account for it, but I am afraid we all, without exception, burst into a roar of laughter which we had considerably difficulty in curbing. After a slight further pause two legs in Air Force blue showed from under the aircraft, followed by the rest of Mr. Churchill in his Air Force uniform as an Air Commodore, looking incredibly cherubic and, of course, with the inevitable cigar. It was my job to be the first to welcome him, and as he shook hands with me he took the wind right out of my sails, by saying: 'Tedder, I have an apology to make to you. I was told you were just a man of nuts and bolts. It was not true, and I was not told the truth. I am sorry.'

I shall never know to what he was referring, but I can only think that it was the occasion when somebody intervened and stopped me coming out to the Middle East as deputy to Longmore. I have always suspected that it was Churchill and Beaverbrook who between them had it cancelled. However, I certainly bore no ill-will. I was disappointed, of course, but fate intervened —and I came just the same.

[1] Churchill: *The Second World War,* vol. IV, p. 412.

Winston was bubbling with exhilaration. He was like a school-boy just out of school and off for a really wonderful holiday. Once the greetings were over we separated and went off to our respective breakfasts. The Prime Minister, of course, was staying at the Embassy, and records his appreciation of the comforts which were made available to him—comforts such as air-conditioning, which were rare in those days. Exhilarated as he undoubtedly was by his escape from the shackles of Whitehall and by the prospect of being for once the man on the spot, he lost no time whatever in getting down to serious business. I was sent for at about eleven o'clock that morning to report to him. He had been esconced in what was normally the ambassadorial bedroom. He had apparently just finished his bath, and, clad in a towel acting as a loin cloth, trailing an electric lead behind him, he was busy tramping across and across the room shaving. A little disconcerting at first.

It was clear that what immediately concerned him was leadership and command throughout the Eighth Army. There was one urgent practical question which required a decision, and that was the command of the Eighth Army itself since, obviously, Auchinleck could not continue indefinitely and also be Commander-in-Chief Middle East. Winston asked for my views. I said I was not in a position to make a firm recommendation. All I could say was that the only general in the Middle East who in my opinion could possibly fill the bill was General Gott. I did not know him personally, but since we had lost O'Connor, Gott alone had acquired the reputation of being a fine leader of men and a very experienced desert fighter. But there were those who said that he was tired after his long spell in the desert, and that it would be wrong to call on him to undertake the terrific task of rebuilding the Eighth Army.

The same day Smuts was due to arrive in time for lunch at the Embassy. He was late, so we sat down, leaving a vacant place beside Lady Lampson. On her other side Mr. Churchill held the floor, absolutely bubbling over with vitality and humour. We had got well on our way into lunch when the door opened, and that dapper little man with the pointed beard and steely, sparkling eyes, came in. I was fascinated to see the change that came over the party. It was no longer a solo but a lively duel, in which there was cut and thrust going on all the time. In their ranging around world problems they happened to come to India, and in particular to Gandhi. 'Gandhi', Smuts declared, 'is inspired by sheer idealism. His appeal is essentially a spiritual one. And that, my dear Winston, is your weakness. It is by facing up to, and overcoming, fear, that you have led the British people to great deeds of courage and endurance; but you have not been able to give them truly spiritual inspiration.' As quick as a flash Churchill retorted: 'Field-Marshal, I take the gravest exception to this dastardly attack on my character. I would have you know that in this past year I have appointed no less than six bishops. If that is not spiritual inspiration, what is?' And then, with a grin to the rest of the party, he said, 'How's that for an adequate answer to an unforgiveable attack on my character?'

That evening, Brooke talked with Churchill. The Prime Minister was fretting that there was to be no offensive action until September. Later that night, he urged on Brooke that Auchinleck must come back to the command of the Middle East and leave the Eighth Army to be taken over by Gott. Brooke argued that he knew Gott to be very tired. Finally, in the early hours, Churchill suggested that Brooke himself should take over the Eighth Army.

The following morning, 4 August, the C.I.G.S. joined us for the Commanders-in-Chief's Conference. We discussed the relative importance of Egypt and the oil supplies of Abadan, and all agreed that in the last resort the oil mattered more than Egypt. If Abadan were lost we must inevitably forfeit Egypt, the command of the Indian Ocean, and the whole position in India and Burma. At noon, Smuts talked with the C.I.G.S. about the command of the Army in the Middle East. Smuts had a good opinion of Auchinleck but thought he selected his subordinates badly, and that some changes were desirable. A little later, Brooke discovered that Auchinleck agreed with him about the necessary changes. General Montgomery should take over the Eighth Army, Corbett should be replaced, 'Jumbo' Wilson would be replaced by Gott, and General Quinan by General Anderson. Brooke has recorded his surprise at hearing that Auchinleck was prepared to accept Montgomery in command of the Eighth Army. He felt serious doubts whether this combination would work, believing that Auchinleck would interfere too much, would ride Montgomery on too tight a rein, and would consequently be liable to put him out of his stride. As the C.I.G.S. was most anxious to place Montgomery in command of the Eighth Army he felt this might mean moving Auchinleck to some other command.

At six o'clock that evening we were summoned to a conference at the Embassy under Churchill's chairmanship. Smuts, Brooke, Wavell, Casey, Auchinleck, Harwood and I attended. Brooke told us of the view taken by the Chiefs of Staff, who thought that if everything went right for the Germans they might be able to advance between three and five divisions on the northern front, supported by two to three hundred aircraft from Tabriz and Astara during October. This force might progress rapidly until the snows set in during December. An advance through Turkey was considered improbable. The Chiefs of Staff did not think that Germany would despatch reinforcements to North Africa while the offensive in Russia was in full blast. They judged that there was a reasonable chance of defeating Rommel in the near future, but unless he could be turned out of Tripolitania, there was little hope of transferring large land forces from the Desert to the northern front.

Churchill observed that so long as the Russians clung on to the Caucasus, he thought we were adequately shielded to the north. He was not yet willing to divert anything from Egypt until the issue had been decided in the Western Desert. With this view general agreement was expressed. When Wavell asked about the chances of a successful offensive in the Western Desert, Auchinleck replied that for the moment the Eighth Army was exhausted, and if he was to destroy the enemy he must wait until his reinforcements were ready in mid-September.

Brooke noted in his dairy that he could see Churchill did not approve Auchinleck's replies:

He is again pressing for an attack before Auchinleck can possibly get ready. I find him almost impossible to argue with on this point.[1]

---

[1] Bryant: *The Turn of the Tide,* p. 441.

After dinner Churchill asked Brooke about his day's work. Brooke soon discovered that it was not approved, and was told that Montgomery could not possibly arrive in time to hurry on the attack. Again, Churchill pressed for the appointment of Gott, to which the C.I.G.S. replied that he had discussed this with Auchinleck, who did not think Gott was up to the job. Brooke said again that he thought Gott was too tired. The question remained undecided.

Very early the next morning, the Prime Minister and the C.I.G.S. were taken on a conducted tour of the battlefield. We all motored to the headquarters of the Eighth Army, Churchill travelling with Auchinleck, while Alan Brooke shared a car with Coningham and me. At the H.Q. we partook of a light breakfast, which was not apparently to Churchill's taste. Later, he found more attractive fare in a lunch at the headquarters of the Desert Air Force. The food, ordered from Shepheard's Hotel, went astray and only arrived in the nick of time. The Prime Minister found this 'a gay occasion in the midst of care—a real oasis in a very large desert.'

I think the Prime Minister was impressed with the spirit and bearing of our men. From his own account of these events he seems to have come to the conclusion that the disasters in the Desert would probably not have happened had Auchinleck not been diverted by considerations of a front too widely extended, and he acknowledged that but for Coningham's activities the 500-mile retreat could never have been accomplished without even greater losses than those we had suffered.[1]

Meanwhile, Brooke had spent the afternoon at Gott's headquarters. Gott himself confessed to the C.I.G.S. that what was needed was some new blood, someone with new ideas and plenty of confidence in them. This served to convince Brooke the more strongly that Gott was temporarily tired and was not the right man to take over the Eighth Army. He recognised that it would not be easy to convince Churchill of this.

The next morning, the Prime Minister told Brooke that he had decided to split up the Middle Eastern Command. A new

[1] Churchill: *The Second World War,* vol. IV, p. 414.

Near Eastern Command would cover the area up to the Canal, and a Middle Eastern Command would include Syria, Palestine, Persia and Iraq. Auchinleck, in whom he had lost confidence, would take over this latter Command. Churchill offered Brooke the Near Eastern Command, with Montgomery as commander of the Eighth Army. Brooke refused at once. He tried, without complete success, to point out to Churchill that the Canal made an impossible boundary, since both Palestine and Syria were based administratively on Egypt. The C.I.G.S. also refused entreaties by Smuts to take over the Near Eastern Command, and at length persuaded him that General Alexander would be a better selection. That evening, Churchill telegraphed to the War Cabinet, recommending the division of the Middle Eastern Command. Auchinleck was to take over the new Middle East Command, Alexander to command the Near East, and Gott the Eighth Army. Brooke did not feel sufficiently convinced of the disadvantages of Gott's appointment to oppose it outright once the Prime Minister had made up his mind. The latter signalled to his colleagues that he did not doubt that the proposed changes would impart a new and vigorous impulse to the Army and restore confidence:

I must emphasise the need for a new start and vehement action to animate the whole of this vast but baffled and somewhat unhinged organisation. The War Cabinet will not fail to realise that a victory over Rommel in August or September may have a decisive effect upon the attitude of the French in North Africa when 'Torch'[1] begins.

It was unfortunately typical of Gott's unassuming character that when he returned to Cairo for two days before taking over the command of the Eighth Army, he made no special request for transport, but merely asked if they could find room for him in one of the routine flights to Cairo. It was certainly not known that he was the Army Commander designate. It was a hundred to one chance that the paths of the solitary Me. 109 and the transport aircraft should have crossed. Whether in fact the old desert warrior would have been able to wind up the rest of the North African campaign as well as, or better than, the new boy from

[1] 'Torch', the invasion of North-West Africa; the successor to 'Gymnast'.

the U.K.—that we can never know. What is certain is that their methods would have varied as much as the two commanders differed.

Immediately we heard of the death of Gott, General Smuts sent for me. He was obviously deeply shocked and intensely disturbed and worried by the news. As he paced to and fro across his room, he shot the question at me: 'Tedder. Has the British Army got no good generals?' To which I replied, repeating what I had told him before in a previous discussion, that I did not know of anyone in the Middle East now that Gott had gone. 'But', I added, 'I have heard of a man called Montgomery whom I do not know personally at all, but I gather he has built up a great reputation as a good trainer'—to which Smuts replied, 'Yes, yes, I have heard of him.' The next thing I heard was that Montgomery had been appointed to take over command of the Eighth Army and was on his way out.

The Cabinet at home agreed only with reluctance to the splitting of the Command, and asked that the nomenclature proposed by Churchill should be changed to the Middle East Command, and the new organisation, the Persia-Iraq Command.

In accordance with the Prime Minister's custom, a letter was sent to Auchinleck offering him this latter post. The document was carried by Colonel Jacob, who wrote in his diary that he felt he was just going to murder an unsuspecting friend. He offered Auchinleck the condolences of Churchill and Brooke on the death of Gott, and then handed him the letter. Auchinleck read it in silence. He remained quite calm. After reflection, he turned down Churchill's suggestion that Iraq and Persia should become a separate Command. 'It would never work,' he said. Nor could he accept the appointment. He had been Commander-in-Chief in India and Commander-in-Chief Middle East. Now he was asked to take a position which was virtually that of one of his own commanders. The fact that he was being moved would indicate to the Army that he had lost the confidence of the Government.

Auchinleck's refusal was conveyed to Cairo by Jacob. This meant that the Prime Minister had not only to work out the details of the proposed new Commands, but also to find yet another soldier to take on the Persia–Iraq Command. According to Brooke's diary, Churchill urged on him at some length that it was essential for Alexander to command both the Middle East and the Eighth Army. The C.I.G.S. tried, without much success, to explain the system of command in the Middle East. Alexander arrived the following morning and consulted with Churchill and Brooke about the organisation of the new Commands. Churchill directed the Middle East Defence Committee to make proposals. As far as the air was concerned, it was assumed throughout that there would be no change in the scope of the Middle East Air Command. The question was how relations between the Air Officer Commanding-in-Chief and the two Army Commanders-in-Chief should now be arranged. We were also asked for our advice as to the exact boundary which should be established between the new Army Commands. Since it was high time to proceed to Moscow, we appointed a sub-committee to go into all these matters in our absence. As air matters would no doubt loom large in the talks with the Russians, it had been decided that I should join the party.

I could not admire the manner of Auchinleck's removal any more than that of Longmore's departure. Towards the end of June, Auchinleck himself had suggested that he might be relieved of his command, perhaps in favour of Alexander. For the moment, that suggestion had been refused. Now, Auchinleck had had to pay a heavy price for his inability to select his senior staff well, or perhaps for the lack of suitable senior generals from whom to select. I admired the way in which he had taken a grip on the critical situation after 25 June and recognised to the full how much the Army's attitude toward the exercise of air-power had improved under his régime. Admittedly, Eighth Army desperately needed leadership and inspiration, but Churchill did Auchinleck an injustice in telegraphing to London a few days later that he was sure we were heading for disaster under him. The Army, the Prime Minister asserted, was reduced to bits and pieces, and oppressed by a sense of bafflement and uncertainty. He went on to allege:

Apparently it was intended in face of heavy attack to retire eastwards to the Delta. Many were looking over their shoulders to make sure of their seat in the lorry and no plain plan of battle or dominating will-power had reached the units.

Certainly I had been deeply conscious of the lack of clear direction in Eighth Army. But I never heard a whisper of any intention after Auchinleck took over that Army on 25 June to retire eastwards; still less did I meet, or hear of, the many who were supposed to be looking over their shoulders to make sure of their seat in the lorry. On the contrary, Rommel's force was spent.

Our fortunes in the Mediterranean, having reached their lowest ebb in the early summer, were now improving, which meant that Rommel's supply position was likely to become even less satisfactory. Malta had not been captured and was beginning to come back into use as an offensive base. The Middle East could expect to receive substantial reinforcements in the immediate future. If only the Russians could hold out in the Caucasus, I felt confident that we could clear the Axis forces from North Africa. I did not believe that the Japanese would be able to take India, and I looked forward to striking hard at Italy, the weak spot of the enemy coalition.

At midnight on 10 August, we drove out of Cairo to the three Liberators waiting at the aerodrome. After a short wait, we took off for Teheran, *en route* for Moscow.

Trip to Moscow–Bird's eye views of Russia–Meeting with Stalin–'The hand of comradeship'–Meetings with the Russian Generals–Second Front arguments–R.A.F. squadrons for the Caucasus?–Kremlin banquet–Beria

WE were about two hours out of Teheran on a northerly course in our Liberator. I was curled up on a bunk, which was more like a stretcher, and had been trying without noticeable success to get some sleep, despite the roar, the vibration, and the cold. I think I must have just managed to doze off when I was aroused by a torch flashing in my face. It was the captain of the aircraft who wanted to speak to me. He apologised, and said he would like to know how important it was that we should go straight through to Moscow.

In a Liberator ahead of us was Mr. Churchill and his personal staff, and we had a useful little collection of V.I.Ps on board, so I asked the captain why he was putting this question. He was rather hesitant, and then said that he had had to feather one of the engines. He could carry on to Moscow quite reasonably on three engines, but he was worried that at the Moscow end there might be great difficulty and delay in getting the necessary spares. I told him bluntly that he was the captain of the aircraft, and what he said must go. It must be his decision, and if his decision was that it would be right to turn back to Teheran, it made no difference how many V.I.Ps we had on board, and I would without hesitation uphold his decision no matter what objections might be raised by our fellow passengers.

So back we went. A very awkward situation. The Prime Minister ahead, on his own except for his purely personal staff, and his military and diplomatic advisers (Alan Brooke, Wavell, Alec Cadogan of the Foreign Office, and myself) at least a day behind. I felt especially sorry for Alec Cadogan. I sensed that he was scared stiff as to what the P.M. might say or do when there was none of the staff with him to keep any sort of check. It was obvious that we must get on our way again as soon as possible. It was equally obvious that we had no reserve aircraft with us, and it would take a matter of days to get one up from the Middle East. The Russians solved our problem for us.

There happened to be at Teheran a Russian Dakota commanded by a colonel whose name I ought to remember, because he was well known for some rather spectacular flights across the North Pole. I think some of my colleagues were a bit dubious about accepting the proposed lift to Moscow, but personally I felt confident that the colonel was a pretty competent pilot, as well as being a very pleasant personality. Our change of horses had its compensations. If we had been in the Liberator we would have been flying at some 15,000 to 20,000 feet; we would have gone straight up the middle of the Caspian Sea and seen virtually nothing of the Caucasus. One of the things we particularly wanted to know at that time was whether the Russians had prepared any defences at the eastern end of the Caucasus between the mountains and the Caspian. It was a time when the German forces were sweeping along the north of the Caucasus and threatened to outflank the mountains. Our Russian pilot flew most of the way at about 500 feet, and, of course, we had a wonderful view of the country. After landing to refuel at Baku we went on, low down, right along the west coast of the Caspian, precisely along the area between the Caspian shores and the mountains where any defences that were made, or to be made, would be, and I was frankly a little excited at this opportunity. Wavell, Alan Brooke and I were seated one behind the other on the port side of the aircraft, and so got a perfect view. In my excitement I went forward, first to Alan Brooke and then to Wavell, to see what they thought of it all, and to see if they could observe any signs of fortifications which were not obvious to me. I must have been unfortunate in the time I chose, because both were fast asleep.

Our Colonel explained that he was not sure how far the Germans had reached, and there was always the possibility of an odd German aircraft exploring as far as the Caspian, so he cut out north-eastward to the mouth of the Volga, and thence north to Kubishev. There were fortunately no signs of any military activity, but the rest of the flight to Moscow via Kubishev was extremely interesting, particularly from a political point of view. As we left the delta of the Volga the very occasional little villages consisted simply of two lines of houses with a very wide street between them, and no sign of any gardens or separate cultivation; nothing but enormous rectangular fields in which the harvesters were still going. In each village one could see the white ruins of the church, and no sign of any tracks leading towards it, then, as one got farther north, one noticed that there were patches—small patches—of cultivation behind each house. The ruined churches were not so ruined, and there were faint signs of tracks leading to and from them. Farther north still, the cultivation behind each house became larger and longer, the churches no longer appeared to be ruined, and the white, bulbous spires appeared undamaged, clearly focal points in the villages.

As we came in sight of the aerodrome at Moscow we could see our reception committee lined up on the tarmac. Naturally we were all intensely interested to see what lay ahead, but in his enthusiasm Alec Cadogan got up from his seat to kneel on the floor and look out of one of the windows. At that moment our Colonel decided to dive straight at the reception committee, followed by a violent zoom before he turned in to land. These unexpected manœuvres sent the unfortunate Cadogan rolling down the floor. There was, however, no damage.

Introductions over, we were wafted off to Stalin's villa, which he had put at the Prime Minister's disposal. It was no small relief to all of us to be united again, and it was quite a cheerful lunch party. Mr. Churchill was on the top of his form. There is no doubt he had had a thoroughly enjoyable time having a *tête-à-tête* with Stalin, and I believe the party had gone on until the early hours. Unfortunately, in his account of it all to us he rather let himself go, speaking of Stalin as just a peasant, whom he, Winston, knew exactly how to tackle. Being fairly certain that the whole villa was a network of microphones, I scribbled '*Méfiez-vous*', and passed it to him. He gave me a glare which I shall never forget, but I am afraid it was too late. The damage was done. According to Churchill, when they met before, Stalin had beeen friendliness personified, but when we went to the official meeting Stalin was from the very outset bitter and rude, and missed no opportunity of showing and expressing utter contempt. Of course, one had to remember that to Stalin, military activities in the Western Desert must have appeared very much small beer— and rather flat beer at that!

I have always felt since then that the P.M's journey to Moscow was one of the most courageous things he did. He knew that Stalin's appeals and demands for the opening of a new front in Western Europe were practically an S.O.S., to meet which Churchill could only offer the landings in North Africa at a later date. As Mr. Churchill described the actual and potential scale of bombing on German cities, Stalin thawed a little. He even became genial, in a somewhat glacial fashion, as Churchill unfolded the plans for the 'Torch' landings in North Africa. The Prime Minister drew the picture of a crocodile, explaining the Allies' intention to attack the soft under-belly. Stalin at once grasped all the implications. 'May God prosper this undertaking', he said irreverently. Mr. Churchill explained that Western Europe would have to wait at least twelve months, if not more, before anything in the nature of invasion would become possible and he did his best to explain to Stalin that to land a mere six divisions in France would be useless. By the time our visit to Moscow took place the strategic bomber offensive was gathering force, and more and more the battle for air superiority, on which all the other operations depended, was beginning to be fought out over Germany, not over England. Mr. Churchill made what play he could out of the bomber offensive and its effect, but I think it was expecting too much to expect that 'Uncle Joe', as we called him, would begin to understand that. After all, we had not a few senior authorities who were equally ignorant. Some, I fear, are still.

During this brief visit to Moscow, a number of the Russians, including Stalin himself, spoke to me with apparent admiration of the gallantry of the Royal Air Force, but I do not for a moment think that they regarded it as having any particular strategic importance.

That evening, we all foregathered in the Kremlin. Stalin had in the meantime rejected Churchill's arguments in a memorandum of frosty tone and doubtful accuracy. It appeared to him and his colleagues that the 'most favourable conditions' existed for the creation in 1942 of a second front in Europe, since all the best German forces had been concentrated in the east, leaving in Europe, so we were told, only inconsiderable forces of inferior quality.

Mr. Churchill repeated his argument about the futility of launching an unsuccessful operation. He also made as much use as possible of the prospective landings in North Africa, and for a moment Stalin's interest was aroused; nevertheless, the whole conference was sour, and never seemed to be getting anywhere, until in the early hours Stalin suddenly said, 'I hope you will honour me by dining with me tomorrow night', to which the Prime Minister retorted immediately: 'I shall be greatly honoured, and I shall leave Moscow at five o'clock the following morning.' I, and the rest of us I think, felt, 'Well, that's that!' and began to collect our papers preparatory to leaving when, suddenly, there was a move from Mr. Churchill—you could almost hear him winding himself up—and for about five minutes he spoke in the most lucid, dramatic, forceful way I have ever heard anybody speak. It was completely impromptu, I think, or it certainly appeared so, and its effect—well, you get some idea of its effect from the fact that the two interpreters, the official British interpreter from the Embassy and Stalin's own personal red-headed little interpreter, Pavlov, turned to look at their notes to find that they had written nothing. They had been so absorbed, and hard-boiled interpreters though they were, they were defeated by the drama of the moment. Alec Cadogan had been making notes and began to read them out, when 'Uncle Joe' put his hand up and said—'No, it does not matter. I do not understand the words, but I like the spirit.' I only wish I could remember the wording of that speech, short as it was, but there are a couple of phrases which did stick in my memory, and which I shall never forget. Mr. Churchill opened by saying: 'I have come round Europe in the midst of my troubles. Yes, Mr. Stalin, I have my troubles as well as you—hoping, hoping, I said, to meet the hand of comradeship' (putting out his hand towards Stalin), 'hoping, I said, to meet the hand of comradeship; and I am bitterly disappointed. I have not met that hand.'

The main military conversations were held on the following day, 15 August. Generals Maxwell and Bradley represented the United States; Voroshilov, Shaposhnikov, and Voronov spoke for Russia; and Brooke, Wavell, and I for Britain. Voroshilov began the first meeting by saying that we should consider the military aspects of the projected Second Front in Europe in 1942. He asked the C.I.G.S. for his observations.

Brooke described how anxious we were to open a Second Front and how strongly the Prime Minister pressed the matter forward. He then explained in great detail how in 1942 it would be impossible with the available resources of armoured divisions and, above all, landing craft, to attempt an amphibious operation of this kind. The Russians seemed quite unable to appreciate the difficulties of the Channel crossing. On several occasions I had to support Brooke's arguments when the Russians made suggestions which completely neglected the fact that in narrow waters the advent of air-power had undermined supremacy at sea.

This part of our talk rambled on for a long time until Brooke said with finality that the British and American staffs did not propose to alter their views. Voroshilov merely remarked that he did not wish to push his opinion beyond a certain point, but he wanted to say, despite all our arguments, that if two great nations like Britain and the U.S.A. were determined to carry out an operation in 1942, it was inconceivable that they could not succeed.

When at the end of these long discussions about the Second Front we attempted to discuss the situation in the Caucasus, Voroshilov merely replied that his instructions were to examine the question of the Second Front only. If the Caucasus situation was of interest to us, he would have to take further instructions before discussing it. Wavell expressed his concern as C.-in-C. India, for the German advance to the south presented an ultimate threat to India's western flank. I remarked that if Air Force squadrons were to go to help Russia in the Caucasus, we must get together very early to lay our plans.

Voroshilov asked how long we should be staying in Moscow, to which Brooke replied that according to Mr. Churchill's present plans we should leave the following morning. Voroshilov then said that he would consult his Government and give a reply that afternoon. He agreed that the German advance did threaten India, but repeated that the best way to hold the Germans on any part of the Russian front would be to open a Second Front in Europe, and a few minutes later, he asked whether we could give any date for the opening of the Second Front in 1943. Brooke replied that it was too early yet. Preparations had begun and were going forward, and the date would be as early as we could possibly make it.

By 6.30 that Saturday evening Voroshilov had received permission to discuss the situation in the Caucasus, and he enquired which particular aspect interested us most. Brooke stuck to general terms, saying that our lines of supply to Russia, through Persia, were threatened by the German advance. We were taking precautionary measures, but it would be extremely helpful to us to know what degree of urgency should be attached to them, and, in particular, whether there was any way in which we could give direct assistance to the Russians.

Voroshilov seemed confident that although the Germans had penetrated some distance south of the River Don, the Russians could protect the supply route. He welcomed the Prime Minister's tentative offer to Stalin of air support, of which he had heard for the first time that day, and said he was sure with the R.A.F's assistance the Russians would not only stop the German advance in the Caucasus, but could finally defeat it. The sooner the squadrons could arrive, the better. Brooke had to interpose at this point the remark that there could be no definite undertaking about the number of squadrons to be sent, or about the date of their arrival. Their move would be dependent on the outcome of the battle in the Western Desert.

I pointed out the importance of getting all the preparations made before the squadrons moved, which Voroshilov said he quite understood, but what he wanted to know was would the help be forthcoming? If the operations in the Middle East were unsuccessful, would the aircraft then be witheld? Could we not make an unconditional offer? This Brooke refused to do. The promise which Churchill had made was conditional on success in the Middle East.

Voroshilov summarised, at last, some facts and figures of the situation in Russia. They had twenty-five divisions on the Caucasus Front, with corresponding air and tank support. He could not give the precise details of this support, for the situation changed so quickly, while the fighting was going on. Although lacking exact information about enemy strength, he thought that including the formations which were turning east towards Stalingrad, the Germans had about half as many divisions again as the Russians. He asserted that the various routes through the the Caucasus Mountains were fortified and held. Preparations had been made to guard against a landing at Batum and the coastal road to Baku was also well held. He was confident that Baku and the Caucasus Mountains would be held until the winter, and in any case the central route through the mountains, which was easily defensible, would become impassable in October. The Russians would value air assistance above all. I said that this was all very well, but that preparations to receive squadrons had so far not been possible at any point north of Teheran, and I was most anxious to get moving. Voroshilov said he had no objection to the beginning of discussions, but it would be necessary to know the exact number of aircraft which would be provided, and whether they would have to be manned by Russian crews. I replied that if a force was sent it would be a complete and balanced one in the proportion of eight fighter squadrons to three light bomber and two medium bomber squadrons, together with a reconnaissance squadron and probably some heavy bombers. Voroshilov observed in an off-hand way that the position appeared to be very indefinite and it hardly seemed worth while preparing the aerodromes on chance, to which I replied that it would be better to have the aerodromes and no aircraft than to have aircraft with no aerodromes.

Marshal Voroshilov said that he did not doubt the sincerity of the offer, but we must realise that the Russians were engaged in many serious battles, and decisions had constantly to be taken. It would be very helpful to have something definite on which reliance could be placed. All the same, he was quite prepared for discussions to start straight away. It would be best to begin work in Moscow and then proceed to the scene of operation.

These proposals would have to be sanctioned by Stalin and Churchill. To this Brooke agreed. General Maxwell, speaking for the Americans, said that he would like General Bradley to take part in the discussions, for the U.S.A. might also provide air assistance.

On this easier note, the meeting ended. Brooke thanked Voroshilov for the information he had provided, and assured him we would do our very best to come to the Russians' assistance as soon as possible. We quite realised the situation. Voroshilov replied courteously that he was grateful for the co-operation offered, and especially for the promise of help in the air. This would be particularly welcome if it came in time and in sufficient strength.

Although this more cordial tone was agreeable to us all, on our side we were struck by the Russians' utter inability to comprehend the essentials of cross-Channel operations. Nor could we feel undue confidence in the information we had been given about the situation in the Caucasus, for it did not tally with what we had seen for ourselves during the flight to Moscow. Of this latter fact, of course, Voroshilov was unaware.

The Russians were bitterly disappointed that we could not offer some direct assistance on the Continent of Europe. Nevertheless, the atmosphere was greatly improved, although at the official banquet that night Stalin was not exactly the soul of tact. He proposed toasts to various people, formations and so on, at about five minute intervals throughout the evening, and we had the Red Army, the Red Navy, the Red Air Force, the Red Intelligence and so on and so on; I should say there were at least a dozen before he came to the British Army, the British Navy and the Royal Air Force. One felt that the toast to the British Army was perfunctory, to say the least, whereas he walked the full length of the table and back, to drink his glass with mine and the toast to the Royal Air Force—all, I think, with deliberate intention of baiting the Prime Minister and Alan Brooke.

At the table I had the good fortune to sit almost opposite Mr. Churchill. He had Pavlov between him and Stalin, and on my right I had a British Embassy interpreter, Mr. Dunlop. A number of times I asked him whether a given translation by Pavlov was correct, to which he replied: 'By and large, yes; but he will make a simple statement into a speech, which very often completely alters the meaning.'

The P.M. was doing his best to make a cheerful party of it, and I was fortunate to be able to overhear a good deal of the conversation. I thought the high spot in the mutual badinage was Churchill talking about his strong support in Parliament and elsewhere for military assistance to the White Russians; and then, to Stalin, he said, 'Have you forgiven me?' Stalin replied, quick as a flash, 'It is not for me to forgive; it is for God to forgive.' I had my own little amusement, too. On my left I had a large, very heavy-looking Russian, and beyond him an American General. At each place at the table there were Lord knows how many glasses, and about four or five different bottles supplied for each. The first toast was given almost as soon as we sat down, which took a lot of people, including myself, by surprise. My Russian neighbour lent across with a bottle to fill one of my glasses, so I very quickly pushed forward a very thin little Vodka glass, the smallest of the lot. As he turned the other side to do the same for the American, the American was not quite quick enough, because he ended up by having a claret glass full of something. The Russian custom for toasts is, of course, no heel taps, and I was very glad I had been able to limit my toast to a tiny little glass, for when I tasted the liquid it was as fiery a brandy as I have ever tasted. My Russian neighbour pressed the American to empty his glass. He gave up and struck at about half-way down; even so, I pitied him. When the next toast came along I watched to see which bottle the Russian used, and I took the same from my collection. It proved to be a most harmless white wine, of which one could have drunk gallons, so I stuck to that.

After we had drunk about six toasts—no heel taps—I noticed my Russian neighbour only half emptied his glass at the seventh, so I remained standing and held my glass upside-down, nudged him and pointed to his glass. He grinned and emptied it properly. At the next toast he did the same, only drank half. I again emptied mine and pointed to his, at which he grinned. At the ninth toast he drained his glass properly and grinned at me, and for the rest of the dinner we went glass for glass. As I said, we could have drunk gallons of it. Poor Alec Cadogan, who was almost opposite me, got very worried and kept shaking his head, pointing to my glass, lifting his elbow and giving other indications that he thought I was going to get tight. He, poor man, had not discovered the secret of the white wine.

As we got up from the table Clark Kerr, the British Ambassador, came over to me and said, 'Do you know what you have done?' I said, 'No, I hope nothing terrible.' The Ambassador replied, 'No. You have done the best job for British diplomacy that's been done since I have been out here.' I was completely defeated by that and said, 'But what do you mean?' to which he replied, 'Do you know who that was sitting on your left, the big fellow who went out from the room with his hand on your shoulder? That was Beria, Head of the O.G.P.U., the Secret Police.'

Apparently, the normal procedure after a banquet like that was to adjourn to watch a film for an hour or so. Mr. Churchill, who by now was getting, not unnaturally, rather peevish, flatly refused and said, 'I am going straight to bed'. Much to our relief, because it gave us the excuse for breaking up the party and getting to bed.

Our return flight was without incident, but when we got back we heard a postscript to our outward flight. When we had had to return to Teheran, with the feathered engine, our crew immediately got down to trying to identify and remedy the trouble. Next day, it appeared that they had done so, and the pilot quite rightly decided to resume his flight to Moscow so that at least he would be available to bring us back. He got about the same distance out from Teheran when a similar thing happened—one engine feathered. Naturally, he returned to Teheran. Meantime a repair crew was on its way from Middle East with spares. Their expert diagnosis of our trouble was that there was a small leak in one of the exhaust pipes from which a tiny jet of flame reached and burnt through the leads to the air screw, causing it to feather. Beyond those leads was a large petrol tank in the wing, which, by about the time of the feathering, would have been some half full of petrol and air, a nice explosive mixture. Had it not been for

the sound judgment of our pilot and the absence of any interference on the part of the V.I.Ps, there might well have been
another one of those unexplained, inexplicable disappearances of
important aircraft.

19 *Churchill's reorganisation–Flow of aircraft to India– Mixed nationalities of our squadrons–Malta convoy from Gibraltar–Timing of 'Torch': London/Washington tug-of-war– Rommel's last bid for the Delta–'Haselden raid' on Tobruk– Rommel in difficulties–Demands from India–Visit to the Desert– The Me. 109G arrives–Montgomery's battle plans–Queensberry Rules– Second Battle of Alamein–Kesselring's views–Rommel in full retreat–'Torch'*

DURING our absence in Moscow, the administration in Cairo had been wrestling with the problems posed by Mr. Churchill's reorganisation, or perhaps it would be more accurate to say disorganisation, of the Command. The small Committee we had set up to go into the problem had proved utterly unable to make any clearcut proposals regarding division of responsibility between the present Command and the new Command in Iraq and Persia. Their suggestions were heavily and rightly criticised by Auchinleck, for they entailed compromise after compromise, and representation throughout G.H.Q. by proxy after proxy, and deputy after deputy—a patchwork organisation which was clearly unacceptable. At this stage India was brought into the debate. It was suggested that India should assume responsibility for Iraq and Persia until a viable separate Command could be formed. In the early stages of the debate there had been no suggestion of altering the position as regards the Air Command, but knowing Wavell's ideas as to the control of air forces, the intrusion of India into the Middle East Command problem immediately gave rise to the threat of a division of the Air Command Middle East. I was determined to fight for continued unity. Any successes that the Air had had during the past two years had been due in no small measure to our flexibility, which enabled us to switch from one part of the Command to another and concentrate where concentration was needed. I regarded that flexibility as absolutely vital. I signalled to Portal:

I am most anxious to find some way of working this fundamentally unsound organisation, but frankly see no prospect of our arriving at such a formula. . . . Most grateful for advice.

who replied at once:

[340]

You have my sympathy in a situation with which I am only too familiar. . . . My only advice is that you should resolutely refuse to be cajoled or pressed into agreeing with what you believe to be unsound. Your reputation fully justifies your taking a firm line, and I will back you to the full.

The argument continued without really making much progress, and I could see that Alan Brooke was beginning to lose patience and intended to try and get a snap decision. He announced in his brisk way that it was now decided that the Command should be split. He was convinced that the new Command must have its own independent air force and that the amount of air strength to be allocated to each Command would be decided by the Chiefs of Staff in London. It seemed to me that now Mr. Churchill was faced with the problem and up against a real hurdle he was not so sure of his ground. He said he would like to give the matter more thought, and he was not wedded to the Indian solution. In any case, he said, the matter must be referred to the War Cabinet. This did not please Brooke, who said it was essential that a solution be reached without delay. At present no one was responsible for dealing with the vital problems of reorganising the Command and preparing for action in Persia and Iraq. Further postponement might be very dangerous. Churchill assured us once again that he was determined Alexander should be relieved of all responsibility for Iraq and Persia, and he fully realised the need for an early decision. He proposed to draft a note setting out the main lines for a solution, which we would consider the next day. In effect, Churchill, after this meeting, abandoned the Indian alternative, and prepared a modified version of his original solution, in which Alexander would be relieved of responsibility for Iraq and Persia, a new Command under General H. M. Wilson taking over on 21 August. The vital issues of flexibility and unity were safe again.

*

On 28 June 1942, the U.S. Army Middle East Air Force was set up under Major-General L. H. Brereton. This act was accompanied by a change of policy by which the Americans decided to establish complete formations of their own aircraft in the Middle

East. I was most anxious lest this decision should cause the flow of U.S. aircraft to the R.A.F. to dry up or fall behind schedule, for in the middle of July, eleven of my fighter squadrons were at no more than half strength. Some were still equipped with Hurricane Is or Tomahawks, types now obsolescent. Nine squadrons enjoyed an existence in name only, for they had no aircraft at all. Between 24 May and 7 July we had lost 202 fighter aircraft on operations. I was informed that I should receive a hundred Kittyhawks in July, with comparable numbers to follow. Baltimores, twin engined light bombers, were to be expected at the rate of about sixty a month. I knew enough already of such promises to take them with a large grain of salt.

Early in August I learned that it had been decided to limit the R.A.F's strength in the Middle East to sixty-five squadrons. The U.S. Army Air Force would have twenty-four, making a grand total of eighty-nine. This did not help me very much with my immediate problem of producing aircraft without which we should scarcely be able to take advantage of the pause imposed upon Rommel by Auchinleck's successful defensive action at the first Battle of Alamein in July. We had been led to expect the arrival of 513 Kittyhawks between April and August. In fact, 251 had been received; and at the end of August a mere fifty-eight were fit for operations. Both Casey and I had long pressed for the diversion of a heavy bomber force to the Middle East, so far without success, and the question was taken up again with Portal in this same month. However, I was promised that no detachment of air forces from Egypt would be made until a decision had been reached against Rommel. In these circumstances Portal, while agreeing that long-range heavy bombers would be desirable in Egypt, did not feel them to be essential. He thought I should probably have to make do with my Wellingtons and two Halifax squadrons. The recovery of Cyrenaica, which was almost a corollary to the defeat of Rommel, would make me far less dependent on the extra range of the Liberators. He added: 'I am absolutely opposed to diverting more heavies from the attack on Germany which is really beginning to have great results.'

As for fighters, Portal assured me that he had just urged again that their despatch should be accelerated, but 'I hope you are not taken in by propaganda speeches about the vast flood of American production. It will be vast, but it is not yet.'

Just as I received this signal, I was asked to despatch Wellingtons, Beauforts, and Liberators to India. I realised the need to build up the Air Force in India as rapidly as possible. On this occasion I asked that the aircraft should be supplied over a period of six weeks, in accordance with the flow of reinforcements arriving in the Middle East from home. Peirse accepted this proposal though he must have been painfully aware how utterly inadequate was his air strength to meet the Japanese.

Less than a month passed before the next serious blow fell. I learned from Portal on 22 September that an American fighter group, originally due to arrive in the Middle East by 1 October, had now been withdrawn altogether from our allocation. The C.A.S. commented:

I fully realise what a blow this will be to you, but now you have probably enough personal experience of Americans to know the difficulties of dealing with them.

He admitted that there was no chance that the four fighter groups due to come to us would be operational in Egypt by January 1943. Every possible pressure was being put on General Arnold, the American Chief of Air Staff, to send Kittyhawks to the Middle East, and Portal understood that in that respect my position would soon improve. At the end of his signal he acknowledged:

Nevertheless, this further failure of Americans to meet their obligations under A.T.P. Agreement is seriously embarrassing, and we will do all we possibly can to make up for it.

A little later it was suggested, for motives I fully understood, that I should meet the Greek desire to form another Greek fighter squadron in the Middle East, and to complete the re-equipment of their other squadrons. However, the substitution of an allied squadron for an R.A.F. squadron seriously affected the mobility and elasticity of my force in a way which was not always understood. Already sixteen of my squadrons were South African Air Force, and in no circumstances could they operate outside Africa, even as far as Sinai or Palestine. Eight of my squadrons

[343]

belonged to the Royal Australian Air Force with a nominal restriction on the areas in which they could operate, and we knew that the Greeks, like the Yugoslav squadrons when they were with us, would be most unwilling, if they did not flatly refuse, to operate away from the Mediterranean. As for the American units which were being further substituted for R.A.F. units, it was difficult at this stage to foretell whether they would succeed in organising themselves to such a degree that they could move to other operational areas. The consequence of all this was that the number of squadrons which I could readily move to the Caucasus or Turkey, the Persian Gulf or Aden, was already sufficiently limited, and the substitution of further squadrons of whatever kind for R.A.F. squadrons was most undesirable.

*

Rommel's success in pushing us back across the Western Desert meant that the only hope of running supplies through to Malta was from Gibraltar. A convoy of fourteen ships set off in August, but only five got through. The rest were lost through enemy air action, as was the aircraft-carrier *Eagle*. Even to pass five ships into Malta in those circumstances was no small achievement. The island had held out all through these months by a combination of bravery, genius for improvisation, high morale and sheer refusal to give in. I had very much hoped that the replacement of General Dobbie would mean a new infusion of fighting spirit in the higher ranks of the Services there. The accounts I received in September, however, were by no means reassuring. Personal intrigues of the kind frequently found under the Dobbie régime had continued under Gort. One small but ludicrous example was set by one of the Gunners who was intent upon building up a name for himself at the expense of the G.O.C., Scobie. This individual did not recognise Scobie as his chief, dealt direct with Gort, and had indeed taken it upon himself to appoint Gort as Air Defence Commander. For the moment, this made no practical difference to the situation, since the anti-aircraft Brigadiers were an exceptionally fine group, and dealt direct with Air Vice Marshal Keith Park, who had now succeeded Lloyd as A.O.C.

While there was no doubt that Gort had done a good deal to organise the domestic side of the island's affairs, the defensive, defeatist atmosphere was more pronounced than ever. Gort apparently told Park at least once a day that he did not wish to be 'in the cooler'. Similar talk about the 'cooler' was becoming habitual amongst some of the other senior people in the Navy and Army. Such an attitude became doubly deplorable at a time when morale among troops and the populace could hardly have been higher.

Malta's fate still depended on our ability to push the enemy far to the west, and eventually out of North Africa altogether.

*

Lord Attlee records that in the autumn of 1941, well before Pearl Harbor, President Roosevelt discussed with him the probable course of the war. Taking down an atlas, Roosevelt put his finger on Algiers: 'That is where I want to have American troops.'[1]

After Pearl Harbor, when the United States had declared war on Germany and Japan, Roosevelt wished to defeat Germany first, using Great Britain as a base, before dealing with Japan.

Some American strategists, notably General Marshall, had urged that a frontal assault should be made against Germany in 1942. When it had become clear that this course was not practical, and after negotiations between Churchill and Roosevelt, the scene of projected operations switched to North Africa. There then ensued a tug-of-war on a minor scale between London and Washington about the timing of the allied operation against North Africa, which was to attack Rommel and his troops from the rear. The Chiefs of Staff in London reasoned that whatever might be the result of Hitler's summer campaign in Russia, the Germans must withdraw large forces for rest and refitting at home during the autumn. As far as air forces were concerned, the date for this process would probably be no later than mid-October, after which the Mediterranean area was likely to be the first to receive Axis reinforcements. Surprise in the North African

[1] Lord Attlee: *As it Happened*, p. 143.

landings was all-important to us. If they were mounted speedily, the enemy might well be deceived as to timing, and deception as to timing might be no less effective than deception as to place. Moreover, October might be a month for critical decisions by the Russians, decisions which might be influenced by allied military action. The longer the delay in launching an attack in Tunisia, the greater the risk that the enemy might forestall us there. The Chiefs of Staff therefore pressed for the earliest possible launching of the operation, preferably in October. Information from Washington showed that the United States Chiefs of Staff were thinking of 7 November as the earliest possible date, although General Marshall preferred a later one. While Churchill was holding his fateful meetings in Cairo early in August, the Chiefs of Staff telegraphed to him that it was perhaps because their United States counterparts were beginning to realise that their troops were not very highly trained, and because it was their first big venture, that there must be no question of failure: 'This mentality makes for delay to ensure that last gaiter button is secure.'

By the end of August the idea of a launching at the end of the first week of October, as desired by the British Chiefs of Staff, had been finally abandoned. General Eisenhower, who was to command the operation, told the British Chiefs of Staff that he was very doubtful whether an assault, even on what he considered an adequate scale, would be possible before 28 October. Churchill made a further effort to persuade Roosevelt that the date should be 14 October, saying he was willing to take any amount of responsibility for running the political risks—with the French in North Africa and the Spaniards—entailed in a North African landing.

However, the opinions of the United States General Staff and of General Eisenhower prevailed. There, for the moment, the matter rested, while preparations for the 'Torch' landings were feverishly pressed ahead. Their value would clearly depend to a large extent on the degree to which we could engage Rommel and push him back. The farther he was compelled to retreat the more effectively and swiftly might the pincers close.

*

The shortages of aircraft, and the severe rate of wastage suffered in the desperate battles of June and July, did not prevent our crews from achieving more than any reasonable man would have deemed possible. Early in September I visited the squadrons in the Western Desert, and reported to Portal on the 7th:

General feeling is that threat to Egypt has been scotched. This has been achieved by astute use of strong positions prepared by previous régime. Difference between this land battle [of Alam Halfa] and previous ones is that in this one soldiers have refused to play enemy game and send tanks against guns. Enemy has been forced to send his tanks against our guns. As regards air battle this has been repetition of previous battle, i.e. intense air attack on enemy concentrations in forward area throughout day and night.

It appeared that the intensity of the air operations had even exceeded that during the worst period of our retreat. The Army commanders I found most outspoken in acknowledging the vital contribution made by air-power. Liaison with the Army in the Western Desert continued to improve under the leadership of Alexander and Montgomery.

The latter had put co-operation with the R.A.F. first in the order of priority, but it appeared that no immediate surge forward by the Army was to be expected:

Immediate prospects not what one could wish. There appears no possibility of following up this success on land [Alam Halfa] while enemy still suffering from what is undoubtedly a severe shock. Have told Alexander and Montgomery that they must not rely on continuance of recent scale of sinkings. After long period of poor luck our ship strikes have had a spell of hardly earned better luck. We will inevitably have our setbacks again. . . .

I thought the enemy would probably revert to heavily escorted convoys with effective smoke screens. The weather would soon deteriorate and as a result Rommel would be able to build up some of his strength. Moreover, I was still gravely worried about the strength of my fighter squadrons. We were desperately short of Spitfires and Kittyhawks, so that the brunt had to be borne by Hurricane squadrons, which were quite outclassed. Casualties were heavy and successes against the enemy relatively few.

[347]

The Americans were already fitting in very well. Brereton had established himself in the Western Desert with Coningham for a time, and his fighter and light bomber pilots had been gradually worked in with our squadrons. They were shaping up well, and before long would begin to be able to operate as units. The heavy bombers had still much to learn. Moreover, the Americans had no replacements of aircraft or crews as yet, and so must inevitably be a wasting asset for some time to come.

This phase marked the end of Rommel's last desperate bid to seize the Delta area, against which he had thrown his tired forces. Our men had flown 674 sorties on 1 September, 806 sorties on 2 September, and 902 on the next day. By the time I sent my signal to Portal on the 7th, Rommel's final attempt to force the Alamein Line had failed.

Portal's reply paid a handsome tribute to the remarkable effort put out by our squadrons. He very much hoped we would manage to go on sinking ships, a process which, besides destroying vital supplies, also made the Axis powers waste air effort on the provision of defensive convoys. As for the future, the C.A.S. telegraphed:

> While sharing your regret that Army cannot immediately attack I must say I would much prefer total defeat and destruction of Rommel *in situ* after short delay rather than yet another fighting retreat to Benghazi starting now and probably ending with us little stronger than him.

He also sent me reassuring news about the despatch of larger numbers of Spitfires in September and October; and expressed himself delighted to hear of our good relations with the Army.

*

During the rest of September, while Alexander and Montgomery were preparing for a forward move in their methodical and deliberate fashion, the only action of note was in the shape of the 'Haselden raid' on Tobruk. This operation, though of little immediate significance in itself, taught some useful lessons. The idea originated from the Navy, who had been intensely anxious to show the White Ensign, and it coincided with a move to make fuller use of the Long Range Desert Group. I took the view that the raid, planned to take place simultaneously from inland and from the sea, was unlikely to achieve much in the way of material effect, but that if it coincided with a breakthrough on our part at Alamein, it might have a valuable psychological and diversionary effect. Having thrown cold water on the scheme from the beginning I finally relented, since the soldiers as well as the sailors were anxious to try it, and were willing to accept the risks. I did not then feel that I could carry my opposition to the extent of refusal.

The operation was controlled from the Combined Operations Room at Alexandria, where I spent two days. The cover attack on Tobruk by the medium and heavy bombers went according to plan. Many eye-witnesses testified to its effectiveness. I could not help being slightly amused when at one stage in the post mortem the effectiveness of this attack was given as an alibi for the inability of the landing parties to get ashore at the right time and the right place owing to the glare of fires and explosions. One party duly reached its objective on the southern shore and held it until after dawn, waiting for the M.T.B. parties, which, with the exception of two, failed to turn up. The seaborne parties were a complete failure. The destroyer parties were very slow in getting the first flight away, with the result that the *Sikh* was badly hit, and the rest of the time seemed to have been spent in trying, unsuccessfully, to get her away.

These failures meant that the destroyers and M.T.Bs. had to try to get back to Alexandria in daylight. An attempt to cover the last destroyer, the *Zulu*, meant offering hostages to fortune by sending ships back into 'Bomb Alley'. Weather conditions, with seven-tenths cloud, made it very difficult for our six Beaufighters to be sure of interception. It appeared that the attack which hit and destroyed the anti-aircraft cruiser *Coventry* caught it completely by surprise. As I told Portal on 20 September:

The result of all this sorry story is of course that the Air Force is blamed for not giving enough fighter cover. The Admiral tried to make an alibi by saying the real trouble was that we had not got enough long-range fighters until I pointed out to him that he knew perfectly well before the operation began what long-range fighters were available (in actual fact they did considerably more sorties than had been reckoned upon) and that no practicably conceivable force of long-range fighters would have been adequate to cover the surface craft which dotted the four hundred miles of sea from Tobruk to Alexandria.

It is clear from this affair that I shall have to produce for record a child's guide in the use of surface craft in the Eastern Mediterranean under present conditions and I am now preparing a paper on these lines.

Indeed, the one tangible success of the sorry operation seemed to be the destruction of some enemy aircraft at Barce.

The only good thing about the affair is that it has at least taught Alexander and Montgomery the real value of these glamorous 'combined operations' and when operations begin again in the Western Desert I think we shall be free from any further fanciful projects of this sort. I have tried to drum it in that the Navy's opportunity will come when we are back at Benghazi. When we are back there we shall need ships and need them badly. The Navy's job in the meantime is to build up its resources and not fritter them away showing the flag.[1]

The virtual failure of the operation did not conceal the essential facts of the situation. Rommel's position, now that he had lost the Battle of Alam Halfa, was a desperate one. His forces were receiving only about one-fifth of the supplies they needed. Most of their transports passed between Sicily and Benghazi, Malta therefore becoming more crucial than ever; and Malta had still not been reduced. Luckily, Tobruk was quite inadequate to the enemy's needs and Rommel was paying the price of success in the Desert, a price we had already paid twice, in the shape of the huge distances between the good ports and the battle-front. He was well over three hundred miles from Tobruk, six hundred from Benghazi, and twelve hundred from Tripoli. Rommel himself acknowledged that the offensive which began on 31 August had failed, because the British positions to the south had been completed in great strength, and his supplies of petrol were not forthcoming.

---

[1] A full account of the Haselden raid can be found in Gordon Landsborough's *Tobruk Commando* (1956).

The continuous and very heavy attacks of the R.A.F., who were practically masters of the air, absolutely pinned my troops to the ground and made impossible any safe deployment or any advance according to schedule.[1]

After the battle was over Rommel wrote that in due course the Allied Air Forces would be able to give his troops and equipment such a pounding that they would be virtually unfit for action. He reasoned that by air supremacy we should secure good reconnaissance reports and should be able to operate more freely and boldly on the ground, since in an emergency the Air Force would be able to delay our opponents until we had taken effective counter-measures, and this process would be accompanied by a speeding up of our own movements.

His supply lines could be put out of use by day, thus causing irretrievable loss of time:

Anyone who has to fight, even with the most modern weapons, against an enemy with complete air superiority, fights like a savage against modern European troops, under the same operational and tactical handicaps and with the same chances of success.[2]

The crucial question for us now was whether Rommel would receive sufficient supplies before the Eighth Army was ready to push him back to the west, and could we do it in time to get convoys through to Malta?

In preparing against our expected offensive, Rommel had to set up defences in the form least vulnerable to our air superiority. Motorised and mechanised formations could no longer bear the main burden of the defensive battle. They were too liable to be disrupted or smashed up by air attack. The Axis forces must try to meet us in fixed positions, constructed for defence against the most modern weapons of war. Rommel wrote:

We had to accept the fact that in future the enemy would be able to delay our operations at will by strong air attacks by day and similar attacks at night with the aid of parachute flares. Experience had taught us that no man could be expected to stay in his vehicle and drive on when attacked by enemy bombers and that it was useless to try to

[1] Young: *Rommel*, p. 272.
[2] Young: *Rommel*, p. 258.

work to a timetable. Our positions had to be constructed so strongly that they could be held by their local garrisons independently and over a long period, without support of operational reserves, until, in spite of the delays caused by the R.A.F., reinforcements could arrive.

British air superiority threw to the winds all our operational and tactical rules, which hitherto had been followed with such success, simply because they could no longer be applied. Without strong air forces of our own there was no answer to the problem of dealing with the enemy air superiority. The strength of the Anglo-American Air Force was, in all the battles to come, the deciding factor.[1]

★

During the visit to Moscow, Mr. Churchill had tentatively and conditionally offered to place some air forces on the southern flank of the Russian armies. It had been agreed that victory in the Western Desert must have priority; but under pressure to open up a Second Front in Europe, the Prime Minister was naturally anxious to show some clear proof of our support for the exertions of the Red Army. Believing firmly that concentration was the key of success, I had always trusted that no thrust to the north should be made until Rommel was finally defeated—unless, of course, Hitler's troops defeated the Russians in the south. As winter drew near we could see that this danger at least was averted for the moment, and I hoped that the idea of placing air forces in the Caucasus might now be abandoned or at least postponed indefinitely. At my instance, the Middle Eastern Commanders-in-Chief signalled to London in this sense, but without success. I wrote to Wilfrid Freeman on 12 October:

The more one thinks about it the more one feels that if the African operations go well we simply must exploit them, as one has been saying for many months. Italy is the weak spot in the Axis at present. We know from past experience that it does not take very much to make her begin to totter. If we hold the African coast and have the forces available, we can begin to pound Italy in a way which I do not think she will be able to stand. Sardinia and Sicily are the next stepping stones. Here to my mind is the real Second Front. From Italy we can

[1] Young: *Rommel*, pp. 258–59.

reach Skoda, and all the other centres of industry and population which have been transferred north-west.

Apart from this strategic appreciation there was a more material reason for my opposition to the Caucasus project. Any forces we could send there would only be a drop in the ocean to the Russians, and as the prospects of salvage and repair would be poor, the rate of wastage would be far higher than that suffered in the Desert. To me it seemed a tragic mistake to make a detachment of that kind just at the time when we should be getting at long last a base for offensive action. Until now the whole Middle Eastern campaign had necessarily been defensive:

It is probably no direct concern of mine, but what one is really afraid of is that the military minds are still hankering after another 1914–18 in France, and that we may make the same mistake as the Germans made when they undertook the Russian land campaign, and in doing so threw away their strongest weapon—air-power.

I had already taken this view in a long private conversation with Smuts on 10 October, and again at the Defence Committee Meeting which he attended the next day. Alexander and Harwood agreed, as did Smuts. When I was alone with him I reminded him of the phrase he used early in 1942—'the air, the architect of victory'—and said I was afraid the old conventions might obscure that great truth.

*

Even as the second battle of El Alamein drew near, the drainage of our aircraft to India continued. General Alexander himself felt anxious that there should be no shortage of aircraft in the Middle East at this critical time. He suggested to the Middle East Defence Committee on 20 October that we should ask that the flow to India be stopped at least until the end of November. Our resources were diminishing and our whole air force was concentrated in Egypt, leaving virtually nothing to protect the other local commands where no threat was developing. The success of operations in North Africa might well lead to the re-opening of the Mediterranean, which would in turn have a direct effect on shipping to India. The Indian front was not for the present active.

If the Japanese did undertake a serious campaign against India, aircraft could quickly be flown there where the ground staffs already existed.

Admiral Harwood, too, was concerned at the shortage of Beaufighter cover for his operations. Indian demands had caused a serious decline in our Beaufighter strength. On 28 October I had no more than seventeen of these aircraft serviceable with which to meet the commitments of providing cover for a convoy to Malta, the 'Torch' landings, and operations against enemy transport, airborne and seaborne.

On receiving these representations, the Chiefs of Staff agreed that I might postpone the despatch of Beaufighters from the Middle East to India until the end of November.

Now, at last, the time had come for the opening of our first sustained offensive in the Middle Eastern campaign. I had pressed Alexander and Montgomery to grasp the nettle at the earliest moment. They had insisted on a policy of consolidation and preparation which seemed to me, if anything, too elaborate and cautious. It was already clear that the new régime was not one which would stake much on a gamble or take inspired risks.

Before the opening of our offensive I went on an extended visit to the Western Desert and 201 Group, where I saw all the commanding officers and most of the air crews. I found them all in first-class fettle. Morale was as high as ever and the standard of performance in the air most satisfying. I wrote to Portal on my return:

I saw one of their 'balbos' [named after the Italian Air Marshal] go off and come back, and it worked like clockwork. 21 Baltimores and B.25's in first-class formation, and about 70 fighters (Hurricanes, Kittyhawks and Kittybombers and a top cover of two sections of Spitfires). The precision with which the party took off and 'rendez-voused' was worthy of Hendon. The return was just as good, the fighters staying overhead until the bombers had landed, the Spitfires having seen the party taken back across the lines turned back to deal effectively with some 109 jackals. The Americans work in very well with our squadrons. They now have their own fighter wing with two squadrons who have already shown up well in combat. Their third fighter squadron which has had more experience, and we can make reasonably mobile, is in one of our own fighter wings and will go forward. They are learning from us, and we are learning from them—I was glad to hear this from both sides.

Thanks to careful husbanding in the last few weeks, we had been able to build up our resources a little. The Hurricane squadrons were now up to strength, and the Kittyhawks nearly so, though one Merlin Kittyhawk squadron was still very weak. Three Spitfire squadrons did not even approach full strength, and I had no reserves for them at all. Only a trickle was coming through from Takoradi, so that there was no hope for the present of building up these three squadrons to full strength, let alone of meeting heavy wastage. Here was a serious handicap indeed, for the Hurricane was badly outclassed, especially since the Me. 109G had started to appear. There was, then, only one real solution:

What we have got to do is to try and knock the enemy air right out of the ring. This is, of course, easier said than done, but you will probably have noticed from other sources that Coningham has already made some progress in this direction. If we can do this, the Hurricane will once again be able to do its job, especially the Tac R [Tactical Reconnaissance] squadrons who, at the moment, have a pretty grim task—since I cannot possibly afford to give them Spitfires.

I was much heartened to discover that co-operation with the Army had further improved, thanks, at least in part, to the lead given by Montgomery on this subject. It was most refreshing to find in Eighth Army Advanced Headquarters the embryo of a real operations room copied directly from our own mobile operations rooms. I took it upon myself to tell the soldiers that it was the first sign I had seen of their being able to collect and sift information about their battle, and consequently the first sign I had seen of their being able to control it. For two years they had been saying that such a thing was impossible. Now they had started it and realised its potentialities I thought it would develop well and make an enormous difference.

The plans for the battle, however, did not seem to be the best that could be devised. I signalled to Portal:

I am not very happy about Montgomery's plans. As I told him, one

[355]

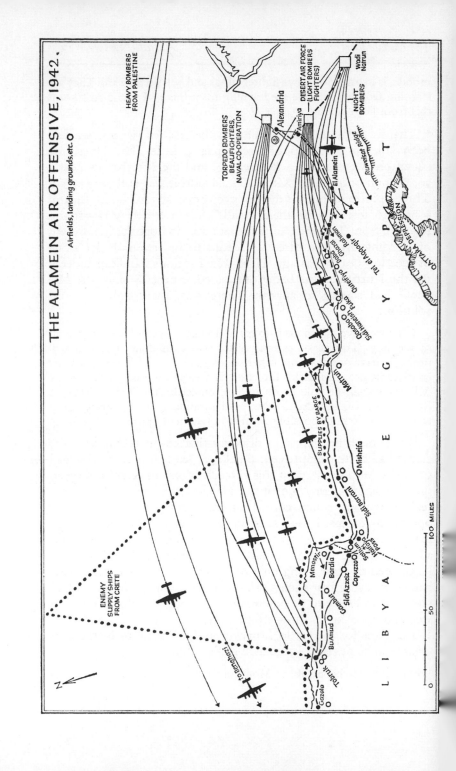

THE ALAMEIN AIR OFFENSIVE, 1942.

Airfields, landing grounds, etc. O

of the main lessons of the past few months has been that the enemy strength has really been broken by the twenty-four hour day of almost incessant air attack allowing him no rest for day after day, interrupting his supplies and food, ammunition, etc., dislocating his communications and control. This factor should, I feel, have been exploited to the utmost in the next battle; having forced him to disperse to a fantastic extent, we cannot, of course, make this attack effective unless he has concentrated again. He will only concentrate if he is threatened on land. We know he is nervous and tense, and any serious-looking threat would almost certainly make him concentrate immediately.

I felt that we should have made such a threat which would have given our air forces an opportunity to hammer the enemy and weaken him for three or four days before the delivery of the vital blow on land. I was afraid that it was now too late to do anything about it:

We shall have a contest on the best Queensbury [sic] Rules lines; the two opponents carefully fattened up in their respective corners, fanned and advised by their seconds up to the last minute until the seconds are ordered out and the gong goes. Of course, from the air point of view, the contest has been going on for some time in the attacks on shipping, lines of communication, and, with the last two or three days, against his air.

The second battle of El Alamein began on land the day after I wrote this letter, 23 October. A most elaborate campaign of deception had successfully misled the enemy's Intelligence. Our superiority in the air had prevented him from making the full reconnaissance which would have revealed our dispositions more accurately. Rommel, who was undergoing hospital treatment in Austria, was asked by Hitler himself at noon on 24 October to return instantly to Africa. This he did; but I think that the battle was already lost. Rommel was inhibited from taking the offensive in the open desert by the disproportion between his own armoured strength and ours, which was being constantly reinforced. His shortage of fuel, as during the battle of Alam Halfa, was acute; and our superiority in the air, the ground-support tactics of our fighters and the resultant tactical limitations on the use of motorised forces severely hampered his effort. Our campaign against the enemy's fighter force, which began on 9 October, undoubtedly proved most effective. 'Mary' Coningham had wisely resisted the temptation to accept his early successes as decisive, and he consistently directed a proportion of his effort towards keeping the enemy air forces down. This policy, coupled with the diversionary effect of attacks on shipping, had nullified the effect of the enemy's air reinforcements. By the end of October, the land fighting had inflicted on Rommel's armour losses which he could not replace. We could not, however, afford to let the time pass without a decision—time was by no means entirely on our side. At Headquarters in Cairo we were all seriously worried by the slow tempo of Montgomery's operations, and the three of us, Casey, Alexander, and myself, agreed to go up to the desert and individually emphasise, not for the first time, the dangers of the situation, in that we might well lose time and with it Malta and the Mediterranean.

When I reached Montgomery's headquarters his visitors from Cairo had been and gone. Montgomery made some reference to 'bellyaching' apparently going on in Cairo. He took me up to his map caravan and showed me his Master Plan for the next operation—'Supercharge'. It scarcely gave any prospect of manœuvre. It was, in fact, what Montgomery described as just a slogging match. I tried to get Montgomery to appreciate the importance of time. Thanks to some very heavy sinkings of tankers we knew that for the present Rommel was critically short of petrol, but it needed only one or two tankers with the skilful use of a smoke screen to get through our blockade, and Rommel would be free again.

Our other danger spot was Malta. If we did not get supply convoys to Malta the population and the garrison would soon be on the verge of starvation and our way through the Mediterranean would be closed. My eloquence on the subject of Malta and of our shipping strikes fell on deaf ears. The only response I got was, 'It's a slogging match.' All I could do was to shrug my shoulders and say, 'Well, it's your battle.'

From the map caravan we walked down together a few yards to the mess tent where Montgomery and I had a very quick lunch. We were just finishing the meal when Montgomery said, 'There is some fresh intelligence regarding Rommel's dispositions. This means a change.' We returned to the maps again. 'Now,' said Montgomery, 'your air crews have been doing a wonderful job in cutting off Rommel's petrol, but they cannot do it every time, and one of these dark nights a tanker will get through and we will have Rommel on the loose again. We do not want that. And now, Malta. Malta, literally starving unless we can get your squadrons back into Cyrenaica so as to get convoys through again. There is no time to spare.'

On 2 November, Montgomery altered the direction of his assault, striking to the south. Our infantry breached the enemy line and the armour began to pour through. Rommel decided on retreat. The next day he received from the Führer the following telegram: 'The position requires that the El Alamein position be held to the last man. There is to be no retreat, not so much as 1 millimetre! Victory or death!'

At the breakthrough, I went at once to the Desert where I found the advanced parties of fighter squadrons already on the road. All the squadrons were in magnificent form and out to kill. The key to success was to get them right forward, swiftly and in long bounds. This was partly a problem for the Army and partly administrative. I was satisfied that the administrative arrangements, based on long experience, were ready. As for the other side of the question, I told Portal:

Coningham and I have repeatedly emphasised importance of long swift moves to Army and am hopeful we shall get what we want. I think it is realised that this is a time when big chances must be taken. Co-operation between fighters and bombers and between British and Americans in Desert is first class, and the operational organisation is working like clockwork, with excellent mutual confidence. Hurricane squadrons doing magnificently loyal work, but are, of course, completely outclassed, and it is hard to tell them they cannot have modern aircraft yet.

Air support for the Army had so far worked extremely well. The liaison with the Army authorities had been excellent, and I sensed an atmosphere of mutual confidence. More disappointing was the discovery on the morning of 5 November that the Army's mobile operations room, of which I had high hopes, was out of action. The six staff officers who should have been manning the centre and recording the hour-to-hour progress of events, were not to be seen. Inquiries subsequently elicited the information that they had all gone forward 'to have a look at the battle'. The fog of war was already developing, but I lived in hopes that this was only a temporary phase. I was able to tell the C.A.S. that the general situation was very satisfactory:

. . . and we should be able to, as indeed we must, maintain present maximum effort. We are all determined not to let enemy get his tail up on the ground or in the air, and if we can get forward in long and rapid stages we should be able to clean up the job.

There could be no doubt that once again air strength played a decisive role. In the last week of October, when our progress was slow, it was the efforts of British and American bombers which broke up an enemy counter-attack on Kidney Ridge before our land forces were engaged. Two days later I received from Churchill this signal:

Many congratulations on the magnificent way in which you are cutting into the enemy in the air, on the ground, and on the sea. Pray give my compliments to Coningham, and also to tell the officers and men who welcomed me so cordially in the Desert. I was sure then that great days lie ahead. Those days have come, and you are all playing a glorious part in them.[1]

I replied:

On behalf all of us I wish to thank you most sincerely for your inspiring message of encouragement. We are all at full throttle and determined to make a job of it.

A day or two later General Alexander telegraphed to the Prime Minister that the R.A.F. had throughout given superb support to the land battle. Our squadrons, he said, were bombing the enemy's retreating columns incessantly. Meanwhile, on 'the other side of the hill', General Kesselring had been gathering some uncomfortable impressions on the spot.

For the first time the R.A.F. has appeared in sufficient strength to be a decisive factor in the battle, but this is probably only the initial phase of the stepping up of Allied air activity which we must expect.

---

[1] Churchill: *The Second World War,* vol. IV, p. 535.

If we do not want to be smashed in the near future by the enemy air forces, now is our very last chance to make a comparable increase in strength.

Of course, we were doing our best to make sure that Kesselring had no chance to effect 'a comparable increase'. This phase of the campaign demonstrated again the unique advantages of air-power as a flexible instrument of war. Aircraft could be switched rapidly from one task to another as the situation demanded. They could be summoned from bases and theatres widely separated. The bombers operated by day and night against Benghazi and Tobruk. Aircraft from Egypt and Malta made carefully co-ordinated attacks against Rommel's seaborne supplies from Europe. Beaufighters blasted trains and transport beyond the range of normal fighters. Torpedo Swordfish loaded with flares ranged the Desert, seeking out targets, and calling up the Wellingtons to deal with them. Fighters covered barges and coastal shipping, so that our seaborne supplies should keep pace with the advance.

While Rommel was in full retreat, General Eisenhower's forces made the 'Torch' landings far behind him, on 8 November. Whilst this lodgement was established, all attention was again focused on the enemy's communications between Southern Europe and Tunisia. Here the advantages of unified air control in what was now the Mediterranean theatre proved their value again. The Middle East Air Forces helped Eisenhower by attacking Tunis, Bizerta, Palermo, and Catania, and the shipping which plied between them. In the three months August to November 1942, over 200,000 tons of Axis shipping were sunk in the Mediterranean. Rommel could scarcely hope to survive such a rate of wastage.

20

Embryo of unified Air Command, Mediterranean–Airfield parties re-enter Tobruk–von Thoma's views–Rommel's views– Benghazi–Army's build-up delays R.A.F. pursuit–Visit to Malta and Algiers–Command chaos–I refuse to advise without authority–Eisenhower's difficulties–Algiers–Sholto Douglas to Cairo–Views on unified command–Churchill: 'Army like a peacock'

I had seriously to consider my personal position. The Secretary of State for Air, Sir Archibald Sinclair, had privately enquired of me whether I thought an early change in the Middle Eastern Air Command was desirable. I was given to understand that I should be wanted at home in the Air Ministry and that I should probably be replaced by Air Chief Marshal Sholto Douglas. In my reply of 8 November I tried, so far as possible, to eliminate my personal feelings and consider only the North African operations. Though the enemy had undoubtedly received a smashing blow I could not regard the campaign as decisive, at least until we were clear of the El Agheila bottleneck. We had already reached there twice and failed on both occasions because we got there too late. Now the vital thing was to keep up at all costs the momentum and pace of the advance:

There are still 500 miles to be traversed. The further we go the more difficult. We ourselves have a grand team determined to push forward as quickly as the land situation permits. I feel sure that unless both we and the Army and Navy achieve impossibilities there is grave risk that we may reach Agheila late and be involved in another stalemate with its consequent risks of yet a third retreat from Benghazi. I feel that having myself twice been in Benghazi already I am in a position to apply the spur not only to my own Command but also to the other Services and the Americans. I do not feel that Sholto Douglas, being a newcomer, will be able to do so with the same force. I would therefore strongly urge that no change be made until the end of the year.

But by then, as we shall see, new possibilities had arisen.

At about the same time I heard of a suggestion that when the battle situation in North Africa was clarified, air operations over the Mediterranean should be placed under the control of a new naval Commander-in-Chief. I protested to Portal on the 14th.

The one outstanding and incontestable lesson of the last eighteen months' operations is that control of sea communications in the Mediterranean has passed to the air. The victory of Matapan was the the last dying flicker of naval supremacy in the Mediterranean, and since May 1941 surface ships have only been able to move precariously at sea at the mercy of hostile air forces and by grace of what fighter cover the available aerodromes make possible. Reasonable security for ships, whether naval or merchant, can only be attained by coast-crawling under fighter cover.

The draft which I had seen placed two naval co-operation commands, one in Central and another in Eastern Mediterranean, under the naval C.-in-C. I asked whether he was also to control the fighters along the North African coast, under whose umbrella all ships would have to creep? Furthermore, the vital element in recent attacks on enemy shipping, and a factor in dealing with enemy naval vessels, had been the long-range heavy bombers. Was the naval C.-in-C. to control them? Was he to decide how air forces were to be switched to the Central Mediterranean, and vice versa, in a theatre where air-power was in indisputable control? The existing organisation by which the A.O.C.-in-C. co-operated with the naval C.-in-C., and concentrated his forces to support the Navy or Army as the situation demanded, had, to the best of my knowledge, worked satisfactorily, so far as the availability of aircraft had permitted.

In my opinion the proposed organisation is a fantastic attempt to put back the clock, and is fundamentally uneconomical and unsound. I would most strongly urge that the matter be considered in the light of the hard facts of the past eighteen months' war in the Mediterranean, and in any case that the M.E. Defence Committee be given an opportunity of expressing their views before any decision is taken.

Portal replied at once that no proposal of this nature had reached the Chiefs of Staff. If it did, his reaction would be exactly the same as mine. He understood the suggestions to emanate from the Admiralty. They had not, at any rate as yet, received the endorsement of the Joint Planners. He was sorry I had been troubled with the matter, but assured me that my views would be most helpful if the proposal ever reached the level of the Chiefs of Staff. Four days later, on 19 November, I learned that proposals of a rather different nature had indeed reached that level. The Joint Planners were looking ahead to the time when the land operations in North Africa had been completed. It was proposed that there should then be set up one naval command for the whole Mediterranean, Red Sea, and Atlantic within six hundred miles of Gibraltar. The commander would be responsible to the Admiralty for all except combined operations in the Western Mediterranean, for which he would be responsible to Eisenhower. The Air command would be split in two. One would come under Eisenhower, and would include American and R.A.F. units based in French Africa except 'coastal aircraft'. The other would be called Middle East and Mediterranean, and would include all air forces based east of the frontier between Tripoli and Tunis, together with all coastal aircraft in the Western Mediterranean and Gibraltar. There would be two Naval sub-commands, and an Air sub-command for the so-called coastal aircraft in the western end of the Mediterranean. A Combined Naval Air Headquarters for the control of the Mediterranean would be established near Eisenhower's headquarters, and would be run by local representatives of the C.-in-C. Mediterranean and the A.O.C.-in-C. Middle East and Mediterranean, who would themselves remain in Cairo.

Portal told me that the Joint Planners seemed to have failed completely to grasp that the war in the Mediterranean would be fought out principally in the air. He thought they had also made a first-class mistake in imagining that particular types of aircraft could be regarded as coastal and segregated from the remainder of the air force. The C.A.S. already knew from my signal of 14 November that I agreed with him on this point.

Admitting that it was easier to criticise than to make acceptable, workable alternative proposals for a difficult task, Portal felt the solution must lie

. . . in centralised Air Command of whole Mediterranean, with eastern and western sub-commands. If Americans will not come in, we must still have two R.A.F. sub-commands, the western ones being lodger units in an area administered by Eisenhower. In that event, co-ordi-nation of strategic use of air forces under directive by Combined

Chiefs of Staff would have to be done by liaison by Eisenhower and A.O.C.-in-C. M.E.

The C.A.S. suggested that I should bring out these points in a report for the Chiefs of Staff. It was particularly important to explode the fallacy of the division of air forces into coastal and others.

The Middle East Defence Committee met on 21 November. For them, I had set out my views in a memorandum. The matters of Naval and Army command did not occupy us for long. It had already been decided that the Naval command in the Mediterranean should be vested in a single C.-in-C. As for the Army Command, the only points for decision were the boundary between the two Commands and the respective spheres of responsibility for operations to the north. Tripoli could be more easily supplied from the west, and the port of Tripoli itself would probably be required by the 'Torch' Command for future operations. Alexander, therefore, felt that Tripolitania should lie in the 'Torch' Command and the boundary should be at Agheila, the best natural defensive position.

Most of our discussion centred on the division of responsibility in the Air Command. We agreed that our object should be to recommend to the Chiefs of Staff the best military solution, irrespective of political considerations about which we were not fully informed. Admiral Harwood said that he had reached very much the same conclusions as I, namely that if the Americans would agree, all air forces in the Mediterranean theatre should come under the control of one A.O.C.-in-C. If the Americans refused this arrangement, at least the British Eastern Air Force should come under the A.O.C.-in-C. Middle East. Harwood urged how necessary it was for the A.O.C.-in-C. to be established alongside the C.-in-C. Mediterranean, who himself would probably be with the American Supreme Commander in the Central Mediterranean. He felt that in these circumstances it would be difficult for the A.O.C.-in-C. to continue to control the air forces on the northern front, and wondered whether it would be possible to establish a separate Air command there.

I replied by recalling the arguments which had taken place when Persia and Iraq were separated from the Middle East. The air forces operating in General Wilson's command were dependent for maintenance upon the base in Egypt. The air forces in the Mediterranean would have to rely very largely on the same base, and I thought it therefore inevitable that operational and administrative control should lie with one A.O.C.-in-C. The extension of the command to the westward, as now proposed, would not in practice add a great deal of responsibility to the A.O.C.-in-C., since under my scheme there would be a sub-command in the west. As for Persia and Iraq, General Wilson would profit in that he would have a call through the A.O.C.-in-C. on greater resources. All questions of major policy would still be decided by the Chiefs of Staff. The A.O.C.-in-C. would naturally establish himself wherever the main centre of activity might be at any one time. If major operations were taking place in the Central Mediterranean, the A.O.C.-in-C. would super-impose an operational headquarters on the sub-command there, leaving a deputy in Cairo, who might change places with him if the centre of activity switched, for example, to the Middle East. The same principle would apply if the northern front were the scene of operations.

The Committee agreed generally with my views and we tele-graphed accordingly to London, recommending that since the Naval command was British, and since the greater proportion of the air forces would be British, the maintenance of which would for many months continue to depend on Egypt, the A.O.C.-in-C. should also be British. If the Americans could not be persuaded to agree to a centralised Air command under a British A.O.C.-in-C., we felt that we should still insist on the maximum possible centralization of control. The British Eastern Air Command in Tunisia should then be placed under the A.O.C.-in-C., leaving the American 12th Air Force under United States command. The British A.O.C.-in-C. and General Eisenhower would co-ordinate the strategic direction of all air forces in the Mediterranean theatre under the ægis of the Combined Chiefs of Staff.

*

Eighth Army was now methodically pursuing the enemy across Cyrenaica. Our air forces, British and American, operated at a full pitch of intensity. After a long period of disappointment, due largely to a lack of training and experience, the American heavy bombers had scored vital successes in the destruction of important ammunition ships in Benghazi and Tobruk. The operation of those ports was seriously affected, and a despairing enemy attempt to reinforce through Benghazi was stopped when an important motor vessel was hit and sunk when approaching the port. The American Kittyhawk and Mitchell squadrons had been operating throughout the battle, and though their pilots had on the whole more flying experience than ours, they had the good sense to work in gradually as individuals and as sections in our squadrons, and as squadrons in our wings: 'They are now,' I told Portal, 'full fledged for war, and have proved themselves fine fighters and loyal comrades.'

Moving forward with the leading troops, our airfield parties re-entered Tobruk on 13 November, and by the next day our fighters were already operating from Gambut, some thirty-five miles east of the harbour. The long-awaited convoys sailed for Malta from Alexandria. By 17 November our squadrons were operating from Gazala, halfway between Tobruk and Derna; and by 19 November from the Martuba airfields in the Cyrenaican bulge. This continual pressing forward not only enabled us to save Malta but also to keep the enemy air forces out of effective operations. Coningham's men had to pass through a test far more severe than was the retreat. They achieved marvels in attacking enemy air transport, which was Rommel's main hope of saving his rearguard, and in harrying the retreating columns of motor transport.

At this time I was deeply interested to read the answers of General Ritter von Thoma to an interrogation about events in North Africa. General von Thoma, Commander of the Afrika Korps, had been captured on 4 November. Asked what the Germans thought about the R.A.F. in the Alamein battle, General von Thoma replied:

We were impressed by the great superiority of your forces. Only a few days before the battle, I had a telephone conversation with Kesselring, who asked me for my opinion about the work of the Luftwaffe. I told him I felt that our chaps were so outnumbered by the English that they seemed to be reduced to a purely defensive role. He replied that this opinion agreed with the reports he had received.

General von Thoma did not know why the Luftwaffe had not made fuller use of the aircraft at its disposal, but thought that one reason was certainly the severe shortage of petrol. As for the part played by the R.A.F. in the whole action, he admitted that the big raids on their airfields before our offensive did great damage and made a profound impression; 'and then, of course, the never-ceasing bombing by day and by night had a terrible effect.' The interrogator also asked whether much damage had been done by ground strafing, and if so, whether the effect was greater in the case of aircraft with cannon or with machine-gun? Von Thoma replied that ground strafing was at times terrific. He did not think it mattered much whether cannon or machine-guns did the more damage:

It all happens so quickly, the planes come down near columns or concentrations and shoot at anything. They are sure to hit something just by spraying their fire, and then you have the added damage caused by panic and confusion. Your bombers put all my batteries out of action, and pounded my H.Q. all night long.

Another authoritative opinion is contained in Rommel's papers. He refers to the overwhelming British strength in heavy tanks, bombers, and artillery with inexhaustible supplies of ammunition and all engaged on a short front at El Alamein.

As a result of the British command of the air and hence of the seas in the Central Mediterranean, and of other reasons detailed elsewhere, the army's supplies were hardly sufficient to enable it to eke out a bare existence even on quiet days. It was out of the question to think of building up. . . .

The British command of the air was complete. There were days when the British flew 800 bomber sorties and 2,500 sorties of fighters, fighter bombers and low-flying aircraft. We, on the other hand, could at the most fly 60 dive-bomber and 100 fighter sorties. This number moreover became continually smaller.[1]

By 19 November our troops were back in Benghazi, for the third time. At some times our squadrons had been operating

---

[1] Young: *Rommel*, p. 278.

from landing grounds well in advance of the covering land forces. We had to use air transport to make up for the Army's inability to provide supplies on the necessary scale. A meeting held by 'Mary' Coningham at Martuba on 20 November showed that the supply position of the Western Desert Air Force was unsatisfactory. Coningham could build up no reserves for the next battle. There was a feeling that the Army were maintaining an unnecessarily large number of personnel in Cyrenaica: 10 Corps, for instance, already had a ration strength of 100,000. Nevertheless, the position was improving, although we were unable, for this same lack of supply, to maintain our medium bomber squadrons in Cyrenaica.

*

Towards the end of the month I spent a day at Malta and a day and a half at Algiers, where General Eisenhower was now established. It seemed to me that the affairs of Malta were running smoothly and well. Rain and wet aerodromes had hampered operations, and I was reluctantly forced to conclude that the aerodromes would not at present stand up to the Liberators which I had hoped to use against Bizerta in support of 'Torch'. Park, the A.O.C. Malta, accompanied me to Algiers, where I met Eisenhower, Admiral Cunningham, and Air Marshal Welsh who was commanding the R.A.F. units in Tunisia. We discussed the co-ordination of our Air effort with their needs. It was generally agreed that we in the Middle East were already doing everything possible to support 'Torch'. To send further units was out of the question for the moment. The landing grounds for the force already available were totally inadequate.

I could not help being deeply disturbed by what I saw and heard. While admitting, in my signal to Portal, that it was outside my province to comment on the conditions, I felt bound to tell him that communications for all Services were practically non-existent except for the archaic French telephone system. The aerodromes were inadequate and heavy rains had bogged down two or three. Dispersal appeared to be non-existent, and the degree of congestion almost unbelievable. There seemed to be little drive to remedy the situation, which was to my mind dangerous in the extreme. The many difficulties were evident enough, but they had to be overcome. The provision of forward landing grounds did not seem to be going ahead and the most advanced fighter aerodrome was some hundred miles from the forward troops.

As for the control of operations, any semblance of a Combined Headquarters had gone. Eisenhower and huge American staffs filled a large hotel which had one or two rooms set aside for Sanders, who had not arrived, Whiteley, the British Army Staff B.G. (he had been B.G.S. with Ritchie in the Western Desert), and Cunningham, who was the live wire in the place. He, however, chose to live in his ship, because it alone had good communications with the outside world. Air Marshal Welsh and his headquarters were some miles out of Algiers, and Doolittle, commanding the U.S. Air, had a separate headquarters in the town. The U.S. Air was running a separate war, and there was an instance on 27 November, when I was in Algiers, when the U.S. Air refused to assist General Anderson's First Army's operations in the north, though Eisenhower assured me that he had given instructions it was to be under Welsh's operational control.

I discussed all these points with Welsh and made such suggestions as I could. I realised that he had to face many difficulties and had not enjoyed proper support from our Army. I cabled to Portal:

In a final private interview with Eisenhower I told him my frank views on the set-up as I saw it, and he said he would do something about it. I expect he will. When I went in to see him he began by saying he was asking for me to go there for a fortnight. He felt there was a lack of drive. I said nothing on the suggestion that I should go there, but said that I felt the lack of drive was probably due to lack of support, *vide* the present arrangement of H.Q.

I realise that my visit was only a cursory one, that there have been, and are, many difficulties, but was frankly concerned at the situation as I saw it. I feel that the whole problem demands firm handling, both from the point of view of the immediate conditions in Algeria and Tunis, and from that of future control of the Mediterranean. I told Cunningham our views about future Air Command in the Mediterranean, and he agreed with them. I feel they ought to be implemented at once.

I recommended that a small operational headquarters from the Middle East should be set up alongside Eisenhower and Cunningham, leaving Welsh free to fight his battle, which for the moment he was quite unable to do. The Middle East, I believed, could help with its experience of mobile organisation, security measures, communications, repair, and salvage:

I am willing to send some individuals over to advise, but without authority feel they can do little. I would most strongly oppose any suggestion that I should go there to advise. Advice without authority and responsibility is useless.

Portal replied on 29 November that he was not entirely surprised by the situation I had described. An advance of three hundred miles had been made in three weeks without any opportunity for preparation or accumulation of supplies and transport. The indeterminate political situation which preoccupied the High Command must have added enormously to the difficulties of all subordinate commanders. Nevertheless, the C.A.S. entirely agreed that the situation must be remedied. He was not clear whether my proposed Middle East operational headquarters with Eisenhower would be executive or advisory. If executive, what would it control? If advisory, what machinery would implement its advice? Neither drive nor firm handling could be applied without sound organisation and a clear definition of responsibility. At present, it seemed that one or the other was essential, as Doolittle's independent air war bore witness. I was asked to elaborate my proposal that one Air command for the whole Mediterranean should be set up at once. Portal confessed he had never thought this would be practicable until the conclusion of the land fighting in Africa. He asked:

Is there any likelihood of Eisenhower agreeing—

    (a) to put all American and British Air Forces under one man,
    (b) to put that man under your command,
    (c) to treat you as an equal in his own theatre of which he is Supreme Commander.

We might hope for (a), but I do not see (b) or (c) happening.

Portal told me that the Admiralty were definitely refusing to have one Naval command in the Mediterranean. This made it even more difficult to press for a single Air command, since Eisenhower would remain Supreme Commander, and there would be no grounds on which to press him to release control of even the British Air in the interests of unified control of the air/sea war. Portal asked me to comment, to say whether I had any indication of Eisenhower's views about future organisation, and also, if possible, whether Cunningham still advocated a unified Naval command.

I agreed at once that clear definition of organisation and responsibility, so far as this was possible with the American set-up, was essential. I thought the A.O.C.-in-C's position in relation to Eisenhower should be the same as Cunningham's, subordinate to the Supreme Commander in respect of operations in Algeria and Tunis, and co-operating with him in air operations over the rest of the Mediterranean. Air Marshal Welsh would be in the same position *vis-à-vis* the A.O.C.-in-C. and the Army as Coningham was in the Western Desert. I had not felt able to discuss these matters specifically with Eisenhower, but saw no reason, in view of his tentative suggestion that I might go there temporarily, to think that he would not accept, or even welcome, such an arrangement:

Relationship between British and American Air Forces must depend largely on personalities. In Middle East they are nominally independent and co-operate; in fact, they are under operational control of myself and Coningham, and frankly acknowledge that situation. Eisenhower told me those had been his instructions as regards Doolittle and Welsh, i.e. that Welsh had operational control of the American Air. I see no reason why this should not work there, as it has here, though at a later stage as the American Air Forces increase, the subordinate commander operating the air in that part of the theatre might well become an American.

I expressed surprise at the attitude now adopted by the Admiralty towards unified Naval command, of which Cunningham was strongly in favour. I could not say whether he would be prepared to press for its institution at once, though I believed he might. In fact he was already exercising such command, for it was at his insistence that naval forces had now been sent from Egypt to Malta.

[372]

A telegram from Portal of 1 December told me of Eisenhower's proposal to the Chiefs of Staff in London that I should go to Algiers for two weeks as his adviser. The C.A.S. telegraphed that the Chiefs of Staff were known to be against this proposal for the reasons given in my signal of 28 November; all the same, they wished to give Eisenhower every possible help. Portal told me that he intended to propose that I should assume command of all air forces in the Mediterranean forthwith. Mr. Churchill was understood to view this prospect favourably. I should be subordinate to Eisenhower for the operation of all the 'Torch' air forces, British and American, and to the Chiefs of Staff for co-ordinating Middle East operations with those of 'Torch' to achieve the enemy's defeat in North Africa as swiftly as might be. Portal went on:

If the above proposal is made and Eisenhower accepts it would you be prepared to move your Advanced Headquarters to Algiers immediately, and take command there personally? I think that Eisenhower would undoubtedly expect this rather than that you should operate from Cairo through any deputy in Algiers.

I replied the same day:

Would be prepared to move H.Q. to Algiers and take command personally. It would, of course, take two or three days to make necessary arrangements. I would also hope that Drummond could return to resume his functions as Deputy as early as possible.

Later that day I received a copy of the signal the Chiefs of Staff sent to Eisenhower proposing the arrangement outlined in Portal's telegram to me. They described it cautiously as 'an alternative arrangement for the temporary purposes of battle which the Chiefs of Staff suggest might be free from any objection if you desire it'. Should this proposal appeal to Eisenhower, the Chiefs of Staff would submit it to the Combined Chiefs of Staff. Eisenhower was told privately that Churchill was understood to favour these proposals and would be prepared to recommend them to Roosevelt.

Eisenhower's reply showed that he thought his situation so serious that only short-term solutions could be considered for the moment. He telegraphed that the Chiefs of Staff's plan might possibly represent the soundest air organisation which could eventually be adopted. However, his problem was immediate and critical and not to be confused, nor its solution postponed, by a deliberate study of an overall system of air command:

I would have been happy, indeed, to have taken Tedder in any capacity, but realising that he has an important and responsible post that did not permit me to request his transfer to this theatre, I asked for his temporary loan so that his great experience and obvious qualities of leadership could be immediately applied to our present situation.

I do not see how he could well serve as commander in two separate theatres which are under separate ground commanders and in both of which special tactical problems exist at this moment. In this view, Cunningham and other principal subordinates concur.

He went on to say that he had taken advantage of the presence in Algiers of General Spaatz to detach him temporarily from command of the Eighth Air Force in the United Kingdom, and appoint him Deputy for Air Operations in the Tunisian theatre. Because there was no time to set up separate communication systems and staff arrangements, Spaatz's position would not be that of a commander.

On seeing this reply, I had little doubt that Eisenhower had somewhat misunderstood the Chiefs of Staff's proposal. He seemed to think that they were suggesting that all the American air forces should be placed under the command of an A.O.C.-in-C. This was not what I had intended. The American air forces in the Middle East were under the command of General Andrews and not under my command, though Andrews accepted my strategic directions. I had intended a similar arrangement for North Africa.

It seemed to me that my case was much reinforced by a request received from Eisenhower on 4 December that a group of B.24s should go to Oran at once, and a squadron of B.17s to Algiers. As it happened, the B.24s and B.17s provided our only effective striking force for attacking Rommel's main port of entry at Tripoli. Their proposed withdrawal to North Africa would limit gravely our ability to strike at the vital supplies on which the whole outcome of the Libyan campaign largely depended. Arrangements had already been made to concentrate the whole

force in the Benghazi area, where they would be in the best position not only to attack Rommel's supply lines, but also the bases
and lines of communication serving the Axis forces in North
Africa. Whenever the opportunity arose to help General Eisenhower's campaign we had taken it. Indeed, on the day when the
signal was received, some of the aircraft were attacking Naples.
We had therefore to recommend that they must be retained under
the control of the Middle East.

The next morning, 5 December, I received a request from Welsh
for more fighters to make up for his heavy losses on the ground,
at which I could hardly be surprised. These events further
emphasised the need for a unified command. When the Middle
East Defence Committee met that day they agreed that it was
essential to establish unified air control as soon as possible. It
was decided to recommend to Churchill and the Chiefs of Staff
that they should press for its establishment at the earliest possible
moment. Tunisia was the key to success of our operations, and
we could not afford to wait for this essential co-ordination.
General Andrews took part in our discussion and said that he fully
agreed with the proposal. To Portal I telegraphed that without
unified command, at least for the R.A.F., we could not get the
best value out of our air forces in support of the two campaigns
now raging:

Practically the whole enemy effort, whether in Tunisia or in Libya,
comes from ports and air bases in Southern Italy and Sicily. The
majority of these are closer to our heavy bomber bases in Cyrenaica
than they are to those at present in use in North Africa. Our air forces
in Malta have played, and are playing, a vital part in these operations,
especially in support of 'Torch'. Close co-ordination of the air operations from the east and from the west is, in my opinion, most urgently
required, and I feel that we have a right to insist on that so far as the
R.A.F. is concerned.

As for Eisenhower's point that the A.O.C.-in-C. could not
serve as commander in two separate theatres under separate
ground commanders, I assumed that he did not realise that I
already controlled air operations in theatres under separate
ground commanders, including those from Malta. I again urged
that I should be relieved of the need to send advisers to Algiers

since I thought advice without executive responsibility to be worse than useless, and with the best will in the world only likely to cause friction. The answer from the C.A.S. showed that we were still talking to some extent at cross purposes. While he agreed with me about unified air command in the Mediterranean, he did not see how it could be fully efficient unless it embraced Americans as well as the R.A.F. Portal said he made no ideological distinction between 'command' and 'control'; evidently Eisenhower did not either. What he meant by either word in this context was the issue of orders or direction for operations and movements. Eisenhower's objections to the Chiefs of Staff's proposals were clearly based on practical grounds rather than those of nationality, and although they thought he was mistaken, his view must be accepted. Since Eisenhower's reasons for turning down the scheme were practical onces, we could make no case for withdrawing from his command or control the R.A.F. squadrons taking part in the 'Torch' campaign. Portal thought that we had the right to insist on close co-ordination between 'Torch' and the Middle East; without unified control this could only be arranged by co-operation. Since we had now offered two staff officers to Eisenhower and he had accepted, they had to be sent. There seemed to Portal to be only one way of carrying the proposal forward:

Only possible further approach to Eisenhower on the subject of co-ordination appears to be a further visit from you, and if you feel it would help, and would care to go, I think it would be a good thing.

This signal had hardly been received when we learnt from London that Eisenhower was asking for the loan of two Wellington squadrons from Bomber Command with the purpose of launching night attacks on Bizerta and Tunis. In view of Eighth Army's success against Rommel and the difficulties of maintaining our squadrons in the forward area, the Chiefs of Staff thought it would be quicker to loan Eisenhower aircraft and crews of two squadrons of Wellingtons from Middle East Command. We replied that Malta was by far the most effective base for attacks on Tunis and Bizerta, since each aircraft could carry out two sorties per night from there. Twenty-four Wellingtons had already been sent to Malta to support 'Torch' and another seven were

flying in that night, 7 December. This left only thirty-two Wellington bombers in Egypt, and we badly needed them to harass the
enemy in support of the Eighth Army. We agreed, however, to
loan one squadron to Eisenhower on the understanding that we
should be able to recall it at short notice. Eisenhower agreed, and
suggested that in order to co-ordinate the air activities of his
forces and mine, I should visit his headquarters for several days
during this critical period. I accepted at once.

The situation was indeed becoming daily more complicated.
Lacking full knowledge of the conditions in North Africa, I
could not adjudicate properly between the many claims now
arriving from Eisenhower and Welsh. I had been asked for, and
had sent, night Beaufighters; had been asked for fighters and had
arranged to make Hurricanes available at Benghazi on call;
had been asked for Wellington squadrons and had offered the
temporary loan of one; had been asked if I could transfer Beauforts and Beaufighter squadrons to North Africa. The operations
from Malta filled a double role; they were closely linked with the
progress of the campaign in Tunisia, but also with other operations
against Rommel's supplies. I telegraphed to Portal on 9 December:

It is daily being made yet more and more evident that the distribution of air forces and the direction of strategic air effort from the
whole of the African coast and from Malta, are matters requiring
almost daily consideration and adjustment, and that that adjustment
can only be properly made by one authority who is in a position to
balance the requirements, the resources and facilities. This does not,
of course, affect the direction of the detailed tactical operations which
are linked with the land operations in Tunisia and Libya.

*

Some six days earlier, Eisenhower had told the Chiefs of Staff
that in the pell-mell race for Tunisia his forces had gone beyond
what he called the 'sustainable limit of air capabilities in support
of ground forces'. The scale of possible air support was not now
sufficient to keep down the hostile strafing and dive-bombing
which were largely responsible for breaking up attempted
advances by the forces on the ground. Eisenhower's air commanders had told him that very shortly, in a week at the outside,

[377]

even air operations on that insufficient scale and under existing conditions would leave them at or near complete breakdown. Advanced operating airfields, the provision of maintenance and stocks of spare parts in the forward areas, establishment of warning services and anti-aircraft guns, all were vitally necessary. A breathing space would be needed. To undertake this policy would mean cutting down air operations in the forward areas. This in turn would reduce ground operations largely to the consolidation of the main gains.

However, provided that Axis reinforcement on the ground could be stopped, the delay of a few days or even more would not be particularly serious, in view of the tremendous distances the forces had already advanced ahead of the anticipated plan. So far, Eisenhower had not been able to prevent such reinforcement, and even if the supply situation east of Algiers were improved there was a definite limit to the rate of build-up and the strength of forces Rommel could sustain in Tunisia. The Supreme Commander hoped to resume the advance as soon as possible, perhaps even by 9 December, in order to take Tunis and throw the enemy back into the Bizerta stronghold, where he might be confined closely while additional reserves were brought up for the kill. All this depended on the weather, for if protracted rain should set in, every airfield available would become unusable except one tiny airfield at Bone, and an all-weather airfield at Maison Blanche.

On 6 December Eisenhower told us that the air casualties for a single day were six Spitfires, ten Bisleys, five P. 38 Lightnings and a Boston, all of them lost because of the mastery in the battlefield area of German fighters. The six Spitfires were lost on the ground through an attempt to use a forward airfield. A plan of 3 December had envisaged the withdrawal of about half the Allied fighters from the forward area in order to minimise losses. Actually, Welsh had been unable to withdraw anything at all because of the ground situation. Thus the possibility of effective air cover during the planned resumption of the advance appeared to be a very slim one.

On the ground, Eisenhower's forces had been repulsed from good positions in front of Tebourza and had lost about forty tanks, to about thirty-three lost by the enemy. Casualties in the front-line formations were heavy and one battalion of the Guards Brigade had been cut off completely.

Eisenhower was not satisfied with the intensity of bomber operations against the ports. On the other hand, the enemy air forces were operating from good airfields in the Bizerta–Tunis area near to the fighting line and with plenty of flak and radar protection, which the Allied air forces had not so far been able to overcome. The exposed character of the barren terrain made enemy operations against the vehicles of the Allied air forces especially effective.

These reports did not provide an attractive prelude for my visit to Algiers. The Middle East Commanders-in-Chief met on 10 December so that I might be fully informed of their views before talking with Eisenhower. It was agreed that I should not make any offer of assistance to reinforce 'Torch' forces unless it were quite certain that the offer could be implemented. The first essential would be to find out exactly what the situation in Tunisia was. If, as had been suggested, a brigade should be sent, it would have to come from Malta. I said that Eisenhower was sure to ask when we thought we could take Tripoli. Alexander refused to commit himself about the outcome of the forthcoming battle at Agheila, nor could he say how far the enemy's situation might be affected by shortage of supplies. Unless the bulk of German forces were destroyed, or unless the enemy did collapse from lack of supplies, Alexander thought it improbable that the capture of Tripoli could be achieved in the next few months by operations from the east alone. The difficulties of attacking the Buerat position were immense. We might be facing a period of stalemate. With this opinion both Admiral Harwood and I agreed.

By 12 December I was in Algiers. Eisenhower held a conference which General Anderson (commanding the First Army), Welsh, Spaatz, and I attended. We reviewed the position which had developed since the beginning of the month.

Eisenhower's hope that the offensive could be resumed about 9 December had been falsified. The forward troops had been engaged in bitter defensive fighting, which caused Anderson to decide on a withdrawal. He determined to move back rather farther than had originally been intended. This movement eventually took place on the evening of 10 December with a minimum of enemy interference, but with the loss of the equipment of at least one battalion of the American Combat Team B. Filthy weather had prevented effective bombing operations, not only because of almost complete cloud cover over every profitable target, but because our bombers were bogged down on their aerodromes. Liberators brought from the United Kingdom several days before had been unable to fly. By an arrangement with me, Eisenhower made a temporary exchange of the Liberator Group for some of Brereton's B.17s. Affairs were so managed that all the primary targets were now placed within range of all the aircraft. I told the meeting that I could accommodate a considerable number of heavy bombers and had ample stocks of fuel and bombs.

The Supreme Commander insisted that if only they were fortunate enough to get a spell of good weather they could do the job. He did not think the enemy's strength in ground forces, except in tanks, had recently increased very much. Anderson said that the enemy employed at least eighty tanks on 10 December, markedly superior to anything we possessed except the Shermans and possibly the Grants. The enemy was lacking in artillery, however. His infantry did not appear to be the best, and in several instances small groups had surrendered voluntarily. The men seemed to have been thrown together without too much training and to have somewhat low morale; on the other hand, the Panzers' morale, and that of the enemy air forces, seemed to be of the highest. Eisenhower now set a target date of 20 December for the renewed advance. He refused to give up the idea of an all-out attempt to win the critical area: 'It is my conviction,' he telegraphed to the Chiefs of Staff, 'that we should strive to avoid settling down to a logistic marathon.'

It was clear enough that the existing air organisation was almost crazy, with two air forces but no effective command. General Spaatz was performing a useful function of co-ordination, though not command. He lacked operational experience and knowledge. One effective commander of both forces was essential, and I had come to believe that the only answer was an American commander with a first-class British deputy. After a long private talk with Eisenhower, I thought he was coming round to the point of agreeing on a unified British Air Command in the Mediterranean, although he still needed very careful handling. One of the Supreme Commander's difficulties was that he had come out to North Africa with the idea that the United Kingdom and North Africa would be from his point of view one theatre. He feared that if North Africa and Libya were linked as one theatre he would lose control over the American air forces in the United Kingdom, from which he hoped to be able to draw reinforcements. I had by now heard that Air Chief Marshal Douglas was already on his way out to the Middle East to replace me in Cairo. I told Portal that I hoped this news could be kept quiet, since I felt that the chances of our getting Eisenhower, or of his getting Washington, to agree to unified air command in the Mediterranean, would be handicapped if it became known that an immediate change in command was impending. I could not conceal from myself that one of the main factors likely to get agreement on this vital proposal was the experience which I happened to have had since December 1940 in the co-ordination of air strength in the Middle East.

As for the immediate situation in Tunisia, communications were unbelievably bad. Peculiar local conditions severely affected wireless communication. The heavy rains had made the situation on the aerodromes equally bad. I saw no quick or easy solution. All this meant that the possibility of achieving any high standard of concentrated air effort in the immediate future was very poor. On these local matters I tried to avoid giving advice and to confine my remarks to basic questions of principle applicable to any operations of this nature. The control of operations of air forces in support of the land battle caused me much disquiet. It seemed to me that General Anderson failed to understand the use and control of aircraft in close support and did not appreciate the handicaps under which the air forces had been operating. My impression was that our squadrons had done magnificently and more than could conceivably have been expected under the conditions. We had shown the Americans the distinction between tactical air operations in support of the land battle and strategic air operations necessarily controlled from the rear, but even Eisenhower failed to realise the immense difficulties under which air operations had been organised and carried out.

On the main issue, my talks with the Supreme Commander proved more promising. I was able to tell the C.A.S. on 16 December:

Think he is firmly hooked, but by no means landed. He is, I think, fully in agreement with the need for unified command in the Mediterranean, but is nervous about his call on U.S. Air Forces in U.K. and about Washington's reactions about putting U.S. Air Forces under British command. As regards the latter, I pointed out that in transferring Heavy Bomber Group to Cyrenaica, he is passing them right out of his command, whereas if A.O.C.-in-C. were in the same position as Cunningham at Algiers, he, Eisenhower, could still have ultimate control.

This marked a distinct, if limited, advance. I again advised Portal that further acquaintance with the R.A.F. set-up in Tunisia had convinced me more firmly than ever that we should only get full value if Middle East resources and experience were fully available for 'Torch'. This could only be achieved if Middle East had command, and I felt we had a right to insist upon it. I believed that parallel U.S. and British Air Commands co-ordinated at Algiers would be feasible if Eisenhower deemed it politically impossible to put the U.S. Air Forces under a British commander.

The next day, 17 December, I asked Portal's permission, which was granted, to return to Cairo that night. I felt that there was much in Tunisia which urgently demanded action, but under present conditions I was helpless to do more than suggest:

The whole affair requires grip and drive. Until, however, impending offensive either takes place or is cancelled, no major reorganisation in forward area appears possible, and in any case, without authority nothing effective can be done. Meantime, have persuaded Welsh to go forward with Anderson.

I then returned to Cairo, taking with me, for the purpose of furthering his education, an American General. I advised Portal by telegraph of the lines on which I thought an Air Officer Commanding-in-Chief should operate. By continuing to control strategic operations in Malta and Libya, he would in North Africa co-ordinate under Eisenhower the operations of the British and American air forces. In the Tunisian theatre the forces would be divided into a tactical short-range force operating in support of land battles, and the strategic force of heavy and medium bombers. I suggested that the tactical force should be commanded by Air Vice Marshal Robb, whose position would be analogous to that of 'Mary' Coningham, while the American, General Doolittle, should command the strategic force with a role parallel to that of 205 Group or the Commanding General U.S. Bomber Command, Middle East. Each commander would have a headquarters alongside that of the appropriate Army Commander. The headquarters of the A.O.C.-in-C. would include administration and supply policy. Since the A.O.C.-in-C. would effect the co-ordination, Spaatz would disappear, as he urgently wished to do.

I told Portal that I believed Eisenhower would agree to the transfer of the Eastern Air Command to the Middle East along these lines. I believed that in our final talk he would have accepted it there and then if I had been willing to say that an immediate change of this kind would materially assist the immediate land operations, but I felt that although it might help, a change at this juncture would be unwise, for it would certainly be produced as an alibi for any failure.

I came away because I felt I had given all the advice I could usefully give, and there was a risk of my coming to be regarded as a regular, but, of course, irresponsible, adviser on actual operations. I felt this to be dangerous, as shown by Anderson remarking to me that the last battle had really been lost because my advice had been taken.

*

On Christmas Day 1942, Eisenhower visited the battlefront in Tunisia. He came to the conclusion that there was no choice but to abandon for the moment the plan for making an all-out effort. It seemed that in the existing conditions any attempt at a major attack would merely court disaster. He had observed four men in a flat grass field trying to extricate a motor cycle which had become bogged down. During the time he watched them they made absolutely no progress at all. This incident was typical of what was occurring on the Allied forces' airfields.

It certainly seemed to the C.I.G.S. in London, and to us in Cairo, that the Eighth Army, after capturing Tripoli, would have to work westward into Tunisia to assist in clearing out the Germans. Alexander thought that Rommel would probably wait until he believed our main attack on the Buerat position was about to develop, when he would withdraw, as he had from Agheila. From 14 January onwards Montgomery expected to possess forces with which he could drive right through to Tripoli in one bound. If the enemy waited to be attacked the onslaught would begin on the night of 19/20 January. One force would attack in the coastal sector and another would turn the enemy flank. In either case, Alexander hoped to reach Tripoli about 1 February. Maintenance was always the principal factor. Admiral Harwood feared that the enemy might try to block the port at Tripoli, and therefore that the date of its reopening was at this stage a pure speculation. He thought that we must allow seven to ten days between the capture of Tripoli and the acceptance of the first ships. Our object would then be to make Tripoli the advanced base and to reduce Benghazi to the tonnage necessary for the maintenance of Army and Air Forces still needed in that area.

*

The Prime Minister was by no means pleased at the slow progress in Tunisia: 'The Army is like a peacock,' he grumbled, 'nearly all tail.'

'The peacock would be a very badly balanced bird without its tail,' replied Alan Brooke.

21

Air Command for 'Torch'–The race for Tunis–Methods of blocking enemy convoys–Casablanca Conference–Mediterranean operations first–Sardinia or Sicily?–Plans for 'Husky'– Roosevelt and Churchill approve Air Command proposals–My new appointment–Increasing American contribution–Allied Air Forces placed under my command–'Gospel according to Montgomery'–Anglo-American marriage: a near divorce!–Churchill on 'Allied Air'–Control of sea communications in the Mediterranean–Mareth Line–Malcolm Clubs–'Mary' v. George– The 'Flax' Plan–Churchill wants 'hot' news–Victories in Tunisia–Team Spirit

EXPERIENCE of battle conditions in Algeria, and his talks with me and others, had by the end of December 1942 convinced General Eisenhower that there must be a single air command in North-West Africa. After long consideration, he decided that General Spaatz should fill this post. The Supreme Commander realised that his solution would not ensure the co-ordination of strategic air activity in the Mediterranean. For the present he wished to organise the bombing effort in that theatre on a basis of co-operation between commands until a better solution could be evolved by the Combined Chiefs of Staff. Neither the Prime Minister nor the Chief of the Air Staff cared much for the idea of placing Spaatz in control of the 'Torch' air forces, for he possessed little experience of the command and administration of a mixed air force in the field. For the sake of obtaining any sort of unification instead of the existing chaos, the Chiefs of Staff agreed that Eisenhower should be allowed to choose his own subordinates, while hoping devoutly that a better system would be created at 'Symbol', the code name given to the forthcoming conference at Casablanca. It was arranged that I should meet the British delegation there. If a unified command were set up, I should probably take it over; otherwise I should return to London, in either event being replaced at Cairo by Sholto Douglas.

Portal instructed me on 5 January not to commit myself in any way, in conversations with Eisenhower, about the reorganisation of the air command for the 'Torch' operations, until I had talked with him at Casablanca. Anything I could do to persuade the Supreme Commander to accept unified control of the air forces in the whole Mediterranean would be invaluable.

Exhaustion after the intensive efforts at the end of 1942 in North-West Africa, coupled with the enemy's ability to concentrate his resources in the Tunisian peninsula, had caused a halt in our advance. There were now massed some 56,000 Axis troops and at least 250 tanks in Tunisia, and his air activity had revived, with damaging attacks on the vital positions at Bone on the coast road. Assaults by land on the French forces had been particularly successful.

The build-up of our ground forces in Tunisia had been much hampered by inadequate communications and a shortage of motor transport so marked that all formations had been practically immobile. This deficiency had not been severely felt so long as it was unnecessary to support a strong battlefront far from the bases; but once we lost the race for Tunis it became critical. The Allied air forces suffered from a lack of landing grounds and poor anti-aircraft defences to protect the existing aerodromes. 'The Luftwaffe,' recorded General Bradley, 'ranged the Tunisian Front almost unmolested. The sound of the aircraft had become the signal to halt and take cover by the roadside.' Any movement on the east-bound roads was subject to repeated air attack, roadsides dotted with 'fox-holes' and scare warnings about Messerschmitts, skull and crossbone notices, and so on—hardly an atmosphere conducive to high morale.

While refusing to consider the picture too dark, Eisenhower was forced to admit that the destruction of any one of the important bridges over the long and precarious line of supply would have almost a decisive effect. Two days later, on 8 January, he advised the Chiefs of Staff that the volume of reinforcement and supply reaching the enemy through the Tunisian ports was a matter for grave concern:

It is an absolute essential that high performance recce aircraft of good endurance able to evade enemy fighters, be provided for recce in the lower Tyrrhenian Sea and the Sicily–Tunisia Channel. Without these our forces both sea and air are blindfolded, and will achieve little or nothing.

On the urgent recommendation of Admiral Cunningham, General Spaatz, and Air Marshal Welsh, Eisenhower therefore asked for the 'immediate despatch of Mosquitos manned by experienced crews, trained in coastal work'.

When I saw this signal, I felt that it did not represent the facts with complete accuracy. Not for the first time had our Admiral made his R.A.F. subordinates dance to his tune. We were all agreed that the volume of supplies reaching the enemy through Tunisian ports was a serious matter. Various factors, principal among them the weather, had caused the situation. Moreover, it seemed entirely misleading to suggest that detection and shadowing south of forty degrees north was a practicable operation in much of the area involved. In my opinion it was not possible to maintain continual reconnaissance over the Sicily–Tunisian channel with any aircraft now available. I had already arranged for some of my torpedo-carrying Wellingtons to transfer from the Middle East to North Africa at the earliest moment, which would probably be in about a fortnight's time.

The appreciation sent by Eisenhower to the Chiefs of Staff gravely over-estimated what was feasible in the way of reconnaissance and shadowing of the enemy's traffic to Tunisia, and far too much reliance was being placed on the results which would be achieved if Mosquitos were made available. I gathered later that the Chiefs of Staff also doubted whether the Mosquito would achieve any better results than the Beaufighter. In any case, Mosquitos were not available for despatch to North Africa. I agreed that naval action by day would be a desperate measure; indeed, it seemed to me it would be a useless waste of ships and men. The only solutions were reasonable weather, submarine action, search and strike by night torpedo aircraft, and attacks by heavy and medium bombers on Tunisian ports, and on Palermo and Naples. Action against shipping to Tunisia had been given first priority at Malta ever since the 'Torch' landings.

For some time the enemy continued to run convoys through to North Africa. As late as 9 February, Air Vice Marshal Lloyd told me that the Tunisian traffic was still not being stopped. Convoys left Naples after midnight, arriving at Palermo at last light the same day; thence by night, sailing close inshore to

Trapani for the passage to Tunisia in daylight. Night attack by Wellingtons off Naples was becoming more difficult and some aircraft were obliged to return to Malta in daylight round Sicily. Attack between Palermo and Trapani by Wellingtons and Beauforts presented serious difficulties too, for the convoys sailed very close inshore against high ground where there was deep water. With the types of aircraft available to us, attack in the Sicilian channel was out of the question on account of the enemy's fighter escort.

*

At the end of the second week in January, the Prime Minister and President Roosevelt, surrounded by a galaxy of Chiefs of Staff and Joint Planners, arrived in Casablanca. Their intention was to work out an Allied strategy for victory against the Axis powers. The British staff presented a united front in comparison with that of their Allies. For this there were, I think, two main reasons. The Americans lacked experience of the complicated and essential staff work to which we had long been inured. Moreover, the various American Service chiefs, especially General Marshall and Admiral King, held their own definite and highly individual views, which did not always coincide. Admiral King had made himself the protagonist of a holding strategy in Europe, believing that the United States should first strike a decisive blow against Japan. General Marshall, on the other hand, had from the start favoured the knock-out blow in Europe. But it had not been easy to convince him of the quite obvious fact that the United States could simply not supply materials in the necessary quantity for a frontal assault on France in 1942. The unity of the British party, which came to Casablanca with a well-prepared series of strategic plans, proved an asset of considerable importance in securing American support. Most of the memoranda written during the Conference itself were the product of the British staffs, with a little assistance from the Americans.

Field-Marshal Dill, after his supersession as C.I.G.S. by Alan Brooke, had established for himself in Washington a unique position. Not only did he enjoy intimate personal relations with General Marshall, but he brought to all his work sympathetic understanding of the Americans' problems. Before the full Conference opened, Dill explained to the British party the preoccupations of our allies. The Americans feared, he told us, that they might become unduly committed in the Mediterranean, and suspected that the British were lukewarm about the Pacific and would not make an all-out effort in that theatre once Germany had been defeated in Europe. This was not to say that they did not believe that Germany was the main enemy, but rather that they did not quite see how she was to be tackled, especially when urgent tasks awaited us in Burma and the Pacific. It also appeared that operations in the Pacific were largely the province of the Navy Department while operations in the rest of the world were left to the War Department. The allocation of resources tended, for this reason, to be haphazard.

The Prime Minister showed from the start that he intended to take his time, discussing everything fully and displaying no impatience. He believed this to be the right way to wean the Americans to the desired point of view. He would work on President Roosevelt as and when the opportunity offered, and in ten days or a fortnight everything would be all right. Mr. Churchill did not conceal that he intended to get agreement on a programme for 1943 which the military staffs might well think beyond the Allied powers, but which he felt was the least that could be thought worthy of the United States and Great Britain. He wanted not only the cleansing of the North African shore, to be followed by the capture of Sicily; but also an attempt at the reconquest of Burma and an invasion of Northern France, perhaps on a moderate scale. The operations in the Pacific should not be of such a magnitude to prevent the fulfilment of the Mediterranean and European programmes. This strategic dilemma was neatly expressed by Portal:

We are in the position of a testator who wished to leave the bulk of his fortune to his mistress. He must, however, leave something to his wife, and his problem is to decide how little he can in decency set apart for her.

I arrived in Casablanca on 14 January with General Alexander. The conference lasted over a week and centred at a very large, modern hotel on the outskirts of Casablanca. It was so secret that once you had passed into the conference you were not allowed out. The hotel was encircled with barbed wire, and there was no external evidence that a conference was taking place. All meals had to be taken in the hotel, which prompted one of my staff to say to Admiral Cunningham that it was exactly like electing a Pope. Admiral Cunningham said, 'Yes, it is. We're in a conclave,' to which the staff officer replied: 'Who do you think will be elected Pope, Roosevelt or Churchill?' Admiral Cunningham retorted, 'It is a matter of complete indifference to me. All I want to know is, who is going to put his hand up and declare when the Pope *is* elected?'

On the following day we attended a meeting between the two political heads and their principal military advisers. First of all, Eisenhower explained the position in North Africa. The Allied forces which had landed in French North Africa, he said, were not a mobile army and possessed little strength for offensive operations. The force had been designed and equipped to capture three ports, an arrangement made necessary because the French attitude had been unknown. It had been hoped to resume the offensive on 22 December, but the weather had been bad and a postponement was the only possibility. It was now planned to make an attempt on Sfax, beginning on 24 January. Eisenhower dilated on the difficulties of keeping the airfields serviceable. Only two were available for fighters, and even these lay a hundred miles from the front line. The Germans, by contrast, had the use of two all-weather airfields in Tunis.

General Alexander described progress by the Eighth Army. He estimated that our casualties in the first twelve days of the battle at El Alamein were about 16,000, and the enemy's between 60,000 and 70,000. If Eighth Army reached Tripoli according to plan it would be quite immobilised until the port was opened. This task would take at best seven or ten days, and at worst up to three months. If three thousand tons of supplies per day could be passed through Tripoli it would be possible to attack the Mareth Line towards the middle of March. Our photographs showed it to be a prepared position though lacking in depth.

I said I thought that convoys could be passed through the

Mediterranean when airfields had been established and the Tunisian tip cleared. As for our air effort in the preceding months, I emphasised that the task had begun during the retreat from Gazala, since which time the enemy air force had been beaten down and great efforts had been made to stop Rommel's supplies. When the focal point of battle had moved to Tunisia, large reinforcements had been sent thither, and to Malta. Eisenhower emphasised the appalling conditions in which our air forces were operating in Tunisia.

The main business of the conference was to decide in which theatre the enemy could be most effectively engaged in 1943. The British representatives argued for the Mediterranean. In the end it did not prove too hard to convert the Americans, for they had no real constructive alternative. Although Admiral King urged an offensive against Japan, the President spoke in favour of Mediterranean operations. In fact, the policy of knocking out Germany first, on which Churchill and Roosevelt had agreed immediately after Pearl Harbor, still held good.

This point decided, which objective should be tackled once the Tunisian campaign was over? The choice lay between Sicily and Sardinia. Here, conflicting currents of opinion served to muddy the waters. The British Joint Planning Staff favoured Sardinia on the grounds that the operation could be launched earlier, that if it were rapidly followed by the occupation of Corsica, the vitals of Italy and Southern France would be laid bare to aerial attack in daytime, and that the capture of Sardinia would, therefore, have a more crushing effect on Italy than would the capture of Sicily. It was argued that if the capture of Sardinia produced the expected effect, Sicily might fall an easy prey soon after. To tackle Sicily would strain our resources to the limit, and might even result in failure. It was the obvious frontal attack for which the enemy would be well prepared. On the other hand, from Tunisia and Malta it would be possible to provide far more powerful support, fighter and bomber, for the assault, than would be possible for the assault on Sardinia and Corsica.

Portal saw the advantages of both courses, but felt on the whole that the aerodromes of Sardinia and Corsica were not sufficiently numerous or good to allow the Allies to reap much benefit from their occupation. The First Sea Lord, Admiral Pound, favoured Sicily if the Americans would produce the necessary naval forces. He did not care much for the idea of an attack on Sardinia. I noted with interest his argument that better air cover could be given to the operations against Sicily from Tunisia and Malta than could be given by aircraft-carriers to landings in Sardinia. The occupation of Sicily would make easier the passage of ships through the Mediterranean. It had been estimated that if thirty ships could be passed through every ten days, the whole traffic round the Cape could be dispensed with. This would mean the release of no fewer than 225 ships for use elsewhere.

The C.I.G.S., Alan Brooke, had no doubts that Sicily was the right choice, being convinced that as fast as the Allies went into the south of Sardinia, enemy reinforcements would pour into the north. He thought the plan for taking Sicily would ensure its quick fall. Reinforcements could only enter through Messina in the north, from which ran only two coastal roads, both of which could be blocked. The Prime Minister, too, favoured Sicily, though less on military than on political grounds. Naturally, he wanted an operation which could be represented to Stalin as something big. It was pointed out that there must be a delay between clearing Tunisia and launching an operation against Sicily. This objection the Prime Minister characteristically overrode by insisting that somehow or other the assault must be made at an early date, though he had not given up the idea of attacks on Burma and on Northern France.

The Americans did not need much persuading. It was agreed, therefore, that Sicily offered us the greater value for the effort involved. An operation for its conquest would be undertaken in 1943 with the objects of making our Mediterranean lines of communication more secure, diverting as much German strength from Russia as possible, intensifying the pressure on Italy, loosening the enemy's hold on the Balkans, and with the hope of securing, at last, Turkey's entry into the war. It was hoped that the operation could be launched during the favourable moon period in June, and if not, at the latest in July. This operation was to be known as 'Husky'. The decision was based on the assumption that North Africa would be cleared by 30 April. The invasion of Italy was not to be a part of this programme, though American forces were to be held in the United Kingdom in readiness for a possible attempt on France in the autumn of 1943.

Once the main strategic decisions had been made, Alexander and I were anxious to return to our posts where there were plenty of immediate problems to meet. Shortly before we were due due to leave Anfa, we were bidden to report to President Roosevelt. Frankly, I was rather disappointed. He asked one or two elementary questions which led to a repetition in brief of our respective reports to the conference. He was quite affable, but beyond expressing his good wishes to us, we did not draw from him the fresh inspiration we had looked for.

To complement the strategic decisions reached at Casablanca, alterations were introduced into the command structure in the Mediterranean. The proposals for the new air command were finally approved by Roosevelt and Churchill on 26 January. An Air Commander-in-Chief for the whole Mediterranean theatre would set up his headquarters at Algiers; under him would serve the Air Officers Commanding North-West Africa, the Middle East, and Malta. He would be subordinate to the Commander-in-Chief Allied Expeditionary Force in North-West Africa in respect of air forces stationed in that particular theatre, and in respect of the operations of other Mediterranean air forces in conjunction with operations conducted in or from North-West Africa. 'Husky' fell within this category. In return, the Commander-in-Chief Allied Expeditionary Forces would give every possible help in the North-West Africa theatre for the operation of Mediterranean air forces.

Now that North-West Africa had become the focal point in the campaign, it was essential to introduce a cohesive structure of air command there. Prolonged discussions brought forth the solution of three sub-commands, one to control heavy and medium bombers with their fighter escorts, another for general reconnaissance and fighter aircraft for the defence of shipping and ports, and the third to specialise in air support for the ground forces. General Spaatz, as Air Officer Commanding North-West

Africa, would have under his direct control supply, maintenance, and repair. Since the closest co-operation between air and ground forces was now recognised by everyone to be crucial, it was laid down that the air officer commanding the air support groups should share an advanced headquarters with a commander who would co-ordinate operations of the three armies in Tunisia, the British First and Eighth Armies, and the American–French forces. To each of the three armies an Army Support Wing would be attached whose commander would act as Air Adviser to the Army Commanders and would direct such air forces as were assigned to them by the Air Support Commander in consultation with the Deputy Supreme Commander. This framework owed a good deal to the methods hammered out by Coningham in the Western Desert. It therefore seemed but natural that he should command the Air Support Forces.

I had by now left Casablanca, and did not wholeheartedly approve every aspect of the new organisation. Experience in the Middle East showed that the organisation proposed for Army support held within it the seeds of trouble. Nevertheless, the cardinal point of having a Mediterranean Air Command was won, and won in time to allow the co-ordination of our forces and the maximum degree of damage to the Axis in the closing stages of the campaign in North Africa.

I was appointed to the post of Air Commander-in-Chief, Mediterranean, Sholto Douglas having already taken over my former position in Cairo. As for the ground forces, it had been agreed that when the Eighth Army fought its way through to Tunisia, it should be placed under Eisenhower's command, with General Alexander as his deputy. No doubt it was felt that Eisenhower could not effectively combine the roles of Supreme Commander and Military Commander.

Alexander and Brooke were in agreement that no premature rush forward should be made until everything was ready for a planned assault by all available forces in North Africa. Eisenhower had favoured the idea of a swift move on Sfax, cutting off Rommel's retreat from the other Axis forces in Tunisia. The Eighth Army, however, was still five hundred miles distant. Probably Brooke feared that we might run all the usual risks of undue dispersal of strength. At Casablanca he had raised the question of a Second Front, suggesting that operations in Italy should be used to divert the Germans from the west in preparation for a full-scale invasion of France. Although this plan was officially adopted, Anglo-American differences reached a sharper pitch on this issue than on any other major matter. To General Marshall the continuation of warfare in the Mediterranean was a sign of British lukewarmness towards the full scale assault on the Reich through France, which alone could secure the defeat of the main enemy. In Alan Brooke's eyes the continued lack of American reinforcements to Europe and the preoccupation with Admiral King's operations in the Pacific, signified American lack of perception.

At this distance of time, there can be no possible doubt that Brooke was right. Not only did we have no hope of acquiring in 1943 sufficient picked and trained troops, with a vast armada of shipping and landing craft for a cross-Channel invasion; even more important, we should not possess until the end of the year the air strength which, wisely used in advance of an assault on France, would ensure its success. It seemed clear to me that our right policy was to clear North Africa first, to take Sicily as a springboard for operations against Italy, the weak spot of the Axis, and to cause in the coming months the maximum devastation of German productive capacity.

*

No one had attempted at Casablanca to hide the fact that the need to pull together the organisation of our air forces in North Africa was urgent. A message from Spaatz told me on 22 January that the situation was by now so critical that part of the new plans must be implemented before the whole had been approved. He asked that 'Mary' Coningham should take over at the earliest possible moment.

The difficulties were not wholly military. The situation in Tunisia was one of the utmost delicacy. Not only had Eisenhower and his staff to steer a course between the contending French factions; there was also the continuing and sometimes embarrassing question of devising an organisation which would produce results without unduly antagonising the Americans. We all realised that without their manpower, wealth, and productive capacity, the war could not be won. Evidently, as their contribution, already large, became dominant, their influence in the making of the critical decisions would grow in proportion. At the same time, we had now been fighting for well over three years and had learned much in a hard school. Undue deference to national susceptibilities on either side might well ruin the joint enterprise in North Africa. Without the Americans' friendliness and willingness to learn, coupled with General Eisenhower's outstanding ability as a co-ordinator and his determination to work most loyally with the British, I do not think that the obstacles could have been surmounted.

In a signal of 12 February, Welsh told the C.A.S. that the Americans were fully alive to the fact that the British were assuming most of the key positions. Suggestions had been heard that Eisenhower was being kicked upstairs while the executive authority appeared to be in British hands. While the situation was accepted, the Americans did not want it to be rubbed in. Spaatz was particularly inclined to bristle easily. It had not escaped his notice that one of the B.B.C's bulletins on the Conference had omitted his name. These were the main elements of the situation when, in February 1943, all the Allied air forces operating in the Mediterranean were brought within the fold of a single organisation and placed under my command. Its structure showed how closely it had been designed to fit the immediate needs of our air forces. Under the new solution, the many elements which made up our air forces were to be combined and employed in concentrations of the highest flexibility, which would be directed from a Central Command at a level which kept in view the needs of the whole theatre.

When I returned to Algiers from Anfa I found that a pilgrimage to Tripoli to hear a gospel according to Montgomery was due to start off the following morning. The changes agreed at Casablanca meant that there was no one with the Eighth Army who was in a position to talk with authority about air action in the Desert during the previous eighteen months, so I thought it advisable that 'Mary' Coningham should accompany Eisenhower's Chief of Staff, General Bedell Smith, to Tripoli. As it transpired I had no need to be worried about Montgomery's view of the exercise of air-power. He had indeed produced a pamphlet of instructions for the troops which, I told Portal, it would be difficult to improve upon; this was not surprising, in view of the fact that the original document had been prepared by 'Mary' Coningham.

I was then able to begin at once the organization of my own headquarters and those of Spaatz and his subordinate commands. This task was not without its pitfalls, as I explained to Portal:

> My own Headquarters has, in spite of all my good intentions, swollen a little, partly, of course, due to the need for combined American and British representation on my staff. I had offered to take [Lieutenant-General Ira] Eaker as my deputy, leaving Wigglesworth as Chief of Staff, and the American [Major-General] Craig, the second deputy Chief of Staff. This suggestion went down very well with Eisenhower and the other Americans. Unfortunately, however, [Lieutenant-General Frank] Andrews has turned it down. I know of no other American whom I could think of in such a post, so I am afraid that suggestion will have to lapse.

The Tactical Air Force under 'Mary' Coningham was to consist of 242 Group covering Northern Tunisia, Twelfth Air Support Command in Central Tunisia, and the Western Desert Air Force in the south. Major-General Doolittle was given the command of the Strategic Air Force made up of all bombers not included in the Tactical Air Force, while Air Vice Marshal Lloyd took over the Coastal Air Force formed from the Coastal Defence Fighter and Group Reconnaissance Units. Long experience determined me to avoid the use of the title 'Air Support Command' for Coningham's charge. I found intense opposition to the title of 'Tunisian Command' and so came to the conclusion that the functional title 'Tactical Air Force 'was the right one. The retention of the title 'Twelfth Air Support Command' in Central Tunisia was a sop to sentiment which I thought it necessary to allow.

I remember Spaatz and I and some seven or eight others, American and British, sealing our agreement over the supper table in Spaatz's villa (every house in those parts appears to be a 'villa'). Throughout the discussion everything had been completely informal, and it was not an occasion for a formal speech. I did, however, wind up the proceedings by congratulating everyone, including myself! I expressed the hope that our work during the past week would set the pattern for the immense challenge which awaited us across the English Channel. I then went on to say:

'You know, we British are intensely proud of our Air Force. We think it is the very best in the world, and that it saved England and the world—all of us. We have our own ways of doing things and I suppose we feel we are justified in keeping these ways. But we also know that you Americans are equally proud of your splendid Air Force, of your magnificent aeroplanes and equipment, and that you feel justified in doing things your way— as well you are. However, it will be the fusion of us, the British, with you, the Americans, that is going to make the very best Air Force in the world.

'And now, gentlemen, this is the last time I shall ever speak of "us", the British, and "you", the Americans. From now on it is "we" together who will function as Allies, even better than either of us alone.'

*

After this, Coningham left for the front. The whole position, as I wrote to Portal, was only too familiar:

. . . Coningham is not going to have an easy time to get rid of the fantastic ideas of soldiers controlling aircraft. There is a lot to be done to get a properly balanced force in the forward area. At present there is a notable lack of day striking forces. The only day striking force at the moment is two very weak Boston squadrons.

I had already had my first spar with Andrew Cunningham, who repeated some sweeping and inaccurate statements about the lack of reconnaissance in the Central Mediterranean, which I was able to refute with evidence. Of course, we had not, and never would have, 'sufficient' reconnaissance and striking forces for day strikes between Sicily, Sardinia, and Naples, though I hoped that we might be able to transfer suitable aircraft from another part of the Mediterranean. The immediate situation, therefore, was unpromising, the prospects for the future brighter. My letter to Portal on 18 February concludes:

The whole situation both from the operational and organisation point of view, is quite incredibly untidy, and it will undoubtedly take a long time to get it tidy. We shall get some headaches in keeping the enemy quiet until we are in a fit state to deal with him properly. One does feel, however, that as far as the air is concerned, we have got the real good-will of the Americans, and we are determined to make a job of it.

Though I now held operational control over all the Allied Air Forces in the Mediterranean, Malta and the Western Desert Command were still administered from Cairo. The whole structure of command, however, remained indefinite, and had it not been for the fact that Sholto Douglas and I were old friends, friction between Cairo and Algiers would have been inevitable. Sholto had originally come out to Cairo to relieve me, but when I was called on to stay in the Mediterranean area and set up a superior headquarters, he was left in an invidious position. This was destined to cause trouble when the Dodecanese once again became the scene of operations.

Meantime, our new joint Anglo-American set-up got down to work smoothly with the minimum of formality. The organisation had worked so well for some three months that it occurred to me we should be well advised to record the whole of our arrangements in detail for the benefit of the Planners in London who were already working on 'Overlord'. This was a foolish mistake on my part. Within a few days of our telling the staffs to draw up a detailed structure, the back hairs began to bristle. Questions of relative ranks and seniority, coupled with national prejudices, threatened a complete break-up of what had been so harmonious. It came to a head at one of my 'morning prayers'. When Spaatz voiced very strong complaints about the way the structure was being developed, it was clear to me that I must take drastic action, and I put the position to him bluntly: 'If you want a divorce, you can have one here and now, repeat now!'

It took only a few minutes for us to decide and agree to call the staffs off and cancel all attempts to formalise our working organisation. In no time the storm clouds had dissipated and the sky was once again clear.

*

The new organisation was brought into effect under conditions which immediately put its value to the test. Less than a fortnight before its establishment, Rommel's retreating army had joined General von Arnim's forces in Tunisia. The opposing air forces were of almost equal strength and the Germans had not yet adopted the policy of economical operation and calculated exposure to which they were later reduced. They had the advantage of operating from runways suitable in all weathers. The winter and early spring of 1943 witnessed the worst weather experienced in North-West Africa for many years, and though our airfields farther west had been brought up to an excellent standard, the advanced landing grounds on the Tunisian borders remained inadequate to our needs and possessed only restricted areas for dispersal. The enemy was able to bomb and strafe these airfields, causing us heavy losses on the ground. Frequent bombing raids were likewise directed against the ports on which we depended.

A bout of pneumonia did not in any way diminish the attention with which Mr. Churchill scrutinised our shortcomings. On 25 February he questioned Portal sharply about what he called the outstanding fact of the moment:

. . . our total failure to build up air superiority in Tunisia considering we have already assigned to this theatre 1,200 American first-line aircraft, 500 British first-line aircraft, the whole of the Middle East first-line aircraft, about 1,000, all with their lavish tails of hundreds and thousands of men and squandering of our shipping. It is to be hoped that Tedder will show some result proportionate to the immense amount of Allied strength devoted to our air effort in Tunisia. The outstanding impression on my mind of the four months since the landing is of the failure and breakdown in the Allied Air.

You have not been able to stop the use of any of the ports or the movements of large forces. When the attack came you could give no support to our troops worth speaking of. Of course, there was always the weather, which, as everyone knows, does not affect the enemy.

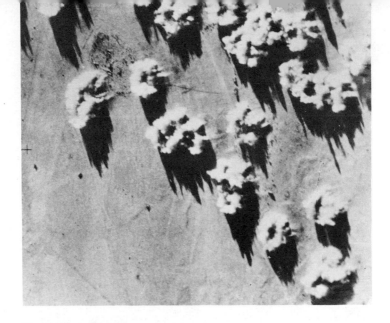

The 'Tedder carpet'

Early morning 'Boston Tea Party', 2 July 1942

Eisenhower, myself, Alexander, Cunningham, and in the rear,
Harold Macmillan, Bedell Smith and Wigglesworth. Algiers 1943

Bray (my P.A.), Craig (U.S.), myself, Wigglesworth, Timberlake
(U.S.)—'we', not 'us' or 'you'. Algiers 1943

The Prime Minister was glad that Air Marshal Welsh had been removed. However, neither this fact nor the heavy bias of the United States relieved the R.A.F. of the need for heart searching and explanations.

As for Tunisia, the C.A.S. explained that the inadequacy of the lines of communication had prevented both the Army and the Air Forces from deploying their full strength. Furthermore, the rate of serviceability of American aircraft had been low, because of failures in their replacement services and maintenance organisation. Portal solemnly assured Mr. Churchill that he had been quite correct in suggesting that bad weather had a one-sided effect, for the reasons that the Germans were based on flat country close to the battle area, whereas the Allies' main air strength was separated from the front by mountainous country. Effective intervention was made difficult in bad weather, when the cloud ceiling over the mountains lay low, and these factors, together with the rawness of the American troops, gave the German dive-bombers their chance.

Though we had admittedly failed so far to cut the enemy's lines of communication by air action, Portal reminded Churchill of the virtual immunity of our own shipping from enemy air attack. Of the 328 ships brought to Algiers and 233 proceeding east of Algiers, between 8 November and 21 January, only fourteen had been sunk by air action. Portal defended Welsh, who had controlled neither the anti-aircraft defences of the airfields, nor the priorities of supply, nor the movements, organisation, and maintenance of the American air units which formed the bulk of his air forces. The C.A.S. warned the Prime Minister that though everything possible was being done to provide the right personnel and material to produce efficiency out of the chaos which still existed, the improvement could only be gradual. Above all, he was certain that until the American Army gained confidence in its own ability to stand up to the Germans, it would display the usual readiness of worsted armies to blame the co-operating air forces.

While this exchange was taking place in London, the enemy had descended to the Western Plain, capturing Thelepte airfield on 17 February. We had managed to remove most of the material

R.A.F. Component of the
MEDITERRANEAN AIR COMMAND
March 1943

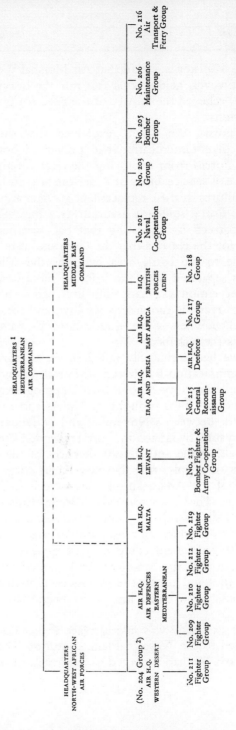

1 Operational Control of Middle East Air Formations.
2 No. 204 Group became Air H.Q. Western Desert under my reorganisation of 1941.

and aircraft in time. The Twelfth Air Support Command, assisted by elements of the Strategic Air Force and a squadron of Hurribombers, was directed against the German troops, armour, and supplies. The whole resources of the Western Desert Air Force kept up diversionary activity in the south, pinning down the German air units in that region. On 26 February, Rommel turned back towards the Tunisian Plain. During von Arnim's attack on the Medjez-el-Bab salient, 242 Group, despite bad flying weather and operating at distances near the limits of its range, flew nearly four thousand sorties. The crisis was barely passed when Rommel attacked again in the south, only to be forced to retreat from the Gafsa area on the second day, in the face of combined activity by the Strategic Air Force and Western Desert Forces.

Complaints from the First Army of insufficient light-bomber support soon reached London. While it was conceded that we had fulfilled our original side of the bargain during the opening phases of 'Torch', the War Office now contended that unforeseen developments in the campaign demanded a larger supporting force. The Americans had promised to contribute 550 aircraft to the Twelfth Air Force. At the present moment only 116 were available for action. Portal could not discover when the Americans intended to remedy these deficiencies and suggested that I should make the strongest representations to Eisenhower, which I did. The C.A.S. wondered whether we could draw upon existing aircraft in the Middle East or whether he could help.

I answered him on the same day, 26 February, that in the past months our lack of success and heavy losses against inferior numbers of enemy aircraft had been due to a lack of the right type of operational control:

Fighters have been frittered away in penny packets to give close cover, bomber and fighter escorts have similarly been frittered away in attacking petty targets, all on the orders of local Army commanders. Under such conditions losses have been high, enemy air has been aggressive and impudent despite inferior numbers, and in consequence effective support of the land battle has been quite unattainable on the scale which should have been possible with the forces available.

. . . the basic remedy is proper organisation and control. This is

[403]

WITH PREJUDICE *January–May 1943*

already beginning to show results which have been noted by the enemy as well as by our troops. Much, however, remains to be done, and it will take time to get the close co-operation here between land and air which we have attained on the other front. No one could be more helpful in this way than Alexander.

An extensive tour of the forward area at the beginning of March reinforced this view. Everything I saw and heard convinced me that the establishment of a joint headquarters by Alexander and 'Mary' Coningham had changed the whole atmosphere and outlook of the British and American land and air forces. The new organisation was working, given all the circumstances, with remarkably little friction. We had now to provide a proper warning system, which at the moment was either thin or non-existent; to arrange for adequate photography and tactical reconnaissance, since we had for some weeks taken practically no photographs in the tactical zone; and to provide extra hitting power.

Returning to Algiers I telegraphed to Portal:

While I have been away my old friend the Admiral has been dogmatising regarding the employment of the air striking force. . . .

Later in the month, when the Eighth Army's assault on the Mareth Line had begun, Spaatz moved up to Constantine, whence he was able to exercise effective control over the Strategical and Tactical Air Forces. This was the key to the whole problem. The Supreme Commander, General Eisenhower, and his Chief of Staff, General Bedell Smith, had accepted our organisation loyally, but, as I wrote to Portal on the 26 March:

They are instinctively antagonistic to it and find it difficult to understand that every General has not a divine right to command his own private air forces, and incidentally a divine inspiration by which he knows better than anyone else how those air forces should be employed. I think most of the Americans who have now seen our organisation working admit that it is sound, and produces better results than their own, but at the back of their minds there is always the bitter feeling which exists amongst them regarding separate air forces.

Before establishing myself in Algiers, I had sent my senior staff officer, Wigglesworth, to serve as a link between me and Eisenhower, but on my arrival at the headquarters at the St. George Hotel, I soon sensed that things were not quite right. Bedell Smith, Chief of Staff to Eisenhower, took an early opportunity to tell me that Wigglesworth would never fit into the combined headquarters—he was not a co-operator. I expressed my regret, but said I thought there must be some mutual misunderstanding, and they ought to allow a little time for things to settle down. It transpired that the trouble had arisen because Bedell Smith considered that everything for Eisenhower must be channelled through him as Chief of Staff. On the other hand I, as Commander-in-Chief, had the absolute right to communicate direct with the Supreme Commander. On this issue neither Bedell Smith nor Wigglesworth was prepared to compromise to the slightest degree, and both of them were by nature and habit blunt and outspoken—fortunately. It was not long before these two loyal staff officers had developed a deep-seated mutual respect and understanding, ultimately akin to affection.

I told Portal of a friendly and valuable discussion with Bedell Smith, who remarked that while he was determined to do everything possible to make the present set-up run smoothly, it did not affect his views about post-war organisation in the United States. So far as he was concerned, a separate air force in America 'would come only over his dead body'. I replied that inter-Service politics in America were no concern of mine, and was able to assure him that I had no intention of engaging in subversive propaganda amongst American personnel.

The difficulties of getting the Americans to understand how we British controlled and commanded air forces and how we worked with the land forces were most pronounced in connection with the advanced planning for 'Husky'. Fortunately, General Patton, who would be the Task Force Commander for 'Husky', was at that moment commanding in south-west Tunisia, where he had the opportunity to see how our system worked. I got 'Mary' Coningham to go and see Patton, and he told me that affairs were shaping well, that Patton was learning a lot and was well pleased. I thought that gradual education was the only possible method, although one not always easy to follow. I was able to write to Portal on 26 March:

There are many things one sees which are wrong and criminally uneconomical, but it would be worse than useless to go at it like a bull in a china shop. The only way in which we can get things really tidied up is by showing the Americans the right way to do things and letting them see where they are wrong and then letting them propose and put into effect the necessary remedies. A lot has already been achieved in this way. . . .

Relations with the Royal Navy revolved around the personality of the Naval Commander-in-Chief, Mediterranean, Admiral Cunningham. Of him I wrote in the same letter:

My old friend and enemy, the Admiral, has of course to be watched like a cat. He has been most helpful and co-operative in many respects, especially over the Gibraltar business in which he is doing his best to get the American Naval Air to be under A.O.C. Gibraltar.

This was a reference to a suggestion from Washington. For more than a year R.A.F. Gibraltar, in co-operation with the Royal Navy, had carried out anti-submarine operations in the area between Gibraltar and Casablanca. In this they had enjoyed considerable success. With the advent of American Naval aircraft into this sphere, the question of their control was reopened. It was suggested that nominal control of anti-submarine operations should be vested in the Allied Commander-in-Chief, Mediterranean. This would mean in effect that the control of R.A.F. Gibraltar would be in the hands of the Flag Officer at Gibraltar, under Cunningham, under Eisenhower. 'I can see no rhyme or reason in all this,' I signalled to London, 'other than the rhymes of the nursery.'

It may be said that all this is academic and that in fact R.A.F. Gib will continue to co-operate with the Navy as they have done and the job will be done. If, however, these questions of control are academic, why do the Admirals and Generals fight for them? If they are not academic, they must actually affect the efficiency of the air operations and I feel we should fight them. Our case is built on solid facts and sound experience.

It was later ruled, with Cunningham's support, that the

existing organisation should continue, the American forces operating under North African Coastal Force control. My report on 26 March on relations with the Navy continued:

On the other hand, of course, every enemy ship which is sunk is sunk by British submarines or mines laid by submarines, and every British ship torpedoed is torpedoed by enemy aircraft. This, however, is all in the game.

Admiral Cunningham considered that he alone was responsible for sea communications in the Mediterranean; or, rather, as he expressed it to me: 'I am the Managing Director and you are the Junior Partner.' I remarked that this was not the first time a Junior Partner had had to shoulder most of the executive responsibility.

*

In Algeria and Tunisia there was no let up for British troops from the squalor and discomfort which marked their living conditions—conditions as bad for morale as the scare-notices on the roadside, and the fox-holes. One noticed that the Americans were very sensitive on this subject—the connection between amenities and morale—so much so that on occasions they seemed to use the two words as meaning the same thing; as for instance when certain American observers reported the Western Desert forces as having low morale, when what they really meant was the complete lack of any official amenities. Consequently, earlier in the year, the Americans took over a large building in the middle of Algiers and rapidly converted it into a first class club with all amenities and with smart American ladies serving. At first, this club, run by the American Red Cross, was open to British troops as well as Americans, but it soon became obvious that that could not continue owing to the numbers. This was a situation which had seeds of trouble, and it worried Eisenhower. It is clear that he got little help from the British Army officers on his staff, and as a result he sent for the Scots lady in charge of British women personnel at his Headquarters, to see whether she could make any suggestions about dealing with the problem. At the same time, I had tackled the British General in charge of 'Q', and consequently in charge of N.A.A.F.I. and all its ways, to tell him that we must have somewhere in Algiers where the chaps could get off the streets. The answer was 'Nothing doing. After all, practically every camp in North Africa has a canteen. What more do you want?' I had no intention of submitting to a brush-off like that, and had a talk with Eisenhower, who told me that he had detailed his Scots lady to try to solve the problem and promised to give a helping hand if it was a question of accommodation. For the rest of the story I cannot do better than to quote the account written by a Press correspondent:

One day in April, a Scots lady was at a luncheon party in Algiers. In the extreme heat the cold beer that was served was welcome. She remarked that she wished the British troops could have similar beer— canned and iced. Her host, M. Roger Capgras, a refugee of France, leaned over and asked if she would care to go with him the next day to the local brewery to see if something could be done. The manager said he would provide the equipment and the beer if permission were given for its distribution; but where could the beer be enjoyed? The Scots lady, later to become Lord Tedder's second wife, saw that she would have to find the R.A.F. men a place which they could call their own— a club and a home. M. Capgras advanced £250, and with this she took over a derelict cafe. For six weeks this dynamic and indomitable lady ordered, threatened and cajoled the Arab workmen. She drove a three-ton truck ten miles out of Algiers at 5.30 each morning to collect them, and stood over them as they painted and hammered away. But at last it was ready.

It was Sir Archibald Sinclair, the then Secretary of State for Air, who suggested that the club should be called after the first V.C.—a posthumous one—of the North African campaign, Wing Commander Malcolm. When I opened the first club by drinking a half-can of that iced beer, I did not make a speech; I merely said, 'This is your Club. Keep it going.' Those few words have set the pattern for the organisation ever since. The clubs are the airmen's clubs, and they therefore have a proprietary interest in them. It was very soon after the opening of the club in Algiers that the troops in Tunis were saying, 'Where's our Malcolm Club?'—the operative word being 'our'. The other key to the success of the Malcolm Clubs has been what we called from the very beginning the 'feminine touch'. Everything depended on the personality of the Club Director. Each girl was hand-picked by that same Scots lady, my wife, and later on by her deputy, and Malcolm Club Girls have become famous throughout the R.A.F.

*

The advantages of our new Command displayed themselves clearly in the next phase of the Tunisian campaign, opening with the American attack on Gafsa in Southern Tunisia on 16 March and Montgomery's assault on the Mareth Line on the Tunisian–Tripolitanian border four days later. Light and medium bombers of the Twelfth Air Support Command rendezvoused for the first time with fighters of the Tactical Air Force on a bombardment mission—a tactical manœuvre which had been developed in the Western Desert during the campaigns of 1942. The day before the assault on the Mareth Line, bombers of Tactical Air Force, with elements of the Strategic Bomber Force, carried out combined attacks on the landing grounds of Tebaga and Gabes, so as to prevent the enemy air from operating against the Eighth Army. Spitfires of the Tactical Air Force covered the return home of our bombers, shooting down many of the pursuing Messerschmitts. By 22 March, the airfields of southern Tunisia were being attacked every fifteen minutes, while the Western Desert Air Force struck against the Kasr Rhilane position. The object of preventing enemy air forces from hindering our land offensives was virtually achieved. No more than five enemy aircraft appeared over the Eighth Army during the first crucial days. By 7 April, the Axis forces had abandoned all their forward aerodromes and were being forced even from Sfax on the coast.

In the last days of March, the Western Desert Air Force helped the first New Zealand Division in its remarkable flanking movement at El Hamma to the tune of five hundred sorties in one and three quarter hours, over an area two or three miles square, and within a thousand yards of the Allied front lines. Our aircraft created havoc amongst the enemy and forced a passage through a wall of Panzers. Although the success of this operation

[409]

depended in part on low visibility and on a large element of surprise, I think it will long remain as a classic example of the power of concentrated air action, for it was even more destructive than the similar operation before El Alamein. The Prime Minister told Parliament on 30 March that the decisive breakthrough of General Freyberg's turning force was 'aided to an extraordinary degree by novel forms of intense air attack, in which many hundreds of British aircraft were simultaneously employed'.

The enemy's last counter-attack in this region, on 6 April at Wadi Akarit, was met by a heavy concentration of fighters and fighter-bombers. That night the German and Italian troops began to stream northwards towards their brief stand at Enfidaville. The retreat was harassed by aircraft of the Western Desert Air Force. When the enemy passed beyond the range of their aircraft, 242 Group joined Twelfth Air Support Command in continuous attack.

The growing experience of Anglo-American co-operation in the air did not mean that everything now went smoothly on the ground. On 1 April I went up from Algiers to visit the squadrons. I landed at Constantine to refuel, when a staff officer dashed up to my aircraft in a great state of excitement. 'Have you seen this?' he asked. 'This' was a signal from 'Mary' Coningham directed to Patton but repeated world-wide, including even the official historian in the Pentagon. Patton's II Corps' G.3 had in his Situation Report recorded: 'Forward troops have been continuously bombed all the morning . . . enemy aircraft have bombed all division C.Ps.' In his signal Coningham pointed out that the number of casualties during the period of the Report was six! He went on to comment:

It is to be assumed that intention was not to stampede local American Air Command into purely defensive action. It is also assumed that there was no intention to adopt discredited practice of using Air Force as an alibi for lack of success on ground. If Sitrep is in earnest and balanced against . . . facts, it can only be assumed that II Corps personnel concerned are not battle-worthy in terms of present operations.

In view of outstandingly efficient and successful work of American Air Command concerned, it is requested that such inaccurate and exaggerated reports should cease. 12 Air Support Command have been instructed not to allow their brilliant and conscientious support of II Corps to be affected by this false cry of wolf.[1]

I knew this was dynamite with a short, fast-burning fuse, and the situation could well have led to a major crisis in Anglo-American relations. Fortunately I was able, despite the bad telephone, to get through direct to Eisenhower. He was obviously deeply concerned. I told him I had instructed Coningham to withdraw and cancel his signal, and to go with me to meet Patton at Gafsa to make a personal apology, and I asked Eisenhower to hold his hand until after our meeting at Gafsa. At Gafsa it was not long before peace had been declared and mutual understanding and good fellowship established, and I was able to report accordingly to Eisenhower. Only afterwards did I learn that 'Ike' had actually drafted a signal to Washington referring to this incident, and saying that since it was obvious he could not control his Allied commanders, he asked to be relieved. That signal never went.

There is a postscript to the meeting at Gafsa. When we had settled it all and the three of us were arm in arm over the odd drink, there was the sudden noise of rifle, machine-gun, and anti-aircraft fire, and three F.W. 190s scooted across about two hundred feet up. I nodded to George Patton, and said 'I always knew you were a good stage manager, but this takes the cake.' Bradley reports that Patton's summing up was: 'If I could find the sonsabitches who flew those planes I'd mail them each a medal.'

Taking the long view, I thought the effect might be good. Patton was now a friend of ours and I thought that the chance of bellyaching signals from the Army would be greatly reduced. But this did not justify Coningham's original signal which inevitably left an unpleasant taste, and was bound to some extent to affect others' assessment of his judgment. Apart from this incident, co-operation between the land and air forces, British and American, was developing well, and I thought the general atmosphere excellent. Even General Anderson had by now changed his tune.

After the withdrawal from the Mareth Line, the Axis air transport effort between Sicily and Tunis had begun to rise from a

[1] Bradley: *A Soldier's Story*, pp. 62–3.

hundred sorties a day to about 250. Towards the end of March I drew up a detailed plan for its suppression, the so-called 'Flax' Plan. It went into effect on 5 April when a total of 287 sorties was flown by aircraft of the Strategic Air Force: 201 enemy aircraft were quickly destroyed, forty of them in combat, for a loss of nine. Attacks on Sicilian and Tunisian aerodromes reaped havoc on ill-dispersed transport aircraft. Five days after the plan took effect, forty-five Ju. 52s and twelve fighters were brought down. On the following day an entire transport convoy of twenty-one Ju. 52s was shot down with five of its escort, followed a few hours later by the destruction of more transport aircraft.

Nevertheless, with the Germans now in full retreat to Enfidaville, they even increased their shuttle service, though with a change of method. Large convoys were flown, not more than twice a day, escorted by short-range fighters at both ends of the crossing. The continuing advance of Eighth Army made it possible for the Western Desert Air Force to operate further forward. The study of intercepted enemy wireless traffic gave us the approximate period during which our chances of massed interception were relatively good. It was arranged that a period of one and a quarter hours should be covered by means of five patrols of fifteen minutes each, overlapping each other by a few minutes, and in an average strength of three Kittyhawk squadrons with a Spitfire squadron as top cover. This effort used up the whole of the Western Desert Fighter Force.

The result was that within three days 106 German transports were shot down. On the late afternoon of 18 April, a convoy of about a hundred Ju. 52s was sighted. Seventy-three of them, with sixteen of their fighter escort, were destroyed. On the following morning twelve more were shot down; and on the 22nd a convoy of twenty-one six-engined Me. 323s was intercepted. All were destroyed, together with sixteen fighters.

Meanwhile, I had received on 20 April a signal from Mr. Churchill complaining of lack of information about recent air operations, and especially referring to the attack of 18 April. The Prime Minister described how highly coloured accounts of the air battle had been sent by correspondents in Algiers, who had the news before His Majesty's Government. He wanted to know how this had happened, and called for a full account of the action. This message was supplemented by a signal from the C.A.S., supporting the Prime Minister's request. He told me that air reports from North Africa usually arrived in London between a day and three days after the event. Because of the scant reports from North Africa, the Air Ministry found it hard to gauge the situation as a whole or to determine what ideas were governing the conduct of the battle by Coningham and Spaatz.

The need for very early reports of really important or novel air operations is shown in the Prime Minister's telegram to you. It is clearly most desirable that we should as often as possible provide him with earliest inside information not available to the Press but which he can give to Parliament in public session. This not only helps the Prime Minister, but is also very good for the Air Force, and since the opportunities are infrequent, I feel we have little excuse for not taking those that occur. Operations on 18th April and those at El Hamma on 26th March are good instances. Prime Minister had nothing on these that had not been skimmed clean in advance by the Press.

Portal asked me to continue my practice of sending home 'Strictly Private' telegrams, which would be shown to no one without my leave. Telegrams to the Air Ministry for Churchill and himself should, whenever possible, be so worded that they could be passed to the other Chiefs of Staff.

In my reply to the Prime Minister I gave an account of the 'Flax' Plan and its working and told him how it happened that he had not received news of the events of 18 April until the morning of 20 April. My first information of our success was gleaned from a short telephone call on a bad line from Spaatz's headquarters on the evening of the 18th. Such facts as we possessed were given to Eisenhower at his morning conference on 19 April, by which time I had gone forward to the battlefront. I explained to Mr. Churchill the extreme difficulty of obtaining full and reliable information from the Western Desert when we had to use communications so rudimentary and at a time when our air efforts were at their height and our progress so rapid. I assured him and Portal that every effort would be made to see that the situation did not recur, and that as communications improved so, also, would the flow of information to London. Churchill replied on 24 April:

I congratulate you all on the brilliant series of operations. Had I received a report in good time I could have made a complimentary reference to this action in the House, which would have been agreeable both to the Royal Air Force and to the United States. As it is, it is only now, five days later, that I have had your account.

During the 'Flax' and post-'Flax' operations, the enemy lost 432 aircraft in the air at a cost to us of about thirty-five aircraft. Thereafter he was reduced to night transport, an operation for which his capacity was limited. During the last nights of the campaign only two aerodromes were available for the few enemy planes that got through. This crippling of the Axis air transport effort played a large part in the enemy's sudden and complete collapse in Tunisia.

Besides playing a major role in the 'Flax' plan, aircraft of the Strategic Air Force continued to bomb enemy installations in Tunisia and in combination with Wellingtons of the Western Desert Air Force and Liberators of the Ninth Air Force, even ranged as far north as Naples. The port areas of Sfax, Sousse, Tunis, La Goulette, and Bizerta were completely devastated; the aerodromes of the region were made unserviceable one after the other; marshalling yards, concentrations of motor transport, bridges, and other targets were repeatedly attacked.

When a pause in the land battle ensued at the end of April we took the opportunity to redirect the whole Western Desert Fighter Force against enemy shipping, while the remainder of the Tactical forces supported the Army. The enemy made a desperate attempt to ensure safe arrival of shipping in Tunisia, but his fighter efforts, though exceptional in scale, failed in their object. On the last day of April, not a single enemy ship arrived in port. In this auspicious way began a new phase in our operations against enemy shipping of all types, similar to recent operations against his air transport. I let Portal know of these successes at once:

The importance of these operations is not merely their effect on current land battles, interrupting enemy supplies, but also indication of our prospects in preventing a Dunkirk. It looks as if the main problem now will be to stop night transit of shipping. This we should be able to do in concert with the Navy.

Both Portal and Churchill sent warm congratulations on this operation, in which, during one day, the enemy had lost three destroyers, a corvette, a ferry boat, an E-boat, and a number of smaller craft. The closing phase of the North African campaign saw the ground and air forces converging on the enemy's bridgeheads. I placed the Twelfth Air Support Command under the operational control of 242 Group, which moved to the extreme north with the American II Corps. The Medjerda river south-west of Tunis formed a boundary between 242 Group and the Western Desert Air Force. From dawn till noon these forces laid down creeping barrages in front of our advancing army. During 6 May over two thousand sorties were flown. By the next morning we knew that the main breakthrough was accomplished. The enemy's forces had been split, one portion lying between Tunis and Bizerta, the other in the region of the Cap Bon Peninsula. The ground situation changed so rapidly that calls for air support could not always be acted upon. Our formations were therefore told to cross the lines and demoralise the enemy further whenever the chance arose.

On 10 May, the northern portion of the enemy forces surrendered. Farther south the Tactical Air Force supported our armour, which, in breaking through the defile at Hamman Lif, separated the main body of the Axis forces from the peninsula and destroyed all hope of a seaborne evacuation. The last groups of Axis troops surrendered on 13 May 1943. The North African shore was cleansed.

I received this message from the Prime Minister:

It is certain the victories in Tunisia would never have been gained without the splendid exertions of the Allied Air Force under your skilful and comprehending direction. Will you tell Spaatz, Coningham, Doolittle and Broadhurst how much their work is admired. The united, efficient and individual devotion to duty which enables so amazing a number of sorties to be made each day is beyond all praise.

The contrast with the events of 1940 could scarcely have been

[415]

more marked. Now, as then, the defeated army wished to escape across the sea; the victors enjoyed air supremacy now as then. But now it was found that evacuation by sea was impossible. Indeed, the Axis forces had been driven in desperation to try and get their men away by air. Some 238,000 German and Italian prisoners fell into our hands.

*

I have always been a firm believer in team work as being the secret of success in any organisation. I was indeed fortunate in the Mediterranean campaign. When I came out to Middle East I brought nobody with me and there were few in the Command of whom I had more than a superficial knowledge, yet within a few days I began to feel that I was one of a team. I think it says much for the *esprit de corps* and morale of the Royal Air Force that it could so quickly develop a fresh team spirit. Both individually and collectively my top team were a strong combination.

Peter Drummond, Deputy C.-in-C., quiet but firm, the ideal and almost perfect deputy, could be completely relied upon to use his judgment and accept responsibility: unfortunately he was later killed in an air crash over the Atlantic. George Pirie, the Air Officer Administration, a dry Scot, was no revolutionary, but thoroughly sound and reliable. He was responsible for the administration of operations from the Western Desert to the Persian Gulf, north to Iraq and Persia and south to the Sudan and East Africa, yet he was very reluctant to hand over to Dawson the maintenance problems normally handled by the A.O.A. Graham Dawson himself, a whirlwind 'action this day' man, intolerant of administrative difficulties, full of originality and initiative in overcoming various obstacles. With the help of one or two of his team from M.A.P. he set up in Egypt a service and repair organisation which literally saved the situation. The story of Dawson's activities in Middle East is an extraordinary, romantic tale of impossibilities. Finally, Wigglesworth, S.A.S.O., a blunt, outspoken Yorkshireman, useful as ballast to the team. He began to come into his own as my Deputy when we moved over to North Africa, and he had to deal with the Americans. This he did with remarkable success, even taming the redoubtable Bedell Smith.

The Desert Air Force was another example of a close-knit team. 'Mary' Coningham the A.O.C. was at times rather a prima donna, but always full of initiative, originality, and courage, and thoughtful for his men. 'Tommy' Elmhirst made his mark as A.O.A. to the Desert Air Force and right-hand man to Coningham. He got some remarkable results in maintaining squadrons in full operation while the Eighth Army were in full retreat. George Beamish, as imperturbable during exciting moments in the desert as he was in Greece and Crete.

One evening, talking with one of my team, we started analysing our organisation, and turning to the question of team spirit I asked, 'What is the secret of team spirit? It appears that we have got it, but how and why?' He said, 'I think it is mainly because we feel that you will back us up. We are encouraged to take risks and accept responsibility, and the knowledge that you will back us if need be just makes all the difference.' To which I remarked, 'I doubt if it is quite so simple as all that!'

Sicily and Italy

FEBRUARY–DECEMBER 1943

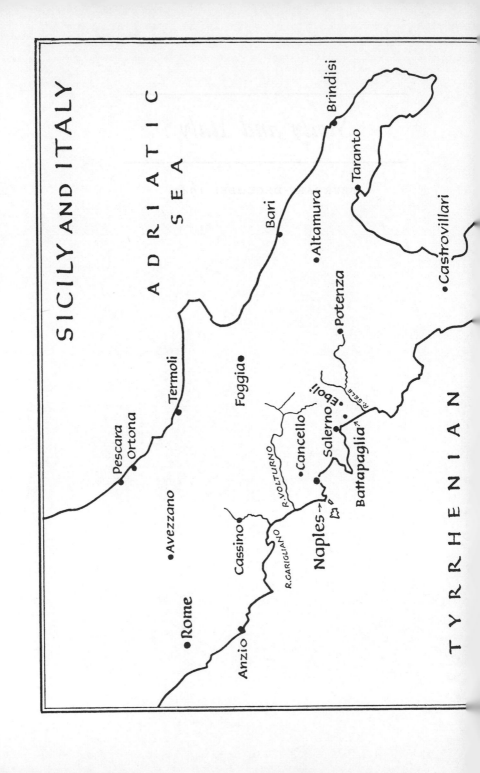

SICILY AND ITALY

ADRIATIC SEA

TYRRHENIAN

Brindisi
Taranto
Castrovillari
Bari
Altamura
Potenza
Pescara
Ortona
Termoli
Foggia
R.SELE
Eboli
Cancello
Salerno
Battapaglia
R.VOLTURNO
Avezzano
Cassino
Naples→
R.GARIGLIANO
Rome
Anzio

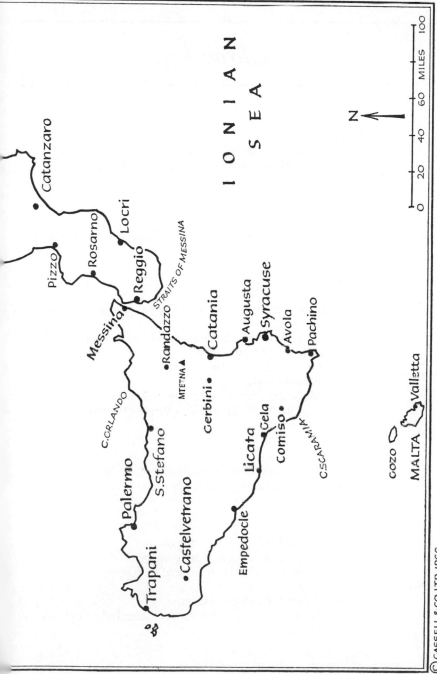

IONIAN SEA

Catanzaro
Locri
Rosarno
Pizzo
Reggio
Messina
STRAITS OF MESSINA
Randazzo
MT. ETNA
Gerbini
Catania
Augusta
Syracuse
Avola
Pachino
C. ORLANDO
Palermo
S. Stefano
Castelvetrano
Trapani
Empedocle
Licata
Gela
Comiso
C. SCARAMIA
GOZO
MALTA
Valletta

N

0   20   40   60   MILES   100

Chronology

1943

September:

10   Germans occupy Rome.
      British capture Salerno.
      British mission lands by parachute on Rhodes.
      Italian fleet arrive at Malta.
11   Allied seaborne force lands at Taranto.
14   Heavy fighting in Salerno.
      R.A.F. makes concentrated attacks along Eboli road.
16   Fierce fighting at Salerno.
      U.S. Fifth and British Eighth Armies link up.

November:

12   Germans land seaborne and airborne forces on Leros.
16   British garrison on Leros surrenders.

Timing and planning of 'Husky'–Pantelleria–Churchill cannot rest 'content'–Rival pleas produce a stalemate–Escape from deadlock Prime-Minister and C.I.G.S. come to North Africa–After Sicily?– Bombing of marshalling yards near Rome–Pantelleria analysis by Professor Zuckerman–Mediterranean campaign 'classic' in use of air-power

OPERATION 'Husky', the invasion of Sicily, was to be the first major landing of the Second World War of seaborne troops in the face of what we believed would be strong and determined enemy opposition. Churchill had directed at Casablanca that the divisions which were to take part should receive intense amphibious training, and that the provision, maintenance, and repair of landing craft should be greatly improved and extended. The Conference had not long been concluded when we began to argue about the date on which 'Husky' could be launched. Eisenhower told the Combined Chiefs of Staff on 11 February of his view that for lack of time for training and preparation an assault on Sicily in June was not likely to succeed. Churchill replied that he hoped this decision need not be taken as final. At Casablanca Roosevelt and he certainly thought that a delay of three months in the middle of the campaigning season between the finish of the Tunisian campaign and the beginning of 'Husky' would be a disaster for the Allies' cause. To the Chiefs of Staff Committee in London, Churchill minuted that even Admiral King was disturbed at this sudden turning down by Eisenhower of the June date. He noted:

It is absolutely necessary to do this operation in June. We shall become a laughing-stock if, during the spring and early summer, no British and American soldiers are firing at any German and Italian soldiers.

The Combined Chiefs of Staff decided that the June period must remain the target date for 'Husky', though Eisenhower was to report an alternative date. He replied to the Prime Minister that he quite realised the importance of launching 'Husky' as soon as possible, but the date would be governed by the schedule of arrival of landing craft. Whereas the landings in North Africa in the previous November had been undertaken against little or no opposition, experience then had strengthened his opinion that a high degree of combined training would be absolutely essential in the face of the opposition to be expected in Sicily, and this could not be attained by the June date. He therefore maintained his opinion that an assault at that period was unlikely to succeed.

Eventually, this question of date resolved itself.

There was, however, a thorn in the side of the Allies in the shape of the island of Pantelleria in the middle of the Sicilian Narrows, some 120 miles from Palermo. We estimated the strength of the Italian garrison at between 8,500 and 11,000 men. Pantelleria had only one beach, five hundred yards long, on which a landing could be made. At first it was believed that a major airborne assault would be necessary for the island's capture. Its seizure would not only remove an embarrassing enemy outpost, cutting across our lines of communication, but would also simplify convoy protection and enable us to station some five fighter squadrons a good deal nearer the Sicilian beaches than would otherwise be possible. Without the use of Pantelleria our initial air effort over the Sicilian beaches of Gela and Licata would be unacceptably small, for they would remain just outside the effective range of many of our fighters. Moreover, if we could take Pantelleria, the installation of radar there would simplify the 'Husky' operations a good deal. On these solid grounds it was decided that the island should be captured.

In the meantime, planning for the 'Husky' operation itself was not proceeding without friction. At a meeting held on 13 March, under Eisenhower's chairmanship, and attended by Cunningham, Alexander (who was to command the ground force) and myself, the main outlines of the initial assault were discussed. It was generally admitted that before 'Husky' could take place at all the enemy's air forces would have to be reduced to an extent which would ensure our supremacy in the air. Axis submarines must be contained sufficiently to prevent losses of our transport vessels. The plan provisionally agreed upon provided for a first phase of two assaults, one against Catania by a British force in the east, and the other against Palermo by an American force in the west. The main problem would be to get the assault troops across the beaches at a time when landing grounds and ports had not been secured. An extensive drop of airborne troops in order to soften resistance behind the beaches was judged the best method. The army required darkness for the landing, the paratroops wanted some moonlight for their drop. This meant, in effect, that the assault must be made with the moon in its second quarter, either between 10 June and 14 June or in a similar period in the following month. Further meetings, however, produced an outline plan, the main feature of which was a series of staggered assaults beginning with the landing of British troops of the Eastern Task Force on beaches extending from south of Syracuse in the east to Gela towards the west, followed by the landing of the American Western Task Force on the beaches in the extreme south-west two days later, and the landing of the remainder three days after that in north-western Sicily immediately west of Palermo. The main body of the Eastern Task Force would be provided by five British divisions, and that of the Western Task Force by four American divisions. This plan, contrary to Eisenhower's original suggestions, meant a considerable dispersion of forces. He had argued that all available force should be concentrated on achieving rapid victory in the south-east, but abandoned this proposal in face of the difficulties of maintenance which would face us unless Palermo were promptly captured. Even before this plan was issued on 25 March, Alexander and Montgomery had convinced Eisenhower that it spread the Allied forces too thinly, and that the British force would not be strong enough for the task of capturing rapidly its immediate objectives, the airfields of the south-east, unless it were reinforced by one additional division. There now ensued a period of some six weeks in which Eisenhower struggled with the dilemma of choosing between two risks; that of being too weak to take the immediate objectives in the south-east on the one hand, and on the other the risk to maintenance if Palermo were sacrificed for the sake of decisive strength elsewhere.

We were agreed that something must be done to strengthen the assault in the south-east. Careful reconnaissance showed that the airfield near Gela was one of the most highly developed, and I particularly insisted that the airfield at Pachino in the extreme south-east must also be captured at once. Failure in the south-east would probably rob the western assault of all chance of even limited success, and even complete success in the west could not retrieve a disaster in the south-east. The salient fact which emerged from our talks was that without early possession of these air-fields the entire plan would prove abortive. Provision for their speedy capture therefore became the guiding principle of our operational plans. It transpired that to find an extra division for the south-east would almost certainly mean the cancellation of the American assault in the south-west, since none of the forces assigned to the north-western landings could be spared. This would be a high price to pay, for the task of this south-western force was to seize airfields which would provide close fighter support for the landings around Palermo three days later. If this were impossible, those landings would have to rely on fighter support based on airfields in the south-east, about twice as far away. This would have the double disadvantage of leaving the south-western fields temporarily in enemy hands and of disrupting the schedule for the attack on Palermo.

These were no doubt the main reasons which made the British Chiefs of Staff especially reluctant to see the south-western assault abandoned. They told the Combined Chiefs of Staff in Washington of their opinion on 25 March, suggesting that some-how an additional division must be provided. The dispute was not satisfactorily resolved. It turned mainly on the availability of landing craft.

On 7 April Eisenhower telegraphed to the Combined Chiefs of Staff and to London that he, Admiral Cunningham, and General Alexander agreed with the view of the planners that the 'Husky' operation offered scant promise of success if the island contained 'substantial well-armed and fully organised German ground troops'. By the term 'substantial' he meant more than two German divisions. He pointed out that the assault must be a frontal one, with the virtual absence of strategic or tactical surprise, and made by a total of some nine divisions against a maximum enemy force of eight divisions, apart from many static battalions. While such an assault should succeed against the Italians, Eisenhower did not consider hopeful the chances of success against a garrison containing a high proportion of German formations. He thought that the dangerous periods would be between D-Day and D-Day Plus 2, when immediate counter-attack might take place, and between D-Plus 3 and D-Plus 6, when the enemy commander in Sicily would have appreciated the location and strength of our landings, and would be able to commit his central reserves to a deliberate counter-attack. 'The above statement of opinion,' Eisenhower telegraphed, 'does *not* affect the intensity of our planning and preparation which are going forward with the utmost vigour.'

These views were not favourably received. On 8 April Churchill minuted that Eisenhower's statement contrasted oddly with the confidence he showed about invading France across the Channel, where he would have to meet a great many more than two German divisions. If the presence of two German divisions was held to be decisive against any operations of an offensive or amphibious character, open to the million men now in French North Africa, it was difficult to see how the war could be carried on:

Months of preparation, sea power and air power in abundance and yet two German divisions are sufficient to knock it all on the head. I do not think we can rest content with such doctrines.

The Prime Minister also noticed that formerly they had been told that it was Alexander and Montgomery who shared Eisenhower's views. Now only Alexander's name was mentioned, and Churchill could not believe that he had expressed himself so crudely. 'It is perfectly clear,' he added, 'that the operations must either be entrusted to someone who believes in them, or abandoned. I trust the Chiefs of Staff will not accept these pusillanimous and defeatist doctrines from whoever they come.' Eisenhower should be asked what he meant by two German divisions and by the eight divisions as against the nine which the Allies would employ. What would be the strength of the enemy divisions?

This is an example of the fatuity of planning staffs playing upon each other's fears, each Service presenting its difficulties at the maximum and Americans and Englishmen vying with each other in the total absence of one directing mind and commanding will power. I regard the matter as serious in the last degree. We have told the Russians that they cannot have their supplies by the northern convoy for the sake of

'Husky', and now 'Husky' is to be abandoned if there are two German Divisions (strength unspecified) in the neighbourhood. What Stalin would think of this when he has 185 German divisions on his front, I cannot imagine.

This Minute was not entirely fair to Eisenhower, since his telegram specifically stated that he would regard substantial German ground troops as meaning more than two German divisions. The Chiefs of Staff immediately said that they agreed with Churchill, and that night, 8 April, a telegram in the same sense, though in slightly less vehement language, was sent to Washington. The United States Chiefs of Staff at once agreed with their British counterparts and signalled accordingly to Eisenhower. He promised in reply that the 'Husky' operation would be prosecuted with all the means at the disposal of his command.

Portal, noticing the absence of my name in Eisenhower's signal, telegraphed to ask whether I had been consulted before the message of 7 April was sent. As it happened, I had been at that time in the Middle East, and Wigglesworth, knowing that I would not be in complete agreement with it, had tried to delay the despatch of the telegram. In the draft seen by him, no names were included. I signalled to Portal on 22 April:

> I had heard this argument about German divisions before, and had questioned this point of view. As, however, it is finally for the Generals to assess the value of their own and enemy troops, I did not, and do not feel I could insist on any official disclaimer so far as I was concerned.

We had to face the probability that our Generals would find the enemy as good as they believed him to be.

Though our attention was still mainly directed to the last stages of the Tunisian campaign, the air commands under my control were preparing for their part in 'Husky'. Malta's effort under Park maintained the standards of intense, devoted exertion which had characterised Lloyd's régime. A new aerodrome at Safi was being constructed, and extensions to three others were ahead of schedule. Aircraft pens, taxi tracks and accommodation, both underground and above the surface, were progressing excellently, and by the end of April Park was able in an emergency to operate an additional ten fighter squadrons.

Agreement had still not been reached, however, on the merits of the 'Husky' plan itself, of which Montgomery wrote to the C.I.G.S.:

A dog's breakfast . . . it breaks every common-sense rule of practical fighting, and would have no chance of success . . . unless someone will face up to this problem and give a decision, there will be a first-class disaster. . . .

On 25 April, I learnt from Sholto Douglas in Cairo that Montgomery proposed to establish his headquarters for 'Husky' in Malta and was most anxious that Air Vice Marshal Broadhurst should be alongside him, in operational control of the air forces supporting the British landings. With this proposal Douglas sympathised. Montgomery, dissatisfied with the arrangements for the photography of Sicily, wished reconnaissance units to be moved promptly to Malta and placed under Broadhurst. I also learned that the General was very perturbed at the continual cutting down of transport aircraft for the parachute troops, particularly as he wished to use the glider brigade from England in addition to three parachute brigades. Douglas explained to him the difficulties about the provision of transport aircraft, and told him that he would be likely to suffer severely if all our transport aircraft were taken off their normal duties for the para-chute role.

Montgomery had, indeed, gone so far as to produce a new plan of his own. I was given an unofficial sight of a signal from Montgomery to Alexander damning the combined plan and making a great play of the desperate fight now being put up by the Germans and Italians, and the possibility of similar oppos-ition, with heavy German reinforcements, in Sicily. Douglas signalled to me on 28 April that Montgomery had told his staff to work from his new plan. They were pressing their opposite numbers in Cairo to do likewise.

All this occurred a bare fortnight after we had overcome Montgomery's objection that the assault on the south-east beaches was not to be mounted in sufficient force and Malta had been induced to accept an extra division. It was this plan which Montgomery had pronounced to be militarily unsound after his unheralded descent upon Cairo. His new scheme did away altogether with the assaults on the south-west beaches, the object of which was to take the south-west group of airfields, and concentrated everything on the assaults in the south-east. Admiral Cunningham objected at once that Montgomery's new plan was unsound since it left three airfields in the occupation of the enemy, except for such force as the R.A.F. could put on to them, while our troops would be landing from a mass of shipping a mere thirty miles off. It also seemed to surrender our greatest asset, that of being able to assault Sicily in numerous places at once and at will.

These proceedings evidently affronted Admiral Cunningham's sense of propriety, for he signalled to the First Sea Lord on 28 April:

I am afraid Montgomery is a bit of a nuisance; he seems to think that all he has to do is to say what is to be done and everyone will dance to the tune of his piping. Alexander appears quite unable to keep him in order. Tedder is also absolutely opposed to this new plan.

But the seriousness of it all is that here we are with no fixed agreed plan, just over two months off 'D'-Day, and the commanders all at sixes and sevens, and even if we do get final agreement, someone will be operating a plan he doesn't fully agree with. Not the way to make the success of a difficult operation.

The next day we held a meeting at Algiers at which Alexander, Cunningham, and I heard Montgomery's case set out by General Oliver Leese, Montgomery being sick. Admiral Ramsay and General Patton were also present. Alexander said that he must accept Montgomery's views since Montgomery was the one who would have to fight the battle. My main points were that I could not accept one-sided action of this kind by an individual commander, affecting the operations by other commanders and fundamentally opposed to the general plan agreed by the Commanders-in-Chief; that the land part of the Eastern Task plan could not be considered without reference, not only to the air and naval aspect of the Eastern Task, but also to the Western Task with which it was closely related; and that Montgomery's

El Aouina.
"Col. Warden's departure.
07.45 27.12.43

'Colonel Warden's' departure from El Aouina, Tunisia, for
Marrakesh after his illness, 27 December 1943

At 12 Air Support HQ, Salerno Bay, 20/21 September 1943

Puddle-jumping back from seeing Patton south of Avranches, 9 August 1944

plan, by ignoring most of the enemy air bases, would leave the expedition and its supplies exposed to a scale of enemy air attack which I thought would be prohibitive and which would gravely prejudice the Western Task. I refused to agree to any plan which diverged from the main principle on which the agreed plan had been built, namely, the immediate attack upon, and early occupation and use of, the main enemy air bases in southeast Sicily. Montgomery's plan would leave thirteen airfields in enemy hands, far more than we could neutralise effectively by air action alone. We had to capture the airfields for our own use at the earliest possible moment.

The views of the Army, on the one hand, and of the R.A.F. and Royal Navy on the other, therefore, conflicted sharply. I signalled to the C.A.S. that Cunningham had strongly supported me on every point from the naval aspect:

> Both of us in difficult position owing to Alexander's sudden volte-face. Must be remembered that Montgomery saw the combined plan and agreed it six weeks ago subject to an additional division. Both Cunningham and I consider that no compromise is possible on this issue.

At the end of our conference it was agreed that General Leese should return and explain our views to Montgomery. I arranged for 'Mary' Coningham to go with him, hoping to give Montgomery a way out by saying that he had not had the air aspect properly put to him. Coningham's first report on their meeting was not, however, promising. He said that Montgomery was obstinate and considered that Eisenhower should visit him and settle the whole affair. Eventually it was arranged that we should all meet at Algiers on 2 May. To Portal I added:

> My personal views are that Montgomery, who, as he has repeatedly assured me, will take 'no risks', is shaken at the thought of the risks inevitable in an operation of this sort. His reaction has been to 'concentrate' Eighth Army in his plan, and so sacrifice the main advantage of an amphibious operation, and at the same time ignore the air aspect. Subject to insistence on the basic principle of the combined plan, we will do all possible to avoid a deadlock. Unfortunately, Alexander has so far shown no sign of putting his foot down, so if Montgomery

proves to be obstinate, a dangerous deadlock is inevitable. Eisenhower and Bedell Smith take a poor view of this affair, and not without justification. Unofficially (since they have not yet been officially involved) they support me and the Admiral.

I also thanked Sholto Douglas for his two signals, pointing out that Montgomery had no competence to lay down any requirements for the organisation or operation of air forces. I had already informed Alexander and told him why I had decided that Park must operate all the air forces from Malta. Evidently Montgomery had been misinformed about the progress of photography and surveys. The need to secure additional transport was admitted, and we had for some time been doing everything possible to get it.

General Montgomery, who was, in his own description of himself, 'a very difficult subordinate', wrote to the C.I.G.S. on 30 April:

> My remarks on the plan have caused a most frightful tornado and it is clear to me that I am regarded as a most unpleasant person. . . . They want me to operate in little brigade-groups all over the place, and I refuse. . . . We cannot go on this way. Unless we get a good plan and a firm plan at once on which we can all work there will be no 'Husky' in July.[1]

By 2 May, Montgomery had produced a revised plan in which he showed that the early capture of the south-eastern airfields in Sicily was vital to the whole project. Everything should, therefore, be concentrated upon it. There was nothing new about this; it was a plan which had been examined weeks before. Personally, I had always favoured it, owing to my doubts about the whole Western Task. The objection was the familiar one of supply, for it had been thought impossible to maintain so large a force from the beaches and the limited harbours in the south-east of the island. The matter was urgently examined afresh, in preparation for a meeting of the three Commanders-in-Chief on 3 May. Meanwhile, I telegraphed to Portal:

> The mental gymnastics of some of our Generals would be amusing if it were not for the effect on their reputation and authority. Appears,

---

[1] Bryant: *The Turn of the Tide*, pp. 33 and 664.

however, there is sporting chance of reasonable escape from the deadlock.

After prolonged conferences, we agreed that the risk should be run. The airfields in the south-east would be secured in the first rush and all available strength in both Task Forces concentrated to ensure that objective. The plan was therefore recast on 3 May on the strategic principle of concentration in the crucial areas. The assaults scheduled for D-Plus 2 in the south-west and for D-Plus 5 near Palermo were abandoned and the whole Western Task Force diverted to the south-eastern assault. In short, we agreed to run the risk about maintenance and supply, as the lesser of two evils. Eisenhower telegraphed to the Combined Chiefs of Staff that all the commanders concerned in the 'Husky' operation had been convinced by the lessons learnt in North Africa of the difficulties of driving Axis troops from mountain positions. The western limit of attack would now include the airfield at Gela and the port of Licata. The American Seventh Army would look after the western assault, and the Eighth Army the eastern assault. It was hoped that this plan would provide us with a strong army able to advance rapidly and cut communications to the westward from Messina, thus isolating the western part of the island. Palermo would be taken at the first possible date. This confirmed Eisenhower's own original view. The British Chiefs of Staff and the Combined Chiefs approved this plan. They thought that the conquest of Sicily, if begun on the target date, 10 July, could be concluded in about a month. Portal believed that the main weakness of the new plan was that the port of Palermo might remain open to Axis reinforcements. He counted on the enormous Allied superiority in the air to neutralise the port and seal off the island.

As we approached D-Day for 'Husky' we had also to look beyond the capture of Sicily. In a paper sent to Eisenhower on 8 May I set out my reasons for supporting an attack on the Italian mainland, which I had long favoured as opposed to one on Sardinia. From the air point of view, I felt that Sardinia would be a tougher nut to crack than Sicily, for the distance of that island from Allied air bases was greater. The alleged advantage that the whole Italian mainland would be placed within easy bombing range was true but misleading, for it was already within range from Tunisia and would soon be so, we hoped, from Sicily. The value of additional bases in Sardinia was more than countered by the additional problems of maintenance and supply. The establishment of air bases in Central Italy would certainly bring within range of the Allied heavy bombers the main industrial centres of the Axis in southern Germany, and also the Rumanian oilfields; but this was not the principal advantage. Our heavy bomber attacks on most of the vital centres in Germany and other Axis countries would be able to use routes which avoided completely the great belt of fighter and anti-aircraft defences set up along the whole northern and north-western approaches. These defences were exacting an increasing toll on the Allied bombing offensive mounted from the United Kingdom, and it would be quite impossible for the enemy to create a similar organisation covering the southern approach. A bomber offensive directed from the south, especially when co-ordinated with that of the United Kingdom, would, therefore, have enormously increased effects, material and moral.

★

Towards the end of May 1943, the Prime Minister again visited North Africa to see for himself our preparations and to discuss the military prospects of the future. Churchill was accompanied by Generals Brooke and Ismay. General Marshall was also present. Our first meeting with the Prime Minister was held on 23 May, and began with a discussion of the impending attack on Pantelleria. This, Churchill thought, would provide a very useful experiment to show the degree to which coastal defences could be neutralised by aerial bombardment. There was a school of thought at home which believed that air forces could knock out coast defences sufficiently to admit of practically unopposed landings. The C.I.G.S. remarked that the difficulty lay in the fact of the time lag between the end of the bombardment and the arrival of the troops. This gave the enemy time to recover. Admiral Cunningham said that eight destroyers would go right in with the landing craft and cover the landings at point-blank range.

[436]

With the Prime Minister satisfied that preparations for 'Husky' were going forward punctually, Eisenhower described a long talk he had had with Alan Brooke on the subject of the general war situation. Brooke had emphasised that the Russian Army was the only land force which could yield decisive results. Any Anglo-American force which could be put upon the Continent was merely a drop in the bucket, and he therefore urged that our efforts must be directed towards diverting German strength from the Russian front. General Eisenhower thought that if the Alllies commanded the air, an Anglo-American force of, say, fifty divisions would probably be able to hold a force of seventy-five divisions on the Continental mainland. If we were going to knock out Italy, we should do so straight after 'Husky' with every means at our disposal. 'Husky' would provide a good indication of the kind of resistance likely to be encountered in Italy itself. Churchill said that there was no chance of putting into Europe an Anglo-American army in any way comparable in size to that of the Russians, who were now holding 218 German divisions on their front.

By 1 May 1944 we should have in the United Kingdom an expeditionary force of twenty-nine divisions, seven of which would have come from North Africa. Britain must be the assembly point of the largest force we could build up, and we must have plans ready to cross the Channel at any time in case the Germans were to crack up. As General Marshall had often pointed out, Northern France was the only theatre in which the vast British Air Force and the United States Air Force in the United Kingdom could be brought into full play. Marshall then said that the United States Chiefs of Staff felt no decision could be made until the result of 'Husky' was determined and the situation in Russia known. The logical approach, according to him, would be to set up two forces, each with its own Staff, in separate places. The first would train for an operation against Sardinia and Corsica, the other for an operation against the Italian mainland. When the situation was sufficiently clear to decide between the two, the necessary force would be made over to the operation in question.

Churchill foresaw that if 'Husky' went too quickly there might be a long period of inactivity. To this Eisenhower replied at once that if 'Husky' were polished off easily he would be willing to go straight for Italy. Alexander agreed with him.

The C.I.G.S. spoke about the hard struggle between the Russians and the Germans now imminent. We should do everything we could to help Russia. Germany was subject to threats at many points in Europe, and our presence in North Africa, with the skilful use of cover plans, had already caused the dispersal of German forces. They could not further decrease their strength either in Russia or in France. The place where German commitments could most easily be reduced was Italy. Our decisions should therefore be based on the result of 'Husky' and the situation at the time of its completion. If the Foot of Italy were packed with troops we must try elsewhere. If Italy were knocked out of the war, Germany would have to replace the twenty-six Italian divisions currently in the Balkans. Germany would also need extra strength at the Brenner Pass, along the Riviera, and on the Spanish and Italian frontiers. Such a dispersal of German forces was exactly what we needed for the cross-Channel operation, and we should do everything we could to aggravate it. The defences on the coast of France, Brooke said, would present no difficulty, unless held by determined men and unless the Germans had mobile reserves with which to counter-attack.

On 31 May we turned to more immediate matters. General Alexander was optimistic about the 'Husky' operations. Our equipment, and the fighting value of our troops, he described as excellent, and our chances of success similarly good, though a fortnight of very bitter fighting might be needed. Once we had a firm grip of the airfields in the south-eastern corner and the ports, we could ignore the remainder of the island for the time being. It should then be possible to cross the Straits of Messina and secure a foothold on the opposite mainland shore, the very wind-pipe of Sicily. It was impossible for us to win a great victory unless 'Husky' was exploited by moving ahead, preferably into Italy.

I thought it right at this point to say that we could not, in the first phase of 'Husky', expect the degree of air superiority attained in the final phases of the Tunisian campaign. The threat from the air to shipping and landing craft should, nevertheless, be greatly eased once we had seized the airfields. A little later, when Alexander remarked that communications in Italy were bad, and getting worse, I pointed out that our air forces had been blasting them for weeks. The pressure on the enemy's wind-pipe was already being exerted.

We met again in Eisenhower's villa in Algiers in the late afternoon of 3 June. The Prime Minister asked me to comment upon air activity in connection with 'Husky'. I replied that our air forces were trying to keep the enemy aircraft down and press them back. We were attacking the enemy's main bases. Several days before we had attacked Bari, from which the enemy moved to Foggia. He had now moved further away still to Piacenza. Our bombing of ports and railways was interfering effectively with shipping and supply lines. Mr. Churchill said that we might discuss the proposal to bomb the marshalling yards near Rome. He had promised the President that Britain would not bomb Rome without agreement between Governments, but he was ready to sanction, even to suggest, the bombardment of marshalling yards. Daylight precision bombing was quite accurate and the yards could quite possibly be attacked with little chance of damage to Rome itself, and none to the Vatican. Marshall agreed. He thought the railway yards were a purely military objective. Their destruction would be of material benefit to the 'Husky' operation, and the psychological effects even more important. The bombing should be undertaken by a very large force of aircraft.

Finally, the Prime Minister said how satisfied he was at the great measure of agreement he had found at these meetings. He did not think we should try at this moment to draw up a formal post-'Husky' plan. It was understood that the matter was in Eisenhower's hands, and he would recommend to the Combined Chiefs of Staff whichever operation seemed best. However, he felt it was generally agreed that it would be best to put Italy out of the war as soon as possible. Our meetings at Algiers had encouraged him most solidly, and he would take home the feeling of confidence and comradeship which characterised actions in this theatre. He had never received so strong an impression of co-operation and control as during this visit. It would be impossible to embark on an undertaking with better augury. He did not want to leave without reaffirming his full confidence in Eisenhower and without expressing his admiration of the manner in which the General had handled his many great problems. Eisenhower replied, characteristically, that any praise which might be given belonged rightly to the officers round the table, and he said with truth that while there might be differences of opinion and discussions in his headquarters, they were never based upon national differences. For the United States Chiefs of Staff, Marshall reinforced the Prime Minister's tribute to the accomplishments and success of Eisenhower and his team. The support given to Eisenhower by the British was deeply appreciated. General Marshall felt that the Germans' greatest discomfort came not so much from their loss of troops as from the fact that Great Britain and the United States had worked so well together.

*

The reduction of Pantelleria was not only a preliminary to the invasion of Sicily. I resolved to make of it a field for experimental study and to find in the operation the answers to many questions which could only be discovered under combat conditions, and which the difficulties of preceding campaigns had given us no real opportunity to pursue.

Pantelleria is but $8\frac{1}{2}$ by $5\frac{1}{2}$ miles in extent, with a rugged terrain. It was defended by fifteen batteries of coastal guns, ground works, and pill-boxes, and possessed a large aerodrome with underground hangars and workshops. We calculated that in addition to the hundred aircraft based on the island, the enemy might be able to bring up a further nine hundred. To oppose this strength, we should be able to operate just over a thousand.

We set out to destroy as far as we could all enemy air interference from the island itself or from Axis territory farther north; to render the port useless and to blockade the island from any reinforcement by sea; to reduce the defences and to study closely what weight of bombs was needed to silence them; to reduce the morale of the garrison by continuous bombardment and to elicit information thereafter by interrogation; and to provide air cover for naval vessels and for the assault or landing craft.

The campaign began on 15 May and was ended by the island's surrender on 11 June. In the first of our aims we were, broadly speaking, successful. We destroyed forty bombers and 196 fighters at a cost to ourselves of sixteen bombers and fifty-seven fighters. By the end of May medium and fighter-bombers had so discouraged enemy shipping that the island was isolated. The last boat to leave had carried away most of the German garrison. The reduction of the coastal batteries began on 30 May. Between that time and the surrender, well over four thousand sorties were flown by all types of aircraft, many of them in such rapid succession that planes were obliged to circle about in the vicinity awaiting their turn to bomb. After 4 June, our men saw no enemy transport nor any attempt to repair the damage done to the guns and their emplacements. The island surrendered twenty minutes before the landing of the assault troops on 11 June. The bulk of the air forces promptly switched their attack to the island of Lampedusa, which capitulated the next morning.

Pantelleria was the first defended place to be reduced to surrender in the Second World War as a result of air and naval bombardment alone. At the time of his surrender signal to Malta on 11 June, the Italian commander was unaware of the imminence of our landing. We found that no telephone lines on the island remained in working order. The roads had generally been rendered impassable, and in some places unrecognisable. Throughout the planning and operations, Professor Solly Zuckerman, a Professor of Anatomy who had been occupied in studying the effects of blast on buildings and the human body, had with my encouragement and support studied the operations and directed research. He made a most thorough analysis of the nature and construction of the defences, the type of bombs and fusing needed, the standards and accuracy of the various types of squadron. On this analysis the bombing programme was organised. During the bombardments Zuckerman made a daily assessment of results on photographic evidence. After the surrender he went at once to the island to examine on the spot the result of our efforts.

His report, dated 20 July 1943, had a more than local significance. Every Italian officer interrogated told us of the complete dislocation of communications. Most of the artillery had been crippled or obliterated. As for the town of Pantelleria, it had been for all practical purposes wiped out. Not a single house escaped bomb damage; and what remained had to be almost entirely demolished before the town could be rebuilt. Yet Italian casualties were light, the total number killed being between a hundred and two hundred, and the total number of wounded about two hundred. This showed, as interrogation confirmed, that most of the populace in the northern half had fled to the central hills, or to the south, and that the Italian battery crews failed to remain at their posts.

Zuckerman found overwhelming evidence that the morale of the civilian population had been shattered by the bombardment, and that the nerves of the garrison also broke. Italian and German prisoners-of-war affirmed that there was nothing to be done under this scale of attack except to relinquish their positions and surrender. It would be fair to say that the effects on morale were so cataclysmic that they alone caused the collapse of the garrison. The coastal defences in the northern half of Pantelleria had been so battered that they had been prevented from offering any serious opposition to an assault. So far as morale was concerned, few had before been asked to stand up to bombing of the intensity experienced around the batteries with an average of a thousand tons per square mile. We learnt nevertheless that the bombing accuracy of the heavy and medium bombers was about half of what we had estimated on the basis of their previous performance against types of stationary targets different from battery positions. The conclusion was that an air operation of this type was possible when relative air superiority was gained and maintained, when careful estimates had been made in advance to show that the available bomber effort could cope with the task, when the defences were not so strong as to be invulnerable to the type of bomb available, and when the forces were allocated and controlled according to a precise plan. Against any but the heaviest type of German coastal defence, it would be unnecessary to estimate for the direct destruction of more than about 20 per cent. of the critical defences in a small region. If these were directly destroyed, the remaining defences would almost certainly be put out of action by secondary causes. Such secondary effects as the destruction of underground cable communications, and of adjacent radar equipment, led Zuckerman to expect that any possibility of co-ordinated defence would be ruled out, even in the case of strong defences of the type which we knew the Germans to be erecting on the northern coast of France.

Here was indeed food for reflection and future action. My only concern was that false conclusions might be drawn from the Pantelleria operation. As I had written to Portal on the 14th:

I have pointed out here again and again right from the beginning that this operation is a most valuable laboratory experiment. The conditions are not such as we are likely to have again, e.g., no enemy air worthy of the name, an extremely limited objective and consequent ability to concentrate a terrific scale of effort on a very small area. Despite all I have said, however, even Eisenhower has now begun to say, can't we possibly do something like this for 'Husky'. In short, I can see Pantelleria becoming a perfect curse to us in this manner.

*

So far, the Mediterranean campaign had provided a complete example of the use of air-power, co-ordinated with land and sea power. Unity of command had given us concentration at the right place and point in time. During our retreat to Alamein in 1942, and up to the time of the battle there, Rommel's supplies to Cyrenaica were interrupted by air action from Malta and Egypt with crippling results. The destruction of petrol and supply ships immediately prior to the battle of El Alamein sealed his fate. During the Tunisian Campaign, the cumulative effect of air attack from North-West Africa, Malta, and the Middle East, on the whole enemy organisation, was the decisive factor in ending the war in North Africa. Attacks on enemy supplies mounted to a crescendo until finally there was virtually an air blockade of the Sicilian Channel, once the advance on land enabled our air forces to fly from central and northern Tunisia. In the final stages, our aircraft gave complete cover to British ships, enabling them to seal the blockade and pick up the stragglers. Now our convoys were able to pass through the Mediterranean, along the North African coast, under the cover of fighter and anti-submarine patrols, with almost negligible losses, despite the fact that enemy bases flanked the route. In North-West Africa, we had made extensive use of ports within a hundred miles of the main enemy fighter bases. Our total losses in shipping on the through-Mediterranean route, between the beginning of the campaign and mid-May, were just over 2 per cent. During the month of April, North African Air Forces sank sixteen enemy vessels and severely damaged thirty-one.

I claimed, with confidence, that these events proved co-operation with, but not subordination to, the Army, to be the right way of employing the Air Force in support of land power. This method had secured for us air superiority in the Libyan and Tunisian battles. As a result, we were not only able to concentrate the main air effort to give direct assistance to the Army, but our land forces were also given a freedom of movement otherwise impossible. The retreat to Alamein and the subsequent advance to Tripoli, with roads packed with transport, could not have been achieved without air superiority. Equally, the final moves in the land battle in Tunisia, when large American and British forces swung across the whole front to effect the decisive concentration, would not have been feasible under conditions existing a few months earlier, before air superiority had been secured. The British and American air forces had become one force, and not two forces co-operating. About five hundred enemy aircraft had been captured on their aerodromes in Northern Tunisia alone. A considerable number of these were already serviceable or could be made so. Since the formation of the Mediterranean Air Command in February, nearly 150,000 tons of merchant shipping had been sunk in Tunisian or Sicilian ports or on the way to North Africa. In the last three weeks before mid-May only one ship was known to have reached North Africa from Italian ports—and this was hit and lay aground off Bizerta.

2 *Air support for 'Husky'–Comparison of air strengths–Dominance of air-power–Invasion of Sicily–Enemy air forces demoralised–Glider and parachute operations: lessons learnt–Plans for 'Avalanche'–Mussolini dismissed–Air concentration on Italian targets–Priorities for air-power again*

OPERATION 'Husky', the invasion of Sicily, provided two lessons in the use of air-power. It showed not only the general principles according to which air strength is exercised, but also the methods by which the whole resources of an Air Force are employed with those of the other Arms in one combined operation. From 15 June 1943 a crescendo of attacks on the enemy's airfields was launched. The movement of the enemy's aircraft from one field to another, the attempts to evade attack by dispersal, the preparation of satellite air strips; all this was watched from day to day. The enemy was harried from field to field. As a result, he was forced more and more to retire upon airfields in Italy. This naturally increased the range at which his fighters had to operate over Sicily and beyond, and caused the progressive weakening of his opposition. The last serious attempt to interfere with our air operations took place on 5 July. By D-Day, 10 July, the enemy did not have a single airfield in Sicily fully operational. The massive and vulnerable armada, amounting to two thousand craft, which carried the invaders, experienced only one enemy air attack, and that was abortive. During the earlier period of assembly, when the ports of North Africa were choked with ships and landing craft, the enemy could not attack effectively. The few night raids which he made suffered heavy losses. We were also able severely to limit his reconnaissance reports, which proved a prime factor in the achievement of surprise.

We could, from our existing bases in Malta and Tunisia, cover the southern half of Sicily. We could not effectively reach the main port, Messina. On the other hand, the capture of the enemy's airfields in the Catania–Gerbini area would make it impossible for him to sustain his air strength within the confines of the island itself. Since there were no airfields of sufficient size in the Toe of Italy, retreat to Naples and Brindisi would be

[445]

unavoidable. It is a measure of the role played by air-power, and now generally acknowledged, that the risk of supplying some of our forces across the open beaches and the rest through only two small ports, was run in order that the vital airfield inland from Gela should fall into our hands at the very earliest moment.

In air operations such as these, the dominating objective is to secure air superiority through the destruction of the enemy's air force. In the case of the 'Husky' assault this meant air superiority without which our landing parties could not be protected. We were able, by surprise, to destroy many aircraft upon the ground. Our problem thereafter resolved itself into finding some way of provoking the enemy into rising from the ground and engaging in combat. To anticipate the narrative for a moment, in the Mediterranean campaign between 6 July and 19 October 1943, the German and Italian Air Forces lost on the ground alone 322 bombers and 268 fighters, as against 207 bombers and 700 fighters destroyed in the air. In addition, we captured over a thousand enemy aircraft.

After the close of the Tunisian campaign the German Air Force showed itself more and more cautious. Much of our effort was devoted to prodding the sensitive points for whose defence the enemy would risk considerable activity in the air. At the beginning of 'Husky', our Intelligence estimated that the Axis air strength amounted to 1,545 operational and reconnaissance aircraft. These were mainly based in Sicily, Sardinia, and the Toe of Italy. We had 1,658 aircraft, and an additional 835 in reconnaissance, transport, and auxiliary strength. Up to the day of the invasion itself, I was much concerned at the fact that enemy aircraft offered so little fight in the air, despite the continuous bombardment to which we were subjecting the targets most vital to his success. I could not help feeling that he might be holding many aircraft in reserve.

The destruction of enemy aircraft is, nevertheless, only one part of the undertaking. The airfields and installations from which they operate must be rendered untenable, too. Before 15 June, we had been very fully occupied in reducing Pantelleria. This operation involved the repeated bombing of Sicilian aerodromes, and really made up the first phase of 'Husky'. The system of airfields in Sicily and Sardinia was complete enough by the end of June to accommodate about six hundred fighters, divided in roughly equal parts between Sardinia, Eastern Sicily, and Western Sicily. When our tactical appreciation was drawn up in March, the enemy had only nineteen airfields in Sicily. By now, he had more than thirty, and we knew from reconnaissance that further expansions were on the way. The fall of Pantelleria accomplished, the Strategic Air Force and the U.S. Ninth Air Force threw the weight of their attack on the main Sicilian airfields. Between 15 and 30 June, these aerodromes alone received well over a thousand tons of bombs. Nearly two hundred enemy aircraft were destroyed on the ground. Others were being transferred to Sardinia and the mainland.

As for seaways and ports, the enemy had long since ceased to venture any considerable convoys in Mediterranean waters. Sicily, however, presented him with a particular problem, for the railway communications on the Italian mainland, already damaged and inadequate, and the limited ferry transport between Reggio in Italy and Messina in Sicily, forced him to risk heavy traffic in the form of small boats in the Tyrrhenian Sea. While hammering away at the airfields, we also paid due attention to this shipping and to the ports. By the end of the month, the harbours of Palermo and Messina had been crippled. Fighters from Malta and North Africa, their sweeps carefully co-ordinated, hunted and assaulted the enemy's shipping, escorted our convoys, and put down the enemy's intermittent responses.

It would be hard to imagine a better demonstration of the flexibility of air-power than that provided by the attacks on airfields in the first nine days of July 1943. From the African mainland, over two thousand sorties were flown against Sicilian aerodromes. In the last week before the 'Husky' landings, the airfields round Gerbini alone received more than 1,320 tons of bombs in thirty-five attacks. The central aerodrome and seven of its nine satellites were made unserviceable. This success was of the highest importance and value to us, for the enemy's main fighter strength had been polarised around Gerbini. The airfields at Comiso, Castelvetrano, and Bocca di Falco were in a similar state to those around Gerbini. The Chief of the German Air

Operations Staff in that theatre had recorded that all the aerodromes, operational airfields and landing grounds on Sicily were
so destroyed by continuous attack that it was only possible to
get this or that airfield in running order again for a short time
by mobilising all available forces, including those of the German
and Italian armies.[1]

*

Now all plans for 'Husky', the largest amphibious operations
of the war up to this point, were ready. I had been unhappy
about the prospects of setting up an effective combined headquarters. We had arranged for combined command posts in
the Bizerta–Tunis area, but the Royal Navy announced that it
was physically impossible for them to get their communications
into Bizerta or that region—I suspect it would have been more
accurate to have stated that it was *traditionally* impossible. This
meant, of course, that the Admiral must (as he had all along
intended) go to Malta during the critical days of the assault. This
in turn meant that Alexander also had to go to Malta, since
quick decisions about calling off a landing here or reinforcing
a landing there had to be made together with the Naval Commander-in-Chief. I had Spaatz, Coningham, Lloyd, and Doolittle
in or near my Command Post which was established on the shore
at La Marsa, looking out to the east over the Mediterranean (I
myself was accommodated in a well-fitted-out German caravan
'collected' in Cap Bon by the R.A.F. Regiment). Neither Coningham nor I could operate our forces from Malta. If I was to exercise
the necessary close control, my subordinate commanders had to
be alongside, with direct communication to the squadrons. All I
could do was to place Wigglesworth as my deputy in Malta, where
he could help to co-ordinate reconnaissance operations from
Cyrenaica, Tripolitania, Malta, and Tunisia. I visited Malta on 8
July to emphasise to Alexander that it was for him and not for me
to allocate priorities of the land targets between the Western and
Eastern Task Force. Feeling some concern about this, I sent
'Mary' Coningham to Malta for a short while during the first

[1] Richards & Saunders: *The Royal Air Force 1939–1945*, vol. 2, p. 306.

landings, so that the point might be watched. Admiral Cunningham seemed quite happy with the arrangements, but the absence of Alexander was indubitably a handicap, especially as he took all his heads of branches with him. I kept an aircraft standing by so that I could be in Malta within two hours.

On the morning of 10 July, the main invasion forces landed in Sicily. It is easy now to forget the scale and scope of this enterprise. The initial assault alone involved 160,000 men, 14,000 vehicles, 600 tanks, and nearly 2,000 guns. This force had been trained, equipped, and embarked at places all over the Mediterranean and even farther afield. Naturally, we could not be sure at the time how successful the air attack had proved. As I have mentioned, I had been slightly concerned at the falling off in the enemy's air activity, lest he might be saving up for the critical stage. By 8.30 a.m. on 10 July, however, our convoys had not been attacked at all from the air. It seemed certain that we had at least reduced the enemy's operational efficiency. We could not maintain continuous fighter cover over all the beaches and ships. Rather, I intended to keep up a certain scale of effort which would attack the German and Italian aircraft wherever they settled. So long as the enemy's air strength could be kept down, our main object was now to interfere with the movement of his reserves and to disorganise his control. I telegraphed that morning to Portal:

The general atmosphere in our Air Forces before the land battle began this morning was that they were on top of the world. There is plenty of hard fighting yet, and the Mediterranean is rough and surprisingly big, but the Force inspires confidence.

On that day, air opposition proved insignificant. It increased on 11 and 12 July, when we shot down fifty-two enemy aircraft, but by the 15th, his air forces were demoralised as far north as Naples.

Our airborne operations, about which I had felt many qualms, were only carried out at considerable cost. On the eastern side, the first glider operation succeeded in its main object of securing a vital bridge south of Syracuse. Partly on account of the high wind, the navigation of the towing aircraft was generally faulty.

A large proportion of the gliders landed in the sea or on the beach. Many of those which reached dry land were more or less damaged on coming to earth, due to the pilots' inexperience of the characteristics of the new glider they were using. Enemy action caused only negligible losses. The second operation in the east, by parachute and glider, also succeeded in its main aim of securing another vital bridge south of Catania, but we suffered heavy losses amongst the second and third waves, largely because of enemy flak. I felt that such losses were inevitable in an area of intense land operations where the aircraft had to fly over a series of airfields all heavily defended. We also had considerable losses from flak from our own ships.

The picture in the west was even less satisfactory. True enough, the first parachute operation did succeed in so far as one compact body of parachute troops happened to be in a position to deal effectively with the German counter-attack at a critical phase of the initial landing. Because of high winds, faulty navigation, and inexperience, the remainder of the parachute troops found themselves scattered over an area some eighty miles in length. The second parachute operation was merely a reinforcement to the first. The landings were supposed to take place in the middle of the battle area. Our aircraft were, in fact, fired upon by friendly ships and land forces throughout the greater part of their passage from Malta, until they were well clear of the Sicilian coast on the return journey. The losses and damage were severe and our parachute troops were fired at before, during, and after the drop. This experience showed the operation to be fundamentally unsound. The aircraft were required to fly along the whole length of an active front at a time when a few enemy aircraft were also operating. The chances of all the ships, and especially all the troops, being adequately warned, were practically nil.

All these operations were executed at night, those on 9/10 July under most unfavourable conditions. They were the first major airborne operations of the Second World War to be carried out in darkness. But in all the circumstances, I told Portal, I thought the degree of success achieved was satisfactory and even surprising:

Air-borne operations have until now been based on fallacious assumption that an operation considerably more difficult than a normal night bomber operation can be carried out efficiently with non-operational aircraft and crews. Provision of operational aircraft and crews in sufficient numbers to carry out any major air-borne operation is clearly impossible. Consequently such operations must be planned with this unavoidable limitation in mind. An air-borne force should be led in by experienced 'path-finders', and should be as concentrated as possible, formations being used.

I recommended that airborne troops should not be directed to land in an area where active operations were in progress, or over a heavily defended area, unless the crucial importance of their objective justified heavy losses. Here were some useful lessons which we were later to turn to good account.

Lord Louis Mountbatten, Chief of Combined Operations, visited the theatre to watch the progress of this battle, and in particular, to observe the co-operation between the three Services. I was entertained to hear from him that in Malta the commanders felt rather sorry for me, for they thought that I was not fully in the picture. Our feeling in North Africa, which was endorsed by Eisenhower who had seen both sides, was that we had the clearer picture of the situation as a whole. I do not think that the separation of the Commanders-in-Chief between the mainland and the island seriously affected our co-ordination. Nevertheless, there was no doubt that it was most undesirable for us to be separated for long periods. This was particularly the case now that the landings were established, when we were all so anxious to push on with the next move, or, rather, to follow up hard. Since 13 July I had been trying to get Alexander to come back with his heads of department so that his headquarters could once again become a live organisation with whom we could do business. Since Mountbatten was about to leave for London, I wrote to Portal:

Operations on the whole have, I think, gone well. Our attacks on aerodromes have undoubtedly been more effective than one expected. The accuracy of some of the bombing has been quite first class. The Lightnings and the Mustangs have been invaluable for freelance work on communications. They are, of course, ideal types for the job. The arrangements for early warning and fighter control on the beaches and forward have been excellent, and you will have noticed the very large number of kills by the night fighters

On D-Plus 4, 13 July, four Allied fighter squadrons were operating from Sicily. By 17 July, the number had risen to sixteen. In the early stages of the assault, the progress of our armies was rapid. But although we strafed the enemy's gun positions and troops by day and night, his skilful use of the geographical features in the northern part of the island reduced his vulnerability to air attack and the progress of our advance, particularly on the eastern side of Sicily, became slower than I had hoped. It became clear that Alan Brooke's prediction of a six weeks' campaign would not be far wide of the mark.

While our fighters destroyed German and Italian aircraft and shipping, the bombers' effort was directed against centres of communication in Sicily and southern Italy. The effect of these attacks was far greater than I had expected, and, I felt sure, was the principal reason for the enemy's inability to control his defences and to counter-attack and reinforce.

By early August we knew that the enemy was preparing to evacuate his forces across the Straits of Messina to the mainland. Again we tried to prevent a 'Dunkirk'. The bombers were directed against bottlenecks around Messina to block the routes to the north-eastern beaches. Night bombers concentrated on those beaches which might be used for evacuation and on possible points of assembly. Meanwhile, the tactical forces continued to operate on lines of communication in the battle area; and the fall of Mussolini in the last week of July gave hope that Italy might be promptly knocked out of the war. In order to provide the Italians with a worthwhile incentive to an early armistice, we began heavy attacks on Naples and other points on the mainland on 1 August. We thought it might even be possible, if the Italians made peace or showed signs of collapse, to launch operation 'Avalanche', an amphibious assault against Naples, from landings at Salerno, in the near future. In the meantime, we had to balance these exciting prospects against the immediate needs of the battle in Sicily. As I signalled to Portal on 4 August:

[452]

One of main problems is and has always been judging the right proportion of effort to direct against enemy air. For the moment we appear to have driven him back so that his fighter effort is almost negligible and his bomber effort hampered by distance. His bomber effort, which had built up, now appears to be going down both in quality and quantity. For time being therefore we should be able to direct most of our effort to support land operation. If, however, political situation renders an early 'Avalanche' operation possible, our effort will again have to be concentrated against enemy air prior to the landing.

Our attempt to prevent another 'Dunkirk', as I had feared, was by no means so successful as in May. The key positions in the north-east of Sicily were well defended. Our crews now had to contend with powerful concentration of flak. This is not to say that the results of their efforts were negligible. On 5 August alone, two merchant vessels, a Siebel ferry and twenty-one barges were destroyed. After this experience, the enemy thought it prudent to confine his evacuation to the hours of darkness, though even then the withdrawal was continually harassed by night fighters and Wellington bombers. Only three miles across the Straits of Messina separated the north-eastern tip of Sicily from the mainland. We found much difficulty in discovering and attacking enemy shipping in this confined space under the shadow of the steep cliffs. Rather more than half the enemy forces in Sicily, mostly Germans, thus escaped, though we took over 160,000 prisoners, and killed more than 30,000 German and Italian troops.

Between 15 June, when the air operations in support of 'Husky' really began, and 17 August, when the Axis forces finally surrendered, 533 enemy aircraft were destroyed in the air. Many more were put out of action on the ground. Almost all the machines captured on Sicilian airfields, amounting to well over a thousand, had suffered damage from bomb splinters. In the same period, 2,000 tons of bombs had been dropped on ports and bases, nearly 7,500 tons on airfields, and no less than 15,500 tons on lines of communication. So intense an effort certainly helped to undermine Italian morale on the island and to prepare the way for the imminent Italian collapse. Here for the first time several air forces, without distinction of nationality, had operated as one. Their contribution to victory in Sicily was capital. On the day after the Axis surrender there I telegraphed to London:

> The outstanding feature of the whole operation was the ability of two air forces—American and British—supported by certain French and Polish units, operating from mainland and island bases covering a front of some 2,000 miles, to integrate their operations and achieve the intense concentration of their effort which contributed vitally to the success of the whole operation.

Even before the assault on Sicily was launched, we were debating what should be our next step. A signal sent from Eisenhower's headquarters at the end of June 1943, which by an error was not shown to me before despatch, suggested that an assault on Sardinia would be preferable to one on the Italian mainland unless we could occupy the Heel of Italy and exploit our success as far as Naples. I had no doubt that the advantages of occupying as large an area as possible in the Toe and Ball, even if we had to fight hard, would far outweigh any which might accrue from the capture of Sardinia. To take and hold even a hundred miles or so on the Italian mainland must shake the wavering morale of the country more deeply than would the occupation of another island. Moreover, we should contain far greater German forces by being on the mainland than by being in Sardinia. This seemed a prime consideration. Even if we were held up in the extreme south of Italy, we should be able to hang on while the air forces pounded away at the communications, industries, and people of Italy. The Axis would then be obliged to bring more air forces to the area. In all probability, Italian resistance would be reduced to such a level that a further advance towards Naples would become feasible. Aerodromes could be developed in the occupied area, and our air superiority would mean that we could render those in the Heel untenable.

In his meetings with us at the end of May and the beginning of June, the Prime Minister had not concealed his fervent belief that only a campaign on the Italian mainland would be worthy of the forces now fighting in the Mediterranean. As the 'Husky' campaign developed, he noticed that 14,000 men of the 26th

German Panzer Division were concentrating just across the Straits of Messina at Reggio. This development, far from inclining him to caution, stimulated his imagination and in a Minute to the Chiefs of Staff on 13 July he said:

The question arises, 'Why should we crawl up the leg like a harvest bug, from the ankle upwards? Let us rather strike at the knee. Once we have established our air-power strongly in the Catania Plain and have occupied Messina etc., why should we not use sea power and air power to land as high up in Italy as air fighter cover from the Catania area warrants? This, of course, would be reinforced and extended by any airfields taken in the Messina area.

Let the Planners immediately prepare the best scheme possible for landing on the Italian west coast with the objective the port of Naples and the march on Rome. Thus to cut and leave behind all Axis forces in Western Sicily and all ditto in the toe, ball, heel, and ankle. It would seem that two or three good divisions could take Naples and produce decisive results, if not on the political attitude of Italy, then upon the capital. Tell the Planners to throw their hat over the fence . . . .

Eisenhower, while by no means opposed to such an operation under the right conditions, was conscious of the absolute need to keep vulnerable shipping under the protection of our own shore-based fighter aircraft. For a large invasion armada to sail directly to Naples or to the northward without the benefit of strong fighter cover would certainly be asking for trouble.

Meanwhile, he was inevitably preoccupied with the obvious intention of the Germans to make a stand in the defensible positions around Mount Etna in Sicily. Eisenhower estimated that Messina might not be captured until mid-August. At a meeting on 17 July, he discussed with Cunningham, Alexander, and me what course we should follow once the whole of Sicily fell into our hands. We were of one mind in believing that Italian morale was such that an attack on the mainland was the best method to exploit the success of 'Husky'. The object would be to force Italy out of the war and to contain the largest possible number of German forces. The possibility of an assault on Naples was to be re-examined at once. On the assumption that large German reinforcement of southern Italy did not take place, we recommended that the war should be carried to the mainland

[455]

as soon as Sicily had been captured, and asked for early approval of this design. It was duly given on 21 July. The Chiefs of Staff added that Eisenhower should extend his amphibious operations northwards as shore-based fighter cover could be made effective.

From my point of view, these various possibilities involved two principal considerations. Before amphibious landings could take place, we must neutralise the enemy's air effort. This process necessarily took time. As it was, most of our squadrons could not be released from operations in Sicily until the enemy surrendered. Landings in the Toe of Italy would need less air support than any alternative, and would be within the range of effective fighter cover. This was the second factor I had to consider. Nevertheless, all my instincts favoured the bolder course. After careful examination I signalled to the C.A.S. on 26 July that I believed a direct attack on Naples to be a practical operation from the air point of view under certain conditions. First of all, we must secure terrain on the north-eastern coast of Sicily where a strip airfield could be made. Then we must concentrate a major strategic effort against the enemy's air forces for three weeks before the actual landing. The whole heavy bomber force must be available for use against targets in Italy. A major airborne effort to take airfields at the earliest moment would be essential.

A meeting of the Commanders-in-Chief that same day filled me with disquiet. The intention of the Army was apparently to make a frontal advance up the north-eastern corner of Sicily, followed by a frontal attack across the Straits. It seemed that the Army were relying on a degree of destruction comparable with that achieved at Pantelleria. It was even estimated that Messina would not be taken until the end of August. The earliest date for further operations would be the end of the first week in September. Since we had just heard of the dismissal of Mussolini on the previous day, 25 July, the possibility of a landing in Naples, to take advantage of a complete collapse in Italy and the withdrawal of German forces, was only to be 'examined'.

As it seemed to me, and as I told the meeting, this was to play the German game:

His object is presumably to hang on bitterly, as long as possible, with a strong rear-guard, so as to give time to organise defences in south Italy. By the methodical frontal attack, with the passage of time required to build up overwhelming material superiority, we are surrendering the initiative to him at a time when we have air superiority and command at sea, and when he has behind him attenuated L. of C. passing through 600 miles of a country which is in the midst of a political upheaval, and which may at any time, or any moment, turn hostile.

To use our whole strategic effort to blast a path through the enemy defences in Sicily must seriously decrease our ability to reduce the enemy's air effort before operations in Italy. Our air forces had now been at full stretch for weeks on end, and because of the slow rate at which air crews were replaced their effectiveness must gradually decline. I felt that at this stage our full strength must be reserved for use against the enemy's air forces.

At this time, although we knew that Mussolini was no longer head of the Italian Government, we could not tell whether his disappearance from office would be followed by an armistice and whether, if it were, the Germans would withdraw from Italy. It seemed highly probable that whatever Italy did, Germany would dispute possession of every inch of the mainland. All the same, there could be no question that the political upheaval there placed a premium on the speedy cleaning-up of the Sicilian campaign and upon operation 'Avalanche', the proposed leapfrog landing at Salerno. On 27 and 28 July, Eisenhower and I talked for many hours about these issues. As usual, he showed himself willing, indeed eager, to undertake any reasonable risk. We took the view that if additional strength could be brought to bear at this crucial point, a handsome dividend might result. Eisenhower therefore appealed to the Combined Chiefs of Staff on 28 July for a temporary doubling of our heavy bomber strength. We both believed that we would then be able practically to paralyse the German air effort in the whole of southern Italy, and to immobilise his German ground units. The chances of success on the mainland would be enhanced beyond measure if we could borrow for a month or five weeks four groups of heavy bombers. We estimated that the availability of shipping and landing craft, the decisive factor in an amphibious operation of this kind, would enable us to launch 'Avalanche' by 9 September.

However, this suggestion came to nothing. Generals Devers and Eaker were consulted and both advised that the diversion of four bomber groups would be disastrous, since the day battle over Germany had now reached a critical stage. On 28 July, the day when Eisenhower's signal was sent, German fighters had for the first time shown a disinclination to attack our bombers. It appeared that other evidence showed the German Air Force to be very hard pressed. It also seemed that although four groups represented only a third of America's heavy bomber force, their removal would mean a reduction in fighting power of more than 50 per cent. Four thousand ground personnel would have to be transferred, together with an enormous quantity of equipment. This move would probably take a month during which time the squadrons would operate at much reduced efficiency. For these understandable reasons, the idea was turned down.

It was already plain enough to me that Eisenhower accepted reasonable risks more willingly than did his British counterparts. As plans for the assault on the Italian mainland went forward during the first days of August, I became deeply concerned lest Alexander and Montgomery should insist upon an attack across the Straits in such strength that the 'Avalanche' operation would become impossible. To 'Mary' Coningham, who was with Montgomery, I telegraphed on 7 August:

The implications of this may affect the length of the war by a year. Evident, however, that on present form 'Alex' will play H.M.V. record if Napoleon insists on his usual frontal attack with no risks. Can you possibly do anything which will result in Napoleon being inspired to propose reductions of, or even abolishing, 'Baytown' [the attack across the Straits of Messina]. I feel this one of the critical decisions in the war, but unless by some means Napoleon can be led to propose, as his own great thought, action which will make 'Avalanche' possible, we shall lose our chance. You have worked the oracle before. Can you do it again?

A meeting which Eisenhower summoned in Tunis three days later disclosed a more satisfactory state of affairs. Everyone now agreed that operation 'Avalanche' must be mounted if it

[458]

were humanly possible. Only the troops and means already employed in Sicily would be used to establish a bridgehead on the Toe of Italy. We should try to avoid placing sizeable forces there, in an area where they could be easily contained. It was recorded by Eisenhower that to act in this way would practically rule out any chance of an operation on the lines of 'Avalanche' that year. This was because the necessary landing craft would have to be used in maintaining over the beaches all the Allied forces in the Toe of Italy.

While preparations for 'Avalanche' therefore went forward, we concentrated our air strength on Italian targets. The area between Naples and the Toe contained in mid-August three German divisions, excluding the Hermann Goering Division which was temporarily in a state of some disarray. In the last days of the Sicilian campaign, some of the Italian units had fought bravely and well. We could not, therefore, discount the possibility of Italian resistance of a serious kind when we landed on the mainland. Eisenhower counted upon air-power to impede the concentration of reinforcements against our landings. The enemy, too, could hardly fail to reason that we were as likely as they to cross from Sicily to Italy. German bomber strength began to build up. On the night of 17 August, about a hundred Ju. 88s raided Bizerta and did some damage, while our Intelligence showed that another German bomber group was entering the area. In all these circumstances, it was a shock to us to be ordered to remove three B.24 Liberator groups from the Mediterranean area. This would reduce our heavy bomber strength to four B.17 Fortress groups and two B.24 groups, both of which were under strength.

Eisenhower at once appealed to the Combined Chiefs of Staff. The best way to keep down the air threat, he said, was to raid the enemy's airfields intensively during the week before 'Avalanche'. Even in the first phases of 'Husky', despite the Allies' great superiority in airpower, we lost a number of ships by enemy bombing and from aerial torpedoes. Yet the 'Avalanche' operation would be infinitely more difficult from the air point of view. Spaatz and I were convinced, as Eisenhower telegraphed, that the immediate loss of these groups would certainly add to the risks of the 'Avalanche' operation. He added that the plans for attack would not be altered, however, as a result of the transfer.

This was bad enough, but we had no choice in the matter. Less than a week later, we learned that three Wellington squadrons would be withdrawn from the Mediterranean on 15 September. I signalled my protest to Portal at once, explaining again that 'Avalanche' involved more risks than 'Husky'. It would be harder to knock out and keep down the enemy air forces and harder to prevent enemy movement on land. Our heavy bomber force would now be one-third less than it had been for 'Husky', while the withdrawal of the Wellingtons would reduce our night bomber effort by more than a third, at what might well prove to be the critical stage of the operation.

This issue placed me in a most difficult position of conflicting loyalties and allegiances. With regret I added to my signal to Portal:

As you know it is not my habit to question Chiefs of Staff decisions, but in this case I feel I have no alternative if this decision is confirmed, but to put the matter to Eisenhower in the strongest possible terms. There is already a tendency in certain Army circles to see increasing dangers and risks from the land point of view. I am more than concerned lest this further reduction of our air strength may not serve as a final excuse for cancelling 'Avalanche'.

I had asked for the loan of these three Wellington squadrons for the six weeks ending 31 July, and quite realised that it would not be easy for Portal to prolong their stay in the Mediterranean. He had, in fact, given a personal promise to 'Bomber' Harris that the squadrons would return to him. I understood how difficult it must be to adjudicate between rival claims, and how hard it was, once units had been transferred from one theatre to another, to secure their recall or replacement. After all, we had had a good deal of experience in this line during my time in the Middle East, where we had not been guiltless ourselves. Nonetheless, we could not doubt that the proposed landings at Salerno would depend for success upon concentrated use of air-power.

Immediately on his return from the Quebec 'Quadrant' Conference, Portal replied that no one without responsibility for the bomber offensive based in the United Kingdom, as well as for the Mediterranean theatre, could form an unbiased view of the rival claims for these three squadrons. He drew my particular attention to three points:

(a) The bombers which are attacking Germany from here are facing extremely heavy fighter opposition and cannot be expected to carry on a full-scale offensive indefinitely without reinforcements. It is this offensive which is largely responsible for the superiority which your Command now enjoys.

(b) Your bomber force on the other hand greatly outnumbers the German fighters, and Allied air superiority has for months past been headline news which has not escaped the notice of our bombers here.

(c) The expected build-up of the G.A.F. in the Mediterranean has completely failed to materialise, and even after withdrawal of 'Tidal-wave' Liberators and Canadian Wellingtons, you will have very great numerical superiority.

If I still felt impelled to make representations to Eisenhower in the light of these facts, Portal thought it important that I should state definitely whether the departure of the Wellington squadrons a week after the Salerno landings would make a really substantial difference to the prospects of success of future operations. If the Chiefs of Staff could be convinced on this point, the date of departure would be doubtless postponed; but, he added rather ominously, in view of our marked numerical superiority, the case should be argued closely and not merely in general terms.

I replied on 2 September that I only challenged the decision about the Wellington squadrons with deep reluctance. I had always done my best to maintain a balanced view about the requirements of my own theatre as related to those of other theatres, and, appreciating the prime importance of the bomber offensive against Germany, had done my best to stop unbalanced demands for increased air strength made by the other two Services. Some parts of Portal's signal I could not accept:

At same time have always realised and have never pretended my view is or could be unbiased. Am however a little surprised to see it is considered that bomber offensive from U.K. is largely responsible for our local superiority when I remember Air Ministry assessment that German fighter wastage in Mediterranean in July was highest monthly total this war and was about three quarters total fighter production. Do not wish press this point since I realise such arguments are unprofitable.

Again I explained how 'Avalanche' differed from 'Husky'. Without air superiority, both operational and in numbers, 'Avalanche' could not succeed. The proper balance between day and night attack was essential. I knew Portal would realise how hard it would be to secure and maintain air superiority at such a distance from our bases. The rapid reinforcement of German divisions in Italy showed plainly that our armies would need all the help we could give them, at least in delaying German concentrations. I thought this problem would remain critical for at least a fortnight after the Salerno landings, and I felt that we could not afford to reduce our night bomber effort so soon. As it seemed to us in the Mediterranean.

. . . there is a tendency to consider the Italian chicken as being already in the pot, whereas in fact it is not yet hatched. Possibly also a tendency to count too much on the military value of an Italian collapse. If H.M.G. still regard the elimination of Italy and the establishment of heavy bomber bases in Central Italy as being effective contributions towards defeating Germany, surely we should concentrate on this immediate object. I suggest that the initiation of heavy bomber attacks from Italy against the 'soft underbelly of the Hun' this autumn, is a contribution towards the main bomber offensive which would more than compensate for a further delay in the rearming of the three Canadian Wellington squadrons.

I knew that Portal would not resent this reply. Nor did he. He answered on 3 September that because it was open to misconstruction he withdrew the remark in his earlier signal to the effect that the air superiority enjoyed by the Mediterranean Command was largely due to the bomber offensive against Germany based in the United Kingdom. What he had meant to indicate was that only about one-sixth of the German fighter force was in the Mediterranean, whereas nearly two-thirds was on the Western Front. Had it not been for the successful battle of the British and American Bomber Commands, reinforcements would have been available for the Mediterranean, and would have seriously interfered with our air superiority there. According to his information, there had not only been no augmentation of the German Air Force in the Mediterranean, but indeed its strength had been reduced by fifty to seventy-five bombers and fighters in the preceding fortnight. As for the hatching of the Italian chicken, the authorities in London had the impression that until recently we in the Mediterranean had not been unduly impressed with the difficulties. Indeed, they had thought at first that we were rather underestimating them. Portal reminded me that the first suggestion of providing escort carriers was made in London, and the despatch of long-range Spitfire tanks, which were already arriving in the Mediterranean, had been his proposal.

A further exchange of friendly signals enabled us to settle this question for the moment. I could not say definitely at this stage whether the squadrons would or would not be essential. Events alone could prove that, and would show how much night effort was required against communications. Our experience had been that night bomber operations against road communications had proved most effective. I hoped to use part of our strength in this way immediately after the 'Avalanche' landings, if the air situation would permit. It was agreed that we should see how events unfolded. If the situation demanded it we should be entitled to ask that the three Wellington squadrons remain after 15 September.

Invasion of Italy–Italian surrender–Salerno and a crisis–Rehabilitation of Italian air forces–'Accolade' rears its head–'Little assistance' required–Three Commanders recommend abandonment of 'Accolade'–'Improvise and dare'–Dangers of unco-ordinated Mediterranean plans–Fall of Cos–Proposed conference for 'Accolade'–Heavy losses–Fall of Leros–Post mortem–Churchill's cable on Leros–German Army's tough resistance–Lessons from attacks on railway targets–Appointment to 'Overlord'

3

ON the night of 2/3 September, British and Canadian troops of Eighth Army crossed the Straits of Messina and landed at Reggio. This was operation 'Baytown'. Later that day, exactly four years after the war began, the agent of the Italian Government, General Castellano, signed the instrument of surrender in an almond grove near Syracuse. This fact remained secret for the moment. Meanwhile, our troops made swift progress up the Toe, reaching Castovillari on 11 September. That day, after a hazardous journey, the naval power of the defeated enemy was delivered into our hands. 'The Italian battle-fleet,' signalled Cunningham to the Admiralty, 'now lies at anchor under the guns of the fortress of Malta.'

Three days earlier, on the evening of 8 September, General Eisenhower had broadcast the news of the Italian surrender. A short while later, Marshal Badoglio, now head of the Italian Government, confirmed these tidings, but any hopes of a swift seizure of Rome, or of a German withdrawal from the peninsula, were soon seen to be doomed. At this moment, our armadas were approaching the Italian coast again. On the morning of 9 September, British troops disembarked at Taranto, and American forces went ashore at Salerno. For ten days the Mediterranean air forces had been preparing the way. After a raid by Wellingtons on Salerno itself during the night of 31 August/1 September, the fires could be seen for sixty miles around. On 2 September we began the systematic bombardment of marshalling yards, while the light bombers busied themselves in attacking troop concentrations, gun emplacements, and an army headquarters. One raid produced a violent explosion believed to be due to a hit on an ammunition dump. From the following day, we attacked enemy airfields consistently. Other assaults were made on bridges and road and rail bottlenecks. On 9 and 10 September co-ordinated attacks were launched upon road and rail junctions and bridges around the Naples area for the express purpose of blocking all lines into and out of Naples and the battle area around Salerno. With the main marshalling yards already blocked by earlier raids, the effort for three days was directed at road junctions surrounding the bridgehead. In this way the supply and reinforcement of the enemy were impeded.

The real crisis of the 'Avalanche' landings at Salerno occurred between 12 and 15 September. For a time, it even seemed that our invading troops would be forced back into the sea, and from the 13th to the 15th, the Strategic Air Force was wholly employed in direct close support of ground operations. Enemy communications and supplies were assaulted without respite. The main roads were literally plastered with bombs. On the night of 14/15 September, the road from Battipaglia to Eboli was buried beneath 237 tons of bombs delivered in one raid by 126 Wellingtons. This was the greatest effort yet made by night bombers in this theatre. It was also the justification for the request we had put to Portal for the retention of the three Canadian Wellington squadrons. I had told him on 11 September, shortly before the main German counter-attack against the centre of our bridgehead was launched, that in my opinion, and in Eisenhower's, we could not afford any reduction in our night bomber effort until the situation was clearer. We asked that the Wellington wing should not be withdrawn for the moment. The Chiefs of Staff, no doubt at Portal's request, agreed. We were able to release them during October. Their retention at this moment may have saved the day.

By 16 September it appeared that the immediate crisis was over. We were now able again to cast our net wider and to attend to profitable targets in the enemy's line of communications. His air effort against our ground and naval forces was by no means extinguished. Prompt counter-attacks and, especially, heavy raids on airfields around Rome and on other suitable targets, caused in a period of three days and two nights the destruction of or damage to no less than 270 enemy aircraft. By now, British and U.S. squadrons were established in southern Italy. This meant a good deal to us, for many of the Tactical Air Force squadrons could begin to pull their weight in the battle area, whereas it had previously been beyond their operational range. The Strategic Forces, by the same token, could return to their normal role of disrupting the enemy's lines of communication. On the crucial day, 15 September, both Strategic and Tactical Air Forces intervened in the battle area itself with a supreme effort. In a period of less than twenty-four hours, the Strategic Air Force alone carried out just on 700 sorties, the vast majority of them in the battle area.

Coningham, who was with the U.S. Fifth Army, signalled on the evening of 16 September: 'No effective enemy attack since bombing 14th, which was probably decisive.' The same evening I received from General Lemnitzer, an American member of Alexander's staff, the following note:

General Clark asks me to express personally his sincere thanks and appreciation for the superb air support given him. He states that he considers it the keystone in breaking up the German attack down the Sele and saving his position. For my own part, I have never heard more unanimous and enthusiastic acclaim from officers and men alike (British and U.S.) than was given the Air Force for its support of 'Avalanche'.

Portal, who had earlier been worried at the lack of detailed information from the Front, signalled:

I never doubted that your squadrons were doing all that was asked of them, but I did at one time wonder whether subordinate commanders were asking enough in view of critical situation on land. I am now reassured. Congratulations and best wishes.

The success of this air effort was recognised on all sides. A couple of days later, a further message from General Clark described the assistance given to the Army on 14 September as a classic example of the effective employment of air-power in close support of ground troops. Eisenhower telegraphed to Washington and to London his conviction that without the concentrated use of naval and air strength we could scarcely have hoped to prevent the enemy from driving our forces into the sea. The enemy forces were not only strong but experienced, and possessed considerable strength in armour. They had every advantage of terrain, for our landing beaches were ringed round by a high range of hills, all in the possession of the enemy. Eisenhower added this general observation about amphibious operations:

I earnestly believe that even given the ground forces necessary to break through the crust of defences of a beach line, there would normally ensue a critical period during which their ability to sustain themselves will depend upon overwhelming air and naval strength to cover them while the ground forces themselves are built up to satisfactory levels.

General Alexander told Spaatz that the tremendous air attacks had not only heightened the morale of ground and naval forces, but had seriously interfered with the enemy's movements, disrupted his communications and prevented the concentration of his forces to launch large-scale counter attacks. Alexander described the air as contributing immeasurably to the success of the Italian operations. I have no doubt that this is true. Air action was by every standard more effective, flexible, and concentrated than naval bombardment, quite apart from the fact that the Navy would not have been able to operate anywhere near the area if our air superiority had been less marked. During a visit to Italy a few days after the crisis passed, I was able to see for myself the results of the bombardments. The whole area round Battipaglia and Eboli was a shambles. Everyone I met, from General Clark downwards, told me that the air effort of the 14th and 15th was decisive. The Strategic Air Forces put forth a greater effort than ever before, and on the 14th alone dropped a thousand tons of bombs. All the squadrons of each air force were fully extended. At Battipaglia, pilots reported flames from explosions as reaching a thousand feet, and the whole town a mass of flames. Almost all the bombs landed either on target or upon or near roads leading to the junctions. While luck had a hand in results of this kind, the general accuracy of bombing was of the highest order.

When at Salerno on 20 September, it was clear to me that the blitz of the 14th had produced an electric effect upon our own troops and a decisive one upon the enemy. The mutual confidence

Istanbul

SEA OF
MARMARA

Salonika

SAMOTHRACE

IMROS

LEMNOS

A E G E A N

N.
SPORADES

MYTILENE

Larissa

SKYROS

E U B O E A

S E A

CHIOS

Izmir

Athens

ANDROS

SAMOS

TENOS

NIKARIA

LEROS

NAXOS

COS

D O D E C A N E S E

CAPE MATAPAN

RHODES

CASTELORIZO

SCARPANTO

Maleme

SUDA BAY

Heraklion

KASOS

Sphakia

C R E T E

M E D I T E R R A N E A N   S E A

N

THE
GREEK ISLANDS

0   20   40   60   80   100   MILES

© CASSELL & CO. LTD. 1966

between all three Services was most marked. During the twenty hours of my stay, I heard about five minutes of anti-aircraft fire against a solitary reconnaissance aircraft. No other enemy aircraft was seen. Our own losses had been unbelievably small. In 1,870 sorties on 14 September we had lost only one aircraft. The enemy's flak defences, which had evidently been quite disorganised, were now beginning to build up again. His air effort, however, was still confined to sporadic raids. It appeared that attacks on enemy aerodromes had not only weakened his forces but pushed him back out of effective range.

The next day, 21 September, I visited Taranto and Brindisi. A number of our squadrons were still waiting to move to the mainland. The difficulty lay in lack of shipping capacity. The programme of advancing the air forces had been pushed back in order to bring over additional troops. At Brindisi I met the Italian Air Minister and his staff and told them that our sole interest was to defeat the Germans. Since they were still in Italy our immediate interest was to push them out. If the Italian Air Force felt likewise, we would do what we could to help them, though their needs must come second to ours and all their air operations must be under our control. I asked that they should collect all aircraft and personnel as soon as possible in the Heel. These conditions were accepted without reserve, though I learned that it might take time to move the Italian Air Force out of Sardinia.

Informing Portal of all this on 22 September, I added:

Our main problem now is to get our forces established in Italy as soon as possible. I wish I saw more immediate prospects of the Army taking early advantage of the enemy's parlous state in Southern Italy.

*

As Mussolini's régime tumbled, the temptation to make a quick bid for possession of the Dodecanese islands became hard to resist. As early as September 1942, the Defence Committee in Cairo had considered whether it would be possible to capture Crete and perhaps the Dodecanese. We decided that before either operation would be feasible, the whole of North Africa must be secured, and the Mediterranean sea route reopened. An invasion

[469]

of Crete and the Dodecanese would entail a large expedition which must detract from the resources which would be needed for the main effort via Sicily. On the other side of the coin, the attractions of Crete and the Dodecanese to us would be much lessened once Cyrenaica had been captured. Moreover, as we had learnt in painful circumstances, to attempt to hold Crete or other islands in the neighbourhood while the Axis remained in control of Greece might become a serious drain on our strength for which no adequate dividend would be received. Short-range fighter cover would be essential:

. . . without the use of bases in Anatolia and/or unless the enemy reserves in the Eastern Mediterranean are reduced to a very low ebb, the capture of Crete or the Dodecanese are impracticable undertakings.

The possibility of using air bases in south-western Anatolia is remote, and on recent experience the provision of short-range fighter cover from aircraft carriers can only result in the loss of the carriers, possibly even before their aircraft come into action.

Had these principles continued to govern the action of the Middle East Commanders-in-Chief in 1943, we should have been spared much unnecessary loss and heart-burning. True, the capture of these islands, if it could be swiftly accomplished, would act as a threat to the Axis position in the Balkans and might even encourage Turkey to side openly with the Allies at long last.

At the end of January 1943, the Prime Minister directed the staffs in Cairo to prepare plans for the capture of Rhodes and the opening of the Ægean. The resources would have to come mainly from the Middle East. In March, the Middle East Joint Planners produced a scheme. Their counterparts in London indicated that operations in the Ægean were not feasible while the 'Husky' campaign was being fought. At this time, 'Husky' was still some four months distant. It was agreed that an operation against Rhodes and other islands could only take place when the German air forces were largely extended elsewhere. Douglas, recognising all the difficulties of the operation, thought that definite plans should be made; the decision whether or not to execute them could only be made in the light of the situation obtaining in the rest

[470]

of the Mediterranean theatre. Recording Churchill's remark that the Middle East had been told to plan for the capture of Rhodes and Scarpanto 'with ingenuity and resource', Douglas hoped this did not mean that it had to be done 'on the cheap' from the air point of view. As he told Portal, we had already had too many lessons in this war about the futility of trying to carry out transpontine operations in the face of heavy air superiority. By late June, our Intelligence showed that the German garrison in the island of Rhodes had now reached a figure of not less than 7,000 and would shortly be at least 8,000. The Middle East Commander-in-Chief, General Wilson, concluded that the plans made to take Rhodes against a German garrison of not more than 4,000 must now be abandoned.

Our whole attention in the next few weeks was occupied with the invasion of Sicily. The fall of Mussolini on 25 July, however, seemed to indicate that Italy might at any moment withdraw from the fight. Mr. Churchill promptly minuted on the 27th:

I suppose that the planners are all keyed up with plans for taking over Rhodes on the assumption that the Italians ask for an Armistice.

What is the composition of the garrison of Rhodes, German and Italian? We ought to get there quite quickly if it is humanly possible, as I need this place as part of the diplomatic approach to Turkey.

The prospect that Italy might drop out of the struggle made operations in the Ægean, for which the code-name was 'Accolade', seem more feasible to the Middle East authorities. There was now some hope that if Italy signed an armistice, the Italian garrisons in the more important islands of the Dodecanese might fight with us to overpower their erstwhile Allies. At the beginning of August, Douglas told me of the opinion which had prevailed at a recent meeting of the Commanders-in-Chief in Cairo. We should be ready to take immediate advantage of any favourable developments in the Balkans and the Ægean which might arise if an Axis withdrawal took place, or if the Italians and Germans started to fight each other, as they might do in Rhodes. There, the Italians greatly outnumbered the Germans. The Middle East was therefore holding ready a small force which could carry out a quick 'Accolade' operation against Rhodes but would be available to go elsewhere if that seemed desirable. These proposals had now been approved by the Chiefs of Staff who had authorised the retention in the Middle East of ships to enable an infantry brigade and an armoured regiment to be embarked forthwith. Douglas, so I learnt, had been asked to carry out a quick 'Accolade' operation in the near future, if the opportunity arose. As he pointed out to me:

> In such circumstances it is almost certain that some air threat from Greece and Crete will still exist; air protection of the convoy will therefore be essential. I will do my utmost to provide all the air forces required from my own resources, but I shall require a little assistance from you.

The 'little assistance' was apparently to consist of four P.38 Lightning squadrons, together with sufficient transport aircraft to lift one parachute battalion group. Douglas explained that he did not see how the operation could be carried out without this because, apart from Beaufighters, he had in the Middle East no fighters with sufficient range to operate in the vicinity of Rhodes from Cyprus. As he could not tell when 'Accolade' would be ordered, it was impossible to say how long the Lightning squadrons must remain in Cyprus. Once the operation was launched, however, he ought to be able to return them within four or five days. If 'Accolade' took place, it would also be essential to neutralise the German air forces in Greece, Crete, and the Ægean. This could only be done by the Ninth Bomber Command, and by the two heavy bomber squadrons, which would have to be released from all other commitments for the purpose during the period of 'Accolade'.

I was naturally anxious to help Douglas and the Middle Eastern Commanders-in-Chief in every possible way, though it seemed to me that the motive of the proposed operation was as much sentimental as military. At this time, we were still in the later stages of the battle for Sicily, after which I hoped for the most rapid exploitation of victory upon the mainland of Italy itself. It was clearly understood that though the Chiefs of Staff had ordered preparations for 'Accolade', the requirements of the Sicilian and

Italian ventures took priority over those of the Eastern Mediterranean. Eisenhower was specifically instructed on 6 August that he should release only those resources which he could spare after meeting his own requirements.

The next day, Eisenhower telegraphed to Cairo that he could provide the troops as requested, with certain landing craft, but after consulting me, he refused to send either the Lightning squadrons or the transport aircraft. The fighters were fully employed escorting the strategic bombers in their primary role of knocking Italy out of the war, and were specifically needed for the proposed 'Avalanche'. All our transport aircraft were more than fully employed.

Alexander, Cunningham, and I were of one mind in advising Eisenhower that the operation against Rhodes, at least, should be promptly abandoned. We could not help fearing that in practice the requirements of 'Accolade' would draw upon resources urgently needed for the main business in hand. In many items, especially anti-aircraft defences, landing craft, and air forces of all kinds, our resources were barely sufficient for present operations, let alone any more. Eisenhower signalled accordingly to London and to Cairo. Again the Middle East Commanders-in-Chief replied that they fully agreed on our main object, and that they were only asking for such limited resources as we could spare. They understood that if there were competition for resources, the operations in the Central Mediterranean must take priority.

Thus, at the moment when Sicily was captured, it seemed that 'Accolade' if it took place at all, would be no more than a minor operation carried out in the wake of a German withdrawal. For the moment, therefore, we concentrated upon speedy preparation for the assaults upon Reggio and Salerno. The Italian surrender of 3 September, announced five days later, seemed to hold out the prospect of a quick and cheap 'Accolade'. For a day or two, the Middle East Commanders-in-Chief had hopes of establishing our forces in Rhodes with the help of the Italian commander, help which was not in the event forthcoming. They also signalled on 7 September that besides the Rhodes operation they were considering the despatch of small parties to other islands held by the Italians, especially Cos. This was welcome news to the Prime Minister, who replied: 'Good. This is a time to play high. Improvise and dare.'

Within a few days it was only too plain that the idea of any operation against Rhodes must be abandoned. The Prime Minister continued to preach boldness. 'This is a time,' he signalled to General Wilson on 13 September, 'to think of Clive and Marlborough, and of Rooke's men taking Gibraltar.'

There was no doubt that if we undertook Ægean operations we should be playing for high stakes. If the Royal Air Force could be established in Rhodes, the Royal Navy could resume control of the Ægean. Turkey, thus reassured, might well enter the war on the Allies' side. The Balkans might erupt in wrath against the invader. A reliable sea route to Russia might well be secured. The Allies might, so to speak, enter Europe through the back door. These advantages seemed so attractive that the evident flaw could easily be overlooked. Once it was established that without serious damage to the Italian operations we could not take Rhodes, the whole 'Accolade' operation was compromised. Without the comparatively good airfields of Rhodes, the Navy could hardly control the Ægean. A glance at the map was sufficient to show that the islands of the Dodecanese lay a long way from our air bases, but close to those of the enemy. Here was the root of the matter.

Apart from Rhodes, now denied us, Cos was the only island possessing a suitable airfield. There, the Italian commander promised co-operation with the Allies, and on 4 September a detachment of six Spitfires was established there. Douglas admitted that this was a policy of risk, but thought it was a time to take risks. If the situation became too sticky, the fighters could be flown out to Cyprus and the ground personnel could slip over to Turkey, whence we could reclaim them in due course. General Wilson attached much importance to Leros, which was unsuitable for air forces. A small number of troops were nevertheless placed there and on Samos. We were able to make these first moves because we had rendered the enemy's airfields in Rhodes temporarily unserviceable. For the moment our shipping, including destroyers, moved freely between Castelorizo, Cos, and Leros, though Douglas acknowledged that such movement would become

much more difficult when the enemy have repaired aerodromes in Rhodes and put air forces there. In the meanwhile we are rushing in fuel and equipment while the going is good. After that we should be able to keep maintenance going at a pinch with supplies from Turkey and by air transport.

Douglas wished that he had a bomber striking force in the Middle East to attack the aerodromes on Rhodes, but realised that this was asking much until the situation in Italy, where we were only just overcoming the Salerno crisis, improved. He asked that I should bear this in mind for the future. I replied on 18 September:

Sorry I have not been able to give more help on Dodecanese. I will certainly not forget it, and if opportunity arises will give you what help I can.

During the next week, further supplies and troops were moved into Cos. Douglas signalled on 25 September that the whole position was 'beginning to look pretty secure'. Meanwhile, the Middle Eastern Commanders-in-Chief had concluded that the capture of Rhodes was necessary to make safe our positions in the islands already occupied. They hoped by this means to endanger the Axis position in Crete, to afford a base for offensive action against sea communications throughout the Ægean which, in conjunction with bombing from the Heel of Italy against land communications, might force the enemy to withdraw from Greece. They proposed an operation to take place about 20 October. For this, certain help from Eisenhower would be necessary.

Eisenhower offered two destroyers, two cruisers, and various other items of assistance, but said that the two L.S.Ts (Landing Ship, Tank) for which the Middle East had asked could only be provided at the direct expense of the build-up in Italy. The Middle East authorities replied that these vessels were essential. In addition, they said that the German air force in the Greece–Ægean area had been considerably strengthened, and now stood, in their estimate, at about 350 aircraft. This meant that the enemy's air effort must be reduced by sustained bombing attacks on airfields around Larissa and Athens. They asked that such attacks should start forthwith; otherwise, even Cos and Leros might become untenable. They also asked again for the four Lightning squadrons in case Cos should be put out of action by heavy-scale attack. The alternative would be aircraft-carriers with extra destroyer escorts. The United States Chiefs of Staff may have suspected that the Ægean operations were intended as the prelude to a serious campaign in the Balkans. At all events, they decided on 6 October that they could not direct Eisenhower to provide for the Eastern Mediterranean equipment needed in Italy. This was the basis on which we had been working throughout.

Even before the American decision was received, serious events had occurred in the Ægean. By 29 September I had to agree that the situation there had so developed as to call for increased air effort from our forces in the Central Mediterranean. The activities of the German bombers and fighters based in the Balkans, and especially in Greece, were reaching such a pitch that we might soon be forced to evacuate the Dodecanese. I agreed that 240 Wing should remain at Douglas's disposal but could not agree to his request that the U.S. Ninth Bomber Force should be sent back to the Benghazi area. They had only just completed their move to Tunisia and were standing by for an attack on aircraft factories at Wiener Neustadt. Without our heavy bombers we could not hammer away at enemy communications into Northern Italy. Aircraft which were just being moved into the Heel, would, I promised, be directed against targets in the Balkans selected by Douglas. I was not hopeful of meeting his request for Lightning squadrons, essential to our impending advance in Italy, and which we could not replace.

All these events, as I told Douglas, showed that operations in any part of the Mediterranean theatre were inseparably connected:

Am very concerned at the way in which the Ægean operations have developed and involved commitments which I have had no prior opportunity of assessing. Moreover, although Ægean is outside Eisenhower's area, operations there and diversion of forces there directly affect his theatre. Procedure by which Commanders-in-Chief,

Middle East, launch operations without full consultation with me and Eisenhower is, I feel, most dangerous. Events have shown what I feel ought to have been evident before, that Balkan operations, particularly from air point of view, are part of those in the rest of the Mediterranean and must be considered as part of that one problem. I do not wish to waste time in criticising the past, and will do my best to help, but I must insist on being kept fully informed as to plans for future operations, so that possible commitments, and consequently moves of and employment of air forces, can be properly balanced.

Douglas's signal, to which this was the reply, had told me that the enemy had 'tickled us up quite smartly at Leros and Cos by formations of up to 25 Ju. 88 with Me. 109 escort. He has succeeded in putting our landing strips at Cos out of action for considerable periods.'

Douglas recognised that unless we could reduce the enemy's effort he might well succeed in rendering the airstrips at Cos untenable. Our footholds in the Dodecanese, and any projected operations against Rhodes, would then be jeopardised. The possession of workable aerodromes in Cos was fundamental to the attack on Rhodes. Portal, not realising for the moment that the decision to put air forces into Cos had been taken independently of me, told us how pleased he was with the forward policy adopted there and how strongly he favoured doing everything possible to build up defensive strength in fighters and anti-aircraft defence. We should fight the German Air Force wherever it went. We could better afford a diversion to the Ægean than they, and wastage inflicted in Greece and the Ægean was just as desirable as wastage inflicted anywhere else. German diversions to this area showed clearly the importance they attached to keeping us at bay there, and thus the value to us of victory.

The Joint Planners in London had already reported that the Middle East Commanders were overestimating the strategic importance of Rhodes. Possession of the island would of itself do nothing to drive the German Air Force out of Greece. Nor did the forces suggested for the operation against Rhodes seem to be sufficient. Further strength could only be provided at the expense of the effort in Italy. The Joint Planners thought it would be better to abandon Cos, Leros, and other islands we had taken, than to divert any proportion of the air effort from its main purpose, the destruction of targets in southern Germany, which was one of the principal reasons for entering upon the Italian campaign. Nevertheless, the collective view of the Chiefs of Staff was very much in line with the opinions Portal had already expressed.

None of this was very helpful to Eisenhower. Our latest Intelligence showed that there already were, or shortly would be, some twenty-four German divisions in Italy. It was clear that the battle there would not be won without a major struggle. Throughout the winter of 1943–44 we should be considerably inferior in ground forces. This disadvantage must be off-set by sustained and continued air attack upon German communications. Eisenhower told the Chiefs of Staff that if it was decided to to carry on with 'Accolade' he would do his utmost, but it could only be at the cost of the campaign in Italy, which would probably 'assume the aspect of a major bitter battle'.

Douglas visited us on 1 and 2 October. Eisenhower and I agreed to increase the weight of attack on enemy aerodromes in Greece, hoping that this might relieve us of the need to send the Lightning squadrons to Cyprus. I also offered Douglas twelve additional Spitfire IXs for Cos. The next morning Eisenhower received a cable from Churchill:

We are much concerned about Cos and are sure you will do all in your power to prevent a vexatious injury to future plans occurring through loss of Cos.

Eisenhower replied that we were already using all our available air-power to this end. That same day I sent two B.24 Groups to Benghazi whence they would attack Greek airfields. This would be in addition to the assaults already being launched from the Heel of Italy. Eisenhower and I felt that such an onslaught by our whole heavy bomber force as well as by B.25 and P.38 groups, should beat down enemy air action to very small proportions and enable the Middle East to intervene effectively in the local battle. But on the very day that all these arrangements were being made, the Middle East Commanders-in-Chief were signalling that the fall of Cos might be expected within twenty-four hours

. . . Owing to great enemy superiority in numbers and weapons and to the fact that we have been unable to prevent his build up.

As long as enemy retains complete air superiority we cannot operate Hunt-Class destroyers in area of operations. Enemy, therefore, has complete control of sea as well as of air in Ægean. This precludes all possibility of reinforcing Cos from Leros or elsewhere, and moreover jeopardises situation of armed forces in Leros and other islands. If Cos falls we must expect early attack on other islands.

The remedy for this situation, they telegraphed, was the immediate provision of assistance on the scale previously asked for. If this were provided, Leros might be held until a successful 'Accolade' enabled us to provide sufficient air support from Rhodes. The loss of the airfields on Cos would clearly make a serious difference to 'Accolade', and in view of the enemy's strength in carriers and other craft, a most generous scale of assistance by bombers and long-range fighters would be essential. Later that day I heard from Churchill:

Cos is highly important, and a reverse there would be most vexatious. I am sure I can rely upon you to turn all your heat from every quarter, especially during this lull in Italy.

I replied the next morning, the 4th:

You have no doubt heard from C.A.S. we are putting maximum effort against enemy in Greece. Anything further I find possible will be done.

As we learnt shortly afterwards, it was already too late to save Cos. The Germans, taking advantage of their air superiority, sent an expedition of three to four thousand men, with tanks and landing craft, to the island, escorted by destroyers. The Government at home do not seem to have been warned by the Middle East Commanders-in-Chief that the enemy possessed effective naval forces in these waters. It appeared that one flotilla of our own destroyers had been withdrawn from the Ægean area in order to escort two battleships to Malta, thus leaving on the whole of the Levant station at the material time only three Hunt-Class destroyers available for immediate use. The Middle East

Commanders had made their dispositions on the assumption that a seaborne operation against Cos would be preceded by the reinforcement of Rhodes and had not realised that the enemy would be able to collect and launch at such short notice an expedition as large as that which took Cos. The Prime Minister expressed keen displeasure.

For the moment, we had to go forward on the assumption that 'Accolade' was still going to be undertaken towards the end of October. So far as I was aware, the participation of elements of the Mediterranean Air Command had never been properly considered. The fall of Cos only made such an assessment more urgent. I set out in detail for Eisenhower's eye the ways in which a determined attack on Rhodes would diminish our air strength in the Italian campaign. In particular, I anticipated a demand for long-range fighters for the purposes of covering convoys and the assault on Rhodes itself. When we remembered the difficulties of providing proper cover over Salerno, I could not help feeling doubtful whether the same type of aircraft, forced to operate at over twice the range, would prove to be of any material value. Certainly we must expect to pay a price in Italy if long-range fighters were diverted to the Eastern Mediterranean. Our Intelligence showed that the enemy had concentrated fighters in the area of Pisa and Leghorn to offer serious opposition to our bombing effort.

Eisenhower replied to me on 6 October that we should undertake no specific commitments for 'Accolade' other than that of blasting the enemy airfields in Greece, which he and I had already agreed was necessary from all points of view. All experience had shown, he said, that when the land forces undertook a major move, a period of more intensive work devolved upon the Air Force. At this time, they anticipated that late October would be a period of intense ground activity, and we knew that our air must be ready to operate then at full pitch. He suggested that I should explain to Portal that while we were sympathetic to the needs of the Middle East we could not meet them at the expense of the Italian campaign. I responded by sending Portal the gist of Eisenhower's message, adding that I agreed with every word of it. I explained how the fall of Cos had completely altered the aspect of the 'Accolade' operation. The latest news from Cairo indicated that the provision of six squadrons of Lightnings or Mustangs had now become an essential feature of the plan. I did not feel that I could advise Eisenhower to leave the Lightning groups in Cyrenaica where they would not be available for their prime duty and where serviceability must fall rapidly since they were operating some three hundred miles from their main base.

The C.I.G.S. had already reached similar conclusions in London. In his diary for 6 October he wrote:

It is quite clear in my mind that with the commitments we have in Italy we should not undertake serious operations in the Ægean.[1]

It has to be remembered, in tracing the final stages of this dismal story, how remote we were from the scene of action. Leros, for instance, lay 390 miles from Cyprus and from Gambut, which was bad enough; but it was also 645 miles from Catania, and 680 from Foggia.

Portal replied to me at once that the Prime Minister had suggested to Eisenhower that a conference should be convened immediately by him in North Africa with his own Commanders-in-Chief and the Middle East Commanders-in-Chief, to study what action should be taken in the Mediterranean. Andrew Cunningham, who had been appointed First Sea Lord on 4 October, was coming out to represent the home Government. Churchill pressed his anxieties both upon Roosevelt and upon Eisenhower. He believed that the Italian and Balkan peninsulas were militarily and politically united, and really constitued one theatre. The diversions of German strength, and especially air strength, to the Eastern Mediterranean, showed what importance the enemy attached to holding that area. The Prime Minister assured the President that he had never wished to send an army into the Balkans, but only by agents, supplies, and Commandos to stimulate the intense guerilla warfare already prevailing there. Rhodes was the key to all this, and he did not feel that the present plan for 'Accolade' was good enough. It was worth at least a first-class division for the initial assault. The policy should not be pursued

[1] Bryant: *Triumph in the West*, p. 50.

at all unless with vigour and celerity, requiring the best troops and adequate means.

Portal telegraphed to me again on 7 October asking me to keep an open mind on the question of air support for 'Accolade'. It would be one thing to undertake an obligation involving an indefinite and perhaps prolonged diversion to the Eastern Mediterranean, but it would surely be a quite different and much easier thing to

. . . undertake to neutralise for a day or two the few airfields from which effective opposition could come, and to provide the fighter cover necessary for the approach, the assault and the battle.

Portal said that he trusted that at the impending conference I should press for the best possible plan to be considered on its merits. This I was certainly willing to do, but I could not help doubting whether a sound operation 'Accolade' could be mounted from the bases in our possession. In replying to Portal, I said that I felt the pressure being put on Eisenhower by higher authority was placing him in a most difficult position. I hoped there was no question of a personal visit by the Prime Minister to the Mediterranean, for I felt it would be most dangerous and might have a disastrous effect on Anglo-American relations. I had already seen Mr. Roosevelt's cold reply to Mr. Churchill's pleadings for support in the Ægean ventures. Roosevelt had refused to force on Eisenhower diversions which would hamper the campaign in Italy and pointed to the Germans' marked superiority in ground troops and Panzer divisions there.

Portal answered that there was no question of any visit by Churchill without the full agreement of Roosevelt, who had been asked to send General Marshall to a conference at Eisenhower's headquarters. If a conference to discuss 'Accolade' under these conditions were denied, a most painful impression would be created at the centre of affairs in London.

However, this crisis did not arise, for Roosevelt, in effect, refused Churchill's suggestion of a high-level conference. It seemed to Alan Brooke that Churchill had worked himself into a frenzy of excitement about an attack on Rhodes, even at the expense of endangering his relations with Roosevelt and the

Americans: certainly Churchill pressed upon 'Jumbo' Wilson the need to claim extra support for 'Accolade'. But the issue had now become largely academic. The conference of the Mediterranean and Middle East Commanders was duly convened at La Marsa on 9 October. During the meetings, news was received of heavy German reinforcement in Italy, and it became clear that a pitched battle must be fought south of Rome. The fullest discussion showed, as Wilson later signalled to Churchill, that if the forces which we all agreed to be necessary for the capture of Rhodes were made available, it could only be at the expense of 'Overlord' in landing-craft, and of the Italian offensive in ships, landing-craft, and aircraft.

There was no doubt in the mind of any one present at this meeting that 'Accolade' could not now be staged effectively. It was clear to me that the Middle East Commanders-in-Chief had no faith in the project and were relieved at the decision. It was not only a question of German reinforcements in Italy. The weather had changed decisively for the worst. In my opinion this was the decisive factor, as I signalled to Portal on the 10th:

Neutralisation of airfields requires heavy and sustained efforts. Weather has already prevented this. For six days B.17s unable to carry out this task. Probability of similar interference by weather increases each week. At Conference project was considered on its merit with great impartiality before repercussions on Italian campaign were examined. In past I have repeatedly pressed for risks to be taken where they appeared reasonable, and will do so again, but in this case I consider project under present conditions is not a reasonable risk.

Our conference had shown in fact that we could hardly hope to take Rhodes until we had established a high degree of air mastery; this could not be achieved unless the bulk of the Mediterranean bomber forces were used; even then, it would take three weeks before the assault. Then there would be a period during which the effort must be sustained in order to get our forces ashore. We simply had not the resources in the Mediterranean to capture both Rhodes and Rome. This decision the Prime Minister accepted.

The Middle East Commanders, realising that the operation

against Rhodes must be postponed, decided that it was still not impossible to retain Leros and Samos. Our hold there however could only be precarious, and heavy losses, especially at sea, might be incurred. This was indeed the case, for in the seven weeks ending 31 October, we had lost in the Ægean operations five destroyers and two submarines, as well as four cruisers and two destroyers damaged.

It would be futile, at this distance of time, to linger over the details of the fall of Leros. Our men held out until the middle of November. During the latter part of October I received many requests for extra support in the air, and always did what I could. In the middle part of the month the weather proved so atrociously bad that it was often impossible to attack the airfields in Greece from which the enemy operated in the Ægean. In addition to other help, I sent to the Middle East two extra squadrons, and left under Douglas's orders the only heavy night bombers in the Mediterranean Command. During October, North African air forces flew more than fifteen hundred sorties against targets in the Balkans.

Nevertheless, we were subject to continual pressure to revise the decisions of the meeting of 9 October. I signalled to Portal on the 31st:

As I see it, the Cos-Leros operation was a gamble for very big political stakes. As I have not full facts, I cannot say how far failure to hold Cos was, or was not, due to weaknesses in planning or execution, but to me it is clear that once Cos had fallen, and effective air cover was no longer possible, one of the main foundations of all Ægean operations had collapsed. The gamble having failed, we are being pressed to throw good money after bad. Douglas presses me to send the B.24 Groups back to Cyrenaica, and to send also the P.38 Groups now in Sardinia. Even the addition of these forces could not, I am quite convinced, especially in current weather conditions, materially affect a situation which is fundamentally unsound, owing mainly to the simple but not quite unalterable facts of geography; i.e. we are attempting to maintain garrison and operate surface ships outside effective range of our own fighter forces, and under the very noses of enemy shore-based aircraft.

The inevitable end came on the evening of 16 November. I

doubt whether in any circumstances it could have been prevented, and certainly luck ran against us. On four successive days, 11–14 November, large numbers of aircraft stood by to bomb the Greek airfields. The weather prevented them from doing anything. Even when the Germans had established themselves in Leros, the tone of the reports reaching me from Cairo was that our troops were holding their own. On the night of the 16th, Mr. Churchill who was approaching Malta by sea on his way to the Cairo and Teheran conference, signalled to me:

I much regret not to see you tonight, as I should have pressed upon you the vital need of sustaining Leros by every possible means. This is much the most important thing that is happening in the Mediterranean in the next few days. I shall have many things to discuss with you when we meet, but I must say now that I do not see how you can disinterest yourself in the fate of Leros.

I had never disinterested myself in the fate of Leros; even less could I disinterest myself in the fate of the Italian campaign, where all the bright hopes of a prompt seizure of Rome and advance to the north had long since disappeared, and where the prospect now seemed to be a slogging match in winter conditions. As for Leros, although we did not know it until the following morning, it had already surrendered by the time the Prime Minister sent his signal to me. General Wilson telegraphed dolefully the next morning that it had been a near thing between success and failure. Four fine battalions had been more or less lost. The Middle East had taken the risk in September with their eyes open, and all would have been well if Rhodes could have been captured. Douglas promptly signalled Portal his strong dissatisfaction with the assistance he had received during the Leros operations, but the result would have been the same, I am sure, if we had doubled or trebled the amount of assistance given him. The strongest squadrons cannot operate without the right facilities and bases. Our only hope in this case, unless Leros could have been maintained entirely by submarine, would have been to operate squadrons promptly from south-west Anatolia. This, of course, involved Turkish consent, a commodity notoriously expensive. I always thought it improbable that we should be able to pay the price, and as it turned out, the bargainings were still in progress when the German assault on Leros began. Our forces there were subjected to merciless and continuous bombardment from the air. Paratroops were landed. In this way, the island's defences were practically cut in half. The only consolation in all this was the damage we had inflicted on the German Air Force. Between 8 September and 22 November, 140 enemy aircraft were destroyed and a further 148 damaged. Of these, the North African air forces destroyed seven in the air, seventeen on the ground, and damaged a further 107.

How could it be that the Air Commander in the Middle East could find himself involved in combined operations in the Ægean with forces quite inadequate for the task, and consequently entirely dependent upon the good will of the Air Commander-in-Chief Mediterranean? Conversely, how could it be that the Supreme Commander Mediterranean and his Air Commander-in-Chief, responsible for a major campaign in Italy and the Central Mediterranean, could be subject to extreme pressure to divert air forces to operations in the Ægean—operations over which they had no control? If the Command set-up was so irrational, it is not surprising that the operations themselves were equally irrational and, therefore, doomed to failure. One would have thought that some of the bitter lessons of Crete would have been sufficiently fresh in mind to have prevented a repetition, and yet, in the sad story of Cos and Leros we had the familiar cries (and justifiable cries) for protection from enemy air attack, complaints of inadequate support from the Air, and heavy casualties in all three Services, because we were compelled once again to attempt the impossible. It seems incredible now, as it seemed then, that after four years' experience of modern war, people forgot that air-power relies on secure bases, weather, and effective radius of action. In the Ægean, as in the previous operations there, the Germans had a string of effective air bases by which the whole area could be covered at medium and short range. Conversely, we had no air bases within some three hundred miles of Cos. The blunt fact is that the whole project was based on the hope that the Italian garrison of Rhodes would turn on and overwhelm the German garrison, thus making two vital airfields available.

One recognises that no precise information could be expected regarding the plan of action to be adopted by the Italians in Rhodes, but equally I have seen no evidence that there had been any special steps taken by our Intelligence.

The operation for the capture of Rhodes, with its perhaps unfortunate name 'Accolade', was a gamble which failed to come off. As a gamble, it did appear to offer possible useful prizes in both the political and military field, but I found it very difficult to see any real justification for it as the odds were heavily against its success. The position of Cos was essentially precarious. The one aerodrome was quite inadequately defended, and it was impossible to instal heavy A.A. and move essential heavy aerodrome equipment. The enemy had, by contrast, a wide selection of conveniently placed airfields in the neighbourhood of Athens, running in a curve south and eastward to Rhodes. The demand that the German air force should be knocked out by attacks by the heavy bombers of the Mediterranean Air Command was quite unrealistic. Such a decisive result called not only for heavy scale attack but also continuity; continuity which was unobtainable owing to the weather conditions over Greece and the Eastern Mediterranean.

*

Until mid-October, our advance in Italy had been relatively swift. The German troops fought a series of delaying actions, but no major battle. After the first week in October, however, German resistance began to steel itself. Evidently we should not take Rome with ease. No doubt one of the enemy's motives was to deny us the use of the airfields there. Our own existing line was not sufficiently deep before Naples and Foggia, where our main air forces were based, for us to contemplate even a temporary stalemate. The arrival of German reinforcements increased the disparity between their strength and Alexander's. I learned from 'Mary' Coningham on 18 October that Alexander had for some two or three days been expressing his disquiet. The Germans now had more than twenty divisons in Italy, with a total of twenty-six in sight. Alexander was unlikely to have this strength even in 1944. On the front in southern Italy, Alexander's eleven divisions were opposed by nine German divisions in a terrain

[487]

favourable to the defence. Without the means of getting round the flank, Alexander said that he saw no reason why we should ever get to Rome. For his part, Coningham had been wondering how it was that the German army were able to fight so successfully without air support and with lacerated communications. The strength of their defences in suitable country seemed to be practically unimpaired so far as day-to-day tactical efficiency in the battle area was concerned. Whether they could mount an offensive without adequate air support was another matter.

Coningham described our air operations as a constant battle against the weather, with the prospect of permanent cloud over the hills in the centre part of the line. On the other hand, we knew on good evidence that the prospects seemed to our opponents even more depressing. General d'Aurelio, who had been on Kesselring's staff for a considerable period, told us that German morale was generally low. Railways were practically at a standstill through bombing and sabotage, and supplies were almost all carried by road. Fuel for motor transport and aircraft was very short. It even appeared that considerable reserve stocks were held on rolling stock, which, because of the danger of bombing, had to be kept in tunnels, thus immobilising the railways and congesting the lines. Heavy losses on airfields, and especially the damage to the main stores park at Cancello, had ruined the German air effort in southern Italy. Our raid on the aircraft factories at Wiener Neustadt had an immediate effect in stopping supplies, particularly of much needed engines. We gathered that General von Richthofen, the German Luftwaffe commander, had decided to conserve his remaining resources and to build up in the rear areas. In fact, he had little choice, since he could not get his supplies forward from the Lombardy Plain in anything like the necessary quantity.

The establishment of airfields in southern Italy had initiated a new phase of the war. We no longer had to rely solely on bases in eastern England to attack the countries of Axis-held Europe. Foggia opened up new possibilities. It was from there that Wiener Neustadt was attacked on 1 October and again later in the month. In the next weeks, targets in Germany, Austria, Czechoslovakia, Rumania, Hungary, Poland, and France were battered. My main object now was to get our strategic forces well forward. The limiting factors were shipping and airfields. Shipping involved a continual fight for priorities, and the maintenance of an expert detective organisation to ensure that these priorities were actually observed in loading and unloading.

I had hoped that the advance of the army and the consequent move forward of the Tactical Air Forces would provide some airfields for the Strategic Air Force. This now appeared unlikely. Alexander was much preoccupied about the shortage of landing-craft, which precluded him from taking advantage of the enemy's inherent weakness, the exposure of his two flanks to turning movements from the sea. On land, the German divisions were blocking the plains and taking advantage of the defensive positions plentifully provided by the mountains. A way had to be found to combine the frontal assault with seaborne landings in the enemy's rear. This meant that landing-craft which, under decisions taken at the Quebec Conference, should have returned immediately to Britain, we thought must be kept back in the Mediterranean. By the end of October, Alexander was reporting that operations in Italy were coming to a standstill. By early November, after much pressure had been applied, the United States Chiefs of Staff consented to allow some tank-landing ships to remain in the Mediterranean until December.

I do not intend to describe these earlier phases of the Italian campaign, over which I exercised little direct control. Although we enjoyed mastery in the air, the terrain, the bravery of the enemy, the difficulties of supply, and the concentration upon the 'Overlord' invasion, scheduled for May 1944, produced a rate of advance which I found disappointingly slow. One lesson of real importance, however, we began to learn. It was this: that concentrated, precise attack upon railway targets scientifically selected would probably produce a degree of disruption and immobility which might make all the difference to the success or failure of the long awaited invasion of France. The clear and detailed reports submitted by Professor Zuckerman convinced me that this was the right method of attack.

The Prime Minister, who had arrived in Tunis and had there succumbed to pneumonia, was sufficiently recovered by Christmas

Eve to hold a long Conference at which Wilson, Alexander, and I joined him to discuss again how we might break the Italian deadlock by an amphibious flanking operation. We were agreed that the landing, at Anzio, must be carried out on a scale which would ensure success, with at least two divisions. The target date would be about 20 January 1944. We felt that the right course would be to delay by up to a month the departure from the Mediterranean of the fifty-six British L.S.Ts now due to leave by 1 February. The Chiefs of Staff, to whom Churchill telegraphed in the early hours of Christmas morning, showed no great zest for this plan. Churchill replied on 26 December that if two full divisions were landed at Anzio, it should be decisive, cutting the communications of all the enemy forces facing the Fifth Army.

The Prime Minister showed himself deeply anxious to clear up the Italian campaign, for the 'Overlord' landings were supposed to be only four and a half months away. Roosevelt agreed to delay the departure of the fifty-six L.S.Ts on condition that 'Overlord' was carried out in May, in accordance with the promise made to Stalin at Teheran.

For me, it was time to return home. Early in December, in a conversation with Churchill at Cairo, Roosevelt nominated Eisenhower to command 'Overlord'. Churchill had later proposed my appointment as Deputy Supreme Commander 'on account of the great part the air will play in this operation'.

The decision to invade Normandy in the early summer of 1944 had been taken on the conditions that Germany could not oppose such a landing with a reserve of more than a dozen mobile divisions, and that Germany's fighter strength in the west should be immobilised. The Prime Minister was right to speak about the great part the Air would play in this operation; for without air-power neither condition would have been fulfilled.

North-West Europe

DECEMBER 1943–MAY 1945

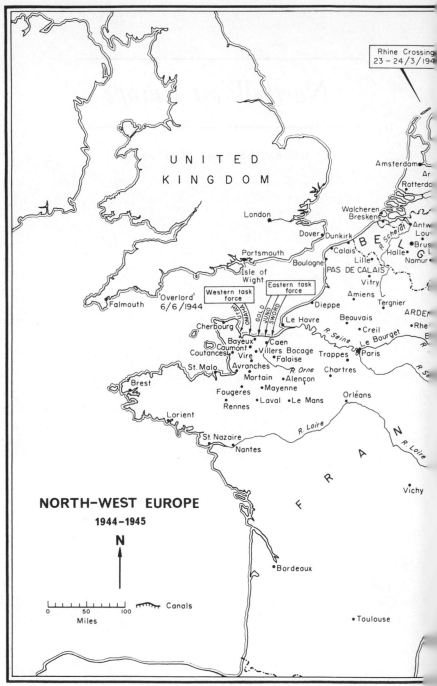

UNITED
KINGDOM

Rhine Crossing
23 – 24/3/194

Amsterdam

Ar
Rotterd

London

Walcheren
Breskens

Dover Dunkirk

Antw
Lou

B E L G I

Portsmouth

Boulogne

Calais

Lille

Halle

Brus
Namur

Isle of
Wight

PAS DE CALAIS

Vitry

Amiens

Tergnier

Falmouth

'Overlord'
6/6/1944

Western task
force

Eastern task
force

Dieppe

Beauvais

Creil

Rhe

ARDE

Cherbourg

UTAH

OMAHA

GOLD

JUNO

SWORD

Le Havre

R. Seine

Le Bourget

E

Bayeux

Caumont

Coutances

Villers Bocage

Caen

Falaise

Trappes

Paris

St. Malo

Vire

Avranches

R. Orne

Chartres

R. Se

Brest

Mortain

Fougeres

Rennes

Alençon

Mayenne

Laval

Le Mans

Orléans

F

R

A

N

Lorient

St. Nazaire

Nantes

R. Loire

R. Loire

Vichy

NORTH–WEST EUROPE

1944–1945

N

0   50   100
Miles

～～～ Canals

Bordeaux

Toulouse

© CASSELL & CO. LTD. 1966

Chronology

1944

July:

8   R.A.F. bomb Caen (2,500 tons).
9   British and Canadians capture Caen.
18   R.A.F. drop 7,000 tons of bombs in area beyond Caen.
20   July Bomb Plot: attempt to assassinate Hitler.
27   U.S. troops break out west of St. Lô.
31   U.S. troops break through at Avranches.

August:

1   British take Le Bény Bocage.
4   U.S. troops take Rennes.
9   Eisenhower's H.Q. set up in France.
11   U.S. troops cross the Loire; German armoured counter-attack ends.
12   Beginning of general retreat of German troops from Normandy; Allies reach Argentan.
14   'Dragoon' landings in south of France.
17   U.S. troops take St. Mâlo, Chartres and Orléans.
    In southern France bridgeheads link up to form 50–mile front.
    Russians reach East Prussian border.
19   U.S. forces under General Patton reach the Seine.
    Allied air forces bomb German armour in Falaise trap.
26   U.S. troops reach the Marne and cross the Seine.
28   Allied troops establish bridgehead over Seine.

September:

3   British liberate Brussels.
4   British troops take Antwerp.
8   First V2 on England.
10   Second Quebec Conference begins.
11   'Overlord' and 'Dragoon' forces link up.
12   U.S. troops cross German border near Aachen.
17   Allied Airborne Army dropped in Holland at Nijmegen, Eindhoven and Arnhem.
25   Withdrawal of airborne forces from Arnhem begins.

October:

21   U.S. troops occupy Aachen.

[495]

1944
November:

4   R.A.F. breaches Dortmund-Ems canal.
20 French Army capture Belfort and reach the Rhine.
24 Allies cross River Saar.
    French Army take Strasbourg.
26 Antwerp open for shipping.

December:

16 Germans launch attack in Ardennes.
19 Field Marshal Montgomery to command all Allied forces north of Ardennes salient, General Bradley all forces to the south.
26 Relief of Bastogne garrison.

1945
January:

2   U.S. troops advance in Ardennes.
16 Ardennes salient eliminated.

February:

4   Yalta Conference opens.
5   New British and Canadian offensive launched towards the Rhine.
13 R.A.F. raid Dresden.
14 U.S.A.A.F. continue raid on Dresden.
22 Operation 'Clarion'. Attack by 9,000 Allied aircraft on central German road and rail communications.

March:

6   U.S. troops reach Rhine north-west of Coblenz.
7   U.S. troops form bridgehead over Rhine at Remagen.
9   U.S. troops occupy Bonn and Bad Godesberg.
10 West bank of Rhine north of the Moselle in Allied hands.
22 Allied bridgehead at Remagen 30 miles long.
23 Rhine crossing by 21 Army Group.
    Allied airborne armies drop on east bank and link up with infantry.
27 Last V2 rocket lands in England.

[496]

1945

March:

29   U.S. troops take Mannheim, Weisbaden, Frankfurt and Aschaffenburg.

30   Russians capture Danzig.

30   Russians cross into Austria.

April:

16   Russians launch attack towards Berlin.

22   U.S. troops enter Czechoslovakia.

23   Russians attack Berlin from south and east.

25   Russian and U.S. forces link up.

May:

1   Hamburg Radio announces death of Hitler.
U.S. and British bridgeheads over the Elbe link up.

2   German armies in Italy surrender at noon.

3   U.S. troops cross River Inn, capture Innsbruck, enter Bohemia and reach the Brenner Pass.
British take Rangoon.

5   German forces in Denmark capitulate.
U.S. troops take Linz.
German armies in south capitulate.
Russians capture Swinemünde and Peenemünde.

7   General Jodl signs instrument of Unconditional Surrender of all German forces at 2.41 A.M.

8   V.E. Day.

Air Command in 'Overlord'–Planning for pre-'Overlord' Air operations–We come to London–First meeting at Norfolk House– Monty's proposal–'Pointblank'–Harris and Spaatz and Transportation Plan–Committee rule–Zuckerman and the time factor–Churchill's ruling–Transportation Plan shown feasible–Strategic operations under my control–Proposed employment of heavy bombers

THE decision that a British airman should be Eisenhower's Deputy Supreme Commander raised complicated issues of command about which the Prime Minister, still convalescing in North Africa after his serious illness, lost no time in telegraphing to London. Both Eisenhower and his Chief of Staff, General Bedell Smith, spoke anxiously to Churchill about the arrangements for air command in 'Overlord'. They did not like the chain of command which put the British and the American Tactical Air Forces under Air Chief Marshal Leigh-Mallory, the Air Commander-in-Chief, whose powers *vis-à-vis* the Bomber commanders, Spaatz and Harris, would have to be defined. According to the Prime Minister's information, Harris had let it be known that he intended to be a real Commander-in-Chief of the Air. The post of Deputy Supreme Commander had been deliberately given to me because of the vast part the Air was to play in the battle for Europe, and Churchill insisted that I must have all the inherent powers:

Tedder with his unique experience and close relation as Deputy to the Supreme Commander, ought to be in fact and in form the complete master of all the air operations. Everything is then quite simple. There need only be one Tactical Air Force which Leigh-Mallory can command. Spaatz will come directly under Eisenhower as his senior officer, and can be told to obey Tedder. There will be no difficulty in arranging between Tedder and Harris. I do not like the idea of Tedder being an officer without portfolio.

In London it was thought that these observations did not do justice to the complexity of the question. The Secretary of State for Air, Sir Archibald Sinclair, at once explained to the Prime Minister by telegram that the British Tactical Air Force under 'Mary'

[499]

Coningham would work with Montgomery's group of armies, while the American Tactical Air Force under Brereton would also be used to support Montgomery in the initial stages of 'Overlord,' but would ultimately work in the main with the American group of armies. Leigh-Mallory, as Commander-in-Chief, would be able to reinforce the one from the other, and was meanwhile in active command of both the British and American Tactical Air Forces. Moreover, he was responsible for the air defence of Great Britain, and in the first stages of 'Overlord' would have to allocate forces between that commitment and the land battle. Leigh-Mallory must be the officer who would integrate with the operation of these Tactical Air Forces the effort of heavy bombers which might be placed at his disposal by the Chiefs of Staff. Sinclair was sure that it would be wrong to derogate from these responsibilities or to blur the line of definition between them and the responsibilities of Eisenhower and myself. Eisenhower would dictate strategy and policy. I should share his responsibility over the whole field of operations by land, sea, and air. The Secretary of State said that he hoped my experience and the confidence felt in my judgment by the Air Staff would ensure that liaison between the various air forces would be effective, and that differences of opinion would be resolved with goodwill:

The Americans want to put Spaatz and Harris directly under Eisenhower. I am convinced that would be a mistake. Not even Tedder has experience of conducting the bomber offensive. Nor, if he is to be an effective deputy over the whole range of land, sea, and air, should he concentrate exclusively on air problems.

The following day, 8 January 1944, the Chiefs of Staff explained to Churchill their view of the differences between command in the Mediterranean and that in the United Kingdom. Whereas in the Mediterranean Eisenhower had been supreme in all military matters, with all the forces under his command, he would while he remained in the United Kingdom be in practice a Task Force Commander. Other forces in Great Britain would further Eisenhower's plans, but would not accompany him to the Continent, and could not be placed under his sole control. Again, my position in the Mediterranean had given me centralised control of all the air forces there. This position at home was, in effect, held by Portal, who was not only responsible for the Royal Air Force but was also the agent for the Combined Chiefs of Staff for the conduct of the strategic bombers until they might be placed under the Supreme Commander. Portal had already relinquished operational control of the forces commanded by Leigh-Mallory. These two officers, therefore, discharged in the United Kingdom the duties I had fulfilled in the Mediterranean.

The Chiefs of Staff agreed entirely with Churchill that I should not be an officer without portfolio and conceived that I should exercise authority over all three Services. They realised that the existence of a Deputy Supreme Commander would make difficult Bedell Smith's position as Chief of Staff. This factor, they thought, explained his attitude and they reminded Churchill that I had been asked for by the Americans, not as a substitute for Leigh-Mallory, but as a Deputy to Eisenhower. I should advise the Supreme Commander on the air aspects of the 'Overlord' plan, should speak in Eisenhower's name to his subordinates on air subjects, and listen to their views. The Chiefs of Staff, like Sinclair, did not contemplate that the Strategic Forces should pass under Eisenhower's command, lock, stock, and barrel.

Churchill agreed at once that this discussion concerned only the forces that had been definitely handed over. The rest would remain under the control of Portal and the Chiefs of Staff. Nevertheless:

I do not know that Tedder is any great authority on war in general, and certainly not in the use of armies and fleets. He has, however, proved himself a master in the use of the Air Force, and this is the task I hoped he would have assigned to him by the Supreme Commander in the same way as Alexander was entrusted with fighting the land battles in Sicily and Italy. As Tedder is only to be a sort of floating kidney, we shall be wasting him and putting more on Leigh-Mallory than in my opinion he can carry.

The Prime Minister said that he felt sure that Eisenhower would raise these matters as soon as he took over. He did. Eisenhower and I had many talks over the problems ahead. As far as I can remember, the point that worried him most was what his relations were going to be with Harris. Harris was by way of being something of a dictator who had very much the reputation of not taking kindly to directions from outside his own command. Eisenhower saw rocks ahead. Bomber Command had a tremendous and greatly responsible role to play in 'Overlord'. If Harris chose to be 'difficult' in his relationships with the Air Ministry, there might well be endless scope for friction. I did my best to reassure Eisenhower by telling him that I was quite certain that if Harris were given specific orders to carry out specific jobs, he would do them loyally. I realised that in giving such a guarantee, I was taking a chance which many people would not have risked, but as events turned out, my estimate of Bomber Command's work, and of its commander, proved to be correct.

*

We had to decide, and promptly, by what methods our air strength could contribute most surely to the re-establishment of the Allied armies in France. To put the matter in its broadest terms, there were two types of target for air attack, point targets and common denominators. Examples of the first category were aluminium plants, ball-bearing plants, molybdenum mines or army headquarters, points from which crucial operations were controlled, or at which vital industries could profitably be attacked. Such targets were tartly dismissed by Sir Arthur Harris as 'panaceas'. Common denominator targets were railways, canals, power plants, oil; that is, targets which were geographically dispersed, the destruction of which would cumulatively affect the whole war situation.

In 1940 the targets laid down for Bomber Command were marshalling yards and oil plants. Unfortunately, our action was so ineffective in attacking these targets that Hamm, one of the biggest railway centres in northern Europe, became a music hall joke. Bomber Command at that time had in fact neither the means nor the technique to attack those targets effectively, and German cities became the main targets for the bomber offensive. In their endeavour to select objectives which could be effectively dealt with, a number of new directives succeeded each other until the Casablanca Conference of 1943, out of which was developed a completely new directive: Our growing bomber force was 'to secure the progressive destruction and dislocation of the German military, industrial, and economic system, and the undermining of the morale of the German people to a point where their capacity for armed resistance is fatally weakened.' This directive was nothing if not comprehensive, and allowed unlimited scope for our differences of interpretation.

While the campaign was being fought out in the Mediterranean the Allied bombers delivered massive attacks on the enemy's towns on a scale hitherto unknown. That these attacks produced severe effects upon the enemy was not disputed. We had now to decide whether the continuation of such attacks would produce by May or June the conditions in which 'Overlord' could be successful, or whether a change of policy would bring us a more substantial dividend. In this respect, the experiences of the Mediterranean campaign provided fresh evidence. At my invitation, Professor Zuckerman had followed his investigations into the bombing of Pantelleria with a detailed analysis of the results produced by air attack on enemy communications in Sicily and Southern Italy. Zuckerman's report showed that planned assaults on a limited number of railway centres had virtually paralysed the system, and the best method of destroying this means of communication was the strategical rather than the tactical method. The most effective course was to destroy repair facilities by heavy bombing of railway centres. It was thought that attempts by tactical air action to achieve an immediate dislocation of movement by rail was unlikely to prove worthwhile except in the battle area. Attacks on rolling stock and locomotives were held to be valuable, but less valuable than the destruction of repair facilities. Only in special circumstances was it thought worthwhile to bomb tunnels or isolated stretches of railway line. All this was well enough; but it did not necessarily help us to decide bombing priorities in the next few months. My experience in the Mediterranean had convinced me of the high value of rail communications as a target for air attack. Moreover, I had complete confidence in Zuckerman's knowledge and judgment. I recognised that there were certain dangers in applying the lessons learnt in North Africa and Italy to the different conditions in northern France, Belgium, Holland, and Germany. Nevertheless, I felt that there

[503]

must be much in the way of the basic principles of railway operations which are of general application, and I therefore suggested to C.A.S. that he get Zuckerman home and put him in touch with the Planners in London.

Meanwhile, the task of planning for 'Overlord' was going steadily forward. The Air Plan, as developed in the summer of 1943, laid down three phases of activity. The first would be the continuation of strategic bombing of Germany, especially of the German aircraft industry; the second phase would be the bombing of targets closely linked with the invasion, especially railway centres, coastal defence installations, harbours, and airfields; the third phase would be direct assistance to the invading ground forces.

Although Leigh-Mallory had, in November, assumed control of the two Tactical Air Forces, by January it was apparent that the scale of air effort needed before and after the 'Overlord' landings would be far beyond the capacity of these forces alone to provide. The Strategic Air Forces must be brought in. As expected, Air Chief Marshal Harris showed himself by no means enthusiastic. Early in the New Year, he stated in writing that the only efficient support which Bomber Command could give to 'Overlord' was the intensification of attacks on industrial centres in Germany. To substitute for this process attacks on other targets such as gun emplacements, beach defences, communications or dumps, would be to

... commit the irremediable error of diverting our best weapon from the military function for which it has been equipped and trained to tasks which it cannot effectively carry out. Though this might give a specious appearance of supporting the Army, in reality it would be the greatest disservice we could do them. It would lead directly to disaster.

This clear-cut opinion was, broadly speaking, shared by General Spaatz, who had just assumed command of the U.S. Strategic Air Forces in Europe.

Not a very promising welcome!

*

It was at this point that Eisenhower, Montgomery, Bedell Smith, and I arrived in London from the Mediterranean. We began at once to study the plans for 'Overlord'. On 21 January 1944, we foregathered at Norfolk House under Eisenhower's chairmanship to compare our impressions. Montgomery, who was to command all the ground forces in the initial stages of 'Overlord', said at once that the planned assault by three divisions was insufficient to obtain a quick success. We must take a port at the earliest possible moment. He pressed that the proposed area of assault in Normandy be extended to include an area of the eastern side of the Cotentin Peninsula. The American forces should be placed to the right and the British to the left, the former to capture Cherbourg, and then drive for the Loire ports, while the British and Canadian forces would deal with the enemy's main strength approaching from the east and south-east. Montgomery thought that we should concentrate on gaining quick control of the main centres of road communication, and should then push our armoured formations deeply between and beyond those centres and deploy them on suitable ground. In this way we should make it difficult for the enemy to bring up his reserves and get them past these armoured formations. He suggested an assault by five divisions, plus one airborne division. The area from Bayeux to the east should be British, and to the west should be American. He confirmed that the air forces should cripple military movement by rail within a radius of 150 miles during the first three weeks of the operation.

Eisenhower agreed with Montgomery that the assault should be strengthened and that Cherbourg should be taken rapidly. He did not want to eliminate the 'Anvil' attack upon southern France unless it were essential. Eisenhower felt that we must not recommend that 'Anvil' be reduced to a mere threat unless we were convinced that 'Overlord' could not otherwise be successfully mounted. He thought, too, that the Combined Chiefs of Staff should not lay down too exact a charter in the arrangements for command. He proposed that Montgomery should be left in sole charge of the ground battle. As long as there was a Tactical Air Force Commander, there must also be a single Ground Commander, and the two must always be together. I was glad to hear so firm an enunciation of the method we had tried and proved in the Mediterranean.

The desire to land on a five-division front presented obvious difficulties. Admiral Ramsay, who had been designated Naval Commander-in-Chief, said that the original plan had been largely satisfactory from his point of view, except that he had doubted the success of the floating 'Mulberry' harbours. According to the plan, two artificial ports had to be completed within seven days. This involved tugging across the Channel more than a million tons of material. Montgomery's new proposal would involve the creation of two more assault forces to lift the additional divisions. Serious congestion would be caused along the south coast, and a good target for enemy bombing or for 'V' weapons would be presented. The two additional assault forces would be late in arriving and late in starting their training. Under the three-division plan, the assault forces would be placed on the central south coast and could sail on a weather forecast of only twenty-four hours. If there were to be five naval assault forces, they must extend as far to the west as Falmouth, whence they would have to sail on a sixty-hour forecast. The additional lift in assault shipping and craft could not be provided in full in May, even if 'Anvil' were postponed, but if 'Overlord' took place in early June the position would be easier.

Leigh-Mallory explained that the air battle had already started. According to his Intelligence, operations against the German Air Force, which went under the code name 'Pointblank', had already caused German fighter production to fall to some 600 per month instead of the 1,000 to 1,500 planned. Nevertheless, the decisive battle in the air would probably not take place until the day of our assault. Then we would fight for air superiority and be likely to achieve it.

For the moment, we had to decide when we should start bombing for 'Overlord' and which targets we should attack. The new plan, based on my Mediterranean experience, was to paralyse the railways by systematic attack on railway centres, and came to be known as the Transportation Plan. This plan was to run like a thread through all the operations up to the end of the war; true, sometimes a very tangled thread—tangled sometimes by deliberate intrigue and sometimes by ignorance and misunderstanding.

Although there were only another three months or so of the pre-'Overlord' period, the situation in London in the middle of February was confused, to say the least. The Prime Minister, the War Cabinet, and the Chiefs of Staff had not yet decided who was to control which portions of which Air Forces, let alone upon what targets these Air Forces should be directed. No agreed bombing policy for the pre-'Overlord' period had been decided, and neither of the bomber commanders, Harris or Spaatz, believed in the Transportation Plan. Leigh-Mallory and I were however putting our weight behind it, although earlier he had been opposed to it.

To bring the Strategic Bomber Forces into the pre-'Overlord' operations, which Leigh-Mallory and I agreed was essential, would mark a transition in the history of Allied air-power. As bomber techniques had improved, the bomber forces had developed a role virtually independent of the Army, the Navy, and the other Air Forces. Until the last days of 1943, the strategic bombers provided the only means by which we could strike heavily at Germany itself. Now we faced the position that unless this comparatively independent role were partially abandoned, 'Overlord', at least in the opinion of those responsible for its planning, could not succeed.

It was still not certain when the operation would take place. Montgomery and the Army planners favoured early May. Early June, however, was the last date at which we could undertake the operation if we were to have any reasonable period of good campaigning weather before the winter set in. In the middle of February Portal and I attended a meeting convened by Leigh-Mallory. Both Harris and Spaatz were present. They thought the Transportation Plan mistaken. They preferred full concentration upon 'Pointblank', the destruction of the German Air Force, which might then be accomplished, or so they thought, before D-Day. We were now evidently approaching the point where 'Pointblank' must be 'married' with 'Overlord'—in other words, the pre-'Overlord' bombing to be carried out by the heavy bombers would take the place of the 'Pointblank' bombing. Spaatz suggested that it would be worthwhile to 'formalise' the committee which was producing the pre-'Overlord' bombing

[507]

plan. Portal agreed, and pointed out that if it were at all possible, the interested parties should come to an agreement amongst themselves before proposals were tabled with the Combined Chiefs of Staff. He suggested that we should get the approval of the Combined Chiefs of Staff for this committeee, with instructions to recommend how pre-'Overlord' requirements could be fitted in with the execution of 'Pointblank'.

This request gave me an opportunity to place before the C.A.S. my deepening doubts about the system by which we were trying to arrive at a decision, and on 22 February I wrote to Portal:

I am afraid that having started as a confirmed optimist I am steadily losing my optimism as to how this is all going to work out. The immediate cause of my loss of optimism is the fact that the examination of plans by the various component parts of the so-called 'Committee' has shown no signs so far of producing any constructive results. I am more and more being forced to the unfortunate conclusion that the two strategic forces are determined not to play. Spaatz has made it abundantly clear that he will not accept orders, or even co-ordination, from Leigh-Mallory, and the only sign of activity from Harris's representatives has been a series of adjustments to the records of their past bombing statistics, with the evident intention of demonstrating that they are quite unequipped and untrained to do anything except mass fire-raising on very large targets.

It was not my habit to take alarm easily, but I was really worried about the present outlook both in respect of planning and of operations.

I do not think that a unified plan can be evolved by a number of independent committees, and I am quite certain that successful operations cannot result from control by committees. As I see it, one of the main lessons of the Mediterranean campaign was not merely the advisability of, but the necessity for, unified command of the Air Force. I know that is Eisenhower's view. I very much fear that if the British Chiefs of Staff and the P.M. are going to take up a position regarding Bomber Command which prevents that unified control, very serious issues will arise affecting Anglo-American co-operation in 'Overlord'. I think everybody in authority, both British and American, realises that it is going to be hard work for all concerned to maintain harmonious co-operation during this next job. A split on the question of the control of air forces might well, since the issues are very clear, precipitate a quite irremediable cleavage.

As I told Portal, I had discussed all these issues with Eisenhower, Spaatz, and Leigh-Mallory, naturally on the basis that the existing arrangements must be made to work. Three days after I sent my letter to Portal, the committee met to consider attacks on enemy rail communications. Leigh-Mallory presided. It was a thoroughly confused discussion, the Minutes of which ran to no less than forty-one printed pages. Critics of the Transportation Plan seemed to assume that we believed the enemy's railway system would be so dislocated as a result of preparatory attacks that the tactical battle would be directly affected. In fact, this was not the main point of the Plan. Our idea was not simply to prevent the Germans from moving ten divisions at the last minute, but to hamper their movement of divisions and the necessary large quantities of supply over a period of months. The railway experts at this meeting declared one and all that the attacks we proposed would cripple the railway system in northern France and Belgium, and that the crippling would become more and more effective as the campaign prolonged itself from weeks into months. Air Commodore Bufton, an habitual non-conformist, argued for the plan of blocking vital points around D-Day itself seemingly on the grounds that we could not rely either on weather or on bombing accuracy in the next couple of months, but could bank on both these factors around D-Day itself. To what extremes can nonconformity descend?

On 28 February, Zuckerman sent me another memorandum. He pointed out that at recent meetings some speakers had stated or implied that to divert effort from the bombing of German towns and industry, and in particular from 'Pointblank' targets, to the preparation for 'Overlord', would be a disaster or a major fallacy, in view of the critical effects which such attacks were already producing upon Germany. The U.S. Strategic Air Forces had been known to state the view that they only wanted another twenty or thirty clear operational days and they would finish the war on their own. We also knew from the frequent pronouncements of Harris and others that Bomber Command believed that what it was achieving deep in the heart of Germany would in time also prove to be the winning factor. 'All this', Zuckerman commented, 'is to some extent justified optimism, and might prove to be in fact true. From our point of view, however, the vital factor is time.'

There could be no question that at one stage in the operation the relative rates of our own and the enemy's build-up may have been a more important factor than gaining a few more degrees of air superiority. There was available a vast mass of evidence about the results of air attacks on Germany between March and December 1943. Zuckerman carried out a thorough and careful survey of the events and came to the conclusion that it was unlikely that when all allowances were made we should achieve in the three-months' period March to May 1944, more than a 7 per cent reduction in the enemy's over-all output. Further, he did not believe that German morale would break as a result of bombing in the next three months.

On 29 February, the Prime Minister intervened on the subject of the organisation arranged for 'Overlord' with which, as he had expected, Eisenhower was not satisfied, and on which he made a most un-Churchillian comment: 'Its structure is certainly awkward-looking.' Mr. Churchill knew that no plan for the support of 'Overlord' had yet been agreed upon by the various air authorities. To bring the matter to a decision, he set down the arrangements he had had in mind throughout. Eisenhower should be Supreme Commander of all the 'Overlord' forces. I should be the 'Aviation Lobe' of Eisenhower's brain. My directive should be 'to use all air forces permanently or temporarily assigned to "Overlord" in the manner which will best fulfil the plan of the Supreme Commander.' In my own right, and as Deputy Supreme Commander, I should be responsible for making an air plan satisfactory to Eisenhower. I must have a suitable staff and the use of the services of the R.A.F. Headquarters staff under Leigh-Mallory. In practice, Leigh-Mallory would execute orders he received from me in Eisenhower's name, whether to prepare plans or to carry them out. I should also, as Deputy Supreme Commander, be empowered to issue orders to Spaatz, Harris, and Sholto Douglas (who had now moved to Coastal Command), in respect of any employment of their forces for 'Overlord' which the Combined Chiefs of Staff had sanctioned. As soon as my plan had been approved by Eisenhower, it would be submitted to the Combined Chiefs of Staff who would do their best to meet its requirements and specify what air forces should be placed at Eisenhower's disposal, and for how long. Churchill ruled:

There can be no question of handing over the British Bomber, Fighter or Coastal Commands as a whole to the Supreme Commander and his Deputy. These Commands have other functions which they discharge under the direction of the C.A.S. .... Agreeably with the plan of the Supreme Command, we shall assign to 'Overlord' such use of these three commands as we may think fit after consultation and in agreement with the United States Chiefs-of-Staff. The Combined Chiefs-of-Staff retain the right to vary the assignments should overriding circumstances render it necessary.

However, the 'Overlord' battle must be the chief care of all concerned, and great risks must be run in every other sphere and theatre in order that nothing should be withheld which could contribute to its success.

It appeared that the Prime Minister was very much disturbed at the idea that Leigh-Mallory should command the strategic forces. Eisenhower explained that he was hopefully waiting for a co-ordinated air plan upon which all could agree, and asked the Prime Minister to do nothing until we had a full chance to make the existing directive work. To Eisenhower, it seemed that Churchill was very impatient, but the Supreme Commander said that if he needed any help, which he did not anticipate, he would come promptly to the Prime Minister.

However [Eisenhower wrote to me] I hope you can push conferences and plans so that we can have an answer quickly. Otherwise the P.M. will be in this thing with both feet. I'm quite prepared, if necessary, to issue an order saying I will exert direct supervision of all air forces—through you—and authorising you to use Headquarters facilities now existing to make control effective. L.M's position would not be changed so far as *assigned* forces are concerned, but those *attached* for definite periods or definite jobs would not come under his *command*.

Churchill, however, had now brought these matters to a head.

The same day, 29 February 1944, the Prime Minister, Eisenhower, Bedell Smith, Portal, and Ismay considered the Minute. Eisenhower accepted that I should make the outline plans, and it was agreed that Harris, Spaatz, and Portal's representative should be at my disposal for this. Eisenhower demurred at anything short of complete operational control of the whole of Bomber Command and the American Strategic Forces. He did not, therefore, welcome Churchill's Minute entirely. He strongly objected to submitting his plan to the Combined Chiefs of Staff. Portal explained that the planning must be considered in two phases. In the first, the strategic bombers could execute the task allotted to them with a loose control and supervision by myself on Eisenhower's behalf. In the tactical phase, starting just before the landings, detailed control by the Supreme Commander would be essential. At least it now appeared that we should soon decide the structure of the Command. What seemed a good deal less certain was whether we should manage to agree on a bombing policy.

A day or two later Leigh-Mallory and his staff proposed a plan which would bring together Strategic and Tactical Air Forces. The 'Pointblank' attacks upon the German Air Force would continue, while enemy communications would be disrupted by assaults on railway centres, and later by the cutting of lines supplying the Normandy area. The objects were to deny air support to the German Army, make it the more vulnerable to our attack from the air, and at the crucial moment of the landing to render the enemy immobile in 'a railway desert'. Neither Spaatz nor Harris approved. Spaatz was especially keen to attack German oil and petrol supplies, for which policy there was indeed a good deal to be said; while Harris would not give up without a struggle the area bombing of German towns. He argued that operational factors made it impossible to accomplish the high-precision bombing of railway centres—oblivious of the fact that at least one Group in his Command was already carrying out precision attacks with great success—and that a relaxation of the attacks on Germany would permit recovery and undo much of the work of the previous two years. Leigh-Mallory sent to the Air Ministry a list of targets which he wished the British bombers to attack.

Most of these were not approved, so Leigh-Mallory put the question before Eisenhower, who in turn passed it to the British Chiefs of Staff. They deputed Portal to examine the whole matter.

Meanwhile, Portal had proposed at the end of February that the practicability of attack on railway centres should be put to the test. A week later, on the night of 6 March, the railway centre at Trappes was devastated by Bomber Command. Not for a month did this centre function again properly. Other yards were quickly attacked in succession. The results showed beyond peradventure that Harris had underestimated the skill of his crews. The Transportation Plan was shown to be feasible. Here was a development of the highest importance, and coming at exactly the right moment. Our capacity to undertake precision bombing, purchased at grim cost, now made it possible for us to advocate with confidence a programme which entirely depended on the accurate delivery of bombs. Once this was understood, the complexities became less hard to resolve. The main question would be one of timing. It was accepted by Spaatz and Harris that immediately before and after the battle their forces must be devoted to the success of 'Overlord'. Leigh-Mallory and I argued, on the other hand, that paralysis of the French railway system could not be achieved in a week or two. Unless we did the job properly, there would be little advantage in trying to do it at all; and if we did decide on the Transportation Plan, it must be carried out with our full resources. Even though the alternative was heavy damage to the German synthetic oil plants, that could not vitally affect the enemy's efforts in time for 'Overlord'.

During the first ten days of March I saw or spoke with Portal almost every day as he struggled to reconcile the difference between Eisenhower's wish for complete control of the heavy bombers and the Prime Minister's ruling that Bomber, Fighter, and Coastal Commands could not be handed over as a whole to Eisenhower or to me. Eisenhower recognised that reservations would in practice exist upon the power of any commander, whether called 'Supreme' or not. It would always be possible for the Combined Chiefs of Staff to impose additional tasks, and for the British Chiefs of Staff to act independently in the case of an unforeseen emergency concerning the safety of Great Britain. The Supreme Commander wished to see such reservations included, and his agreement with them noted in the records; but he did not want to put them in the specific directive to the Supreme Commander. I put these arguments to the C.A.S. on 9 March. He seemed willing to accept them. With Eisenhower's agreement, Portal therefore minuted to the Prime Minister on 10 March that the strategic air plan for 'Overlord' was now in my hands as Eisenhower's agent. I was dealing with Spaatz and Harris over their parts in the plan. It was Eisenhower's intention, with which Portal agreed, that the co-ordination of operations for the strategic plan should be under my control, with such reference to Eisenhower as he desired. The tactical plan around the D-Day assault involving the use of all air forces assigned to 'Overlord', including strategic bombers, coastal aircraft, and the Fleet Air Arm contingent, would be prepared and co-ordinated by Leigh-Mallory under my supervision. Portal wrote to Mr. Churchill:

Neither General Eisenhower nor I consider that the assignment of strategic bombers for the purpose of executing either plan . . . can be made on the basis of allocating a proportion of the forces, or of their effort, to him.

Rather, he went on, it was now intended to continue 'Pointblank' in parallel with other air operations more directly aimed at the support of 'Overlord'. The plans themselves must regulate the proportion of total effort absorbed by each task. The Combined Chiefs of Staff should therefore be asked to assign to Eisenhower such use of the strategic bombers as might be necessary to execute the 'Overlord' and 'Pointblank' plans, retaining the right to impose additional tasks. If these plans were approved, the effect would be that between dates to be decided by the Combined Chiefs of Staff, both the Strategic Bomber Forces would be at the operational disposal of Eisenhower for the purposes of the strategic and tactical plans. Once 'Overlord' was established on the Continent, the directive for employment of the Strategic Bomber Forces would be reviewed.

Mr. Churchill minuted: 'I think this is very satisfactory.'

The proposals were put to the Combined Chiefs of Staff in a

signal of 13 March, which pointed out that air operations in support of 'Overlord' were being planned, and that some preparatory operations were already in progress as a corollary to 'Pointblank'. Shortly, 'Overlord' must take precedence over 'Pointblank'. It was proposed that when Portal and Eisenhower approved the air programme, the responsibility for supervising air operations out of Great Britain of all forces engaged in the programme, together with any other air forces that might be made available, should devolve upon Eisenhower. The Strategic Air Forces were only to come under Eisenhower's direction when a plan for the air support of 'Overlord' had been approved. Even though the question was now becoming so urgent, this day still appeared to be somewhat distant.

I agree with Montgomery on priorities–Oil v. Transportation–
War Office opposition–Arguments on casualties amongst French
civilians–Portal's views on air attack on communications–Bufton the
non-conformist–More controversy over possible casualties–Reference to
Roosevelt–Decision after three months–Defence Committee Meetings and Chiefs
of Staff

2

WHEN the principal 'Overlord' commanders met on 10
March 1944, there appeared to be general agreement
that the best methods of employing our Strategic Air
Forces in those three months before D-Day would be first the
destruction of the German Air Force as laid down in 'Pointblank', and secondly the disruption of the French transportation
system. Within a couple of days of that meeting, two memoranda
had been circulated, one from the U.S. Air Force and one from the
Air Ministry, both of them largely occupied in erecting 'Aunt
Sallies'. The case against the Transportation Plan rested on two
main planks—neither of them being in accord with the facts.
The first proposition was that the French and Belgian railway
systems were by no means fully stretched, and that their ability
to repair was virtually unlimited. The second proposition was that
the essential military traffic in Northern France represented only a
small percentage of the existing traffic, and that, therefore, only
a small proportion of the railway system need be kept in working
order. On the former point, there had evidently been a complete
failure to appreciate the intensity, variety and far-reaching
nature of damage caused by a serious attack on an important
railway centre. As for the latter point, it was stated in the American
paper that military traffic in Axis Europe would not at its maximum be more than one-fifth of the total traffic. On the American
plan I felt

... that the German Air Force (which should include the bomber aircraft production) should remain as absolute first priority. I am frankly
sceptical of the oil plan, partly because we have been led up that garden
path before, partly because the targets are in difficult areas (six of them
in the Ruhr, where we have been assured that the Americans could not
do precision bombing on railway targets because of flak and smoke, and
the most important ones in the areas south and southwest of Berlin,

where penetration is most difficult), and partly because I am not sure as to the real vulnerability of the new synthetic oil plants, where the enemy has presumably taken immense precautions against an air attack by means of dispersal, protection, etc. I am even less impressed by the arguments advanced for the tank targets as a help for 'Overlord'.

Portal, while refusing at this stage to take sides in the controversy, fully agreed with me that the German Air Force should remain an absolute priority. He was not at all sure that we should not find that to wipe out the German Air Force would take the whole available Strategic Bomber effort, and that if this could be done we should not have an 'Overlord' operation to tackle but something on the lines of a police operation, where swift mobile columns could readily penetrate and subdue a tottering Nazi empire. Even if this latter assumption were not true, Portal doubted whether the Germans could stage an effective counter-attack against 'Overlord' if their air force had been wiped out beforehand.

I felt a good deal less sanguine than did the C.A.S. about the possibility of knocking out the German Air Force in time. In any case, I was sure that any such policy was too much of a gamble. We were now approaching the end of March. D-Day was to be at the beginning of June. We could not stake everything on attacking the German Air Force at this late date.

General Montgomery asked that before D-Day the air forces should try to knock out the enemy air force, to destroy and disrupt communications so as to impose delay on enemy movement towards the landing ground, to mislead the enemy as to the real point of attack, and to assault such targets as coastal batteries and oil installations. This order of priorities accorded very much with my own views. I had by now received from the Joint Intelligence Committee a document on enemy rail movements which, if accepted, would have ruled out the dislocation which the Army commanders demanded. The paper made two main assumptions; first, that essential military movements by rail could be cut down to an extremely low figure, and second, that all other rail movement could be dispensed with indefinitely. The enemy was estimated, for no apparent reason, to possess some two months' stocks ready for intensive operations. The movement

[517]

of traffic for the enemy forces in the Normandy area, however, certainly did not suggest that the Germans felt able to sit back with ample stocks. We knew, from reconnaissance and from Intelligence sources, that the enemy's road and rail transport was already strained. We also knew beyond doubt that the enemy hoped he might be able to keep open the three main routes from the east by manning those routes entirely with German personnel. The Joint Intelligence Committee, like the Intelligence section of the Air Ministry and General Spaatz's staff, failed to appreciate how complex an organisation is a railway system, and how air-power's main characteristic, its flexibility, made it possible to retain the initiative. I was also surprised to find in this document an estimate for the German Air Force's required supplies around D-Day which was considerably less than they were already receiving. The whole basis of the figures, as I told Portal at once, seemed to me academically unrealistic. To talk of military traffic in a strictly limited way was quite misleading. Moreover:

If the country in which an army is operating is not kept alive, it will itself become a heavy commitment on that army. Neptune area [Normandy] is not self-supporting, and I am certain the Hun cannot afford to turn off the tap. Incidentally, in all these calculations the J.I.C. make no allowance whatever for any transverse traffic, either of military or para-military needs.

Against such calculations we had to put concrete evidence already obtained after attacks on railway centres. A comparatively light assault on Tergnier had resulted in a seven days' delay in the movement southwards of an S.S. division. At Amiens, the strong attack on the night of 15/16 March brought railway working to a complete standstill. A week later, access to the marshalling yard was still barred. On the night of 23 March a strong attack on Creil laid both the engine sheds flat. Both lines to Paris and the lines to Beauvais were cut at least twenty times. The attack on the night of 13/14 March at Le Mans proved so effective that ten days later normal operation was still suspended and only 50 per cent. of the sidings had been repaired. The attack at Trappes had caused the immobilisation of some sixty loco-motives, and even at the end of March only one half of the marshalling yard was available for traffic. At that time, nearly a month after the original attack, the standards carrying the electric cables over the main line had still not been re-erected, although the line was open for steam working. All these results had been secured by bombing of a comparatively unplanned nature.

We had now reached the point where, if the Transportation Plan were to have a chance of success at all, the issue must be decided. On 24 March I sent to Portal a memorandum on the employment of the Allied Air Forces in support of 'Overlord'. I recounted General Montgomery's requirements, to which Operation 'Pointblank' was already making an essential and direct contribution. Moreover, it was sapping the enemy's general and industrial strength, and on all counts should continue. What was now required was an adjustment of 'Pointblank'. We could only derive full value from our immense air-power, our strongest single asset, if this target system were based

... on one common object towards which all the available air forces can be directed. We would waste much of our power if the U.S. Strategic Air Forces were to operate against one system of objectives, Bomber Command against another, and the A.E.A.F. against yet another. Concentration against one common system, by both day and night, is essential.

The choice lay between Spaatz's Oil Plan and the Transportation Plan. No one could doubt that in view of the proved ability of the American Strategic Forces to carry out precision bombing deep in Germany the Oil Plan would ultimately produce grave effects on the whole German war effort. I did not think, however, that such effects would be produced in time.

On 25 March there was, I had hoped, to be the crucial meeting with the final decisions. Unfortunately, although the military decision was made it proved only to be the first of a series of hard-fought verbal battles, and at which one was severely handicapped by the fact that most of those taking part in the discussions were, naturally enough, totally ignorant of the complexities of railway working. Portal said he felt sure that everyone agreed that the execution of the Plan would have a most serious effect on the efficiency of the enemy's railway system.

We must, however, be certain that what remained would not be adequate for the amount of movement which the enemy would find necessary in the first few weeks after the landings. A long discussion followed. Eisenhower supported the Plan, saying that in his view the question for a decision was this; the first five or six weeks of 'Overlord' would be a most critical period for our armies, and we must take every possible step to make sure that they got ashore and stayed there. The greatest contribution that he could imagine the air forces making to this was that they should hinder the enemy's movement. If the preparatory bombing held out hopes that enemy movement would be hampered, he thought it would be worthwhile. In default of any alternative plan which would produce greater results, or even equal results, he thought the Transportation Plan should be adopted.

General Kennedy of the War Office (Intelligence) agreed with Eisenhower's diagnosis of the problem, but said he thought that his prescription was wrong. Kennedy thought that since frequent and heavy attacks on railway targets in Italy had not produced a significant interference with strategic movement there, it was doubtful whether this method would produce any better results in France. The War Office put forward an extraordinary proposal that the policy should be rather to concentrate on delaying enemy movements after 'Overlord'. They also felt that a less ambitious plan was called for, a plan aimed at a smaller area and carried out shortly before D-Day. Kennedy thought the plan should be re-examined in consultation with the War Office experts on the working of military railways. This aroused Eisenhower, who again weighed in to the effect that all he had read had convinced him that apart from the attack on the German Air Force, only the Transportation Plan offered the air forces a reasonable chance of making an important contribution to the land battle in the first vital weeks after the landing. He agreed that the War Office Staff should be consulted, but added that in his view it was only necessary 'to show that there would be some reduction, however small, in military movement to justify adopting the plan, provided that there were no alternative available.'

Spaatz argued his familiar case about oil, but had to admit, when questioned by Portal, that there would be no noticeable effect until four or five months after putting the plan into action. Harris doubted whether there was time for him to complete his programme now in the short period remaining. He wanted to continue attacking cities in Eastern Germany as long as the hours of darkness made it possible. He also raised the question of high casualties. Portal put the point to Churchill in a Minute a few days later:

> In the execution of this Plan very heavy casualties among civilians living near the main railway centres in occupied territory will be unavoidable, however careful we may be over the actual bombing. Eisenhower realises this and I understand that he is going to propose that warnings should be issued to all civilians living near railway centres advising them to move. I hope you will agree that since the requirements of 'Overlord' are paramount, the Plan must go ahead after due warning has been given.[1]

At long last a decision on the bombing plan was arrived at on a military level. Eisenhower's authority as Supreme Commander, coupled with his definite view of the most valuable contribution which air-power could make, virtually settled the matter. It was also clear that the C.A.S. now thought that the Transportation Plan offered more prospect of success than any other.

It now went before the War Cabinet with a list of more than seventy railway targets in France and Belgium. The Bomber Command estimate of high civilian casualties, perhaps between 80,000 and 160,000, caused the Cabinet on 3 April to take an adverse view. It was decided that the Defence Committee must consider the matter later that week. The Cabinet feared that to inflict death and injury upon scores of thousands of friendly civilians might bring much hatred upon the Allied Air Forces. The Ministers were by no means convinced that the military advantages would outweigh the obvious political drawbacks. 'The argument for concentration on these particular targets', Churchill wrote to Eisenhower, 'is very nicely balanced on military grounds.'

[1] Ehrman: *Grand Strategy,* vol. V, p. 297.

Eisenhower consulted me about his reply. We fully understood that the weight of argument which had been brought against the bombing of railway centres in occupied territory was, indeed, heavy, but in our view other considerations were even weightier:

We must never forget that one of the fundamental factors leading to the decision for undertaking 'Overlord' was the conviction that our overpowering Air Force would make feasible an operation which might otherwise be considered extremely hazardous, if not foolhardy. . . . I and my military advisers have become convinced that the bombing of these centres will increase our chances for success in the critical battle, and unless this could be proved to be an erroneous conclusion, I do not see how we can fail to proceed with the programme. I admit that warnings will probably do very little in evacuating people from the points we intend to hit. On the other hand I personally believe that estimates of probable casualties have been grossly exaggerated.

The French people are now slaves. Only a successful 'Overlord' can free them. No one has a greater stake in the success of that operation than have the French. . . . I think it would be sheer folly to abstain from doing anything that can increase in any measure our chances for success in 'Overlord.'

Eisenhower had understood from a recent conversation with Churchill that it was intended to invite General de Gaulle to come to London soon. The Supreme Commander thought that the General should be able to explain the matter to the French nation in such a way that they would accept these bombings as a necessary sacrifice. This note went to the Prime Minister on 5 April. That night I attended the first of a series of meetings, lasting over the next month, at which the fate of the Transportation Plan was decided. We foregathered at 10.30 p.m. in the Defence Map Room, two floors below ground, in the Cabinet Offices. The Prime Minister presided. My memorandum, asking for permission to attack railway centres, had been circulated in advance, together with the report on probable reactions of French and Belgian opinion. Churchill said that even if rail communications were essential, he was not convinced that the effects which would be achieved by attacks on rail centres would justify the slaughtering of masses of friendly French allies who were burning to help us when the day came, and who showed their friendly feelings by giving unstinted help to our airmen forced down among them. He did not say that we should not bomb the railways, but before we did so we must be convinced that the advantages counted for more than the political drawbacks.

Portal said that though he had formerly been against the Plan, he had been so impressed after discussing with me and with Zuckerman the results achieved by bombing in the Mediterranean campaign, that he had told Leigh-Mallory to study the possibilities of such attacks for 'Overlord'. He suggested that if the railways were sufficiently dislocated to delay even by one week the arrival of, say, nine divisions, this might well turn the scales. I said that all my experience had convinced me of the value of systematic air attack on communications. Everything that I had heard since returning home had confirmed the view that the lessons learned in North Africa were applicable to 'Overlord'. As regards the French railway system, there were indications that it was far from being in a sound condition, and as for the effect on French morale, we had already received from French railway personnel details of the results of the attacks. In many instances these reports even suggested other railway centres which could profitably be attacked. Air Commodore Bufton argued that good results under the present Plan could only be achieved in clear weather, and suitable opportunities were not therefore very numerous. He would prefer to direct the effort against targets which would produce a definite effect on the efficiency of the German Air Force. Large training centres and ammunition dumps were another possible target. In this way the bomber forces could be occupied until they were needed for the tactical plan of cutting certain key communications.

Portal observed that he had at first agreed with Bufton's views, but as a result of testing the soundness of the Transportation Plan he now felt strongly that there was no suitable alternative and no other one comparable. The estimate of the number of civilian casualties had been made by the Operational Research section at Bomber Command and was based on a number of false premises. No allowance, for instance, had been made for any move of the population away from the target areas, and it had been assumed that all the bombs carried on unsuccessful missions would cause civilian casualties. Moreover, the total number of casualties estimated included even those slightly injured.

The C.I.G.S., Sir Alan Brooke, doubted if the success we were likely to achieve would justify the effort. Until 'Overlord' was launched, he felt that attacks would be better concentrated on the German Air Force. Sir Andrew Cunningham, however, said in his usual forthright way that there seemed to be no doubt that attacks on railways on the scale we contemplated would make a material contribution to 'Overlord'. He knew of no worthwhile alternative, and favoured the attack provided that warning was given to the civilian population. By this time most of the Ministers had weighed in against the Plan, though the grounds of their opposition varied. The Foreign Secretary, Mr. Eden, thought that the attacks would be a different matter if carried out in the heat of battle, but if launched well in advance of 'Overlord' would be of very great value to enemy propaganda, and would produce a grave effect on French and Belgian public opinion. After the war, he said, we should have to live in a Europe which was already looking to Russia more than he would wish. He thought that the road system of France would be almost adequate to support the relatively small enemy forces which would be put against 'Overlord', and that targets like camps and dumps would be more attractive than railway centres.[1]

Sinclair, however, argued on the same lines as Portal. No one had suggested a better plan, but the deciding factor should be the soldiers' opinion. If they thought that the destruction of communications would be a valuable contribution to 'Overlord', the political implications should be faced. The Prime Minister again suggested that oil targets should be attacked. Portal pointed out at once that if there were no 'Overlord' then he would agree that oil was the right target, but since the enemy had in France sufficient stocks of oil to sustain operations for some months, the loss of the Rumanian oilfields would not affect 'Overlord'. Once 'Overlord' was assured, oil would be the right objective.

[1] Avon: *The Eden Memoirs: The Reckoning,* pp. 448–9.

After some hours of discussion on these lines, Churchill said he did not propose that we should arrive at a firm decision that night. I should talk over the matter with Eisenhower in the light of what had been said, and should consider whether the Plan could be revised to exclude those targets where the risk to the civilian population was greatest.

By 12 April I was able to tell Portal that we had done this, although it might still be necessary to attack them at the time of the assault. A revised estimate of casualties likely to be inflicted in all attacks, including those in southern France, and based on experience in Great Britain and in the Mediterranean, showed a total of about 16,000 killed and injured. This figure made no allowance for evacuation which at home and in the Mediterranean had mounted to at least 50 per cent. of the population. The casualties announced by Vichy sources for attacks just carried out near Paris and Lille were 148 and 156 killed, compared with our estimates of 420 and 500 respectively. I wrote to Portal:

I must emphasise that the systematic execution of this plan and the progressive dislocation of the enemy controlled railway system which is its object, are essential preliminaries to the actual assault. Only if the railway system feeding the Neptune area has already been gravely disorganised, can we hope, at the time of the assault, effectively to interfere with the enemy's movement and concentration, and so gain the time which will be a vital factor in the opening phase of the campaign.

In a memorandum to the War Cabinet, Portal repeated the terms of my paper, and recommended the adoption of the new plan. At 10.30 p.m. on the 13th, the Defence Committee foregathered again in the Map Room. Portal told Churchill that according to our present information 549 civilians had been killed and 873 injured in eleven out of thirteen attacks on French railway targets. This information was derived from Radio Paris or Vichy broadcasts, and the total of injured no doubt included the slightly injured. Vichy sources were unlikely to minimise casualties, and even according to them the number of killed had been less than half that estimated by us, showing either that our figures were on the high side, or possibly that evacuation had already started. The Prime Minister's remarks were largely on the lines of those he had made at the meeting on the 5th. He had always thought the first estimate of casualties exaggerated, and was prepared to accept the revised estimate; but he was still not convinced of the strategic merits of the plan, and did not think it would have a material effect on the battle.

In theory, it was possible for me to issue a directive to Spaatz and Harris, for Eisenhower had been granted powers to direct the Strategic Air Force. In practice, it was not easy to do so at once because of the War Cabinet's opinion. At a meeting under my chairmanship, held on 15 April, we were told that Churchill's formal approval had not yet been given for the issue of the directive. I objected to any further delay, and after a discussion we decided that Eisenhower would issue it without waiting for formal approval. We should add a paragraph to the effect that the political aspects of the plan would be kept under continuous supervision.

For the next few days, bad weather prevented any large-scale operations on transportation targets, but they were resumed on the night of 18 April with excellent results. The next night we met again at 10.30 to review the situation. Portal told the Defence Committee that casualties were smaller than had been estimated, and I said that we were receiving Intelligence to show that attacks on railway centres were already having considerable effect. For example, on 9 February 250 French trains had been detained in sidings. By 20 March, this figure had risen to 540.

The Prime Minister again wondered whether the military effects of the Transportation Plan would make the suffering worthwhile. He asked about the possibility of attacking synthetic oil plants. Portal and I repeated once again that this policy could not be expected to be effective in time for 'Overlord'. Several Ministers then said in effect that though they had no great belief in the plan we had better continue with it for another week and see what happened. Sinclair again argued doughtily in favour of the attacks on railway centres. He pointed out that a Vichy broadcast that very day had attacked Frenchmen for finding excuses for the Allied bomber crews, and had suggested that a number of them were regarding the fires in Paris as a 'torch of victory'.

[526]

Although the C.I.G.S. again pleaded for an early decision and said that he felt it would be fundamentally wrong to change the plan now, Churchill said that he did not think a firm decision could be taken at this point, though admitting that the longer a decision was deferred the stronger became the case for continuing the Transportation Plan. It was difficult to judge the efficacy of the policy. He still did not believe that it would prevent the enemy from moving his troops. The casualty rate might increase to such an extent that the plan would become politically quite impossible. We had therefore better meet and review it at the end of a further week. Meantime I had agreed with Spaatz that the U.S. Eighth Air Force should attack some oil targets in limited numbers. He had expressed to me some concern that the present attacks, even on German Air Force factories, were not bringing the Germans into the air. Since it was important to reduce the enemy's air strength before 'Overlord', we decided to see what effect would be produced by attack on a few oil targets. A little later I arranged with Harris that Bomber Command should also attack some oil targets when other more urgent tasks made it possible.

The Defence Committee met again on the night of 26 April with the Chiefs of Staff present. Eisenhower and I had gone to the west of England to see a rehearsal for the 'Overlord' landings. Air Vice Marshal Robb represented me. Zuckerman was also present. I gathered that the Prime Minister began by reading out a large number of memoranda which summarised broadcasts from Continental sources about our bombing of railways, and he argued again that we should build up a volume of dull hatred in France which would affect our relations with that country for many years to come. His concern would be less if he were convinced of the merits of the plan. Portal pointed out that Montgomery attached great importance to the enemy's tactical railway communications being attacked near the 'Overlord' date and that such attacks were scheduled to start some three weeks before D-Day. Even if it were decided to abandon the present policy, tactical attacks should be permitted in the period just before the assault.

Eventually, it was decided that the Prime Minister would put the whole question to the War Cabinet the next day. Meanwhile, Portal would prepare a list of railway centres where it was estimated that attacks would cause less than a hundred fatal casualties, while I was to be told to consider what alternative plan should be adopted if the present one were abandoned.

At the War Cabinet on the following day it was agreed that the Transportation Plan should now be revised to include attacks only on railway centres where the estimated casualties did not exceed 100 to 150. Meanwhile, Churchill would telegraph to Roosevelt after seeing Eisenhower. On 29 April the Supreme Commander received from the Prime Minister a note of the conclusions reached by the Cabinet on 27 April, together with a summary of the arguments which had weighed with them. These arguments ran on familiar lines. The Government did not feel sure that the Transportation Plan would actually bring great military advantages. Would it not, the Prime Minister asked, be a good thing to invite the American Air Force, perhaps in conjunction with the Directorate of Bombing Operations in the Air Ministry, to produce a plan within the next few days for employing the Strategic Air Forces in such a way that not more than, say, a hundred French lives should be sacrificed on any target? If this plan proved to be vastly inferior to the Transportation Plan, the arguments in favour of the latter would be strengthened, and the Government could be more easily convinced that the political disadvantages must be overridden.

Eisenhower asked me to draft a reply for him. I pointed out that in deference to the strong political objections raised by the Cabinet, instructions had already been given that some of the targets should be attacked at a later stage of the operation, although this postponement affected the full efficacy of the plan. Any plan for the full use of our air-power meant civilian casualties. These had been accepted in the past when we had attacked submarine bases and factories. Railway centres had always been recognised as legitimate military targets. Although the Prime Minister's letter stated that the Transportation Plan involved the death of ten to fifteen thousand Frenchmen, this estimate assumed that there would be no evacuation despite our specific warnings. However, experience had already shown that even if Vichy

The Team, Algiers, 1942 (Portal, Eisenhower, and myself)

From the train *en route* to Moscow, 13 January 1945

Berlin, the Brandenburg Tor, 9 May 1945

figures were accepted, casualties had been considerably less in the aggregate than our estimate. A number of our attacks had also caused very heavy casualties to German personnel. I explained once again that

> . . . the object of the whole operation is so to weaken and disorganise the railway system as a whole, that, at the critical time of the assault, German rail movements can be effectively delayed, and the rapid concentration of their forces against the lodgement area prevented. Time is the vital factor during the period immediately following the assault. The delay which would be involved by enforced use of motor transport in place of railway transport, would, in itself, be of inestimable value.

> To limit the operation to centres where casualties were estimated at 100 to 150 would emasculate the whole plan. Such a limitation must presumably apply to all air operations before the assault, including essential tactical operations in the last two or three weeks when there would be an extensive programme of bombing operations against military targets over a wide area. Many of these attacks would inevitably cause death and injury. The plans for 'Overlord' had been based on the assumption that our over-whelming air-power would prepare the way for the assault. If our hands were to be tied in the way now suggested, the perils of an undertaking already hazardous would be much increased.

Eisenhower sent this document, with only minor changes of wording, to Churchill on 2 May. It was considered by the War Cabinet that night. The Prime Minister spoke of the Supreme Commander's onerous responsibility. Care should be taken not to add to his burdens unnecessarily. Very great consequences might follow from interference with his plan on political grounds. He, the Prime Minister, had not fully realised that our use of air-power before 'Overlord' would assume so cruel and remorse-less a form. Great slaughter would inevitably result from the planned air attacks. The Foreign Secretary was still perturbed at the possible reactions on European opinion. After the war, Eastern Europe and the Balkans would be largely dominated by Russia, whereas the peoples of Western Europe would look to us. If the present attacks continued, they might well regard us with hatred.

He was not convinced that a decision in favour of the Transportation Plan was a matter of victory or defeat.

On this occasion Alan Brooke supported the Transportation Plan more vigorously. He had no doubt that the plan would make it more difficult for the enemy to move his forces. Now that so much effort had been devoted to it, it would be unwise to change to a new policy. Eventually, it was agreed that the Prime Minister should consider further the air plan for support of 'Overlord'.

I had already visited Field-Marshal Smuts, who was in London at this time, and had told him of the Cabinet's reactions to the Transportation Plan. He said that the political considerations must yield to the military arguments. I gathered from Portal on 3 May that Smuts had spoken in strong though indirect support of this view. That night, with Leigh-Mallory and Bufton, I attended the last of this series of meetings of the Defence Committee. It was evident that the Ministers had not fully realised that attacks on railway centres were only a feature of the broad policy of air support for 'Overlord'. Leigh-Mallory estimated that in the month remaining before D-Day, some 35 to 40 per cent. of the bomber effort would be devoted to railway targets.

The Prime Minister feared propaganda to the effect that while the Russian and German armies advanced bravely despite the lack of air superiority, the British and Americans relied on ruthless employment of air-power regardless of the cost in civilian life. It might also be said that the British were the greatest offenders because they scattered their bombs over wide areas by night, whereas the Americans carried out precision bombing by day. 'You will smear', said the Prime Minister, 'the good name of the Royal Air Force across the world.'

It was proposed that the Cabinet should communicate their views to the President and to the State Department so as to ensure that the Americans accepted their share of responsibility. It was admitted that so far French reaction had been good. Churchill asked me whether I would be content with a plan under which the number of civilians killed in attacks on railway centres up to D-Day did not exceed ten thousand. I replied that it was most difficult to make an accurate estimate of casualties, but I thought the number killed so far was probably between three and four thousand, and I was hopeful that the full plan could be implemented without exceeding the ten thousand limit.

Meanwhile, we continued to receive news of the destruction of ammunition and troop trains. The extent to which the Germans were importing personnel to help in running the railways was indicated by a report that in one of our attacks on Creil, a direct hit on a shelter had killed twenty-five people, of whom eighteen were Germans.

Lord Cherwell thought that bridges might be suitable alternative targets. I remarked that bridges could be repaired fairly quickly. The average of the most optimistic estimates was that destruction of a bridge would prevent traffic for fourteen days. Such attacks would therefore have to be confined to the period of a fortnight before the assault. For security reasons, many of the important bridges could not be attacked until D-Day itself. After various Ministers had repeated well-known points of view, the Prime Minister said that the War Cabinet should draw up a paper for transmission to the State Department, while he would telegraph to Roosevelt. To kill some ten thousand Frenchmen before D-Day was likely to have a serious effect on European relations. On the other hand, if 'Overlord' were successful, it might, by shortening the war, save the lives of millions. It was decided that action should be taken on these lines; that I should review the railway plan to ensure that not more than ten thousand civilians were killed, and that I should report the course of the discussion and the conclusions to the Supreme Commander. This I did, while Churchill invited Roosevelt to consider the matter from the highest political standpoint. He told the President that the War Cabinet were unanimous in their anxiety about 'these French slaughters', even on a reduced scale, and also in their doubts 'as to whether almost as good military results could not be produced by other methods. Whatever is settled between us, we are quite willing to share responsibilities with you.'

Roosevelt replied, in effect, that the military considerations must dominate. No possibility of alleviating French opinion must be overlooked, always provided that our effectiveness against the enemy was not reduced at this crucial time:

However regrettable the attendant loss of civilian lives is, I am not prepared to impose from this distance any restriction on military action by the responsible commanders that in their opinion might militate against the success of 'Overlord' or cause additional loss of life to our Allied forces of invasion.

As Churchill observes, this was decisive. The weight of casualties to French civilians continued to be less than had been feared, and:

The sealing off of the Normandy battlefield from reinforcements by rail may well have been the greatest direct contribution that the bomber forces could make to 'Overlord'. The price was paid.[1]

Roosevelt's attitude, then, had at last decided a question which had agitated our counsels for the better part of three months. I shall never forget those meetings in the Map Room when we wrangled for hours about the Transportation Plan. Even at the end of them, I was far from sure that the Prime Minister fully understood our purpose. I could not help noticing, as the meetings dragged on into the early hours, and the decisions were postponed from week to week, how tired he was and how the rush of events since 1940 had undermined even his strength. Many years later, I read with interest Alan Brooke's opinion, formed at the same time, that the Prime Minister was failing fast. Churchill himself confessed to the C.I.G.S. on 7 May that he was no longer the man he had been.[2]

I also had occasion during these weeks to observe the three Chiefs of Staff, sometimes at their morning meetings and at the gatherings of the Defence Committee. I thought that Brooke was a better chairman of the Chiefs of Staff than Dill had been, because he argued less over details; but it seemed to me that the C.A.S. provided the real brains. Brooke would often fume, rattling off in his staccato fashion objections and complaints about Churchill's impossible demands. When he had finished,

---

[1] Churchill: *The Second World War,* vol. V, pp. 466–8.
[2] Bryant: *Triumph in the West,* p. 187.

Portal would quietly point out how by a concession here and an alteration there an agreed policy could quickly be reached without the sacrifice of essentials. Churchill himself is reported to have said: 'Portal has everything.'

*'French railway system is in complete chaos'–Casualty calculations–
'Mary' Coningham's team–V-weapons–First stage of Plan nearly
complete–I review air campaign–Decision to drop 82nd Airborne
Division at 'Utah'–weather conferences–Go!–'A classic example'*

BY this time, early in May 1944, there could be no substantial
doubt that our attacks were producing the most serious
effects. Colonel Hoeffner, who managed Rundstedt's rail
transport in France, reported the situation to be critical. The
German armies there needed a hundred trains per day from home.
In April, the average had been sixty. By early May it was thirty-
two. Coal had now to be brought from the Saar instead of from
Belgium. By the middle of the month, seventy of the ninety-nine
targets selected for attack had received attention from our air
forces. Forty of these targets had been destroyed or rendered more
or less inoperative. Thirty more had been in most cases seriously
damaged. None of the targets in southern France and southern
Germany allocated for attack by the U.S. Fifteenth Air Force had
yet been assaulted. In general, the degree of destruction achieved
was high. Through-lines had been blocked for periods varying
between thirty-six hours and thirteen days. We estimated that a
servicing capacity for four thousand locomotives had been
destroyed or seriously damaged. Fourteen ammunition trains had
been exploded. In a report of 15 May, the German Transport
Ministry observed that the recent raids had caused the systematic
breakdown of all main lines:

> Large-scale strategic movement of German troops by rail is practi-
> cally impossible at the present time, and must remain so while attacks
> are maintained at the present intensity. . . . In assessing the situation as a
> whole it must further be borne in mind that, owing to the widespread
> destruction and damage of important construction and repair shops, the
> maintenance and overhaul of locomotives has been considerably
> disorganised; this causes further critical dislocation of traffic.[1]

The growing incidence of destruction was, as we expected,
reflected in the reports of European radio stations and newspapers.
Propaganda on Paris, Vichy, and Brussels radio made the most of

[1] Ellis: *Victory in the West,* vol. 1, p. 111.

casualties to innocent civilians and damage to their property. Secret reports from our agents in France generally indicated that our bombing had been accurate and French morale had remained high. The commentator on Radio Vichy thought it worth while to deny on 13 May that the French transportation system had suffered material damage. The communiqué of the German High Command on the previous day had stated that the continued strong attacks by Anglo-American bombers might be considered as preparation for the invasion. An appeal that we should desist, addressed by French Cardinals to the British and American Episcopate, featured largely in enemy-controlled propaganda. According to Vichy Radio, a night raid on Lille caused 173 deaths, and another on Epinal 185 deaths.

The changes of attitude adopted by such sources proved most revealing. At first, in mid-April, the raids were called a 'campaign of wilful terrorism aimed at civilians without any military object, and having no connection with operations on land'. A little later, the raids were admitted to be a preliminary to invasion. During May, a third point of emphasis developed. German-controlled sources did not now deny the importance of the military objectives at which the raids were aimed, but held that they did not justify the incidental damage to civilians and their property on account of the inefficiency of our bombing; but we did not have to wait long for outright confirmation of the value of the plan. For example, the commentator on Radio Paris at lunchtime on 23 May said:

The French railway system is in complete chaos. The Allies have successfully pulverised into rubble whole marshalling yards. They have destroyed countless locomotives and have made scores of railway stations unuseable.

The rest of the destructive work which could not be done by the Allied pilots has been accomplished by experienced squads of saboteurs, who have blown up railway tracks and directed attacks against goods trains and other rolling stock.

It was also admitted at the same time that saboteurs had put out of action the whole hydro-electric system in France, and had forced the Government to introduce fresh electricity cuts. Because vital locks and other facilities had also been destroyed, rivers and canals could no longer be used for transport. Thus the transportation system in France was being described as being a desolate sight

. . . and the temper of the population, especially that of Paris, is rising because no food is available, nobody can travel, and there are restrictions in the use of electricity. Frenchmen are blaming the Germans for all this misery which has descended on France.

Two days before this report was broadcast, Mr. Churchill had minuted to me:

Railroad bombing. How does your score stand now, and are you keeping well within the limits you mentioned?

I received a similar enquiry from Portal. I replied to Mr. Churchill that while it was most difficult to give a really reliable estimate, our information indicated that casualties were well within the limits. The Axis reports showed that so far 6,062 civilians had been killed. This indicated that the casualties inflicted, even as judged by the enemy, were some 40 per cent. below our estimates. On the other side, some 2,450 Germans had been killed, including 285 of the three hundred railway specialists despatched from Germany to repair Creil:

One report says that at Clignancourt 400 Germans, celebrating Hitler's birthday, are still under the ruins. Another valuable dividend has been the considerable number of ammunition trains that have been blown up.

I told the C.A.S. that this question was now becoming complicated by casualties arising from attacks on other targets. There was, also, always the possibility of some gross error, though I thought there was now little risk of this with Bomber Command. They had learned a great deal about precision and concentration of bombing and were being extremely careful if there were any risk of bad mistakes. On two or three occasions, whole parties had come back with their bombs. I thought that if we escaped such a gross error, and if the Germans at Vichy did not suddenly decide to launch a special propaganda campaign, we ought to be able to keep within the limit of ten thousand. We had a good deal of evidence to show that there had been extensive evacuation from the neighbourhood of these centres. The Prime Minister accepted this position, and minuted that there was no need to discontinue the plan, though we should keep up warnings to civilians whenever possible. This we had been doing for some time, although it meant accepting higher losses among our bomber crews.

I had already instructed the bomber commanders that at this stage it was more important to watch the enemy carefully and hit him where it would hurt most, than to cling to any prearranged plan. We must strike at the railway system as it was being used, not merely in accordance with the Transportation Plan as it was written. The growing dislocation of the French and Belgian railway systems rendered other targets, especially engines, rolling stock, and now bridges, the more vulnerable. On 21 May the intense attack upon them had begun, when 750 aircraft flew against such targets in France, and five hundred fighters of the Eighth Air Force attacked them in Germany. The rail and road bridges began to receive attention. Though expert opinion, with which I had concurred, had earlier held these targets to be relatively unprofitable for attack, our bomber crews now surpassed even their own high standards. All these attacks had to be mounted without revealing the direction of the invasion, less than three weeks distant. Meanwhile, the Luftwaffe put up virtually no opposition and repeated sorties against launching sites ensured that the onslaught of V-weapons did not hamper the preparations for 'Overlord'.

With 2nd T.A.F. 'Mary' Coningham was successful in putting into practice the lessons of North Africa. His headquarters, jointly staffed by American and R.A.F. officers, included representatives of 21 Army Group. It was Coningham's suggestion that fighter-bombers would probably attack bridges more successfully than heavy bombers. This began on 24 May and was undertaken by the U.S. Ninth Air Force under Brereton, who was to work with him and whose acquaintance he had made in the days of the North African campaign. Of the twenty-four Seine bridges between Paris and the sea, eighteen were smashed by D-Day and the other six blocked. Bridges over other rivers received like treatment.

The Air Staff had known from careful photographic reconnaissance that the flying-bomb offensive by V.1s was timed to begin in December 1943, with two salvoes of sixty or seventy bombs arriving simultaneously on London in the late evening and early morning. We were able, by expert interpretation, to discover all the salient facts. At the crucial moment, our bombers ruined the launching sites. It had taken the enemy six months to build new and simpler launching sites. By then, the Transportation Plan was depriving him of the bombs themselves and of other vital items of supply.

Our reconnaissance showed, too, that rockets were being built. The V.2 rocket launching pads and the V.1 flying bomb sites, known to us as ski sites, were grouped mainly in the Cherbourg Peninsula and in the Pas de Calais area, and by December 1943, sixty-three ski sites and five rocket sites had been identified. Before D-Day our air forces had dropped some 40,000 tons of bombs against these sites, when a total of ninety-three were knocked out, and it was estimated that there were never more than ten ski sites in a condition to fire. The Germans rapidly built modified sites which we had little opportunity to attack before D-Day itself, but it was not until 12 June 1944 that the first flying bomb could be launched against Britain.

By now, enemy propaganda had reached a new pitch of intensity. At the end of May, Radio Paris accused us of causing nearly four thousand deaths and eight thousand casualties in a period of forty-eight hours. In the meantime, the Prime Minister had been shocked to find out that I had not received regularly the Intelligence reports prepared each day almost entirely from Axis-controlled sources about the reactions in Europe to the bombing offensive. He minuted to me on 28 May that he could give no assurance for the moment that the air forces had done more good than harm. He asked me to see him in the coming week. I replied that we fully appreciated that intensified enemy propaganda was a very serious political factor, and I assured him that it was being constantly borne in mind by those who had to conduct these operations. That part of the Transportation Plan which entailed heavy attacks on railway centres was now practically complete. Le Bourget remained the only centre of this kind which had not been attacked, an adherence to the War Cabinet's ruling on acceptable civilian casualties, and we should not touch it unless it seemed to be essential from the Army's point of view. Most of our effort was now occupied with the tactical phase of cutting communications by attack on bridges, engines, tracks and junctions. It was in this operation that 2 Group of 2nd T.A.F. played a significant part.

By 30 May, I had received a further gloomy Minute from the Prime Minister, whose tone was, however, a little more friendly. He did not agree that we had chosen the best targets. I was much concerned that the Prime Minister should take so literally the unfiltered poison provided by the Intelligence summaries of European reaction. He seemed to set great store on what was, after all, pure enemy propaganda. I felt as good as certain that the figures of casualties being put out by Vichy and Berlin were grossly exaggerated. However, the plan was now nearly complete. General Montgomery and 21 Army Group were pressing for an attack on Le Bourget, but for the moment I postponed it again.

In reply to Mr. Churchill I pointed out that the figures of alleged casualties given by Axis sources up to the end of May were 10,776. Many discrepancies were evident. One report on the attack at Nimes, said: 'Civilian casualties high', while the broadcast figure was a mere 150. Another report on an attack at Marseilles said that civilian casualties were 'considerable', while the broadcast figure was no less than 1,500:

It is also to be noted that the first broadcast figure for Lyons was 50. The subsequent one has been brought up to '700 or more'. I feel there are considerable grounds for suspecting distortion of the facts.

In a second memorandum of the same day, 1 June, I tried to warn Churchill against unconditional acceptance of the daily Intelligence summary. I sent him a sheaf of reports from our agents in France. One of them said, for instance:

It would take one person alone whole days to count the wagons which at first sight seemed to run into hundreds—a complete hotchpotch, wheels and axles 100 metres from the chassis, and the bodies of the wagons reduced to atoms.
An indescribable chaos reigns in the coal and goods yards.

Another report said that the locomotive depot at Saint Pierre des Corps was reduced to dust. All the sidings were unfit for use. Two thousand men had been conscripted to make repairs.

The local people are unanimous in considering this one of the least cruel and most effective raids; only eight deaths have been reported. . . .

The opinion of the marshalling yard staff is very satisfactory; everyone had time to get away, and the damage to the railway installations is considered perfect in its way.

At this stage, just before 'Overlord' was launched, I reviewed the whole air campaign for the Prime Minister. Our action against the German Air Force had consisted mainly of deep penetration by day into Germany, and attack on airfields in occupied territory by day and night. The deep penetrations were intended to destroy German Air Force productive capacity at the factories and the repair depots, and to destroy the Luftwaffe in combat. Enemy fighter reaction in the air had decreased sharply, and it seemed probable to me that he was doing everything possible to conserve strength. Thus, heavy bomber attacks had been switched to oil targets in the hope that their importance would force the enemy to battle. To some extent, this tactic was successful, and the enemy had suffered heavy fighter casualties. Although the Germans thought an attack in northern France to be imminent, they still kept back the great bulk of their fighter forces to defend the Fatherland. Our attacks on airfields in occupied territory had not, in general, caused much heavy damage, though they had enforced very wide dispersal with consequent loss of efficiency.

The object of the Transportation Plan was to disrupt and dislocate all movement by attacking the railway network at its most sensitive points, and when one disrupted a railway centre, i.e. a control centre, one was cutting communications and destroying rolling stock. These were merely incidental contributions towards the main aim of general dislocation. All but two of the selected railway centres had now, on 1 June, been attacked with satisfactory results. By the end of April, over a thousand trains, even after drastic reductions of traffic, were immobilised. On 2 May, German Air Force units had been warned that if they were needed to concentrate in Northern France to repel an invasion, they must be prepared to move by road, since movement by rail might no longer be possible. The German Commander-in-Chief in the west reported on 8 May that the attacks on railways had already achieved the interruption of supply and troop movements. The attacks on rail centres in the South of France had disrupted supplies and reinforcements to Italy. The three main tank depots and re-equipment centres in France and Holland, and the main tank assembly plant near Magdeburg, had been successfully blitzed, as had ammunition dumps and an explosives factory in France. The programme against enemy radar installations which had been assigned to 83 and 84 Groups T.A.F. was almost complete, and most of those covering the approach and assault area had been put out of action. Fighter Command, which from November 1943 was known as Air Defence of Great Britain, had been almost completely successful in preventing enemy aircraft flying over southern England, and by so doing concealed both the direction and date of invasion. Under Sholto Douglas, Coastal Command had been keeping a constant watch on movements of enemy shipping, and up to 31 May there had been only twenty-two U-boat sightings, six of which resulted in a sinking.

To sum up, the preparatory air phase of the 'Overlord' Campaign is now almost complete. The operations have, in all their various aspects, constituted a single plan of campaign, each part dovetailing into the whole. Though we already know that in certain respects success has been achieved, the ultimate test is to come.

*

The War Cabinet's anxiety to restrict bombing to targets where few civilian casualties would be caused, had delayed or ruled out attacks on several important centres. This fact the enemy was not slow to recognise. Le Bourget, one of our original targets of highest priority was never attacked at all, and provided throughout the main leak for military movement to Normandy.

Of the 65,000 tons of bombs dropped on transportation targets, 45,000 were delivered by Bomber Command. Sixty-two of the

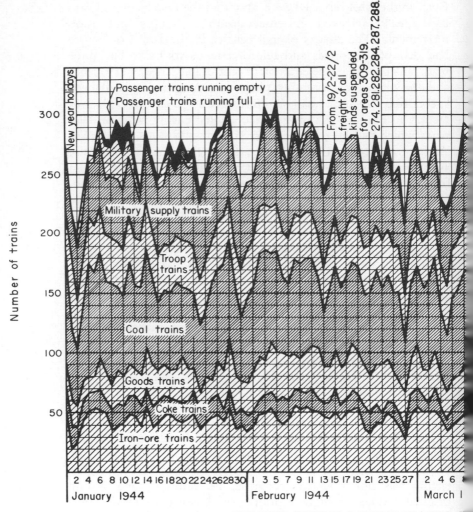

CAPTURED GERMAN RAILWAY TRAFFIC G

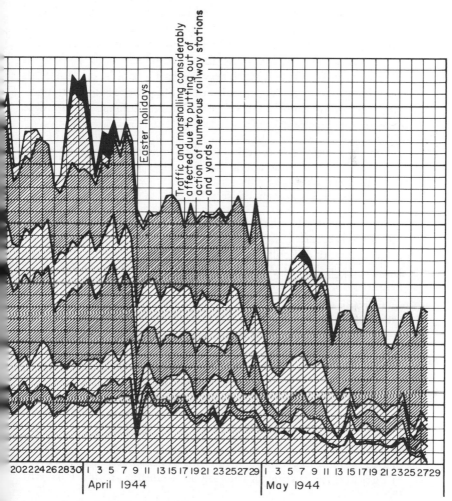

Easter holidays

Traffic and marshalling considerably affected due to putting out of action of numerous railway stations and yards

20 22 24 26 28 30 | 1 3 5 7 9 11 13 15 17 19 21 23 25 27 29 | 1 3 5 7 9 11 13 15 17 19 21 23 25 27 29

April 1944

May 1944

ING PRE-'OVERLORD' TRAIN MOVEMENTS

targets were so badly damaged by D-Day that no further heavy
bomber attacks were necessary. By now, just before D-Day,
only three marshalling yards in the area we had attacked were
working to full capacity, one of which was Le Bourget. Several
were only working to 2 per cent. of their capacity, and others at
varying figures up to 10 per cent. Only four were working above
50 per cent. capacity, including the three which were working at
full capacity. Our Intelligence services had got hold of comments
made by French railway officials about the progress of our operations. Some of them were of considerable interest to me. One
head of a department said:

> If we, who belong to the S.N.C.F., had to practise a sabotage of the
> same character, we would not do any better. Disorganisation is progres-
> sive and irreparable. The Allies make work necessary, and know how
> to adjust their raids to await the repercussions of previous raids.

As General Zimmerman, a senior German staff officer,
acknowledged after the war, troop movements by train became
more and more difficult, until at last the reinforcement of the coast
had to be carried out almost entirely by road. When the Seine and
Loire bridges were methodically destroyed, even movement by
road became very slow. Meanwhile, the bases available to the
Luftwaffe were being pushed as far back as Paris.[1]

The Germans' air reconnaissance was so spasmodic that they
could get no clear picture of the point we had chosen for the
assault. They were, of course, studying winds and tides in a nervous fashion, constantly ordering men hither and thither to meet
possible threats of invasion. The bombing of the railways and
bridges had not in any way disclosed fresh information about the
point at which we intended to strike. The attacks on railway
centres might equally indicate an intention to land in the region
of Le Havre or in Normandy or, with the destruction of the Seine
bridges and the cutting of the Grande Ceinture around Paris, the
Pas de Calais.

Naturally, we employed every possible ruse to confuse the
Germans. We attacked more points outside the landing area

[1] Westphal (ed.): *The Fatal Decisions,* p. 182.

than within it. We hoped to indicate that the main blow would fall not in Normandy but in the Calais area.

*

The battle of wits and strength would now be decided within a few hours. In these last stages, some agonising decisions had to be made. The brunt of responsibility fell upon Eisenhower as Supreme Commander. Leigh-Mallory and his staff believed that airborne operations in the Cherbourg Peninsula, without which the American attack on the Utah Beach must be abandoned, might result in complete failure. Estimated losses as high as 75 and 80 per cent. were spoken of. We had news of the arrival of a fresh German division in the Cherbourg area. General Bradley said flatly that he would not land on the Utah Beach without the support of the U.S. 82nd Airborne Division. Leigh-Mallory exclaimed at a meeting on 27 May that this would mean the virtual destruction of two airborne divisions. On 29 May, in Eisenhower's absence, I presided over the Supreme Commander's conference, and ruled that the 82nd Division must be landed. Leigh-Mallory said, in effect, that it was impossible; Montgomery said, or rather, his Chief of Staff, General de Guingand said on his behalf, that it was essential. We decided that 21 Army Group's requirements must be met, irrespective of casualties. Later, Leigh-Mallory pressed his view on the Supreme Commander. Eisenhower ruled that the decision to proceed must be maintained.

The timing of D-Day itself was dictated by a combination of meteorological factors. The men and vehicles could land only at low tide when the obstacles which the Germans had been feverishly placing upon the beaches would be uncovered. The preliminary bombardment needed some forty minutes of daylight. The airborne forces could not be landed with any reasonable prospects of success except in moonlight conditions. The armada must be able to cross the waters under protection of darkness. More than two million men were involved in this vast operation. Only on 5, 6, and 7 June would all these factors coincide.

In May, the weather had been favourable. Early in that month,

[543]

which would have provided another suitable time for the landings, both Smuts and Montgomery had told me how much they regretted that we were not crossing the Channel then. The weather was perfect, and the longer we waited the greater the German's opportunity to prepare their defences. At the crucial moment in early June, we received our first news of an unfavourable change in the weather. I spent all day at Portsmouth on 2 June. Eisenhower had called a conference there. It appeared that the good weather might break at exactly the wrong moment for us. The next day, Saturday 3 June, we foregathered again at the headquarters of Admiral Ramsay, Southwick House, north of Portsmouth. All the principal commanders were there. Eisenhower presided. We sat in the Mess Room, which was large, with a table at one end, and easy chairs at the other. On three sides of the room the walls were lined with bookcases, most of which stood forlorn and empty. We did not sit round the table, but occupied the easy chairs and listened to an exposition of the weather as it was likely to affect us. The senior meteorologist, Group Captain Stagg, told us that evening that the long period of settled conditions was breaking up. The outlook for D-Day and the succeeding days was most unpromising. We were given to understand that the type of weather we should expect was such that forecasting more than twenty-four hours ahead would be a most hazardous undertaking. The high-pressure system which covered southern England and part of the Continent was being replaced by depressions. Stagg and his colleagues were agreed that on 4 and 5 June there would be an increase in the wind force up to Force 5 in places, with warm, moist air from the south-west bringing heavy cloud conditions with a base at about 500 feet, though occasionally, perhaps, right down to sea level. It was clear that these conditions ruled out 5 June as D-Day. After a long discussion we decided to meet again at 4.30 a.m. on 4 June. In the meanwhile, one of the United States Task Forces, sailing from ports in the West Country, would be allowed to proceed, and would not be recalled until our next meeting had confirmed the bad weather.

Early on the Sunday morning we met again. Although there were some hopes of a slight improvement, D-Day was definitely postponed. One of the principal reasons was that while sea conditions would be manageable, the air forces would not be able to carry out their programme. Montgomery, knowing full well that weather conditions would prevent the air forces from giving any real support, amazingly asserted his willingness on the part of the Army to take the risk. I disagreed, and opted for a postponement. Eisenhower remarked that the whole operation was taking place with forces which, in comparison with enemy strength, were not overwhelmingly powerful. The operation, he said, was only feasible in its present form because of our very great air superiority. If the air could not operate, then the operation must be postponed. He asked whether anybody disagreed with his view. There came no reply.

Orders were immediately issued to the ships which had already left port. By miracles of improvisation they contrived to return and refuel in time. At our second meeting that same Sunday, Stagg described a marked change in the weather. The front giving rain and low cloud was passing away and should start to clear in our area in two to three hours. This clearance should last throughout Monday, 5 June, and up to about 7 a.m. on Tuesday, 6 June. Winds, which had now reached Force 6 in some places, would moderate by 5 June. It appeared that the weather conditions on Monday night would be suitable for the heavy bombers to operate, though operation later in the morning would be curtailed by large areas of heavy cloud. Ramsay said that 'Admiral Kirk [commanding the American Task Forces, including that from the West Country ports] must be told within the next half hour if 'Overlord' is to take place on Tuesday. If he is told it is on, and his forces sail and are then recalled, they will not be ready again for Wednesday morning. Therefore, a further postponement would be for forty-eight hours.'

Leigh-Mallory said he thought it would be likely to be only a moderate night and Bomber Command would have great difficulty in getting their markers down and in doing useful bombing. Several people said that Leigh-Mallory was being unduly pessimistic. I agreed with him that operations of the heavy and medium bombers were going to be chancey, but observed that it was a question of making the best use of gaps in the weather.

Eisenhower said simply that if instructions were not given

now, the operation could not take place on 6 June. At about 9.45, he said: 'I am quite positive that the order must be given.'

It was given accordingly. We met for a few minutes at 4.15 a.m. on 5 June. Another weather chart had come in, and it contained nothing to alter the decision of the previous night. One of our party pressed for a longer forecast, to which Group Captain Stagg replied: 'No. If I were to do that I would be a guesser and not a meteorologist.'

'Overlord' was launched beyond recall.

*

When Eisenhower said at the meeting on 4 June that 'Overlord' was feasible in its present form only because of our very great air superiority, he spoke no more than the literal truth. He might have added that it was not simply a question of air superiority but of air-power, which can be exercised in its full form only after air superiority has been gained. The battle for air superiority was largely won, though we did not yet know how completely; what was now to be proved was that our exercise of the air-power which air superiority made possible, had achieved for us the results we had claimed. Those results were bought at a heavy price. Between 1 April and D-Day, the British and American air forces lost about two thousand aircraft and more than twelve thousand officers and men. Nevertheless, we had at our disposal air strength on a scale which would have seemed inconceivable in the early years of the war. It amounted to more than eleven thousand aircraft. On the night of 5 June and on D-Day itself, our crews flew some fourteen thousand sorties.

We could hardly have foreseen, when we were battling for our lives in 1940 and 1941, that we should be able to assemble a multitude of ships all along the south coast of England, and convey men in their hundreds and thousands across the Channel without presenting the most enticing targets to enemy air-power. Yet this is what we had been able to do. A comparison suggests itself. Air superiority is the difference between the unhindered passage of our shipping across the Channel to the beaches of Normandy and the continual harassment our coastal shipping had suffered in the early days of the War. 'The history of war', wrote

Stalin to Churchill a day or two later, 'knows no other like undertaking from the point of view of its scale, its vast conception and its masterly execution.' As for our exercise of air-power, a German who was feeling the brunt of our attacks, one Captain Mössel, provided his own tribute. He understood what the new dimension meant to warfare when he wrote at the end of May 1944:

We are experiencing a classic example of the air war on an extensive scale, its aim being to decide the war in the air above Germany. I have observed that a number of officers still do not realise the danger of this form of warfare. They still maintain the attitude that they are *Herren Offiziere*, who bring wars to an end by occupying the territory of the enemy. That he should find it possible to overpower his adversary by cutting off his communications by sea, by destroying his armament factories, by paralysing his means of transport and by reducing his towns and villages to ruin has not yet become clear to them. What war in the air or war on the sea means is still beyond their comprehension.[1]

---

[1] Saunders, *The Royal Air Force* 1939–1945, vol. 3, p. 100.

4   D-Day–Bolstering morale with bombs–To Normandy with Ike–
Tactical use of heavies (Cassino?)–Eisenhower: 'Constant aggressiveness'–Montgomery's dilatory methods–Eisenhower gives Montgomery
blank cheque–Montgomery's directive of 30 June–Warning against
blank cheque for Air Support–Montgomery's directive of 10 July, after the fall
of Caen–Montgomery and the Air commanders–Attempt on Hitler's life–
Eisenhower: 'Time is vital'–Need to take risks–Montgomery's directive of 21
July–German view of British forces–'had for suckers'–Bradley's offensive,
25 July–Breakthrough accomplished–The Falaise 'pocket'–Operation 'Dragoon'

DURING the night of 5 June 1944, the five fleets carrying
our troops and their equipment met off the coast of the
Isle of Wight and turned towards Normandy. Despite the
intense activity of the Royal Navy, whose vessels were sweeping
clear the path of the armada, the Germans failed to recognise
the immediacy and the strength of the blow. As the ships closed
towards the French coast, our airborne assault and the air-strike
forces went in. Coastal defences had to be attacked when the
airborne forces were about to land, though other batteries in the
centre of the invasion area were not bombed until the early hours
of 6 June. More than a thousand bombers were deployed against
the coastal installations, dropping some five thousand tons of
bombs.

By dawn, the work of the heavy bombers was, for the moment,
accomplished. They withdrew as the naval bombardment began.
A shield of day fighters appeared over the many vessels crowding
towards the beaches. The weather was a little better than Group
Captain Stagg had ventured to forecast. The wind had moderated,
the cloud was well broken and its base was not lower than 4,000
feet, ideally suited for airborne operations. In the hour before the
landings, large areas of temporarily clear sky provided the right
conditions for precision bombing of the shore defences and our
medium and light bombers carried through with the task unhindered, although from subsequent examination it was difficult
to assess what effects the operation had had.

While these events moved forward, we in London eagerly
awaited each scrap of information. The first reports from the

Army Headquarters and from Coningham were favourable. The airborne operations, however, were not a complete success as only one-sixth of the force landed on their correct drop zones, but casualties were less than anticipated. I believed that we had achieved tactical surprise, in part because the enemy had not been expecting us in such conditions. That we had not been expected, and that our ships had been able to cross to Normandy without loss from air attack, indicated how great a degree of advantage was conferred upon the power with air supremacy. During the day, the King and the Prime Minister arrived to see our War Room. Both were satisfied with the early promise of the assault. The same day, the Prime Minister heard from Stalin that the Soviet forces' summer offensive would begin towards the middle of June on one of the important sectors of their Front. This would become a general offensive at the end of June and during July.

As our forces established their bridgehead, we expected at every moment that the Luftwaffe's reply would begin in real earnest, but, as in the case of Sicily, we did not realise how thoroughly we had done our job. We had estimated that the German Air Force would be able to carry out between six and seven hundred sorties per day over the area of the landings, whereas in the event it proved that they were unable to manage more than two hundred.

We had three immediate objectives in Normandy. The first task was for the assault divisions to get ashore and build up a beachhead. They must deal with the expected counter-attacks. The Second British Army under General Dempsey would push rapidly towards the country south and south-east of Caen and Falaise, where airfields could be built quickly. Moreover, this was the only area really suitable for the deployment of tanks in the whole region of the invasion. The task of the American First Army, led by General Bradley, would be to secure the peninsula and especially the port facilities of Cherbourg.

If our strongest card, overwhelming air-power, was to be played effectively and promptly, we had to have airfields in France, and at a meeting of the principal commanders on 10 March, Leigh-Mallory had stressed the importance of this. He thought at that stage that the heaviest air fighting would probably take place in the Seine area. We must therefore, have enough airfields around Caen and the areas west of Paris to operate over the Seine in strength. In the original 'Overlord' plans, this need had been fully recognised. The timetable had provided for the capture of the Caen airfields in the fortnight following D-Day, and of the further group west of Paris by about a month from D-Day. The revised plan did not seem to cater in the same degree for the early capture of the airfields south-east of Caen.

Montgomery explained that his plan now was to maintain a very firm left-wing to bar the progress of enemy formations advancing from the east, while our mobile armoured formations would press forward in a southerly direction. Before we extended ourselves to the east, we should ensure that we had formed a firm base.

In these first days of the assault, the task of the Tactical Air Forces under 'Mary' Coningham was to attack enemy airfields and to block roads leading to the beachhead, in order to prevent the rapid arrival of reinforcements. Leigh-Mallory, under my general supervision, directed the policy of the Allied Expeditionary Air Forces and, during the critical days of the assault, of the large strategical forces which had been specially assigned. He was also responsible for working out bombing plans and for choosing targets for the Expeditionary Air Forces.

For the first few days, all went well. The reaction of the German Air Forces was almost unbelievably sluggish, although we had reports on 10 June that two-thirds of the German fighter strength had left the Reich for Normandy. That day, the Prime Minister telephoned me to say that he was pleased with the progress of 'Overlord': 'I have my eyes on Cherbourg.'

It was soon clear that the enemy would try to reinforce his forward troops with units and supplies from north-east France and Belgium, using lines of communication across the Seine. This meant that the Germans must pin down our left flank by holding the Caen–Falaise area. From the outset, fighting was stubborn on that front. One of the British armoured divisions, the 7th, pushing out on the right of the Second Army, ran into a resistance so fierce that it was in danger of being surrounded.

Only with the aid of artillery support from the U.S. 5 Corps on its right could the division extricate itself in good order. However, until we could make a real move forward in the region of Caen, we could not deploy our full air or tank strength, nor could we menace the enemy-held Channel coast and take its ports.

By 12 June when the Supreme Commander saw General Bradley for the second time since the landings, it was beginning to look doubtful whether we should immediately take the areas on our left flank which we had considered so important to success. Bradley's U.S. First Army was making some progress towards Cherbourg. He had previously estimated that he might take the town in ten days if he were extremely lucky, or in a month if he were less lucky. In fact, it took twenty days after the landing.

Meanwhile, the two invasion Task Forces had been landing their follow-up troops, but the front remained very constricted, and all the fighting formed part of one tactical battle. General Montgomery co-ordinated the whole land battle and was to continue in that role until the British and American Army Groups had been built up to their full strength. They would then split, each under its own commander, and break out, or so we hoped, into mobile warfare. For me, that day could not come soon enough. I was sure that the possession of overwhelming air-power, and its use before 'Overlord' to disrupt the railway network which the enemy would have to use, had placed in our hands a weapon of the utmost value. Our right course was to strike as boldly and swiftly as possible while the enemy was feeling the effects of the paralysis of the railways and our constant harassing of his movements by road. The longer we delayed in securing the area round Caen and beyond it, the less became our chances of victory in 1944. The German commanders seem to have been in little doubt about the effect on their prospects of our dominance in the air. Rommel reported on 12 June that operations in Normandy would be

... rendered exceptionally difficult and even partially impossible by the extraordinarily strong and in some respects overwhelming superiority of the Allied Air Force and by the effect of heavy naval artillery.... The enemy has complete control over the battle area and up to sixty miles behind the front. Almost all transport on roads and in open country is prevented by day by strong fighter-bomber and bomber formations. Movements of our troops in the battle area by day are also almost completely stopped, while the enemy can move freely. . . . This crippling and destructive operation of the enemy Air Force. . . .[1]

When a week had passed since D-Day without the capture of Caen, it became clear to us at S.H.A.E.F. that the hopes of a rapid breakthrough on the left were now remote. At our usual meeting on the morning of 14 June, Coningham disturbed any remaining complacency by announcing that his information on the situation in France did not agree with what we had just been given. He said that the 7th Armoured Division had suffered a severe setback, and described the situation as being near crisis. We decided to put in what I described as 'a terrific air punch' against targets near the battle line, largely for the purpose of bolstering morale. Later in the day I talked with Eisenhower and told him what had been said at the meeting. We decided that we would at once go to France to see whether there really was a crisis.

We flew by Fortress to Normandy the next morning. Meanwhile, at the usual commanders' meeting, Leigh-Mallory produced a scheme for the use of heavy bombers on tactical targets to assist the army. Someone murmured 'Cassino'.

It was in these circumstances that on arrival at General Dempsey's Second Army headquarters I found in session a joint Army/Air conference. The purpose was to consider the tactical use of heavy bombers on the lines that Leigh-Mallory had agreed. Neither Spaatz nor Coningham was represented. I was much disturbed at these developments, and found Coningham, who happened to be in Normandy that day, incensed. I agreed with General Dempsey that Coningham and his staff should consider the proposal for this use of the bombers, and report back. This was speedily done and the operation was cancelled. Later in the day, I confirmed to Montgomery that his opposite number was Coningham, and Dempsey's was Air Vice Marshal Harry Broadhurst (83 Group). Montgomery seemed relieved to have this confirmation. As for the military crisis, it was apparent to Eisen-

[1] Young: *Rommel,* pp. 205–6.

hower and to me that it was over-emphasised. One reason for the virtually static nature of the front at this time was our shortage of ammunition. Nevertheless, Coningham announced at our meeting the next morning at Stanmore: 'The Army plan has failed.'

Both Eisenhower and I assured Montgomery of the fullest air support for ground operations. Three days after our visit, on 18 June, Montgomery issued a directive in which he again ordered an all-out offensive towards Caen. The enemy's resistance in this sector remained stiff. German concern for the Caen area was so great that for the moment all available Panzer divisions were concentrated there. Eisenhower kept up a considerable correspondence by telegraph and letter with Montgomery. He also made sure, by enquiries to me and others, that all air strength necessary to any phase of the ground battle should be instantly available. The burden of the Supreme Commander's messages was the need for constant aggressiveness, in order to deny to the enemy time and opportunity to seal us off with the aid of artificial defences. We pushed forward into the battle zone every fighting unit we could move. As early as 18 June, Eisenhower told Montgomery by letter of his personal efforts to push forward fighting units and ammunition at the expense of all other types of personnel and stores. He added: 'I thoroughly believe you are going to crack the enemy a good one.'

A day later, however, a gale of hurricane strength began. Four days elapsed before the landing of men and supplies could be resumed. The sea routes between the beachhead and England were severed. Of the two artificial harbours one was ruined, the other damaged; many vessels lay stranded. As General Eisenhower has observed, conditions would have been ideal for a German counter-offensive, except for the effectiveness of the air campaign to isolate the battlefield. 'Here, as always,' he wrote, 'was emphasised the decisive influence of air power in the ground battle.'[1]

As the days slipped by, I could not help being worried about Montgomery's methods of conducting the battle. The principle which we had proved after painful experience in the Mediterranean—that the Army and Air commanders should live side by

[1] Eisenhower: *Crusade in Europe*, p. 286.

side, and decide their policies together—had been allowed to lapse. The reason in this case was the lack of suitable communications in Normandy which would permit Coningham to control the air forces from Montgomery's headquarters. Because we had not secured the areas south and south-east of Caen, where airfields could speedily be used, our air forces were still largely based in Great Britain. I also feared that our delay in attacking, for whatever reasons, would allow the enemy to assemble a reserve and thus to overcome the good effects of the Transportation Plan. After lunch on 22 June I put these fears to Eisenhower, who had planned to visit Normandy soon. Later in the day Coningham rang after returning from the battlefield, to express his fears about Montgomery's dilatory methods. The present delay in building up our strength on account of the gales in the Channel, was, in Coningham's opinion, an excuse but not a reason for inaction on the left flank.

Eisenhower had been disturbed by some incidents which revealed confusion in combined Air/Ground operations. There had been a few reports of Allied aircraft being fired at from our own lines. It was alleged that on some occasions our aircraft had fired upon, or bombed, Allied troops. The Supreme Commander, with his habitual good sense, told me that he thought these errors had been of such limited extent that we must not let them sour relations between the Services. He was particularly anxious that any such occurrences should not discourage the Army from calling upon the air forces for maximum assistance, or the air forces from being ready to render it. He hoped that I would make it my special province to keep in the closest possible touch with Montgomery, not only to see that the requests of 21 Army Group were satisfied, but also to see that they had asked for every practicable kind of air support. Eisenhower urged me to communicate directly with Montgomery, by telegram or in person, whenever I thought fit.

I decided to visit Montgomery very soon. At this moment, just as the Americans were about to take Cherbourg, the British attack on the east flank began. The Supreme Commander telegraphed at once to Montgomery:

Please do not hesitate to make the maximum demands for any air assistance that can possibly be useful to you. Whenever there is any legitimate opportunity we must blast the enemy with everything we have . . . I am sure that Bradley understands the necessity of hitting hard and incessantly.

Montgomery replied that once the attack had started in real earnest 'I will continue battling on the Eastern flank until one of us cracks, and it will not be us'.

There was certainly every reason for us to move at once, for we were receiving Intelligence which showed that the enemy was assembling armoured forces, though painfully and laboriously, for a counter-attack. The railway line between Nancy, Vitry, and Paris had not been cut, a serious gap left by the Eighth Air Force in the execution of the Transportation Plan. This was not a time at which we could afford bad relations between the ground and air forces. I went to France to see Montgomery on 29 June. Immediately on my return I talked with Eisenhower, from whom I gathered that Montgomery had suggested that Coningham was being too critical and somewhat unco-operative. I still felt that the matter would not be satisfactorily settled until the Army and Air commanders lived side by side. The next day, 1 July, Eisenhower told me that he was also worried at Montgomery's dilatory behaviour outside Caen, and at the frankness of Coningham's criticisms of the Army. I was given to understand that Montgomery and his Chief of Staff, de Guingand, would not be unduly upset at the removal of Coningham. I replied that this would be a disaster, and that Coningham's frankness was justified.

Now that the Americans had taken Cherbourg, while we had failed to take Caen, it became clear that a breakthrough must be accomplished on the right in order that mobile warfare might be established and the whole Front loosened up.

On 27 June Mr. Churchill minuted to me:

I should be glad if you would let me know what airfields you have working on the other side, and to what extent they are being used for basing squadrons as well as for refuelling.

I had to report in reply that our progress was well behind schedule. Up to the morning of 27 June we had thirty-five fighter and fighter-bomber squadrons based in France, together with three squadrons of the Ninth Air Force giving cover over the beaches:

There are five strips serviceable in the British sector, and eight on the American side, all of which have been made by the engineers. No captured airfields are yet available.

We have had to withdraw from 2 strips in the east under shell fire, and, on the American side, 3 strips included in the above figure have become temporarily unserviceable owing to the number of Dakotas we have had to use to fly in emergency ammunition.

The programme for airfields was 27 by D plus 24, with 81 squadrons. The bad weather on the beaches and the lack of elbow room ashore has led to the move-over being phased back, and we shall be considerably behind programme.

After his visit to Bradley on 24 June, when it was evident that we should soon have Cherbourg, Eisenhower made up his mind that the full weight of American strength should be used to break out into the open country on our right. On 30 June, Montgomery issued a directive which showed clearly the intention to hold on the left and break through with the American forces. No doubt he judged that this would be the most economical course, in view of the strength which the Germans had thrown against our eastern flank. In his directive, Montgomery maintained that his broad policy had always been to draw the main enemy forces into battle on the east, and to fight them there, so that our affairs on the western flank could proceed the more easily. This policy had been very successful, but:

It is on the western flank that territorial gains are essential at this stage, as we require space on that side for the development of our administration.

The policy, indeed, had been so successful, Montgomery wrote, that the British Second Army was now opposed by a formidable array of German panzer divisions, eight of which had already been identified. It was clear that Hitler had reinforced the Normandy Front strongly and that a full-blooded counter-attack seemed imminent. This he welcomed. Our tactics must remain unchanged:

(a) *To retain the initiative.*
We shall do this only by offensive action. On no account must

we remain inactive. Without the initiative we cannot win.

(b) *To have no setbacks.*

This is very important on the eastern flank; the enemy has concentrated great strength here and he must not be allowed to use it successfully. A setback on the eastern flank might have direct repercussions on the quick development of our plans for the western flank.

The main tasks of the British Second Army would therefore be to hold the enemy's forces in the area between Caen and Villers Bocage, to suffer no setbacks, and to develop operations for the capture of Caen 'as opportunity offers—and the sooner the better'. Meanwhile, the U.S. First Army should develop an offensive southwards on the right flank, beginning on 3 July. This Army would then pivot to its left in the region of Caumont, and swing south and east on to the general line Caumont–Vire–Mortain–Fougères. When the base of the peninsula at Avranches was reached, the right-hand corps (8 Corps) would turn westwards into Brittany and move towards Rennes and Saint Malo. The remainder of that army would make as rapidly as possible towards Laval, Mayenne, Le Mans, and Alençon.

This document, placing the capture of Caen after consolidation and the avoidance of setbacks, was not received with much enthusiasm at S.H.A.E.F. We hoped that Eisenhower, who was at this moment visiting Montgomery, would insist on an early attack. However, on the Supreme Commander's return I found him still very worried about Montgomery's relations with the air forces. In essence, the situation was that Montgomery thought the Air not vigorous enough in support of the immediate battle, while Coningham continued to be sharply critical of the Army's slow progress. I agreed with Coningham that the Army did not seem prepared to fight its own battles. After I had talked over these matters with Eisenhower and Bedell Smith on 6 July, it was agreed that the Supreme Commander should draft a letter which would tell Montgomery tactfully to get moving.

By the next morning a draft was ready. It said that for Montgomery's attack 'all resources of the Air would be available', until I insisted that the Air could not, and must not, be turned on thus glibly and vaguely in support of the Army, which would never move unless prepared to fight its way with its own weapons. Eisenhower's final letter, sent off later that day, pointed out that when 'Overlord' was undertaken, the Air Forces had been asked to obtain air superiority and to delay the arrival of enemy reinforcements. Both these requests had been met. Our build-up of strength had gone ahead rapidly, and we were approaching the limit of our available resources. Thereafter the enemy might well increase his relative strength. We must examine every method, therefore, of expanding our beachhead and getting more room for manœuvre before the enemy could attain substantial equality in infantry, tanks, and artillery. On the left, we should by all means secure territory to protect the beach from enemy fire, and suitable airfields. On the right we must take additional small ports on the north side of the Brittany coast, and break out into the open where our superiority could be used. The letter went on:

I am familiar with your plan for generally holding firmly with your left, attracting thereto all of the enemy armour, while your right pushes down the peninsula and threatens the rear and flank of the forces facing the Second British Army. However, the advance on the right has been slow and laborious, due not only to the nature of the country and the impossibility of employing air and artillery with maximum effectiveness, but to the arrival on that Front of reinforcements. . . .

Eisenhower passed on information received from the Intelligence Services that some German infantry had arrived on the front opposite the British Army, allowing the enemy to withdraw certain Panzer elements for regrouping and the establishment of a reserve. He thought therefore that every possible effort should be made to prevent a stalemate, or the necessity of fighting a major battle with the slight depth we still held in the bridgehead. A full-dress attack on the left flank, supported by all our resources, had not yet been attempted. For this we should need some good weather so that the Air could give the maximum assistance. Through Coningham and Harry Broadhurst, Montgomery would have available all the air-power that could be used, even if it were thought necessary to resort to area bombing to soften up the defence:

I will back you up to the limit in any effort you may decide upon to prevent a deadlock, and will do my best to phase forward any unit you might find necessary. For example, if you could use in any attack on your left flank an American Armoured Division, I would be glad to make it available and get it in to you as soon as possible.

. . . Please be assured that I will produce everything that is humanly possible to assist you in any plan that promises to get us the elbow room we need. The Air and everything else will be available.

This letter reflected Eisenhower's conviction that whereas attacks by the British Second Army had recently been made on a scale of two or three divisions only, a co-ordinated attack with our whole strength would put the left flank in motion. Asked on 8 July what I thought of the present Army plans and attacks, I could only reply: 'Company exercises.' That day I phoned Portal, who told me about his visit to Normandy on 7 July. He too was disturbed at the lack of progress by the Army. The problem was Montgomery, who could be 'neither removed nor moved' to action. Later that day, Generals Morgan and Gale, Deputy Chief of Staff and Senior Administrative officer respectively, spoke to me of their apprehensions about the slow pace of our advance. Gale pointed out that unless we could get a second deep-water port his build-up would collapse. I gathered from Morgan that the Prime Minister was alive to the danger. To a member of my staff I remarked during the afternoon that in war all advantages are but questions of time. Unless we seized our opportunity at once, Germany would recover from the paralysis of industry, which bombing had helped to bring about. There were indications that her industry was being put rapidly underground.

Just at this moment, the British Second Army was launching its attacks on Caen. At the Stanmore meeting on 7 July, Leigh-Mallory revealed that Bomber Command was to support Montgomery's attack. I felt that the plans had not been adequately worked out in detail, but did not oppose them. Later that day, I told Leigh-Mallory that he was in danger of leading the Army up the garden path by his sweeping assurances of help. I felt that the limitations of air support on the battlefield were not sufficiently understood; neither was the full scope of the role of air-power

[559]

outside the battle area sufficiently appreciated by the Army, or by Leigh-Mallory.

In less than an hour, the Allied Air Forces dropped over six thousand tons of bombs in front of our armies. By nightfall on 9 July, the enemy had been pushed back across the River Orne, which flows between Caen and Faubourg de Vaucelles. We now needed an early advance across the Orne to provide airfield capacity, and elbow room for the Tactical Air Forces. In a directive issued to his subordinate commanders on 10 July, however, Montgomery stated that now Caen had been captured, our tactical situation on the eastern flank was very good. His broad policy would remain unchanged. It was to draw the main enemy forces into battle on the eastern flank and to fight them there, so that our affairs on the west might proceed the more easily; in spite of Montgomery's directive the enemy had now been able to bring up reinforcements to oppose the U.S. First Army.

It was important, Montgomery wrote, to speed up our advance on the western flank. We must gain possession of the Brittany Peninsula, for if its capture were long delayed we should be greatly hampered in developing our full strength. He continued:

Having captured Caen and thus secured a sound position on our eastern flank, we must now gain depth and space in our lodgement area. We require space for manœuvre, for administrative purposes and for airfields.

It appeared to Montgomery that we were now so strong and well situated that we could attack the Germans hard and continuously. So long as we killed or captured them in large numbers, our left flank was doing what was needed. The Second British Army would hold Caen securely

. . . and our positions in the bridgehead east of the River Orne to the north of Caen, will be maintained, and improved as opportunity offers.

The Faubourg de Vaucelles, lying on the south side of the Orne opposite Caen, will be secured and a bridgehead thus gained, if this can be done without undue losses; I am not prepared to have *heavy* casualties to obtain this bridgehead over the Orne, as we shall have plenty elsewhere.

This plan, therefore, did not give priority to that early advance

A toast in Russian to the signing of the ratification of
Unconditional Surrender. Berlin, 8 May 1945. Zhukov and
Spaatz on my left

eastwards across the Orne which would provide airfield capacity. The plan looked rather to a cautious advance south and westwards, where the terrain was less favourable for airfield development. The emphasis was placed on the capture of Brittany and on its potential port capacity, which would be used to build up strength before the real advance to the east should begin. It seemed clear to me that Montgomery did not attach sufficient importance to the pressing time factor. Few weeks of summer remained. Our urgent need was to get across the Seine. On the evening before the attack on Caen, we had been assured in an official telephone message from 21 Army Group that the object was to 'drive right through Caen and establish a bridgehead beyond the Orne'. This bridgehead we had still not attained. It now appeared that even a very limited bridgehead across the river would not be attempted unless it could be gained without undue losses. The enemy's critical shortage of fuel and motor transport and of other supplies did not seem to have played much, if any, part in the formation of the plan. I told Eisenhower on 11 July that in my view Montgomery's directive was most unsatisfactory. It seemed to be a repetition of the 'Company exercises' to which I had objected a day or two before.

However, a new signal from Montgomery arrived which seemed to give evidence of a change of mind. We gathered that Operation 'Goodwood' would soon be launched, its purpose being to break into the area south-east of Caen. Eisenhower and I decided that the reply should be worded in such a way as to make it clear that we expected Montgomery to go ahead, even if the weather ruled out full air support. Eisenhower sent off an enthusiastic message on 13 July. He assured Montgomery that all possible air support would be given. All the senior airmen were in full agreement because the operation would be 'a brilliant stroke which will knock loose our present shackles. Every plane available will be ready for such a purpose.'

I signalled to Montgomery the same day that I fully endorsed Eisenhower's message. All the air forces would be full out to support the 'Goodwood' plan to the utmost of their ability. Both Eisenhower and I were immeasurably happier at this turn of events. Montgomery seemed to have accepted the view that even if the weather prevented the fullest deployment of our air-power, he should go forward. Eisenhower thought that at last our whole front line would act aggressively against the enemy so that he would be the more vulnerable to a sharp thrust. Montgomery replied to my signal:

Three things important.

First: To hold the ring between now and 18 July and delay enemy moves towards lodgement area to greatest extent possible.

Second: To examine every means so that the Air can play its part on 18th and 19th July even if weather is not 100 per cent.

Third: Plan if successful promises to be decisive, and therefore necessary that the Air Forces bring full weight to bear.

Montgomery placed so much importance on 'Goodwood' that he asked S.H.A.E.F. to be especially careful in suppressing news and newspaper speculation about it. Preceded by tactical bombing on a large scale, it duly went forward on the morning of 18 July. First reports showed that the bombing was successful and a breakthrough achieved, but our exploitation of the opportunity, as so often before, lagged behind the early promise. It was apparent, and not for the first time, that Dempsey's advance had been rigidly restricted. Before I left my office that evening, I phoned Portal and Eisenhower to tell them that in my view it was not rapid enough. Our armour had penetrated only some three miles beyond the line of the morning's bombardment. By 19 July it was clear that the Germans were now in a position to prevent us advancing. Our three armoured divisions, the 11th, 7th, and Guards, had been counter-attacked from several directions. The advance came to a halt.

On 20 July, I spoke to Portal about the Army's failure. We were agreed in regarding Montgomery as the cause. We also talked about the control of the Strategic Air Forces. Portal felt that the time was drawing near when their control could revert to the Combined Chiefs of Staff exercised through himself. Second, and more immediate, was the problem of Leigh-Mallory's flirtation with Montgomery at Coningham's expense. I said: 'In these circumstances, Leigh-Mallory has no time for the direction of the Strategic Forces, and I, at S.H.A.E.F., will have to do that.'

Although I frequently conferred with Eisenhower in these

days, I did not normally keep a record of our conversations. According to the diary of Eisenhower's aide, Captain Butcher, I told the Supreme Commander on the evening of 19 July that Montgomery had, in effect, stopped his armour from going farther. Later, I am reported as saying that the British Chiefs of Staff would 'support any recommendation that Ike might care to make with respect to Monty for not succeeding in going places with his big three-armoured division push.'

I am sure that this record is misleading, for although I strongly disapproved of Montgomery's action, it was quite beyond my powers to speak in the name of the British Chiefs of Staff. Indeed, the chairman of the Chiefs of Staff Committee, Alan Brooke, gave Montgomery strong support. Brooke warned Montgomery of Churchill's tendency to listen to suggestions that he was not prepared to take risks. Montgomery himself is recorded in Brooke's diary as being 'in grand form and delighted with his success east of Caen'.[1]

I had a shrewd idea that Bradley had been urging Eisenhower, now that it was clear there was going to be no breakthrough on the British Front, to plan a break-out on the western flank. It was refreshing to hear of at least a possibility of breaking the deadlock. Welcome though it was, there was one element of doubt, and I asked Alan Brooke for his personal opinion of the prospects. As usual with him, he was very blunt. He said, 'I know the bocage country well from my boyhood days, and they will never get through it.'

My experience of British generals during this war (with the notable exception of O'Connor) had been that they would initially choose the straight-ahead line of attack and only adopt the famous right hook when compelled to do so. It was, indeed, unusual for me to accept an opinion such as that the C.I.G.S. proffered, and it was not without some quiet amusement that I later observed that the official military historian had pilloried me for having adopted the C.I.G.S's view. It served me right.

★

My immediate problem was to place on a more solid footing

[1] Bryant: *Triumph in the West*, p. 235.

the arrangements for control of our Air Forces. Leigh-Mallory, though earnest, zealous, and brave, did not inspire confidence as Commander of the Allied Expeditionary Air Forces. It seemed to me that he was insufficiently firm in explaining to the Army authorities the limitations of air-power in direct support of the ground battle. A few days before 'Overlord', I had told Leigh-Mallory that I did not approve of the tactical air plan and especially of the proposed attacks on towns to establish road-blocks. I thought the German Air Force could profitably receive more attention. Leigh-Mallory, however, considered that direct support to the Army was the first priority, and that our fighters could keep the Luftwaffe quiet. Later, he complained of my criticisms, which had been made at the usual morning meeting of Air commanders. I replied on the day of 'Overlord' itself by telling him not to be so silly. A leader must be ready to take criticism. Already the conflict of view between the American authorities and Leigh-Mallory about bombing priorities was becoming very marked. I did succeed in inducing him to forget the plan of making road-blocks. Spaatz, however, told me on 7 June that he was unhappy about the daily meetings at Stanmore. Too little consideration was given to the American proposal to intensify attacks against airfields used by the enemy. I did my best before the meeting the next morning, to explain gently to Leigh-Mallory that a less brusque manner would pay dividends. The Americans, with whom on this point I sympathised, pressed again for more systematic attacks on German airfields. Leigh-Mallory maintained his preference for attacks on railways and roads, but did go so far as to ask Doolittle for an airfield plan. For a time the atmosphere at the Stanmore meetings improved. Leigh-Mallory talked less, and gave the others more opportunity to present their opinions.

Nevertheless I was rapidly coming to believe that the whole system of controlling the air forces must be reorganised. I felt that the Headquarters of the Allied Expeditionary Air Forces could be eliminated, or, at any rate, largely reduced. The Americans, led by Spaatz, wanted Leigh-Mallory removed. Even Harris, who co-operated most loyally, was very irritated at the delay at A.E.A.F. Headquarters in giving him his targets for each night's bombing. The incidents in mid-June, when Leigh-Mallory sent a committee to Montgomery's headquarters without asking Spaatz for a representative, have been described. A month later, I could not help feeling that Leigh-Mallory's large assurances to Montgomery encouraged the unhealthy tendency of the Army to rely on air-power for support of a kind which it could not really confer. Zuckerman's preliminary report on the bombing of Caen during the first combined operation indicated that it had been of little value except to morale, and one of the lesssons which he drew on that occasion was that the Army machine had not informed its various cogs correctly about the purpose of the heavy bombardment which was laid on as a prelude to the assault. By now it was evident that Leigh-Mallory wanted to run the air side of the battle. I felt that if this were so, he could not control the Strategic Forces, which I must take over. On 13 July I told Leigh-Mallory that if he became in effect Air Commander for the battle, I should have to take over the Strategic Forces. On this, he said that he would think the matter over again. Leigh-Mallory's weakness was his desire to interfere with subordinate commanders. I told him that his job was not to command but to command in chief. 'Mary' Coningham and Brereton knew more about the tactical employment of air forces than he or I. Our job was to control, not the Tactical or Strategic Air Forces, but their commanders. This was the background to the crisis in relations between Montgomery and the Air commanders, and to my conversation with Portal on 20 July. In a further talk on 22 July, Portal agreed with me that Leigh-Mallory could not fight the battle and control the strategic bombers. I had already taken over from Leigh-Mallory the responsibility for the attacks on 'Crossbow' V2 sites and Spaatz showed clearly that he would do all he could to prevent Leigh-Mallory from controlling the Strategic Air Forces.

For the moment, these matters had to remain in suspense. Early on the morning of 21 July, we received news of the attempt on Hitler's life by certain members of the German High Command. I saw the Supreme Commander at once, and told him that Montgomery's failure to take action earlier had lost us the opportunity offered by the attempt on Hitler's life. I asked him to act at once

[565]

with Montgomery. Eisenhower agreed to do so, and said he would prepare a Paper. I intended, if the Supreme Commander would not act firmly, to put my views in writing to the British Chiefs of Staff. I told Eisenhower that his own people would be thinking that he had sold them to the British if he continued to support Montgomery without protest. Later, I attended Bedell Smith's morning meeting, and, thinking of the threat from 'V'-weapons, remarked: 'Unless we get the Pas de Calais quickly, southern England will have a bad time.' When Bedell Smith replied that we should not get there soon, I said: 'Then we must change our leaders for men who will get us there.'

During that afternoon of 21 July, a copy of Eisenhower's letter to Montgomery arrived at my office. I was disappointed that I had not seen it before despatch. The Supreme Commander recalled that in a letter of 8 July, Montgomery had insisted that we must get the Brittany Peninsula, that we must not be hemmed in to a relatively small area, and that we must engage the enemy in battle. He also recalled Montgomery's directive of 10 July, in which it was stated that we were so strong and well situated that we could attack the Germans 'hard and continuously in the relentless pursuit of our objectives. This will be done by both First and Second Armies.' This, Eisenhower wrote, was exactly his own view. So far as he could tell, we were now relatively stronger than we could probably hope to be at any time in the near future. 'Time is vital,' he wrote, 'we must not only have the Brittany Peninsula—we must have it quickly. So we must hit with everything.'

In late June, Eisenhower went on, when Bradley's U.S. Third Army was cleaning up around Cherbourg, the British Second Army was trying to prevent any movement of German troops from the eastern to the western flank, so that when the U.S. First Army turned southward it would have the best possible conditions for a rapid advance to the base of the peninsula. The Second Army was not entirely successful, and would have not been except by means of a definite and continuing offensive. Since then, despite all his aggressiveness, Bradley's advance to the southward had been disappointingly slow. Again, when armoured divisions of Second Army broke through the enemy's forward lines, Eisenhower had been extremely hopeful and optimistic. 'I thought that at last we had him and were going to roll him up. That did not come about.'

Now we were pinning our immediate hopes on Bradley's attack, which should begin very shortly, but the country was unsuitable, and the enemy strong at the point of main assault. The Supreme Commander thought it more than ever important that we should be aggressive along the whole front. Now that the advances near Caen had partially eliminated the need for a defensive attitude, he felt Montgomery must insist that Dempsey keep up the strength of his attacks. As Bradley's move started, Dempsey's should be intensified until he gained the space and airfields we needed. The enemy had no big reserves immediately available, so we did not need to fear, at this moment, a great counter-offensive.

As soon as I read this letter, I commented to my personal Staff Officer that it was 'not strong enough. Montgomery can evade it. It contains no order.' I could not help fearing that in this dangerous situation, Montgomery, while welcoming the terms of the letter, might fail to carry out its implications. To me it seemed imperative that we attacked early on both fronts, aiming at deep penetration and a rapid exploitation. Three factors dictated this course. The first was political. That night I wrote:

> The crisis in Germany, the growing war weariness in this country [Britain], and the emergence of the flying-bomb with the probability of the long-range Rocket, afford us our opportunity and indicate our danger. If we strike effectively now, we hit an enemy, the higher direction of whose military machine is suffering from some confusion.

> If we postpone indefinitely our effective attack, his military direction will recover its poise, while the nervous strain on the civilian population of this country will be growing more serious.

The second factor was operational, as Eisenhower had, indeed, pointed out to Montgomery. Thanks to the success of our build-up and the failure of the enemy's, both due to air superiority, our relative strengths showed a remarkable preponderance of men and machines in our favour. This situation could not last indefinitely. The third factor was administrative. We hardly had enough room, at the height of summer, to manœuvre our forces in the territories so far captured. Unless we could increase that area and obtain more port capacity, I did not think we should have the communications, or the space, to maintain our forces during the winter. All the evidence available to me indicated a serious lack of fighting leadership in the higher direction of the British armies in Normandy. I thought Montgomery should be invited to review his present corps and divisional commanders with the object of weeding out ruthlessly the inert and incompetent, and substituting for them men prepared, when occasion demanded, to take risks.

On 22 July, Montgomery replied to Eisenhower's letter that there was not, and never had been, any intention to stop offensive operations on the eastern flank. Montgomery had also issued a new directive to his commanders. I told Eisenhower in a letter of 23 July that I could see in the new directive little indication that Montgomery appreciated the vital importance of time, which Eisenhower had emphasised in his letter of the 21st. Nor could I see any indication of the bold offensive action which the time factor demanded and our strength justified. I was shocked by the satisfaction with the situation which the directive expressed. Apart from the initial success of the 'Overlord' landings, I could see no grounds for satisfaction with the operations in the eastern sector. For weeks after the landings, while our build-up proceeded, the enemy struggled from hand to mouth with inadequate forces, split up in bits and pieces along the line, disorganised in command and short of material and weapons. On the west, despite the difficulties of the terrain, we had been able to widen the beachhead and clear the Cotentin Peninsula:

> On the eastern flank, despite our overwhelming superiority, we were apparently unable to exploit our advantage, and now, more than six weeks after the landing, one of our beaches, and the only port of any size, is still under enemy shell-fire.
>
> I cannot forget, either, that one of the original objects underlying the selection of the point of attack was the seizure of the good airfield ground South East as well as North West of Caen, that the Airfield programme which should have been completed by D plus 40, is still only half complete, and some of the airfields are still under shell-fire. These are no grounds for satisfaction.

[568]

It is clear that in the recent operation to the South of Caen, there was no intention to make that operation the decisive one which you so clearly indicated as necessary in your letters and signals to General Montgomery. An overwhelming air bombardment opened the door, but there was no immediate determined deep penetration while the door remained open, and we are now little beyond the furthest bomb craters.

In the new directive issued by Montgomery, I saw a return to the previous plan. A limited extension of the line round our eastern flank was to be made. Once we had done this we were to keep the part of the front east of the River Orne

. . . as active as possible with the resources available; the enemy must be led to believe that we are contemplating a major advance towards Falaise and Argentan, and he must be induced to build up his main strength to the East of the River Orne, so that our affairs on the Western flank can proceed with greater speed.

I told Eisenhower that I had no faith in such a plan. Experience had shown that the enemy could not be prevented from moving his forces from one flank to another by such means. Very probably, the 9th and 10th S.S. Panzer Divisions would be found shortly facing General Bradley's attack in the west. While I had every faith in Bradley and his commanders, I did not think we could expect rapid moves in that area because of the nature of the terrain. On the other hand, the country in which wide and rapid sweeps could be made was that lying to the south-east of Caen. I felt that some more specific action was needed if we were not finally to lose our initial advantage and the opportunities of decisive victory which it offered. I therefore urged again that Eisenhower himself should form a Tactical Headquarters in France, and take control of the two Army Groups, thus putting an end to an arrangement by which 21 Army Group had operational control over General Bradley's forces. Until this could be done, I suggested that Montgomery's directives should give clear and unmistakable orders for decisive, energetic action.

Fearing a division on national lines, and apprehending that Eisenhower might feel difficulty in giving such orders to a British General, I wrote to the Supreme Commander:

I know you will appreciate that I do not write this through any

weakening of my complete confidence in you; on the contrary, I write
it because I realise the difficulties of Allied Command and in the hope
that the expression of my views as your immediate British subordinate
may be of some assistance to you and to support you in any action
you may consider the situation demands.

Portal had already seen, and agreed with, the broad terms of
this letter. Eisenhower wrote to Montgomery that they were
apparently in complete agreement that a vigorous persistent
offensive should be sustained by both armies. A general offensive
was further indicated at this moment because of the evidence
we were now receiving that the enemy had to use S.S. troops to
ensure effectiveness in other units. There was clearly confusion
and doubt in the ranks of the Germans which we should exploit.

I had heard from a number of sources that the Americans were
beginning to criticise Eisenhower for being too 'soft' in his
relations with the British. They were inclined to cite his toleration
of Montgomery's dilatoriness as an example. On the night of
24 July, 'Mary' Coningham dined with me. He said that Montgomery had talked with the Prime Minister for an hour, and
'had him in the bag'. However, Montgomery had changed his
tune towards Coningham, and had decided that they should
once more work closely together.

At this point there fell into our hands a German document
which gave the enemy's view of the British Second Army's methods
of fighting. Army Intelligence in the Second Army had the courage to circulate it. I found it most illuminating. The report said
that the tactical principles of the British troops were that a
thorough reconnaissance carried out mainly by aircraft and tanks
preceded every engagement. This reconnaissance was usually
supported by intensive harassing fire from artillery. British
attacks took place on principle only after a barrage of anything
up to three hours. 'A successful break-in by the enemy is almost
never exploited to pursuit. If our own troops are ready near the
front for a local counter-attack, the ground is immediately
regained.' The enemy drew the conclusion that they should
occupy the main line of resistance very thinly, holding behind
every sector a local reserve supported by tanks, ready to advance
as soon as the artillery fire lifted. 'It is best to attack the English,

who are very sensitive to close combat and flank attack, at their weakest moment—that is, when they have to fight without their artillery.'

The report described the fighting morale of the British infantry as being not very great:

They rely largely on the artillery and air force support. In the case of well-directed artillery fire by us they often abandon their position in flight. The enemy is extraordinarily nervous of close combat. Whenever the enemy infantry is energetically engaged, they mostly retreat or surrender.

On all days of action the Germans noted the strongest concentration of fire, with great expenditure of ammunition. There was never any deception by artillery fire as to the main point of the effort. On the contrary, the main effort of the artillery was always directed where the breakthrough was intended. The report also drew attention to the continual attack on this particular division's advance by single and twin-engined fighters. Convoys, vehicles, and important cross roads were destroyed. Special attention was paid to fuel and supply vehicles:

There was no resistance by our own aircraft, and therefore the enemy had undisturbed opportunity for flying low in search of our supply routes. Since 13 June artillery reconnaissance has been used, and fighter-bombers and fighters against our anti-aircraft and artillery positions. . . . Enemy bomber forces do not allow themselves to be dispersed by accurate anti-aircraft fire once they have concentrated for their attack.

As I wrote to my old protector and friend, Lord Trenchard, on 25 July, I thought that from the point of view of the air battle and the strategic air operations, things were going smoothly and well, but in the last affair I felt that we had all, including Eisenhower and myself, been

. . . had for suckers. I do not believe there was the slightest intention to make a clean breakthrough. Moreover, as has happened before, deliberate and cold-blooded endeavours are being made in high quarters in Normandy to hide the facts. I am determined to get at the facts if I possibly can, but I can see only too well that there is every prospect that awkward ones will be either drowned or doctored.

By now, Eisenhower had decided in principle to set up a Tactical Headquarters in Normandy. At a meeting with him and Leigh-Mallory on 26 July, I said again that if Leigh-Mallory went forward to control the battle I should take over the Strategic Air Forces. Leigh-Mallory exclaimed in his hot-blooded way that I continually foiled him. Eisenhower studiously ignored the incident. He said that he was anxious that I should examine the use of heavy bombers in support of ground forces. Bedell Smith, Leigh-Mallory and I considered this proposal the next day. The Supreme Commander was anxious that I should convene a meeting of the Army Commanders to elucidate the lessons learned from the attacks by Montgomery and Bradley which had been preceded by 'set-piece' bombing. As Bedell Smith remarked: 'We now possess a power of breakthrough; we must learn how to use it.' I thought it was essential to follow up the bombing quickly before the enemy had time to recover. If necessary, the safety margin of the Army had to be reduced and the risk of casualties from our own bombing accepted. Generals Spaatz and Eaker, to whom I also spoke, expressed their doubts about the use of heavy bombers in direct support of the Army. Eaker went so far as to say that they should be used only in a combined operation such as an actual landing. Spaatz's opinion was less extreme. He feared that too frequent a use of heavy bombers in direct support would act as a drug and and eventually provoke an antidote.

After the fall of Cherbourg it took Bradley several days to rearrange his forces ready for the main attack. It was slow and hard fighting in constricted areas. Bradley and his unit commanders were not only resolute, but the fighting qualities of the troops were superb. On the morning of 25 July he opened the assault which led to the breakthrough from the Cherbourg Peninsula across the St. Lô–Perrier line. Eisenhower, speaking as the responsible American commander, assured Bradley that he took sole responsibility for the necessary price of victory. A breakthrough at this juncture would minimise the cost:

General Montgomery's plan calls for a vigorous and continuing offensive by the other armies in the line, thus allowing you to pursue every advantage with an ardour verging on recklessness, and with all your troops, without fear of a major counter-offensive from the forces the enemy now has on this front. All these attacks are mutually supporting, and if Second Army should secure a breakthrough simultaneously with yours, the results will be incalculable.

A tremendous weight of air attack was thrown in. Inevitably some of the bombs fell on our own troops—a three-star American General was one of the casualties—and S.H.A.E.F. were kept busy working to prevent the destruction of the confidence between the ground and air forces. For the first day the progress was slow. On 26 July, however, the breakthrough was accomplished and the American armoured forces rushed southwards towards Coutances and Avranches and beyond. Meanwhile, Eisenhower was appealing to Churchill for vigorous action on Montgomery's part. The Supreme Commander mentioned stories appearing in the American Press to the effect that S.H.A.E.F. were sparing British forces at the expense of the Americans, who were suffering all the casualties. It was decided that the C.I.G.S. should dine with Churchill, Eisenhower, and Bedell Smith on 27 July. Alan Brooke thought that this meeting did 'a lot of good'. He offered to go over with Eisenhower to Normandy if this would assist in handling Montgomery. It seemed to the C.I.G.S. that the strategy in Normandy was a straightforward matter. The British forces on the left must hold and draw the Germans on to themselves while the Americans swung up to open the Brittany Peninsula. The trouble came with the Press reports that the Americans were bearing all the brunt of the war.

In a letter to Montgomery the next day, Brooke commented that Eisenhower clearly considered that Dempsey should be doing

... more than he does; it is equally clear that Ike has the very vaguest conception of war! I drew his attention to what your basic strategy had been, i.e. to hold with your left and draw Germans on to the flank whilst you pushed with your right. I explained how in my mind this conception was being carried out, that the bulk of the armour had continuously been kept against the British. He could not refute these arguments, and then asked whether I did not consider that we were in a position to launch major offensives on each front simultaneously.

I told him that in view of the fact that the German density in Normandy was $2\frac{1}{2}$ times that on the Russian front whilst our superiority in strength was only in the nature of some 25% as compared to 300% Russian superiority on Eastern front, I did not consider that we were in a position to launch an all-out offensive along the whole front. Such a procedure would definitely not fit in with our strategy of mopping up Brest by swinging forward western flank. . . .

Now, as a result of all this talking and the actual situation on your front, I feel personally quite certain that Dempsey must attack *at the earliest possible* moment on a large scale. We must not allow German forces to move from his front to Bradley's front or we shall give more cause than ever for criticism. I shall watch this end and keep you informed, but do not neglect this point; it is an important one at present. . . .[1]

I cannot feel that Brooke's letter to Montgomery does justice either to Eisenhower or to the facts. To say that Eisenhower knew nothing about strategy is manifestly unfair; to reduce to a bald figure of 25 per cent. our superiority in France did not reflect our overwhelming strength in the air; and to dismiss as impossible the simultaneous launching of major offensives on each front and then to urge a full-scale attack by Dempsey, seems to be a self-contradictory policy. Eisenhower and I had long wanted offensives on both fronts, not least for the reason given in the last paragraph of Brooke's letter. Indeed, before he received it, Montgomery had adopted the policy of full-out attack. He had already telegraphed to Eisenhower:

I have ordered Dempsey to throw all caution overboard, and to take any risks he likes, and to accept any casualties, and to step on the gas for Vire.

By 31 July, Bradley's attack had penetrated so far that Eisenhower told Montgomery:

Bradley has plenty of Infantry Units to rush into forward area to consolidate all gains, and permit armour to continue thrusting and surrounding enemy. With Canadian Army fighting intensively to

---

[1] Bryant: *Triumph in the West*, pp. 243–5.

prevent enemy movement away from Caen area, Dempsey's attack, coupled with Bradley's, will clean up the area west of Orne once and for all.

Two days later, Eisenhower told Montgomery that German resistance seemed to have disintegrated materially in the region of Avranches. Our armoured and mobile columns would therefore want to operate boldly against the enemy's flanks. All the commanders should be aware of the fact that in emergency, supplies could be dropped by air.

From the region of Mortain the Germans tried to counter-attack towards Avranches to cut Bradley's line of communications. Both Bradley and Eisenhower saw the opportunity to swing round from the south against the flank of the German attack. To obtain the forces for this, troops had to be taken from the very spot which faced the German attack. Eisenhower happened to be at Bradley's headquarters when this move was discussed, and approved it there and then. He told Bradley that if the Germans should temporarily break through from Mortain to Avranches and thus cut off the southward thrust, we could give the advance forces two thousand tons of supply per day by air. However, the German counter-attack was bravely withstood and the American enveloping movement and the British attack on the left finally resulted in the cooping up of large German forces in what we came to call 'the Falaise pocket'.

In the earlier stages of this offensive, Bradley was undecided whether to put a strong force into the Brittany Peninsula, or whether to put our main strength into exploiting the break-through. Again, Eisenhower happened to be at his headquarters, and decided that the right policy was to make another and wider envelopment of the enemy forces towards the Seine and even the east of Paris. By mid-August a large number of German troops were almost sealed off in the pocket. Our full air strength was used against the trapped German divisions. The Allied crews took the fullest advantage of the excellent targets provided by the massed, confused enemy formations. The American forces sped onwards towards Paris, liberated on 24 August. The enemy had lost in the campaign of Normandy the better part of half a million men, and a mass of equipment.

This was the work of a man of whom Brooke said, 'Ike knows nothing about strategy'.[1]

*

In the meantime, another front had been opened by landings in the south of France. Operation 'Dragoon', formerly known as 'Anvil', had been postponed when it became clear that it could not be mounted simultaneously with 'Overlord'. Neither Churchill nor the British Chiefs of Staff had felt much enthusiasm for this operation. Eisenhower and the American Chiefs of Staff, on the other hand, supported it firmly. At intervals it was argued that since we should soon have the Brittany ports we should not need Marseilles; that the forces allocated to 'Dragoon' could be better used elsewhere; that 'Dragoon' could not be made to dovetail with 'Overlord'; that in any case the 'Dragoon' offensive would proceed but slowly. Eisenhower contended that the capture of ports in Southern France would improve our supply position, since American ships would not then have to pass through British ports; that a successful offensive in Southern France would prove an extra prong to the general onslaught upon the Reich; that it would draw off a number of German divisions from northern France; that 'Dragoon' and 'Overlord' together would cut off large German forces in south-west France; that 'Dragoon' would protect the right flank of 'Overlord'; and that the 'Dragoon' forces would advance north of Lyons within six weeks of the landing. In these views both Admiral Ramsay and I strongly supported the Supreme Commander. The United States Chiefs of Staff refused to accept the commitment of our resources in the Mediterranean to large-scale operations in Northern Italy or in the Balkans. This virtually decided the question. 'Dragoon' was eventually launched on 15 August. Its rapid progress justified our highest hopes.

[1] Bryant: *Triumph in the West*, p. 243.

5

IN carrying this narrative forward towards the end of August, I have anticipated the story in certain vital aspects. 'Overlord' had not long been under way when we began to receive detailed confirmation of the fact that the Transportation Plan had dislocated the French railway system. After D-Day, when we could attack any target without prejudicing security, air attacks were directed against bridges over the Seine and Loire and in the Paris–Orléans gap; against bridges in those areas of France and Belgium where disruption of rail traffic would mean serious congestion near the battle area; and against rail centres and junctions which our Intelligence sources suggested were either centres for entraining or points directly concerned with major military movement. In these operations, Bomber Command dropped about 50 per cent. more tons of bombs than all the other air forces put together.

As the battle progressed after 6 June, we realised ever more clearly that the enemy's divisions in the line were not at full strength and that his forces were moving up in driblets. Within the Seine–Loire area, the railways were almost paralysed, and only one division, whose move originated within the area, used rail transport to any appreciable extent. Even then, our bombing on the trains of its leading units obliged them to detrain and cost serious losses in equipment and ammunition. Armoured vehicles and tanks were obliged to progress as best they could by road, a process which often damaged them seriously before they reached the battle area. Many enemy units were delayed for lack of petrol and shortage of motor transport. They made long journeys by bicycle and by marching on foot. Early in the month of June a considerable number of German troops did, indeed, manage to cross the Loire by rail and road bridges, although those travelling by rail did not appear to have got much further north than Le Mans. In the case of the Seine, it was a different story. All the road and rail bridges between Paris and the sea had been cut or blocked by 6 June and were kept out of action thereafter. Rail

[577]

traffic was, therefore, canalised into the Paris–Orléans gap, and very little rail movement of troops was reported west of Paris. Trains could still get through to Paris from the east, but even here the capacity of the railways was so reduced that they could not deal even with the highest priority military traffic, let alone with anything else. The bulk of the 9th and 10th S.S. Panzer Divisions from Poland were obliged to detrain as far east as Nancy and Bar-le-Duc.

After Paris was entered, we set up a research unit, with French help, in the railway offices of the Gare du Nord. It immediately became apparent that attacks on stations along specific main lines produced a state of creeping paralysis. A captured German General attributed the difficulties experienced in moving reinforcements to the Normandy battle to the skill and the scientific employment of the Allied bombers. The destruction by air attack of bridges, and the laborious ferry crossings enforced upon some of the Panzer divisions, caused particular difficulties. Other statements showed clearly that the enemy's belated withdrawal was rendered no less difficult by the same means, at a time when the few escape routes were overloaded with German traffic streaming away from the battlefront. The same General emphasised the effect of Allied air attack on the supply situation. All he could do, on receipt of repeated orders to counter-attack, was to report that such action was made impossible by the lack of fuel and ammunition. These commodities had to be fetched from dumps, some of which were as remote as the east bank of the Marne, along routes patrolled by our fighter-bombers, and loaded with German traffic moving in the opposite direction. Another German senior officer said simply that France, the country in which all means of transportation were interrupted, had defeated the Germans.

Von Rundstedt, shortly before his supersession, issued on 20 June a document entitled 'Experiences from the Invasion Battles of Normandy'. Our Intelligence services soon obtained a copy. It included this revealing sentence:

Within $2\frac{1}{2}$ days, at a depth from the enemy bridgehead of about 65 miles, 29,000 enemy sorties were counted; of these, about 2,300 aircraft a day dive-bomb and strafe every movement on the ground, even a single soldier.

Another document which soon came into our hands was the telephone journal of the German Seventh Army. It revealed that communications had broken down from the start. At midnight on 6 June, one division reported that there were no communications at all between the divisions, the regiments, and the battalions. On 8 June, the Seventh Army complained that it had no communication with and therefore no knowledge of the movements of, 2 Panzer Corps and its divisions. On 13 June, 47 Panzer Corps was in position a whole day awaiting orders but out of touch with Seventh Army Headquarters. The journal contained many complaints about lack of fuel. When extra forces were moved into the battle area they could not be supplied. In answer to complaints on 13 June, the Quartermaster-General stated that the nearest fuel dump with available supplies was at Nantes. We learned from other sources of Intelligence of the effect of Allied bombing on the Germans' capacity to move quickly: 265th Infantry Division came in part from Lorient by bicycle because of the shortage of petrol. To add insult to injury, even the movement by bicycle was interrupted by bombing. In equally bad straits was 275th Infantry Division, because the trains were bombed and the French had seized all the available horses. One company took a whole week to move 150 miles. The wide dispersal of marching columns to avoid attack delayed their organisation for fighting when they did at last reach the battle area. All three railway routes selected for moving the 1st S.S. Panzer Division from Belgium were blocked in turn by bombing, and it took a week to reach Paris from Louvain because railway routes were cut. From Le Havre, 346th Infantry Division moved by bicycle and then had to be ferried over the Seine because the bridges had been destroyed. Up to fourteen days were taken to effect moves from southern or eastern France to Normandy, and up to nine days for moves from the Pas de Calais. By the end of July, in short, the combined effect of air attack and to a lesser extent French sabotage had made the rapid transfer of troops by rail impossible. By now, dispersion of rail movement was necessary well to the east of Paris. It took 9th and 10th S.S. Panzer Divisions as long to get from eastern France to Normandy as they had taken to get from Poland to eastern France. They had to cover the last few hundred miles by road.

These attacks were not, of course, our only preoccupation. Much attention had to be diverted to the threat from flying-bombs and rockets. The flying-bomb attacks opened up in real earnest on the evening of 15 June. When the first reports came in, we were inclined at S.H.A.E.F. to treat them with some detachment, refusing to allow the new threat to overshadow 'Overlord'. The enemy had chosen his moment well, for the main sites in the Pas de Calais were cloud-covered. On the evening of 16 June, I attended a meeting which the Prime Minister had summoned to consider the 'Crossbow' operations. Churchill refused to allow these developments to upset our concentration on the battle in Normandy. Our attitude could not be maintained for long, however. By the morning of Sunday 18 June the situation was more serious. Eisenhower ruled that the air forces' first priority must now be 'Crossbow'. He minuted to me later that day:

These targets are to take first priority over everything except the urgent requirements of the battle; this priority to obtain until we can be certain that we have definitely gotten the upper hand of this particular menace.

This directive I showed to Churchill at a meeting which he called to discuss 'Crossbow' that evening. We had now received Intelligence that the Germans were ready to use the rocket sites as well. Not until the vile weather of mid-June had abated were we able to aim really vigorous air blows against the sites. From 23 June the offensive went forward with full vigour.

It was not always easy to steer a course between the conflicting demands of the battle, of the oil targets, of the 'Crossbow' sites and of the general 'Pointblank' attack upon the German Air Force. Both Harris and Spaatz co-operated in executing the decisions reached by superior authority; but both were, not unnaturally, anxious to return to the kind of operation which seemed to them to offer the prospect of decisive, early triumph. In a memorandum to the Supreme Commander on 28 June,

Spaatz urged that now 'Overlord' was under way, a policy decision was necessary. He thought that on days when the weather made visual bombings over Germany possible, we should concentrate on operations 'designed to deny the German Armies the means to continue resistance'. This object, and the neutralisation of the Luftwaffe, should take priority over all others with only two exceptions: first, a major emergency in the land battle, and second, operations against the big rocket-firing installations. Spaatz believed that unless we were confronted with such a major emergency, the results obtained from the tactical use of heavy bombers would not give as much support to 'Overlord' as the use of the same amount of force against critical targets in Germany.

Eisenhower ruled that the 'Crossbow' targets must remain our first priority. When the entire strategic forces could not be used against 'Crossbow' we should attack the aircraft industry, oil, and the production of ball-bearings and vehicles. All targets must give way to any land battle which required the use of strategic air forces.

Though the unseasonable weather continued to hamper air operations against the 'Crossbow' sites, I advised that air action could reduce, but not exterminate, the menace. I thought at the beginning of July that we could manage to keep the German effort within the present limits, which were serious enough. I advised strongly against the idea of reprisals, with which the Prime Minister was toying. Portal, too, was disturbed by a proposal for a public announcement that if attacks by flying-bombs persisted, we would retaliate by wiping out certain named towns in Germany. He thought it would be a mistake to enter into what would amount to negotiation with the enemy, for such a course would provide the Germans with invaluable proof that the flying-bombs were achieving success, and that their decision to start the attacks had been right. He did not think that the Germans would alter their decision out of consideration for the population of towns which had no important part to play in the war effort. Moreover, to bomb German towns on such a scale would represent a very serious diversion of effort from those objectives connected with Germany's power to sustain the war, such as communications and oil, and from the battle in France. He remarked to his colleagues in the Chiefs of Staff committee that the launching sites were so easy to repair that we had now given higher priority to the supply sites and storage dumps. In recent weeks, some 40 per cent. of the whole bomber effort had been employed against 'Crossbow' targets. To achieve retaliation on the scale suggested would need not less than five thousand sorties in fine weather. The C.I.G.S. agreed that we should not take more of our bomber effort away from targets of military import-ance, though we should watch for new developments which might indicate an increase in the weight of attack, and particularly for any sign of employment of the rockets. Portal's information was that German production of flying-bombs seemed unlikely to exceed 1,200 per month. Moreover, their problem of maintain-ing a flow of components from the factories to the launching sites might become critical. The Chiefs of Staff therefore decided on no immediate action. On reading the record of this discussion, Eisenhower minuted to me:

> As I have before indicated, I am opposed to retaliation as a method of stopping this business—at least, until every other thing has been tried and failed. Please continue to oppose.

The Chiefs of Staff on 5 July rejected entirely the use of gas against 'Crossbow' installations, and also, for the time being, bombing attacks on small towns. They did not wish to rule out this latter possibility for all time, and reported accordingly to the Prime Minister. Again Eisenhower minuted that for the time being, at least, he refused to be a party to so-called retaliation by the use of gas: 'Let's, for God's sake, keep our eyes on the ball and use some sense.'

I have mentioned already that one of the principal reasons for my anxiety that we should take an early offensive in Normandy, was the desire to overrun the 'Crossbow' sites. Although a high priority was devoted to their reduction in July, attacks by flying-bombs on Southern England caused a good deal of heart-burning in London. Portal told me on 28 July that the Air Ministry was coming under heavy fire from what he delicately termed 'certain not too well informed quarters of the Government' about the percentage of bomber effort being devoted to 'Crossbow'. He wrote that he did not clearly understand which authority decided what portion of available effort on any given day should be directed against particular targets. On some days, the needs of the battle would obviously determine what was available for use elsewhere. There must still, however, be considerable scope for decision, especially on days when the requirements of the land battle were small or non-existent. He asked me to confirm that there had been no alteration in Eisenhower's directive that 'Crossbow' had complete priority, subject only to the needs of the battle.

I had for some time been much dissatisfied with the quality of the Air Ministry's Intelligence organisation, which still failed to see the merits of the Transportation Plan and which was not now providing the strategical forces with timely information of the right quality about 'Crossbow'. It was clear to me and to Sir Henry Tizard, whom I visited at Oxford on 9 July, that the implications of the flying-bomb mattered much more than the immediate inconvenience it was causing. Later that day, I asked the Deputy Chief of the Air Staff, Air Chief Marshal Bottomley, whether we were proposing to make flying-bombs, on which the Americans had already started. Bottomley asked 'What will be their application in our hands?' to which I replied: 'In their present form they are a toy; but their development will profoundly affect both war and peace.'

In answer to Portal on 6 August I said that there had been no alteration in the priority allotted to 'Crossbow'. The daily allocation of targets was settled at the meeting each morning over which Leigh-Mallory presided and which I usually attended. The fact that more bomber effort had not been devoted to 'Crossbow' was due to a combination of the weather, which had only given us very fleeting opportunities, and lack of useful targets. As our Intelligence improved, I hoped we should be able to evolve a more satisfactory target system. Until then, I feared that our efforts were bound to be rather piecemeal and unsatisfactory.

By now, the success of the offensives launched by Bradley and Montgomery offered some hope that we should soon reach the only really reliable solution by overrunning the launching sites. In mid-August, a material reduction in the 'Crossbow' effort was noticeable. This, I thought, was due to the enemy's enormous difficulties in transport, now that his armies were in precipitate retreat. If the fighting stabilised, the enemy would have an opportunity again to transport supplies for the flying-bomb sites, and the effort would then increase. I emphasised to the Air commanders the high importance of bombing liquid oxygen plants, of which there were about six in range of our bombers. Both the rockets and the flying-bombs were dependent on this source.

By this time, flying-bombs had killed rather more than 5,000 people, had seriously injured more than 15,000, slightly injured some 20,000 and had destroyed some 30,000 dwellings. These figures, it might be thought, offered ample justification for the continued offensive against 'Crossbow' sites. However, the problem was not a simple one. Air Chief Marshal Harris pointed out on 18 August the extreme difficulty of bombing accurately the flying-bomb and rocket installations. Against these targets Bomber Command had already carried out nearly ten thousand sorties, losing the better part of 100 aircraft and 650 personnel. Nearly 36,000 tons of bombs had been dropped, quite apart from the vast effort made against the same targets by the Americans. Harris did not think that we had achieved a result commensurate with the effort. On the other hand, this scale of attack, combined with the needs of the battle, had caused us to take virtually the whole of Bomber Command and much of the American effort away from German targets for some $3\frac{1}{2}$ months. If the situation were allowed to go on in this way we should have to do all over again what we had already achieved in the progressive destruction of Germany's industrial capacity. The only real and effective answer to the flying-bomb and rocket, in Harris's view, was to increase the weight of the offensive against Germany and make it increasingly impossible for the enemy to produce the needful war material. The aim should be to destroy German resources and facilities until the armed forces were disarmed and the whole country collapsed. The American bomber forces had been built up to such an extent that they considerably exceeded the first line strength of Bomber Command, and had, for the first time, adequate reserves of material and personnel. A combined Anglo-American offensive against Germany, Harris argued, could produce results far more effective than those secured in 1943. The Allied heavy bomber forces could eradicate any German town except Berlin, in a combined, though not necessarily simultaneous, attack. In the process, the German night-fighter force would be annihilated, and the remains of the day-fighter force would soon be destroyed.

A few days after this memorandum was received, Anglo-American troops were in Paris. Northern France and Belgium were soon liberated. Harris's arguments, in so far as they related to the 'Crossbow' sites, were therefore soon reduced to irrelevance by the swift onrush of events. The gathering momentum of the offensive on land overran the rocket sites in the Pas de Calais and elsewhere. The other part of Harris's policy, however, relating to the right employment of our overwhelming strategical forces, was a factor of high importance in the argument soon to begin afresh. For the moment, the strategic forces devoted their effort to oil, communications, the German Air Force, and area bombing of German towns.

*

At this point, we may pause to measure the effect of air-power on the campaign in France. As we have seen, the air offensive against the transportation before D-Day had produced a state of virtual paralysis in the railway system of northern France and Belgium. This was the air's decisive contribution to that wide complex of operations by which Allied military strength was re-established in Western Europe. After D-Day the continued attacks on transport by road and rail, the harassment of even the smallest enemy movement, the onslaught against the 'Crossbow' sites, the direct intervention in the ground battle, and the continued assault upon Germany's productive capacity, meant the difference to us between a precarious foothold and a swift advance. By this, I do not mean to say that air-power had won the battle alone; but I was at the time, and remain, confident that without the exercise of air-power which our superiority in the skies made possible, victory could not have been won. Between 6 June and the end of August, the crews of the Allied Air Forces had flown nearly half a million sorties.

6

Exchanges between Eisenhower and Montgomery–Eisenhower's re-arrangement of command structure–Montgomery's vision of Berlin– Meeting at S.H.A.E.F.–General view of European strategy– Inadequate ports–Antwerp

ON 1 September, Eisenhower assumed operational control of the Allied Forces in France and S.H.A.E.F. was set up in Versailles. Montgomery surrendered his position as Ground Force Commander and now directed the Northern Group of Armies (21 Army Group), while General Bradley assumed control of the Central Group of Armies (12 Army Group), which now consisted of First and Third American Armies under Generals Hodges and Patton.

At this time, a mood of optimism prevailed. I gathered that the War Cabinet had taken it upon themselves to decide that the war would be over by Christmas. This atmosphere coincided with, and was partly induced by, a spate of victories which, I was sure, gave the misleading impression of premature collapse. The triumph in France, the Russian successes north of the Carpathians, the recent plot against Hitler's life, the purges inside Germany, caused many to believe that the end of the war was in sight, perhaps in a mere matter of weeks. Soon we discovered differently. The Russians had to stop at the Vistula, the Italian campaign seemed to be bogged down again, the thrust at Arnhem was soon to fail. These reverses, or pauses, meant that the war would inevitably continue into 1945; moreover, they indicated in my view that the German effort was not yet spent.

I was glad that Eisenhower had now moved from Britain to France. One of the most disturbing features of the campaign in recent weeks had been the uninhibited boosting at home of the British Army at the expense of the Americans. From what I heard at S.H.A.E.F., I could not help fearing that this process was sowing the seeds of a grave split between the Allies. For the moment, the Americans were being extremely reticent and generous, largely on account of Eisenhower's fine attitude, but, as I wrote to Lord Trenchard:

Sooner or later they will come into the open, and if the British public believe all they are being told now, they will not like being told a very different story by the Americans. It is a dangerous situation and may become a tragic one. However, perhaps coming events may cover up the past. . . .

Eisenhower's immediate concern was to allot tasks to the different armies. In his directive of 3 September, the Supreme Commander ruled that the Northern Group of Armies and that part of the Central Group operating north-west of the Ardennes, were to take Antwerp, reach the Siegfried Line covering the Ruhr and then seize the Ruhr. The other part of the Central Group of Armies should take Brest, protect the southern flank of the Expeditionary Force, occupy swiftly the section of the Siegfried Line covering the Saar, and then seize Frankfurt:

It is important that this operation should start as soon as possible, in order to forestall the enemy in this sector, but troops of Central Group of Armies operating against the North-west of the Ardennes must first be adequately supported.

Meanwhile, on 4 September, Montgomery had telegraphed to the Supreme Commander:

I consider we have now reached a stage where one really powerful and full-blooded thrust towards Berlin is likely to get there and thus end the German war.

We have *not* enough maintenance resources for two full-blooded thrusts.

The selected thrust must have all the maintenance resources it needs without any qualification, and any other operation must do the best it can with what is left over.

There are only two possible thrusts, one via the Ruhr and the other via Metz and the Saar.

In my opinion the thrust likely to give the best and quickest results is the northern one via the Ruhr.

Montgomery added that time was vital, and a decision about the selected thrust must be made at once: to attempt a compromise solution and split our resources so that neither thrust was a full-blooded one would prolong the war. He considered the problem viewed in this light, 'as very simple and clear-cut'. He felt sure the Supreme Commander would agree that a decision on the above lines was required at once. Perhaps Eisenhower would like to come and discuss it?

Eisenhower replied on 5 September that while he agreed with Montgomery's conception of the powerful and full-blooded thrust towards Berlin, he did not agree 'that it should be initiated at this moment to the exclusion of all other manœuvres'.

In Eisenhower's view, we must immediately exploit our success in destroying the bulk of the German Army in the west by breaching the Siegfried Line, crossing the Rhine on a wide front, and seizing the Saar and the Ruhr. This he intended to do with all possible speed. Once this process was accomplished, we should have a stranglehold on two of Germany's main industrial areas, and should thus largely destroy her capacity to wage war. This policy could also assist in cutting off forces which were now in retreat from south-western France:

> Moreover, it will give us freedom of action to strike in any direction and will force the enemy to disperse, over a wide area, such forces as he may be able to assemble for the defence of the West.

> While we are advancing, we will be opening the ports of Havre and Antwerp, which are essential to sustain a powerful thrust deep into Germany. No reallocation of our present resources would be adequate to sustain a thrust to Berlin.

Eisenhower's intention was, therefore, initially to occupy the Saar and Ruhr. By the time we had these areas, Havre and Antwerp should be available to maintain one or both of the thrusts mentioned by Montgomery. 'In this connection,' Eisenhower telegraphed:

> I have always given, and still give, priority to the Ruhr and the northern route of advance. . . . Locomotives and rolling stock are today being allocated on the basis of this priority to maintain the momentum of the advance of your forces, and those of Bradley northwest of the Ardennes. Please let me know at once your further maintenance requirements for the advance to, and occupation of, the Ruhr.

The crucial points of this telegram are the insistence that we could not make a thrust deep into Germany without deep-water ports, especially Havre and Antwerp; and that no matter what degree of priority we gave Montgomery from our existing resources, his armies could not without other sources of supply reach Berlin. A week or two earlier, on 19 August, Montgomery had met the Foreign Secretary, Eden, and had asked what help we could expect in the use of Belgian harbours and from the civilian population. He explained to Eden that the Channel ports 'had not the capacity he needed, and that if the battle unrolled as he planned, he must have the use of Antwerp'.[1]

On account of poor communications, Eisenhower's message was much delayed in reaching Montgomery, and by 7 September only the second half had been decyphered. Montgomery replied at once that his maintenance was 'stretched to the limit'. His transport system was based on operating 150 miles from the ports, but he was at present more than three hundred miles from Bayeux. In order to save transport he had cut down his intake into France to six thousand tons a day

... which is half what I consume, and I cannot go on for long like this. It is clear, therefore, that based as I am at present on Bayeux, I cannot capture the Ruhr. As soon as I have a Pas de Calais port working I would then require about 2,500 additional 3-ton lorries plus an assured air-lift averaging minimum 1,000 tons a day to enable me to get to the Ruhr and finally Berlin. I submit . . . that a reallocation of our present resources of every description would be adequate to get one thrust to Berlin.

Montgomery asked again whether Eisenhower could come to see him. The Supreme Commander, who was recovering from a slight accident, promised to come as soon as possible. He added that although maintenance was everywhere stretched to the limit, over hundreds of miles of sketchy communications, we must speedily push up 'all along the Front to cut off retreating enemy and concentrate in preparation for the big final thrust'.

As he telegraphed to the Combined Chiefs of Staff, Eisenhower thought the best opportunity of defeating the Germans in the west lay in striking at the Ruhr and the Saar, confident that the enemy would concentrate the remainder of his available forces to defend these essential areas. The first operation was to break the Siegfried Line and seize crossings over the Rhine. The main effort would be on the left. Then the Allied armies would prepare

[1] Avon: *The Eden Memoirs*: *The Reckoning*, pp. 468–9.

logistically and otherwise for a deep penetration into Germany. Reverting again to the crucial question of supply, Eisenhower warned that the German occupation of the islands at the mouth of the Scheldt was certain to delay our use of Antwerp and would, therefore, vitally influence the full development of Allied strategy. Once Antwerp had been seized, the armies operating north-west of the Ardennes and the Northern Group of Armies would breach the sector of the Siegfried Line which covered the Ruhr, and would seize that area. He wished to retain freedom of action to strike in any direction so far as the logistical situation permitted. Until we had the Channel ports and the railway lines leading from them in full working order, our supply situation was stretched to breaking point. The advance across the Siegfried Line meant a gamble which Eisenhower was prepared to take in order to exploit the disorganised state of the German armies in the west.

In their reply of 12 September, the Combined Chiefs of Staff approved these proposals, drawing the Supreme Commander's attention to the advantages of the northern line of approach into Germany and the need to open up the north-west ports, particularly Antwerp and Rotterdam, before the bad weather set in.

Eisenhower's view, with which I entirely agreed, was that it was fantastic to talk of marching to Berlin with an army which was still drawing the great bulk of its supplies over beaches north of Bayeux. The urgent matter was the Channel ports, especially Antwerp, on account of its capacity to store oil in bulk. 'Robbing the American Peter, who is fed from Cherbourg, will certainly not get the British Paul to Berlin. Patton's Army has been nearly immobilised by shortage of supplies for days.'

On 10 September I went to Brussels with Eisenhower, in whose aircraft Montgomery joined us. In our discussion, Eisenhower explained again the precarious nature of our supply system and the need to gain the use of Antwerp promptly. He thought that without railway bridges across the Rhine, and without plentiful supplies, we could not maintain in Germany a force capable of penetrating to Berlin. To Portal I telegraphed that in our conference at Brussels

... the advance to Berlin was not discussed as a serious issue, nor do I think it was so intended. The real issue is the degree of priority given to the American Corps operating on Montgomery's right flank, and the extent to which Montgomery controls its operations. On this there was useful discussion, and I expect Eisenhower will clear this with Bradley tomorrow. Montgomery, however, made great play over word 'priority' and insisted that his interpretation of the word implies absolute priority, if necessary to the exclusion of all other operations. Argument on such a basis obviously futile, and Eisenhower made it clear that he could not accept such an interpretation. We must fight with both hands at present, and a moment for the left hook had not come yet and could not come until Northern Army Group maintenance was based securely on the Channel Ports.

I feel the discussion cleared the air, though Montgomery will, of course, be dissatisfied in not getting a blank cheque. It will help to ensure that the Ruhr thrust does get the proper priority which we all feel it should have.

In his Memoirs, Eisenhower observed, justly it seems to me, that Montgomery was acquainted only with the situation in his own sector. He understood that to support his proposal would have meant stopping dead for weeks all units except those of 21 Army Group. 'But he did not understand the impossible situation that would have developed along the rest of our great front when he, having outrun the possibility of maintenance, was forced to stop or withdraw.'[1]

Having conferred with Bradley and Ramsay, Eisenhower was confirmed in his conviction that the early capture of deep-water ports and improved facilities for maintenance were prerequisites for a final assault on Germany proper. Our situation was that any stretch of seven or ten days of bad weather in the Channel, a condition which grew increasingly likely as winter drew near, would paralyse our activites and make the maintenance of our forces, even in defensive roles, extremely difficult. From the very beginning of the 'Overlord' plan, we had thought it essential to gain deep-water ports. Communications on the mainland must also be improved. Without these steps, a swift advance by adequate forces, which would depend on bulk oil,

[1] Eisenhower: *Crusade in Europe*, p. 336.

transport, and ammunition, was not a feasible operation of war. Having pointed this out to the principal commanders in a signal of 13 September, Eisenhower explained that the general plan was still to gain the Rhine, secure bridgeheads across it, seize the Ruhr and concentrate for a final non-stop drive into Germany. While these operations were proceeding, the Northern Group of Armies must promptly secure the approaches to Antwerp or Rotterdam, and additional Channel ports. The Central Group of Armies must reduce Brest so that it might be available for staging troops. The Southern Group of Armies must join up with the right of the Central Group so that the supply lines leading from Marseilles might help to support the Central Group as soon as surplus capacity could be made available.

In the immediate future, the Northern Group of Armies would advance to seize a bridgehead over the Rhine and would prepare to take the Ruhr. Eisenhower had already promised Montgomery additional maintenance for this purpose. The Central Group of Armies would push only so far as to hold adequate bridgeheads beyond the Moselle, and thus create a threat to the German forces, preventing them from reinforcing farther north by taking away troops from the area of Metz. As soon as this was accomplished, all available resources of the Central Group must be given to supporting the drive of the U.S. First Army to seize bridgeheads near Cologne and Bonn. This latter operation would be a preliminary stage in the capture of the Ruhr. Once the Northern Group of Armies and the U.S. First Army had taken bridgeheads across the Rhine, the U.S. Third Army would advance through the Saar and do likewise. If sufficient maintenance became available for the U.S. Third Army, it would move forward at once. Once the Moselle bridgeheads had been won, operations on the left would take priority until the Rhine bridgeheads were attained. The only exceptions would be that the other forces must have adequate maintenance for security and continuous reconnaissance, and also that the necessary supplies must be devoted to securing and developing ports. On 15 September, Eisenhower wrote optimistically to Montgomery that he hoped we should soon be in possession of the Ruhr, the Saar, and the Frankfurt area. He thought that the Germans would make a stand in defence of the Ruhr and Frankfurt, and be sharply defeated. Their dwindling forces would probably try to check our advance on the remaining important objectives in Germany by attacks which should create opportunities for us to round up the last remnants of the German Army in the west.

Clearly [the letter continued], Berlin is the main prize, and the prize in defence of which the enemy is likely to concentrate the bulk of his forces. There is no doubt whatsoever, in my mind, that we should concentrate all our energies and resources on a rapid thrust to Berlin.

However, our strategy would have to be co-ordinated with that of the Russians, and we must therefore consider alternatives. The areas of the northern ports, of Hanover and Brunswick, Leipzig and Dresden, Regensburg and Munich might all be of economic or political significance. We could not, therefore, determine precisely our objectives until nearer the time of their attainment. Eisenhower wished

. . . to move on Berlin by the most direct and expeditious route, with combined U.S.–British Forces, supported by other available forces, moving through key centres and occupying strategic areas on the flanks, all in one co-ordinated, concerted operation. It is not possible at this stage to indicate the timing of these thrusts or their strengths.

Montgomery answered on 18 September that everything turned on the administrative situation. The vital factor was time, and what we had to do, we must do quickly. He did not think that a concerted operation, with all the available land armies moving forward into Germany, could be quickly carried out. But

forces adequate in strength for the job in hand could be supplied and maintained, provided the general axis of advance was suitable, and provided these forces had complete priority in all repects as regards maintenance.

Montgomery thought that the Ruhr was the best objective, that we should then march on Berlin by the northern route, where the ports lay and where we could use our sea-power to the best advantage. For this advance, 21 Army Group, plus the U.S. First Army of nine divisions, would be adequate, so long as they received everything necessary in the matter of maintenance. The other armies must do the best they could with what was left over. If the Supreme Commander thought that the right axis of advance was by Frankfurt and Central Germany, Montgomery suggested that 12 Army Group should be used and should receive all necessary maintenance. To this, Eisenhower rejoined that he had never implied that he was considering an advance into Germany with all the armies moving abreast. He again pointed out that he too preferred the route to Berlin via the Ruhr as the best line of advance; but only the early capture of the approaches to Antwerp would enable that flank to be adequately supplied. It was not possible for all the divisions, except those of 21 Army Group and about nine of 12 Army Group, to stop where they were, nor could we strip transport and everything else from these divisions to support a single knife-like drive towards Berlin. We must marshal our strength along the western borders of Germany, if possible to the Rhine, ensure adequate maintenance by getting Antwerp working at full blast, and then carry out the drive Montgomery suggested.

I merely want to make sure that when you start leading your Army Group in its thrust on to Berlin, and Bradley starts driving with his left to support you, our other forces are in position to assure the success of that drive.

Otherwise the main thrust itself would have to drop off so much of its strength to protect its rear and its flanks that very soon the drive would peter out.

Eisenhower assured Montgomery that he had given preference to the left all the way through this campaign. 'All other forces have been fighting with a halter around their necks in the way of supplies.' Some of Bradley's forces were to be moved so that General Hodges (commanding the U.S. First Army) could concentrate his full strength on the left in his drive forward towards the Rhine. When we got to the Rhine, Bradley's next concern would be to put a strong army on his left to accompany Montgomery to Berlin.

These assurances did not meet Montgomery's point of view. He replied at once that his concept was not the same as Eisenhower's. He had always wanted to stop the right and go on with the left, but the right had been allowed to go on so far that it had outstripped its maintenance and we had lost flexibility. Now Eisenhower apparently wanted to go still farther with the right, and said that all Bradley's Army Group would move forward sufficiently to be a supporting position for the main drive. He, Montgomery, thought that the right flank of 12 Army Group should be given a very direct order to halt.

The net result of the matter, in my opinion, is that if you want to get the Ruhr you will have to put every single thing into the left hook and stop everything else. It is my opinion that if this is not done, then you will not get the Ruhr.

Eisenhower, therefore, summoned a meeting in the War Room at S.H.A.E.F. on the afternoon of 22 September. The Supreme Commander presided. Ramsay, Leigh-Mallory, Spaatz, Bradley, and I were present. Montgomery did not come, but was represented by Freddie de Guingand. Our position in the north at this point was not entirely a happy one, for operation 'Market Garden', the airborne thrust against Arnhem, had been launched on 17 September with indifferent success. Montgomery has since charged, in his Memoirs, that the operation was not regarded at Supreme Headquarters as the spearhead of a major Allied movement in the north, designed to isolate and finally to occupy the Ruhr. This must be a matter of opinion. So far as I knew at the time, Eisenhower made every possible effort to give Montgomery the necessary supply. The weather was most unfavourable to us, the airborne forces at Arnhem itself landed too far away from the vital bridge, but above all the operation committed the 'spearhead' to a single line of approach to a single objective, which allowed the Germans to concentrate easily against it. However, at this stage, 22 September, the outcome was not known.

At the meeting, Eisenhower said he wished everyone to make a clear distinction between the logistical requirements for attaining the objectives already mentioned in existing orders (which included seizing the Ruhr and breaching the Siegfried Line) and the requirements for a final drive to Berlin. He laid it down that he wanted everybody to accept the fact that the possession of 'an additional deep-water port on our north flank was an indispensable pre-requisite for the final drive deep into Germany'.

De Guingand, on Montgomery's behalf, outlined the plan of 21 Army Group for attacking the Ruhr from the north. It would be necessary to employ three corps in that effort. He wondered whether 12 Army Group could take over the sector occupied by the British 8 Corps. After some talk, Eisenhower approved the envelopment of the Ruhr from the north by 21 Army Group, supported by the U.S. First Army, as the main effort of 'the present phase of operations'. He also approved the change in the boundary between 21 and 12 Army Groups. 12 Army Group should continue its thrusts as far as its current resources permitted towards Cologne and Bonn, and would seize any favourable opportunity of crossing the Rhine and attacking the Ruhr from the south when the maintenance situation permitted. The rest of 12 Army Group should not take more aggressive action than was permitted by the maintenance situation after the full requirements of the main effort had been met. 21 Army Group must open the port of Antwerp as a matter of urgency, and develop the operations culminating in a strong attack on the Ruhr from the north. 6 Army Group would continue operations for the capture of Mulhausen and Strasbourg, since these attacks would not divert resources from the other Army Groups.

After this meeting, de Guingand telegraphed to Montgomery, so it appears, that Eisenhower had supported his plan 100 per cent. This was not an entirely accurate way of recording the decisions reached. From the start, both Eisenhower and I had wanted, as I had signalled to Portal on 10 September, to give priority and proper weight to the thrust against the Ruhr. We understood just as well as Montgomery the crucial significance of the Ruhr in the German economy. Indeed, that factor had long since entered into our planning of air operations. At the same time, as the messages quoted in this chapter will show, we had both insisted from the start that without Antwerp we could not get to Berlin. As Montgomery admits in his Memoirs, he made the bad mistake of underestimating the difficulties of opening up the approaches to Antwerp. He thought, wrongly, that the Canadian Army could do it while 21 Army Group was making for the Ruhr.[1]

---

[1] Montgomery: *Memoirs*, p. 297.

Moreover, this meeting at Versailles did not decide to halt the other forces. What we tried to do was to give reasonable priority to any effort which was likely to seal off the Ruhr from Germany, but so to marshal our other strength along the western borders of the Reich that the swiftest advantage could be taken of any German collapse. At the same time, if we were forestalled in the north, we should by this method have alternative lines of approach.

By the end of September, we had taken Brest, Le Havre, and Boulogne. The enemy still had Lorient, St. Nazaire, Calais, and Dunkirk. The Central and the Southern Group of Armies, the latter fresh from the success of the 'Dragoon' landings, had met, and had produced a continuous Allied line from the North Sea to the Mediterranean. In September, though this front had moved steadily east, its rate of advance in most regions had declined as the enemy's resistance increased. Except in the Low Countries, the Germans had now established a relatively stable front, roughly speaking co-terminous with their frontier. The campaign in France, we estimated, had cost the enemy about a million men and untold quantities of equipment. Such losses could not be made good, but could be mitigated. Every possible step to this end was being taken by Hitler's Government, and, as Eisenhower telegraphed to the Combined Chiefs of Staff at the end of September, we could discern no signs of a collapse in morale or in the will to defend Germany.

What remained of the enemy's armour had been mainly concentrated in the region of Aachen and south of Nancy. We thought that reinforcements from Germany might number some ten divisions in the course of October. It became clear that the enemy's real policy was to defend the western frontier of the Reich for as long as possible. The line chosen in the first place was that running from the water obstacles in Holland to the Moselle, the Vosges and then the Rhine. The Supreme Commander thought that the Germans might well attempt counter-attacks to restore the situation at those points where this line had been breached.

It must be remembered that we still did not have control of Antwerp. Our communications and lines of supply were strained to the limit. The advance and deployment of divisions were thereby restricted. Eisenhower, in his message to the Chiefs of Staff, described the opening up of the port of Antwerp as 'a matter of transcendent importance' which might not be completed before November. The use of Le Havre, primarily for American supply, would certainly shorten the line of communications and relieve some of the present congestion. We were making every effort to ease the supply situation by importing rolling stock and redeveloping the railways of France and Belgium. Air supply was in use on a large scale. Even some of our strategic bombers were being used for this purpose, while the transport aircraft were employed on airborne operations. Air supply over considerable distances was extremely costly. In some cases it was costing us one and a half gallons of 100-octane gasolene to deliver one gallon of 80-octane motor fuel to the forward depots.

Eisenhower assured the Chiefs of Staff that his general intention remained unaltered. He wished to press on with all speed to destroy the German armed forces and to advance deep into Germany, and he had not

. . . deviated from my opinion that the best means of doing so is to strike the Ruhr and the Saar, throwing the greater weight against the Ruhr.

The capture of the Ruhr by the Northern Group of Armies, and by the First United States Army, is the main effort of the present phase of operations.

The Northern Group of Armies is responsible for opening the port of Antwerp as a matter of great urgency. The possession of Antwerp and its approaches is essential to sustain the drive deep into Germany.

At the end of the first week in October, Montgomery signalled to Eisenhower that he could not continue the planned operations to gain the line of the Rhine unless more maintenance were granted. Eisenhower replied on 8 October that the plan for co-ordinated attack to the Rhine must be postponed until strength could be brought up, which must come from the United States divisions on the beach. Nevertheless:

Plans of both Army Groups must retain as first mission the gaining of the line of the Rhine north of Bonn as quickly as humanly possible.

Bradley and Montgomery replied that the tempo of their

operations towards the Rhine must be reduced until we could improve the maintenance situation. Montgomery proposed to stop the operations towards the Ruhr and to concentrate on opening up the approaches to Antwerp. To this Eisenhower rejoined:

Unless we have Antwerp producing by the middle of November, entire operations will come to a standstill.

I must emphasise that, of all our operations on our entire front from Switzerland to the Channel, I consider Antwerp of first importance.

In his Memoirs, Montgomery has made a good deal of play with the apparent contradiction contained in these two telegrams. I think that it is fairly simply explained. In sending his message of 8 October, Eisenhower assumed, as he and I had done all along, that whatever else happened Montgomery would concentrate on opening up Antwerp. No one could say that we had not emphasised the point sufficiently by conversation and signal. It was subject to that priority, I know, that Eisenhower said both Army Groups must retain as their first mission the gaining of the Rhine.

Later in the month, Eisenhower turned down Montgomery's suggestion that one man could direct the land battle along the whole front. The Supreme Commander himself must 'adjust the larger boundaries to tasks commensurate to the several Groups operating in the several areas'. After a meeting with Montgomery at Brussels on 18 October, the Supreme Commander refused to be moved from his policy of extended advance. In a directive of 28 October, Eisenhower recognised that the Germans had imposed a pause. Antwerp must be secured, as it was a few days later, though we did not have the use of the port until 28 November. His general plan was still to make the main effort in the north, to defeat the enemy west of the Rhine, and to secure bridgeheads; then to take the Ruhr and penetrate deep into Germany; to destroy the enemy in the Saar and to be ready to advance from there. In the south we should use as fully as possible maintenance from the Mediterranean, and act aggressively in order first to defeat the enemy west of the Rhine and then to cross into the Reich.

In many of these transactions of September and October, I played only a secondary part, since I spent almost as much time in

Great Britain as I did in France. I was never able to convince myself that at any stage until we held Antwerp, Montgomery really believed that we could march a sizeable Army to Berlin with our existing resources of supply and maintenance. I therefore supported Eisenhower's policy.

7
German reports on Allied air attacks–Direction of bomber
offensive returns to C.C.S.–Quebec Conference–Effect of new directive–
Decision in 1944?–Portal's reaction–'drugged with bombs'–How to
end the war–Operations 'patchwork quilt'–Enemy communications
primary objectives–Dislocation of German rail system–New Target Committee–
Oil as prime target–My proposals of 25 October–Directive of 1 November–
Harris's views–Pattern of air offensive established–Brooke supports Montgomery's
attack on Eisenhower–Proposed converging attack into Frankfurt/Kassel–
Montgomery wants Command bounded by Ardennes–Hitler's last fling

I T will be recalled that the first directive to Bomber Command
in 1940 had specified rail communications and oil as the priority
targets, though we were at the time quite incapable of hitting
them. In the succeeding years we had kept the Germans' oil
situation under careful review. Germany depended a good deal
on captured stocks as sources of supply. Even these had been
barely sufficient to meet the heavy consumption of the campaigns
in Russia and the Mediterranean between 1941 and 1943. By the
latter year, plans for the establishment of synthetic oil plants were
coming to fruition. At about the same time, the Allies began to
close the ring around the Reich. At last our bombers were within
reach of the plants in Germany, Austria, Hungary, and Rumania.
In May 1944 I confirmed with Spaatz and Harris that some of our
effort should now be devoted to oil targets. The Fifteenth U.S. Air
Force, based in Italy, operated against plants in Rumania,
Hungary, Czechoslovakia, Austria, and even as far away as
Poland and Silesia. I had always thought that there was much to
be said for the 'Oil Plan', though for the immediate purposes of
'Overlord' the Transportation Plan had to come first. Once the
raids on oil targets began to build up, we soon had evidence of
their effect on Germany's capacity to sustain a war on several
fronts. Though we did not know it at the time, Speer had reported
to the Führer as early as 30 May, with a certain rueful humour:

With the attacks on the hydrogenation plants, systematic bombing
raids on economic targets have started at the most dangerous point.
The only hope is that the enemy, too, has got an Air Staff. Only if it

had as little comprehension of economic targets as ours would there be some hope that after a few attacks on this decisive economic target it would turn its attentions elsewhere.

At the end of June, Speer again reported losses of aviation fuel on a scale up to 90 per cent., and warned that unless repairs could be effected more rapidly and protection improved, it would be impossible to cover the most urgent needs for the Wehrmacht by September. In other words, from that time onwards there would be an unbridgeable gap between consumption and production which must lead to tragic results. His report at the end of July showed that in consequence of air attack on refineries and synthetic oil plants, production of aviation spirit had declined from 175,000 tons in April to 156,000 tons in May, 53,000 tons in June and 29,000 tons in July. The production of carburettor and diesel fuel showed a similar decline, though not as yet on so spectacular a scale. By late August, Speer was writing dolefully about the successful Allied attacks on German chemical works. The three hydrogenation plants had been brought to a complete standstill for some weeks. The effects of these new raids would be felt throughout the chemical industry. Production of aviation spirit in August had fallen to a mere 12,000 tons, and could not rise in September above 10,000 to 15,000 tons. This figure compared with an estimated production of 101,000 tons. The fuel situation, indeed, was so bad, Speer went on, that offensive moves at the front would no longer be possible in October. The only hope was defence of the key plants and points of the Fatherland by the 'flower of the Luftwaffe'. However, renewed attacks proved so effective that between 10 September and 16 September no aviation spirit was produced at all.

It was not only in high circles of the German Government that the oil offensive was providing food for reflection. In a memorandum circulated to his colleagues just before the Quebec Conference in September, Portal argued that the critical phase of 'Overlord' was now passed. The need for the Strategic Air Forces to support the land battle directly would be at most intermittent. The system by which since April the Supreme Allied Commander had directed the Strategic Air Forces did not seem to Portal entirely satisfactory. The co-ordination of strategic bombing with the Russians, a problem which daily assumed greater importance, could only be dealt with in Moscow where the Anglo-American mission under the direction of the Combined Chiefs of Staff must negotiate directly with the Soviet High Command. For the purposes of 'Pointblank', Eisenhower had directed operations in accordance with target priorities laid down by the Air Staffs. In practice, as it seemed to Portal, difficulties had arisen in ensuring through this method that the priorities for 'Pointblank' attacks were properly observed by the operational commands. Control of the strategic bomber forces should therefore revert to the Combined Chiefs of Staff. An illustration of the need to centralise control again was provided by the offensive against oil targets. It had become abundantly plain that the enemy was faced with an increasingly critical situation in respect of oil. To exploit these difficulties fully, Portal wrote, it was essential that the attack on oil resources should be pressed at the maximum intensity. To ensure that the bomber effort was available, control must be exercised directly through the British and American Air Staffs, who had jointly acquired experience of planning and developing the combined bomber offensive.

The Combined Chiefs of Staff, viewing the war as a whole, would also be in the best position to appreciate the psychological moment when overwhelming attack on German morale might be expected to precipitate collapse. In addition, the move of Eisenhower's headquarters to France made the reversion of control from him to the Combined Chiefs of Staff a matter of urgency. He was now separated from the Air Staffs in Great Britain on whom he normally depended, and from all the authorities to whom the Air Staffs looked for guidance.

The American view, in broad terms, was that reversion to control by separate commands would involve the uneconomical use of our resources. The Quebec Conference produced a compromise whereby control of the Strategic Air Forces was again vested in the Combined Chiefs of Staff, represented for this purpose by Portal and Arnold. They, in turn, delegated their powers to the D.C.A.S., Air Marshal Bottomley, and to Spaatz. The effect of this decision was therefore to remove from Eisenhower, and in practice from myself, the day-to-day superintendence of our strategic bomber effort. So far as my views of its proper use were concerned, the results were less far-reaching than they might otherwise have been. On 13 September, just before the Quebec Conference reached its decision, I had conferred with Bottomley. I decided that the employment of the Strategic Air Forces would continue to be in full support of the land battle in the final phase of the assault on Germany. Oil targets would have first priority. Second priority would be given to the German transportation systems by rail and water, in particular those leading to the Ruhr and through it, with attention also being paid to similar targets in the Saar. As objectives near to the battle-front were dealt with, attacks would be carried out on targets progressively deeper into Germany. Equal priority with transportation targets would be accorded to motor transport and tractor plants, ordnance plants, and depots. The German Air Force would take third priority. If attacks on the first and second priority targets did not produce enough reaction from the Luftwaffe to enable us to weaken it continuously, we might have to lay on special attacks. I thought that damage to the rail and water transportation systems would oblige the enemy to make greater use of his roads which were not included in the list of priorities. The continuous successes against oil targets, and action by the Tactical Air Forces, should bring about the desired degree of dislocation while not disrupting our own subsequent advances on the ground.

Although, therefore, control of the Strategic Forces passed out of my hands shortly after this meeting, the directive issued by Bottomley to the Strategic Air Forces on 25 September was, in theory at any rate, satisfactory to me. It accorded first priority to oil, and equal second priority to the German transportation system, tank and motor vehicle production plants, and ordnance depots. Action against the German Air Force was allotted no definite priority. The result in practice was less satisfactory. It was admitted in the Directive that if bad weather ruled out precision bombing, area attacks would be undertaken. In fact, Bomber Command reverted in October largely to area attack, while the U.S. Eighth Air Force spent nearly one half of its efforts on marshalling yards and the remainder on a number of other targets. Only 6 per cent. of Bomber Command's effort in October was devoted to oil targets.

It was still hoped by some that the Allies would triumph by Christmas. At an informal meeting of the United States Chiefs of Staff in mid-October, General Marshall said that he felt the Combined Chiefs of Staff should decide whether we were going to achieve victory in Europe in 1944 or whether military policy should be directed on the assumption that victory would not be won until well into the succeeding year. If all were agreed to aim at a decision in 1944, it might be desirable to redirect our main air effort so as to contribute more to the immediate issue on the battlefield, leaving targets of longer-term interest to look after themselves. For instance, if the synthetic oil industry could be reduced to a point from which it could hardly recover in three months, the effort being directed against it could be diverted in the main to targets of more immediate significance to the German Army. Marshall made it clear that in his view the right answer was to go all out for a decision in 1944. Portal told me of all this at once. Although Marshall mentioned among the longer-term targets only the oil industry, he might also include in that category tank and motor transport factories, airfields, railway transport centres and industry in general.

Portal had recently told me in conversation that he would be against measures of the kind proposed by Marshall. He did not believe that we could afford to let Germany take care of itself and thought that the proper application of the Strategic Air Forces to targets behind the front was more likely to shorten the war than their application to the battlefield. He wrote:

I believe that the constant application of heavy bomber power to the land battle, when it is not essential and when its only purpose is to save casualties, must eventually lead to the demoralisation of the army. If one division captures an objective with strong heavy bomber support and loses only a few men, other divisions will naturally be reluctant to attack without similar support, and we shall sooner or later reach a stage where almost the whole of the heavy bomber effort has to be frittered away in small packets if the army is to attack at all.

Portal asked me to let him have a paper on the subject. It was possible, though he thought it unlikely, that Marshall desired a

[605]

concentration on some short-term transportation plan instead of concentration on oil and industry. It would be dangerous, the C.A.S. believed, to apply wholesale to Germany the lessons of France. He asked for my conclusions on this point, too. I replied on 25 October:

As you are aware, the British Army have for months now been allowed to feel that they can, at any time, call on heavy bomber effort, and it will be laid on practically without question.

We are now, I am afraid, beginning to see the results in precisely that demoralisation of which you speak. The repeated calls by the Canadian Army for heavy bomber effort to deal with a part-worn battery on Walcheren, and the evacuation of Breskens because of intermittent harassing fire from this battery, is in my opinion only too clear an example. It is going to be extremely difficult to get things back on to a proper footing. You can see the argument, i.e. Antwerp is vital, Antwerp cannot be used without Walcheren, Walcheren is vital, every possible effort must be directed towards Walcheren, therefore Bomber Command should continue to pour bombs into the mud.

I am doing my best to get things straight, but I am sure you will realise that, the Army having been drugged with bombs, it is going to be a difficult process to cure the drug addicts—particularly since the troops are undoubtedly getting pretty tired.

I entirely agreed with Portal that it would be most foolish to leave Germany to take care of herself. If my memory of our conversation was correct, Portal had agreed that our attacks on oil plants should keep the time scale in mind. Our object should not be to destroy completely each source of fuel, but to prevent production. If a plant had been put out of action for a month or two, it should be left. In fact, the oil programme should now largely be one of policing, except in instances where we had reason to believe that the plants were really producing oil. I also told Portal that I had for some time been very uneasy about the progress of the bombing offensive. My appeals to the Planners had not produced any answer based on a full analysis of the whole situation. I knew that my views would not be acceptable in some quarters, but, as I wrote to Portal:

I feel that the time for debates and compromises is past. In my opinion we can only make the full weight of air power felt if we set all our various air forces to work at once towards one common objective; if we do that, I believe that air power will be decisive—and quickly.

There were, as it seemed to me, two ways of ending the war. One was by land invasion, and the other by breaking the enemy's power and control behind the lines. I did not believe that these two courses were alternative or conflicting. Rather, they were complementary. Nor did I think that we should shorten the war either by concentrating our whole effort on the ground battle or by putting the full weight of our strategic bomber power against political and industrial targets within the Reich. The main objective of the land campaign was the Ruhr. The Army Groups had by now made it clear that they wanted the air forces to interrupt enemy supply and reinforcement across the Rhine. As a secondary objective, they wanted us to reduce drastically the enemy's capacity to withdraw heavy equipment across that river. Up to the last week in October, the strategic bombers' contribution to this end had been the attack on oil, on the Dortmund–Ems Canal and occasional assaults upon ordnance and motor transport depots. The Tactical Air Forces had made attacks on railway lines and trains and on bridges, though in the latter case with little result. As I wrote to Portal:

> I am not satisfied that, on these lines, we are using our air power really effectively. The various types of operations should fit into one comprehensive pattern, whereas I feel that at present they are more like a patchwork quilt.

As for the air attack on Germany itself, I felt that again our efforts were rather disconnected. We were attacking more or less simultaneously oil, cities, depots, marshalling yards, canals, and factories. In this I could discern no comprehensive or economical use of our overwhelming air strength. It seemed to me that the urgent task was to find a target the attack on which would affect the whole economic viability of Germany. Such a target existed:

> The one common factor in the whole German war effort, from the political control down to the supply of troops in the front line, is communications. Leaving on one side signal communications as

being relatively invulnerable to air attack, rail, road, and water communications are the one common denominator. The city populations may have gone underground but without surface communications they will starve. Industries may have gone underground but their lifelines remain on the surface. Industries have been dispersed, but the more they have been dispersed the more they depend on good communications. Governmental control depends to a very great extent on efficient road and rail communications as is only too evident today in Belgium and France. The army's dependence on communications needs no comment.

In my opinion our primary air objective should be the enemy's communications. Road, water, and rail are interdependent and complementary, and our air operations should play on that fact. The present oil plan is the key to movement by road and air, and, moreover, directly affects operations in the battle areas. It is supplemented by fighter attacks on M.T. The river and canal system in Western Europe has been examined and targets indicated. The successful attack on the Dortmund–Ems Canal is being followed up by attacks on further vulnerable points. The practicability of mining the Rhine, and thus stopping the extensive barge traffic, is being examined.

On the other hand, we had done little in the way of systematic attack against the enemy's rail system except to send the fighter-bombers to cut lines. There had also been a certain amount of effort devoted to shooting up trains. It was only in the last few days that these operations had begun to show some dividend, and yet it was now abundantly clear from French and German railway records that it had been the heavy attacks on railway centres and marshalling yards which mainly paralysed the rail system in northern France, and that the effect of such attacks was far more rapid and final than had been anticipated.

In the Overture to this book I have referred to the handicap which we had suffered through lack of any adequate means for testing weapons. Once hostilities had broken out, however, it was possible to study the effects of enemy weapons and in due course of our own weapons. As soon as we began to advance along the North African shore we passed over the scene of recent fighting and were able to study the effect of our operations. It was then that I had asked for some operational research scientists who were used to analysing varied evidence. Professor Zuckerman was chosen, and it was a fortunate day when he was sent out to the Mediterranean. As has been seen, his services became of incalculable value. The subjection of Pantelleria by bombing, which was controlled by Professor Zuckerman, was an interesting experiment, but as I have previously remarked I was not altogether happy about it. I feared that it would be only too easy for people to draw their own obvious conclusion that it should be possible by sheer weight of bombs to blast a way through any defences. I am fairly certain that some of the demands for masses of heavy bombers were based on the desire to emulate Pantelleria. It was later, when we occupied Sicily, that we began to acquire invaluable evidence for application into Europe. I remember one day going to Palermo to see a Bombing Survey Unit which Zuckerman had set up there with some thirty young Italian railway personnel. They were amassing basic railway records which showed an ever-increasing paralysis of railway movement. Already it was clear that the paralysis was spreading deep into southern Italy.

A similar survey of the French railway system was then called for, and a Bombing Survey Unit was set up in France as soon as it could get into the Normandy bridgehead. When Paris was liberated, this unit established itself in the Gare du Nord with the assistance of French railway officials. Soon after we had settled in at Versailles where Eisenhower and I shared the Petit Trianon, Zuckerman dashed in in a great state of excitement. He had something to show me. These were the daily railway records made by the Germans from the moment Brussels was taken by them in 1940 until they were thrown out in 1944. They were in the form of long rolls of graph paper rather like wall-paper. Zuckerman had picked them up from one of our Intelligence officers who did not realise their significance. I happened to be upstairs with Eisenhower, so Zuckerman had to wait. Meantime he showed the papers to Scarman, my staff officer, and one or two others, who were all excited at what they saw. When I came into the room after my meeting with Eisenhower, Zuckerman started unrolling the charts on the carpet in the ante-room to my office. I remember that I got down on my knees on the floor, and after examining them and realising their significance, turned to him and said, 'Zuck, is your German good enough to serve as an interpreter?' It was following on this 'discovery' that I summoned a meeting in Versailles of the Bomber Chiefs of Staff and told them, not for the first time. that they had been wrong about the communications offensive.

I agreed with Portal's views that it was essential not to apply too literally to Germany the lessons of France and Belgium, but I agreed with his conclusion for a different reason. In the enemy territories the enemy had been able to maintain military traffic at the expense of all non-military and economic traffic. In the Reich itself, however, all loss of traffic was a dead loss to the war effort. In France and Belgium we knew the enemy had prepared for the kind of attack we meted out by bringing in large bodies of special labour and railway workers. In Germany now all indications were that the man-power which had not been thrown into the Army was fully employed on digging defences. Even the normal personnel of the railways had been drastically combed out. In France and Belgium all the available repair and salvage material and personnel could be concentrated on patching up the railways, whereas in Germany such facilities were already overstrained in repairing and salvaging factories and public services. In France and Belgium, again, our programme of attack on rail centres had been severely limited by the need to avoid civilian casualties. We should not be deterred by any such scruple from attacking German rail centres.

It did not seem to me necessary to spread our attacks broadcast all over the German rail system. I was convinced that with Germany in her existing condition we could obtain 'immediate results which have every prospect of being decisive'.

Our main strategic concentration should be against the Ruhr; against its rail centres, oil targets, the canal system, and the centres of population. With such a system we should be able to maintain the attack under all conditions in which heavy bombers could operate. Such a scheme would take account of the operations of the Tactical Air Forces against trains, embankments, and bridges, which would then be complementary to the strategic operations, and would have far better prospects of producing immediate effect than in the past when the heart of the rail system had been relatively untouched. The Strategic and Tactical Air Forces would, in a word, then be operating towards one objective. I believed, and so advised Portal, that the execution of a co-ordinated campaign against the communication system of Western Germany on these lines would soon produce a state of chaos which would vitally affect not only the immediate battle on the West Wall, but also the whole German war effort.

Both Eisenhower and Bedell Smith agreed in substance with this argument, provided that the emphasis of our attack remained on oil. The Intelligence Services at S.H.A.E.F. also agreed completely that, next to oil, transportation was the most important target for the strategic bombers. But the Supreme Commander told me on 27 October that he understood Marshall had the backing of the American Chiefs of Staff in requesting that all bomber effort be directed to the immediate assistance of the battle. Should this order be given to S.H.A.E.F., Eisenhower and I agreed that the best way of executing it would be to carry on with bombing on the lines indicated in my memorandum. At a meeting later the same day, I subjected the Director of Bombing Operations, Air Commodore Bufton, to a heavy cross-examination when he defended the prevailing directive. The net effect of our meeting, which was also attended by Spaatz, Bottomley, and Robb, was an agreement to amend the existing Directive so that oil should remain the first priority with transportation and rail centres in particular as the second priority. The next day, Portal, who was visiting our Headquarters as Eisenhower's guest, said that he thought my paper was the right answer to Marshall's request for air support to the armies.

These discussions had some influence, I believe, on the course of the strategic bomber offensive. During the month of October, a new body, known as the Combined Strategic Targets Committee, had been set up under the joint chairmanship of Air Commodore Bufton and Colonel Maxwell, his counterpart in the American Strategic Air Forces in Europe. S.H.A.E.F., Bomber Command and U.S. Eighth Air Force were also represented. The object was to fuse operational and technical advice. Bottomley and Spaatz would be advised accordingly about priorities, about any changes found to be necessary in the directives, and about proposals from S.H.A.E.F. and elsewhere which involved the use of strategic bomber forces. It was no secret that most members of this committee, and especially the joint chairmen, favoured oil as the prime target. At a meeting of some members of the committee, held on 24 October, the day before I submitted my paper, it was alleged that excepting the zone immediately behind the battle, the enemy's rail facilities were so vastly in excess of his military requirements that no appreciable effect could possibly be achieved within the envisaged time period, the ninety days in which, so it was hoped, the war would be won.

As I expected, it was felt in the Air Ministry that my proposals of 25 October would probably conflict in practice with the oil plan. The Air Staff, and especially Air Commodore Bufton, were convinced that heavy attacks on oil plants were called for, in view of the desperate efforts the Germans were making to get such plants back into working order after each raid. However, towards the end of the month, the Combined Strategic Targets Committee did recommend that the attack on transport should now be carried into German territory. On 1 November, new directives were issued to the Strategic Air Forces. Oil was to have first priority, and transportation alone the second priority. Thus the necessary concentration was to some degree achieved, though area bombing continued for some time.

On the same day, Air Chief Marshal Harris, to whom Portal had passed a copy of my memorandum, told the C.A.S. that the war had already been shortened by concentrating bomber effort for the past three years against all potential industrial targets within Germany, and would have been shortened a good deal further by the same means but for the large diversions of bomber effort which had necessarily, and in some cases unnecessarily, been made during the past nine months. None the less, he agreed with me that we must now find a happy medium between assisting the armies and continuing the effective bombing of Germany. Experience in France showed that when the armies got stuck, the only means of getting them started again was by concentrated tactical bombing with heavy bombers. He argued that my recommendations about targets were largely in line with the policy followed by Bomber Command. The main concentration had been against the Ruhr whenever conditions made it economical, and the targets selected had been oil targets, rail centres, canal systems, and the major centres of population. The result had been that ten major oil plants in the Ruhr, the Dortmund–Ems Canal, and some of the main dams had been put out of action and kept out of action. In addition, area bombing of Essen, Duisburg, Cologne, Dusseldorf, and Dortmund had been undertaken. It was not tactically feasible, Harris wrote, to go on hammering away at the same area or the same type of target, day in day out, night in night out, without making the task of the defenders too simple. He wanted to impress most strongly on everyone that in the conduct of the bomber offensive it was seldom possible to bomb what we wanted to bomb. What was bombed was generally the nearest target to the top of the priority list available at the material time, in the light of weather, tactical, and other factors. A further difficulty in building up the offensive into the 'real comprehensive pattern' for which I had called, was the number of cooks now engaged in stirring the broth. 'During the last few weeks,' Harris wrote characteristically, 'every panacea-monger and "me too expert", to many of whom we had already (we hoped) given the quietus in the past, has raised his head again.' The Admiralty had resuscitated a U-boat threat, the ball-bearing experts had become vocal, even Special Operations Executive had raised its 'bloody head' and produced what he hoped was 'its final death rattle'. Since the middle of 1943, Bomber Command had virtually destroyed, Harris claimed, forty-five of the leading sixty German cities. In spite of 'invasion diversions', they had managed to keep up, or even exceed, the average of two and a half cities devastated each month. There were few industrial centres of population now intact. It seemed to him that except for pin-point targets more suited to day bombing, the Ruhr was nearly knocked out. This process could be completed without depriving the Army of the support it needed; and, in his view, such completion would do more towards accelerating the defeat of Germany than the armies had yet done, or would do.

These extreme claims for the effectiveness of air-power Portal tactfully refused to admit. He replied that:

In the light of all available intelligence I feel that the whole war situation is poised on 'oil' as on a knife edge, and that by a real concentration of effort at this time we might well push it over on the right side.

Harris replied that he fully agreed about the urgency and effectiveness of the oil plan, an opinion he did not entirely maintain—at least in practice.

The growing weight of attack against the German transportation system began to be felt. Speer reported to his master in mid-October about the severe crisis in the communication system of western and southern Germany brought about by air attack. Early the next month he was of the opinion that a continuation of the attacks on the Reichsbahn might result in 'a production catastrophe of decisive significance for the futher conduct of the war'.

The real pattern of the Allied air offensive was now being established. The oil plants and the communication system were not alternative but complementary targets. A successful and sustained attack upon them meant that Germany would soon lose the war. As the last flickers of the Luftwaffe's power faded away, our forces concentrated against these two types of target. The Strategic and the Tactical Air Forces, the former now again under the Combined Chiefs of Staff, and the latter under my direction since Leigh-Mallory's departure to be Commander-in-Chief Far East in early October, devoted their efforts to the same ends. Of course, the land battle could by no means be neglected, but by concentration on the Ruhr we served both the purpose of preparing the way for our armies and of cutting off from Germany her most important industrial area. The oil plants, rail centres, especially those feeding the Ruhr, a few viaducts, bridges, and trains, were attacked with gusto. The paralysis was clearly spreading. Our reconnaissance showed huge stocks of coal piled up at the pits because the railway system could no longer distribute it. Factories and industries all over Germany began to stagnate or to cease production. The shortage of gas and electricity was soon critical.

It was my task to see that the Tactical Air Forces' activities dovetailed as neatly as posssible with those of the Strategic Air Forces. In a memorandum of 23 November, I described for the

benefit of the Army Group and the Tactical Air Force commanders, the policy underlying the operations of the Strategic
Bomber Forces. Now that the enemy had lost Rumania to the
Russian advance, we estimated that less than 25 per cent. of his
previous oil production remained available. We had abundant
evidence to show that the shortage of gasolene had limited, and
was limiting, to a critical extent, the operation of German
armoured divisions, motor transport, and aircraft. We knew that
the Germans had given the highest priority to the repair of their
oil installations, a sure proof that our attacks were directed in the
right quarters. Experience had shown that they were capable of
remarkable achievements in this direction. We had therefore to
make sure that the main synthetic oil plants were constantly kept
out of action. I recognised that with the onset of winter and the
bad weather, the strategic bomber forces would be faced with a
formidable task in maintaining this pressure by visual bombing.
I therefore instructed that the Tactical Air Forces should help by
attacking oil targets whenever the direct requirements of the
land battle would allow. There were some targets—as, for instance,
concentrations of tank cars in storage depots and on the railways—
which the tactical forces could attack much more economically
than the bomber forces.

As for the attack on communications, our object was to delay
and disrupt the supply and reinforcements of the German
armies, to disorganise enemy war production, which, because of
widespread dispersal, depended more than ever on good communications, and generally to weaken the central control of the
whole German war machine. When the attack on the oil targets
was not operationally possible, the strategic bomber forces
were now to concentrate their effort against rail and water
communications in Germany, particularly in the 150-mile belt
of Germany which extended east from the Rhine as far as 10
degrees east. The object would be very much the same as the
object of the Transportation Plan; to destroy servicing facilities, marshalling yards, and junctions, and interrupt the main
canals.

Of the cumulative effect of these targets on Germany's capacity
to fight, I shall write in the next chapter. Here, it is sufficient to

notice that Speer had no doubt what our policy was going to mean to Germany. He warned Hitler in December:

The enemy has recognised that systematic attacks on our communications may have a most decisive effect in all spheres on our conduct of the war.

He told his staff that their troubles in the months to come were dictated by the situation in the communications system which had recently deteriorated 'to a quite exceptional extent'. He also paid us the compliment of saying that the men who worked out the Allied plans for attack understood something about German economic life. 'We were fortunate', Speer added, 'that the enemy did not put this far-reaching plan into effect until about six or nine months ago.'

The progress of the land battle was still slow. Early in November, it will be recalled, the approaches to Antwerp had at long last been cleared. It became evident that the Germans intended to fight a major battle west of the Rhine, using the Siegfried Line as a basis for defence. 12 Army Group began to concentrate all available strength in the Aachen area. Limited advances were recorded, but in general the offensive ordered by Eisenhower at the end of October fizzled out in the bad weather. Sometimes the shortage of ammunition was acute, and the advance by Patton was not properly co-ordinated with that of Bradley's armies. Field-Marshal Montgomery saw in these events a confirmation of the rightness of his view that everything should long since have been concentrated on one blow. The Chiefs of Staff evidently felt that Eisenhower had no grip on the battle. Alan Brooke's diary records that they discussed at some length on 20 November the unsatisfactory state of affairs in France

. . . where Eisenhower completely fails as Commander. Bedell Smith lives back in Paris quite out of touch; as a result the war is drifting in a rudderless condition. Had a long and despondent letter about it from Montgomery over the week-end. Am preparing a case, as we shall have to take it up with the Americans before long.

This letter from Montgomery had reported that he had neither seen, nor spoken with Eisenhower since 18 October, and had met him but four times since the campaign in Normandy was won:

He is at a Forward Headquarters at Rheims. The Directives he issues from there have no relation to the practical necessities of the battle. It is quite impossible for me to carry out my present orders. . . . Eisenhower should himself take a proper control of operations or he should appoint someone else to do this. If we go drifting along as at present we are merely playing into the enemy's hands, and the war will go on indefinitely. . . . He has never commanded anything before in his whole career; now, for the first time, he has elected to take direct command of very large-scale operations and he does not know how to do it.

Montgomery told the C.I.G.S. that he thought the only way to finish the German war was to concentrate in great strength at a selected spot, with fresh divisions ready to exploit success. He asked whether he should again raise the matter with Eisenhower. Brooke advised strongly that he should not. He felt that the Command organisation and the present strategy on the Western Front would shortly show themselves to be so deficient that the strongest representations could be made in Washington. The C.I.G.S. also felt certain that in view of the Americans' preponderance in strength, they would insist that any Land Commander appointed should be an American.

Brooke's solution was that Bradley should be appointed Commander of the Land Forces, with myself as Air Commander working closely with him. The Front would be divided into two Groups of Armies, one north of the Ardennes under Montgomery, and one south under Patton. Eisenhower would resume the true functions of a Supreme Commander. He put this proposition to Mr. Churchill, who was also worried at the course of events on the Western Front. The Prime Minister doubted the need for a Land Forces Commander. Brooke thought, nevertheless, that he had succeeded in pointing out that control must be taken out of Eisenhower's hands, and the best plan would be to repeat what had been done in Tunisia, where Alexander had been brought in as Eisenhower's deputy to command the Land Forces for him.[1]

When Eisenhower visited him on 28 November, Montgomery said that the plan contained in the Directive of 28 October had failed, and that we had suffered a strategic reverse. Eisenhower

[1] Bryant: *Triumph in the West,* pp. 333–6.

apparently agreed. Montgomery said that we must have a new plan, in which we should get away from the doctrine of attacking all along the front, and must concentrate our resources on a selected vital thrust. Again, Eisenhower apparently agreed. Montgomery said that it seemed a pity Eisenhower did not have Bradley as Land Force Commander to take off him the work of running operations on land. With this the Supreme Commander disagreed. Montgomery proposed that he should command north of the Ardennes and Bradley to the south. Eisenhower said he thought there would be difficulties about this, since the main objective lay in the northern zones, but he would be quite prepared to put in a strong Army Group under Bradley north of the Ardennes, and to put Bradley under Montgomery's operational command. This talk went on in a friendly manner for some three hours, and Montgomery thought that he had proved to Eisenhower

... that we had definitely failed and must make new plan and next time we must quite definitely not (repeat not) fail. He admitted a grave mistake has been made and in my opinion is prepared to go almost any length to succeed next time.

After a further talk the next morning, Montgomery recorded his conviction that Eisenhower would never agree to the appointment of a Land Force Commander for the whole front. If he reverted to the system which had operated in Normandy, it would mean that Montgomery would in reality be in operational charge and would be able to influence the whole land battle by direct approach to Eisenhower. Brooke recorded in his diary that if all this materialised

... we shall be all right, but I have fears of Ike going back when he has discussed with Bedell Smith, Tedder, etc.[1]

Meanwhile, Montgomery had taken the precaution of recording in a letter what seemed to him to be the main points agreed in his conversation with Eisenhower. The Supreme Commander's reply, however, indicated that Eisenhower's understanding of the conversation was not entirely consonant with Montgomery's.

[1] Bryant: *Triumph in the West*, pp. 342–5.

Just at this time I happened to be in London where, on 2 December, I discussed with Portal whether or not an overall Ground Force Commander was necessary. The C.A.S. mentioned discussions he had recently had with Montgomery, and his belief that Montgomery was right in pressing for this appointment to be made. I gathered that the Chiefs of Staff agreed with Montgomery in feeling that there was some unnecessary frittering away and dispersal of effort which could be eliminated if one mind controlled the whole matter. This whole subject had occupied my attention and thoughts for some time. I told Portal that I did not think the appointment was essential, and that in my view Eisenhower could do the job. I described the moves which were now on foot to enable Eisenhower to maintain closer control over the Army Group Commanders.

At this point in early December, Eisenhower was most anxious to use what reasonable weather remained to the fullest advantage. The attacks begun in the first and second weeks of November had by now eliminated, according to our Intelligence, some 120,000 Germans in the area of Aachen, where 12 Army Group had concentrated a good deal of strength, and there was a definite threat to further advance because of the German capacity to flood the Roer River by breaching the dams. It might be necessary for us to pause while we captured the dam sites. Meanwhile, as Eisenhower told the Chiefs of Staff on 3 December, the operations in the south would go forward so long as the prospects continued good, with the possible hope of making a major breach in the Siegfried Line. The bad weather encountered from mid-September had denied us the full use of the air force and had made manœuvre by tanks impossible in some sectors, and extremely laborious in others. We must go forward as long as any worthwhile results were being achieved, and yet at the same time plan for the decisive campaign to take place at the earliest moment when the weather would allow full development and application of our power. 'In a way it is a repetition of the winter we spent in Tunisia, but on a vastly greater scale.'

In the same message, Eisenhower said that it still appeared to him that the best line for the major effort would be to the north of the Ruhr. To conduct that attack, 21 Army Group would need

[619]

at least one very strong American Army working with it. There were two points indicated for offensive action by forces to the south in support of that operation. These were the Cologne–Bonn and the Frankfurt areas. The first was a very unfavourable spot for crossing the Rhine, while the Frankfurt area would be the best region south of the Ruhr for an attack which involved crossing the river and then pushing rapidly north-east, driving towards a common point in conjunction with the attack in the north.

Four days later, Bradley, Eisenhower and I travelled to Maastricht to meet Montgomery. Eisenhower said that the object of our meeting was to exchange views about the future conduct of the campaign so that the Staffs could get to work. He emphasised the heavy rate of attrition which our present operations were forcing on the enemy—a rate very much greater than our own. The Germans could not afford losses on such a scale, and if the Russians launched a major winter offensive, attrition at this rate might have decisive results. Our current operations must continue as long as they paid real dividends. As for crossing the Rhine, he was advised that the present and prospective floods were quite exceptional, and it might not be possible to effect a major crossing until May. Montgomery was then asked for his views about subsequent operations. He replied that the future plan must meet two requirements; it must cut off the Ruhr from Germany, and it must force the enemy into the mobile warfare in which he would be defeated because of shortage of material and fuel. The only area in which such a mobile war could be waged was north of the Ruhr. All our available effort must be concentrated, therefore, on the drive across the Rhine north of the Ruhr, and operations on the rest of the Front should be purely containing ones. It also transpired that Montgomery was thinking of a strong attack by American armies across the Rhine in the neighbourhood of Bonn, but it was not clear whether, once this bridgehead was established, the subsequent drive would be northwards, parallel with the Rhine, or north-eastwards to link with the northern attack. Eisenhower agreed that the main object was to cut off the Ruhr and to get the enemy on the move, but said that according to his information the country east and north-east of Bonn was

quite unfit for mobile warfare. Movement on the line Frankfurt–
Kassel, on the other hand, seemed to be quite practical. A crossing
at Bonn might be a useful subsidiary. He refused to check the
present operations on the Saar Front, and if they reached
the Rhine he thought there would be great advantage in making
the main supporting thrust on the line Frankfurt–Kassel. If we
thus launched the converging attacks from widely separate points,
we should exploit the enemy's greatest weakness, immobility,
and his inability to switch forces across a wide front. However,
he would be glad for the Staffs to look at both alternatives.

Montgomery refused to agree that a thrust from Frankfurt
had any prospect of success. If it were undertaken, he said,
neither it nor the thrust north of the Ruhr would be sufficiently
strong. The difference of view about this Frankfurt–Kassel
thrust, he insisted, was fundamental. Eisenhower disagreed. The
basic conception was the same, a main drive north of the Ruhr
supported by a converging attack from a point south of the Ruhr.
The only difference was the point of origin of the secondary
thrust, and in any case this must depend not only on the study of
the alternatives by the Staffs, but on the progress of operations
on the Saar Front.

On the question of command, Montgomery said that in his
view, all operations north of the Ardennes should be under one
Command, and all south of the Ardennes under another. Eisenhower retorted that Command boundaries should be determined
by the nature of operations in front of the line, and not by geographical factors behind it. It was agreed that we were not
intending to operate in the Ruhr itself, and the Ruhr, therefore,
offered the most logical and practical boundary. The main
attack north of the Ruhr would come under 21 Army Group, the
supporting drive south would come under 12 Army Group,
covered on the right flank by 6 Army Group. Montgomery
insisted that this was a second fundamental difference of view,
and reiterated that all operations north of the Ardennes should
come under one commander. Again Eisenhower refused.

As for the future, we were all agreed that the pressure must be
kept up throughout the winter, and if possible, the enemy cleared
back to the Rhine; that the main object was to seal off the Ruhr

from the rest of Germany, and thereby make the enemy fight; that the main attack should be north of the Ruhr, and that the starting point of the converging attack from the south could not yet be decided.

It appeared to Montgomery that Eisenhower had changed his mind on all the main points which he thought had been agreed at their meeting on 28 November. He wrote to Alan Brooke that:

I personally regard the whole thing as quite dreadful. I can see no good coming out of this business. Eisenhower and Bradley have their eyes firmly fixed on Frankfurt, and the route thence to Kassel. We shall split our resources and our strength, and we shall fail.

As for Eisenhower, Bradley, and myself, Montgomery described himself as having played a lone hand against the three of us:

They all arrived to-day and went away together. It is therefore fairly clear that any points I made which caused Eisenhower to wobble will have been put right by Bradley and Tedder on the three-hour drive back to Luxembourg. . . . I can do no more myself. . . . If we want the war to end within any reasonable period you have to get Eisenhower's hand taken off the land battle. I regret to say that in my opinion he just doesn't know what he is doing. And you will have to see that Bradley's influence is curbed.[1]

Very soon after this, Eisenhower and I were invited to meet the Prime Minister and the Chiefs of Staff in London. We fore-gathered at 6 p.m. on 12 December in the Map Room. Mr. Churchill presided, and all the Chiefs of Staff attended. Eisenhower explained that during the winter he hoped to keep up the pressure on the enemy, and if possible to clear him back to the Rhine, both in the north between Nijmegen and Bonn, and in the south to the south-west of Frankfurt. In 1945, he proposed to launch strong converging attacks from widely separated areas. These would probably not take place before May. One attack was to be carried out north of the Ruhr by 21 Army Group with an American Army of ten divisions, and the other on the line Frankfurt–Kassel by 12 Army Group. The possibility of a sub-sidiary attack in the Bonn area was also being considered. Brooke

[1] Bryant: *Triumph in the West*, pp. 349–50.

strongly objected to this plan, and said that it violated the principle of concentration, a violation which had resulted in current failures. He said it was impossible to undertake this double invasion of Germany with the limited forces we had.

Later we all dined with the Prime Minister at 10 Downing Street. Brooke advanced the same arguments again, but could not persuade either Churchill or Eisenhower. Both Churchill and the Supreme Commander thought that the difference was one of emphasis, and that the matter would probably be resolved after the Staffs had studied the problem. According to Brooke's diary, he seriously thought of resigning, since Churchill did not seem to attach any importance to his views. The next day, however, the Prime Minister told him that at dinner the previous evening he had felt obliged to support Eisenhower, his guest, one American against five others, with only myself to support him. After a meeting of the Cabinet, who were depressed that it might be May before we crossed the Rhine, Brooke was asked to prepare a paper on the broad strategic situation. This document argued that despite lip service, the Quebec Directive, with its stress on the northern advance, had not been followed. Nor could Eisenhower hope to command by the spring enough strength to make a successful attack on two fronts.

Eisenhower and I did not know of these developments at the time. We had returned to our headquarters on 14 December. During a meeting with General Bradley two days later, a report arrived that a German counter-offensive of some weight had opened along the 5 Corps front in the Eifel district. Further Intelligence later in the day proved to be so important that Bradley decided to return immediately to his own headquarters. By the morning of 17 December it was clear that a German counter-offensive had started and that it had all the appearances of being a major effort. We were told that seventeen divisions were committed, and that the armoured elements had already penetrated some distance. S.H.A.E.F. were caught unawares, the Intelligence services having told us that Sixth Panzer Army was being held in reserve, but having failed to give any indication of its early use. The Ardennes offensive, Hitler's last great fling, had begun.

[623]

8   *Counter-attack in the Ardennes–Bastogne–New Command set-up–
Mr. Churchill's gesture–Western Front and Russian Front–Air-
power halts German offensive–Eisenhower and Montgomery arrange
counter-attacks–Juin threatens to withdraw–Montgomery's 'interesting'
battle–British Press stirs the pot–German evidence of efficacy of Allied air-
power–Effect of Ardennes offensive*

BY early December 1944, the U.S. Ninth Army had reached the Roer River, with the U.S. First Army conforming more slowly. Bradley thought it imprudent to try to cross the river while the dams remained intact, especially since Sixth Panzer Army was known to have moved west of the Rhine. Repeated attempts to breach the Roer dams by air action had failed, as we feared. First Army, therefore, launched on 13 December a new attack to capture them. All the operations in November and early December were accompanied by worse weather than had been known in these regions for many years. Farther to the south, the offensive of the U.S. Third Army towards the Saar, beginning at the end of the first week in November, had progressed swiftly. By 2 December, a substantial stretch of the Saar River had been closed to enemy traffic. Eisenhower hoped that the Third Army would achieve victory there, but decided that a time limit must be set. The final attack was due to begin on 19 December. Regardless of results, divisions were thereafter to be transferred to the north. The southern group of armies had taken the offensive on 13 November. A week later the French First Army had reached the Rhine. By 27 November, French armour had taken Strasbourg, a victory of the highest significance for France. This concentration around Aachen and in the Saar involved us in a calculated risk. The Eifel sector of some seventy-five miles between Trier and Monschau was held by no more than four divisions. It was not a region which contained strategic objectives of high importance, or large depots; moreover, the terrain was judged to be difficult. The bad weather made photographic reconnaissance, on which we relied heavily, difficult and often impossible. Our Intelligence was at fault in supposing that the Germans did not possess the transport or the fuel for a major offensive operation, for despite the lack of aerial reconnaissance, the U.S. 12 Army Group had received some reports which should have suggested the impending stroke.

On the 8th I went up to Luxemburg to Bradley's headquarters for a meeting with Eisenhower and Bradley. One wall in the big room was plastered with a map showing the whole of Bradley's 12 Army Group's front from north to south. The relative weakness in the centre did not go unnoticed, but Bradley was confident that there were adequate forces which could be drawn up from the south should the Germans attempt anything.

At all events, on 16 December von Rundstedt thrust through the Ardennes at the weakest point in our lines. For the moment, the scanty American forces were brusquely swept aside. No doubt the enemy's immediate intention was to seize the Meuse crossings between Namur and Liège. Some twenty-four nominal German divisions were employed. Against this we had immediately available three infantry divisions and one armoured division in the line. These troops, though by-passed and divided by the German thrust, fought most valiantly and denied the enemy the important area of St. Vith. Two American airborne divisions, moved from the reserve in the area of Rheims on 18 December, helped to hold back the German advance. One of these divisions, reinforced by armour, held out in the important road centre at Bastogne, though attacked incessantly and surrounded completely. This feat was made possible by concentrated effort on the part of our fighter-bombers. Supply was carried by air. Aircraft ferrying in further troops achieved the better part of a thousand sorties despite air opposition from a rallied Luftwaffe and the abominable weather.

For a time, some confusion reigned. It appeared that Bradley's own headquarters at Luxemburg was endangered, and that the lifeline of our Northern Forces through Antwerp might be severed. On 19 December I accompanied Eisenhower to Verdun, where we met Generals Devers, Bradley, and Patton. Eisenhower at once set the tone of our gathering by remarking: 'The present situation is to be regarded as one of opportunity for us and not of disaster. There will be only cheerful faces at this conference table.'

We were agreed that the counter-attack must go in at the earliest moment. The whole front south of the Moselle passed at once to strict defence. All penetrations across the Saar River were given up. While Devers was to take over most of the U.S. Third Army Front, Patton would move northwards with six divisions, organising a major counter blow for 23 or 24 December. We realised that our weakest spot was in the direction of Namur. The enemy was expected to attack with armoured forces near Monschau to broaden his penetration of our lines, and might launch a secondary attack from the region of Trier. The Germans might also try to attack to the north of the U.S. Ninth Army but Montgomery had reserves capable of dealing with such a blow: 'The general plan', Eisenhower telegraphed to the Chiefs-of-Staff, 'is to plug the holes in the north and launch a co-ordinated attack from the south.'

Eisenhower, when he knew of the strength of the enemy's effort and its dividing effect on the communications within our Central Group of Armies, understood at once that it would not be practicable for one commander to handle the American forces to the north and the south of the large salient which the Germans were carving out. He fixed a boundary running through the breach in our lines and put all forces to the north of it under the operational command of Montgomery, while Bradley took command in the south. Every available man was sent to defend the Meuse crossings. The Liège–Namur section was especially vital, since many of our main lines of communication and signal installations lay there.

On the day when these decisions were taken, 20 December, I attended a meeting which Eisenhower called to consider the situation as it had developed. The Supreme Commander had talked with Bradley during the night by telephone, and asked whether all preparations had been made to establish road blocks if necessary. He was assured that this had been done. General Kenneth Strong, the British head of Eisenhower's Intelligence staff, thought that the enemy had committed everything to this thrust, which was now moving due west and not north-west towards Liège and Namur, as we had previously expected. The Supreme Commander said that we must not allow the importance of the Aachen area to deter us from adopting the best line of defence wherever it might be. By telephone, he asked Bradley: 'Where is the line you can hold the best and cheapest? I don't care how far back it is.'

At this stage, the weather conditions were so bad that air forces were more or less grounded, much to the annoyance of General Hodges of the U.S. First Army, and the German thrust continued to progress. We hoped that our own concentrations might be made secretly because the enemy would be denied air reconnaissance, and felt sure that if this could be achieved, we could surprise and defeat the Germans. Later, the work of our air forces, and especially of Bomber Command, was beyond praise. Harris's men made a telling attack on Trier on 19 December, although heavy fog clouded their bases and their objectives. At Eisenhower's request, I telegraphed warm congratulations to the Commander-in-Chief, Bomber Command, who replied:

> Very many thanks for the generous message from the Supreme Commander, which has been passed on to all concerned.
> You can count on us in any weather short of the impossible.

On this document, Eisenhower minuted: 'Goddamit, they have already achieved the impossible.'

On 21 December, Eisenhower held another meeting. He had again spoken to Bradley by telephone, and confirmed the new command arrangements. Bradley told us that supplies were still getting through to the U.S. 7th Armoured and 106th Divisions, which were putting up a magnificent fight. He thought this stand must have upset materially the enemy's plans in the northern part of the thrust. Montgomery had telegraphed that he saw no reason to give up the ground in the Aachen area, which had been so hardly won. During our discussion, I, like several others, expressed some concern lest the counter-attack which Bradley was mounting might be a piecemeal affair similar to the German counter-attacks in Normandy. This might happen if the two divisions which were on their way were put into a battle without awaiting the build-up of greater strength. But we all agreed that it was important to hold Bastogne, and Eisenhower directed that a counter-attack for this purpose was to be limited, and not to be allowed to spread. In fact, it would be for the purpose of establishing a firm *point d'appui* for the main counter-offensive. Eisenhower said that he feared the impetuous Patton would talk Bradley into allowing him to attack at once with the object of going right through, and without awaiting the co-ordinated counter-offensive.

To the Prime Minister, as usual, these disagreeable events acted as a stimulus. On 22 December he telegraphed to Eisenhower that as a mark of confidence in him as Supreme Commander the following announcement would be made at once:

In order to sustain and nourish our Armies in line, His Majesty's Government have decided to make available in the coming months additional fighting men. A large part will be found by new call-up from civil life. Some will be obtained by transfer to the Army from the Royal Navy and the Royal Air Force. More will be found from the Army itself by further combing out and retraining of units and individuals who have hitherto been engaged in static forms of defence or in administration services. The total to be provided above previous plans will amount to quarter of a million men.

The weather now began to improve, which meant that our strongest card could be played again. Air action soon produced a paralysing effect on movement in and around the battle area. The Strategic Air Forces battered the marshalling yards east of the Rhine and blocked nodal points. The medium and light bombers of the Tactical Air Forces co-ordinated their effort with that of the heavy bombers, destroying bridges, headquarters, dumps, and other targets in the battle area. Fighter-bombers ranged far and wide in and beyond the battle front, creating havoc in enemy movement by road and rail. We soon knew from enemy prisoners how efficiently we had managed to starve their forces of fuel, food, and ammunition. On Christmas Eve, a well-concerted attack on German airfields reduced the growing activity of the Luftwaffe, and thereby afforded our fighter-bombers even greater opportunities for concentrating on the exercise of air-power rather than the gaining of air superiority. By 26 December, the U.S. Third Army had linked up with the gallant garrison in Bastogne and checked the enemy's advance on that flank. This attack also served to draw enemy forces from the north of the salient. By the time that we managed to halt the enemy's forward rush, he had breached a gap in our front some forty-five miles wide. His forward troops had got within four miles of the Meuse. By Boxing Day, however, our additional reserves had reached the area and there was no fear of losing it.

Throughout this anxious Christmas period we received reports almost every hour about the fighting in the salient. Now that the weather had allowed us to exercise our strength in the air, the news became a little brighter. On Boxing Day, at a meeting held in Bedell Smith's office, he told us that Hodges had only been able to meet the enemy's threat against First Army because of the air support he had been given. We understood Bradley to be very disturbed by the results of his meeting with Montgomery on the previous day. He found Montgomery taking a purely defensive view. Bradley wanted to move his headquarters northwards and take over his two armies again.

At another meeting under Eisenhower's chairmanship later the same day, I urged, as usual, the need to hit back smartly. The weather might not last, and we already had a good deal of evidence that the enemy was running short of supplies. Robb gave us the latest news from the Second Tactical Air Force. It appeared that Montgomery had a new plan. 'Praise God from whom all blessings flow,' said Eisenhower.

By the afternoon, when we met again, General Bradley had turned up. He told us of his immediate plans to strengthen the southern flank of the salient and then to attack. His axis of attack would run north-eastwards from the Bastogne area, and not north-eastwards from the shoulder of the salient as Patton had wished. He did not wish the 101st Airborne Division to be relieved, and generally exuded confidence.

My own comment, in a letter written on 22 December 1944 was: 'The fact that the Hun has stuck his neck out is, from the point of view of shortening the whole business, the best thing that could happen. It may make months of difference. But he might have waited until after Xmas!'

*

On 21 December, five days after the Ardennes offensive began, Eisenhower had telegraphed to the Combined Chiefs of

Staff that we had recently noticed a tendency for German divisions formed or reforming in the east of the Reich to move to the Western Front. The arrival of these divisions, Eisenhower signalled

... obviously influences the events in my area, and if this trend continues it will affect the decisions which I have to make regarding future strategy in the west. I therefore consider it essential that we should obtain from the Russians at the earliest possible moment some indication of their strategical and tactical intentions. If, for instance, it is the Russian intention to launch a major offensive in the course of this or next month, knowledge of the fact would be of the utmost importance to me, and I would condition my plans accordingly. Can anything be done to effect this co-ordination?

I am aware that a request of this nature would inevitably entail my giving reciprocal information to the Russians, which I am quite ready to do.

Up to this stage, the Russians had shown themselves entirely unwilling to impart to us even basic information. The Combined Chiefs of Staff agreed with Eisenhower's suggestion, but felt quite certain that the Russian High Command would commit nothing to writing, and that the only way of obtaining information would be by means of a visit to Moscow by a very high-ranking officer from S.H.A.E.F. They were sure that on a question of this importance the Military Mission in Moscow would get nowhere. They were, therefore, proposing to the Prime Minister that a joint approach by himself and Roosevelt to Stalin should be made. It would be left to Eisenhower to decide which officer should go to Moscow. The President and the Prime Minister acted promptly on this advice. By Boxing Day, Stalin had agreed that a staff officer should visit him to discuss the situation on the Western Front and its relationship to the Russian Front; and to arrange for the exchange of information which was essential to the co-ordination of our efforts. Eisenhower asked me to lead this Mission. I agreed at once. It was arranged that I would go to London for a day or so and would then set off for Moscow. Meanwhile, the daily meetings continued. On 29 December, General Whiteley, who had just visited 21 Army Group with Eisenhower, told us that a counter-attack from the north flank was planned to begin either on 1 January or immediately after the expected German attack in that region. We understood that Montgomery did not want to mix up British and American units, and was quite certain that the enemy was going to attack U.S. First Army. I said that I thought I would delay my departure for Moscow until Montgomery had decided to attack. Otherwise, Stalin would put us through the hoop.

'What makes me so Goddam mad,' said Bedell Smith, 'is that Monty won't talk in the presence of anyone else. He gets Ike into a corner alone.' Whiteley observed that he and de Guingand had tried to take part in the talks, but were excluded. A little later the same morning, Eisenhower himself confirmed his understanding that Montgomery would attack by 1 January if he were not attacked himself. It seemed to the Supreme Commander that the best axis of attack from the south would be from Bastogne. Both Bedell Smith and I objected, pointing out that this would be to attack from the tip of the salient, whereas if we struck from the flank farther east we would stand to gain far greater results. For the purposes of my mission in Moscow, Eisenhower said that our intentions were to eliminate the salient, to pin down the panzer armies in battle now, and try to destroy them west of the Rhine, to drive on with all our strength on the main axis Prum–Bonn, and to come out of the whole affair with sufficient reserves to allow Montgomery's original plan of a thrust from the north towards Krefeld to take place. After we had cleaned up the Ardennes offensive, we should have many divisions to rehabilitate. The fact that we were dependent on the Channel ports limited our use of further forces in the European theatre. Communications and supply difficulties would not allow us to contemplate a thrust through Bavaria to join up with the Russians working north from Hungary. 'The basic thing,' Eisenhower said, 'is to defeat the German armies west of the Rhine; for this, everything must be concentrated to get to the Rhine from Bonn northwards.'

The part played by the air forces in halting the German offensive became clearer every day. On 29 December, the 2nd Tactical Air Force operated with outstanding success in the area of Munster, when twenty-nine locomotives were destroyed and thirty-six damaged, together with large numbers of wagons and motor vehicles. In the battle, the 2nd Tactical Air Force had shot down thirty-two enemy aircraft. Sixteen of these were destroyed by one Norwegian squadron. Desperate measures were taken to overcome the unfavourable weather conditions. Generally, only a short period of time elapsed between the clearance of morning fog over the English east coast bases of the U.S. Eighth Air Force and the closing in of evening fog. The heavy bombers took great risks to get off and land under these conditions, losing many aircraft and crews in the process. It was most difficult to identify small targets in the battle area from great heights in these conditions. However, photographs of the targets and of the marshalling yards supplying the area of the German offensive showed that immense damage had been done.

Eisenhower understood Montgomery to believe that unless he had control of all the armies down to the Moselle, everything would fall flat. Montgomery also thought that Bradley had made a mess of the Ardennes situation. Bedell Smith and the Supreme Commander agreed that while Montgomery had quickly restored the situation on the north flank in the U.S. First Army area, he was far behind Bradley when it came to the need for taking rapid offensive action. Even if Montgomery were given the wider control of Bradley's Army Group, Eisenhower understood that he would insist on remaining in active command of 21 Army Group. Montgomery had apparently told the Supreme Commander that there was no one else fit to hold the job, and that in any case the British public would not stand for a change. By the time that these discussions took place, I was already in London preparing for my visit to Russia, on which, after being delayed by the weather, I set off on 1 January.

On 31 December, Freddie de Guingand had arrived at S.H.A.E.F. There seemed to be a delay in mounting Montgomery's attack from the north. De Guingand advanced some explanations. It was impossible to switch suddenly from defensive positions to offensive without careful preparation. In any case, we had apparently got the enemy 'on the run like a wet hen from one side of the salient to the other'; time was on our side, and we should let the Germans exhaust themselves and then counterattack. Nothing could be worse than an ill-prepared attack.

Reserves must be collected and disposed. Bedell Smith pointed out that after Eisenhower had met Montgomery he had clearly understood that an attack would be launched by Montgomery immediately after an attack on him, and certainly not later than 1 January. De Guingand said that Eisenhower must have got hold of the wrong end of the stick. An effort was then made to find a signal confirming the arrangements, but de Guingand said: 'Knowing Monty, the last thing he would do is to commit himself on paper.' A little later he said: 'You know Monty, and I am doing all I can to boost him.'

At a meeting in Eisenhower's office later the same day, 31 December, de Guingand repeated the arguments for a delay. Eisenhower remarked that he had been clearly told by Montgomery that he would attack by 1 January at the latest. De Guingand refused to commit himself to a date, but suggested that the attack might be mounted by 2 or 3 January.

It appeared that co-ordination between 21 Army Group and 12 Army Group was quite lacking. Bradley had now launched his attack from the Bastogne area on the full understanding that Montgomery would move from the north on or before 1 January. No German attack on the north had taken place, but one of the panzer divisions being held for it had been switched southwards to hold up Bradley. If Montgomery did not attack soon, the enemy might be able to hold up Bradley and then switch his strength back to the northwards, retaining the initiative which he would lose at once if we used all our strength in a co-ordinated movement.

I need not describe in detail the events of the first part of January, which took place while I was trying to get to Moscow. In the first few days of the month, the situation caused Eisenhower and his staff much anxiety. At one point, a withdrawal from the Plain of Alsace to the Vosges was considered. The thought of abandoning Strasbourg again to the Germans brought tears to the eyes of General Juin, the French First Army Commander. Eisenhower ordered that the Alsace Plain must be held if it were humanly possible. Withdrawal from one corner of the front north of Strasbourg was found to be necessary. On the news of this, General Juin threatened to remove the French Army from Eisenhower's

[633]

control. Bedell Smith, in reporting this interview, said: 'Juin said things to me last night for which, if he had been an American, I would have socked him on the jaw.'

Quite apart from the possible withdrawal of the French Army from Eisenhower's command, there were three or four hundred thousand French citizens in the area who would be the subject of the worst reprisals by the Germans if we had to retreat. These considerations were forcefully urged upon Eisenhower by de Gaulle.

Montgomery's counter-attack eventually went in on 3 January and gathered strength thereafter. Eisenhower, who had already been told by Marshall that the appointment of a British officer with operational control over Bradley would be unacceptable, had let Montgomery know by letter that he could not agree that one Army Group Commander should fight his own battle and give orders to another Army Group Commander. The Supreme Commander had been working on a plan by which, when the enemy had been defeated in the salient, everything should be concentrated for the destruction of the Germans north of the Prum–Bonn Axis. The plan also provided for the concentration of strength north of the Ruhr when the Rhine was crossed. The Ninth U.S. Army would be placed under the operational command of 21 Army Group. As soon as the reduction of the Ardennes salient permitted, the Headquarters of 12 Army Group would move north, close to those of 21 Army Group. The two commanders would effect 'any detailed or emergency co-ordination required along Army Group boundaries in the north . . . with power of decision vested in C.G., 21 Army Group'. What must now be prevented was the stabilisation of the salient with infantry, which would permit the enemy to use his panzer forces at will on any part of the front. 'We must regain the initiative,' Eisenhower wrote, 'and speed and energy are essential.' He also told Montgomery that he would deplore the development

. . . of such an unbridgeable group of convictions between us that we would have to present our differences to the Combined Chiefs-of-Staff. The confusion and debate that would follow would certainly damage the goodwill and devotion to a common cause that have made this Allied Force unique in history.

For the moment this cleared the air. The British Chiefs of Staff, however, signalled to Washington on 6 January that in their view the conduct of the campaign had suffered from a lack of proper co-ordination at the top ever since one commander had ceased to be in charge of all the ground forces. They thought that one man should be given the power of operational control and co-ordination of all the forces employed for the northern thrust. The Chiefs of Staff admitted that they had been as surprised as anybody by von Rundstedt's counter-offensive. His quick initial successes, however, had gone a long way to confirm their misgivings. As a result of the dispersion of effort between north and south, the enemy had caught us off balance with our forces scattered, and with no reserves available to deal with the emergency. The Chiefs of Staff did not think that Eisenhower would have available sufficient forces for a movement of double envelopment which he seemed to intend. It was therefore important to decide on one major thrust, which should be in the north.

This signal was privately placed before Marshall on 9 January. His immediate reaction was that it would be unwise for the Combined Chiefs of Staff to imply that the present situation was in any way due to Eisenhower's mishandling. The best thing was to avoid criticism, which could be directed against both British and American. He regarded the present command arrangements as a temporary expedient to meet the Ardennes emergency. Marshall also indicated fairly strongly that the Americans were inclined to question Montgomery's handling of some of the situations with which he had been faced, for example, Antwerp *vis à vis* Arnhem. These potential disagreements at the highest level coincided with a period of actual disagreements at a lower one. On 5 January, de Guingand had telephoned to S.H.A.E.F. to ask whether it could be announced in the Press that Montgomery was in command of the American First and Ninth Armies. Eisenhower ruled that the time was inopportune and that de Guingand should be told that the announcement would be made when the situation in the salient was under full control and the two armies were drawing near to each other. The repercussions of such an announcement in America were obvious. Later in the day, Robb learnt from the headquarters of the 2nd

Tactical Air Force that the announcement of Montgomery's command was being made in Brussels that afternoon. He was asked whether Coningham's control of the two American Air Forces could also be made public. The source of the leakage was not known to S.H.A.E.F.

In a Press conference given on 7 January, Montgomery described how Eisenhower had placed him in command of the whole northern front. He emphasised that the repulse of the German onslaught had been an Anglo-American effort, but somewhat unfortunately went on to describe the battle as 'most interesting. I think, possibly, one of the most interesting and tricky battles I have ever handled, with great issues at stake.'

Montgomery expressed his admiration for the fighting qualities of the American soldier, and said how grieved he was to see uncomplimentary articles about Eisenhower in the British Press. However, the subsequent handling of Montgomery's statements by the British newspapers and by the B.B.C. caused a crisis. The Prime Minister telephoned several times to Eisenhower, who said that Bradley was most upset. He proposed to award the Bronze Star to Bradley with a citation drawing attention to his fighting qualities, and to the work of the American Armies in bearing the brunt of the German offensive. At the daily meeting on 9 January, the Supreme Commander remarked that censorship was a two-edged weapon. Anything withheld by the censors immediately acquired news value, and the Press, by innuendo or other means, invariably circumvented it. It seemed to him that the reaction of the American Press to the statements in the British newspapers would be to exaggerate the United States point of view. There would be no end to the statements which the Press of the two countries would make in reply to each other. He also remarked: 'For two and a half years I have been trying to get the Press to talk of "Allied" operations, but look what has happened.'

When de Guingand saw the British reporters in Brussels on 9 January, they were able to prove to him that their articles had given a balanced view of the picture, but that their editors had been responsible for the flaming headlines which told the British public that Montgomery had defeated the Germans in the salient. It was also learned that the radio station at Arnhem, then in German hands, had intercepted some of the despatches and had re-written them with an anti-American slant. They had then been put out and mistaken for B.B.C. broadcasts.

By this time, the enemy had begun to withdraw from the western end of the salient, though still resisting on the northern and southern flanks. The concentrated air attack on communications had played a most material part in ensuring the failure of the Ardennes offensive. But this was only part of the story. Early in November, Speer had reported that the continuous attacks against the Ruhr were having

. . . the most serious effect on our entire armament and war production. In addition to the bombing of production plants in the Ruhr, the systematic attacks carried out on railway installations are largely responsible for the critical situation. While the former can result in an appreciable drop in our total war output, the disruption of our communications may well lead to a production crisis which will gravely jeopardise our capacity to continue the war.

Speer also warned Hitler that a labour force of fifty thousand foreign prisoners had been transferred from trench digging to the repair of damage caused to the German transport system by Allied air-power. Even the German armaments industry must give up thirty thousand men for the same purpose and to restore badly hit industries in the Ruhr, while 10 per cent. of the total number of miners had been withdrawn for immediate relief work. To defend transport centres, anti-aircraft guns had to be taken away from important arms factories, even in the Ruhr itself. Speer pointed to the desperate and growing shortage of coal; to the attacks on blast furnaces, intended to destroy Germany's steel-making capacity; to the growing isolation of the Ruhr from the areas it formerly supplied. In sum:

In the long run the loss of the industrial area of Rhineland–Westphalia would be a mortal blow to the German economy and to the conduct of the war.

In actual fact, at the present time the Ruhr area can be completely written off as far as the German economy is concerned except for goods still manufactured within the inner network. . . . We shall do

[637]

everything within our power to win the battle of the Ruhr, the outcome of which will determine the fate of our Reich.[1]

By the end of November, our air forces had destroyed the
Weser–Ems and Mittelland Canals just when they had been
repaired. This process was later to be repeated, and deprived the
Germans of the opportunity to transfer goods from rail to water
transport. The transport situation in the Ruhr meant that coal
supplies were already a third below what had previously been
considered the irreducible minimum needed to keep the armament
and war production industries alive. Those industries were now
receiving no more than a sixth or a seventh of their former
supplies. Nor were these the only effects; despite operation
'Pointblank', German production of fighter aircraft rose steadily,
indeed swiftly, in 1944. After the war, Speer was asked to explain
how it was that the Luftwaffe nevertheless grew weaker in offensive power. He replied:

The answer to that was simple—the Allies destroyed the aircraft
as soon as they were made. These instances show how the attack on
communications, apart from the immediate tactical effect on the battle,
helped to destroy Germany's capacity to make armaments and therefore to make war.

After the Germans had launched their assault on 16 December
our air forces concentrated against enemy communications
leading up to the Ardennes. The immediate effect of these air
operations was shown by the fact that when the assault began,
rail traffic was reaching Stadtkyll and Bitburg. A fortnight
later, all supplies had to be fetched from the right bank of the
Rhine. The rail system was vital, for motor transport was
limited in capacity. Moreover, it could only be used to about
30 per cent. of that capacity, because air attack forced the lorries
to proceed at night, and without lights. Under interrogation,
Speer pointed out that the Ardennes offensive was ordered to
begin, though fuel was lacking; the equipment for bridge
building lay far to the rear, and the whole supply organisation
was insufficient to reach the distant goal of the operation. 'With-

[1] Webster & Frankland: *The Strategic Air Offensive Against Germany
1939–1945*, vol. 4, pp. 349-56.

out any doubt,' he added, 'the lack of supplies was due to the transport difficulties caused by air attack.'[1]

Air-power was also ranging farther afield. Hitler tried to bring divisions from Norway to the Western Front. Shipping was provided to move two or three divisions per month. By the early spring, because of attack and mining from the air, only one division was moved in six weeks. By April the movement was negligible. Small wonder that the Commander of the German Fighter Force remarked ruefully that the fighting had degenerated into a 'Wild West Show put on by the Allies'.

The strategic offensive against oil had been showing good progress. By early December, synthetic plants in West Germany had been so battered that their production was negligible and repair work on them rendered most difficult, while some had been put out of action because destruction of communications had denied them raw materials. The synthetic plants in central and eastern Germany were obviously our next targets. In the first week of December, seven of the eleven plants in these areas were attacked. This process was carried on despite the appalling weather, until the third week in December. The U.S. Fifteenth Air Force based in the Mediterranean took its full part. We soon had Intelligence to show that even after some very careful hoarding of oil supplies for the Ardennes offensive, the German staffs had in their planning been forced to rely on the hope of capturing Allied stocks of fuel. Yet there was no denying that the offensive had had a serious effect on our campaign. The planned onslaught against the Ruhr and the Saar had to be curtailed. The Strategic Air Forces were, of course, drawn into the immediate battle area. The targets we especially desired to attack in Germany—oil plants, communications, and the production of jet aircraft— were virtually unmolested for a month. Our own casualties were not far short of 80,000, though we estimated the enemy's losses at about 120,000. This was in addition to his loss of some six hundred tanks and heavy guns, and about 1,600 aircraft. We realised that after nearly a month of full-scale effort, the enemy's fuel stocks must be reduced to the bare minimum.

[1] Webster & Frankland: *The Strategic Air Offensive Against Germany 1939–1945*, vol. 4, p. 381.

Our converging attacks from the northern and southern flanks
of the salient finally met on 16 January. The Germans had fought
with great stubbornness and fanaticism. Eisenhower telegraphed
to the Chiefs of Staff on 7 January that the situation would be
much relieved if the Russians launched a large offensive, for Germany's weakness of fighting on three fronts would then be fully
exploited, and she would have to divide her resources. If the
Russians did not intend to attack we might be faced in the west with
the arrival of new divisions from Russia and from other fronts.
There was even a prospect that if the Germans could hold any
Russian attack, perhaps by giving up ground, until the thaw in
March, they might then be able to switch a considerable number of
divisions to the west before we were able to undertake a major
offensive there. It was to clarify these crucial issues that I had
been sent to Moscow.

*Russians and a bomb line–Journey to Moscow–The Crimea–Stalin–
Stalin on Western Front plans–Major Birse sums up–My Russian
speech–An American base in Russia*

OUR military, not to say political, relations with the Russians seemed most unpromising. Efforts had been going forward for some months, as the pincers of the Allied and Russian attacks closed upon Germany, to establish a bomb line. Early in November, fighters of the U.S. Fifteenth Air Force had by mistake, attacked Russian troops, an error which had caused the Chiefs of Staff to direct that a temporary bomb line must be established until we enjoyed effective liaison with the Russians. This latter commodity proved elusive. Perhaps because the Russians did not understand the principles of strategic bombing, they had proposed a bomb line which was unsatisfactory, and which hampered our operations in south-eastern Europe. Proposals and counter-proposals were bandied about between the Russians and the Allies, while the cumbersome machinery of consultation through the Military Mission in Moscow made it virtually impossible to adjust the bomb lines promptly to suit the ebb and flow of battle. At the time of my visit to Stalin that January, there was no agreed strategic bomb line, since the latest Russian proposal to establish a line north of the Balkans was unacceptable. When the American Eighth Air Force had the opportunity to attack targets east of the proposed line, it was our policy to let the Russians know of our intention, indicating the general area and probable date, but giving no information about specific targets. Several pieces of evidence had come to light which showed that the Russians might now become a little more friendly. What the Allies wanted was a method of establishing a bomb line, not at the highest level between Washington, London, and Moscow, but by direct liaison with commanders in the field.

However, this was only one of our difficulties. The Russians had never shown any keenness to allow a foreigner to work at any of their Army headquarters, and at the beginning of January had sent a flat refusal to our request for the acceptance of Air liaison officers. We were told that in the Russian view this step

[641]

was unnecessary. Liaison could be effected satisfactorily through Moscow. For over three months we had been pressing the Russians without success to allow facilities on their airfields for our bomber aircraft crippled in operations over eastern Europe. The Russian High Command had disapproved of our dropping supplies into Poland on the grounds that such supplies fell into the hands of the Germans, or of partisans who were hostile to the Red Army. There was a good deal of truth in this, because the partisans to whom we were sending supplies looked to London and were not kindly disposed to the Russians. Our formal application to Moscow for Italian-based aircraft to fly over Russian-occupied territory to Poland was refused. Nevertheless, our aircraft were ordered to take the risk, and up to the time of my visit the Russians had made no forcible reaction. Only one visit by the R.A.F. section of the Military Mission to operational units of the Russian Air Force had been allowed in a period of eighteen months. Though we had given the Soviets vast quantities of supplies, including hundreds of our own aircraft of almost every type, they had refused to let us have even samples. The file containing these and many other examples of Russian unhelpfulness was given to me before I left.

I have mentioned already that my journey from London eventually began on 1 January. So bad was the weather and so many the difficulties that five days later I had got no farther than Naples, whence I signalled to Eisenhower suggesting that I might return to S.H.A.E.F. to await reasonable conditions. He telegraphed back assuring me that the air situation was well in hand, and that he would prefer me to proceed. Meanwhile, we had been unable to obtain any useful information through the Military Mission in Moscow about the Russian plans. Hearing of my slow progress, Mr. Churchill said to the Supreme Commander: 'You may find many delays on the staff level, but I expect Stalin would tell me if I asked him. Shall I try?'

Eisenhower said that he would be very glad if the Prime Minister would do this. Churchill therefore cabled to Stalin that the battle in the west was very heavy. At any time large decisions might be called for. Stalin would know from his own experience how very anxious was the position when a broad front had to be defended after temporary loss of the initiative. Eisenhower greatly wished, and needed to know in outline, what the Russians planned to do, for this affected all our major decisions. In case I had still not got to Moscow, Churchill would be grateful if Stalin could let him know 'whether we can count on a major Russian offensive on the Vistula front, or elsewhere, during January. . . .'

Stalin received this message on the evening of 7 January; it is a measure of his powers of decision and of his place in the Russian State that he was able to reply the same evening. Stalin telegraphed that the Russians were preparing an offensive, though the weather was for the moment unfavourable. Nevertheless, in view of the position of Britain and the United States on the Western Front, the Soviet High Command had decided

. . . to accelerate the completion of our preparation, and, regardless of the weather, to commence large-scale offensive operations against the Germans along the whole Central Front not later than the second half of January. You may rest assured that we shall do everything possible to render assistance to the glorious forces of our Allies.[1]

My journey eastward was chequered by various unforeseen delays. Caserta was the first stop after Naples, and I have a very chilly recollection of the huge, gaunt, pretentious palace in which the Allied Headquarters had ensconced themselves—self-confessed 'birds of passage'. Despite my impatience to get on with the job, and despite the inevitable melancholy of a palace that had so obviously seen its best days, I did make the most of my opportunity to enjoy the magnificent views from the hilltops around.

My next stop had a special reason for engraving itself on my memory. We had landed at Cairo West to refuel and proceed north about midnight. I drove out to the aerodrome about 11 p.m. to be greeted by something of an atmosphere. Apparently, only one or two minutes before I arrived, somebody had noticed the sound of running water. I myself could hear it as my car stopped. The 'water' was 100 octane-petrol pouring from one of the main tanks in the fuselage of our York. It appeared that one of the tanks had sprung a bad leak which the bullet-proof lining

---

[1] Churchill: *The Second World War*, vol. VI, pp. 242–3.

had failed to seal. Fortunately so, for the journey from Cairo to the Crimea was over the mountains of Anatolia—notorious for their turbulent conditions. Had the leak not disclosed itself until we were well on our way, the odds are that in the very rough conditions which we did in fact experience en route to the Crimea, it would have then sprung badly, and our prospects in the winter night over the mountains or the Black Sea would have been doubtful, to say the least.

We landed on a grim, bleak, featureless Crimean plain on which two or three timber huts were the only sign of human habitation. A small reception party greeted me, including, to my relief, a British Naval officer who was a qualified interpreter. Amongst the others was the commander of the Russian Air Forces covering the Black Sea. Strangely enough there was no snow lying, but the cold was raw, and we were glad to get out of the wind into the warm log cabin, where a table had been laid and the inevitable bottle and glasses set out ready for action. Food, which I found difficult to identify, appeared at intervals throughout the day, laced with unlimited supplies of Crimean wine, fortunately not quite so lethal as vodka, but nearly so—and by the evening the last of my Russian hosts had collapsed. I, myself, as last man in—or perhaps I should say last man out—rather than accept the hospitality of some rather doubtful-looking bunks next door, opted for a bench in the room where we had dined and wined, and my R.A.F. batman, Pearce, earned undying fame in his own estimation by insisting upon removing my heavy flying boots for me.

I had, in the meantime, been having intermittent arguments with the Russian commander about my onward progress. The Russians insisted that the weather was quite unfit to fly through to Moscow, and that in due course they would arrange a train. For this I would have to wait until late the following evening. The next morning, my hosts offered to take me to see the country. The alternatives were a trip to Sevastopol, and through and over the mountains to the south coast of the Crimea. I chose the former for historical reasons. I am glad to have seen Sevastopol, or Sevastópol as the Russians call it, though, except for its associations, it is a singularly uninspiring spot to visit on an early January day. However, I made a small and uninspired sketch near Balaclava which is only distinguished by the autograph in Russian script of the Russian A.O.C., Black Sea. *En route* there we passed through a small town nestling on the slopes of the foothills. Scarcely any signs of ruins, and yet it appeared to be dead; one only saw two or three individuals altogether. Discreet enquiries from us elicited a story (perhaps indiscreet) that the local population had been found guilty of collaboration, and had been removed to somewhere in the remoter parts of Siberia—a sinister sidelight on the Stalin régime.

The train, when it arrived after dusk, proved to be surprisingly comfortable, having one of the standard *wagon-lit* coaches. The rate of progress was slow and monotonous. Once away from the Crimea, we ran into the Russian mid-winter—mile after mile of featureless snow, with, every now and then, lines of snow fences. Periodically we would stop at a station, where there would be a small crowd of peasants, most of whom were offering eggs, a chicken or two, and other more mysterious provisions. Many of our fellow travellers in the other coaches made the most of the opportunity to walk on the platform—a welcome relief from being cooped up in the very 'hard' coaches.

The railway terminus at Moscow was much like any important European station; a small bevy of officials to meet us—a Marshal, a Colonel-General, a Lieutenant-General, a Major-General, and a Captain, and representatives of the British and American Missions. The British Ambassador was away, so his chargé-d'affaires took his place. Averell Harriman was present as head of the American Mission. We got down to business at once, deciding who should accompany me, and getting the general form. There was some difference of opinion as to who should accompany me to meet Stalin. Harriman, in particular, was very insistent in expressing his view that he and a British diplomat should. He pressed the point very strongly, saying that when I sat down at Stalin's conference table I would find Molotov opposite me, and would immediately get into deep water. It was difficult for me to take any line different from that taken by representatives on the spot. I had thought over the matter very thoroughly and come to the conclusion that I was purely a military man concerned with military affairs, and I would make that clear from the start. If Molotov was present and tried to talk politics, I would close up. I am afraid that at the time Harriman was rather annoyed with me, and I hope that as things turned out I was forgiven.

In the event, with me were the American Generals Bull and Betts, two members of the Allied Military Mission, Major-General Deane and Admiral Archer, and Stalin had his Army Chief of Staff, Antonov. He had his usual little interpreter, Pavlov, and we had the British Embassy interpreter, Major Birse. Stalin took his customary place at the end of a long table, opposite me; a blank seat on his right, where I had seen Molotov sitting during the Churchill conversations, and then Antonov.

The series of anterooms on the way to Stalin's own room, appeared the same as they had at the time of the Churchill visit, but I must admit a slight feeling of awkwardness as I noticed each guard, as I passed him, cast a suspicious eye upon one or two small wooden boxes which I had under my arm, despite the fact that I had unwrapped them so that they could be seen for what they were, cigar boxes. I noticed one change in Stalin's office. On one wall, there were three or four life-sized paintings. In 1942, the portraits had been those of Karl Marx, Engels, and others. In 1945, they were of four field-marshals from Russian military history, including Suvarov. There was also a change as regards Stalin himself. In 1942, he had been very much a civilian in his grey smock, breeches, and field boots. In 1945 he was in full sail as a field-marshal, suitably hung with red stars and similar appropriate decoration.

As we were ushered in, Stalin came down from his desk at the end of the room, and greeted me. We exchanged opening pleasantries. He twitted me with having taken so long to get to Moscow, to which I replied with a rude remark about Russian weather which had necessitated my coming up by train, adding that had I been allowed to, I would have come by air without a thought. I then offered him the boxes of cigars, with General Eisenhower's compliments. He took his pipe out of his mouth, pointed to the cigars on the table, and said, 'When do they go off?'—to which I appeared to flinch, looked at my wristwatch, and said, 'They do not go off until I have gone.' The small joke went well. We then got straight down to business.

In view of my previous experiences, I expected to have to spend hours fencing before digging out the information for which I had come. Stalin promptly opened by taking the wind completely out of my sails. He said, 'I know why you have come. You want to know what we are doing and are going to do,' upon which he spread a map on the table, and clearly and concisely, and as it later appeared accurately, he described not only current operations but also future intentions as far as the Oder. He said that the Red Army was now engaged in a large-scale offensive. This offensive had been prepared over a month and held in abeyance, waiting for weather conditions. Meantime, however, he had been aware of the German attack on the Western Front. He had understood the situation at once, and in view of the Allied need he had decided to launch the operation regardless of the weather, beginning on 12 January.

Stalin asked whether Eisenhower believed the Germans' claim that they had frustrated the Allied offensive for a maximum period of six months and a minimum of two months. In reply, I described our plans, and said that we were now assured by the engineers that the best time for crossing the Rhine was in the spring between early March and mid-April. I described the Allied air effort and particularly the strategic bombing of oil, rail, and water targets. The strategic problem which would affect both the Russians and ourselves, was that of timing of operations in the spring, when the weather might prevent the Russians' progress and at the same time allow us to cross the Rhine. Stalin asked: 'Are you implying that the Allies may have to wait until the summer before undertaking offensive operations across the Rhine?'

I assured him that we had no intention of letting up. I explained the intention of a secondary thrust through Frankfurt. Stalin asked, too, about the Allies' estimate of German strategic ground force reserves. He remarked that the great value of the Budapest operations had been that they attracted fifteen German divisions, six of them armoured. The enemy now had twelve armoured divisions to the south of Budapest, a very stupid disposition, in his opinion, since that left them with no trained reserves whatever. In reply to my question, Stalin said that the organisation of German artillery was very weak. According to him, the Germans habitually used their tanks as artillery. This habit he regarded as a symptom of their deterioration and of a growing inability to think offensively. We agreed that German Air Force personnel were suffering from lack of training, perhaps enforced by the shortage of petrol; and that while many German pilots were still willing to fight hard, there were comparatively few who knew how to do it.

I then asked: 'Will it be possible to keep the Hun anxious in the period when weather conditions on the Eastern Front rule out large-scale operations from mid-March to late May?'

Stalin retorted that it would: 'I cannot guarantee a full-scale offensive in this period, but we have organised units and provided methods for keeping the Germans stirred up and at strength on the Eastern Front.'

It was a question of dealing short, sharp blows, with two or three infantry regiments backed up by heavy artillery. Though the German communication system allowed rapid movement between the fronts, he was sure that nothing would move from east to west during the spring thaw. His first assumption was incorrect, since we knew that the Germans were having great difficulty in moving forces from one front to the other.

'In my opinion,' Stalin went on, 'the war will not end before the summer; there is no will inside Germany around which opposition to the Hitler régime can coalesce. The final break will very probably be produced by famine. We must not forget, however, that the Germans are frugal and enduring. They have more stubbornness than brains. In fact, they should not have undertaken the Ardennes offensive; that was very stupid of them.'

Stalin thought that even now the Germans must be moving forces from the west. If they did not, they could not resist in the east. When the better weather came and the German Air Force of two thousand planes was confronted with ten thousand Russian planes, their situation would be even more unsatisfactory. When he enquired about our strategic reserves, I explained why our forces in Alsace had necessarily been weakened to provide strength for the counter-offensive to the point where our hold on

Strasbourg might become precarious. Stalin replied that while Strasbourg might not be of great military value, its recapture by the Germans would give them great political and psychological capital. The Allies would be wise to maintain at least ten divisions in strategic reserve.

Throughout the meeting I was most impressed by Stalin's knowledge of his subject. An example was his comment on one of the current plans in the west, particularly of the proposed main drive north of the Ruhr. 'Yes', he remarked, 'it is obvious; it is obvious to us; it is also obvious to the Germans. Difficult country is not so obvious.' Stalin showed great interest in Antwerp and whether the port was in full operation again. He also showed interest in the air campaign against the German synthetic oil plants and its widespread effects. I pointed out that Blechhammer Synthetic Oil Plant was at extreme range for the British and American bombers from the west, and, consequently, had so far escaped attack, but on the other hand, it was at short range from Russian bomber bases. Stalin did not wait for me to underline the obvious deduction. This was the only moment when one saw a flash of his awe-inspiring anger, as he rounded on Antonov in a menacing manner to ask why this key-point had not been attacked. Antonov went pale, and rose rather shakily to his feet to reply. I saw no particular advantage in pushing his head under the hammer; so I intervened by saying that I would, of course, give Antonov all the technical and topographical details necessary. (To the best of my knowledge, this had been done some months previously.) This incident gave an impressive glimpse of the fear which ruled the régime.

Apart from that event, our exchanges were frank and friendly, with an occasional touch of humour. On one occasion, after Pavlov had interpreted a rather involved argument, Stalin turned quickly towards Birse and said, 'Did Pavlov interpret me properly?' to which Birse had no hesitation in saying, 'Yes, very well.' 'There you are,' commented Stalin, 'these interpreters always hang together—or should!'

At the end of our meeting, Stalin said, in essence: 'We have no treaty, but we are comrades. It is proper, and also sound, selfish policy, that we should help each other in times of difficulty. It would be foolish for me to stand aside and let the Germans annihilate you; they would only turn back on me when you were disposed of. Similarly it is to your interest to do everything possible to keep the Germans from annihilating me.'

He then asked to be told when I was leaving, so that he might have time to reply to a letter from Eisenhower which I had brought. I thanked him for the way in which he had received my visit. Stalin replied: 'I am embarrassed by your expression of gratitude.'

Major Birse, who had wide experience of interpreting at Anglo-Russian meetings, noted that this was an occasion when, from the very beginning, Stalin appeared to be in the best of humours. Perhaps the capture of Kielce that very day had played its part. Since the Marshal's habit was never to pay fulsome compliments, or to indulge in rhetoric, my avoidance of both was held to be a point in my favour. Stalin's reactions, in Major Birse's experience, might be judged from his expression, his manner of speech, his humour or lack of it, his handling of the interpreters, and his method of ending a meeting. Birse thought that Stalin genuinely welcomed my visit and seemed to like me and my endeavour to go straight to the point. Throughout the interview he had looked pleased, and the interpreter noticed no signs of the ill-humour which had on other occasions announced its presence by a knitting together of the eyebrows and a steely look in the eyes. Nor did he show signs of boredom, which had been frequently observed on other occasions. It had to be remembered that Stalin had been playing a new role, as a military leader, for only three and a half years. He had been mentioned in the same breath as Napoleon and Alexander the Great, and did not appear to object to such comparisons. It must, therefore, have been gratifying to receive the visit of a fighting man, deputy to the Supreme Allied Commander. There was evidence that while the Russians had little use for the British Army, they were full of admiration for, and perhaps envy of, the Royal Navy, and had the greatest respect for the Royal Air Force. Birse noted Stalin's particular interest in my account of our air effort, and of the devastated area behind the front in Normandy and the repetition of the process on the Rhine. He was impressed by our intelligence of the German petrol shortage and the need to bomb oil plants. The Marshal seemed pleased to learn Germany's oil output was but 30 per cent. of normal, and that tanks were being captured with no petrol in them. His interjections during my report were meant to be helpful, and the fact that he had so early in the interview disclosed the Red Army's plan was significant. 'This was meeting us more than halfway,' Major Birse wrote, 'judging by the way such problems have been treated in the past.'

Only when Stalin referred to the suspected transfer of German divisions to the east from the Western Front did he raise suspicion in Birse's mind about his appreciation of the relative size of the tasks. His attitude towards the Russian interpreter, Pavlov, was paternal and without sign of impatience. In Birse's view:

> The entire absence of recrimination, belittlement of our effort or bitterness, the Marshal's readiness to lay his cards on the table while recognising the importance of our plans, make me think that this has been one of the most satisfactory and encouraging meetings with Marshal Stalin.

Immediately after the conference, Stalin wrote to Eisenhower:

> In my opinion both sides have exchanged information of an exhaustive nature which will be very useful. I do not doubt that the offensive of the Soviet troops which is developing in a satisfactory manner, in spite of unfavourable weather, will oblige the Germans to divide their reserves with the result that they will have to renounce their offensive in the west. This will ease the position of the Allied troops, and, as I hope, will accelerate preparations for your intended offensives.
>
> I wish you and the forces led by you every success.

I had four remaining hurdles to surmount—a formal dinner which might well have been called a banquet; a visit to the Bolshoi to see *Prince Igor*; a small drinking party with the generals; and finally, but by no means the least, the obstacles which one after another seemed certain to keep me in Moscow indefinitely. The dinner followed the normal pattern except that it was entirely military. The preparation of my speech had helped me to pass the time on the train journey from the Crimea which might otherwise have been tedious. I wrote the gist of my few sentences in English and got my two interpreters, English and Russian, to translate it into Russian word by word, then sentence by sentence, and finally I repeated the whole thing again and again until I had got it word and sound perfect:

'On behalf of General Eisenhower and the armed forces of the West which I have the honour to represent, I thank you for your Toast. For years now you and we have together been fighting one war but separate battles against the common enemy. But, now, as we draw the noose tighter, more and more our separate campaigns are becoming one campaign, and our battles will become one battle. That is why I am here. We feel that we have reached the stage when commanders should meet and know each other's minds. No one is more sorry than General Eisenhower that he felt he could not leave the Western Front at this moment. I hope this meeting is only the first of a series which will end in Berlin.

'I give you a Toast: Victory, early and complete, and may we soon meet—not in Moscow, Teheran, Cairo, Paris, or London—but in the ruins of what was Berlin.'

'Предлагаю тост: за победу, скорую и полную, и за нашу встречу, не в Москве, Тегеране, Каире, Париже или Лондоне, а среди развалин того, что было Берлином.'

At the dinner party I managed to get it off without muffing, and undoubtedly it made a hit with my hosts. It so happened that the Toast which I proposed proved to have an element of prophecy in it. My next meeting with the Russians in May 1945 was in Berlin, which was certainly in ruins, to witness the last act of surrender.

Prince Igor and the Bolshoi Theatre were naturally magnificent, the brilliance and luxury of the decor and costumes making a remarkable contrast to the drab dullness of the packed audience. Even the two or three ladies who made up our party in the principal box were dressed entirely in black, lacking even the red handkerchief which appeared to be *de rigueur* in the streets. Light conversation was not easy, but it was interesting to hear from our own interpreter that the presence of wives at an official party was a complete innovation. The party with the Air generals at mid-day on the 16th was quite light-hearted.

It was when first one difficulty and then another cropped up attending our departure that I began to wonder if I had been unduly optimistic and our visit had been too successful to be true; difficulties such as clearances for our freedom of passage right through, operational clearance, weather clearance, and difficulties with the local control. Meantime, our York was waiting for us. The final snag was that the Russian pilot who was detailed to go with us tried to insist that he must fly the aircraft. It began to appear almost like calling for some rough stuff. I told the Russian that our pilot was the captain of his ship and any attempt to override his authority would not be in any way tolerated! However, we let him sit in the second pilot's seat, ensconced a Russian wireless operator with knowledge of all the necessary codes, and finally a singularly unglamorous woman, who may have been booked down as a 'navigator' but whom I suspected to be a girl friend of the Russian pilot. We finally cleared these hurdles, but not without some quite strong language on my part; apparently one had to use parade-ground manners to get through.

By contrast, our passage south was very peaceful—most of it over a layer of thin snow-clouds. Our first stop was at Poltava, which had been set aside as a refuelling base for the American heavies. Poltava was a small oasis—or, perhaps, rather an outpost —of the west. Cloudless evening sky, and cold that caught one's breath. It was interesting to hear of the experience of the American party. When they first arrived, the local townspeople gave them a completely unrestrained welcome, asked them into their homes, and so forth. Gradually the atmosphere changed, for which the Americans could see no reason. Apparently at first the Americans had passed on to the Russians all the various glossy American journals until the order came that these publications were not to be circulated amongst the local populace. Gradually the ring closed in, until the American set-up was completely wired in and isolated from the rest of Russia. I can only imagine that the Russian authorities were afraid that all those wonderful pictures of glamour and luxury would serve to seduce the Russians.

In view of the fact that the Russian offensive had started before

I had even got to Moscow, General Morgan, adopting the famous wartime slogan, signalled to me: 'Was your journey really necessary?' Adopting his mood, I replied: 'No.'

Nevertheless, I could not doubt that my first-hand knowledge of Russian plans would prove of high value at S.H.A.E.F.

Eisenhower's plan for operations in 1945–Operations 'Grenade' and 'Veritable'–Area bombing–Threat of jet fighters–German cities as targets for strategic air forces–Proposal to post me to U.K.–Germany's growing shortages–Aim to isolate the Ruhr–Operation 'Clarion'–Operation 'Bugle'–Fallacies of war by committees–Preparations for crossing the Rhine

BEFORE I reached Moscow, the Combined Chiefs of Staff had asked Eisenhower to submit an appreciation and detailed plans for the operations of 1945. The Supreme Commander was anxious that since the British Chiefs of Staff had already declared their views to be closely in line with Montgomery's, the Combined Chiefs should not pre-judge the issues before his opinions had been heard. The enemy's probing attacks in Alsace continued to cause much heart-burning at S.H.A.E.F. General Eisenhower became impatient at the failure to deal with the threat to Strasbourg.

'What gets me, honest to God,' he said at a meeting on 18 January, 'is when two of their panzer divisions are loose, we sit around and get scared.' Bedell Smith retorted that we had a right to be scared when a motor transport battalion crossed the Rhine in boats, and established a small bridgehead into which a division at once appeared. Eisenhower said he could not see where the 10th or 11th Panzer Divisions could be thrown in anywhere along our front to make a cataclysmic difference. That day, Eisenhower ordered that the Southern Group of Armies should promptly attack the enemy penetrations in Alsace. Success here would release forces for employment north of the Moselle, where Eisenhower intended to launch strong offensives in order to regain the strategic initiative. The Central Group of Armies would continue its offensive to take advantage of the enemy's unfavourable position in the Ardennes. They would seize any opportunity to reach the Siegfried Line, and, if successful, advance to the north-east. This attack would be pressed with all possible vigour so long as there was a reasonable chance of securing decisive success; but as an alternative, we must be prepared to pass quickly to the defensive in this sector and to attack in the sector of the Northern Group of Armies. Montgomery and Bradley would complete preparations for this offensive in the north, but not in such a way to weaken the operations in the Ardennes. They should plan to reach the Rhine north of Dusseldorf. This offensive would be launched with the minimum delay if and when Eisenhower decided not to continue with the offensive in the Ardennes. The northern attack would comprise operation 'Veritable'—a move southwards from the Reichswald—and operation 'Grenade'—the drive towards Dusseldorf—both under command of the Northern Group of Armies. The U.S. Ninth Army would remain under operational control of 21 Army Group and would be built up to a total of twelve divisions for operation 'Grenade'.

Montgomery hoped, and maintained it had been agreed, that the Ardennes operations should be closed down so that strength could be concentrated for 'Veritable'. It seemed to him that Eisenhower's directive of 18 January showed that Bradley was once more 'going off on his own line', and that indecision and patchwork had taken the place of a clear and decisive plan. Eisenhower's proposals to the Chiefs of Staff, sent a day or two later, attracted the unfavourable notice of the C.I.G.S., who thought that the Supreme Commander was still trying to back the northern advance as well as the move on Frankfurt and that he would not have the strength to carry out both operations.

It was just at this point that I returned to S.H.A.E.F. There I found the headquarters staff disturbed at the fact that the threat to Strasbourg was still not averted. It seemed to me that we were not exploiting our advantages to the full. The enemy appeared to have the initiative and to be playing on us, yet we could move our divisions far more easily than he. Our motor transport could move, thanks to air superiority, bumper to bumper, day and night. The enemy's situation was far different. On 22 January our air forces had a particularly successful day against his transport. The U.S. Ninth Air Force, with the aid of the 2nd Tactical Air Force, had destroyed huge numbers of lorries and wagons. On one line, they blew up an ammunition train which left a crater three hundred yards long. The main concern at our meeting the next day, however, was still the situation in the area of the Sixth Army Group. Eisenhower said: 'I'm beginning to think we must get cleaned up in the south, even if it is going to hold up the offensives in the north.'

He referred to the running sore to the south of Strasbourg, where we had reinforced heavily and were being pushed back. It was proposed that we might go on the defensive in the Ardennes, where Patton was at that moment following up the enemy's withdrawal with typical dash. Five divisions could then be allotted to General Devers to finish off the enemy in the Colmar pocket. Eisenhower said this was like using a sledgehammer to crack a nut, but it was explained that the possible move of five divisions was suggested on the assumption that we might have to relieve all the French forces in the Colmar area. 'God! We have certainly been let down by the French,' said Eisenhower.

He spoke to Bradley about the situation in the Ardennes. The latter thought it would be a grave mistake to give up the offensive for the moment. Eisenhower was inclined to agree, since this was at that moment the only part of the front on which we were taking positive action and getting results. I questioned the policy, however, and asked what it was going to achieve. The offensive was aimed at Euskirchen, but even when it had crossed the Siegfried Line there was still much country in the Ardennes to traverse, and there could be no rapid exploitation. The clash was between those who favoured a continuance of the Ardennes offensive, which Bradley described as a 'going concern', with great possibilities, and the preparation of a heavy all-out assault in the north. I preferred the latter course, but Eisenhower was under great pressure to adopt the first. He had twice given preference to the north and said 'No' to the American Army Group commanders and Patton. On neither occasion was any decisive result achieved.

I felt that we should take advantage of the Russian offensive. A measure of its effect on our situation may be deduced from the deliberations in the highest circles at home. On 12 January, the War Cabinet had discussed the possibility that the war in Europe would not end before 31 December 1945. Ten days later, the Chiefs of Staff observed that the Russian offensive had transformed the situation. On the most optimistic basis, the war would be over by mid-April. A more reasonable date would be mid-June and at the worst it would be early November. Though Bradley repeated his certainty that his attacks would go through the Siegfried Line, their continuance might well affect the timing of operation 'Veritable'. Since this latter offensive was the main attack, with fresh troops, I felt that nothing should now be allowed to delay it. I urged this course again at the Supreme Commander's meeting on 25 January, pointing out that the Russian offensive would probably have to stop in a month or so on account of the weather. The northern part of our front was the only place where the Germans could be struck really hard, and was also the only place where we had fresh troops in the form of 30 Corps.

I pressed these views on Eisenhower, while our full air-power was used to paralyse German movement behind the Front near Strasbourg. On the last day of January, General Bradley arrived at S.H.A.E.F. Eisenhower at once called a conference to discuss 'Veritable' and 'Grenade'. Bradley made it abundantly plain that since the Ardennes offensive and the subsequent publicity of Montgomery's handling of it, friendly and intimate co-operation between him and the Field-Marshal was out of the question. He stressed strongly the political importance in the United States of giving the big thrust to an American Commander. At present, his troops, and to some extent their families, were either indignantly loyal to him or had had their confidence in the leadership severely shaken. Neither reaction, he said, was healthy. After a good deal of discussion, Bradley accepted his part in 'Grenade'.

It was fairly clear from this meeting that American pressure would not allow Eisenhower to put everything in the north to the exclusion of effort further south. The Supreme Commander assured the Combined Chiefs of Staff, who were assembled at Malta before moving on to the Yalta Conference, that he would seize the Rhine crossings in the north immediately it was feasible and without waiting to close the Rhine throughout its length. This movement would be undertaken as soon as the situation in the south allowed him to collect the necessary forces without running needless risk. This helped to mollify the British Chiefs of Staff. Their American counterparts pointed out at the Malta meeting that the southern advance was not intended to compete with the thrust in the north, but must be sufficiently strong to draw off German forces which would protect the important area around Frankfurt, and to provide an alternative axis if the main effort failed. Since it was impossible in any case to use in the north more than thirty-six divisions, with ten in reserve, twelve could be allotted to the subsidiary advance. Bedell Smith, who attended this meeting, proved most helpful in explaining clearly Eisenhower's intentions.

The Allied air forces had continued to exert unrelenting pressure againt Germany's waning strength. The strategic bombers attacked the petroleum industry as their first priority, and lines of communication as the second. Special emphasis was placed upon the Ruhr. The observance of these priorities, and our preoccupation with the Ardennes offensive, had allowed the Luftwaffe to recover a good deal of fighting strength. The enemy had developed his fighter force at the expense of other branches of the Luftwaffe, and had turned to the rapid development of jet fighters. We had a good deal of evidence that the Germans intended to produce these on a large scale. Even by January 1945, a considerable number were operating. They were disconcertingly superior in speed and armament to our conventional fighters, and even more important, to our unarmed reconnaissance aircraft. We therefore decided to use the strategic effort to neutralise the threat from jet aircraft by knocking out the facilities for producing them, the training centres for their pilots and the airfields on which they were based.

Although the control of the strategic forces had reverted to the Combined Chiefs of Staff, Air Marshal Bottomley, to whom their powers were in practice delegated, continued to consult me. At the end of January, he visited S.H.A.E.F. There, with General Spaatz, we discussed the best use of our strategic power. It seemed to us that the main synthetic oil plants should hold first priority for all the Strategic Air Forces. Whenever weather conditions made it possible, precision bombing by day would be carried out against them. The next targets in order of priority were Berlin, Leipzig, Dresden, and other cities where heavy attack would hasten civilian evacuation from the east, and the subsequent confusion hamper the movement of reinforcements from other fronts. Spaatz had already ordered that day attacks should be made on Berlin whenever the weather permitted. This priority was one which was dictated by the changing features of the battle in Europe. As we took up the line of the Rhine, and the Russians moved to the eastern borders of the Reich, it had become more than ever important to deny the use of interior lines of communication to the Germans. The Russians were perfectly conscious of the importance of this plan, and a day or two after my discussions with Bottomley they asked at Yalta that we should prevent the Germans from moving troops eastwards. In particular, we were asked to paralyse Berlin and Leipzig. By the time we received this request, one great daylight raid had just been mounted against Berlin, on 3 February.

The third priority was now attack on communications, and especially on those which were necessary to the movement of major reinforcements to the east, and those which affected land operations. The Strategic Air Forces based in the United Kingdom were operating particularly against targets in the area Ruhr–Cologne–Kassel. The Fifteenth Air Force was told to pay special attention to any sign of transfer of forces, and would attack communications as necessary. Jet targets and communications in Southern Germany would also be attended to. The strategic day fighters, after escorting the bombers, would attack rail movements on the main routes of reinforcement to the east. These orders are an example of the way in which we tried to use our air-power in a co-ordinated manner, not simply to bring Germany to the point of economic, and therefore of military collapse, but also to make sure we suffered no major setback on land.

All this was well enough; but I had never agreed that a reversion to control of the strategic forces by the Combined Chiefs of Staff from S.H.A.E.F. would produce more efficient direction, and months of experience confirmed me in that view. To issue the orders from the remote heights was one thing, but to ensure their speedy and efficient observance was quite another. The Air Ministry's Intelligence services were by no means faultless, and I could not feel a great deal of confidence in the system of trying to run a war by committees.

*

To the best of my recollection, it was in the last days of January that I first became aware that I might be superseded as Deputy Supreme Commander. The Prime Minister, regretfully convinced that the Italian Front must now become a subordinate theatre, felt that Alexander could hardly be left there commanding small forces. It appeared that I was also wanted back at the Air Ministry, presumably in order to become Portal's deputy. In the early hours of 4 January, therefore, the Prime Minister suggested that in view of all this, Alexander might take my place as Eisenhower's Deputy Supreme Commander. To the C.I.G.S. this seemed, as he wrote in his diary

. . . a sound move and one which might assist in keeping Ike on the rails in the future.

Brooke was apparently asked to sound out Eisenhower's views. It appears, however, that after lunch on the same day, 4 January, Churchill suggested to Eisenhower that Alexander might replace me. According to Brooke's account, the Supreme Commander said he would welcome Alexander. Field-Marshal Montgomery, who was consulted by Brooke the next day, said that he was 'all for such a plan which might go some way towards putting matters straight'.[1]

At this stage I had left on my long visit to Moscow, and I heard nothing of these events at the time. On 29 January, however, after I had returned to S.H.A.E.F., I saw General Eisenhower, who had been to Marseilles to consult with Marshall. I had done my best, in view of the urgent need for Eisenhower's presence in France, to ensure that he should not be summoned to the meetings at Malta and Yalta, and I had even persuaded Mr. Harry Hopkins to cable President Roosevelt in this sense. Whether for this or for other reasons, Eisenhower was not summoned to the meetings, and Bedell Smith deputised for him there. On returning from Marseilles, Eisenhower discussed with me the whole problem of the Command, admitting that he had asked for Alexander. I was given to understand that the Prime Minister had requested my release, and Eisenhower explained in his characteristic, kindly manner, that he did not want to stand in my way.

[1] Bryant: *Triumph in the West*, pp. 375–6.

Admiral Leahy, who was present at the Malta meetings, records that on 2 February, the Prime Minister twice spoke of Alexander's replacing me as Deputy Supreme Commander. Mr. Churchill remarked that the activities in Italy were much less important than before. Tito no longer needed the Allies' help. According to Leahy's account Roosevelt had no great objection to the proposed change, which, they agreed, should be made in the next six weeks.[1]

On the same day, 2 February, Brooke's diary records that Churchill had told him how, in the opinion of Roosevelt and Marshall, my replacement by Alexander might produce repercussions in the United States. It might be thought that Alexander was being put in to support Eisenhower after a failure in the Ardennes. In about six weeks' time, however, when new offensive operations would have begun, and the Ardennes operation would be fading into the background, they would be quite prepared for the change. Montgomery, apparently forgetting that he had been consulted about, and had welcomed, my proposed replacement, records in his Memoirs his amazement that the question of a ground force commander was reopened in February 1945 by the Prime Minister. Montgomery remarks that my role as Deputy Supreme Commander was never very clear to him, and that I, being an airman, finally found myself employed to co-ordinate the air operations. In his opinion, this was not what I had originally been intended to do, but it was what I came to do 'because of the never-ceasing rows between the lords of the air, each with his own strategic conceptions and with great jealousies between them'. These observations are hardly fair to the Air commanders. Montgomery does admit, however, that 'the Generals were little better'. This is to put the matter mildly. At all events, Montgomery was apparently consulted privately by Churchill and by Brooke about the proposal that Alexander should replace me. He answered immediately that if Alexander were brought to S.H.A.E.F., there would be storms both in the Press and with the American Generals. This is presumably an accurate record of what he said; it is also the exact reverse of what he had said in the previous month.

[1] Leahy: *I Was There,* pp. 346–7.

At a meeting in mid-February, therefore, Montgomery assured Eisenhower that he now regarded the Command arrangements as satisfactory. He understood the Supreme Commander himself wished to handle the land operations and to command the three Army Groups. Montgomery's own front was to make the main effort, and Eisenhower had placed an American Army under the command of 21 Army Group. Montgomery hoped that this Command situation would remain unchanged until the war was over, which should be in the spring.[1]

The next day, 15 February, Eisenhower discussed with me again the proposed changes. He intended to write to the Chiefs of Staff stating the conditions under which he would accept Alexander. Alexander's functions, if he came to S.H.A.E.F., would be political and economic, but not military. As Eisenhower said: 'I will have nobody standing between me and my Group Commanders.'

This latter point was enunciated clearly in the letter which Eisenhower sent off a day or two later. He laid it down that he, Eisenhower, ran the campaign, while I handled air problems and was responsible for administration in the rear areas and for looking after such matters as the Control Commission for Germany. This, apart from the Air, is what Alexander would do if he came to S.H.A.E.F. Moreover, if I were replaced, there would be much speculation about the reasons for the change. American commanders might suspect that the British were resorting to pressure in order to get their policy adopted.

A fortnight or so afterwards, Eisenhower again spoke at length to Montgomery about Alexander's possible appointment as Deputy Supreme Commander. Montgomery remarked that if Alexander now took over this office, it would be resented in 'certain American quarters'. It would be better to avoid at all costs any further friction. The German war would soon be won, and Alexander might as well remain in Italy, while I saw the war through to the end as Deputy Supreme Commander. Eisenhower agreed with him entirely. Churchill, who visited S.H.A.E.F. early in March, was given the same view, firmly expressed by

[1] *Compare* Bryant: *Triumph in the West*, p. 402 *and* Montgomery: *Memoirs*, pp. 233–5.

[663]

Eisenhower. Churchill seemed to be impressed, and promised to give the matter further thought. A few days later, he ruled that the whole idea should now be dropped.[1]

*

The progress of our forces during February and March was a good deal more rapid than had been anticipated. It had been originally planned to launch 'Veritable' on 8 February. Despite Montgomery's fears and the diversions in the south, this operation went forward on time. It had been planned that operation 'Grenade' would follow on 10 February, but the Germans flooded the Roer and delayed this latter operation until 23 February. In launching these movements to clear the enemy from the area west of the Rhine, we had new advantages. The Russians had overrun Silesia, an area which possessed its own supplies of coal and iron. German morale was not what it had been. The failure of the Ardennes offensive, the growing shortage of vital equipment and supplies and the repeated hammerings from the air, took their toll. As the C.I.G.S. acknowledged after the war, we could take greater liberties in these conditions. An advance on a wider front, he admitted, might present advantages; once the Ardennes offensive had been repulsed, Germany was as good as defeated. No serious opposition was likely to be encountered, the double attack might soon become a pursuit and as such fully justified.[2]

It was my task to use the air weapon to ease the forward path of the armies. According to our Intelligence, five and a half years of war had left Germany with three major weaknesses which we could exploit to help the ground forces—fuel, transport, and deficiences in certain items of equipment. Because of the Russian offensive, virtually all the industrial output of Upper Silesia was lost. It was an area which had been relatively immune from our bombing and, therefore, progressively more important in the German economy. The effects of this loss were to reduce the supplies of hard coal available in the rest of Germany by about

---

[1] Montgomery: *Memoiors*, p. 326
[2] Bryant: *Triumph in the West*, p. 398.

35 per cent., and the supplies of finished steel by about 25 per cent. Our Intelligence at S.H.A.E.F. told me in early February that Germany's present output of steel, even assuming the most drastic and rigid economies, could not meet the needs of her armament production. The German railways had drawn nearly half their coal supplies from Silesia, while public services such as gas and electricity now became almost entirely dependent on steel and coal from the Ruhr, an area which we were bombing daily. The loss of Silesia had come at a time when coal shipments from the Ruhr were normally heavy and when the two main canals linking the Ruhr with Central Germany were both frozen over and cut by Allied air action.

The upshot of this state of affairs was that most of Germany's remaining industrial output now depended on the smooth working of communications in the very limited area which linked the Ruhr with the rest of Germany. We had therefore an excellent opportunity to supplement our attacks on the enemy's dwindling oil production by attacks on transport in this area. It was the Army Intelligence services, be it noted, who told me that the best support the Strategic Air Forces could give the Allied ground forces was to press home the attack on oil plants, then to attack communications round the Ruhr, and only third in order of priority to attack the important tank assembly plants. By the third week in February, our evidence indicated that even for so vital an undertaking as the Ardennes offensive, petrol had been diluted as much as 70 per cent. with crude Benzol, and even then only very limited supplies had been available. Now, in order to cope with the demands in the east, the Western and Italian Fronts were being starved of fuel.

It must be understood that when the Germans were lined up along their Western border, as they now were, their situation in respect of transport was different from that which had obtained nearly a year before in France. In Western Germany, the enemy had available a dense and thereby vulnerable rail and road network. This fact faced us with difficult decisions of policy. If we decided that we should cut bridges to hamper the German war effort, the obvious line for such an attack was along the Rhine; but there were, over that river, no fewer than twenty-nine rail bridges, thirty-four road bridges and more than a hundred ferry crossings. Many of the bridges were so strong that they would withstand anything except very heavy bombs which our fighter bombers and medium bombers could scarcely deliver. I therefore decided that we should concentrate on the rail system, In this task, the medium and fighter bombers could be used to the full, as well as the strategic bombers. The latter were mainly used to attack the larger rail centres and against certain bridges and viaducts. We evolved a plan by drawing a line of interdiction, running in a rough curve to the south from Bremen to the Rhine at Coblenz. Along this line lay some eighteen rail bridges and viaducts, the destruction of which would cut every main railway line leading from the Ruhr to the rest of the Reich. We calculated that three of these lines were of paramount importance, for between them they carried half the rail traffic to and from the Ruhr. Moreover, as I had urged, Montgomery's offensive in the north was to have priority. If we could disrupt systematically the rail centres in that area, his crossing of the Rhine would be helped, for the ability of the enemy to deploy ground forces in the rear areas would be much hampered. A series of planned attacks on these eighteen bridges and viaducts was therefore begun on 21 February.

At the same time, of course, we maintained our shield over the Allied armies. The slow pace of our advance in its early stages, which was largely dictated by conditions on the ground, was not allowed to present the enemy with tempting targets. On the contrary, the German transport was so thoroughly hunted that even motor-cyclists could not proceed without danger.

On 22 February, operation 'Clarion' was flung against the German railways. Though it did not, in my view, pay dividends proportionate to the enormous effort entailed, it did provide a good example of air-power used on the largest scale. The object was to destroy in one massive blitz as much as possible of the enemy's transportation system, to reduce the excess capacity of that system and to render him more vulnerable to onslaughts directed against particular points. On this one day, about nine thousand aircraft operated from all sides, from Italy, France, Belgium, Holland, and Great Britain. Railways, canals, and vehicles were attacked on a scale never known at any other time of the war.

The next day, 23 February, the enemy, distracted by 'Veritable' and reeling from the heaviest blow yet delivered against his communications, had to face operation 'Grenade'. In the upshot, the River Rhine was rapidly closed from Krefeld to Cologne and subsequently, largely on account of two brilliant operations by the American First and Third Armies, from Cologne to Coblenz. The First Army found the railway bridge at Remagen intact and exploited the unexpected good fortune with a swiftness which overcame the enemy. General Patton, displaying his habitual speed off the mark, closed the River Moselle from Trier to Coblenz with one small gap in the middle. It was in these circumstances that by 11 March, with our situation transformed, we found ourselves along the Rhine from Nijmegen to Coblenz and across it at Remagen.

In the meantime, General Spaatz, much encouraged by the success of operation 'Clarion', expressed himself as anxious to repeat the dose. He was most impressed by the fact that the widespread confusion caused by 'Clarion' must have enforced large-scale dispersal. For reasons which I have already explained, I favoured a more restricted attack, concentrated in space and time, and designed to isolate the Ruhr. With the support of the Intelligence Section of S.H.A.E.F., I pressed in early March for an operation known as 'Bugle', and thought that we might mount a series of attacks, some widespread, some concentrated. The enemy would then not know from day to day how to prepare against such attacks. After a good deal of persuasion, Spaatz agreed, somewhat reluctantly.

Air Marshal Bottomley signalled from London that it was agreed that 'Bugle' should be mounted, on condition that it did not prejudice the attack on major oil targets in Central Germany, and that any synthetic oil plants actually or potentially active in the Ruhr were included amongst our targets. For the purposes of this operation, communications targets in the Ruhr might take precedence over Benzol plants. It was thought the operation should take place at the earliest opportunity. The Communications Working Committee of the Combined Strategic Targets

Committee, so I was told, would nominate communications targets for the strategic bombers, in consultation with my staff, so that the selection might conform to our tactical plans. The Working Committee would also assist the American forces and S.H.A.E.F. as required. I was asked to undertake the detailed planning of this operation in conjunction with the Eighth Air Force, and with S.H.A.E.F. and the Americans.

The D.C.A.S. also signalled that operation 'Clarion' had involved a switch of pressure from an area already under strain to areas in which the potential for repairs had been little affected, and which were not related to specific military operations. Past experience suggested that a communications network selected for attack should be limited in size and readily accessible, so that the necessary intensity could be maintained. I was told that the Joint Intelligence Committee had reached the conclusion that while they had no information to show the effects of the 'Clarion' attacks on German capacity to resist, they knew that attacks on the German oil system in the last ten months had affected every branch of Germany's war effort, and had seriously hampered even very important military operations. Bottomley therefore doubted the wisdom of continuing widespread attacks, and said that they should certainly not be allowed to interfere with the oil offensive. The Joint Intelligence Committee had also been examining the effect of interrupting the supply of coal from the Ruhr to the rest of Germany, and had decided that German war production was being seriously reduced, and the transport system seriously dislocated, by the shortage of coal. This shortage was due in the east and north to the loss of Silesian supplies, and in the west mainly to the bombing of communications. If supplies of coal from the Ruhr could be cut off completely, a fall in war production would take place in most other parts of Germany. If the cutting off of coal supplies from the Ruhr were accompanied or preceded by the loss of the remainder of the Silesian coalfields, the complete disorganisation of Germany's war effort would be accomplished in a matter of a few weeks. Bottomley thought, therefore, that if mass attacks on communications were undertaken again, they should be designed to affect to the utmost the movement of supplies, and especially of coal, to and from the Ruhr. Operation

'Bugle' seemed to meet this requirement. He therefore favoured it, and agreed to marshalling yards as the aiming points.

By a clerical error, a signal reporting a meeting of Air Commanders on 1 March, when we had agreed on 'Bugle', had not been addressed to the Air Ministry. Bottomley assumed that in spite of the form and wording of the telegram, it was a suggested plan of operations rather than an order, at least in respect of the Strategical Forces. He telegraphed:

> Assuming General Spaatz' concurrence in the plan generally, we have signalled Bomber Command asking them through their Advanced Headquarters at S.H.A.E.F. to co-operate in drawing up the detailed plan. Agreed that time and date should finally be decided by U.S.S.-T.A.F. in conjunction with S.H.A.E.F. and Advanced Headquarters Bomber Command.
>
> Communications Working Committee of C.S.T.C. will nominate communications targets for strategic bombers in consultation with staffs of U.S.S.T.A.F., S.H.A.E.F. and Bomber Command as necessary to ensure selection suitable to tactical plans.

I found these signals more than a little ridiculous. The failure to send to the Air Ministry at once the signal about the meeting of 1 March was simply a mistake, which was soon rectified. I had always insisted most carefully that the Executive Authority of the Combined Strategic Targets Committee should be recognised in relation to all operations which were not directly concerned with the ground battle. But as we advanced nearer and nearer to the centre of Germany, it was becoming ever more difficult to draw a clear line between strategic operations directly affecting, and those indirectly affecting, the land battle. The proposed 'Bugle' would have an effect on the battle as direct as any of the strategic operations before D-Day. I prepared a telegram to Bottomley:

> The fact that the operations of the immense Strategic Air Forces are supposed to be directed by a Committee advised by a series of Committees and Sub-Committees, is so remarkable and constitutes such a unique method of conducting military operations, that there is no risk of its being forgotten.

Though I later substituted for this telegram a slightly more temperate version, my view remained unaltered. I naturally agreed with the Air Ministry that 'Bugle' offered better prospects than a repetition of 'Clarion'. On a short visit to London between 9 and 12 March, I found that both Portal and Bottomley agreed that we should mount 'Bugle' as quickly as possible and follow it with a repeat performance. We were also agreed that while weather permitted, priority must be given to the oil targets. For a few days, the weather prevented the launching of 'Bugle'. Bomber Command, however, was able to launch two daylight attacks on Essen and Dortmund. The bomb load was the heaviest dropped in any single raid, with over 4,500 tons on each target. In return, the Luftwaffe made desperate efforts, with the use of jets, to reduce the Remagen bridgehead, but without success.

On my return to S.H.A.E.F. from London, there awaited me Intelligence reports which showed the desperate situation to which Germany had been reduced. Rundstedt, appealing for an all-out defence of the Ruhr, said:

> As your womenfolk at home now require Westphalian coal to replace the produce of overrun Silesian coalfields, so we require more weapons from the Ruhr factories to compensate for the loss of the armament factories of Silesia.

It was estimated that German production of gasolene was running at a mere 14 per cent. of its former level. This situation was reflected at the front. In the west, despite greatly reduced needs because of the transfer of formations eastwards, and the use of large quantities of Benzol, the fuel situation had steadily grown worse. According to our information, the situation on the eastern front was little better. Because of the difficulties of transportation by rail and water, industrial stoppages at plants in and outside the Ruhr had become widespread. The main cause was lack of power, because sufficient quantities of coal could no longer be transported from the Ruhr. Our Intelligence services had detected a drop in the output of finished munitions because consignments of shell cases failed to arrive. There was evidence of a shortage of explosives. It was probable that tank and other assembly plants, which were equally dependent on the regular supply of components from the Ruhr, would be similarly affected. The military effects of all this were evident. We knew that the Germans were finding much difficulty in moving supplies to the front west of the Ruhr. Motor transport was being used on a large scale to relieve the damaged railways.

This information, and much more to the same effect, confirmed my view that the attack on the Ruhr and its approaches was paying good dividends. As early as 22 February, the vital viaduct at Bielefeld had been hit. It was finally destroyed on 14 March. Five days later, the Arnsberg viaduct was wrecked. None of the three main routes leading out of the Ruhr could now be used. Between 21 February and 24 March—the day of the Rhine assault crossing in the north—our forces made forty-two attacks on the eighteen vital bridges and viaducts. By the latter date, ten of them were destroyed, three were damaged and impassable, and one partly destroyed. Two more had come within range of our artillery. Only two of the bridges were therefore rated as passable. Whenever necessary, the attack on the Dortmund–Ems and Mittelland canals was kept up. The enemy made repeated efforts to repair the damage, but as soon as the repairs were completed we attacked again. These results provided the justification for operation 'Bugle'.

In preparing for the crossing of the Rhine, the tasks which the air forces had to fulfil were, with important differences of emphasis, similar to those successfully accomplished before and during 'Overlord'. First, we had to clear the enemy from the skies, especially at the places selected for the crossing and at the points chosen for the airborne landings. Anti-aircraft defences had to be smashed, the transport aircraft carrying paratroops had to be protected, the ground forces sustained in battle, and the enemy prevented from reinforcing. Montgomery urged that heavy bombing should begin several days before the assault on 24 March, on the grounds that although surprise would by this method be lost, it would be lost anyway, given the size and scale of the invasion. While the plans were being made, the air forces were sealing off the Ruhr by the full-scale onslaught on communications. Some twenty-one nominal German divisions were cooped up in that region.

Some members of the staff at S.H.A.E.F. argued that such assaults had more economic than military significance. But I insisted that a policy of cutting off the Ruhr, combined with the well-proven method of attacking railway centres in the Ruhr itself, would be of the highest value in preventing quick German reinforcement when Montgomery's forces crossed the river. The success of the attacks on bridges and viaducts was so marked that little justification was called for. Bomber Command, the American Eighth and Ninth Air Forces, and the 2nd Tactical Air Force, literally ruined the rail system of the Ruhr in the month before Montgomery's assault. Nor did roads, motor vehicles or barracks escape their notice.

On the night before the crossing of the Rhine, the effect of combined shelling and air attacks on the town of Wesel, about to be assaulted by our troops, was overwhelming. The place was more or less wrecked and the remnants were speedily captured by the 1st Commando Brigade. By 24 March, the Ruhr was isolated, a week before the ground forces surrounded the area. The air operations on the crucial day of the crossing were carried out with negligible opposition from the Luftwaffe. After the first day or two, the German ground forces put up only feeble resistance.

I think it fair to say that the events of February and March had provided a good deal of justification for Eisenhower's refusal to concentrate everything in the north. As he pointed out to the Combined Chiefs of Staff on 24 March, the recent victories west of the Rhine had resulted, as we had planned, in the destruction of a large proportion of the enemy's forces on the Western Front. He thought that the situation now presented the opportunities for which we had struggled and which we must seize boldly. The dash and daring displayed in the American First and Third Army sectors had brought us two bridgeheads which could be consolidated and expanded rapidly

. . . to support a major thrust which will assist the northern operations and make our exploitation more effective. While we are continuing to plan for and to be ready to meet stern resistance, it is my personal belief that the enemy's strength on the Western Front is becoming so stretched, that penetrations and advances will soon be limited only by our own maintenance. There is already deployed in the north all the strength that can be effectively maintained east of the Rhine for the next few weeks, and I am directing the most vigorous action on all fronts. I intend to reinforce every success with the utmost speed.

In order to isolate the Ruhr, the Supreme Commander directed on 25 March that the forces of Bradley and Montgomery were to make contact in the area Paderborn–Kassel, to clean up the enclosed area and to prepare for further advance: 6 Army Group would meanwhile protect the southern flank.

According to the best estimates we could obtain at the time, the Germans had lost on the Western Front between 1 October and 16 December 1944 about 350,000 casualties and prisoners. This represented about 25 per cent. of the average enemy fighting strength in the west during this period, but at the same time reinforcements continued to arrive in numbers more than sufficient to balance the losses. Nevertheless, without this battle of attrition, there would have been some ninety German divisions on the Western Front when the Ardennes offensive was launched; instead, there were only about seventy. Between 17 January and 7 February 1945, a period of some three weeks, a further 90,000 losses were inflicted on the enemy. The Russian offensive drew five infantry and seven panzer-type divisions to the east. In the period between 8 February and 31 March, Germany lost half a million dead and prisoners. In sum, the Allies had inflicted over a million casualties in smashing the Germany Army in the west between 1 October 1944 and the end of March 1945.

This was the war which could be seen and measured on the ground; but, as Mr. Churchill acknowledged, the Allied air forces played a part of supreme importance in breaking the last great German stand in the west.[1]

In the month of March alone, Bomber Command and the United States Eighth Air Force dropped more than 130,000 tons of bombs, well over the tonnage dropped in the whole of 1942. In the middle of March, Speer reported to his Führer that the figures of coal deliveries from the Ruhr meant that supplies for

[1] Churchill: *The Second World War*, vol. VI, p. 359.

shipping, for the railways, for gas and electricity, for food, and for armaments, could no longer be assured by any means:

The final collapse of the German economy can therefore be counted on with certainty within four to eight weeks. . . . After this collapse, even military continuation of the war will become impossible.

This was the unseen campaign.

I I
Russians near Berlin–Eisenhower writes to Stalin–Marshall refuses to stop Eisenhower's signal–Eisenhower: 'Berlin no longer important'–Churchill disagrees–Churchill introduces political factor–Prime Minister soothes F.D.R.–And blames me!–No more burning cities–German armed forces surrender–I join Russians in Berlin to sign the ratification of surrender–Cairo to Berlin

BY the time that Montgomery's attack across the Rhine was launched, the Russians were within thirty-five miles of Berlin. For obvious reasons, Eisenhower was most anxious to know the Russian plans. He therefore sent to Stalin on 28 March a personal message which was not shown to me before despatch. The Supreme Commander explained how his immediate intention was to encircle and destroy the enemy forces defending the Ruhr, and to isolate the area from the west of Germany. This object would be accomplished by mounting offensives round the north of the Ruhr and from Frankfurt through Kassel, until the ring was closed. He thought this phase would end in later April or even earlier. The next task would be to cut the enemy's remaining forces by joining hands with the advancing Russian armies.

For my forces, the best axis on which to effect this junction would be Erfurt–Leipzig–Dresden; moreover, I believe, this is the area to which the main German Governmental Departments are being moved. It is along this axis that I propose to place my main effort. In addition, as soon as the situation allows, a secondary advance will be made to effect a junction with your forces in the Regensburg–Linz area, thereby preventing the consolidation of German resistance in a redoubt in southern Germany.

Before he decided firmly on future plans, Eisenhower wished to co-ordinate them as closely as might be with those of the Russians, in respect of direction and timing. He asked whether Stalin could let him know his intentions, and how far the operations outlined in the telegram conformed with Russia's probable action? This message, which Eisenhower sent for purely military reasons, caused consternation in London. The C.I.G.S. noted that Eisenhower had no business to address Stalin direct. Such communications should go through the Combined Chiefs of

[675]

Staff. Moreover, the telegram seemed to Brooke to be unintelligible and to imply a change of plan. The Chiefs of Staff tried to have Eisenhower's message stopped, believing that we should adhere to the policy of a main thrust across the plains of north-west Germany to take Berlin. By this means, German ports in the west and north could be opened up, giving us a good line of communication by sea to and from Germany and severing all German communications with Holland. The U-boat war would be annulled to a great extent. The Allies would then be free to move into Denmark, to open a line of communication with Sweden and to use nearly two million tons of shipping lying idle in Swedish ports. Frantic cables were exchanged between London, Washington, and S.H.A.E.F. General Marshall told 'Jumbo' Wilson (who had replaced Dill after the latter's death in Washington) that the main object was to defeat the German armies. and that if this were accomplished, ports and the like would fall into our hands automatically. He recalled the remarks he had made in the closed session of the Combined Chiefs of Staff at Malta, and felt that the campaign should not be run by a committee. He refused pointblank to do anything which would undermine Eisenhower's authority with the Russians, and said it would now, in any case, be too late to stop his message from reaching Stalin.

The opinion of the British Chiefs of Staff was not improved when they learned unofficially on 29 March that Eisenhower proposed to remove the American Ninth Army from the control of Montgomery's 21 Army Group in order to give extra weight to the central advance through Leipzig. This meant, in their view, that the main weight of the Allied thrust would be shifted to the south and would leave 21 Army Group with a much wider front to cover. They thought that the consequence would be the slowing up of Montgomery's advance and delay in the capture of the northern ports. The United States Chiefs of Staff, on the other hand, thought that Eisenhower's communication with the Russians had been necessary in view of the rapid advances into Germany from both sides. Nor would they discredit or lower the prestige of a highly successful commander by sending a modification of his signal. If there were to be modifications, they had better be sent by Eisenhower. They thought that the course of action he had outlined to Stalin was in accord with the agreed strategy. Their information was that Eisenhower was deploying east of the Rhine and north of the Ruhr the greatest number of forces which could be used there. They felt confident that Eisenhower's policy would secure the ports and the other objectives desired by the British Chiefs of Staff more quickly and more decisively than the course of action they urged.

Eisenhower had meanwhile explained his motives in full to Marshall. He pointed out that he had already been instructed to deal directly with the Russians about military co-ordination. There was no change in basic strategy. The British Chiefs of Staff had always protested against his determination to open up the Frankfurt route, because they thought it would be futile and would draw strength away from the northern attack. From the beginning, even before D-Day, he had explained to his staff and senior officers, his plan of linking up the primary and secondary efforts in the Kassel area, after which one great thrust would be made to the eastward. This main effort should be towards Leipzig, in which region was concentrated most of Germany's remaining industrial capacity, and to which area we believed the German Ministries to be moving:

My plan does not, repeat not, draw Montgomery's British and Canadian forces to the southward. You will note that his right flank will push forward along the general line Hanover–Wittenberg.

Following the principle which Brooke had always urged, Eisenhower was determined to concentrate on one major thrust. All that his plan involved was to place the Ninth U.S. Army under Bradley for the phase of operations during which the central forces would advance from Kassel to the Leipzig region— unless, of course, the Russian forces should be met to the westward of that area. After that, the position would be consolidated, and his plan showed that the Ninth Army might again have to move up to assist the British and Canadians in clearing the whole coast-line west of Lubeck. He fully understood the advantages of gaining the northern coast-line at the earliest moment. It seemed to Eisenhower, furthermore:

[677]

. . . that Berlin itself is no longer a particularly important objective. Its usefulness to the German has been largely destroyed, and even his Government is preparing to move to another area. What is now important is to gather up our forces for a single drive, and this will more quickly bring about the fall of Berlin, the relief of Norway, and the acquisition of the shipping and the Swedish ports than will the scattering around of our effort. . . . I should like to point out that the so-called 'good ground' in Northern Germany is not very good at this time of year. That region is not only badly cut up with waterways, but in it the ground during this part of the year is very wet and not so favourable for rapid movement as is the higher plateau over which I am preparing to launch the main effort. Moreover, if, as we expect, the German continues the widespread destruction of bridges, experience has shown that it is better to advance across the head waters than to be faced by the main streams.

Eisenhower also explained his intentions fully to Churchill, who replied that he feared Montgomery's front might be so stretched that the offensive role assigned to him might peter out. He did not know why, if the enemy's resistance weakened, we should not cross the Elbe and advance as far eastward as possible:

This has an important political bearing, as the Russian Army of the south seems certain to enter Vienna and overrun Austria. If we deliberately leave Berlin to them, even if it should be in our grasp, the double event may strengthen their conviction, already apparent, that they have done everything.

The Prime Minister did not consider that Berlin had lost its military, and certainly not its political, significance. Its fall would have a profound psychological effect on German resistance everywhere. The idea that the capture of Dresden and junction with the Russians there would be a superior gain, did not commend itself to him. He would greatly prefer persistence in the plan that the U.S. Ninth Army should march with 21 Army Group to the Elbe and beyond to Berlin. This would not be

. . . in any way inconsistent with the great central thrust which you are now so rightly developing as the result of the brilliant operation of your armies south of the Ruhr. It only shifts the weight of one army to the northernmost flank, and this avoids the relegation of His Majesty's Forces to an unexpected restricted sphere.

Both Eisenhower and I had always taken the view that considerations of politics were outside our sphere of responsibility. It was for the British and American Governments to determine the degree to which political considerations should outweigh, or balance, the dictates of military strategy. Until now, very late in the day, we had not been instructed to take particular points as far east as possible in order to forestall the Russians. As Eisenhower at once remarked to Churchill, his telegram had introduced

... a new idea respecting political importance of the early attainment of particular objectives. I clearly see your point in this matter.

The only difference between Churchill's suggestion and Eisenhower's plan, in the Supreme Commander's eyes, was one of timing, which might yet prove to be unimportant. This would depend on the amount of resistance we met. The Supreme Commander must concentrate first in the centre to gain the position he needed. He thought that the next move after that would be for Montgomery to cross the Elbe, reinforced as necessary by American troops, and reach a line which included Lubeck on the coast. If German resistance should crumble, there would be little, if any, difference in time between gaining the central position and crossing the Elbe. On the other hand, if resistance tended to stiffen, it would be vitally necessary to concentrate and not to try and carry out all the projects at once. Eisenhower signalled to the Prime Minister:

I am disturbed if not hurt, that you should suggest any thought on my part to 'relegate His Majesty's Forces to an unexpected restricted sphere'. Nothing is further from my mind, and I think my record over $2\frac{1}{2}$ years of commanding Allied Forces should eliminate any such idea.

The Prime Minister had by now sent a long and soothing telegram to Roosevelt expressing full confidence in Eisenhower, but emphasising again the high strategic and psychological importance of Berlin. Churchill wondered whether, if the Russians got the idea that they had made the overwhelming contribution to the common victory, this might not lead them into a mood which would raise formidable difficulties in the future. He considered that from the political standpoint we should march as far east into

Germany as possible and that should Berlin be in our grasp we should take it. This course also appeared to him to be sound on military grounds.

On 2 April, we received Stalin's reply to Eisenhower's message. He said that the plan to cut the German forces by joining up with the Russian armies entirely coincided with the intention of the Soviet High Command. Stalin agreed that the right place to join up would be in the area of Erfurt, Leipzig, and Dresden. The main blow of the Soviet forces would be delivered in that direction. Since Berlin had lost its former strategic importance, the Soviet High Command would allot secondary forces to its capture. The plan to form a second ring by joining up Soviet and Allied forces in the area of Vienna, Linz, and Regensburg, was also approved by the Soviet High Command. Stalin added that the beginning of the main blow by the Soviet forces would be timed for about the middle of May.

This latter information, as Marshall told Wilson, was somewhat unexpected. He had hoped that Anglo-American forces would reach Berlin by the end of April. He did not think Eisenhower's central thrust should go farther east than Leipzig; after that, it should be directed towards Berlin. The British Chiefs of Staff's reaction to Stalin's telegram was that the delay of his main drive until mid-May strengthened the case to maintain the thrust in the north, and particularly towards Berlin. Stalin had not indicated to Eisenhower the date on which the so-called secondary forces of the Soviet High Command would move towards Berlin. The British Chiefs of Staff 'could not exclude the possibility that Stalin intended to take Berlin himself, and to keep the Allies out of it as long as possible'. The United States Chiefs of Staff replied that the psychological and political advantages which might accrue from the possible capture of Berlin ahead of the Russians should not override the dominant military consideration, the destruction and dismemberment of the German armed forces. They thought that Eisenhower should be allowed to continue to correspond directly with Stalin, and that he alone could conduct the battle in the rapidly changing circumstances. Their British counterparts retorted that admittedly Eisenhower alone could conduct the battle from day to day, but he fought that battle in accordance with broad strategy laid down by the Combined Chiefs of Staff.

I had attended the meeting of the British Chiefs of Staff in London on 3 April. I have no record now of what passed, though according to Alan Brooke's diary I explained that Eisenhower had been forced to wire immediately to Stalin, since Montgomery had put forth a directive with which the Supreme Commander did not agree. Brooke said, according to his own record, that he was 'astonished Ike found it necessary to call on Stalin in order to control Monty'. Moreover, he could not accept this excuse, as the boundaries of 21 Army Group and the U.S. Ninth Army remained the same in Eisenhower's order and in Montgomery's, the only difference being the transfer of the Ninth Army from Montgomery to Bradley. Rather more than a week later, Mr. Churchill, in a Minute to the Chiefs of Staff, abused me for allowing Eisenhower to telegraph directly to Stalin without reference to London. In so writing, the Prime Minister seemed to Brooke to be

forgetting that he himself had entirely undermined Tedder's position by continually communicating direct with Ike and cutting Tedder out. . . .[1]

*

We now realised that the end of the war was in sight. It is my purpose here not to describe the now familiar military operations of the last month or so, but to distinguish the role played by air-power in the concluding stages. After I had consulted with Portal and Bottomley on 9 April, it was ruled that Bomber Command should undertake no more bombing designed solely to obliterate industrial areas. There might still be special circumstances when enemy resistance could best be destroyed by this method, but in general the main object of the Strategic Bomber Force would now be to give direct assistance to the land campaign. I was much concerned lest, during this last period of the battle, we should allow ourselves to wander from the agreed bombing policy. The evidence concerning the serious state of enemy rail communications, and their vital importance to him, accumulated

[1] Bryant: *Triumph in the West,* p. 446.

every day. Now that a heavy blow had been struck at the Luft-waffe, I thought that all our efforts should be concentrated against rail communications, especially in the area of Halle–Leipzig. This was the largest remaining industrial area in German hands and the most important nodal point in Germany. East–west and north–south traffic passed through it. Bottomley agreed that the current directive should be amended, though the effort against oil, which was not now great, should be maintained. He agreed that at this stage the application of the strategic bombing effort, except against oil targets and the Luftwaffe, should be guided mainly by the needs of S.H.A.E.F. This rule this prevailed for the last month of the war.

The armies were now advancing rapidly. By mid-April Eisen-hower was considering how to sub-divide the enemy's remaining forces and capture the areas where the Germans might make a last stand. For these purposes, he thought the best way to divide the enemy in north would be to drive forward to Lubeck, and in the south to join up with the Russians on the axis of their advance down the Danube valley. It would also be most desirable to make the thrust to Berlin, since the enemy might group forces around the capital and its fall would have a great effect on the morale of the enemy and of our own peoples. In this respect Eisenhower adopted, at least in part, the views which Churchill had urged on him. The main areas where the enemy could offer prolonged resistance were the national redoubt in the south and Norway in the north. Into the former area we must break before the enemy could man it properly, and in the north we must nego-tiate with Sweden and then liberate Denmark as a method of setting Norway free. As the Supreme Commander summarised his intention:

The essence of my plan is to stop on the Elbe and clean up my flanks. . . . While it is true that we have seized a small bridgehead over the Elbe, it must be remembered that only our spearheads are up to the river and our centre of gravity is well back of there.

A few days later, Eisenhower told Marshall that the Red Army was in a perfect position to 'clean out' Czechoslovakia. It seemed that the Russians would certainly reach Prague before we could. His intention was to destroy any remaining organised resistance by the Germans. If a move by the Allies into Czechoslovakia was then indicated as desirable, we should probably take Pilsen and Karlsbad, joining up with the Russians:

I shall not attempt any move I deem militarily unwise merely to gain a political prize, unless I receive specific orders from the C.C.S.

Such specific orders were not received by S.H.A.E.F. For the failure to take Prague, Eisenhower has been much blamed. For myself, I doubt whether the capture of that city would have prevented the eventual incorporation of Czechoslovakia in Stalin's empire. Much more probably, we should have withdrawn our troops quickly, after which overwhelming Russian strength would no doubt have asserted itself soon.

On the evening of 4 May, the German armed forces in Holland, North-West Germany, and Denmark, surrendered to Montgomery, who had reached Lubeck on 2 May and had sealed off Denmark just before the Russians arrived. On 5 May, German plenipotentiaties arrived at S.H.A.E.F. to discuss surrender terms. It transpired that they were not authorised to sign any capitulation. They were allowed, therefore, to send a message to the German General Staff asking that a representative with full powers should come to S.H.A.E.F. at once. Next day, Colonel General Jodl, Chief of Staff of the Wehrmacht, came to negotiate the surrender. The talks went on throughout the afternoon and evening. In the early hours of 7 May the formal instruments were signed. Later we received signals from Moscow. It was decided that I should go to Berlin, accompanied by French representatives and S.H.A.E.F. staff officers, to sign with the Russians and Field-Marshal Keitel a ratification of the surrender just agreed at Rheims. We would all meet in the remains of Berlin on 8 May.

I had precisely two hours in which to get off with my colleagues at 8.30 a.m. The party consisted of myself as head of the delegation, Spaatz representing the U.S.A., de Lattre de Tassigny representing France, Leslie Scarman my secretary, and finally Philip Wintle, my pilot and personal assistant. We were to land at Stendahl to join up with a party of Germans from the north and rendezvous there at 11 a.m. with some Russian fighters who were to escort us to Tempelhof. The three German delegates were Field-Marshal

[683]

Keitel, Admiral Friedeburg, and Air Marshal Stumpf. We arrived at Stendahl in plenty of time, so much so that after about three-quarters of an hour of waiting we had almost given up, and were making quite uncomplimentary remarks about Russian punctuality. In the event, they were punctual to the minute—the Russian minute. They, quite naturally, were operating to their time instead of to G.M.T., and it was not without a certain element of relief that we saw their fighters come over in good formation, waiting for us. One could not help thinking that some of their young fighter boys would probably still be a bit light on the trigger. When we got near Tempelhof, on the southern side of Berlin, we could see the city still burning. The yellowish smoke enveloped all and there was an acrid, bitter smell of burning. There was a Russian Guard of Honour lined up on the aerodrome, and having looked at them, I quite sympathised at the Germans being scared stiff. I do not think I have ever seen a tougher, more primitive lot; short, stocky little fellows, with their Slav ancestry very self-evident, and as tough as you can make them. At the Guard of Honour I noticed there were three national flags but not the fourth—the French, an omission which I felt would be useful in the discussions I was to have with General Zhukov. And I did, in fact, use this omission as an invaluable debating point.

The Berlin through which we drove showed little evidence of the bombing, just here and there a burnt-out shell of a house, but apart from that, it gave one a weird impression of being in some sort of coma. The only sign of life was in the queues at water standpipes in the streets. The headquarters to which we were taken was, or had been, an Engineering College, with one or two largish villas grouped round it. When we arrived nobody seemed to know, or to care, anything about us. We were shown into a long corridor with benches all round the walls, occupied by a motley collection of people looking very much like panel patients awaiting their turn. I waited for about five minutes and then got hold of a man who looked as if he had some sort of authority, and told him I wished to be taken to see General Zhukov at once. He demurred, and said the General was very busy, to which I replied I was equally busy and wished to see the General at once. A little quiet insistence was necessary before I obtained entry to the General's office. Zhukov was very apologetic that I had been kept waiting. To tell the truth, I suspect we had arrived much earlier than he had expected, and that in fact they were not fully briefed.

I had brought with me a Draft Instrument of Surrender similar to that which was used at Rheims. Zhuhov had obviously never seen such a document or anything like it, so when one remembers the deeply suspicious nature of the Russians it is not surprising that it took the best part of twelve hours, most of it spent standing in Zhukov's office, to sort out the outstanding issues, each of which had to be argued out *ad nauseam*. Some of the issues were quite serious, and there was one proposed amendment which would have handed over the Germans completely to the Russians. I had a feeling that the presence, or absence, of M. Vishinsky was a potent factor which determined the progress, or lack of it, in our negotiations. On one occasion when Vishinsky was not in the office Zhukov put his hand on my shoulder and said, 'Please believe me, I am not trying to be difficult, but we must get this right now otherwise there will be trouble later.' Later on in the day, when we appeared to have reached an impasse over whether or not the signatures of the French and American representatives should be allowed to appear on the document, I ventured to dig Vishinsky gently in the ribs and remark, 'It does not look as though we are going to get our ration of vodka and caviare.' Vishinsky replied, 'Will you excuse me?' and walked out of the room. He came back a few minutes later with some paper with writing on it, which he gave to Zhukov. Zhukov glanced at it, gave a laugh, and the one outstanding difficulty was solved— Spaatz and de Lattre de Tassigny signed under the signatures of myself and Zhukov as witnesses.

It was past eleven o'clock when we were ready to present the terms to the Germans. We gathered in a long room which would hold a couple of hundred people. At one end there was a head table where I sat down with Zhukov, Spaatz, de Lattre, and Vishinsky. As we were taking our seats I gave an order for the German delegation to be brought in. Keitel, the Field-Marshal, led the way, tall and arrogant, holding his baton high and looking in every way the personification of the horrid blend of Nazi and Prussian. I held up the Instrument of Surrender and asked Keitel if he had read it, understood it, and agreed it. He gave his assent, came forward and signed, followed by the Admiral and the Air Marshal. Keitel then tried to make some protest at there not having been time for outlying troops to have been notified. We were certainly not going to agree to anything which would delay the completion of the formal surrender, and I ordered them to withdraw.

There then occurred a scene of disorder which surprised me, knowing the Russian care for protocol. At least fifty photographers of all sorts started climbing over the chairs, the tables—and us. We literally had to fight our way into the open air. It was past midnight before we could get the signatures completed. An hour later we returned to the room where the surrender had been signed, to find it all fully laid out for a large-scale banquet—and that meant six hours at least. There were bottles beside each plate—red wine, white wine, champagne, vodka, and brandy—as lethal a loading as one could imagine. It was not surprising that there were a number of alcoholic casualties. I was glad to note that none of them was British.

Before our return to Tempelhof at 7.30 that morning I asked to be taken right through the middle of Berlin, down the Unter den Linden, through the Brandenburg Tor, already surmounted by red flags, and to the Reichs Chancellery. The Reichs Chancellery was a shambles with half the ceiling scattered over the floor. Amongst the rubble were two or three of the swastika banners which had hung above the doorway to Hitler's office. The Russian officer escorting us pointed at one of these swastikas, and then at me, and it eventually found a place of dishonour in the Imperial War Museum in London.

After taking the salute from the Russian Guard of Honour I was able to join my, by now, somnolent colleagues on my Dakota. I relaxed in the co-pilot's seat and watched with satisfaction a final display of Allied air superiority as typified by the victory rolls being carried out by our escorting Yak fighters. The journey from Cairo to Berlin had been long and arduous, but at that particular moment I felt that it had certainly been very necessary!

[686]

Summing-up

IT is our custom and our history to find ourselves involved in war for which we are inadequately equipped and suffering from that mental inertia which lays us open to the charge of habitually thinking in terms of the last war but one. The war which broke out in 1939 found us running true to form. At that time the very idea of air warfare as such was new—very new indeed when considered in relation to the history of war as a whole.

The four years of the Mediterranean campaign provided us with a clear step-by-step demonstration of the development of air-power and its relationship to land and sea forces, and introduced in rather brutal terms the new factor of air superiority and its effect on the operations of the land and sea forces. To attain that position air forces must be adequately equipped, trained for battle and securely based. When we lost airfields, as we did in Greece and Crete and also in certain phases in the Western Desert, we lost the initiative both on land and sea.

One of the outstanding characteristics of air-power proved to be its flexibility and the terrific concentration made possible by a unified air command—a unity only achieved by a faith born of mutual understanding between all branches and ranks of the air forces. This spirit is summed up in my final Order of the Day to all ranks of the Allied Air Forces in the Mediterranean on 12 May 1943:

'By magnificent team work between nationalities, commands, units, officers, and men from Teheran to Takoradi, from Morocco to the Indian Ocean, you have, together with your comrades on land and sea, thrown the enemy out of Africa. You have shown the world the unity and strength of air power. . . .'

It was there in Africa that first the British and then the Americans learnt how to fight a war in which action by land, air, and sea was closely integrated, and but for the lessons learnt there victory in Europe would not have been gained so speedily or at

[687]

such little cost. There was little that was cheerful or exhilarating about the last stages of the war except the wonderful spirit which existed throughout the Allied team, and for which we should be eternally grateful to General Eisenhower. It is twenty-five years since General Smuts, another Allied leader and one of the world's greatest statesmen, pointed to the rough road ahead with these words:

'I am not worried about the war; it will be difficult but we shall win it; it is after the war that worries me. Mark you, it will take years and years of patience, courage, and faith.'

Operation Codenames

ACCOLADE   Proposed operation against Rhodes, 1943. Later abandoned.

ACROBAT   Projected British advance from Cyrenaica into Tripolitania, early 1942.

ANVIL   Allied landings in Southern France, 1944. See 'Dragoon'.

AVALANCHE   Allied invasion of Italy (Salerno), September 1943.

BATTLEAXE   Operation to relieve Tobruk, Western Desert, June 1941.

BAYTOWN   Eighth Army assault on the Toe of Italy, 3 September 1943.

BUGLE ⎫   Widespread air attacks on communications
CLARION ⎭   throughout Central Germany, February 1945.

CROSSBOW   The committee (later the attack) on V-weapon launching sites.

CRUSADER   British offensive in Cyrenaica, November 1941.

DRAGOON   Final name for 'Anvil'—Allied landings in Southern France, 15 August 1944.

FLAX   Plan for the suppression of Axis air transport between Sicily and Tunis, 5 April 1943.

GOODWOOD   British Second Army's attack south-east of Caen, 18–21 July 1944.

GRENADE   The United States Ninth Army's offensive in conjunction with 'Veritable', which see—February 1945.

GYMNAST   Original plan for Anglo-American operation which eventually became 'Torch', which see.

HARPOON   Cover operations for convoys from U.K. to Malta 1942.

HUSKY   Allied invasion of Sicily, 10–17 July 1943.

MARKET   Airborne leapfrog operation from the Meuse–
GARDEN   Escaut Canal to Arnhem.

NEPTUNE   The amphibious operations within 'Overlord'.

[689]

OVERLORD	Allied re-entry into North-West Europe, June 1944.
POINTBLANK	The attack on German fighter forces and the industry upon which they depended, 1943–4.
SUPERCHARGE	Breakthrough plan at the 2nd El Alamein.
TORCH	Allied invasion in French North Africa, November 1942. See 'Gymnast'.
VERITABLE	Offensive by Canadian First Army on the Rhineland, in conjunction with 'Grenade', which see— February 1945.
VIGOROUS	Covering operations for convoy from Eastern Mediterranean to Malta, June 1942.

Bibliography of Sources

BOOKS QUOTED OR REFERRED TO IN THE TEXT

ATTLEE, EARL C. R., *As It Happened* (Viking, 1954).
AVON, EARL OF, *The Eden Memoirs: The Reckoning* (Cassell, 1965).
BRADLEY, GENERAL OMAR N., *A Soldier's Story of the Allied Campaigns from Tunis to the Elbe* (Holt, 1951).
BRYANT, SIR ARTHUR, *The Alanbrooke Diaries* (Doubleday).
    The Turn of the Tide (1957).
    Triumph in the West (1959).
CASEY, LORD, *Personal Experience 1939-1946* (McKay, 1963).
CHURCHILL, WINSTON S., *The Second World War* (Houghton Mifflin).
    III. *The Grand Alliance* (1950).
    IV. *The Hinge of Fate* (1951).
    V. *Closing the Ring* (1952).
    VI. *Triumph and Tragedy* (1954).
CONNELL, JOHN, *Auchinleck* (Cassell, 1959).
————, *Wavell, Soldier and Scholar* (Collins, 1964).
CUNNINGHAM, ADMIRAL LORD, *A Sailor's Odyssey* (Hutchinson, 1951).
EISENHOWER, GENERAL DWIGHT D., *Crusade in Europe* (Doubleday, 1948).
LANDSBOROUGH, GORDON, *Tobruk Commando* (Cassell, 1956).
LEAHY, ADMIRAL W. D., *I Was There* (McGraw-Hill, 1950).
LIDDELL HART, CAPTAIN B. H., *The Tanks*, Vol. II (Cassell, 1959).
————, ed., *The Rommel Papers* (Harcourt, 1953).
LLOYD, AIR MARSHAL SIR HUGH, *Briefed to Attack* (Hodder & Stoughton, 1949).
MONTGOMERY, FIELD-MARSHAL THE VISCOUNT, *Memoirs* (World, 1958).

TEDDER, A. W., *Air Power in War* (Hodder & Stoughton, 1948).
————, *The Navy of the Restoration* (Cambridge University Press, 1916).
WESTPHAL, GENERAL S. C. T., ed., *The Fatal Decisions* (Michael Joseph, 1956).
YOUNG, DESMOND, *Rommel* (Harper, 1950).

OFFICIAL HISTORIES OF THE SECOND WORLD WAR
published by Her Majesty's Stationery Office

BUTLER, J. R. M.: *Grand Strategy*, vol. II, 1957.
EHRMAN, J. P. W.: *Grand Strategy*, vol. V, 1956.
ELLIS, MAJOR L. F.: *Victory in the West*, vol. I, 1962.
PLAYFAIR, I. S. O.: *The Mediterranean and Middle East*:
  II. *The Germans Came to the Help of Their Ally*, 1962.
  III. *British Fortunes Reach Their Lowest Ebb*, 1960.
(*a*) RICHARDS, D. G., & (*b*) SAUNDERS, H. ST. G.: *The Royal Air Force 1939–1945*:
  2 (*a* & *b*). *The Fight Assails*, 1953.
  3 (*b*). *The Fight is Won*, 1954.
ROSKILL, CAPTAIN S. W.: *The War at Sea 1939–1945*:
  I. *The Defensive*, 1954.
WEBSTER, SIR CHARLES, & FRANKLAND, N.: *The Strategic Air Offensive Against Germany 1939–1945*:
  4. *Annexes and Appendixes*, 1961.

Index

Index

Index

DATE DUE

6/16.17			
MY 11 17			
GAYLORD			PRINTED IN U.S.A.